Advance Praise for *A Darkness Ablaze*

"Joe Houts has done a valuable service in publishing the Civil War letters and diary of his great-grandfather, Dr. John Hendricks Kinyoun, a most remarkable man. These will provide important new insights into the traumas faced by those who served in the medical field during this great conflict which divided the nation."

— **Dr. William E. Parrish, Professor Emeritus, Mississippi State University,**

"Joseph K. Houts, Jr., has provided a three-dimensional picture of his ancestor, Dr. John H. Kinyoun, a picture that allows us to look inside the man at his heart and soul. This book is the result of a promise Houts made to his grandmother, Mrs. Alice Kinyoun Houts, a well-known genealogist and historian in her own right.

The author has transcribed letters from Dr. John Hendricks Kinyoun to his wife. To these, he adds his own comments, and historical and biographical notes which enhance the material and allow greater insight into the experiences of Dr. Kinyoun after the battles, on the home front, and in the political arena as seen through the eyes of this highly educated doctor from the Piedmont section of North Carolina.

All in all, it is a fitting tribute to Dr. John H. Kinyoun, a humanitarian who tried his best to save lives under primitive medical conditions. This book also adds to our understanding of the participants in the War for Southern Independence and their views about that war and their own unique situation."

— **Frances H. Casstevens, Historian, Yadkinville, North Carolina**

"Like all books of soldiers' letters, each offers a special insight on that man's impression of the war, particular battles, and their own branch of service. Being that Dr. Kinyoun was in the probably relatively small Confederate medical service from North Carolina, his reminiscences are important, as very few documents exist pertaining to this aspect of combat operations. While the letters do not provide any major revelations about the Civil War, they do hold a special place for researchers on this subject matter."

— **Chris Calkins, Chief of Interpretation, Petersburg National Battlefield**

Publications of Platte Purchase Publishers

Saint Joseph Series

On the Winds of Destiny by Jacqueline Lewin & Marilyn Taylor
Old Saint Jo by Sheridan A. Logan
Rare and Scarce Saint Joseph Books, Pamphlets, and Music by J. Marshall White

Children's Discovery Series

The Elephant Way by Joyce Rochambeau

Civil War Series

A Darkness Ablaze by Joseph K. Houts, Jr.
As the Mockingbird Sang by Suzanne S. Lehr

Others

Midland Empire Studies: An Interdisciplinary Review of The St. Joseph Museums Inc.

Dedicated to a true friend and a true servant of God,
My Friend,
Major Mark Martsolf,
The Salvation Army

Flag of the Sixty-Sixth North Carolina Infantry Regiment.
From the author's collection.

A Darkness Ablaze

The Civil War Medical Diary and Wartime Experiences of Dr. John Hendricks Kinyoun, Sixty-Sixth North Carolina Infantry Regiment

by

Joseph Kinyoun Houts, Jr.

"Committed to Civic Engagement"

Platte Purchase Publishers
A Division of
The St. Joseph Museums Inc.
St. Joseph, Missouri

Editor, Alberto C. Meloni
Executive Director
The St. Joseph Museums Inc.

Production Manager, Sarah Elder
Curator of Collections
The St. Joseph Museums Inc.

Editorial Assistant, Jacqueline Lewin
Assistant Director for External Affairs
The St. Joseph Museums Inc.

Library of Congress Control Number (LCCN) 2005907850
Houts, Jr., Joseph Kinyoun

A Darkness Ablaze: The Civil War Medical Diary and Wartime Experiences of Dr. John Hendricks Kinyoun, Sixty-Sixth North Carolina Infantry Regiment by Joseph Kinyoun Houts, Jr..—1st. Ed. (Platte Purchase Publishers/Civil War Series). Summary: Contains the Medical Diary and Letters of Dr. John Hendricks Kinyoun, C.S.A., from the American Civil War years of 1863-1865, with an Introduction and five Chapters about Kinyoun's life, view of the war, and Civil War medical practices written by the author Joseph Kinyoun Houts, Jr.

ISBN: 0972535365

1. Platte Purchase Publishers (MO) — Adult History
2. St. Joseph Museums Inc. (MO) — American History
3. American Civil War — Medical History/Diary/Letters
4. Confederacy — Medical History/North Carolina
5. North Carolina — History/Civil War
6. Medicine — History/American/Civil War

Printed in U.S.A. by
BookMasters, Inc.
Mansfield, Ohio

PREFACE

At long last, family histories have become recognized as a most essential element of our understanding of the human historical drama. As a result of the history profession's varied initiatives, fondly remembered as history "From the Bottom Up" and "From the Inside Out," family history is now taught and practiced as at least a legitimate, if not an absolute necessity, to learning about the past and who we are, why we are, and how we got to where we're at. Once upon a time, only the wealthy and/or bluebloods made sure that their genealogies were researched and preserved for posterity. The "dispossessed" were left only with oral history, a very poor substitute at best, given the existing literacy levels, as a means of preserving their family heritage. But, in spite of all the advances in our understanding of both the importance of such knowledge and the means whereby it can be acquired, it is still amazing how so few individuals can provide specific, accurate, and factual historical details about their ancestry. Most families never have the one member from each generation who is deemed responsible for acquiring, preserving, and teaching the family's human saga. In even rarer cases does a family anoint one of its own to interpret for the rest what their past historical experiences mean and how it has led all of them to their present circumstances.

The family of Joseph Kinyoun Houts, Jr., was twice blessed in their efforts to know and maintain their family history; first with Joseph's grandmother, Alice Kinyoun Houts, who was determined to preserve all evidence of the family's past, and second, with Joseph himself, who, although discouraged from becoming a professional historian as opposed to a lawyer, was nevertheless anointed and inspired by his grandmother to tell the stories for which the material evidence gave testimony. And what stories they are that Mr. Houts, Jr., has so generously agreed to share with his entire family and, most fortunately, with the rest of us. The American Civil War and John Hendricks Kinyoun's role in the conflict, as viewed through his letters and medical diary, cannot be overlooked by anyone who wishes to understand that event so often dubbed "The Second American Revolution." Nor can anyone dismiss such primary evidence, who is interested in the history of medicine and the contributions made to the profession and the world through America's Civil War. Joseph Kinyoun Houts, Jr., presents and interprets the events and their human participants, especially his ancestors, with a historian's care, a relative's pride, a familial tradition bearer's reverence, and a human being's desire to share his family's stories as a means to further a deeper understanding within all of us of our communal historical past.

With the advent of the Civil War Sesquicentennial celebrations, Platte Purchase Publishers is proud to make this work available to its readers. In fact, in the coming years, it is looking forward to numerous publications on the Civil War, thereby initiating efforts at a Series. And, Mr. Hout's publication is a most fitting title to commence that effort.

Such works as this, above and beyond their historical and interpretive value, might stand for all of us as beacons of how we too must shoulder the responsibility within our families for the perservation and the recounting of our own unique stories. For they cumulatively record and reveal tales with which we can identify when at last we choose to admit we are all one people, all one human family.

Alberto C. Meloni
St. Joseph, Missouri, 2005

ACKNOWLEDGEMENTS

As with the majority of any undertakings, the final product can only be accomplished through the help of others. Without question, this book could not have been completed without the generosity and guidance of many individuals and in particular my family; Noreen, Joe III, and Katie, plus my countless friends. First and foremost, special recognition belongs to my grandmother, Alice Kinyoun Houts, a lady of remarkable talent and foresight. She entrusted to me one of her most cherished possessions, the Civil War Medical Diary of her grandfather, John Hendricks Kinyoun. Besides grandmother, I owe him a great debt of gratitude for writing the Diary and preserving it through the remainder of his life. Absent this and grandmother's subsequent safekeeping, the document would have probably been lost to the ages in some forgotten corner of an attic.

Many thanks go to Dr. Wallace "Wally" McDonald, who assisted me immensely through the use of his medical books and particularly in reviewing and editing the Medical Glossary presented in the Appendix. The good doctor has been a great supporter of my efforts in this project and was never too busy to lend a helping hand. Thanks Wally, you are a genuine good friend. I would also like to thank Frances H. Casstevens, a long lost Kinyoun relative from North Carolina, who helped me immensely with background information. Frances was kind enough to read my manuscript and provide an endorsement. My thanks also go to Chris Calkins of the Petersburg National Battlefield for his review and testimony of my book. Further, I thank Susan Provost Beller for letting me use material from her book entitled, *Civil War Medicine in the Civil War*, which contains a picture of one of one of Dr. Kinyoun's medical cases. In addition, I want to thank Marshall White of the *St. Joseph News-Press* for his critique of the manuscript. Marshall has always been very supportive of all my Civil War endeavors.

In addition, a special acknowledgement must be extended to Alberto Meloni, Director of The St. Joseph Museums Inc. and its Platte Purchase Publishers for agreeing to publish my book.

As in my previous book, I owe a great deal of gratitude to Dr. William E. Parrish, my former history professor at Westminster College in Fulton, Missouri. He was good enough to review my final draft and provide an endorsement. I am deeply indebted to you, Bill for everything you have done.

I would like to thank everyone for your help, support, and suggestions while I was writing this book. I apologize for any possible errors and/or omissions.

Besides everyone else, there is a special group of friends I want to thank; my co-workers at Commerce Bank. Their encouragement and support has led me to continue in my passion for history. Thanks fellow employees, you will always be considered family.

I again want to thank my immediate family. Writing a book is no small task and in the process schedules still have to be met and time reserved to one's home front. Although, not without a little grumbling, my wife and children have been very patient over the last few years, while I secluded myself off into a writer's world. Also, I want to thank my sister, Trish Reeves, and her two children, Caroline Petrie and Jeremiah, who have been enthusiastic about my efforts and offered a great deal of support.

Finally, I come to my dear Dad. Several years ago, I remember telling him about writing my first book and remembering his response to be somewhat mild at best. Knowing him well as I do, he probably thought I was just talking big once again. Plus, he is from the "Show Me State." The Missouri State motto has always been his standard-bearer, meaning, "seeing is believing." However, one night when he was over for dinner I pointed to a table, where I had placed about 150 printed pages of the manuscript. I commented to him that it represented my progress to date, and suddenly out of his normal character, he seemed to awaken and realize my previous statement about writing a book was in fact true. On its publication, I gave him the first copy, of which he diligently read in the course of a short week and upon finishing was very complimentary.

Shortly thereafter, I told him of my plans for a second book about the family. He was most encouraging, although I felt he appeared a little shocked at his son attempting another manuscript, yet so soon. Within a brief period though, he once again understood my seriousness. To his credit, he has been an able research assistant. He has gone through many of the old family papers finding new information and various photographs. His contribution alone has added significantly to this project. After fifty-two years Dad, what can I ever say, but thanks again, you have always been my very best friend.

Joseph Kinyoun Houts, Jr.
St. Joseph, Missouri, 2005

Table of Contents

Kinyoun Family Coat of Arms.
Note original English spelling of name.
From the author's collection

INTRODUCTION

Of all my many childhood memories in recalling those times when I was either sick or injured, two in particular have stood out as the most horrific. The first such experience occurred prior to my entering grade school. It was in the winter, and I had contracted the ever dreaded and to some extent life threatening German Measles. I can still vividly recall the high fever, chills, vomiting, and the thought I would never get better. I cried until it hurt more to cry, than to lay in total stillness and silence. The family doctor had been by the house several times to assess my condition, which had continued to steadily decline. The cramps were unforgiving, and my fever would not break. Red spots checkered my skin. The decision had been made between my parents and the doctor to wait and see what morning brought. If the fever had not receded, then I was to be taken to the hospital. My mother sat by my bed most of the night. Fortunately, the fever did break by dawn, and I remembered waking up soaking wet. Both parents were greatly relieved, and I would dare say the doctor, too, since he no longer had to come to our house in the middle of the night. Although I was going to survive, the thought, and better yet the feeling, of almost dying has never left my memory.

The second such experience occurred during my Second Grade. One early fall Saturday morning, my mother directed my father to take me to get my hair cut at Chet's Barbershop. I did not like getting my hair cut. Even today, I do not enjoy going through this process. It just has always seemed to be one of those maintenance issues, which will never go away, kind of like cutting the grass once a week during the summer. It looks great for a few days, and then you have to cut it all over again. On the day in question though, I was happily planted in front of the television set watching my favorite cartoon show, "Mighty Mouse." I was in no mood to go to the barbershop, although I did always enjoy the Bazooka bubble gum given out afterwards, dependent, of course, upon my good behavior. On this day, I was more resistant, and father was somewhat grouchy about my attitude. He and mother had had a late night out with their friends, which I suspect added to his joyfulness.

Well, I headed out the door with him, and we were both silent towards each other. Being somewhat frazzled now, he lost track of what he was doing. He opened the door to the front seat, and I stated bluntly my desire to sit alone in the back seat away from him. Some words were exchanged, and in the process he accidentally slammed the front passenger door on two of my right fingers. The pain was excruciating beyond imagination. I promptly screamed bloody murder, which not only brought mother outdoors with her tongue lashing wildly at father, but also a sizable lot of the neighbors appeared in witness to this heinous experience, much to my parents' dismay.

Imagine, open child abuse on Ashland Avenue in broad daylight, plus a screaming child to boot. How Embarrassing! So off we went to the Thompson, Brumm and Knepper Clinic, Inc., one of my Dad's clients. He was a lawyer, you know. The diagnosis was simple; surgically remove the fingernails. Even after the surgery, I will never forget the pain. My parents, feeling sorry about the accident, took me to Benny Magoon's Delicatessen afterwards and bought me my favorite lunch. It consisted of a bowl of chili accompanied by a pepperbeef and Swiss cheese sandwich with mayo on an onion roll. Father had a gin martini and mother stared at him with her piercing baby blue cold eyes. You could almost see her look frosting his cocktail glass. Needless to say, at least for the moment, I avoided getting a haircut. All things aside though, the experience of pain through disease and injury opened my eyes to the frailty of life and the consequences of exposure and accidents. In my cases, I was afforded anesthesia, pain relief medicines, antibiotics, a clean operating room, and recovery environment. However, only a hundred years previously, men in both the Union and Confederate armies during the American Civil War would die from a minor scratch after it had become infected. Of sad parallel, common childhood diseases would in themselves alone account for many of the illnesses afflicting and eventually killing the enlistees. Unfortunately, only a few years would transpire before medical science could comprehend and alter its general practices in a form adequate enough to address the needs of the patient and combat the invisible world of microorganisms. The educated physicians of the period knew illnesses were caused by disease. However, even with all this knowledge, this generation of medical practitioners could not explain, nor sufficiently comprehend, the seclusive habitat and transient nature of germs and how to achieve their scientific eradication.

Which brings me to the point of why I wrote this book. I have always been intrigued with the intricacies of medicine and its ability to cure the sick, refortify the lame, and give hope to the soul. This passion stemmed from my grandmother, Alice Kinyoun Houts, whose grandfather, father, and a brother were all doctors. I have long been a fan of the Civil War, and grandmother could see this interest in me when I was very young. Wetting my appetite further, she would tell me many stories about our family's role in the conflict. She allowed how her kinfolk had supported the Glorious South, whereas her husband (my grandfather) had the disgrace to be related to those dreaded Yankees. Even worse, grandfather was one of those nasty Republicans.

She was a proud lady, and, as a genealogist, had become an expert on the family's lineage Through the generations, she safely kept stacks of papers and personal items once owned by our ancestors. Since I was the first male grandchild to carry on the family name (even though of Northern extraction) and, in particular, her maiden name as my middle name, I always felt to be her pet. Understand, I do not intend any disrespect to my cousins, and it probably was not true, but it was my impression while growing up. In any event, she did show and give me many of the family's Civil War effects. Grandmother's greatest prize was the Civil War Medical Diary of her grandfather, John Hendricks Kinyoun, who, among other wartime assignments, was the regimental surgeon for the Sixty-Sixth North Carolina Infantry Regiment from 1863 to 1865. In a letter to me, dated March 6, 1968, she wrote a summary of his life and war experiences. In the last paragraph though, she directed that "After school is out I [Joe Houts, Jr.] am going to aid my grandmother in the deciphering and making a readable copy of his [Dr. John Kinyoun's] War time [*sic*] Diary, so it can be more easily typed and several copies made."

In the summer of 1968, I visited her for several weeks, and at various times we examined the Diary. However, we got distracted by other activities, such as going to the movies and out to lunch, which left her desired task unfinished. As the years went by, we both talked about the document with the intent of completing the project. However, seeing the years were fading in her life, she willed the document to me in hopes I would someday accomplish this endeavor. Unfortunately, she passed away in 1974, my senior year in college. The Diary had been wrapped in brown wrapping paper and addressed to me for safekeeping. At the time, I was twenty-one years old and proceeding to law school. I returned home to a career in banking with a new wife, followed by two children. During this period the Diary lay untouched, I simply did not have the time for any outside interests while trying to raise a family and succeed in the business world.

Then one day, I happened across a dust-covered bundle in a remote corner of the house, where I had casually tucked away several personal items from younger days. The package was bound in faded yellow twine, and on the front contained the inscription, " John H. Kinyoun Assistant Surgeon General Confederate Army Hospital Records for Joseph K. Houts Jr." I instantly recalled this gift from grandmother and decided the time had come to fulfill her wish. The problem though was that I was in the final stages of writing my first book, *Quantrill's Thieves*, which also dealt with her side of the family. Before long, however, I completed this book, freeing me to pursue the Diary. In examining the document, I found its condition to be generally stable, except for the binding and various minor blemishes attributed to its age. I could not help reflecting back upon the magnificent history this document had gone through. Here it was, 2002 and the diary's age was almost three times in length as my present life, a feat totally within itself. Suddenly, I appreciated why this journal had meant so much to her and to the medical history of our country.

That being said, it is best if I let this book do its own speaking. Besides grandmother's wish for the Diary, I had one as well; to present it to the public. My hope is that it might finally answer those questions as to the fate of the soldiers who served with the Sixty-Sixth North Carolina Infantry Regiment. I especially want this document to afford some honor to those men for their service and to those who died, whether from disease or battle. Family members, although removed by many years and generations, might now be able to learn the truth concerning their ancestors from a medical perspective. I have never liked the word "closure," because in the case of those who have fallen or died the only end has been for the victim, not the living. Unfortunately, those remaining have always been left living the nightmare of a loved one's loss the rest of their lives. Hopefully, while not providing closure, the Diary will at least bear a little comfort to present and subsequent generations as to what really happened to the men of the Sixty-Sixth.

Capt. John H. Kinyoun with his son, Joseph James Kinyoun. In 1887, Joseph Kinyoun founded the National Institutes of Health, Staten Island, New York
From the author's collection.

CHAPTER I

"A DARKNESS"

"In him was life, and the life was the light of man.
The light shines in the darkness,
And the darkness has not overcome it."

John 1:5

Shiloh, April 6-7, 1862

The terrible sounds of the cannonade could still be heard thundering through the early night, asserting each foe's claim to the day's contested battlefield. Echoing whisps of gunfire streaked across the sky amid the urgency of commanding voices bellowing orders at a hurried pace. But the most common noise on this congested scene occurred from the ever-lingering groans and cries of the wounded and dying, lying scattered about this now hallowed ground. At dawn, the Confederate Army had launched a sweeping attack upon the field and forced the Union Army to the banks of the Tennessee River. However, reinforcements had arrived for the North, and the tide slowly turned in favor of the Union command. What at first had been considered a great Confederate victory had most decidedly resulted in defeat. As to the men of both armies, the toll in casualties had become unspeakable. Although in a military sense the battle was over, the battle from a medical standpoint, to treat and save the wounded was just beginning. Of sad irony, more victims would probably be vanquished because of primitive medical standards, lack of trained personnel, and infectious diseases than all the thousands of death volleys cast these two early budding days of spring.

Young Corporal Isaiah B. Keuppers had run away from his home in the middle part of Alabama at the first call to arms in defense of the newly created Confederate nation.[1] He was only 15 and, although too young to enlist legally, he was a fair size of a lad for his age and easily passed the scrutiny of the enlistment sergeant. Early on as a soldier, he more than proved his ability and eagerness to fight and kill the ever-hated Yankee. Because of his spirit, and in part due to signs of leadership, he was promoted to the rank of corporal in the first week of January 1862. His commanding sergeant told him it was kind of a New Year's present. Keuppers, elated at his newfound military status, wrote his parents about their son's whereabouts and service to the country, for the first time since running away. Of special mention was the promotion. His parents were excited to hear from him, but at the same time disappointed in his actions. However, the Keuppers were not unlike many other Southern families during this period, in having a son leave home to join the war effort. Isaiah told his folks about the skirmishes he had fought in and how on one occasion he had even carried the flag or "colors" into battle, never dropping it once. All seemed well for Corporal Keuppers, until the morning of April 6, 1862.

On that day, the corporal and his unit had been brought forward to be part of the lead Confederate surprise attack on Union forces under the command of Ulysses S. Grant. The general and his army held a position on a little known port on the Tennessee River called Pittsburg Landing. It was dawn, and the hope had been not only to surprise the sleeping Union Army, but to drive them into the river, thereby regaining control of the state for the South. Keuppers was positioned at the end of his column, and, as the sun broke above the morn, he, along with his comrades, was ordered to advance forward at a double-quick pace. Within minutes, they were upon the slowly rising Northern troops, and with immediate precision gunned them down in their tracks, many not even making it out of their tents.

Isaiah ran in front of his outfit dodging fire at every third step. However, as he crested a small hill, a well-placed Minié ball from a retreating Yankee pierced his chest. The pain was excruciating, and he tumbled headlong into a tangled heap. The sensation of death raced through his mind, as blood and watery yellow fluids of bile poured from his now exposed lungs. He rolled over onto his back gasping for breath, but with each beat of his now failing heart the inner linings of this cavity secreted more discharge from the wound. Dirt and blood had initially plugged the opening, which further inhibited the passage of air. However, with the probe of his finger he managed to clear some of the embedded debris. Foam had begun to rise from his throat and breach his quivering lips. In time, his mind began to drift backward to childhood memories, when as a boy he could remember the sweet moments of his mother's affections.

All night he languished in pain and semiconsciousness, growing weaker at every minute as his body began the final transition from life. Smells emerged from his wound, indicating the initial onset of infection caused by the thousands of microorganisms that had set in. As a new morning broke upon the horizon, he had, for some unknown reason, survived the night. Rain had moved in overnight and washed some of the ooze seeping from his chest. The shivers had been relentless, and his body convulsed at uneven intervals. The cold had also accompanied the rain, and at times he pleaded for the sight of his Maker.

In the distance, he once again heard the renewal of combat between the armies. Suddenly, a horde of strangers swept upon the area where he lay. The sun was in his eyes, but he could faintly see a man standing above him. As his eyes slowly focused, he saw a silhouette of a Union soldier, leaning overhead, panting heavily with a musket aimed inches from his head. He heard the soldier begin to cry openly, saying "Oh My God!" "Oh My God!" "Isaiah! What has happened to you." Corporal Keuppers also cried, but in a soft and begging moan for help, asking for mercy though and not salvation. The soldier knelt beside him and lifted his head, so he could have a drink of water. Isaiah again pleaded for mercy, asking the man to end his misery, for he knew death awaited him and he did not want to suffer anymore. He repeated the request several times, and finally, just as he expected an answer, a bullet from the Yankee's gun slammed his brains into the ground.

It was a blessing for the now dead Isaiah Benjamin Keuppers for within a day or two, he most likely would have died from either his injury or the disease brewing within the wound. However, the truly tragic aspect in this man's passing was not in his dying, but in the fact it had been hastened by his cousin Josiah Keuppers, who knew upon seeing his kin, there was no point in his living any longer. As Josiah turned to walk away, another shot rang out from a concealed Confederate sharpshooter perched atop a nearby tree. Instantly, he pitched backwards and fell upon his cousin. He was now dead, too. In a few days, both men would be buried together in a shallow unmarked, wet grave, leaving their families to wonder forever as to their eventual fate. [2]

Besides the young corporal and his cousin, many other men died in the battle of Shiloh. One of the most notable casualties of the day was Confederate Gen. Albert Sidney Johnston, who had been wounded by a bullet in the leg, severing the femoral artery. He subsequently perished by bleeding to death. Earlier, he had dispatched his chief surgeon, David W. Yandell, to the aid of the countless fallen, in particular to assist a contingent of wounded Yankee prisoners.[3] By this act of humanity, he most likely had sacrificed his own life. Johnston would be only one of thousands to die by neglect or uninformed and inappropriate medical attention, a condition affecting both sides of this great conflict.

The Rebellion had been raging just over a year, and the strain upon the country's medical resources had become clearly evident in these early battles. But why had this happened? Civilization had purportedly made amazing leaps in its industrialization and manufacturing technology of the period, even in spite of the great geopolitical, social and economic upheavals of the century. Unfortunately, war has always represented mankind's worst form of diplomacy, leaving the average citizen to wonder why greater pains have not been taken through the ages to stop this dreaded act. More importantly though, why had there not been significant strides made in the art and science of healing? As the Civil War progressed, the medical profession began, for once, to understand some very basic and fundamental facts in the caring and handling of the sick and wounded.

Not all was achieved during this horrific experience, but at the very least the seeds to future advances were to some extent finally planted. It could be said the profession was cloaked in darkness, but out of this ghastly upheaval a light began to shine and transform this darkness into the reality of present day science. Many individuals during this conflict added to a change, not only in the thinking, but also in the processes of coping with the burden of overwhelming casualties. One such individual was Dr. John Hendricks Kinyoun of the Sixty-Sixth North Carolina Infantry Regiment. In addition to being the regimental surgeon, he kept during his service what has become known as the Kinyoun Medical Diary, hereinafter referred to as the Kinyoun Diary or Diary. He had only been a doctor for five years until this appointment, and had not been in a position to practice his new profession. By the end of the war though, he regrettably would be one of the most seasoned doctors in the country, experiencing daily the traumas, horrors, and agony of those he labored to save in an environment devoid of the true reality in treating patients.

Before his role can be evaluated, a general knowledge of the era needs to be set forth. A period when doctors were so very close to fully understanding the ways of modern medicine, but tragically for the victims of this dreadful contest, not close enough. In looking at this time, it must be asked, what were the standards within this field before and during this period of darkness? Consequently, how did this war forever change the treatment of disease and injuries? Did in fact a new light begin to shine, which would bring hope to sufferers of its long shadows?

Early Nineteenth Century Medicine

Throughout the course of history, people have been confronted with the destructive elements of disease, its origins, multiple facets, and cures. Disease has constantly ravaged civilization in the form of plagues, epidemics, and in particular, as an appendage of war. In the middle of the nineteenth century, doctors and health boards overall had a limited perception about the treatment of disease, common injuries and, worse yet, combat casualties. The men of the American medical profession to a large degree lacked the scientific ability to properly detect and administer to the needs of the sick and dying. In many instances, medicine in America could at best be placed as lying somewhere between a misunderstanding and a charade.[4]

On the other hand, the European medical community had been making some important advances in understanding the origins of disease during the period leading to and following the American Civil War. Although it would still be many years before their discoveries would bring results, they were beginning to recognize medicine more as a science than as a practice of trial and error. By comparison, American doctors and medical personnel were at best in an embryonic state of knowledge. Many individuals would simply proclaim themselves a doctor without any formal medical training. In some cases, they would be known as fakes and quacks who distributed worthless concoctions in a bottle. These putative doctors promised loudly that their bottled brews or mystical skills were a cure-all for every ailment of the mind and body. Even those having a medical background were far from what would be considered qualified. Those people having an education might have only read a single book or attended classroom lectures for as little as two months, let alone participated in any laboratory studies.[5] The giants of modern medicine, Drs. Pasteur, Koch, Lister, and other pioneers of the period did not appear on the horizon until the last quarter of the nineteenth century, long after the needs of the Civil War.[6]

Today, medicine has jumped enormous hurdles. If not for the microscope and the learning achieved through laboratories, medicine as a whole would still be in its dark ages. Did the Civil War move medicine in a new direction? Most pointedly it did and in several important ways. If nothing else, it operated as a catalyst for what was to yet occur within the field. Although advancements were made as a result of the war, none were particularly of a purely scientific basis. Not to be slighted, the accomplishments made resulted more from the hypothesis of common sense than through today's standards of medical research and application. Probably, the greatest achievement occurred in the concept that sanitation, ventilation, and nutritional food should be given to the patient. Overall, sanitation would be the most valuable of these three benchmarks because it provided clean air and food. In other words, the idea of applying cleanliness to patients by Southern and Northern doctors enhanced their survival rate. It was not always a common practice, but the more sanitized an environment, the greater probability of recovery.[7]

Ironically, Dr. Kinyoun and his numerous peers would leave a recognizable mark on the advancement of medicine. It would not be achieved necessarily on a scientific platform, but in the future discoveries made by the profession, including those of his son Dr. Joseph James Kinyoun of the Marine Hospital Service thirty years later. Dr. Joseph Kinyoun did study under Drs. Pasteur and Koch. He would establish the first laboratory in New York City, which has evolved into today's National Institutes of Health, now located in Washington, D.C. Of added note, besides specializing in pathology and microbiology, he knew the importance of sanitation, which most likely had been derived from knowing about his father's wartime experiences.[8]

Early Medical Standards and Practices of The Confederacy

After the South had seceded and formed the Confederate States of America, the presumption shared by both the North and South was that the impending conflict would be short-lived. Most individuals, including the politicians and the military on each side, thought only a few battles would be needed to decide the outcome of this American crisis. To everyone's surprise, such would not be the case, especially as the sun set in northern Virginia after the First Battle of Manassas (Bull Run) on July 21, 1861. The Union Army that day seemed poised and ready for victory, and, at first, the field of battle seemed to be theirs. However, as events unfolded, the South would be the victor as the Northern troops fled in horror at their defeat, racing towards their capital of Washington, D.C., in search of sanctuary.[9] Each nation had misjudged the situation, for the war would last until the middle of 1865, bringing four years of darkness and despair upon the land.

By the end of this great conflict, the South alone would mobilize upwards of 750,000 men to serve in its army and navy, and 258,000 would perish either from their wounds or, more often, disease. It has been estimated 1 out of 3 deaths occurred in battle, whereas disease accounted for the remaining two-thirds.[10] All told, each soldier or sailor would be sick six times during the war, bringing the combined caseload of battle wounds, accidents, and diseases to a staggering estimate of 4,500,000.[11] Without question, the South saw itself overwhelmed with the situation. As previously stated, the medical community had very little if any training. Some medical literature existed, but most of it had not been updated, and overall, medical education decreased up to the 1850s.[12] Of some importance though, the use of the lancet and scalpel in surgical procedures proved to be of valuable service in attending to the countless number of casualties. These instruments had been borrowed from the French, which again highlighted European medical advancements.[13]

Even prior to the First Battle of Manassas, the Confederacy had undertaken measures to provide for the general health and well being of its soldiers. On February 26, 1861, the Provisional Confederate Congress at Montgomery, Alabama, the first capital of the government, introduced a bill entitled an "Act for the Establishment and Organization of a General Staff for the Army of the Confederate States of America."[14] Eight days after Confederate President Jefferson Davis' inauguration, the bill was enacted into law. The statute called for one surgeon general, four surgeons, and six assistant surgeons, with the ranks of colonel, major and captain, respectively. The surgeon general would receive an annual salary of $3,000, with surgeons receiving $200 to $162 per month and assistant surgeons$150 to $110 per month. In addition, all would receive housing and fuel as part of their payment.[15]

Over time, new legislation would be enacted restructuring and expanding the medical service in order to better provide for the troops. However, regardless of those initial efforts to address organizational matters and prepare for battle casualties, disease alone invaded both armies of the North and South early on and wreaked havoc among the new recruits. By May 1861, it became rampant among the various enlistment camps. Never before had so many young men been forced together from all regions of the country. With them, they brought numerous infectious diseases, especially childhood illnesses like the measles and mumps. Other diseases like malaria, smallpox, and typhoid fever also spread like wildfire among them, causing many to die before ever seeing the light of battle, a tragedy within itself. The reason for this devastating occurrence was the lack of immunity in their bodies to these vicious organisms, as well as the lack of adequate sanitation in the camps.[16]

Outside of disease, probably the greatest compounding factor to a soldier's death involved the initial care afforded him after being wounded. First, it became important that a victim receive attention quickly, which, in most circumstances did not occur as a result of the magnitude of battlefield injuries. Second, if a soldier remained untreated for the first 24 hours, then in all probability he would eventually die from the injury. In many battles, the wounded lay on the field for periods at least that long before a truce would be called in order to remove the fallen. Clearly however, the most contributing factor to death centered on issues surrounding general sanitation. Of dangerous consequence, the finger proved to be the most common probe instrument used by doctors as an examination tool. Surgical gloves and masks, even if heard of, were not used in most cases, and medical instruments were rarely cleaned between operations. Doctors and other medical personnel were known not to have changed their blood-soaked clothing until the end of the day. One surgeon documented, " We operated in old, blood-stained and pus-stained coats."[17] As seen by these primitive and unsanitary procedures, one can easily understand how infectious disease claimed so many lives.[18]

Besides the poor quality of general operating procedures, other factors contributed to the plight of not only the wounded but also the everyday soldier.

The general conditions of the environment profoundly affected one's well-being. Camps were overcrowded, shelters were often cramped, poorly ventilated, wet, and cold, which led to a whole host of problems. At times, food and water were not only tainted but also totally lacking in nutritional value at times, which could cause diarrhea, dysentery, and scurvy.[19] The food became so bad at Winder Hospital in Richmond that the patients revolted by throwing it all over the ward.[20] Overall, these conditions arose out of the ignorance concerning basic sanitation, which caused the most problems. The preparation of food was poor, and water would come from streams and rivers instead of sterile ground wells.[21] It has been noted that on occasion a latrine would be placed or men would bathe upstream from where a hospital or camp drew its water.[22] Alcoholism and depression bred out of these conditions. Even weather became a common enemy, especially the cold and rain. It seemed to advance an already deplorable condition by operating as a conduit for the further spread of disease.[23]

Another contributing factor to loss of life resulted from the advancements in mankind's killing apparatuses. The most deadly component of the war can probably be attributed to the invention of the Minié ball or bullet. It had been designed in 1849 by Capts. Henri Gustave Delvigne and Claude-Etienne Minié of France. The bullet consisted primarily of lead and had a conicle design with several grooved rings around the body and a hollow base. The rings allowed it to load easier and travel at a farther and straighter distance. The use of lead caused it to pan out upon impact, causing a shattering effect when striking bones and internal organs. In most cases, where the missile had hit a limb, the appendage would have to be amputated because the underlying bone was devoid of future composition.[24] As a whole, bullets accounted for nearly 250,000 of all casualties, North and South, with 108,000 being credited to the Minié ball.[25] Other advancements included the use of rifling in the manufacture or conversion of smooth bored muskets and artillery pieces. Rifling involved a procedure where the bore was drilled with rings inside the barrel allowing for improved firing range and accuracy. Also, the use of countless types of shells, fuses, and powder configurations profoundly added to the total number of wounded;[26] 12,500 from shell fragments and 359 from cannon balls.[27]

Efforts were utilized to treat and save a wounded limb, but in many cases, due to a lack of antibiotics, the wound would become infected, especially from gangrene, resulting in amputation. The effect of a successful amputation was in most cases devastating to the soldier, denying the individual the use of one and sometimes multiple limbs. Such outcomes would leave the person without the ability to seek gainful employment and, in effect, leave him to the generosity of family or the charity of society. It should be recognized that America in the 1860s was predominately an agrarian nation. If an individual did not have the physical ability to work the land as a farmer, rancher, or laborer, then, absent an advanced education, he would most likely forever remain dependent upon others. As the war progressed. a new procedure was introduced called "resection." Instead of a total amputation, the limb would be resectioned back together after removing the wounded or infected area. Although not an attractive sight, it still allowed many who would otherwise be incapacitated to have the ability to remain semi-productive citizens.[28]

Enlightenment

As war became imminent and subsequently erupted, and with casualties increasing beyond imagination, the Confederate government and several forward thinking individuals began to make changes within the medical system to better address the situation. The first of many changes was to expand the administrative staff overseeing the medical care within the army and navy. Two additional laws were enacted on March 6, 1861. The first established medical officers for the army, and the second created a pay scale. In addition, the President could appoint one surgeon and one assistant surgeon per volunteer regiment or militia unit. The appointments were for as long as the doctors were needed, making their enlistment closed ended.[29] On May 16, 1861, the Confederate Congress increased the number of surgeons from four to six and the number of assistant surgeons from six to fourteen. Within three months Congress realized this was far short of the need and authorized President Davis to appoint as many surgeons and assistant surgeons as deemed necessary.[30]

In April 1863, another attempt took place to restructure the Medical Corps, but without explanation the bill expired in Congress. One interesting clause of the measure elevated the surgeon general's position to the equivalent of a brigadier general at the corresponding pay level.[31] By 1864, the medical department had been restructured again, turning it into a defined bureaucracy, complete with various checks and balances over the country's military medical operations. At this point, the administrative staff consisted of six medical officers, including the surgeon seneral, in his office, alone.[32] Also, there were eighteen surgeons acting "as medical directors in the field and supervising the work of medical officers there."[33] Five medical boards had been established by this time in the conflict, which were entrusted with examining the qualifications of prospective surgeons and assistant surgeons subject to promotion.[34]

During the course of the war, 3,344 surgeons would serve in the Confederate army or navy. Of those, 3,237 would serve the army and 107 the navy. The army had one surgeon general, 1,242 surgeons and 1,994 assistant surgeons. The navy had twenty-six surgeons, thirteen passed assistant surgeons, sixty-three assistant surgeons, five assistant surgeons of the war, with the army's surgeon general in charge. Supplementing these ranks were countless "contract surgeons;" employed outside the military to assist as needs dictated, usually after a large engagement or near encampments.[35]

The cost for not only the employ of medical staff, but for all medical appropriations during the war amounted to a staggering $76,000,000, with the army receiving $74,000,000 to the navy's $2,000,000. The Union, on the other hand had only spent $47,352,000.[36] The significant difference between each side's allocations could be explained by several theories. First, most of the battles fought during the Civil War took place on Confederate territory, thereby placing and leaving most all the casualties in and to the South for treatment. As a result of this situation, the South, in turn, probably had to hire many more contract surgeons than the North. In many instances, wounded Federal soldiers were left in the care and custody of the South because they had either been captured, their armies had retreated, or Union forces were unable to cope with them as they further advanced in a campaign. Also, the Confederacy experienced runaway inflation, which drove up the price of medical care. Supplies were limited, and those imported from Europe became scarce with the Union blockade of Southern ports.

Another factor arising out of the conflict involved the creation and administration of hospitals. In 1861, the Confederate Congress had only appropriated $50,000 for hospitals. But, by the spring of 1862, the situation had changed considerably, due probably in large part to Maj. Gen. George B. McClellan's advance on the Confederate capital of Richmond during his Peninsular Campaign. Another reason stemmed from Gen. Robert E. Lee's subsequent rout of McClellan's forces in the Seven Days counteroffensive campaign in the early summer of 1862. During this period, Richmond had twenty hospitals with a combined capacity of handling thousands of patients.[37] However, Congress further recognized in September 1862 that more was needed in the care of the young nation's casualties. In that month, it enacted legislation entitled "An act to better provide for the sick and wounded of the army in hospitals." The measure mandated increased personnel, better living conditions, and rations for the patients.[38]

At the war's start, officials reported sanitation within the hospitals as being deplorable. The overcongestion of the troops led to a proliferation of communicable diseases, caused largely by the lack of proper air ventilation and the spoiling of common water sources because of the improper handling of human and animal wastes.[39] The situation did improve, and by 1863 appropriations were increasing to meet the ever-growing influx and demands of the sick and wounded, along with a new round of legislation further addressing this area.[40] Richmond became the medical center for the South because of its numerous hospitals and its location as the country's medical department.[41] The most notable facility was the Chimborazo Hospital, which could house 8,000 individuals, and in the course of its existence, treated 76,000 patients. In addition, the hospital had five ice and soup houses, a brewery with a capacity of 400 kegs, a bakery which could produce 10,000 loaves of bread daily, 200 head of diary cattle, and several goats. It had the distinction of being the largest military hospital during the war.[42] The Winder Hospital also became an important complex, being able to accommodate a caseload of 5,000 individuals.[43] By war's end, there would be 154 hospitals, compared to barely a handful at its beginning.[44]

The Surgeons

The most prominent of all the Confederate surgeons was Samuel Preston Moore, appointed by President Jefferson Davis as the surgeon general on July 30, 1861.[45] He succeeded two previous doctors as the head medical administrator for the Confederacy and would remain in this position until the end of the war. Without question, this individual did more to advance the wartime medical needs of the South than anyone else. Moore had graduated in 1834 from the South Carolina Medical College. In his early career, he served several western tours of duty and participated in the Mexican War. A native of Charleston, he was considered a highly experienced doctor.[46] Described as, "intelligent, thorough, impartial and industrious,"[47] he was also known as a great organizer and a good administrator, just the individual needed to overcome the country's monumental medical problems. Further, Moore had a reputation as a disciplinarian and believed others in his command should be of the same demeanor.

Moore established many new procedures for Confederate medicine. He set the format of today's general hospital and created a system of medical boards for the purpose of screening prospective surgeons and assessing their abilities in the field. In addition, through his efforts a medical journal was established, the *Confederate States Medical and Surgical Journal*, and published from January 1864 to February 1865. Another important element of his administration involved the requirement that each surgeon keep a log of his sick and wounded. Some surgeons did this, but in the heat of battle and confronted with the countless casualties, it oftentimes fell by the wayside. Those doctors maintaining logs or medical records were often lax in their preparation, much to the criticism of Surgeon General Moore. However, as time would soon prove, the practice of medical documentation would become a critical element, not only in the advancement of medicine, but more important in the treatment of the afflicted.[48]

Although Moore proved quite able to complete the initial challenges of bringing together the semblance of a medical department and accompanying network, the lack of knowledge and training of those surgeons in the field was another story. The South found itself confronted with a lack of all the major essentials with which to wage a sustained confrontation against its opponent. Its most precious commodity, manpower, paled in size, when compared to the North's burgeoning population. In particular, a lack of doctors plagued the South, and, of those available, many were deficient in training and experience. Doctors were oftentimes referred to as ignorant, neglectful, drunk, incompetent, and vague.[49] Several accounts have claimed doctors drank a lot during battles and while performing operations.[50] In some cases, the wounded were known to have raised their gun against an approaching surgeon, out of fear he would do more harm than good. One commentary about the situation stated that doctors killed more men than all of Lincoln's armies.[51]

However, even in light of these criticisms, the Confederate Medical Corps dealt with a caseload and working conditions beyond modern day imagination. For example, following the battle of Murfreesboro, Tennessee, from December 31, 1862, to January 2, 1863, battlefield hospitals became so overcrowded with wounded that many were sent for care to Chattanooga, Tennessee.[52] The conditions were so bad, especially for the doctors, "Some surgeons working at the depot stood so long that their boots had to be cut from their swollen feet."[53] Obviously there were faults with a portion of the South's doctors, but in reality more comments have actually been made in support of their enormous efforts, than to the contrary. Not all were drunks, and most performed their work with great dedication and compassion.[54] On one occasion, a doctor reportedly even captured a stand of colors during a battle.[55] As a whole, they were described as, "a group of courageous men,"[56] whose efforts to the war were significant.[57] The doctors had a horrendous task before them. It was not their fault that medical science had lagged behind the demands of the period. Considering what they did know, and faced with the burdens before them, it could be said their accomplishments were just short of being miraculous.

Their circumstances were often not any better than those of the patients they served. Doctors, too, died of infectious diseases and wounds sustained in battle while treating the fallen. During cold weather, their fingers would sometimes freeze while performing their duties and had to be thawed with warm water.[58] One can only imagine the horror experienced by these individuals, day in and day out, amputating limbs and heaping the remains into large bloody piles outside the operating tents, which then became covered with flies and swarming rodents gnawing away eagerly at the mound. Moreover, the constant smell of death and decomposing body parts and fluids would make the strongest of men prone to drink, if not vomit, and possibly become insane due to the constant exposure. Even before an engagement, they had to ready themselves and their supplies knowing what lay ahead. In some cases, they had to advance into the line of fire in order to provide treatment. Of one small comfort, captured doctors were not considered combatants and accordingly were seldom sent to prisoner of war camps. This arrangement had been worked out between Generals McClellan and Lee prior to the Seven Days Campaign in June 1862.[59]

Union Medical Situation

The Union Army experienced much of the same medical growing pains that the Confederacy did in its efforts to administer to their wounded. That being said, the entrenched Northern army medical establishment proved to be very resistive in changing its procedures to accommodate its casualties. At the war's outset, Dr. Thomas Lawson commanded the Union Medical Corps as the surgeon general. He had served in the department since the presidency of John Quincy Adams, and throughout his tenure seemed more concerned with penny pinching the costs of supplies than in fostering in needed changes. Lawson died on May 15, 1861, and Dr. Clement Alexander Finley became his successor. Finley was a career surgeon and had risen to second in command of the army's medical service. On June 13, 1861, President Lincoln signed into law the creation of the United States Sanitary Commission (USSC) . It emerged largely as a response to Lawson's ignoring, and his lack of comprehension for, the severity of the situation facing him. The Commission wanted to provide better medical standards for the soldiers, and in part, to prevent the nation from experiencing the same horrors experienced by Europe during the recent Crimean War.[60]

Unfortunately, ignorance, jealousy, and politics played heavily upon the North's ability to administer the medical department consistently. In time, Surgeon General Finley was relieved of duty by legislation passed on April 16, 1862, and replaced by Dr. William Alexander Hammond, the choice of the Sanitary Commission, on April 25, 1862. Hammond pushed through many reforms, but fell into disfavor with the medical establishment and Edwin M. Stanton, the Secretary of War. In November 1863, Hammond met the fate of his predecessor. Col. Joseph K. Barnes became the acting surgeon general, followed by his official appointment in August 1864. Barnes remained in charge until the war's conclusion, and he continued on a path of reform much like Hammond.[61]

On the western scene, a similar situation arose especially once the casualties rolled in after the battle of Wilson's Creek, Missouri, in August 1861. By

September, Gen. John C. Fremont, the western Union commander, issued General Order #139 creating the Western Sanitary Commission (WSC), which had been lobbied for by prominent St. Louis citizen Rev. William Greenleaf Eliot. Initially, it ran into conflict with the USSC, but through Eliot's efforts managed to retain its separate identity. The WSC served many useful purposes, promoting clean hospitals, railroad ambulances, hospital boats, and tried to address the plight of the many newly freed slaves, as Union armies in the West advanced deeper into Southern territory. During the war it attended to thousands of soldiers and raised $770,000, in addition to receiving and distributing over $3,500,000 in donated supplies. In contrast to the USSC, which dissolved at the war's conclusion, the WSC remained in existence for another twenty-one years, until Eliot's death in 1886.[62]

Of sad consequence to the everyday soldiers, struggling to survive from battle to battle, the early bickering and misguidance of the medical high command contributed to their illnesses and prolonged their misery. Fortunately, the public made important inroads for the soldiers' well-being through the creation of sanitary commissions, although they were not without their own problems.[63] In the beginning, the Northern army medical command did not follow the progressive measures undertaken by the Confederacy's Surgeon General Samuel Preston Moore.[64] It wasted precious time and energy in attending to the needs of its casualties because of its administrative bungling, and needlessly sacrificed many of its brave men due to such ineptness. Of all the other military advantages weighing in favor of the Union army, its medical department's initial reactions to the medical needs of the troops were a great disappointment.[65]

After a bumpy start the Union Medical Corps became more efficient and learned to better deal with the load of its patients. By war's end it would employ over 11,000 doctors, comprising seven units. Outside of its early administrative problems, hiring competent physicians caused many headaches, much like in the South. The North, also had no better field of doctors from which to select. In time, the situation would change, whereby standards and review processes were put in place to gauge a doctor's competency. This enhanced the patient's survival rate.[66]

Some medical advances were made that had a profound effect on the patient. One example involved Dr. John Sublett Logan, who had enlisted as a contract surgeon on October 25, 1861, attached to United States Army Hospital located in Louisville, Kentucky. He had previously graduated from the Kentucky School of Medicine in 1859, afterwards attending the Jefferson Medical College in Philadelphia, Pennsylvania, for further graduate work. Logan worked in and administered several hospitals during his war years. While assigned to Hospital 13 in Louisville during 1863, the doctor developed a new treatment application for gangrene. It consisted of using bromine on the infected area, and it met with success in arresting this disease. The surgeon general even recognized the doctor's discovery and its importance. Unfortunately, Logan resigned from the army on April 14, 1864, in order to pursue other interests. However, his discovery helped abate probably the most dreaded of all post injury illnesses that had resulted in the loss of many lives.[67]

At the start of the war, the North's medical profession had little regard for sanitation and hygiene, but eventually, through reforms and the urgency of the Sanitary Commission, conditions improved for the sick and wounded. Clean and nutritious food, well ventilated hospitals, and a greater use of such measures as sterile bandages also aided the victim's recovery. Many of these same discoveries and applications were being detected and applied by Southern doctors. However, the North did exceed its rival in other areas. It passed legislation for an ambulance service and had at its disposal sanitary commissions to augment the government's efforts. Further, its hospital network and distribution of medical supplies became very proficient. But, of all lessons to be learned, the most notable were sanitation, ventilation, and clean food for the troops and their ailments.[68]

A Lasting Imprint

All in all, the Confederate medical service did the best it could under the circumstances, and in many cases it tried to improve its services, especially in the areas of sanitation, ventilation, and nutrition. Other important advances were derived out of the war, most notably the keeping of medical logs as to the state of health for not only the sick and wounded, but for the average soldier as well. In time, this accounting would become a standard medical procedure. The current basis of hospitals also originated during this period. The layout of these early care facilities would become an important prototype for the future, which stressed fresh air and cleanliness. There would still be a long road ahead before the refinements of modern medicine became truly visible. More wars would come and go, but in the interim important changes took hold, all for the betterment of the patient. The Civil War would not be the country's last conflict to address these imperfections of society. Nevertheless, at least one great achievement came out of this American tragedy. Simply, a new beginning in the understanding and application of everyday medical practices emerged, a feat truly significant in its own right, which forever left a lasting imprint on the medical profession.

CHAPTER II

"YADKIN COUNTY BOY"

The Land

All lands have a certain provenance unto themselves where the vastness, uniqueness, and the special harvest within define their character. Even the most desolate of places can produce life and sustain its eternal existence. The more common composition contains a variety of elements, which bring forth a new birth with each season, giving the environment not only a balance of what has passed before, but the unfolding of challenges yet to test the present. The ultimate bounty of any soil has been to bear subsistence in all of its many complexities. When examining the productivity from an area, the conventional acknowledgement as to its worth has generally rested in the quality and abundance of its produce. However, the real value of a setting cannot be totally derived from the yield, but more in the making of its people, who for the most part have been molded by their initial roots.

Yadkin County, North Carolina, lies nestled in the Piedmont Region of the state. The word "Yadkin" originates from several possible sources. One version derives from an early scouting party into the area, where the adventurers came upon a settlement called "Yattken Towne" located on the "Yattken River." Several others claim the name was fashioned from the river named "Yattken,"which encompassed a wider area than the present-day county.[1] But local folklore suggests its being a creation of the Siouan dialect, meaning a "place of big trees" or as called by some, the "big tree."[2] The Indian name though seems the most appropriate because it truly described the land, a place where the forests rolled endlessly to the lower levels of the coast and then back again to the higher plateaus of the Appalachians. It appeared like an ocean of enduring greenery.

Before the colonists entered the region, it teemed with an abundant assortment of bounty. Fish and wildlife were particularly plentiful, consisting of turkey, beaver, squirrel, deer, raccoon, muskrat, and mink. Other animals included mountain lions, bears, wolves, elk, and bison. Trout, catfish, and bass ran freely in the streams and rivers. The soil was rich on both sides of the Yadkin River, which allowed for many forms of farming, providing crops of pumpkins, corn, potatoes, and of special import, tobacco. Most spectacular though, from which its name may have sprung, were the trees dotting the terrain, composed principally of red and white oaks, followed by hickory stretching before the naked eye for miles.[3] Being part of the Piedmont, the county drifted at variance in elevation having an average of 1,000 feet above sea level to a high altitiude surpassing 1,500 feet.[4] Yadkin truly represented a place of great opportunity for not only the brave colonists, who would eventually set foot within its boundaries, but also for the young American pioneers following the Revolutionary War.

The People

The life of any land has always been the breath of its people. For a region yet untouched by European civilization, Yadkin overflowed with people at the dawn of colonization. A wilderness brimming with game hosted a Native American population of equal merit, for within the state were 6,000 Cherokee, 1,200 Cheraw, 500 Keyauwee, and 500 Catawba, including the Waxhaw and Sugeree, as well as the Tutelo and Saponi. There were approximately 12,500 Native Americans inhabiting the region.[5] The Indians had existed on this land since time began, and it had produced for them all the necessities of their society. It would seem as if they had been given an eternal right to claim this land of plenty, forever unto themselves. But, as the white man began to peek beyond his coastal confines, a transition would soon follow, forever changing this once truly opulent paradise.

The area saw its first white men in 1673, when a noted trader by the name of Abraham Wood based at Fort Henry, Virginia, which would become the future city of Petersburg, sent a scouting party to the region in hopes of expanding trade with the Indians. James Needham and Gabriel Arthur, both of English descent, led the delegation. The men crossed the Blue Ridge Mountains and gazed upon the Great Smokey Mountains, while on their nine day journey. Arthur, reported on June 18, that his expedition had broken away and ventured south along a trail called the "Trading Path," later to be known as the "Great Wagon Trail." Eventually, they came upon a hollow called the Shallow Ford, which lay before the Yadkin River. By this feat, he and his party had become, in all likelihood, the first white explorers to enter upon this once isolated ground. However, not until 1748, did white settlers come into the county. The first two individuals were Morgan Bryan and George Forbush. Bryan, a Quaker, from Pennsylvania, brought his family to the area and secured a land grant for his claim as recorded on October 27, 1752. The region probably attracted Bryan because he was an Indian trader. Forbush was originally from Maryland and, at one point, had staked roots in Pennsylvania followed by Virginia. The two men did not necessarily come together, but were related through Forbush's daughter, Mary, who wed one of Bryan's sons.[6] Therefore, an initial bond existed between the two families, which no doubt helped forge their mutual survival in this new, but imposing, wilderness.

Other colonists journeyed to theYadkin area during this period, and by 1750, migration increased from the eastern seaboard.[7] The surnames of these newcomers consisted of Davis, Carter, Cresson, Linville, and most notably, a man named Squire Boone, the father of Daniel Boone. The legacy of Daniel Boone, as the country's greatest frontiersman, outside of maybe Meriwether Lewis, William Clark, and Kit Carson remains true even to the present-day. Boone was full grown by the time his family moved to the region.[8] On August 14, 1756, he married Rebecca Bryan, the granddaughter of the county's first settler Morgan. As history would soon show, he moved about frequently, but on many occasions would return to the county.[9] While residing in Davie County, which adjoins Yadkin, he would set out to find an opening over the Appalachian Mountains for migration into the heartland of the country. He would find the previously discovered Cumberland Gap which opened the wilderness of Kentucky. The Gap had been discovered by Dr. Thomas Walker in 1750 while on an exploring expedition in the employ of the Loyal Land Company of Virginia. However, it was Boone, along with two other adventurers by the names of John Stewart and John Findley, who rediscovered the opening in 1769, eventually leading to the settlement of Kentucky and its subsequent statehood. Daniel Boone would accomplish many other notable achievements during his lifetime, but this event probably did more to make him an American folk hero than any other.[10] Finally, he would take up roots in Missouri, where he would die at the age of 86 in St. Charles County on September 26, 1820. In 1845, his body was disinterred and reburied in Frankfort, Kentucky.[11]

In time, the area would become a diverse mixture of numerous European Americans. Most prominent were the English and Welsh from Virginia, the Germans from Pennsylvania, and the Ulster Scots and Quakers hailing from the eastern regions of North Carolina.[12] The newcomers, of course, would begin to leave their own mark upon the land by planting crops, fighting with the Indians, and building forts in order to protect themselves.[13] They also brought their own version of spirituality through their varied religions. The main influences were the Baptists, Methodists, and Quakers. On a lesser note, but of equal importance and within the tight boundaries of faith, the first Masonic Lodge was created in Huntsville, North Carolina, on January 20, 1795, and appropriately called the "Shallow Ford Lodge." Later, it would be renamed "Unanimity Lodge No. 34" and moved to Rockford.[14]

As migration increased, so did the area's population. By 1850 the region, which would soon become Yadkin County, totaled 9,222 individuals, one-half the population of Surry County.[15] On December 28, 1850, Yadkin County was officially established by the North Carolina General Assembly. It was formed out of several present-day counties, primarily the area south and west of the Yadkin River, comprising that portion of Surry County known as "Little Surry."[16] For this reason, half of the 1850 census contained a portion of Surry. On the surface, growth appeared steady, but not rapid. By the eve of the Civil War in 1860, the population of Yadkin County had increased to 10,714. However, when the census was taken in 1870 the population had decreased to 10,697,[17] which at first glance does not appear to be a major fluctuation. But, read in the light of the aftermath of the war, it did measure some importance concerning the effects of the conflict on the county. Between census periods, the decline amounted to only seventeen individuals, which in normal times may not have amounted to much of a difference. Between 1850 and 1860, from a purely number-to-number perspective, the population had increased by 1,492 . It should be remembered, though, that half of the 1850 figure included one-half of Surry County or roughly 9,222 people. If the difference between the two census intervals and a deduction for the other county can be brought back into the equation, then a whole new meaning can be seen in the census of 1870. First by adding the real growth between 1850 and 1860 of 1,492, to the 1870 census, the population should have been 12,206, assuming the same growth rate. The war, though, changed everything. It scarred the land, it scarred the people, and it hindered the county's growth by 14.10 percent, notwithstanding the untold number of casualties from the war. Of special note, it must be recognized many returning soldiers found the county in shambles and totally lacking of any semblance of law and order. In short, many packed up their belongings and moved west.

The Doctor

Family Beginnings and Early Years

The Kinyoun family arrived in Yadkin County from Pennsylvania sometime between 1783 and 1785.[18] Their name has had several different spellings. Most common has been "Kenyon," followed by "Kinyon."[19] In all likelihood, each version has some universal connection or ancestry. The family immigrated from England in 1777, with Joel Kinyoun being the first arrival. He joined Gen. George Washington's colonial army, eventually being promoted to the position of assistant paymaster.[20] His parents were Daniel and Isabelle Etheridge Kinyoun. Joel moved to North Carolina after the Revolutionary War and settled in Currituck County along with his wife, Lorey Gregory Kinyoun. They were the grandparents of Dr. John Hendricks Kinyoun. Lorey predeceased Joel on March 3, 1798, in Currituck County, and he died sometime around 1822 in Rowan County. Next in line was the doctor's father James Kinyoun, a farmer, born on February 4, 1804, in Currituck County, who, on February 12, 1824, married Mary Hendricks, born on October 19, 1801, in Rowan County. Mary died on April 19, 1856 in Rowan County, followed by James on September 19, 1857, in Davie County.[21]

Dr. John Hendricks Kinyoun was born on October 4, 1825, in Davie County.[22] At some point, he moved to Yadkin County, where he resided until after the Civil War.[23] Little has been found concerning his early childhood. One thing has become certain though, and that was his extensive education. He must have been an exceptional student as a young child. At the age of twenty, he attended the Jonesville Academy for five months, followed by two years at the Mocksville Academy. From there, he spent a year at Wake Forest College in North Carolina, followed by his enrollment at Columbia College in Washington, D.C. He eventually graduated with honors from Union College of Schenectady, New York, receiving an A.B. degree. [24] This degree is today's equivalent of a Bachelor of Arts.

Being somewhat of an entrepreneur and obviously wanting to stay within the world of academia, Kinyoun founded a school named the East Bend Academy in Yadkin County upon returning home after graduation. As stated by one individual, it was " located in as fine and healthy a region as there is in our state [North Carolina]."[25] The Academy commenced operations in 1855 and remained in existence for fifty years. On its' opening, he had one associate to assist him by the name of Joseph A. Creel, a Baptist minister. The academy served as a private school for young girls and boys. Within a short period, it flourished rapidly and had an enrollment of 250 students by 1859. Admission costs ranged from $5.00 for reading to $17.00 for instruction in engineering.[26] Traditional courses of the time characterized the curriculum, which consisted of, "English, French, Italian and Spanish, modern languages, and Latin and Greek, ancient languages. The courses included such classics as Caesar's Commentaries, the Latin Testament, and extensive writings from Virgil and Cicero."[27]

While administering the academy, the doctor began the study of law under the tutelage of Judge Richmond M. Pearson, also from Yadkin County, who during the war would serve as a justice on the North Carolina Supreme Court.[28] Kinyoun received his law degree from Columbia University and received admittance to the state bar sometime in the mid-1850s. However, after a brief period of practice, he tired of the work, believing it not to be an honorable profession. Accordingly, not to be detoured in finding a career, he entered Bellevue Medical School in New York City, graduating in 1859, with honors. Once again, he returned to his home county and, on March 12, 1859, began practicing medicine.[29]

At the start of the Civil War, Kinyoun would be one of twelve doctors in the county, and he became known for his particular style of medical application in maintaining extensive logs of patients and those supplies disbursed in their treatment.[30] As soon witnessed by his wartime service, record keeping would not only become his trademark but ultimately a requirement of all Confederate military doctors. During this period, the doctor took as his bride Elizabeth Ann Conrad, exchanging their vows on December 18, 1856, with the Reverend William Turner officiating at the ceremony. She was the daughter of John Joseph and Keziah Harding Conrad,[31] one of the more prominent families of the county, who were slaveholders.[32] John and Elizabeth would have seven children, named as follows in the order of their birth: Mary Elizabeth, Joseph James, Lula Alice, Flora Ridings, Estelle Keziah, Nellie, and John Conrad. Three of the children died before the age of five; Mary Elizabeth, Nellie, and John Conrad.[33]

Aside from all the terrain and genealogy which went into the making of this man, a simple fact remained; he arose above the challenges confronting him. Born into an agrarian family, he most likely would have been bound to the same earth as his forefathers, except for his inner stirrings. His continuing inclination towards knowledge made him a new kind of explorer onto a new and expanding plateau. He was different from those of his own kind, who had ventured westward from the sea in hopes of finding a new, virgin, yet fertile land to work. Kinyoun symbolized a special outcrop of the "American Experience." This young man sought a better understanding for not only himself, but of his surroundings. However, he along with a new generation of similar young countrymen would become a new wave of pioneers. These were a folk not of the same pretense of those before them, but the beginning cornerstone of a new generation of Americans. They were determined to expand a dream beyond a simple plot of land. John Hendricks Kinyoun and many others like him embodied a new breed on the eve of the Civil War.

The Hollow Drumbeats Of War

The drumbeats of war have beckoned forth the youngest and best of each new generation. Unfortunately, wars have always seemed to follow a set pattern of recruitment. The inherent problem with them has been the span of time between conflicts. Just as the horrors of one engagement have faded from memory, another conflict has erupted, bringing into its merciless clutches the next contingent of eager budding patriots. As a result of this recurring, but often ignored and ill gotten lesson, roughly 15 billion individuals have perished as a result of war, accompanied by all of its attendant calamities.[34] It could be said with the sincerest of empathy, that nature, even at its most civilized state, has never advanced beyond the consumption of its own creation.

With the conclusion of the War of 1812, the United States finally won its right to stand among all nations as a country unto itself, free of its colonial past, the trappings of the British Empire, and living in post revolution freedom. A new sense of confidence was now instilled, whereby the country could go onward as a fledgling equal among the world's powers. One contradiction remained and that was the very essence of the country's existence as set forth in the Declaration of Independence, the Constitution and the Bill of Rights, "that all men are created equal." A profound statement, which truly defined this new nation, except for its greatest omission and oversight. This neglect was the enslavement of tens of thousands of blacks, who had been forcibly transplanted to the American continent as sub-human servants, in the eyes of their kidnappers.

In testimony to this dilemma, a dramatic event would occur upon the national stage in 1859, and within the confines of just over a year, it brought the country to the brink of civil war. The incident involved John Brown's raid on the United States Armory at Harper's Ferry, Virginia, on October 16. Brown had become infamous for his rabid style of abolition during the Missouri-Kansas Border War between 1854 to 1859, a conflict that sought to make Kansas either a free or slave state within the Union. He achieved notoriety early in the conflict when he and several of his sons butchered five supposedly pro-slavery farmers in retaliation for a raid on Lawrence, Kansas, by Missouri Border Ruffians on May 24, 1856.[35] The South condemned his actions, but in the North, he became the symbolic radical leader behind the national movement to free all slaves across the land.

At Harper's Ferry, Brown attempted to seize its armaments and equip a 200,000 man slave army. His intention was to march upon the South, liberating all the indentured within his path and most likely killing all white slaveholders. Such an occurrence had taken place in 1831, when a black slave preacher named Nat Turner led an unsuccessful revolt in Virginia. The rebellion was eventually put down, but at the cost of over 51 whites and the hanging of Turner. Ever since this uprising, the South had had a psychosis about this reccurring, especially in those slave states where the slave population exceeded or equaled that of the slaveholders. With Brown's raid, the South once again found itself suffocating with fear over the possibility of another slave insurrection and the thought of being murdered in their very beds by their servants. A chilling thought. Federal troops overtook Brown at Harper's Ferry. He was arrested, tried, convicted, and sentenced to death by hanging, which was carried out on December 2, 1859.[36]

Unfortunately, the execution of John Brown did not calm the fears of the South, nor soften the North's abolitionists. The North felt betrayed by Brown's death because the trial took place in the Southern slave state of Virginia, which caused many Northerners to believe a fair and impartial setting had not been afforded to the accused. As a result, the country took the final steps towards polarization. The newly formed Republican Party chose Abraham Lincoln of Illinois as their candidate for president in the 1860 election. The Democratic Party, predominantly of the South, could not formulate a united party ticket, which led to a splintering and the emergence of several other candidates. With this factionalism, the South viewed its partnership within the Union nearing an end, especially in the event of a Lincoln victory.[37] As fate would determine, he won the election, and within a month, the country began to unravel, with South Carolina's secession on December 20, 1860, followed by ten other slave states, including North Carolina on May 10, 1861.[38]

In truth, North Carolina did not necessarily want secession. If anything, it may have felt an obligation to stand behind its fellow slave states after the Confederate victory at Fort Sumter, South Carolina, on April 14, 1861. Secession may have been prompted by President Lincoln's call for 75,000 Federal volunteers for a ninety-day enlistment period in order to put down the rebellion, following the attack on Fort Sumter. Historians have debated this fact as the reason why North Carolina, along with Virginia, Tennessee, and Arkansas left the Union. The thought of Federal troops going across their territory to attack and subjugate another state led to their decision to join the Confederacy. This would soon prove to be a painful course for North Carolina because by war's end, it contributed the most troops in defense of the "Cause," in comparison to all the other Southern states. Consequently, it's suffering was increased by the shear number of its troops and the resulting demands on its citizens.[39]

The Twenty-Eighth North Carolina Infantry Regiment

Kinyoun enlisted into the Twenty-Eighth North Carolina Infantry Regiment on June 18, 1861, shortly after his state's secession. His fellow soldiers elected him captain of Company F, which in due course would become known as "The Yadkin Boys," in honor of their home county.[40] The company conducted its military training near the grounds of his East Bend Academy. As captain, he kept a special small leather-bound notebook, measuring 3 ¾ x 5 ¾ inches, inside of which he listed each man's height and other pertinent information about the men under his charge. Of particular interest, he did not list his height or those of 1st Lt. T.V. Apperson, 2nd Lt. Jno. H. Poindexter, or 3rd Lt. W.A. Marler, the officers of the company. Most of the soldiers were of average height around 5 feet 10 inches, with one individual as short as 5 feet 4 inches and two topping out at 6 feet 2 inches.[41] In addition, he maintained records on the outfit's marching positions and times, noting, "common time was 90 paces; quick time, 110 paces, and double time quick step, 165 paces."[42] Lastly, the booklet contained a log of various items, mainly food, donated to the company by friends and family over a period of roughly thirty days, between July 19 and August 17, 1861. The assortment of gifts were varied and included such things as three baked chickens, ten fruit pies, two gallons of whiskey, beans, one mutton, two and one-half gallons of cordial, one peck of beets, nine pounds of bacon, two gallons of cucumbers, one bucket of pickles, three and one-half gallons of whiskey, nine chickens, countless loafs of bread, and a lot of dry wood.[43]

To say the least, the troops were well supplied in this early part of the war, especially as to whiskey. Their diet appeared varied and assorted, almost gourmet in its content. However, as the conflict stretched into more months and years, these plentiful staples would soon become more like luxuries. The home front found itself ill prepared to support and supply a 750,000 man army and at the same time provide for their own needs. Few men remained to plant and harvest the crops. Further, as the Union Army invaded the South, they laid waste to planted lands in order to prevent the produce from reaching the Confederate soldiers and sustaining the war effort.

In the beginning, the provisions seemed good and reflected the patriotism of the population. One other observation from this list of men's heights, marching paces, and bounty can also be gleaned from Kinyoun's early documentation of general rudimentary information. For some reason, he felt compelled to compile this data concerning his company. Obviously, his educational background, coupled with having been a school superintendent, doctor, and a lawyer, influenced this routine course of conduct. As a result of this environment, it can be understood how the eventual evolution of his Medical Diary became such a well-formulated record. It could be surmised, that humans have always been a product of their own setting.

The regiment had an initial enlistment of 1,199 men,[44] and was referred to as the "Mountain Boys."[45] Kinyoun's Company F had a total of 152 original enlistees. Many of the recruits were related as either brothers, cousins, or otherwise, which was not an uncommon occurrence in other companies and even regiments. The captain would command several of his own relatives within the unit. Of special mention, one person composed a battle hymn about the Twenty-Eighth Regiment sung to the popular tune of "Dixie Land." The last stanza went, "When Kinyoun comes with his Yadkin Boys, He'll put an end to the Yankees' joys."[46] During this early stage of the conflict, although a doctor, Kinyoun served as a combatant rather than a provider of medical services.[47] Company F fought in some of the more significant battles of the conflict. These included, but were not limited to, Ox Hill, Cedar Run, Gaines Mill, Chancellorsville, and Gettysburg. At Gettysburg, on July 3, 1863, they advanced on the "Angle" which climaxed in the infamous "Pickett's Charge,"[48] where twelve men were killed and ninety-two wounded in the assault.[49] The "Angle" has also become synonymous with the saying, "The High Water Mark of the Confederacy." This phrase means the highest point north the Confederate army advanced into Northern territory during the course of the war.[50]

Fortunately for the captain, he had previously left the company and missed the battle of Gettysburg. For some unknown reason, Kinyoun tendered his resignation from the company on March 28, 1862, to become effective on April 2, 1862.[51] However, one explanation has surfaced that might shed light on his leaving the command. It has been documented he did not necessarily quit, but was voted out as captain by his own men. Apparently, an individual named Apperson disliked him and conspired to become his replacement, because of a mutual contempt between them. There were three such men in the company by this last name, Capt. T. or Thomas V. Apperson, P. A. Apperson and John A. Apperson. Odds would support Capt. T. V. Apperson as the party in question, since he was second in command of the company under Kinyoun.[52]

Accordingly, his service with the unit lasted roughly nine months. When formed, the regiment had been transferred to Wilmington, North Carolina. Most of their duties were light in nature and centered around guarding railroad bridges on the Wilmington and Weldon lines, coupled with some post chores. On one particular occasion, they paraded through the city, and as written by a reporter for the *Wilmington Journal,* "Almost as we go to press the Twenty-eighth Regiment moves-down Second Street, with steady tramp, the long line of their bayonets gleaming in the sun, and the firm bearing of the men indicative of determination and giving promise of gallant service when called upon."[53] Other praises would be bestowed on the outfit, and it could almost be said the war appeared remotely distant. However, by the spring of 1862 things began to change when the Union Army invaded the state from the coast. The Twenth-Eighth transferred into action following the aftermath of the battle at New Bern on March 14 and assisted with the Confederate retreat. After this engagement the regiment went through a reorganization process.[54] Kinyoun may have been removed from command at this point, or he left on his own accord. Regardless of the reason, his leaving became a blessing, because it caused him to miss the Gettysburg campaign. Consequently, this change may have saved his life, in light of the regiment's position on the last day of that horrific battle.

Winder Hospital Service

After his departure from Company F, Kinyoun served as a doctor at the Winder Hospital from April 1862 to August 1863, and possibly several others located in Richmond, Virginia. He may have administered a hospital as far away as Vicksburg, Mississippi. His new assignment was reported to be similar in stature to the South's largest hospital, Chimborazo, also located in the Confederacy's capital. Winder Hospital opened sometime in April 1862, which roughly coincided with Kinyoun leaving the Twenty-Eighth North Carolina Infantry Regiment the month before. The facility and its complex comprised 125 acres and contained six divisions, with each having a separate medical officer in charge. It could provide services for upwards of 5,000 patients.[55] Concerning its amenities, there were few places for the sick and wounded in comparison. A description of the time stated it had, "the most approved Russian steam plunge, and shower baths, water closets, a bakery, an icehouse, a sixteen-acre hospital garden worked by convalescents, and sixty-nine cows. Two canal boats were used to obtain additional food for the inmates."[56] The hospital would serve the South well, although there has been a varied report as to its quality of food, but on the other hand, it's extensive sanitation practices received some credit.[57]

In 1863, Winder armed 300 of its more fit patients and sent them to the army for guard duty, in order to bolster the lack of manpower in the Confederacy.[58] However, as the war dragged on and the casualties increased, the government decided, at the urgency of General Lee, to close the hospital and several others so as to provide more medical personnel in the field. To the South's great misfortune, Winder caught fire on January 31, 1864, and seven wards were destroyed at a cost of $50,000,[59] ironically the same amount as the South's initial appropriation in 1861 for all its hospitals.[60]

It should be remembered that Gen. George B. McClellan commenced the Union Army's Peninsular Campaign against Richmond in the early spring of 1862, which led to a tremendous influx of casualties for the South. If the general could have succeeded in his plan and captured the Confederate capital, then the war might have ended earlier. With this onslaught, the South generated all its vital resources towards stopping the Union army. Obviously, Kinyoun witnessed McClellan's assault and may have thought his services could have been of greater value to the Confederacy as a doctor at the newly constructed Winder medical center. Regardless of the whys, he remained stationed there for over a year, and through its enormous caseload, he most likely gained a significant amount of invaluable experience for what lay before him.

The Sixty-Sixth North Carolina Infantry Regiment

At some point, whether by his own designs and wishes or merely because of the dictates of the war, the doctor embarked upon yet another military role. In all likelihood, he may have left Winder Hospital at General Lee's insistence for more medical officers to be sent into the field to cope with the ever-growing number of casualties. One thing remained certain; the shortage of men and supplies now being experienced by the Confederacy. In July alone, the country had lost countless men at the battles of Gettysburg and Vicksburg. Gettysburg accounted for more casualties, whereas Vicksburg resulted more in a greater total loss of manpower. This loss may have been more costly because with its surrender, the South was now cut in half by the North's control of the Mississippi River, denying it of needed men and supplies from the Trans-Mississippi Region. As a way to alleviate this dilemma, in early August 1863, James A. Seddon, Confederate Secretary of War, issued an order to consolidate several units into a new regiment designated as the Sixty-Sixth North Carolina Infantry Regiment. The order was rescinded however, largely because such a decree ran contrary to established military protocol. Later the same month, another attempt failed because the order tried to place troops together from different states, begging a question of state sovereignty or as more commonly called "states rights," the leading cause of the war. But, on October 2, by way of a special order, the regiment was officially mustered into service as the Sixty-Sixth again, composed of the Eighth Partisan Rangers Battalion, the Thirteenth Infantry Battalion, and Blackmer's Company, also known as the First Company A, Salisbury Prison Guard. Although another definitive source has held the First Company A did not join the unit.[61] The command structure consisted of Col. Alexander D. Moore as its chief officer, accompanied by Lt. Col. John H. Nethercutt, Maj. Clement G. Wright, W. G. Williams as adjutant and John H. Kinyoun, Assistant Surgeon, as his initial staff officers. Over the course of the next twenty months Kinyoun would write his Medical Diary.[62]

The regiment had in excess of 1,100 men, and it established an impressive record during its two years of existence. In early October, it became attached to Brig. Gen. James G. Martin's brigade and moved to the region of Cape Fear along the North Carolina coast. It remained in that area until the middle of February 1864. Towards the end of March, the army transferred the Sixty-Sixth to Weldon and then Plymouth, followed by a move to Tarboro. Eventually arriving at Petersburg, Virginia, around May 12, the regiment was attached to Hoke's Division in Kirkland's Brigade and immediately put on picket duty outside the city's limits. Shortly thereafter, on May 13 and 16, it came under enemy fire for the first time at Port Walthal Junction, and reports stated, it acted "gallantly" on each occasion.[63]

After this engagement, the unit fought at Bermuda Hundred, north of the James River, and for the first time, sustained significant casualties. The Sixty-Sixth remained in this position until June 1, when it was hurriedly rushed to the battle of Cold Harbor in support of General Lee's counter measures to curtail General Grant's maneuvers to capture Richmond. Grant made a headlong charge against the well-entrenched and barricaded Confederates on June 2, and within the shadow of a few minutes, sustained over 7,000 casualties.[64] This attack would be known as one of the most costly mistakes of the rebellion. The Sixty-Sixth was at the forefront of this assault, but fortunately did not suffer many losses. But the next day on June 3, the last day of the confrontation, a bullet struck Colonel Moore in the neck, mortally wounding him. With his death, John H. Nethercutt became the regimental colonel.[65]

The unit stayed at Cold Harbor for roughly another ten days. On June 14, it moved, along with the rest of Hoke's Division, to Petersburg, arriving on June 16. The transfer occurred in response to General Grant's further press south from Cold Harbor. General Lee sensed Grant's intentions and dispatched troops to the city in hopes of avoiding its capture, which would have been devastating to Lee's defenses at Richmond. Petersburg was a very important railroad connection, and its loss would in effect leave Richmond without this vital line of supply. Therefore, the defense of this city equaled the capital in importance from a strategic standpoint.[66]

On its arrival at Petersburg, the regiment immediately saw action by repeated charges from Union troops. Each time, they were successful in holding out against superior forces and in driving the enemy back. Grant continued to press the Confederate lines for almost a week.[67] In one charge, he lost upwards of 700 men, which Dr. Kinyoun described to his wife in one of his letters. After several more assaults, the general realized the futility in his tactics and settled in for a siege of the city, just as he had done earlier at Vicksburg. Grant may have been concerned about more frontal attacks because of his recent debacle at Cold Harbor. Another staggering loss in Union men could have signaled dire consequences, not only for the campaign but his leadership as well.[68]

The Sixty-Sixth remained at Petersburg throughout most of the rest of the year. It participated in numerous skirmishes during this period and witnessed a most terrible daily bombardment from the besieging Union forces. At the battle of the Crater on July 30, the regiment reportedly was sent into the mêlée to help avert a Union breakthrough in the Confederate lines. Another significant encounter occurred during their involvement at the battle of Fort Harrison, north of the James

River near Richmond, on September 30. Unfortunately, the attack was ill planned and executed, leading to a stalemate between the sides. Fort Harrison represented a strategic position in the siege's defenses and probably on account of this factor, the troops remained there as a counter balance to the Union forces occupying this stronghold.[69]

Finally, on December 22, the unit received orders commanding it to Wilmington, North Carolina, by way of train. The trip turned out to be very cold and uncomfortable for the troops. On arrival, it proceeded to Sugar Loaf near Fort Fisher, in defense of the last open seaport in the Confederacy, which had still not been closed by the Union naval blockade. For the next three weeks, the Sixty-Sixth participated in the defense of the fort in hopes of preventing its capture. However, on January 15, 1865, the North seized this last bastion of Southern international commerce. The regiment held its position, but on February 18 retreated to Wilmington. Unfortunately, in short order, the Union army advanced upon them, resulting in the city's abandonment on February 22, incidentally the birthday of George Washington.[70]

The Final Days and Surrender

On March 7, 1865, the regiment arrived at Kinston, North Carolina, and, over the next few days, fought in several skirmishes. Two major encounters occurred, the first at Southwest Creek followed by Wise's Fork (Wyse Fork). The latter resulted in a slaughter of Hoke's forces. From these battles, the unit moved back to Kinston, and then in a few days continued to Goldsboro, and later to Bentonville, where it participated in the last major battle of the Civil War. Confederate Gen. Joseph E. Johnston had recently been directed to pull together several displaced regiments and form a new army to confront Union Gen. William T. Sherman's march through the Carolinas. The Sixty-Sixth, now consolidated into this new fighting force, clashed with Sherman's army at the battle of Bentonville from March 19-21, 1865. Johnston, being outnumbered, outgunned and outmaneuvered during the conflict, pulled his troops from the area. On the evening of March 21, the regiment, along with the rest of Hoke's Division, retreated to Smithfield, North Carolina.[71]

At Smithfield, Johnston attempted to regroup his beleaguered forces, waiting for Sherman's next advance. Apparently, Sherman was equally tired, and the Confederates were able to gain three weeks of relative quiet. However, on April 10, the Union general headed out from his position near Bentonville and once again began the pursuit of Johnston. Within three days Sherman had captured Smithfield and Raleigh, the state capital. There, word reached them of Lee's surrender several days earlier on April 9 at Appomattox Courthouse, Virginia.[72]

Within a few days, Johnston realized the obvious and commenced negotiations with Sherman for the surrender of Johnston's forces. During this period, the devastating news of Lee's surrender created a mass exodus of desertions among Johnston's ranks. Colonel Nethercutt surmised that the Sixty-Sixth had in effect already laid down their arms with General Lee on April 9, because the regiment still technically belonged to the Army of Northern Virginia. In any event, Johnston saw the writing on the wall and surrendered his army on April 26 at Durham Station, North Carolina, which effectively ended the Civil War. Dr. Kinyoun also surrendered at this time. By the end of May, the Sixty-Sixth had disbanded, and of those remaining, a total of sixty-four men or less than 1 percent of the unit's original strength, had been paroled and told to go home, a mere shadow of its once proud 1,100 plus members.[73]

The True Meaning of Freedom

Any experience on the scale of the Civil War will bring out many special moments and revelations, when confronted with such terrible, trying, and moving challenges. As will be subsequently seen in **Chapter III *"Abraham The First,"*** the best examples of those feelings for Dr. Kinyoun have been set forth by way of a study of his letters sent home to his wife. Besides these documents, the doctor made a personal observation upon returning home. The paper has been included because it captures his initial reactions to the South's defeat in Yadkin County. It should be noted he refers to his father-in-law, Joseph Conrad, as "grandfather," a patronage of the times. Limited editing has been done in order to enhance its readability, but not so as to diminish the insightful reflection of the times. In cases where the writing could not be discerned, three dashes have been inserted.

The importance of this essay is that it exemplifies the realities now confronting all sectors of the civilian populace. The African American has finally been freed, and the consequence of this new element in Southern society has a stark new meaning upon all its citizens. Sadly though, the long sought freedom of the slaves does not carry with it any type of constructive transition. For now, they must find a place for themselves in this white dominated country. In particular, these new emancipates were almost left totally stranded to support themselves. They had no monetary savings, no assets, formal education, personal possessions, or any significant job skills by which to make a living. Everything on or about them, including the very clothes on their back, belonged to their master. Yes, they were now free and rightfully so, but plainly and painfully, it revealed the price of such an accomplishment was nothing more than a very hard beginning.

The document contains two parts. The first sets forth an account of what the doctor encountered upon his arrival home and how the freedom of the former slaves has impacted the white man's former way of life. The second portion has a more personal and truly human side to the consequence of freedom, as witnessed by Kinyoun, upon the slaves being told about their newfound freedom. One can see the anger, confusion, and hesitation experienced by both whites and blacks at the slaves' liberation. Without question, a new revolution had taken place, not only in a military sense, but also and more important in a social and economic sense, which forever changed the nation in the early spring of 1865.

An Incident of the Emancipation

It was in the summer following the disbanding of the Confederate forces, when one by one of the remnant of the gallant band came home to take up anew [their work in building up their homes] the burdens of civil responsibilities. They found but little left, it was a sad spectacle, houses burned, plantations devastated, labor system completely disorganized – ruin and desolation on every hand. It was discouragement from the very first.

The soldier and those too old to go to war, thought that the establishment of the military government in the seceding states – made no good, and that the victorious Yankee not content with fighting it out on the field with sword and musket saw yet another opportunity to punish and humiliate the Southern people. That this fear was unfounded in our section was soon apparent. The Negro, who had been quiet and peaceful, all during the four years of strife, should now become arrogant – insolent - and ---on mischief was not remembered.

It had its beginning at the time and following General Stoneman's invasion through North Carolina, wherein much property was destroyed, or confiscated. Nearly if not all the planters living in the line of his march was made to suffer in many ways. All the horses and mules were taken – and here and there the jaded and worn out mounts were turned loose. Many of the young Negro men, some through inclination others through persuasion went with the army – and for a time were not heard of, but after a while, tiring of their new found freedom, they began to return. As soon as they did, began to preach the gospel of freedom – and to stir up all the animosities which had been engendered by the presence of the Union Soldier.

It was natural that the whites would attempt to repress such, as it was feared another uprising as occurred in Haiti and Jamaica would be reenacted. As a consequence, many a good citizen was haled [*sic*]before a military tribunal to answer the charge made by some of those bigoted Negroes. The majority of these were fairly investigated and the decision made by it was nearly always made in the best interests of the community, and unless the act was of the most flagrant nature, it was not taken cognizance of.

Things were drifting along in this manner for some time when my grand father [*sic*] Joseph Conrad, one day sent word for all the blacks to come to the front porch. After a little while they began to saunter in until at last nearly all were present. Uncles Sam and Stephen sat on the front steps and then Dawn, Rans, Jerry and Amos and --- with their wives and numerous progeny – extending themselves in a semicircle all around them. Grandfather told them that he had something of importance to say to them and he wanted all to listen closely to what he had to say. He said that General Lee had surrendered to the Union Army and the war was ended. He then took a paper and read to them President Lincoln's Emancipation Proclamation and when finished reading told one and all that they were free, that he had no further authority over them and they could now do whatever they pleased, and more over must --- for themselves.

He said this is all, - slowly they dispersed, some muttering to themselves – or asking questions one to another about their freedom. Uncle Stephen hobbled away with the crowd leaving Uncle Sam, setting just where he was. He say, "Mar's [*sic* – Master] Joe, You say ise [*sic*-I am] free?" "Yes Sam you are just as free as I am." "Does you mean to say dat [*sic*- that] old Sam has to go to work, and make his own libbin [*sic* – living]?" "Yes Sam that's what your President Lincoln says – you must now look out for yourself. The war is over, the Confederates lost, and whatever Mr. Lincoln says we must all do."

Uncle Sam sat in a deep study – presently he looked up, scratching --- white wool and says, " Mar's [*sic*—Master] Joe who raised you? Who played with you went fishin and hunted with you, and took care of you when yous [*sic* – you was] a boy – waznt it [*sic* – was not] me?" Grandfather says, "Yes Sam." "haint [*sic* – have not] I always been with you ever since you were a baby – and haint [*sic* – have not] I nursed you when you were sick?" Again came the reply, "Yes Sam." "does you goes and says dat [*sic* – that] ise [*sic* – I am] free and has to go to work as old as is, and has to leave you and Miss Betsy?"

"Now look-a hear Mar's [*sic* – Master] Joe ise [*sic* – I am] gonin [*sic* – going] to tell you right now I aint [*sic*] a gonin [*sic* – going] to do it, de [*sic* – the] rest of de [*sic* – the] fool niggers can go – and go where ---day [*sic* – they] pleases – but for me Ise [*sic* – I am] gonin [*sic* – going] to stay right here – and you has to take care of me."

Tears were slowly trickling down the old man's face, his voice was choked, his head was bowed down as with a great load. Grandfather bowed only at the last --- "Yes Sam" – and tears were falling. I could not then appreciate just what the --- of all of it meant. To see Uncle Sam and Grandfather crying was something I never knew before. Finally Grandfather said, "Sam you can stay here as long as you want and I will take care of you." And he did.

The chief mourner at Grandfather's funeral was his Negro boy companion, his adviser and his life long faithful friend, Uncle Sam.[74]

After the War

With the war over, the soldiers who participated in this long and horrible conflict returned home to loved ones and friends. For those soldiers in the Union Army, their homecoming was filled with joy in the victory and the ability, for those not severely maimed by the experience, to begin anew. Not so for their beaten counterparts, the Confederate soldiers, for most of this war had transpired on Southern soil, leaving the land scarred for decades. In many areas, the houses had been destroyed, the fields laid to waste, and the livestock either stolen or run off. The once proud South now mirrored a mere shadow and a faded memory of itself.[75]

Yadkin County had suffered, too, especially in the end when Union Maj. Gen. George H. Stoneman destroyed portions of the county as part of Sherman's invading horde in April 1865.[76] Its wounds were not as deep as other parts of the former Confederacy, but it had definitely changed in comparison, prior to secession. Sadly, Dr. Kinyoun may have lost more than some of the other returning "Yadkin Boys." At some point in the early stages of the conflict, his house had burned to the ground. Only a few surviving personal items had been retrieved from the blaze, which possibly included some of his letters home to Mrs. Kinyoun. Other soldiers returned to nothing, too, but at least they were able to return, as opposed to the countless men who died.

Seeing things devastated and the countryside now overrun with Northern carpetbaggers, freed slaves, and a whole host of other radical changes, Kinyoun packed up the family's belongings and, accompanied by his wife and children, Joseph and Lula, moved to Johnson County, Missouri, in either 1866 or 1868.[77] Why he chose this particular county has remained a mystery and almost an irony, because it had experienced a large amount of bloodshed and civil unrest during the war. It had been one of the major counties supplying partisans who belonged to the most notorious of all the guerrilla leaders, William Clarke Quantrill.[78] For Kinyoun to take up new roots in this place almost bordered on the bizarre because it, too, had been ravaged in many ways. On arriving in Johnson County, the doctor settled the family in a little town lying directly east of the county seat, Warrensburg, by the name of Centerview.

Although a physician, he initially split rails for a living in order to feed his family. Imagine a guy, who was a professional by trade, having just spent four horrific years facing death daily and living in the worst of all possible human conditions, and being forced to abandon his place of birth. Next, imagine a doctor, out of necessity, having to embark upon one of the hardest of physical tasks as a means of support, absent maybe the digging of ditches. In today's world, such a path would be considered amazing, if not unbelievable.[79]

In time, he started practicing medicine again, and, in short order, his practice mushroomed, due in part to his being the only doctor within a radius of forty miles.[80] Unfortunately, his wife Elizabeth died of pneumonia in 1872. Dr. Kinyoun took a second wife by marrying Mrs. Martha E. (Carmichael) Hammond, whose husband had been killed during the Civil War.[81] Although they never had any children, she proved to be a good stepmother to the Kinyoun offspring.[82] Kinyoun maintained correspondence with his family and friends in Yadkin County. In one letter, the doctor spoke about a large grasshopper plague in 1875. To his surprise, the newspaper in Winston, North Carolina, printed the story.[83]

During the 1890s, the United Daughters of the Confederacy bestowed upon him the prestigious Southern Cross of Honor, reserved for those veterans of the long ago South, who had offered commendable service to their former country.[84] Another interesting aspect surrounded his apparent interest in following national and international current events. Kinyoun was a Baptist by faith and a Democrat by politics.[85] In time, he became active in the community and served as president of the Warrensburg State Normal School for a term of six years. Of further notice, he at one time served as the mayor of Centerview.[86]

The doctor was highly regarded in and around Johnson County, and upon his passing, on July 27, 1903, the testimonies to his character were overflowing.[87] The Masonic Corinthian Lodge No. 262, A.F.A.M., with the Rev. Frank Russell officiating, administered the funeral service on behalf of the family.[88] As a final farewell to the good doctor, the lodge enacted this final testament in recognition of their fallen brother:

In Memory of Dr. Kinyoun

On Monday night members of Corinthian Lodge No. 262, A.F.A.M. adopted the following resolutions on the death of their late Brother, Dr. J. H. Kinyoun of Centerview:

Whereas, It has pleased Almighty God in His inscrutable providence to take from the walks of men our aged Brother John H. Kinyoun who died at his home in Centerview, Missouri. July 27, 1903.

Resolved: That in the death of Brother Kinyoun his family has lost a beloved husband and father, this Lodge a worthy member, and society a respected citizen.

Resolved: That we, his Brothers, ever bear him in fraternal remembrance, emulating his virtues, and devote ourselves, to the time honored tradition of our fraternity.

Resolved: That we extend to the bereaved family of Brother Kinyoun our sincere sympathy in their sorrow, commanding them to the loving care of The All-Wise God of Grace and Comfort.

Resolved: That a copy of these resolutions be placed upon the record of this Lodge, a typewritten copy be tendered the family, and a copy each be handed the county papers with request that they be published.

Respectfully Submitted.

G. J. Donnell
W. R. Delaney
W. R. Shipp.[89]

It could be said many men go to their graves barely knowing themselves, but believing they had lived the best life possible within their means. Other men may think they knew themselves, but in truth never believed for sure. But, John Hendricks Kinyoun may rightfully have believed, he lived his life to the fullest, in light of his surroundings.

CHAPTER III

"ABRAHAM THE FIRST"

Historians have always prized old letters, especially those from wartime experiences, viewing them as a true expression of a period's sentiments. The following correspondence written by Dr. Kinyoun to his wife, Elizabeth Ann, offers some very revealing insights about the Civil War. In all, six letters have survived, but with only two being complete. Unfortunately, through the course of time, they have become brittle as well as appear to be fire damaged. The Kinyoun household in Yadkin County, North Carolina, did burn to the ground early in the war, but prior to the date of this correspondence. There must have been another fire, because four of the letters contain burn marks. Surprisingly though, even with this defect the bulk of the lot has remained fairly readable. The most important factor, however, is their dates. In each case, the damage did not erase the date logged at the top by the doctor. Therefore, at least their age has been legitimized by this ever so subtle detail.

Probably, the most noteworthy thing about these transcriptions can be understood from the old adage of "People come and go in this world, but words will always last forever." Nothing could be more insightful to the true sentiments of a soldier in the field during this dark period in American history than those set forth in these writings by this Confederate surgeon. These writings have been presented as an accompaniment to the Diary. Between them, a clearer image of this man's experiences and ability to maintain his medical accounting of sick and wounded can be seen and the lengths he took to achieve this task. A feat in itself, let alone the knowledge contained in each set of documents aptly depicts his state of mind as well as his accomplishments.

Before viewing the letters, it should be understood that the doctor wrote them in a somewhat choppy style. At the end of a sentence, he would insert a comma, followed by a dash, and then capitalize the next beginning thought as a new sentence. The letters have been edited in order to make them more readable. Specifically, where a comma has been inserted, combined with a dash and beginning capitalization, all has been changed to reflect a complete thought. However, periodically a dash was correctly used as a rite of transition, and it has been left in place.

The word [*sic]* has been inserted followed by a clarifying word, signifying a variance between present-day grammar and spelling. Further, words have been put between brackets [ ] in order to smooth out the writing. Concerning his spelling, at times it has an archaic format, in particular the words "cannot," "something," " a while," and a few others. Where this has occurred, the proper spelling has been inserted, instead of denoting the error by using the word [*sic*], so as to make it's reading easier. Another distinguishing feature within the letters is Dr. Kinyoun's capitalizing and underlining of words, as a form of seriousness and often as a point of anxiousness. None of these alterations have been made to change the content of these documents in anyway.

One must understand the conditions in which they were written. Most likely, the letters were drafted under the rather stark elements of weather. The doctor may have been ill, hungry, and tired at the end of his daily routine. Given the workload of patients he dealt with, it can be assumed there were never enough moments to think ahead or compose beforehand any precise or orderly collected thoughts. By the same token, he probably did not have the time to proofread their contents because of his surroundings. In deciphering them, the handwriting has a general legibility. However, in a few instances the words were not discernable, and therefore, three dashes, "---" have been set forth, meaning an unknown. In addition, the transcribed word or phrase may be in error because the writing has been scribbled, leading to a best guess. But, taken as a whole, these expressions of a soldier's inner conscience from the past have provided a true revelation of what goes through an individual's mind when thrust into a state of war.

Concerning those letters damaged by the fire, an ellipsis " . . ." followed by the term "Burned" denotes the beginning of a destroyed section of the letter. The word "Restart" followed by another ellipsis ". . ." marks the end of the damaged section and the continuation of the letter. Occasionally, words have been placed between brackets, [ ] to complete a missing or burned phrase, word, or section.

In order to fully understand these letters and their meaning, a format has been devised with the intent of enhancing the reader's comprehension. Hopefully, this layout will not only clarify the obvious contents, but also what they meant in light of the political and military developments occurring during the war. First, the actual letter has been set forth in the section titled "**ORIGINAL,**" where the actual document has been presented. Next follows the "**TRANSCRIPTION**" section where the original has been transcribed into a clearer text. Lastly, an "**ANALYSIS**" has been presented explaining the actual or underlying meaning behind the doctor's reflections, discussing his hopes, anxieties, and observations. Of no surprise to the student of this great conflict, one will find an amazing parallel between these letters and present-day classroom teachings, and those discussions set forth in American History books about the country's second revolution.

ORIGINAL

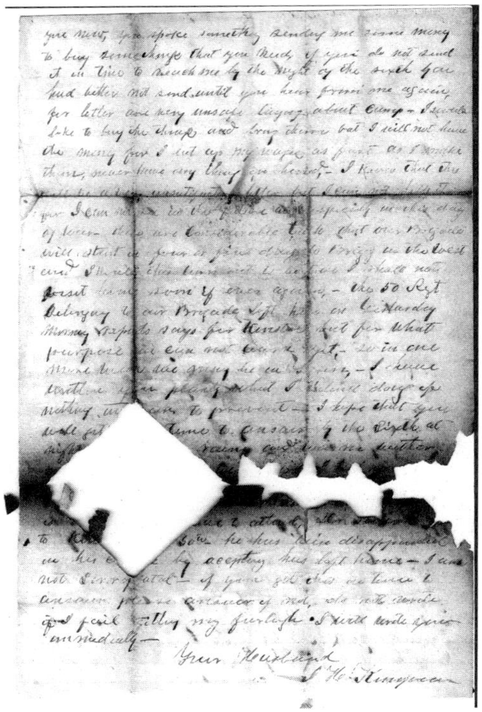

TRANSCRIPTION

Camp 66 NC Regiment
Martin's Brigade
Nov 29, 1863

My dear and beloved Wife

I have concluded to write you this morning though I have not a word that would interest [you] in the least. We hear very little and see nothing as we are in the woods surrounded by a swamp and creek and have chills a plenty of them. I feel some better this morning and getting better of my Jaundice, though not well yet. I have the sinus headache about twice per week lately.

You have heard of Bragg's defeat or fall back? I fear that we have been worsted badly at this battle. This means the war [will be] longer and longer for we have to fight it out.

The principal reason of my writing you this letter this morning [is] that I intend trying for a furlough to come home and my calculation is "---" succeed in getting it approved to start from Wilmington on the moorning of the Seventh, Monday "---" and would like for you to ". . ." Burned. Restart ". . ." the colonel will approve my "---" but doubt whether Gen Martin "---", for I have an Asst Surgeon that Martin does not like much, and had him removed from the 50th Regt and [Dr.] Potter put here, though I inted to try him myself and if I feel I must fail, I will fail trying.

I want ot come home very badly in this month; it is all in darkness at present. The reason I wrote you now, you spoke something [about] sending me some money to buy some things that you need, if you do not send it in time to reach me by the night of the sixth you had better not send until you hear from me again, for letters are very unsafe laying about Camp. I would like to buy the things and bring them but I will not have the money for I eat up my wages as fast as I make them, never have anyting in hand. I know that this will be a very unsatisfactory letter, but I cannot help it for I cannot see in the futhere and especially in this day of war.

There are [is] considerable talk that our Brigade will start in four or five days to Bragg in the West and should this turn out to be true I shall not "---" home soon if ever again. The 50th Regt belonging to our Brigade left here on yesterday morning, reportssay from Kinston, but for what purposes we cannot learn yet. So in one more week we may be in Tenn.

I have written you plenty what I intend doing if nothing intervenes to prevent. I hope that you will get the time to answer by the sixth ". . ." Burned. Restart " . . ." Dr. Potter is going to Kinston [with the] 50th, he has been disappointed in his orders by accepting, [but] has left hence. I am not sorry at all. If you get this in time to answer, please answer, if not, do not send. If I fail getting my furlough, I will write you immediately.

Your Husband
J H Kinyoun

ANALYSIS

The doctor begins this letter by commenting to his wife of nothing to write about. He does mention his somewhat ill health, in particular having the "chills," which could mean a malaria condition such as intermittent fever. Kinyoun also discloses he has jaundice, a common affliction during the war. Next, he asks her if she has heard the bad news concerning the break through of Union forces under Gen. Ulysses S. Grant from the siege of Chattanooga, Tennessee, in late November. The loss of this battle for the city will eventually lead to Gen. William T. Sherman's campaign for Atlanta, Georgia, culminating in his March to the Sea in late 1864.[1] One interesting observation concerning this question lies in the speed of communication between Chattanooga's capitulation and the date of his letter. The time frame between both represents only a few days. This represented a remarkable achievement, given the unsophisticated nature of communication at this period in the country's history.

Continuing, Dr. Kinyoun states he will be seeking a furlough home, if at all possible. He has been assigned a new assistant surgeon named Potter who has fallen into disfavor with Maj. Gen. James Green Martin. The general was from North Carolina and was credited with raising more troops during the war's first year than any other Confederate state. In addition, his soldiers were the best supplied.[2] The doctor next states he may have to stay put, leaving the impression of having to deal with the newly transferred physician. His thoughts then drift back to the prospect of coming home. Apparently, Mrs. Kinyoun had written him previously, hoping he might be able to secure some needed supplies for the family's well-being. This could have been possible because during the war, the soldiers were in part expected, and compelled out of necessity, to supply themselves. In order to fulfill this requirement, purveyors or sutlers would follow the troops and their encampments selling them every possible ware.[3] The doctor might have been able to purchase those items for her through this process. Not unlike the troops, the home front experienced many shortages and discomforts as well.

However, he remains uncertain as to his furlough. He further relates not having any money and cautions her not to send any money prior to the night before his leaving because others might steal his mail while away.

The remainder of the letter returns to the war effort and the possibility he may be transferred with the regiment to Tennessee, in order to shore up Gen. Braxton Bragg's beaten forces,[4] which might result in his death. He does refocus on the present and expresses in a roundabout manner his dislike for Dr. Potter, who has been transferred to the Fiftieth Regiment. The letter concludes by again hoping for a furlough. Kinyoun's last passage states he will contact her immediately, if it does receive approval, leaving one with the thought that this war of now almost three years seems to be wearing greatly on this man. Based on the tone of the following correspondence and its close proximity to the date of this writing, it appears unlikely he was granted leave to visit his family.

ORIGINAL

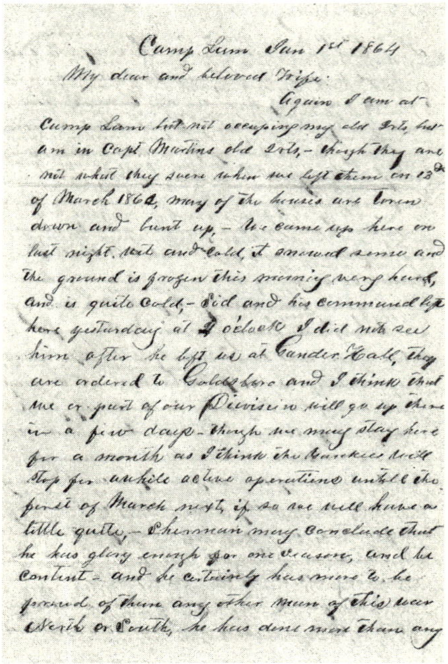
Camp Lam Jan 1st 1864
My dear and beloved Wife:
Again I am at
Camp Lam but not occupying my old Qrts, but
am in Capt Martins old Qrts, - though they are
not what they were when we left them on 13th
of March 1864, many of the houses are torn
down and burnt up, - We came up here on
last night, wet and cold, it snowed some and
the ground is frozen this morning very hard,
and is quite cold, - Sid and his command left
here yesterday at 2 o'clock I did not see
him after he left us at Cander Hall, they
are ordered to Goldsboro and I think that
we or part of our Division will go up there
in a few days - though we may stay here
for a month as I think the Yankees will
stop for awhile active operations untill the
first of March next, if so we will have a
little quite, - Sherman may conclude that
he has glory enough for one season, and be
content - and he certainly has more to be
proud of than any other man of this war
North or South, he has done more than any

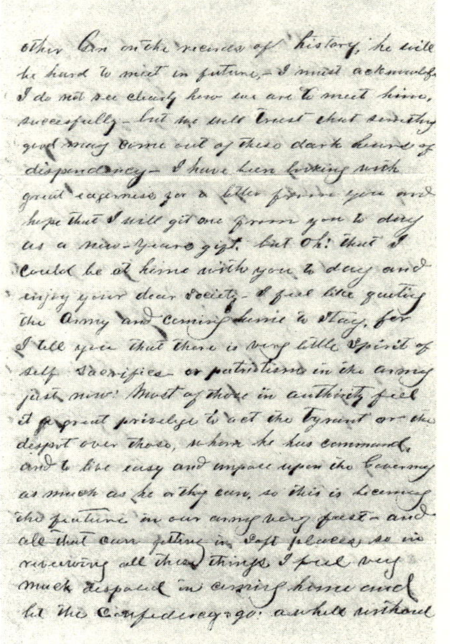
other Gen on the records of history, he will
be hard to meet in future, - I must acknowledge
I do not see clearly how we are to meet him,
successfully - but we will trust that something
good may come out of these dark hours of
dispondancy - I have been looking with
great eagerness for a letter from you and
hope that I will get one from you to day
as a new-years gift. but Oh! that I
could be at home with you to day and
enjoy your dear society - I feel like quiting
the Army and coming home to stay, for
I tell you that there is very little spirit of
self sacrifice - or patriotism in the army
just now: Most of those in authority feel
it a great privelige to act the tyrant or the
despot over those, whom he has command,
and to live easy and impose upon the Government
as much as he or they can, so this is becoming
the feature in our army very fast - and
all that can getting in soft places, so in
reviewing all these things I feel very
much desposed in coming home and
let the Confederacy go: awhile without

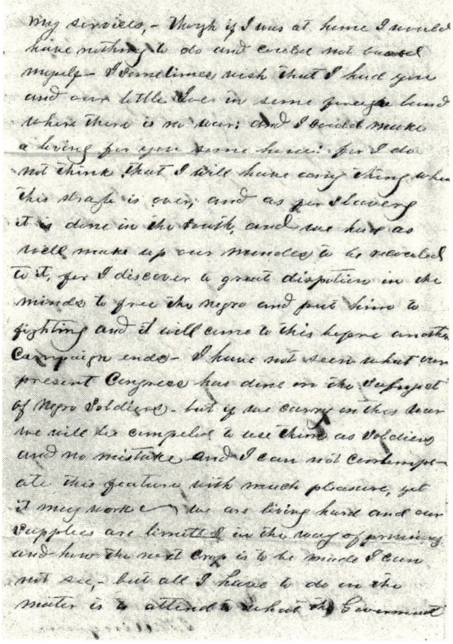
my services, - though if I was at home I would
have nothing to do and could not travel
myself - I sometimes wish that I had you
and our little ones in some foreign land
where there is no war: and I could make
a living for you some how: for I do
not think that I will have any thing when
this strafe is over, and as for slavery
it is done in the South, and we had as
well make up our minds to be reconciled
to it, for I discover a great disposition in the
minds to free the negro and put him to
fighting and it will come to this before another
Campaign ends - I have not seen what our
present Congress has done on the subject
of Negro Soldiers - but if we carry on this war
we will be compelled to use them as soldiers
and no mistake. And I can not contemplate
ate this feature with much pleasure, yet
it may work - We are living hard and our
supplies are limitted in the way of provisions
and how the next crop is to be made I can
not see, - but all I have to do in the
matter is to attend to what the Government

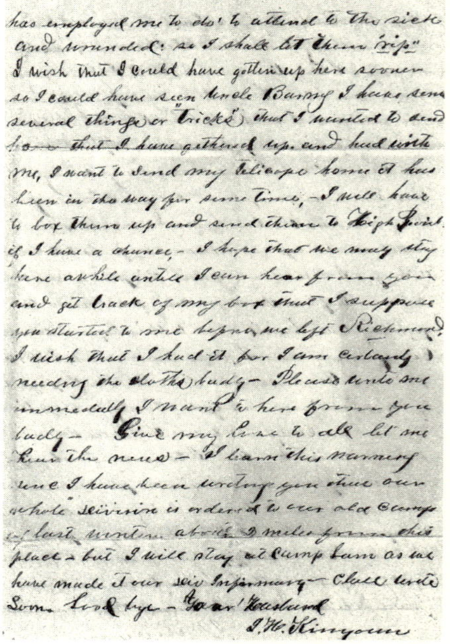
has employed me to do: to attend to the sick
and wounded: so I shall let them "rip"
I wish that I could have gotten up here sooner
so I could have seen Uncle Barny I have some
several things (or "tricks") that I wanted to send
home that I have gathered up. and had with
me, I want to send my Telicope home it has
been in the way for some time, - I will have
to box them up and send them to High Point
if I have a chance, - I hope that we may stay
here awhile untill I can hear from you
and get track of my box that I suppose
you started to me before we left Richmond.
I wish that I had it for I am certainly
needing the clothes badly - Please write me
immediatly I want to here from you
badly - Give my love to all let me
hear the news - I learn this morning
since I have been writing you that our
whole division is ordered to our old camp
of last winter about 2 miles from this
place - but I will stay at Camp Lam as we
have made it our sick Infirmary - Shall write
soon. Good bye - Your Husband
J. W. Kinyoun

TRANSCRIPTION

Camp Lam Jan 1864

My dear and beloved Wife

Again I am at Camp Lam but not occupying my old qrts. [quarters], but I am in Capt Martins old qrts., though they are not what they were when we left them on 13 of March 1862. Many of the houses are toren [*sic*] down and bunt [*sic*-burned] up. We came up here on last night, wet and cold, it snowed some and the ground is frozen this morning very hard, and is quite cold. Sid [also known as Sidney] and his command left here yesterday at 2 o'clock I did not see him after he left us at Camden Hall. They are ordered to Goldsboro and I think that we or part of our Division will go up there in a few days.

Though we may stay here for a month as I think the Yankees will stop for a while active operations until the first of March next, if so we will have a little quite [*sic*-quiet]. Sherman may conclude that he has glory enough for one season, and be content-and he certainly has more to be proud of than any other man of this war North or South, he has done more than any other Gen on the records of history, he will be hard to meet in the future. I must acknowledge, I do not see clearly how we are to meet him, successfully – but we will trust that something good may come out of these dark hours of despondency.

I have been looking with great eagerness for a letter from you and hope that I will get one from you today as a new years gift. But Oh! That I could be at home with you today and enjoy your dear society. I feel like quiting [*sic*] the Army and coming home to stay, for I tell you that there is very little spirit of self sacrifice [*sic*] or patriotism in the Army just now! Most of those in authority feel it a great privilege to act the tyrant or despot over those, whom he has command, and to live easy and impose upon the governing as much as he or they can, so this is becoming the picture in our army very fast – and all that our getting in soft places, so in remembering all these things I feel very much disposed in coming home and let the Confederacy go, a while without my services. Though, if I was home I would have nothing to do and oculd not "---" myself.

I sometimes wish that I had you and our little Joe [his son Joseph James Kinyoun] in some far away land where there is no war, and I could make a living for you somehow for I do not think that I will have anything until this sacrifice is over. And as per slavery, it is done in the South, and we had as well make up our minds to be resolved to it, for I discover a great disposition in the minds to free the Negro and put him to fighting and it will come to this before another campaign ends. I have not seen what our present Congress has done on the "---" of Negro soldiers, but if we carry on this war we will be compelled to use them as soldiers and no mistake and I can not contemplate this feature with much pleasure, yet it may work.

We are living hard and our supplies are united in the way of provisions and how the next Crop is to be made I cannot see - but all I have to do in the matter is to attend what the government has employed me to do, to attend to the sick and wounded: so I shall let them "---". I wish that I could have gotten here sooner so I could have seen Uncle Barney. I have some several things or "Tricks" that I wanted to send home that I have gathered up and I have with me. I want to send my telescope home it has been in the way for sometime. I will have to box them up and send them to High Point, if I have a chance. I hope that we merely stay here a while until I can hear from you and get track of my box that I suppose you started to [send] me before we left Richmond. I wish that I had it for I am certainly needing the cloths badly. Please send some immediately, I want to here [sic] from you badly. Give my love to all and let me here [sic] the news. I learn this morning since I have been writing you that our whole division is ordered to our old Camp of last winter about 2 miles from this place – but I will stay at Camp Lam as we have made it our Div Infirmary. Please write soon. Goodbye – your husband

J. H. Kinyoun

ANALYSIS

As with most all individuals, New Year's Day has a way of making us reflective of the past, but more importantly mindful of the future. By this letter dated January 1864, Dr. Kinyoun was no different. In the first part of it, he writes that his regiment has been assigned to winter quarters. The housing has fallen into disrepair, the weather has soured, and he has missed the opportunity of seeing Sid [Sidney]. This individual appears frequently in his correspondence. Sid may have been Sidney Francis Conrad, a cousin and the son of John Joseph and Keziah Harding Conrad. He served in Company F of the Seventieth North Carolina Infantry Regiment.[5] Continuing on and of some surprise, the doctor expresses an admiration for Union Gen. William T. Sherman, believing him to be the best general of either army. He points out the South will have a difficult time in containing him, once hostilities pick up in the spring. As the year 1864 would soon demonstrate, this opinion of the general will ring true, as Sherman marches through the Deep South in the fall, after the collapse of Atlanta, Georgia, on September 2.[6] This is a rather remarkable insight because the general, although known, had not yet achieved household name status.

The doctor somewhat in the same negative tone, then speaks of deserting and returning home, which seems amazing for a medical officer, or one who has given an oath to put others above self. This statement alone reveals the growing desperate situation confronting the Confederacy, especially in the minds of its defenders. Some of this sentiment can possibly be attributed to his loneliness, combined with the bleakness of winter, and the prospects of a never ending war. However, of particular interest, he complains about the officers treatment of the regular soldier. Kinyoun states they act like "tyrants" and "despots." Armies and navies have oftentimes fallen victim to the arrogance of their commanders, resulting in desertions, uprisings, and mutinies.

Of astonishing revelation, he writes of one dramatic way to stop the future advance of Northern troops. He recommends the slaves be freed and put into arms.

The doctor indicates others, probably fellow soldiers, feel the same way, and the sooner the Confederate Congress acts, the better for the Cause. Although, he does point out not to truly like the idea. Again, expressing his predictions, he states that such will happen before the end of another campaign. By this comment, he might be saying the South needs more manpower or possibly he has begun to realize victory may be doomed absent such an event. A fact well known, the North had a much larger population and could more easily fill the depleted ranks of its armies, as opposed to the South. Even with this advantage the North had begun theprocess of mustering African Americans in defense of the Union, especially noticeable after President Lincoln issued the Emancipation Proclamation in late 1862, and put into effect January 1, 1863. By this period in the war, the casualties had become horrific on both sides. However, the South had a limited reserve of men to resupply its empty ranks after each devastating battle.

Another reason behind this statement, in 1862 and 1863, the Confederacy had labored for foreign diplomatic recognition, in particular from England and France. To some degree, these countries initially did support the South, but the issue of slavery and the South's inability to secure a decisive victory on Northern territory prevented this event from occurring. Maybe, Kinyoun was hoping such a change in his nation's politics might still gain them foreign recognition and possible military intervention. As time would show, foreign recognition never materialized, but in the waning days of the Confederacy, an act was passed seeking to enlist the slaves.[7]

In the final passages of the letter, he reiterates the severity of camp conditions and the scarcity of supplies. He has resigned himself at this point to fulfill his duty as a doctor and administer "to the sick and wounded," instead of deserting as expressed earlier. By this time in the war, the South was being slowly strangled to death by the Union naval blockade, which explains to some degree the lack of provisions. The blockade originated in part out of Union General in Chief Winfield Scott's Anaconda Plan. One of its elements called for the combined usage of the navy and army in sealing off all Southern ports and internal waterways, thereby suffocating the Confederacy, as if in the death clutches of the large snake bearing its name.[8] Other reasons for the shortage stemmed from the Confederacy's lack of a large manufacturing complex to sustain its war efforts. The South's economic base was agrarian, opposed to the more industrialized North. Sadly, Kinyoun looks to home, as opposed to the army, for clothes and other needed articles of subsistence.

The doctor mentions something about what he called "tricks" and wanted to send it or them home. The meaning of "tricks" has escaped definition. Possibly, he had procured some type of illegal contraband against army regulations. Kinyoun states he will be sending home his telescope, which demonstrates by its possession, he was more advanced scientifically than some of his peers. However by returning it, he most likely has become too busy to star gaze as a pastime or lost interest, given his surroundings. In closing his letter, he asks for news from the home front, gives his love to all, and at the same time, states his unit has been moved to another location near the Divisional Infirmary.

ORIGINAL

Camp 66th NC Regt
March 8th 1864

My dear and beloved Wife:

I again seat myself to
write you a line, though I passed my usual time of
writing, I had nothing of interest to write and I have not
been a much of a condition to write you, as I have
been afflicted with torticollis or wry neck or
plainer still "Crick in the neck" - I have been troubled
with it considerably but have the consolation of know
ing it not to be very dangerous and think that I will
soon be well again of this affliction, - I had the happiness
of receiving your short but interesting letter by yesterday
mail written on the third of the present month, - it
was interesting because it brought the glad tidings
of yours and [illegible] good health, this is the happiest
moments that I ~~[illegible]~~ enjoy in camp to learn that
you are well, and I was also delighted to see in it
that you thought that Sidney would visit me before
a great while, I would be very glad to see some one
from home for this I scarcely ever see in this command
I am rather unfortunately situated in this respect, it
is much more pleasant to be in a command where some
visit the neighborhood but such is not my case in this,
We are getting a long very well here in camp, our
regiment is reenlisting for forty years or during
the war, I do not think that we will be called on
by our Congress or our County to renew our enlistment, for should it continue until the forty years

are out the most of us will be old enough to quite the
arts of war and return our mother dust, though I
do most ardently think the struggle will be over or the
most of it this year, and my reasons for so thinking
are that I think that Abraham the first will allow
an election to come off in the North nex Nov and
should he be defeated, I think they will commence
reflecting upon the magnitude of the war and the greate
difficulty attending our subjugation and will make
us some propositions for settlement, but should
he be elected and not defeated I can not see where
the end will be - for if he is re-elected the Democr
ats of the North will supporte his administration as
they have done all the time - the war will grow more
and more cruelle longer it continues, there will
be very little mercy shown on either side from
this out, - that premeditated and uncivilized raid
on Richmond with a pledge to murder Jeff Davis
and Cabinett, is inexcusable and should not escape
punishment by our authorities, and we should make
all that we take pay the out rage! - We have
one more brigade sent down to this place Gen
Kempers Virginia Brigade they have gone down
the river to Smithville near Fort Caswell. There
is still a rumor that we will be sent off in
a few weeks but it is only rumor, we can not
say what will be done - I still think that we
ought to be sent out in more active servce for
this Brigade has never seen any service yet

We are having fine weather though entirely too dry
having very little rain, I fear that we will have
too much rain in the months of April & May again.
We are having much talk in camp about W. W. Holden
being or anouncing himself as a candidate for the
next Governor of North Carolina - I hope that Vance
will agree to run against him though it is talked
that Vance will not run, but I think he will and
if he does we shall beat mr Holden, - there is a
great cry in the Army, if Governer Vance will put
in to the army all the Melitia officers and Magestrates
Constables & Debuty Sheriff between 18 & 45 he
will secure the vote of the whole Army from our
State, I hope that he may give up some of these
useles Characters that have been doing nothing so
long at home for the Army - and make them take
their arms awhile and let them learn the difference between
staying at Home speculating and marching the soldiers
march - I was glad to hear of the flourishing condition
of your school I hope that you will do much good in
teaching the young idea how to shoot, - I hope that
you enjoy yourself in teaching for I know well that
I would enjoy it so much better than in this miserable
life in which I am placed Oh! deliver me from
this idle camp life, you have no pleasure in any
thing, save discharging your duty, - the balance is
irksome and demoralizing and enervating to all
of a mans nature, - I feel like that I would take
much delight in doing any thing that would be work
if I could only have a country independent once more

I was glad to learn that Joe had paid a visit
to Salem, - I must suppose that he saw much to
talk about, and tell him he must build him
a Gasometer against I can come home again. -
I hope if Sidney does not get to come that
you will write me, and give me a long letter -
there are many conscripts coming in to the
camps a long now - Judge Pearson has desided
the Substitute clause of the Law and has went
against all others judges that have desided
on the subject - he will be sick of this yet - and
will give thousands that he had given a different
opinion - I have not recieved any letter from
Lemuel yet - cannot hear a word from
him. - I written Eliza last week -
I will close - though I hope that I may have the
happiness of seeing Sid before long
Give my love to all our family -

Your husband
John H [illegible]

TRANSCRIPTION

Camp 66th NC Regt

March 8th 1864

My dear and beloved Wife:

I again seat myself to write you a line, though I passed my usual time of writing. I had nothing of interest to write and I have not been a [in] much of a condition to write you, as I have been afflicted with tortibollia or dog neck or plainer still "Crick in the neck." I have been troubled with it considerably, but have the consolation of knowing it not to be very dangerous and think that I will soon be well again of this affliction.

I had the happiness of receiving your short but interesting letter by yesterday mail written in the third of the present month. It was interesting because it brought the good tidings of yours and Joe [*sic* – Joe's] good health. This is the happiest moments that I enjoy in camp to learn that you are well, and I was also delighted to see in it that you thought that Sidney would visit me before a great while. I would be very glad to see some one from home for this I scarcely ever see in this command. I am rather unfortunately situated in this respect, it is much more pleasant to be in command where some visit the neighborhood, but such is not my case in this.

We are getting a long very well here in camp, our regiment is reenlisting for forty years or during the war. I do not think that we will be called on by our Congress or our Country to renew our enlistment, for should it continue until the forty years are out the most of us will be old enough to quite [sic-quit] the arts of war and return our mothers dust. Though I do most certainly think the struggle will be over or the most of it this year, and my reasons for so thinking are that I think the Abraham the First will "---" an election to come off in the North next Nov and should he be defeated. I think they will commence reflecting upon the magnitude of the war and the great difficulty attending our subjugation and will make us some propositions for settlement, but should he be elected and not defeated I cannot see where the end will be – for if he is re-elected the Democrats of the North will support his administration as they have done all the time. The war will grow more and more "---" longer to continue. There will be very little mercy shown on either side from this out.

That premeditated and uncivilized raid on Richmond with a pledge to Murder Jeff Davis and Cabinet, is inexcusable and should not escape punishment by our authorities and we should make all that we take pay the outrage! –

We have one more brigade sent down to this place, Gen Kemper's Virginia Brigade they have gone down the river to Smithville near Fort Caswell. There is still a rumor that we will be sent off in a few weeks but it is only rumor, we cannot say what will be done. I still think that we ought to be sent out in more active service, this Brigade has never seen any service yet.

We are having fine weather through entirely two days having very little rain, I fear that we will have too much rain in the months of April & May again. We are having much talk in camp about W. H. Holden being or announcing himself as a candidate for the next Governor of North Carolina. I hope that Vance will agree to run against him though it is talked that Vance will not run, but I think he will and if he does, we shall beat Mr. Holden. There is a great cry in the Army, if Governor Vance will put into the Army all the Militia officers and Magistrates, Constables & Deputy Sheriffs between 18 & 45 he will scare the lot of the whole Army from our state. I hope that he may give up some of these useless characters that have been doing nothing so long at home for the Army – and make them take their armies a while and let them learn the difference between staying at home speculating and marching to soldiers march.

I was glad to hear of the flourishing condition of your school I hope that you will do more good on teaching the young, the idea how to "---" . – I hope that you enjoy yourself in teaching for I know well that I would enjoy it so much better than in this miserable life in which I am placed. Oh! Deliver me from this idle camp life, you have no pleasure in anything, save discharging your duty. The balance is inhumane and demoralizing and "---" to all of a man's nature. I feel like that I would take much delight in doing any thing that would be work, if I could only have a Country independent once more.

I was glad to learn that Joe had passed a "---" to "---". I must suppose that he saw much to talk about, and tell him he must build "---" a "---" against I can come home again. I hope if Sidney does not get to come that you will write me, and give me a long letter. There are many conscripts coming in to the Camp "---". Judge Pearson has decided the Substitute Clause of the Law and has went against all those judges that have deseded [*sic*-descended] in the subject – he will be sick of this yet – and will give thousands that he had given a different opinion. I have not received any letter from Samuel yet, "---" hear a word from him. – I written [*sic*-wrote] Eliza last week. I will close – though I hope that I may have the happiness of seeing Sid before long.

Give my love to all our family.

Your husband
John H. Kinyoun

ANALYSIS

The doctor commences this letter by stating to his wife that his delay in writing has been due to an illness. Although having been ill, he seems more positive or even happy in his thoughts, glad to know his wife and son Joe are in good health. He comments his pleasure to learn that Sidney may soon visit and wishes he could see other people as well. Camp life has improved since January, which could be attributed to the passing of winter and the arrival of better conditions or weather. Of some humor though, he comments that most of his regiment has reenlisted for forty years, which would make everyone a very old man at the end of such time. On a different note, he expresses some hope for a political solution to the conflict should Abraham Lincoln not be reelected as president. However, he remarks that, if "Abraham the First," as he calls Lincoln, would be successful in his election bid, then the situation will progressively worsen. Kinyoun points out the Northern Democrats will rally behind Lincoln, until the war ends one way or another. In truth, Lincoln was in jeopardy of not winning a second term. The prolonged struggle and mounting casualties made him an unlikely survivor. Even as late as July and August, with Northern troops bogged down at Petersburg, Virginia, and in northwestern Georgia in the campaign for Atlanta, his chances seemed slight at best. It was not until the fall of Atlanta, that the North's conscience changed, leaving it to believe victory might be at long last possible, which reaffirmed their faith in Lincoln and secured his reelection.[9]

Kinyoun expresses his outrage at an assassination attempt upon Confederate President Jefferson Davis. The doctor, in this passage, was referring to the ill-fated raid on Richmond, Virginia, between February 28 and March 4, 1864, by Maj. Gen. Hugh Judson Kilpatrick and Col. Ulric Dahlgren. Dahlgren was killed during the campaign. Reportedly, documents were found on the colonel's body outlining a plot to assassinate the Confederate president. This discovery became public on March 5, as published in the *Richmond Daily Examiner,* and further enraged the South. Obviously, Kinyoun was expressing the same sentiment.[10]

The doctor then writes of the deployment of another brigade, but points to their lack of experience and comments they should be sent out on patrols to gain experience. Politics enters his thoughts again, as he addresses the question of who will be the next governor of North Carolina, W. H. [*sic* W. W.] Holden or incumbent Zebulon B. Vance. Governor Vance appears to be his candidate, but he states the governor should compel the local magistrates, constables, and deputy sheriffs into the Confederate ranks. The issue of the peace officers' worth to the home front had been of some question within the state and, as the doctor comments; they would be of greater service to the war effort, if on active duty. Vance would win, but Holden would become governor in the early reconstruction era.[11]

The letter returns to a more personal moment. He writes about the boring nature of camp life and longs to be free of its confinement. Apparently, he had just received correspondence from his wife, talking about the success of her school and the antics of son Joe. Prior to the war, Kinyoun had operated a school, so possibly during the war, she had followed in his footsteps.[12] Once again, he hopes Sidney will soon visit him. Camp life was extremely grueling, conditions were poor, supplies in short order, and idleness never ending, unless a unit was sent into combat. Kinyoun obviously did not enjoy the everyday mundane routine of military service. Although, as historians of this period have also noted, nor did anyone else.

On concluding, the doctor once more delves into the political situation at home. He speaks about the Substitute Law and a recent ruling by Chief Justice Richmond Pearson, under whom he once studied law. Apparently, Kinyoun did not agree with the opinion and thinks the judge, too, will eventually regret the decision. Substitute laws were a unique form of wartime legislation, whereby one individual could buy his way out of military service by paying another to substitute for him. Hence, the word "substitute" evolved as the name for these types of laws during the war.[13]

ORIGINAL

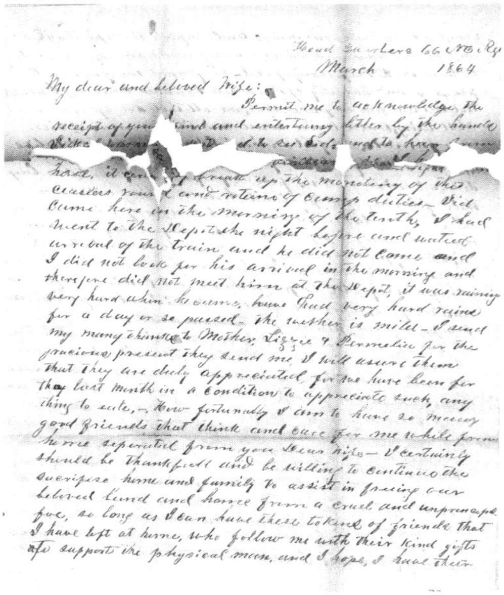

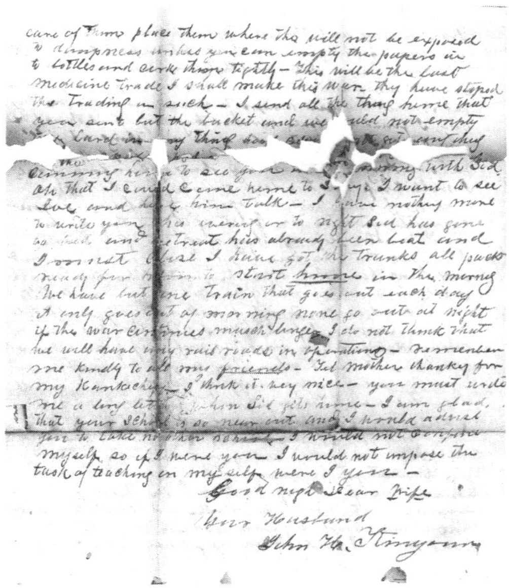

TRANSCRIPTION

Head Quarters 66 NC Regt.

March 1864

My dear and beloved Wife:

Permit me to acknowledge the receiving of your kind and entertaining letter by the hands [of] Sid "---" was "---" to see Sid and to hear from "…" Burned. Restart "…" heard, it can only break up the monotony of this ceaseless round and routine of Camp duties. Sid came here in the morning of the tenth, I had. I had went [gone] to the Depot night before and waited arrival of the train and he did not come and I did not look for his arrival in the morning and therefore did not meet him at the Depot, it was raining very hard when he came, have had very hard rains for a day or so passed.

The weather is mild – I send my many thanks to Mother, Lizzie and Permelia for the gracious present they sent me. I will assure them that they are duly appreciated for we have been for the last month in a condition to appreciate such, anything to eat. Now fortunately, I am to have so many good friends that think and care for me while from home separated from you Dear Wife. I certainly should be thankful and be willing to continue the sacrifice [of] home and family to assist in freeing our beloved land and home from a cruel and unprincipled foe, so long as I can have these tokens of friends that I left at home, who follow me with their kind gifts to support the physical man, and I hope, I have their prayers to sustain, encourage and support the spiritual and inner man. What our army needs nearly as much or more than their daily food – they need the fervent prayers and humility of the whole Christian Church. I would [wish] that this war was only over that, we all that are spared and still living, could come home and the reunion with our families. "---" feel us though, I would "--- to live "…" Burned.

Restart "…" desire to destroy all the private property that they can lay their filching and puntated [sic-punitive] hands [on]. They will soon or later be over taken in their high course of wickedness. There has [have] never [been] a people that have escaped a just and righteous punishment for their base and cruel deeds, then if mine never has escape how will the Yanks escape. They will be punished and I think before another fall, they will have administered a potion [*sic*-portion] and I hope a great potion [*sic*-portion] of it.

I have been around with Sid some, we went to the Theater two nights, one night I saw Hamlet played and the next celebrated play called the "Honey Moon". Sid seemed to be well pleased, though he will tell you all about it, when he gets home. He leaves in the morning I wish that he could have stayed longer with us, but he said that he had made arrangements to meet the buggy at High Point. I think that Sid has some notion to come to this regiment, though I did not persuade him for

"---" take his own choice as we do our "---" in life.

Sid gave me one hundred dollars that you sent by him for me to buy you some things, so today [Monday] I and Dr. Wiseman went down to Town today and thought that we would buy our wives something to send home, but we failed. I thought that I would get you that dress that you wrote me about sometime since, but they did not have a piece of Calico that I would buy for a Negro to wear, so I did not buy any. I found "---" nor had they any spool thread of "---" not "---" you anything at "..." Burned. Restart "..." in sending "---" so many things of comfort to me. I will keep the hundred dollars that Sid give me and will wait an opportunity of buying you something after the first of April, they do not want to trade anything now, until after April. I believe that they have layed [*sic*] their goods away and will bring them out after the first of the next month. I will try to get my money changed for small bills, five and under, though it will be a difficult job in this Town. I feel like I wish that we had no money at all for it is aggravating anyway you "---" it, you cannot keep it when you want to buy anything and now you cannot get it off of hand, so it is a pest.

I send [sent] your cloth in "---", it is not as good a piece as I want, but it was the best I could get. There is not a piece of it in Town, in fact there are very few goods here now. I send [sent] you some empty bottles and you can interpret the meaning without saying that you can in the first opportunity return them full of something to eat or rather to drink. I made some "---" since a purchase of some medicines bought them with some funds. I send [sent] them up, please take good care of them, place them where they will not be exposed to dampness, unless you can empty the papers into the bottles and cork them tightly. This will be the last medicine trade I will make this war. They have stopped the trading in such. I send [sent] all the things home that you sent, but the bucket and we could not empty the lard in anything "---" could "---" not get anything "..." Burned.

Restart "..." coming here to see you in the morning with Sid. Oh, that I could come home to stay. I want to see Joe and hear him talk. I know nothing more to write you this evening. Tonight Sid has gone to bed and retreat has already been beat and I must close, I have to get the trunks all packed ready for him to start <u>home</u> in the morning. We have but one train that goes out each day, it only goes out of morning, none go out at night, if the war continues much longer I do not think that we will have any railroads in operation.

Remember me kindly to all my <u>friends</u>. Tell mother thank you for my handkerchiefs. I think it very nice – you must write me a long letter when Sid gets home. I am glad that your school is so new out and I would advise you take no other school. I would not confine myself so, if I were you. I would not impose the task of teaching on myself, were I you.

Good night Dear Wife
Your Husband
John H. Kinyoun

ANALYSIS

Unfortunately, this letter and the next two were severely damaged by fire. All three of these documents have had the middle section destroyed, leaving each letter in two parts. Although in a poor state of condition, it has remained readable to a great extent. In this correspondence, dated sometime in March, which can be inferred to be after March 10 by a reference in the second sentence, the doctor begins by expressing his anticipation of seeing Sid. He also expresses gratitude for receiving a few supplies from other family members and friends. Next, Kinyoun goes into a spiritual spiel about praying for him, mankind in general, and the soldiers within the army. As in several of his other writings, he wants to come home and wishes the war were over.

The doctor then goes into quite a narration about his visit with Sid. Both men appear to be very close, and they enjoyed some free time by attending two plays. However, he mentions that Sid will be leaving in the morning. During his visit, Sid had given him $100 from Mrs. Kinyoun. The doctor tells her he went shopping with Dr. Wiseman to buy her a dress, but nothing was available. It appears supplies are low in the shops or the merchants might be withholding their wares for prices to increase, considering the Confederacy's runaway inflation. He does buy her some material though and sends it home. However, in discussing the quality of the fabric called calico, he states how it was of such poor condition that he would not "buy for a Negro to wear." A very degrading statement, but sadly, probably a very true statement of the times, reflecting the majority of many

Southerner's thoughts and opinions. Although the South seceded from the Union based on the principle of "states rights," still the most important "right" behind secession was their wanting to keep the "right" or institution of slavery.

Of some interest, he speaks about sending some bottles home for his wife to use in both their procurements of medicine. Apparently with his own funds, the doctor has been buying drugs or medication with which to treat his patients. He states that the trade business in these types of supplies has dried up, and accordingly, he will not attempt any more dealings. By this time in the war, the effects of the Union naval blockade were being sorely felt, as evidenced not only in the lack of material goods, such as clothing, but also in medical supplies. Within nine months, all Confederate ports will be either blockaded or under Union Army control, with the port of Wilmington, North Carolina, being the last to fall on February 22, 1865.[14] Of some irony, Kinyoun's regiment under the command of Maj. Gen. Robert F. Hoke would eventually be transferred from Petersburg to Wilmington to aid in its defenses.[15]

The letter concludes with his packing Sid's belongings for his return trip and stating his desire to come home and see their son Joe. Of some note, he comments that the railroads have become unreliable and may cease operating. Rail service was very important to the war efforts of both sides. Historians have stated it was one of the first times in history they were used as a major tactical component in engaging an adversary.[16] But, as a result of the Union naval blockade and a reallocation of the South's industrial resources, such as steel, they rapidly fell into disrepair.

In parting, he advises her to give up her school and, in essence, enjoy life. This statement, although probably well intentioned, has a perplexing tone. On the one hand, he has done his noble duty, but on the other hand, the Kinyoun family has undergone extreme hardships in their own right, all because of his absence. Most wives today would probably have a very different reaction to such a patronizing statement.

ORIGINAL

them threaten to distroy the city and they
Gen ~~Bush~~ Bushrod Johnson Command
carried and taken back from the Yanks
some of our works and captured some
7 hundred prisoners and among
them Brig Gen, - we will have a blody
time in a very few days more and
perhaps a few hours more - The most of
Grants Army is this side of the James and
it is thought he will make his great and
final effort to take Richmond, I hope
that he will most stagnanly fail - this must
be shortly - they are pressing us both
sides of Petersburge, I will write you
in a short time again - I have just
received your and Sidy letters
I will write him as soon as I can and
find him or his adress - I will
[illegible] [illegible] badly I cannot [illegible] more

Hare's Farm 2 miles of
Petersburge June 17th 1864

My dear and beloved Wife:

Permit me this morning
to write you a word, though I have nothing
incouraging to write you, from the fact I
am very unwell to day I came near dieing
last night, had "Cholera Morbus" I do not remember ever being so sick as I was last
night, but thank God that I am better this
morning. I have not been ~~off~~ off duty a
moment yet, I am here in three hundred
yards in rear of my Regt, though I have
a tolerable safe place I think though we
are some times under a most tereffic
shelling and showers of minnies, I have
not been injured as yet, though my coat
has been cut by a fragment of shell. -
I have been alone with my [illegible] at
[illegible]

have the 42d regiment to attend to alone
as Dr. Wiseman is sick and at
Petersburge, and that Virginian, Rennes
has not been to the front yet, I would
not if I were Col have such a man in
charge of a Regiment - he is of no acount
I do not think Dr. Wiseman is very
sick though I have not seen him for
several days - had dysentery, -
I suppose before you get this, that you will have
red the results of this great battle, that are
raging at present, - we came here night before
last and found the enemy in possession
of a part of ~~our~~ our works and have the
most commanding position around the
town, we have regained a potion of
the works we lossed on the 15th by the
[illegible] of Raney of the Virginia Wise
[illegible] was run out and [illegible] two

that the Yankees held of ours, - they open
the fight on yesterday evening they formed
in three lines of Battle and charge our
possition, we repulsed them three times
killing several of them though it was not
with such slaughter as we made of them
at Gaines Mill, - they have been firing very
heavely all day up to this hour, I think
that they will attempt to carry our works
this evening by storm again, but our boys
are determined to hold their position at
all hazzards, we have a good fighting
division and good Brigade - things
rather look gloomy around this place
at present, but Beuregard & Lee is in
fine spirits, the Yankees have one
one Whitworth Gun and have been
shelling the town last night and
and to day though they [illegible] [illegible]

Hare's Farm 2 miles of
Petersburg June 17 1864

My dear and beloved Wife:

Permit me this morning to write you a word, though I have nothing encouraging to write you, from the fact I am very unwell today. I came near dying last night, had "Cholera Morbus." I do not remember ever being so sick as I was last night, but thank God that I am better this morning.

I have not been off duty yet. I am here in [with] three hundred guards in rear of my Regt., though I have a tolerable safe place, I think though we are sometimes under a most terrific shelling and showers of minnees [sic-Minié]. I have not been injured yet, though my coat has been cut by a fragment of a shell. I have been alone with my " . . ." Burned. Restart " . . ." have the 43rd regiment to attend to also as Dr. Wiseman is sick and at Petersburg, and that – "---", "---" I has not been to the front yet, I would not, if I were col. have such a man in charge of a regiment. He is of no accident. I do not think Dr. Wiseman is very sick though I have not seen him for several days-had Dysentery.

I suppose before you get this, that you will have read the results of this great battle[s], that are raging at present. We came here night before last and found the enemy in possession of a part of our works [earthen work fortifications] and have the most commanding position around the town. We have regained a portion of the works we lossed [lost] of the works on the 14th by the "---" of Bravery of The Virginians. " . . ." Burned. Restart " . . ." that the Yankees [get] hold of ours. They opened the fight on yesterday evening. They formed in three lines of battle and charged our position. We repulsed them three times killing several of them though it was not with such slaughter as we made of them at Gaines Mill. They have been firing very heavily all day up to this hour. I think that they will attempt to carry our works this evening by storm again, but our boys are determined to hold their position at all hazards. We have a good fighting division and good

Brigade.

Things rather look gloomy around this place at present, but Beauregard and Lee is [are] in fine spirits. The Yankees have one Whitworth gun and have been shelling the town last night and today though they are " . . ." Burned. Restart " . . ." him threaten to destroy the city and "---" Gen Bushrod Johnson's command carried and taken back from the Yanks some of our works and captured some 7 hundred prisoners and among them a Brg Gen. We will have a bloody time in a very few days more and perhaps a few hours more. The most of Grant's Army is [on] this side of the James [River], and it is thought he will make his great and final effort to take Richmond. I hope he will most significantly fail.

This must be shortly [short]-they are pressing us both sides of Petersburg. I will write you in a short time again. I have just received yours and Sidney's letters. I will write as soon as I can and fine him or his address. I will "---" badly I cannot write more now "..." Burned

Your husband
John H. Kinyoun

ANALYSIS

The doctor begins this writing by telling Mrs. Kinyoun of his near death experience with cholera the night before. Cholera was and has remained to this day a very dreaded and deadly disease, attributed in large part, but not exclusively, to poor and inadequate sanitation. Although sick, he has had to stay on duty because fellow surgeon, Dr. Wiseman, has been in poor health, too, but with dysentery, a debilitating and fatal illness in itself.

For the most part, the rest of the letter addresses his experiences at the early battles for Petersburg, Virginia. In the first week of May, newly appointed Union General in Chief Ulysses S. Grant, commenced his spring campaign with the combined purposes of defeating General Lee's Army of Northern Virginia, capturing the Confederate capital of Richmond, Virginia, and ending the war.

Within a month's time, Grant had engaged Lee's forces at the battles of the Wilderness, Spotsylvania, and Cold Harbor with devastating losses on both sides. By the first of June, Grant had pushed Lee to the outskirts of Richmond and the railroad junction further south at Petersburg. Initially, Grant attempted to take the city by force, but the Confederates managed to hold on, which ultimately led Grant to besiege the city for approximately ten months, before its fall.[17]

Kinyoun's letter notes that Grant's troops have tried to storm their fortifications only to be beaten back. On several occasions, both sides jostled for competing positions, and he states one attack was sorely repulsed. The doctor comments though, that not such a whopping was given the Yankees since Gaines Mills, Virginia. This battle took place during Lee's Seven Days Campaign in late June 1862, which relieved the beleaguered capital of Richmond from capture by Union Gen. George B. McClellan in his failed Peninsular Campaign.[18] The doctor has been serving in the rear ranks, but, even though removed, had a shell fragment tear through his frock coat. It appears as if the Yankees were raining artillery shells and bullets upon their defenses at a constant pace.

As Kinyoun described, the Union Army had been firing on them using a Whitworth cannon, a breech-loading weapon, which through this design allowed for a faster discharge of its deadly payload.[19] The doctor may have been confused about the presence of this type of cannon. It has been documented that Whitworths' were not used by Union forces at Petersburg. Although the Confederates did possess two such artillery pieces, they had used them in hopes of dislodging the North's behemoth mortar called the "Dictator," initially placed on a railroad car because of its size.[20]

Besides these comments on the battle, he also states how 700 Northern prisoners were taken in an attack lead by Confederate Gen. Bushrod Rust Johnson with the added bonus of capturing a Union brigadier general. Johnson led quite a remarkable career with the army. On January 24, 1862, he was captured only to escape and be wounded severely at the battle of Shiloh in April of the same year.

Originally serving in Tennessee, the army transferred him to the Eastern Theater, where his forces bore the initial brunt of defending the trenches at Petersburg.[21] One authority has stated a brigadier general was not captured during this period.[22] Therefore, either Kinyoun was misinformed or either side did not properly document the general's capture.

Kinyoun next gives Grant's location as being on one side of the James River and how he thinks the general will still try to take Richmond. He closes the letter stating they are under attack again.

ORIGINAL

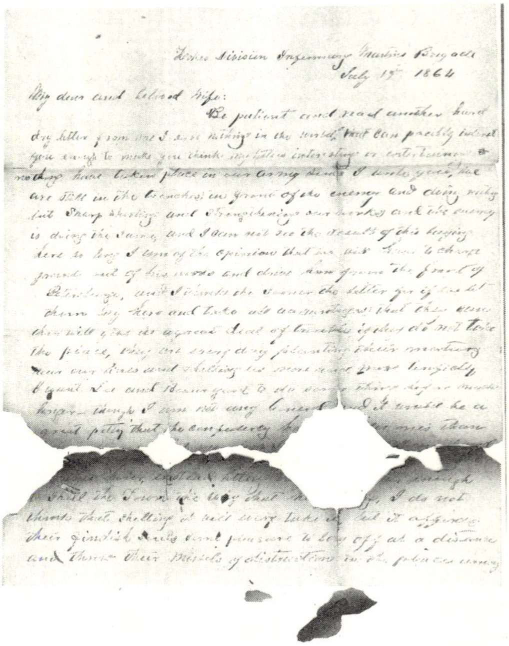

TRANSCRIPTION

Hoke's Division Infirmary

Martin's Brigade

July 19, 1864

My dear and beloved Wife:

Be patient and read another hard day letter from me, I have nothing in the world, that can possibly interest you enough to make you think my letter interesting or entertaining. As nothing has taken place in our Army since I wrote you. We are still in the trenches in front of the enemy and doing nothing, but sharpshooting and strengthening our works and the enemy is doing the same, and I cannot see the result of laying here so long, I am of the opinion that we will have to charge Grant out of his works and drive him from the front of Petersburg, and I think the sooner the better, for if we let them lay here and take all advantages, that they can, they will give us a great deal of trouble, if they do not take the place, they are every day planting their mortars near our lines and shelling us more and more terrifically.

I want Lee and Beauregard to do something before much longer. Though I am not any General and it would be a great petty [sic] that the Confederacy "..." Burned. Restart "..." this hour, instead of letting "---" enough to shell the Town "---", I do not think shelling it will ever take it, but it offers their findish [*sic*-fiendish] souls some pleasure to lay off at a distance and throw their missles [*sic*] of distruction [*sic*] in the place, among a parcel of women and helpless children, without any notice whatever of their intentions of shelling the place, though understanding their low and devilish inclinations and brutish nature we were somewhat prepared for their shelling the place and therefore there have not been very many casualties occurred in Town, since they made their appearance before the city – though to Town you could not imagine how they could throw so many shells in the place and not hurt anyone, for the streets are full of people. Women, children and Army all the day long – the inhabitants have grown quite use to the bursting and screaming of shells, it is surprising how careless that people can become of danger. To look at it from a human point of view, this life is a mere chance or accident anyway, but the Great Providence has all to <u>do</u> with <u>all</u> the unseen and incomprehensible mysteries of this and the future. And we therefore need not trouble ourselves about the results of actions, if we only do our duty to the best of our knowledge and "---" that we have of duty, this is nearly all or quite all, that we may be concerned about the doing of our duty. This is the first "---" <u>do our duty</u>, and the results will be right " . . . " Burned.

Restart " . . ." had been captured by the enemy and had "---" escape by an adventure of swimming a river. I was glad to learn that he had escaped their hands so luckily.

I am very anxious to get a letter from you stating all about the officer and other things of home. The mail is coming through now and I am expecting a letter from you every day as it comes in each day. The Weldon Road [railroad] is done, but the Danville is not and I learn that it will be some time before it will be in running order, though I hope it will be sooner than reported for we are needing the use of the road very badly just now, to get in supplies we are living very hard just now again, but I do not think it will last long.

We are getting new flour now, I want you all to have the wheat thrashed out soon so we can have something better for breakfast than coarse cornbread, it certainly goes very rough this morning. We still draw sugar and coffee, but it is not much to live on, yet it does the Army a great deal of good as a stimulant. The men need some stimulant of some kind, what Whiskey I get, I make me bitters of wild cherry and dogwood strong. I make about four gallons every third day and put some whiskey in it and treat my sick each morning and I can see that it does my men more good than all the rest of the medicine that I give them. I have a man whose business it is to get the "---" and make the Tea and I have a forty gallon "---" full all the "…" Burned. Restart "…" and another thing "---" for the men to them is "---" and the other or some of them drink the whiskey and these men do not see it, but enough of my practice.

I have not so many sick men in the command as I sometime a day ago. I hope in a short time to have very few sick.

We are having a beautiful rain today, it has been raining gently all the morning has "---" the dust ended - the air and washed it out clean so we can breath[e] clean again, how great full [*sic*-grateful] this rain, it has been so long since it rained any for us, over seven weeks. The Yanks are as glad of this rain as we are.

We have heard [nothing] very late of Early "---" [Confederate Gen. Jubal A. Early]. We received here was that he had crossed the Potomac [River] on his return from Maryland with all his body of cattle and horses. Though I did not learn at what point he recrossed [*sic*]. I hope that he may have good luck in getting back safe to our lines with all he brought out.

There is talk in our lines here this morning that Gen Lee intends charging Grant's works here today or tomorrow, though I do not know whether there is any grounds for the report. If he contemplates such a thing, now is the best time to do it for in a few days, Grant will [be] stronger than he now is, for those troops that Grant sent up to defend Washington City [D.C.] against Early will be back and we will have them to contend with. Though I dread for us to have to charge the works for they are very strong and must cost us a great deal of life to take him. I cannot say how it will "---", though if Lee has determined to "---" the Yankee army "---" at a heavy lost. I wish "…" Burned. Restart "…" We left Plymouth on 7 of May and we have been fighting and under fire of the enemy 66 days with [without] any rest "—" we stand it much longer – but we must stand it long enough to whip the Yanks.

I have no new [news] as you have learned by reading this much, excuse me for I have told you all I know about the war. I am well. Give my love to all, write me soon and often, tell Joe to write me – and kick as many bullies as he wants.

Your Husband

J. H. Kinyoun

ANALYSIS

The last of Dr. Kinyoun's six letters addresses the battle conditions during the siege of Petersburg, Virginia. Of some note, eleven days after this letter, the battle of the Crater would take place on July 30, and the Sixty-Sixth would be instrumental in stopping the Yankee break through.[23] By now both sides were bogged down in trench warfare. He indicates his boredom with the situation, but at the same time reveals the dangerous nature emanating from the battle by the constant harassment of flying artillery shells and pot shots from hidden sharpshooters. The letter is full of war news, and his opinion about the handling of the situation. His writing has a sense of urgency in its tone, whereby he has become increasingly impatient with the siege, and Generals Lee and Beauregard, and their do-nothing approach. With this thought, the phrase "the best defense is a good offense" must run through the man's thoughts. In particular, he complains that General Grant's forces have been growing stronger by the day, and the

Confederates should take some type of aggressive action before the opposing side's numbers become overwhelming.

As he writes, Union heavy artillery has been brought forward to continue in the daily pounding of the Confederate defenses. His letter states mortars are being used against their lines. In fact, only a single mortar was used during the siege, given the name "Dictator." It could hurl thirteen inch shells and originally rested on a flat bed railroad car. Later, it would be moved to a wooden platform. Its purpose was to extricate the Southern troops located on higher ground north of the Appomattox River. Regular artillery could not effectively reach their elevated position.[24]

The doctor's dislike and bitterness over the North's conduct of the artillery campaign can be noted from his reference to them as "fiendish souls." He comments about the total disregard for the lives of women and children by the Yankees' bombardments, but allows how the populace has lapsed into a state of complacency about the endless shelling. As the siege dragged on, Grant's strategy focused on bombarding the entrenched Confederates into submission. Although the residents of Petersburg and its defenders believed the artillery to be solely directed at the city, this was in fact not true. Grant mainly wanted to destroy the fortifications and the railroads. The town did receive many barrages, but by accident and not design. The Southerners had been forced from their initial defenses of two and a half miles east of the city within the battle's first few days, pushing back to a half mile. Upon besieging it, and engaging its artillery on the city's defenses, many of the shells over-shot and landed inside the town damaging 600 buildings. Surprisingly, only six civilian casualties were reported, which correlates with the doctor's statement concerning injuries from the countless shelling.[25]

Following these comments, he seems to drift into the spiritual side of the war, as he did in another letter, stating it was more or less God's will as to how things will work out, stressing one must still "do his duty." By this statement, it almost sounds as if he had resigned himself to the South's eventual defeat, although at the same time fearing such a result, he had made up his mind to stay the course. Kinyoun proceeds to degrade the Yankees and talks about an escape, which took place, but the name of the individual was burned beyond recognition.

The letter next travels back and forth on various minor topics. However, he mentions the plight of the railroads, in particular the Weldon Railroad and how important it has become to keep another line open for badly needed supplies. Grant strategically moved against the Weldon tracks, because its destruction would cut provisions to the city and its defenders. The general in large part attacked Petersburg, located approximately twenty miles south of Richmond, so as to sever its rail lines and stop the entry of provisions in the hope of shortening the capital's life.[26]

From this point, he focuses on another important military development, Confederate Gen. Jubal A. Early's raid on Washington, D.C., in the first part of July 1864. Unfortunately for the South, Early failed in his attempt to capture the city, due mainly in part to being distracted and diverted to a battle at Monocacy, Maryland, on July 9. He won the battle, but by this act, Union troops gained a window of opportunity to reinforce the capital and prevent its capture. The general had been sent north by Lee through the Shenandoah Valley, in hopes of seizing the Federal capital and forcing Grant to redirect his troop buildup at Petersburg. However, Early missed the chance and commenced his retreat back to Virginia on July 12.[27]

Kinyoun recognizes the diversion of Grant's troops to Washington City, as it was called during the war, and complains to his wife that an opportunity exists for Lee to quickly attack Grant before these troops returned to Petersburg. Lee, though, did not seize the moment because in many respects his troop strength and reserves had been greatly exhausted by Grant's relentless march south, commencing in early May.[28] Kinyoun even acknowledges this fact by stating the army has been on the move since May 7, fighting a total of sixty-six days straight.

In many respects, this reflected Grant's overall strategy to constantly engage the South with his superior number of troops and supplies, depleting the Confederacy, at every opportunity, of its resources to sustain the war.

On a different note, the doctor speaks about the general supplies or rations of the army, noting that the cornbread, or sometimes called "pone,"[28] was of a poor quality and there was little else to consume except some sugar and coffee. Of interest, he states whiskey was of service to the men, not only as a stimulant, but also as a medication for his patients. During the war, the use of whiskey or alcohol as a medication was somewhat common. However, its medical effects were anything but helpful in arresting disease or injury, although it could alleviate pain. Finally, Kinyoun wishes his wife well and tells her to have son Joe kick some bullies, probably just an expression of the times, but of some irony considering the doctor's station.

SUMMARY

Probably the best characterization of Dr. Kinyoun's letters might be that of looming gloom. Their time span covers approximately nine months from November 1863 to July 1864, and although containing some uplifting references, overall they portray a sense of despair and longing. Unfortunately, the Kinyoun Genealogical Papers do not contain any correspondence from the early or last days of the war. Obviously, during the final stage of the conflict Kinyoun would have most likely exhibited despair and frustration at the Confederacy's impending defeat. However, those earlier ones might have shown a more upbeat tone, especially during the Army of Northern Virginia's successive string of victories, prior to the battle at Gettysburg, Pennsylvania, July 1-3, 1863, and the fall of Vicksburg, Mississippi, on July 4 of the same year. The letters are after these great battles, but before the South's ultimate end in April 1865. But, with these documents, the true feelings of a seasoned veteran of three years of fighting, and attending to the sick and wounded come forward in a somewhat darkened light. To all soldiers, wars have always held two promises for its participants, the first being personal survival and the second being victory. Rarely would one yearn for the opposite. Sadly though, both attainments have never been blessed with being synonymous. In the doctor's case, he survived, but the purpose for which he fought was lost.

All in all, these documents add insight and reinforcement to the actual events of this short, but horrific period. Camp life, disease, and shortages are frequently mentioned throughout. Conditions can be summed up as deplorable. The Union naval blockade, destruction of railroads, and the lack of a significant industrial-based economy left the South with little hope of sustaining a long war and adequately supplying its thousands of troops on a regular basis. The doctor highlights these limitations and almost benignly writes his wife to assist in his procurement of medicines for the patients, therein providing a disheartening example of how the Confederacy was so ill equipped to protect its very instrument of survival, the army. Unfortunately, the situation would only worsen as the conflict progressed. One can almost sense the severity of the soldier's plight in the doctor's writings, especially his constant desire to come home and forsake the war.

Of special interest was his knowledge and understanding of the combined military and political scenarios constantly facing the new country, and its quest for independence. Being highly educated, as both a lawyer and a doctor, he recognized the consequences of each battle's defeat and how it would affect the course of the war. To say the least, Kinyoun was opinionated as to the conduct of various politicians, military officials, and troop movements. Being a loyal Southerner, he makes a shocking statement in stating the slaves should be freed and put into the Confederacy's diminishing ranks as soldiers. In addition, he notes the slaves will be eventually released from bondage in the future anyhow, implying why not use them now in service to the "Cause." In itself, these revelations represent an important comment and observation. The doctor has been fighting for the South since the conflict's beginning in order to preserve a certain way of life, in particular, the institution of slavery, although cleverly cloaked under the disguise of "states rights." Now, after almost three bloody years of fighting, the issue had become less important as opposed to Southern liberty. This is an amazing transformation, yet, in another letter he degrades the Negro, when writing about the quality of a sewing fabric, saying, in essence, it is not deserving of a black person to wear as a potential garment. A truly sad comment, which indicates that the issue was not totally so much about indentured oppression, as it was about the perceived inferiority of a race. To an impartial mind, this is better known as racism. Unfortunately, as American History has so painfully demonstrated, it has remained an agonizing and unrelenting shadow upon the land to this day.

CHAPTER IV

IN DIES - "EVERYDAY"

The word " diary" has its origin in Latin, derived from the term Dies, *meaning day. Even in modern times, it continues to mean a recording of daily events and observations set forth or transcribed in a diary or journal. The purpose of this process has been to save the day's reflections for subsequent reference and study.*

The Diary

Throughout the ages, persons have set upon countless ways to record their everyday existence. The earliest such forms of expression can still be seen today in European and Native American caves, where ancient sketches have depicted hunting scenes and battles of long ago. As civilization slowly advanced, new techniques evolved, not only in the recording of events, but also in the emergence of oral and written communication. The Egyptians developed the alphabet of hieroglyphics, and the Babylonian King Hammurabi conceived the first legal code, followed by advances made through the Greeks, Romans, and the derivative Romance languages. Other parts of the world, in the Far East and the African continent, established their own basis of speech and preservation of interaction. All of these progressions have represented major steps in an ever changing and expanding network of cultural posterity and testimony to a society's past and heritage. Today, the microchip and the computer have moved forward at such rapid paces that new products of technology have often become obsolete upon their very introduction into the marketplace. Where once ill clad primeval people etched their happenings on moss covered cave walls or animal hides, now business attired workers simply press an electronic button to talk, write, and save the day's hallowed moments.

In many ways, Dr. Kinyoun's Diary holds the same distinction in this long line of recording, by being a bridge to the future in medical knowledge and advancement. Early in the organization of the Confederate Medical Department,

Surgeon General Samuel P. Moore ordered the recording of statistical information, in the form of a journal, concerning the medical well-being of the army's troops .[1] Kinyoun was no stranger to record keeping, as evidenced by his logs at the East Bend Academy and while serving as captain of the Twenty-Eighth North Carolina Infantry Regiment before becoming a Confederate doctor.[2] Many other surgeons kept extensive journals documenting their day-to-day activities and treatment of the sick and wounded.[3] Others were more lax in this requirement, leaving some to question the value of their service and their ultimate impact on patients. In several cases, the journals, diaries, and medical papers of numerous doctors have been preserved and now rest in the custody of family descendants, private collectors, educational institutions, and museums.[4] Fortunately, the Kinyoun Medical Diary has been handed down to the present and escaped being discarded by subsequent generations. As stated in the Introduction, the doctor's granddaughter greatly treasured this unique statement of the past and made sure her grandson shared the same appreciation. It was her profound hope that someday the two of them would publish the document, so it could be examined by others, who were left in doubt as to the wartime service, experiences, or death of their loved ones. Unfortunately, she passed away before this dream could be realized. However, because of this desire, the Diary, as she called it, has been reproduced here in full for present-day researchers and genealogists of Civil War history.

The Diary covers the period from September 1863, the regiment's formation, to April 1865, when the Civil War came to a conclusion. Upon examination, the document can be seen as a testament to the doctor's education and experience. It has been carefully transcribed in his handwriting and sets forth an accounting of the regiment's casualties and sickly. It is roughly 191 pages. These sheets have the purpose of narrating the month's sequence of patients. The journal has a general readability to it, due in large part to the handwriting's legibility. In a few instances, the pages have faded with time, or the ink has smeared, or run because of condensation. But for the most part, the names have been clearly logged onto each sheet, allowing for them to be easily discernable.

All told the Diary has five sections. The first and most extensive is the day-to-day logging of patients and their various afflictions, whether from disease or the result of battle injuries. The first section has the general title of "Register Sick and Wounded of Sixty Sixth Regt North Carolina Troops." Periodically, the doctor has strayed from the heading, by adding, abbreviating, or deleting a word from this format. As combat increased, he added the word, "Killed" to the title. Under this segment, as a starting point, every page has a set layout with several variances. He documented his information on a monthly basis and has so identified each period by the month and year. Next, lines and boxes have been drawn for the insertion and recording of daily information across the printed paper in the form of a rough spreadsheet. The first column has been titled "Number" written in the left-hand top section followed by boxes headed with "Name," "Rank," "Regiment," "Company," "Complaint/Diagnosis," "Date," and "Remarks." As the pace of the war quickened in the spring of 1864, other sections were inserted to catalog the day's routine. Those added headings include "Admitted," "Readmitted," Returned To Duty," and "Sent To General Hospital." Prior to May 1864, the regiment had been mainly positioned in North Carolina. However, with the advance of Gen. Ulysses S. Grant and his forces upon Gen. Robert E. Lee's Confederate Army of Northern Virginia in the early part of this month, the unit was thrust into the vortex of containing this advance of the Northern forces. It was during this period that the Diary took on a different configuration. By the time Grant's forces were threatening Richmond, Dr. Kinyoun's regiment had been transferred north to this theater of action.[5] Consequently, the recording of casualties can be seen in the Diary from this point onwards in the war.

The next major section has been titled, "Morning Reports," which sets forth categories as to the whereabouts of soldiers, as a summary total per grouping. Following these reports, the doctor has compiled a log labeled," Return of Medical and Hospital Property, received, expended, and remaining on hand at – for the –

ending [month and year]." It has been further broken down by sub-sections designated as "Articles," "Recd. Since last return," "expended with the sick," "On hand," and "Remarks." An extensive amount of supplies has been documented within these sections. Next, he has a "Summary" of diseases, followed by several pages highlighted by the heading "Special Diseases," which has a listing of the illnesses and the number of men afflicted by the diseases he diagnosed in their treatment. All these divisions within the manual have added greatly to its understanding and to knowing the plight of those soldiers serving in the unit. The extent of the Diary also has special meaning in its affirmation of the organizational abilities of Dr. Kinyoun. Without question, he seriously performed his duties under the gravest of circumstances, and through this dedication has left future generations a vast treasure of information.

The Stories Within

On analyzing the journal, the reader will discover a whole host of diseases, conditions, and battle wounds. The Diary catalogs the daily ailments of the troops. In some cases, definite patterns of affliction can be easily seen while flipping through the pages. Intermittent Fever, more commonly known as Malaria, occurred on a frequent basis, and to some degree, it appeared to have a contagious aspect because it was documented as affecting many men within the same company. Probably, the most prevalent ailment was diarrhea with a fever. Starting on June 27, 1864, while participating in the siege of Petersburg, Virginia, upwards of 170 patients were listed with this condition, representing approximately 16 percent of the entire regiment. Most likely, the outfit contracted the disease, due to either tainted water or food, a common occurrence during the conflict. Dysentery was also very common, which has similar traits to diarrhea. What a wretched experience it would have been to be among these men, where the smell, refuse, and the feasting flies would have sickened the strongest of individuals.

Other interesting ailments were the various forms of venereal disease.

Syphilis, gonorrhea, and other genital diseases were not uncommon, leaving one to surmise the rigors of war were not without sexual contact and its consequences. Other conditions abounded, but the second largest medical causality resulted from those men wounded in combat. Kinyoun would record the wound and the medical procedure taken, but tragedically, one can turn ahead several pages and see where the victim died. As seen many times in the "Remarks" section, the doctor would send his patient to a nearby general hospital for further treatment. Hospitals, as a rule, offered a greater chance for recovery than the exposed confines of the open field.

In documenting battle injuries, the doctor wrote very descriptive entries to catalog the extent of the casualty. An entry made on June 18, 1864, stated Lt. Col. J. H. Nethercutt, who had just succeeded Col. Alexander D. Moore after his death on June 3 as the regimental commander, had been wounded by a, "Contusion of face by shell," further noted as "Severe." On January 19, 1865, the Diary read Benton Jeffreys of Company A was, "Killed in action by [a] shell." In another case, J. M. Euda [Eudy] of Company G was, "Wounded right arm above elbow, flesh, slightly, by Minie Ball," on March 8, 1865. He was transferred to, "G. H. [general hospital] Raleigh, N. C. by surgeon at Hospital Infirmary Goldsboro N. C. thence to Genl Hospital Goldsboro N. C." For the most part, these young and gallant men survived the horrible experiences of encampment and battle. To many, to die in battle lessened the continuing and agonizing experiences of bodily devastation from disease, with the dread of its reappearance and lingering incapacitation and misery. Their tragic fate would only be to live again and be sucked into the furnaces of a continuing physical and mental hell, by another disease or battle injury. The enormity of the Civil War, as seen by the Kinyoun Diary, represented not only a watershed of the suffering within his charge, but of a new beginning, which in short order would transform America's medical knowledge.

However, all considerations aside, the most unique aspect of the Diary is its correlation to the battles the regiment fought in comparison to the doctor's corresponding logs for the same month. The engagements have a direct link to his documentation of combat casualties. At the same time, when the unit was not engaged, the entries dropped off considerably or reverted back to more of a chronicle of various diseases. It can be said the Sixty-Sixth had somewhat of a mild wartime experience early on in the war. But, with the advent of spring in 1864, until the war's conclusion for them in late April 1865, they were faced monthly with some type of military action, as borne witness by the Diary. In order to better recognize this correlation, a time line sets forth the regiment's military encounters in relation to monthly medical notations in the journal.

Diary Month	**Period of Battles**
May 1864	May 12, 1864-Petersburg, VA May 13, 1864-Port Walthal Junction,VA -Bermuda Hundred, VA
June 1864 July 1864 August 1864 September 1864	June 1-3, 1864-Cold Harbor, VA June 16-Sept. 1864-Petersburg, VA
September 1864 October 1864 November 1864 December 1864	September 30.-December 1864-Fort Harrison, VA December 22, 1864-Wilimington, NC
January 1865	January 15, 1865-Fort Fisher, NC
February 1865	February 18-22, 1865-Fall of Wilmington, NC
March 1865	March 7, 1865-Kinston, NC -Southwest Creek, NC -Wise's (Wyse) Fork, NC March 19-21, 1865-Bentonville, NC
April 1865	April 26, 1865-Surrender at Durham Station, NC

Another interesting consideration is to examine the number of patients documented for each separate month. The doctor has cataloged his information on a monthly basis, which in effect has the same purpose, as if they were chapters of a book. Viewing them as chapters, as opposed to raw medical data has the effect of creating a story for each month. On examining each period and comparing it to the actions and movement of the regiment, several conclusions can be drawn from this analysis, bearing a unique consequence to the other. As an aid in deciphering this information, each month has been listed, followed by the number of soldiers treated for the period.

Month	Number
September 1863	115
October 1863	124
November 1863	170
December 1863	162
January 1864	289
February 1864	214
Marhc 1864	85
April 1864	176
May 1864	336
June 1864	133
July 1864	182
August 1864	188
September 1864	183
October 1864	144
November 1864	51
December 1864	79
January 1865	93
February 1865	81
March 1865	100
April 1865	42
TOTAL	**2,947**

After reviewing the above month-to-month entries, the most apparent fact is in the twenty month total of patients, a staggering 2,947 victims out of an initial total regimental strength of 1,100 men. Roughly, a 268% disease, injury, or casualty rate for every soldier in the unit. Or more simply stated, each man became afflicted on average, a little over two and one-half times during the twenty month span of the Sixty-Sixth. Without question, this exposure represented an abnormally high rate. Another noticeable feature has been in the seasonal aspect of the entries. In September of 1863, the tabulation numbered 115, but for each month thereafter in the year, except for a small dip in December, the numbers increased steadily. This change was probably attributed, in large part, to the onset of diseases caused by cold weather. As will be recalled in Dr. Kinyoun's letter home to his wife on New Year's Day 1864, he complained about the harshness of the conditions, which obviously persisted and led to a compounding of illnesses. As seen by the January total, there were 289 reported cases. On the other hand, in the early spring, the doctor in another letter reported how the climate had moderated and was improving in March 1864. Again, the numbers for the period have offered the same correlation, where the total was only 85. A spike occurred in April, but once summer arrived, the numbers decreased overall, except for a new element to the equation.

In May 1864, the regiment entered the forefront of the fighting, and instead of the season being a rebirth of new growth, bounty, and prosperity, it became a killing field. Unfortunately, this new element would remain unabated from thence forward, only to be culminated by the war's bitter end. As General Grant continuously pushed southward, the fledgling and embattled Confederacy would now pay dearly in the irreplaceable expense of its greatest asset, its soldiers. Although the South's downward spiral to defeat began with Grant's determination to bleed it of its most valuable commodity, the Sixty-Sixth did not always participate in day-to-day combat. On several occasions, it had a reprieve from the daily attacks, especially when the unit served more as a guard unit from late September 1864 until late December 1864 at Fort Harrison, outside Richmond, Virginia. When examining the totals for October, November, and December, a marked decline in casualties and illnesses can be seen in the monthly figures. In all likelihood, the troops repositioning greatly altered the previous steady stream of log entries up to this point.

Even with this, three remaining bits of information can be gleaned from these numbers. First, as the war entered its last year, the total number of patients dropped significantly in comparison to the previous months. The reason for this decline can be found in the doctor's comments concerning them. Starting back in the fall of 1864, the casualties and resulting diseases had increased, and in order to effectively deal with their treatment, the doctor had sent many of the soldiers to a general hospital, detailed them, or placed them on furlough. Not knowing the complexities of wounds and disease, probably many of these men either died or were unable to regain their strength and return to the unit as a combatant. In effect, the supply of viable manpower had begun to rapidly decrease without any substitution, because the South had few if any men left to effectively provide in its defense. Second, given the dire straits now facing the Confederates and the continual advancement of Union forces on all its borders, many soldiers simply deserted. A common disease for all armies has historically been this factor, when the end has started to make its appearance. The third most telltale fact from these numbers can only be seen in June 1864, when the highest total was achieved of 336 cases. In this month, Grant lost 7,000 of his own troops in a frontal attack at Cold Harbor. It became a turning point in the war, for it showed his resolve to sacrifice a superior contingent of troops in order to win. Previous Union commanders would have retreated at such a staggering loss. But, Grant was different and knew he had the reserves and resources to replace them, whereas the Confederacy did not have such assets. One last point; statistics have always been fascinating to view on the surface, however, when examined in relation to their meanings, oftentimes a more haunting picture will emerge, such as in Dr. Kinyoun's Diary, for their true importance has always lain more from within than from without.

Grandmother's Wishes

As a supplement in understanding the Diary, appendixes have been attached as a reference guide. They have been broken down into several sections, with each titled as follows,"Appendix 1 - Rosters" which includes rosters for Company F, Twenty-Eighth North Carolina Infantry Regiment and the Sixty-Sixth North Carolina Infantry Regiment, "Appendix 2 - Medical Glossary," "Appendix 3 - Dr. Kinyoun's Medical Diary," and "Appendix 4 - Photographs." Only Appendix 3 and the roster for the Sixty-Sixth in Appendis 1 have a relationship to the Diary. The rosters have been incorporated into Appendix 1 in order to provide easy access when trying to locate an individual's name. Although "Company F" has nothing to do with the Diary, it was added to this section so as to educate the reader about those men serving under Kinyoun, their captain during his first command. Appendix 4 features photographs of Dr. Kinyoun during his Confederate service and his later years, as well as that of his family and home.

The Medical Glossary has an important role in understanding the illnesses and injuries of the troops listed in the Diary. It should be understood, however, that not all the diseases set forth in the journal have a corresponding term or definition in the glossary. In several cases, as a result of the handwriting, condition of the paper, or the ink, an entry could not be deciphered with any discernable recognition. Also, several medical terms could not be found in any dictionary, and others utilized have since been changed in spelling, or their use as medical terminology has been discontinued in today's scientific world. Such terms from the past and their subsequent discontinuance of usage have been referred to as "archaic." In reading the glossary terms, the current day spelling has been set forth in bold type first, followed by the Diary's version. The phrase [*sic*] has been placed by the recorded entry, designating its variance from today's common spelling. Occasionally, the common terminology for the medical term can be found immediately after the archaic translation.

Accordingly, in compliance with grandmother's belated wishes, the Diary has been reproduced and set forth in full in Appendix 3.

CHAPTER V

"ABLAZE"

The Homecoming

Dr. Kinyoun gently snapped the horse's reigns, and, in an instant, he and his few possessions, after four years of war, headed home to Yadkin County. After surrendering at Durham Station, he was lucky enough to find an able horse and an old buckboard in which to make the journey. As he slowly embarked upon this final path, his mind moved backwards across the many years of service and remarkable experiences in his support of the now vanquished Confederacy. He appeared to be again reliving each moment. The friends, the loneliness, and the constant longing to be with his family in peace ran through his thoughts. Within a day, he would rejoin these loved ones, but as the beast of his passage trotted towards this reunion, the memories began to haunt him, questioning the purpose of the past and what still lay ahead.

After a few days merriment and recuperating with the family, he went to the parlor and started to unpack his trunk. There was not much left of his once proud uniform, it was badly weathered, but still had a single button with the initials "C.S.A." inscribed on the front, representing the former Confederate States of America. Next, he removed the crimson sash, which bedecked his butternut uniform. Following these retrievals, he carefully unloaded his army regulations manual and an odd assortment of Confederate money and bonds, now useless as a currency. Finally, at the bottom, Captain Kinyoun brought out his Medical Diary, the only proof of his whereabouts and service to the "Lost Cause." Tears began trickling down his cheeks, as the painful memories of the war transcended his thoughts, wondering what good, if any, had transpired from this great conflict. Visions of all the sick, the wounded, and the dead pounded his conscience, with the questions being asked over and over, "What had been the purpose?" "What had been achieved after all this bloodshed?" and lastly, "What had he done of value during this period and why had he gone to war?" Terrible questions, always asked too late in all such civilian and political upheavals.

In nineteenth century America, and elsewhere in the world, patriotism and the spirit of revolution were almost synonymous. During these periods, rarely did one ever second-guess his decision upon entering into an adverse situation of the magnitude of the Civil War. For the most part, it had been weighed against the moment, as if by impulse requiring an immediate choice. Only afterwards, when all the realities have come home, did the individual come to the realization it may have been, at best, pointless. John Hendricks Kinyoun probably faced these same inner reflections, as did many other retiring Southern and Northern veterans. In his case, the Civil War had been a complexity of sorts. At its inception, he served as a combatant. However, as the conflict progressed in lives and time, the doctor applied his pre-war profession to the betterment of the rebellion, in an attempt to save and mend lives. Although being a very small footnote to this great crisis, his Diary would now stand as a testament to his efforts to appease the horrors of war. Yet, as he probably well knew, it would be a sad statement to the waste and decimation of a whole generation. A bitter eclipse, which encompassed a vast contingent of patriotic men and women caught up in the unfurling passions of a regrettable episode in the evolution of a young nation.

The Simple Reality

For the most part, the Diary served many purposes. In particular, it represented a recording of those men who had been sick, wounded, or who had eventually died from their wartime experiences. As will be recalled, Confederate

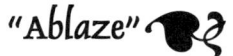

Surgeon General Moore impressed upon his officer medical corps the importance of maintaining articulate documentation of those in their charge.[1] Dr. Kinyoun followed his commander's order with great dedication, combined with accompanying substance and procedure. Even after the war, he kept extensive records as to his patients' illnesses, progression, and ultimate well-being. By this subtle practice, he and his profession created a new process, called documentation. Probably, the surgeon general should be thanked for making this a regulation. However, Kinyoun had already immersed himself into this habit. As a young doctor at the conflict's beginning, he made this function a requirement and it most likely became a routine from then on. Upon his death, these pre-war records were donated in 1970 to the Western Historical Manuscript Collection, University of Missouri, located in Columbia, by his granddaughter, Alice Kinyoun Houts.[2] But even without such an order, it would be more than fair to say the good doctor would most likely have kept the same type of extensive journal. It should be remembered, throughout his early careers as a teacher and while a captain of Company F in the Twenty-Eighth North Carolina Infantry Regiment, he maintained very thorough records

However, in the total scheme of things, is the Diary of medical significance? Better yet, given the emerging, but primitive standards of the time, was it even necessary? And lastly, does it really provide any meaningful purpose or insight into the administration of medicine during this period?

Concerning its importance, the Diary has its pluses and minuses with the positives outweighing the negatives. That this document has survived for over 140 years can, in itself, be called noteworthy. And yes, it also has the omnipresence of being perhaps a prize from the past, as demonstrated by all the intricacies set forth between its covers. Up to this point in medical history, the rudimentary logging of raw data about a patient's condition and outcome had been scarce. With his journal, present generations can now learn about the plight of these soldiers and their treatment. Because of Surgeon General Moore's record keeping mandate, a new procedure became instilled into the profession, as evidenced by Kinyoun's work.

The doctor did not act alone in his diligence to this command; many others kept just as extensive logs. Probably the most notable was Dr. Samuel H. Stout, who served as the chief hospital administrator for the Army of the Tennessee. By war's end, he had amassed a collection weighing upwards of 1,500 pounds.[3] This was probably the most immense statement to one man's actions and recollections during the war. Without question, Kinyoun's Diary has little semblance to such an assemblage as Stout's. However, in its own right, on a more down to earth level, the Diary has just as much value, and possibly more so, in that it has addressed the afflictions of the everyday soldier.

Beyond this recognition, it also answers the question of its necessity. All too often, the parallel query in the aftermath of wars has concerned those not surviving, but more pointedly, "What ever happened to my son, husband, or father? How and where did they die and where are they buried?" Hopefully, this journal will finally offer a long lost partial answer as to the fate of those brave men, who never returned home to their loved ones. To the immediate family of those who succumbed, it obviously has arrived too late in answer. And therefore, because of this factor, it was necessary, offering in effect an obituary of the how, when, and where of the fallen. But, it also was necessary from a scientific standpoint. For the document has a transcending aspect, which in essence can be said to represent a bridge from the past to the beginnings of modern medicine.

By its recordings, an invaluable insight into the period's medical techniques and administration has been preserved as a connecting link to present day medical practitioners. As seen by this process, the treatment of patients had a certain continuity. Whereas before, the progression of an individual's illness and outcome was left largely undocumented, now a format had been put in place, chronicling the disease and initial treatment. For once, an attending or a subsequent physician would have an accounting of those procedures and remedies attempted upon the sick and injured with a notation as to the results. Truly, this represented a most important medical development. As one of the outgrowths of this war, such as the recognition of sanitation, ventilation, and nutritious food, records have now become an almost overwhelming part of the daily recovery process.

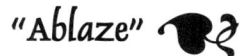

However, in the larger scope of things, the Diary represents a small step forward in relation to the many other medical advancements of the war. Without question, the achievements in this area were more recognizable by the accomplishments of men like Moore and Stout. Other doctors in the Confederate service made major contributions, as well as many Northern physicians. Obviously, Dr. Kinyoun and his journal pale in comparison to these other benchmarks. His real significance though, rests more in the posterity of his actions than in any startling discovery. Very few Civil War medical diaries remain in existence, which in itself makes it important. It stands as lasting proof to a change in the way medicine was being approached in regards to the care of those in need, as directed by one doctor's superior and his faithful execution of that order. Many examples of this type of duty can be found today in testimony to this new approach in health care. Therefore, it does say, how a new trend in medical history transpired with the keeping of a simple ordinary log, or better yet, a history of the patient.

An Intervening Light

Although advancements in medicine have been made, unfortunately a dark side has emerged out of these developments. Medicine, or better yet, science has now evolved into a very diverse and complex academy of learning. Sadly, science has achieved the ability to alter the structure of diseases, making them ever more lethal and contagious. It has actually become a whole new industry known as biological or chemical warfare, where microorganisms and chemical elements can be mutated into other more deadly forms. These new organisms have been made resilient to existing vaccines and antibiotics, thereby leaving the human species totally exposed to their ravages. Throughout the ages, wars have had a certain irony about themselves, especially as seen in the Civil War. Though the war was merciless, the care and treatment of the sick and wounded took on special meaning and importance. However, as civilization and its conflicts have entered a new millennium, the scientific good obtained from these tragedies has in turn been used to make wars even more ominous. The Cold War and all its ghastly overtones of nuclear annihilation may dim in comparison to a biological confrontation. The lessons of destruction from a chemical war, as experienced during World War I, should be reason enough to mind the horrors of such an engagement. Truly, these weapons of mass destruction will only hasten the world's unnecessary demise.

War and medicine have historically gone hand in hand. Progress has been made out of the most terrible of all possible situations, and with any luck, will continue on such a path. In 1861, when the first salvos of gunfire were exchanged between the North and South, American medicine was in its infancy, or at best covered in a thin veil of darkness. By its end, new ideas and techniques had come forth, putting this science on the road to modernization. In effect, a light was beginning to shine through the darkness, out of a country ablaze in death and destruction. One can only forever hope, if war must always be accompanied by medicine, the latter will never be used as the destroyer, rather than being the savior. Only time will truly tell.

If nothing else, the medical accounting as set forth in Dr. Kinyoun's Diary, with all its untold statements, will at last serve as a lesson to the consequences of killing one's enemies for the sake of an unresolved issue. He would have wanted it to be used for constructive purposes, as well as for its professional. Hopefully, when everything else has reached its worst in potential, the words of the disciple John will be heeded and continue to bring civilization forward, where darkness can and will be defeated by an intervening light.

Appendix I
Rosters

Twenty-Eighth North Carolina Infantry Regiment Company F [1]

Officers

Captain John H. Kenyon [Kinyoun]
Captain Thomas V. Apperson
First Lieutenant John T. Conrad
Second Lieutenant W.A. Marler
Second Lieutenant J.G. Truelove
Second Lieutenant John H. Cornelius
Second Lieutenant James M. Starling

Noncommissioned Officers

John F. Fletcher
John C. Kelly
R. M. Logan
R. Martin
G.D. Williams

Privates

B.F. Adams
E.J. Adams
Ira Alderman
John A. Apperson
P.A. Apperson
Alfred Bean
Wiley Bean
A.E. Beard
H.C. Becker
John C. Brown
G.W. Blakely
J.R. Bowvender
H.T. Brann
W.J. Brinkley
J.K.P. Brown
John A. Carter
L.L. Chamberlain
Benjamin Colvard
J.S. Colvard
T.E. Colvard
W.M. Colvard
A.E. Cornelius
R.S. Cozzens
S.D. Creson
Jesse Davis
T.W. Davis
A. Dickerson
W.S. Dixon
John H. Donath
Anderson Douglas
J.F. Flinn
W. C. Flinn
Francis Gough
W. D. Hale
James S. Hall
Lewis W. Hall

T.G. Hall
William M. Haynes
W. L. Head
Richard Hunt
R. H. Hutchins
S. G. Hutchins
David W. Jayne
D.W. Joyner
John T. Joyner
Timothy Joyner
Eugene Kettle
Joseph Kittle
James M. Kirk
Peter Lay
P.H. Lynch
Pleasant Lynch
Richard Logan
James N. Marler
Joseph F. Marler
Gilbert Martin
John V. Matthew
Bennett Martin
John H. Martin
Wm. A. Marler
John McCollins
Nicholas Mickles
Benj. Murphy
F.A. Myers
G.D. Myers
Wm. H. Myers
J.W. Nance
George Neal
M.L. Nichols
H.J. Norman
Nicholas Patts
Benjamin A. Phillips
W.A. Phillips
I.C. Poindexter
John H. Poindexter
C.A. Poindexter
A.H. Potts
Cyrus Queen
R.M. Rash
A.W. Roberts
G.W. Shepherd
G.W. Shipwush
— Speer
Alexander Speer
James D. Speer
W.A. Speer
Lewis H. Spier
M.D. Spillman
W. H. Spillman
Wm. Spillman
C.C. Sprinkle
J.M. Starling
C. Strickland
S.B. Strickland
James W. Tacket
Thomas E. Tacket
Francis Taylor
W.C. Taylor
R.D. Ticker
James G. Truelove
Larken H. Vestal
Thomas P. Webb
W.W. Welsh
James A. Wishern
T.H. Wooten
Andrew Yarborough

Killed in Action

T.G. Bowvender [Bovender] at Chancellorsville
James D. Conrad at Gettysburg
Daniel Davis at Cedar Run
Lewis Donathan at Cedar Run
Wm. Donathan at Ox Hill
Alexander Fortner at Gettysburg
Thomas R. Hicks at Gaines Mill
Milton Murrah at Chancellorsville
Wm. Pettit at Ox Hill
A.M. Womack at Gaines Mill

Missing in Action

Azariah Brown
Joseph Chaplin [Choplin]
Sidney Chaplin [Choplin]
W.D. Kelly
Caston Kettle
John W. Tackett

Died

W.H. Apperson
G.W. Bowvender [Bovender]
J.M. Brann
Squire Brown
J.F. Brown
L.M. Cornelius
Lemuel Cozzens
J.W. Freeman
B.C. Head
John S. Joyner
H.A. Logan
Hiram Mitchell
Abraham Murphy
J.W. Nocholson
Wm. Norman
Robert Roas
W.H. Spence
Franklin Tacket

Sixty-Sixth North Carolina Infantry Regiment Roster [2]

Regimental Officers

Colonel Alexander Duncan Moore, Killed: June 3, 1864
Colonel/Lieutenant Colonel J.H. Nethercutt
Lieutenant Colonel/Major Clement G. Wright, Died: March 13, 1864
Major David S. Davis
Adjutant W.G. Williams
Ensign Roderick Sugg
A. Q. M. W. C. Jordan

Surgeon J. H. Kinyoun
Assistant Surgeon S. Eves
Assistant Surgeon T. S. Fox

Sergeant Major W. B. Wright
Q. M. Sergeant John Wiseman
Ordnance Sergeant W. B. Stansell
Com. Sergeant R.P . James

Hospital Steward W. P. Teague

Drum Major C. Austin
Musician – Bartollomer
Musician J. Bragg
Musician M. Bragg
Musician J. D. Carnington
Musician G. Carter
Musician J.C. Carter
Musician C. Darden
Musician – Edwards
Musician L. Evans
Musician J. P. Garris
Musician W. Genkins
Musician J. S. Gooch
Musician J.J. Griffin
Musician P. Griffin
Musician S. Griffin
Musician G.W. Hall
Musician D.M. Hix
Musician C. L. Koonce
Musician W. C. R. Loftin
Musician W. Massey
Musician John Murphy
Musician – Myers
Musician John Smith
Musician F. Spruce
Musician B. F. Stancell
Musician E. D. Suggs
Musician W. B. Wright

Companies

Company A
Orange County

Officers

Captain Joseph W. Latta,
Captain/First Lieutenant Albert C. Faucett
First Lieutenant/Second Lieutenant James G. Latta,
Second Lieutenant John C. Lynch, Killed: July 4, 1864 near Salisbury, Virginia
Second Lieutenant/Second Sergeant George B. Pearce

Noncommissioned Officers

First Sergeant John Couch
Second Sergeant George B. Pearce
Third Sergeant William R. Scarlett
Fourth Sergeant John Hall
Fifth Sergeant Isaac D. Whitaker
First Corporal William G. Couch
Second Corporal James D. Horner
Third Corporal John W. Rhew
Fourth Corporal James H. Browning

Privates:

Nelson Baldwin
James Barbee
William J. Barnes, Promoted to Sergeant
William Barrow
William J. Blackwood
Nash Booths
Andrew J. Borland, Detailed
George W. Brockwell
James Brockwell
Gaston Browning
John W. Browning
Moses Browning
Sidney Browning, Killed: May 18, 1864
William Browning, Died: July 19, 1864
H.H. Cardin
William H. Cardin, Wounded: May 1864
James T. Carrington, Wounded: July 4, 1864
John D. Carrington, Transferred
Richard Carrington
W.P. Carrington, Discharged: August 14, 1864
James Cates
John M. Cates
Robert Cates
Thomas Cates, Wounded: June 3, 1864
William Cates
William J. Cates
Willie E. Cates
L.C. Chisenhall, Killed: May 20, 1861
Sidney Chisenhall
C. Chrismand
James N. Christian, Wounded: July 30, 1864

William D. Cole
Benjamin Correll, Died: July 15, 1863
George Couch
Nathan Couch, Wounded
Thomas J. Couch. Killed: January 23, 1864 or 1865
David W. Couch
William Couch
Robert Crabtree
William R. Crabtree
C. D. Dannagan, Killed: June 3, 1864
James T. Dixon
David Faucett, Died: August 5, 1864
Thomas Faucett
James W. Garrard
Skidmore J. Garrett, Detailed
Willie P. Gates, Detailed
Bryant Glenn
Hillman Glenn
William C. Glenn
William T. Glenn
George Gresham
Andrew Hall
Gaston Hampton
Charles M. Herndon, Wounded: July 3, 1864
James E. Hicks
Gaston W. Hill
John A. Holloway
Little D. Horner, Detailed
Moses W. Horner
Dupree Howell
Jesse W. James, Wounded: May 20,1864
John T. James, Promoted to Corporal
Thomas N. James
Benton Jeffreys
Durell Johnson
Wm. A. King, Died: June 24, 1864
John Kirkland, Died: July 20, 1864
Phillips W. Latta, Died: August 18, 1864
William Latta
Cadmus H. Lyon
William F. Mahon
Fielding Mangum
William S. Mayes
Simeon McFarland
Abel R. Mitchell
James Monk, Detailed
Green Phipps, Wounded: May 20, 1863
S.P. Phipps, Promoted Corporal
Simeon Phipps
John Pool
Ransom Pool, Wounded: May 18, 1864
Rufus Pool
Herbert Proctor, Died: July 3, 1864
John Proctor
Silas M. Rhew
Willaim Rhew
William Rhew (not a duplication)
Thomas J. Riley
William L. Riley
Andrew J. Rhodes
George A. Rhodes
James C. Scarlett
Charles Simpson
William Simpson
William Simpson, Jr.
John W. Smith
John W. Stanly
Samuel M. Strayhorn
Albert A. Tate
William Teasley
F. M. Thompson, Wounded: February 23, 1864
Henry Urnsted
Moses Vicker
Henry H. Walker, Died: August 18. 1864
John A. Walker
Chesley P. Warren
James W. Watson
A.J. Whitaker
James A. Whitaker
William W. Wolford

James Woods, Died: August 12, 1864
James M. Woods
James M. Woods, Jr.
John Woods, Died: July 4, 1864
John M. Woods
William M. Woods

Company B
Nash and Franklin Counties

Officers

Captain Passun Nicholas, Prisoner: July 20, 1863; Died: Johnson's Island, Ohio
Captain/First Lieutenant Winfield S. Mitchell
Second Lieutenant/Private W. A. Moore, Promoted From Ranks, Resigned
Second Lieutenant David. N. Sills
Second Lieutenant J. B. Bunting, Jr.

Noncommissioned Officers

First Sergeant G.H. Pitts
Second Sergeant J.H. Pitts
Third Sergeant J.P. Tucker
Fourth Sergeant J J. Wiggs
Fifth Sergeant T.C. May
First Corporal J.J. Griffin
Second Corporal C.H.C. Bunting
Third Corporal J.J. Wester
Fourth Corporal J.C. Baker

Privates

G.R. Acree
John Alford
Simeon Baker
G. W. Bartholomew
N. Bartholomew
Merritt Batchelor
Rufus Batchelor, Died: Richmond, Virginia
William Bennett
J.A. Bowden
J.W. Bowden
M.B. Bowden
R.T.D. Bowden
W.B. Bowden
J.R. Braswell
David Bunn
T.B. Bunting
J.M. Champion
A.J. Collins
G.W. Collins
G.W. Cook
J.B. Cook
Stephen Cook
G.W. Coppedge
Hiram Coppedge
J.N. Coppedge
Jordan Coppedge
Joseph Coppedge

J.H. Culvard
W.T. Davis
E. Dorsey
J.O. Edwards
W.H. Edwards
J.H. Fuller
Thomas Gay
J.S. Gooch
R.F. Griffin
P. Griffin
Joseph Harper
A. D. Hines
Edmond House
Fenner Jones
Samuel Joyner
Richard Joyner
W.B. Lancaster
J.F. Leonard
J.J. Leonard, Jr.
J.J. Leonard, Sr.
G.E. Matthews
James Matthews
J.I. May
S.W. May
William A. Moore, Promoted to Second Lieutenant
J.C. Mullins
J.M. Murphey
J.N. Nelms
J.H. Odorm
Joseph Perry
J.B. Privett
J.G. Sillis
O.C. Stallings
John Stiles
M.C. Strickland
G.W. Thomas, Sr.
C.W. Thomas, Jr.
Samuel Thomas
H.H. Todd
J.H. Todd
Benjamin Upchurch
W.P. Weathers
B.E. Wester, Discharged: February 22, 1864
E. Wester
T.C. Wester
E.C. Wiggins
Bennett Wood
Henry Wood
J.H. Wood
W.H. Wood
J.W. Williams
S.J. Yelverton

Company C
Wayne and Lenoir Counties

Officers

Major/Captain David S. Davis
First Lieutenant R. E. Davis
First Lieutenant/Private J. B. Herring
Second Lieutenant James Williams, Jr.
Second Lieutenant Jesse Holland

Noncommissioned Officers

First Sergeant R.W. Herring
Second Sergeant James Canley
Third Sergeant W.I. Phillips
Fourth Sergeant W.B. Cox
Fifth Sergeant Isaac Casey
Fist Corporal J.R. Wade, Prisoner
Second Corporal L.W. Phillips
Third Corporal Lemuel Brown, Prisoner
Fourth Corporal A.B. Herring

Privates

Perry Anderson
Jackson Basden
Joseph Benton
James Bishop
Jacob Botts
Jesse Boyett
Hardy Brown
John Brown
H.M. Brown
John Canley, Discharged
Thomas Canley
Jacob Cox
John Cunningham
Bryant Davenport
Burwell Davis
Daniel Davis
James Davis
John Davis
C.B. Deal
James Duncan
Hugh Galagher
Ichabod Grant
Jesse Hardy
B.I. Herring
George Herring
J.B. Herring, Promoted to First Lieutenant
I.R. Herring
S.B. Herring
Henry Herring
Robin Hinson, Detailed
T.R. Hill, Discharged
Zach Hill
Reding Hines
J.I. Hines
J.H. Hines
H.L. Horn
C.C. James
R.P. James
W.H. Kennedy, Prisoner
G.D. Kearney, Prisoner
Benjamin Lanier

J.L. Lanier
Zebulon Lanier
Graham Lee
E.E. Leltner, Detailed
A.R. Miller, Detailed, Q. M. S.
Riley Mobley
Orlen Mobley
W.L. Parker, Prisoner
N.J. Phillips, Prisoner
W.I. Phillips, Prisoner
William Powell
J.W. Quinn
Henry Register
J. Rayner, Prisoner
Isaac Sanderlin
Jere Sanderlin, Prisoner
Enoch Sasser
Isaac Strout
Job Strout
Richard Strout
Levi Sutton
J.A. Sutton
A.W. Taylor
Q.M. Tharrington
G. Tindall
John Tindall
J.W. Thigpen
David Vaughan
D.H. Wade
J.R. Waller
M.G. Waller
Davis Williams
Edward Williams, Promoted to Corporal, Prisoner
Law Williams

Company D
Jones and Lenoir Counties

Officers

Captain W. T. Robinson
First Lieutenant T. H. Kearney
Second Lieutenant William A. W. Askew
Second Lieutenant Lewis Bynum

Noncommissioned Officers

First Sergeant D. W. Hood
Second Sergeant Richard Isler
Third Sergeant J. L. Hardy
Fourth Sergeant Lemuel Fields
Fifth Sergeant E. J. Barrow
First Corporal W. L. Wiggins, Promoted to Sergeant
Second Corporal Thomas Sutton
Third Corporal Joseph Bragg
Fourth Corporal Simpson Harper

Privates

Lewis Alagood
Edward Arnold
James Arnold
John Arnold
Stephen Arnold
Elijah Arthur
Amos Askew
Benjamin Askew
Thomas Avery, Detailed
J.M. Bragg
J.J. Brock
F.I. Bryant, Detailed
T.I. Bryant, Detailed
John Bynum
J.B. Callton
Thomas Cameron, Detailed
J.B. Carter, Promoted Corporal
C.W. Demon
Joel Dixon
Simson Dixon
Cullen Doyerty, Detailed
W.H. Doyerty
Isaac Dudley, Prisoner
Stephen Dudley, Prisoner
Thomas Dudley, Prisoner
John B. Evans
Edward Goldwin
James Goldwin
Frederick Grady, Died Of Wounds
William Grady
J.A. Hadock
W.O. Hadock
K. Harper, Promoted to Corporal
W.A. Haswell
A.J. Haswell
L. Howland
George Ipock
Samuel Ipock
D.T. Jackson, Prisoner
A.H. Jones
Frederick Jones, Detailed
David Jones, Prisoner
Stephen Jones
Absalom Kinsey, Prisoner
A. Littleton, Prisoner
David Marvins
W.C. May
J.J. May
W.H. McGhee, Prisoner
Frederick McKoy
James Moore
W.F. Moore, Prisoner
Wright Moore, Detailed
E.I. Newbolt
T.E. Outlaw
C. Pringle, Detailed
George Parker
J.C. Parker
W. Prescott, Prisoner
G.A. Richardson, Prisoner
William Simpson, Prisoner
J. J. Sumerlin
Cicero Taylor
D.H. Taylor
Jeremiah Thomas, Prisoner
James Thigpen
John Turner
Simeon Turner
Elisha Walters
John Weeks, Detailed
William Weeks
L.W. Wood, Detailed
Awner Worthington
Benjamin White
Frederick White, Detailed
James Yates
John Yates

Company E
Lenoir and Carteret Counties

Officers

Captain Guilford W. Cox
Captain/Second Lieutenant Steven S. Quinerly
First Lieutenant Ivan K. Witherington
First Lieutenant/Second Sergeant W. M. Dennis
Second Lieutenant William I. Grimmet
Second Lieutenant/Private John Hall
Second Lieutenant/Fifth Sergeant John E. Taylor, Promoted From Ranks, Wounded

Noncommissioned Officers

First Sergeant James S. May
Second Sergeant William N. Dennis
Third Sergeant James D. Witherington, Wounded
Fourth Sergeant Robert R. Hill
Fifth Sergeant John E. Taylor
First Corporal William G. Dudley
Second Corporal F.M. Gwaltney
Third Corporal L.K. Witherington, Promoted Sergeant
Fourth Corporal C.M. Davis

Privates

John Albert, Detailed
Josiah Aldridge, Detailed
James Barbee
L.B. Besney, Promoted Corporal
Pinkney Boon
William Bowers
James W. Boyette
James T. Bradley
Jesse Braxton
Franklin Brown
Jesse Brown, Wounded
Robert Bryan
Frederick Cox
John M. Cox
Joseph Cox, Wounded
William C. Cox
W.R. Crabtree
Phineas Davenport, Prisoner
John W. Dawson
Willie Dawson
Forney Dupree
Jesse F. Dupree, Detailed
Lewis Edwards, Wounded
Norfleet Fountain
John C. Garner
F. M. Gaultney, Died Of Disease At Home: September 7, 1864
Rufus Glancy
William Glancy, Detailed
James D. Gould, Died Of Disease: July 18, 1863
Thomas Gray
John Hall, Promoted Second Lieutenant
Abram Hardie
John A. Hardie
Ira Heath
Richard Higgins
Robert P. Hill, Wounded

Marion Hines
William Howard
William Howard, Died Of Wound:
August 15, 1864
John Irving
James M. Jarell
Joseph Jenkins
William L. Jones, Detailed
Allen Jones, Detailed
Alexander Jones, Detailed
Frank Jump
Lafayette Kirkman
Richard Lee
N.J. McPherson
Allen Moore, Detailed
Eason G. Moore
Matthew Nelson
Kincy Nobles
Wiley Parker
Lenoir Pate, Wounded
Gatlin Pate
Alfred Powell
Robert Quinn
James E. Quinnerly, Died: July 2, 1863
T.J. Riley
W.L. Riley
T.M. Ross
Alexander Rouse, Detailed
John Simpkins, Detailed
Henry Smith, Died: September 4, 1864
John Smith, Detailed
Joseph Smith, Wounded: September 29,
1864
Benjamin F. Stokes
Edward Stokes, Detailed
Guilford Stokes
Cyrus Strickland
James N. Sugg
John Sutton
Richard Sutton
David Warlis
Augustus Waters
Jesse Waters
W.D. Waters
J.W. Watson
S.O. Watson
Spencer C. Watson
Lewis C. White, Died At Richmond:
August 1864
W.L. White, Detailed
John L. Williams, Wounded: July 30,
1864
Robert Wilson

Company F
Jones and Lenoir Counties

Officers

Major/Captain John H. Nethercutt
Captain/First Lieutenant Willis/Willie J. Raspberry/Rasberry
Captain/Second Lieutenant Chris D. Foy
Second Lieutenant Frank Foy
Second Lieutenant S. Sidney Carter

Noncommissioned Officers

First Sergeant James T. Witherington
Second Sergeant Philemon Bender
Third Sergeant Jackson H. Kinsey
Fourth Sergeant Luby Harper
Fifth Sergeant Amos W. Askew
First Corporal Lewis Bynum
Second Corporal Joseph F. Brock
Third Corporal David W. Hood
Fourth Corporal Lewis A. Barfield

Privates

Owen Adams, Died: March 7, 1863
Ivey Andrew, Detailed
Edward Arnold
James Arnold
John Arnold
Stephen Arnold
Thomas Avery
Joseph B. Banks
Lewis A. Barfield, Detailed
Richard S. Becton, Promoted Fifth Sergeant
Elijah A. Bell, Promoted Corporal
Matthew Bowen
Andrew J. Brittain
John J. Brock, Transferred From A. & R.R. Bridge Co., May 16, 1862
Frederick J. Bryan
Lewis C. Bryan
Thomas J. Bryan
Mitchell Busick
John Bynum
James B. Carlton
Thomas Case, Transferred From A. & R.R. Bridge Co., May 16, 1862
John Corner
E.L. Curren
James W. Dawson
James W. Dawson (probably duplicate)
Robert Dawson
Cullen Doherty
Henry Doherty
William K. Doherty
Thomas E. Dudley
William T. Duvall, Detailed
Calvin Etheridge
John B. Evans
Joseph Evans
Joseph B. Ferrands
James O. Frazzell
Charles Freeman
Lewis Freeman
John Futrell

Burwell Ginn, Transferred to10th Regiment Artillery: August 20, 1862
Carny Gooding
Council Gooding
John Gooding
Moses Gooding
John A. Haddock
William G. Haddock
George W. Hal, (probably Hall)
Alexander H. Hamilton
Epenetus Hardy
Franklin Harper, Promoted to Corporal
D.H. Harrison
Reuben Hood
James L. Howland
C.J. Huffman
W.B. Huffman, Wounded: April 16, 1863
Lewis Humphrey
William G. Ipoch
Richard Irvin
Wm. Irving
Joseph H. Jolly
A.H. Jones
A.J. Jones, Promoted to Corporal
Everett Jones
Frederick Jones
J.B. Jones
James Jones
Jesse Jones
W.L. Kilpatrick
David King
Ivey King
Samuel King, Wounded: April 17, 1863
John C. Koonce
J.B.C. Lane
Barney Leary
Robert Leary
H. Wood Levin
Arthur Littleton
Andrew J. Loftin, Transferred From A. & N.C.R.R. Bridge, May 15, 1862
Thomas J. Loftin
William Lorans
James Metts
William Metts
Bennett Mizengo
J.C. Moore
James Moore
Stephen Moore
William Moore
Wright Moore
Richard Morgan
Stephen Morgan
J.R. Murphy, Detailed
John Murphy
E.J. Newbold
Joseph H. Nunn, Promoted to Corporal
T. E. Outlaw
S.P.E. Pennington
Alexander J. Rasberry
Allen Rasberry
G.A. Richardson
William Robertson, Transferred to Tenth Regiment Artillery, August 12, 1862
Charles Sawyer
Edmund E. Sherar
Alfred Simmons
John W. Simmons, Transferred From Bridge Company, May 15, 1862
Simeon Simmons, Transferred from Bridge Company, May 15, 1862
John Small
Sylvester Small
Bartemus Smith
C.C. Smith, Wounded, April 1863
J.W. Smith
Titus B. Smith
Fennel Smith
John L. Stanley
James A. Stanly, Prisoner
Thomas Stilly
E. D. Sugg
Hardy Sugg

R. P. Sugg
Owen Sullivan
Owen Sullivan (probably duplicate)
Jesse J. Summerlin
John Sullivan
J. P. Taylor
Jesse Taylor
Lewis Taylor
James Thigpen, Transferred from A & N.C.R.R. Bridge Co., May 15, 1862
William J. Tilgham
George P. Turner, Died: April 21, 1863
James B. Turner
John Turner, Transferred from A & N.C.R.R. Bridge Co., May 15, 1862
Silas Venters
Everett S. Whaley
John Whaley, Killed, April 17, 1863
Benjamin White
Frederick White
Haywood A. White, Detailed
Needham M. White
S.J. White
Forney Wilcox
Furnifold Wilcox
William Wilcox
Joseph H. Williams
Abner Witherington
James G. Witherington
James W. Witherington
John H. Witherington
Shade W. Witherington
Levi W. Wood

Company G
Lenoir County

Officers

Captain E. B. Blackmer, Resigned, September 5, 1864
First Lieutenant W.J./G. Williams
Second Lieutenant W.C. Brandon
Second Lieutenant J.W. Walker

Noncommissioned Officers

First Sergeant J.M. Burton
Second Sergeant B.R. Bagget
Third Sergeant F.A. Layton
Fourth Sergeant W.T. Griffin
Fifth Sergeant William Brown
First Corporal J.F. Payne
Second Corporal J.T. Foster
Third Corporal N.J. Griffin
Fourth Corporal J.I. Miller
Musician J.C. Austin
Musician S.C. Griffin
Musician D.M. Hicks

Privates:

A. Allgood
A. Brown
W.S. Badget, Promoted to Sergeant
J.J. Barringer
J.W. Baxter, Promoted Corporal, Died at Home, October 8, 1864
P.H. Cain
A. Carter
William Carter

H.F. Chirod
G.A. Cobble
R.H. Cook
H.H. Crews
James Cross
H.H. Cyrus
J.H. Dennis
C.S. Dennis
J.M. Eudy(Euda)
J.N. Foster
J.H. Fraley
J.M. Fults
J.W. Garner, Promoted to Corporal
D.B. Gheen
G.H. Ghun
D. Gibble
G.W. Gibble
H.C. Gibble
J. Gibble
W. Gibble
W.C. Gibson
D. Graves
N.J. Griffin
James Harris
H. Harrison
A. Hedgecock
E.W. Hunt
H. Hunt
W. Jenkins
G.P. Johnson
I.H. Johnson
H.H. Kimmer
W.D. Lanler
F.M. Leslie
F.M. Leslie, (not a duplicate)
W. Livingood
J.M. Loftin
W. Loftin
C.A.G. Miller, Promoted to Corporal; Prisoner at St. Petersburg: August 13, 1864
J.C. Martin
J.P. Martin
M.C. Myers
W.A. Myers, Promoted to Corporal
J.M. Overcash
W. Overcash
A.A. Owens
J.D. Pealer
J.M.C. Peninger
R.A. Plumer
M. Potts
W.A. Reavy
W.L. Recks
B.A. Rose
T.A. P. Roseman
C.N. Sain
Nathan Sain
E. Shaw
W.A. Suping
S.W. Solomon
H.J. Shuping
S. Speight
J.S. Spurgeon
V.D. Swain
G.W. Thomas
W.T. Thomason
W.H. Thrift, Died at Home, October 5, 1864
F.E. Vanhoy
William Vanhoy
W.M. Wallace
C.C. Ward
R. Weaver
T. Windsor
W.H. Windsor

Company H
Duplin and Onslow Counties

Officers

Captain James G. Davis
First Lieutenant Willis W. Cherry
Second Lieutenant Robert J. Swinson
Second Lieutenant Edward Williamson

Noncommissioned Officers

First Sergeant Charles C. Croom
First Sergeant John P. Miller
Second Sergeant Roderick P. Sugg
Third Sergeant Isham Sholar
Fourth Sergeant Joseph H. Nunn
First Corporal Franklin Harper, Promoted to Sergeant
Second Corporal John Holland
Third Corporal James W. Dawson, Promoted to Sergeant
R. H. Jones (no rank)

Privates

J.S. Amon
D.F. Barber
G.W. Bell
John M. Bostic
J.W. Bowen
E.D. Brinson
O.W. Brittain, Detailed
L.J. Brock
J.W. Brown
Owen Brown
P.I. Bryant
Cason Capps
James C. Daniel
John Davenport
J.J. Edwards
L.H. Emory
Charles Freeman
John Gurganus
Lewis Hall
Burwell Ham, Discharged, October 22, 1864
Joel Ham
J. O. Harrison
J.M. Henderson
S.W. Henderson
S.M. Hines
L.L. Humphrey
J.G. Hunter, Died of Disease, October 22, 1864
J. E. Hunter
Charles Holland
M. M. Jones
W.H. Kennedy
Thomas Kilpatrick
A.G. Kornegay, Promoted Corporal
I.L. Lanier
H.I. Lee
John Murphy
Daniel Padgett
G.W. Pierce
J.C. Rayner
J.B. Rhodes
Gaston Roe
J.W. Rouse, Detailed

J.B. Royall
John Royall
John Sanderson
Levi Sanderson, Detailed
Lewis Sanderson, Detailed
J.A. Sandlin
J.M. Shehan
A.E. Simmons
Bryant Smith
David Spence
Ferdinand Spence
E.D. Sugg
Benjamin Sumerlin
Lemuel Sumerlin
Aurke Swinson
Jesse Swinson, Transferred
J.J. Thigpen
Kenan Thigpen, Died Of Disease: August 23, 1864
Elza Taylor
W J. Taylor
N.W. Tetterton
C.G. Thomas
H.G. Thomas
Frederick Whaley
Rigden Whaley
Sebastian Whaley
W.B. Whaley
William Whitman
H.N. Wilkins
Benjamin Williams
Jesse Williams, Died Of Wound: August 12, 1864

Company I
Wayne, Onslow, and Jones Counties

Officers

Captain Jesse P. Williams
First Lieutenant Josiah W. Smith, Resigned: September 2, 1864
Second Lieutenant Silas W. Venters
Second Lieutenant Luby Harper

Noncommissioned Officers

First Sergeant L. Williamson
Second Sergeant George T. Bennett
Third Sergeant James B. Jones
Fourth Sergeant Cicero Taylor, Detailed
Fifth Sergeant Thomas Uzzell
First Corporal Matthew Uzzell
Second Corporal James Hayward, Promoted to Sergeant
Second Corporal Jacob G. Rhodes
Fourth Corporal Allen Wooten
Musician Calvin Darden

Privates

Marshall Branch
Christopher Brinson
Levi J. Brock
Richard Brown
C.H. Churchwell
John Coley
William Copeland
Calvin Deans
Henderson Deans
James Elmore
John Futrell
Dawson Ginn
Benjamin N. Gurganus
George W. Gurganus
Hezekiah Ham
William H. Ham, Promoted to Musician
William H. Harrison
Thomas J. Hewitt
Abram H. Hill, Discharged, October 10, 1864
Lemuel Hill
Parrott N. Hill
Lewis Jackson
Luke Jarman
Rigden Jarman
William Jarvis
William Jones
Jacob G. Kennedy
Owen H. Kennedy, Promoted to Sergeant
Asa King
Thomas King
John F. Koonce
Gray Lewis
William Landing
Hosea Marshburn
Kenan Marshburn
Moses Marshburn
Bennett Millard
John A. Miller, Detailed
Wesley Morton
James Nettercutt

Sheridan F. Nickens
Joseph W. Outlaw, Detailed
Needham B. Outlaw
Edgar Parker
William Pate, Died: September 6, 1864
Henry Radford
John Register
William Revis
John L. Roberts
Robert(s) Sandling
Wiley Sasser
John A. Scisson
Anson Shephard
Calvin Smith
Henry G. Smith
Charles Southerland, Died, October 22, 1864
Abner Sullivan
Elijah Sumersill
Jesse Swinson
Major Swinson
John Sykes
James B. Turner
John B. Taylor
John P. Taylor
Levi Taylor
L.H. Tull
Charles Vaughan
William Vaughan
J.N.B. Vick, Detailed
Y. D. Vinson
Thomas White
C. S. Witherington, Detailed
L. J. Wolfe

Company K
Wayne and New Hanover Counties

Officers

Captain William C. Freeman
Captain John P. Sykes
First Lieutenant E.F. Gilbert
First Lieutenant/Private Alvin Bagley (Bailey), Promoted From Ranks
First Lieutenant/Fourth Sergeant John J. Massey, Promoted From Sergeant
Second Lieutenant J.T. Sykes
Second Lieutenant Wm R. Privett
Second Lieutenant Alvin Bailey, (could be duplicate of Bagley/Bailey)
Second Lieutenant/Private D.J. Knowles, Promoted from Ranks

Noncommissioned Officers

First Sergeant O.L. Jackson
Second Sergeant B.F. Stancill
Third Sergeant C.C. Stancill
Fourth Sergeant John J. Massey, Promoted to First Lieutenant
Fifth Sergeant Edwin Darnes
First Corporal T.W. Ellis
Second Corporal J.P. Garris
Third Corporal B.F. Whitney (Third Sergeant)
Fourth Corporal J.G. Rowe

Privates

Henry Anderson
Ezekiel Bagley
Alfred Bailey
Alvin Bailey (Bagley), Promoted to First Lieutenant
John W. Bailey
Reddin Bailey
W.W. Bailey
Clinton Barnes, Died of Wound: August 15, 1864
J.J. Barrington
Benjamin Bradley
Levi Bradley
David Brock, Died: September 13, 1864
Richard Brown
R.C. Bryant
Benjamin K. Byrd
J.A. Boswell
J.T. Boswell, Promoted to Sergeant
W.W. Bland
John Capps
William Capps
Wiley Cornish
James W. Cox
J.H. Crawford
L.H. Crawford
D.H. Creech
Larkin Creech, Prisoner: June 19, 1861
Thomas Croft
William H. Croom, Detailed
Everett Dickson
James W. Edwards
A.J. Ellis, Wounded: September 1, 1864
Charles W. Ellison
Elisha Evans
J.D. Evans
P.R. Farmer, Promoted Corporal
Mosses Farmer
James Florey
Bryant Glisson
B.B. Hamilton
Claudius Hemant
George Hill, Detailed
W.F. Hill
Christopher Hines
Thomas Hines, Prisoner: June 12, 1864
Henry Howell
Jethro Howell
C.W. Huggins
Joseph Hughes, Discharged: August 10, 1863
S.S. Ingram
O.L. Jackson
William Jackson
J.G. Jennett
J.W. Johnson
M.T. Johnson, Transferred: August 16, 1863
W.D. Jones
D.J. Knowles, Promoted to Second Lieutenant
James A. King, Detailed
Jonas Lamb
Thomas J. Lamb
David Lane
J.M. Lane
John Lane
John W. Lane, Promoted to Corporal
Littleton Langston
David Lewis
B.G. Massey
D.F. Massey
W.C. Massey
West Massey
William Massey
Nowell Mathis
Wells Mathis
H.W. McLorem, Detailed
L.L. Merritt
James J. Millard
Bennett Millard
Demsey Newell
Nathan Oldham, Prisoner Corporal

A.W. Oliver
H.N. Oliver
W.B. Oliver
T.T. Oliver
Wesley Oliver
George F. Parker
Wiley Parker, Jr.
Wiley Parker, Sr., Detailed
Van H. Pate
D.J. Pittman
James Price
N.G. Price
N.W. Roberts
W.W. Rogers
J.G. Rowe
A.G. Ruffin
William Sasser
D.A. Sellers
John Smith
W.J. Spencer
J.J. Stallings
J.T. Stallings, Prisoner: July 17, 1864
W.H. Stallings, Prisoner: July 17, 1864
J.H. Stancill
W.B. Stancill
D.K. Stanly
John Summerlin
Levi Taylor
R.H. Tomlinson
W.H. Tomlinson, Died: October 15, 1864
Hillard Turner
Willis Waller
Benjamin F. Waters, Detailed
Erastus Wellons
J.T. Whittey
Nathan Wiggs, Promoted to Sergeant and Died In Hospital: October 27, 1864
E.W. Williamson
David Winborn
D.D. Woodard, Died At Raleigh: August 9, 1863
Joseph Woodard
Richard Woodard, Died September 1, 1864
Willie B. Wright

Appendix 2
Medical Glossary

MEDICAL GLOSSARY

Following are the most commonly used medical terms in Dr. Kinyoun's Diary and the most recognized throughout the Civil War.

Abscess/Absys [*sic*] – a localized collection of pus within the body, which can be attributed to a bacterial infection.

Anasarca – large amounts of localized fluids; generalized edema-swelling; dropsy.

Anemic – resulting from the condition of anemia, constituting a deficiency and/or a reduction in the red blood cell elements in the hemoglobin. Affliction evidenced by lack of strength associated with contraction of disease and its effects, or in war-depleted acute blood as a result of a wound(s).

Ankylosis/Ancholsis[*sic*] – the immobility of a joint, such as an ankle, or connection due to an injury, disease, or operation; bent.

Anthrax – an infectious disease caused by spore forming bacterium; transmitted to humans through herbaceous animals; often fatal.

Apoplexy – archaic term for a stroke.

Asthma – recurrent attacks of wheezing and shortness of breath. It can be an allergic reaction to various factors resulting in an inflammation of the air passages. However, there are other causes for allergic reaction, such as colds.

Bacteria – disease causing microorganisms.

Bilious/Billorsa [*sic*] /Billiosa [*sic*] aka Bile – excess production of bile from the liver.

Bronchitis – affliction and/or infection/inflammation of the bronchial tubes. Several variations exist of this disease, most notably acute and chronic. Symptoms include, but not limited to, fever, coughing, and bringing up sputum.

Catarrh – a pulmonary infection, which can be in the head, as well, resulting in a discharge from a mucous membrane, evidenced by mucous drainage and cough.

Cephalgia/Cephalagia [*sic*] – headache.

Chicken Pox aka Varicella – a highly contagious viral disease commonly known or classified as a "Childhood Disease," but may affect adults. Fever, chills, and skin eruptions known as pox are characteristics of the illness.

Chills – a shivering or shaking condition, whereby the body experiences a sense of coldness, often associated with such illnesses as **Malaria, Smallpox**, and other diseases having a high fever.

Cholera – associated with warmer climates, an acute intestinal infection resulting in vomiting, coupled with massive **Diarrhea** and severe cramping; attributed to feces contaminated water source, and may result in death from fluid loss.

Colic – abdominal pain.

Consumption – archaic term for the disease known as **Tuberculosis.**

Continuance/Continuance Fever – a persistent fever.

Contract Surgeon/Doctor – a paid, non-military surgeon and/or doctor to supplement military medical needs. Usually hired in areas of battle to assist in administering to the wounded. Usually paid higher than military doctors and, in some cases, were purported frauds lacking any medical background.

Contusion – bruise.

Cystirrhagia/Cystorrhagia – inner bleeding from the bladder**.**

Cystitis – bladder and/or urinary tract infection.

Debility/Debilitus [*sic*] – to be infirm and/or in a weakened state; also known as asthenia.

Dia – meaning through, also as a prefix meaning across, between, or apart.

Diarrhea – a liquefied and more frequent discharge of feces, may be combined with a fever, and caused by tainted food and/or water.

Diphtheria – an acute upper respiratory infection characterized by a covering of the throat by a false membrane, which can ultimately lead to death.

Disease – illness and/or sickness which may be caused by a microorganism/germ, may result in death or extensive convalescence, recuperation or period of recovery. A general deviation from the normal state of health.

Dyspepsia – indigestion, abdominal discomfort, belching.

Dysentery – a disease resulting in the inflammation of the large intestine, followed by severe abdominal pain and discharge of bloody mucous through bowels in the form of **Diarrhea**.

Emesis/Emesia/Emesnia [*sic*] - act of vomiting.

Epilepsy – a disorder of the brain, which may result in seizures, loss of consciousness, and mobility.

Febris/Fever – an increase in the body's temperature from its normal level.

Fistula – an abnormal connection or passageway between organs or blood vessels that do not connect, or that leads to the skin.

Frostbite – a freezing of the extremities, most notably the limbs, and in particular, the toes, fingers, ears, face, and nose. It is a result of overexposure to cold temperature, and if left untreated, can lead to gangrene and eventual amputation.

Furunculus/Furuncle/Furunculosis – a boil in the skin caused by a staph infection.

Gangrene – death of tissue, usually in limbs, accompanied by a putrid smell. A condition resulting in the loss of blood and accompanying oxygen to afflicted area. Amputation was a common remedy in treatment in order to save patient, prior to the introduction of antibiotics.

Gastritis/Gastretis [*sic*] – a condition resulting in the inflammation of the stomach.

Germ(s) – a microorganism capable of causing a disease.

Gonorrhea – sexually transmitted disease causing pain and persistent discharge in the genital tracts, also known as the "clap."

Hemorrhage – a large amount of bleeding from a blood vessel.

Hemorrhoid/Hemoroid [*sic*] aka Piles – painful swelling of veins within the anus.

Hepatitis – an inflammation of the liver, with three varying degrees of severity, commonly known as **Hepatitis A**, **Hepatitis B**, and **Hepatitis C.** Hepatitis D, E, F, and G have also been identified.

Hernia – a break in a cavity wall of the intestine, brain, or other body area causing a protrusion.

Herpes – any of several inflammatory diseases of the skin, resulting in blisters of the mucous membranes and skin. These diseases come in many forms, including chicken pox, shingles and genital herpes.

Hospital – a facility where the sick and wounded are taken or transferred to for the treatment of their disease and injury by medical personnel. A hospital may be as simplistic as a tent, or as comprehensive as a building.

Inflammation – a localized protective response of the body where heat, redness, swelling, and pain occurs.

Intermittent/Intermitance [*sic*] aka Intermittent Fever – an illness or condition occurring at separated intervals, also associated with reccurring fever similar to, or associated with, **Malaria**.

Jaundice (Icterus/Icturus) – a condition resulting from the presence of bile pigment in tissue and bilirubin in the blood, characterized by a yellowing of skin pigmentation.

Lumbago – lower back and/or upper buttock pain.

Malaria aka Ague – an infectious disease commonly transmitted by mosquitoes, resulting in a recurring high fever, sweating, and shaking chills.

Measles (Rubella/Rubeola) – a highly contagious viral disease often termed as a "Childhood Disease," affecting all ages, absent a vaccination. High fever and a red rash are common indications of illness.

Nephralgic – kidney pain.

Nephritis/Nephretis [*sic*] – inflammation of the kidney.

Neuralgia – pain extending along the path of a nerve.

Orchitis – an inflammatory condition of the scrotum, or sack containing the testes.

Paralysis/Paralisis [*sic*] – inability to move, a condition attributed to either injury or disease.

Paronychia/Paronchia [*sic*] – an inflammation of the skin folds around the nail.

Phlegmasia – an archaic reference to the word inflammation.

Phlegmon – a spreading inflammation, due to strep infection.

Phthisis/Pthisis [*sic*] – aggressively wasting or consumptive condition; archaic term for pulmonary **Tuberculosis.**

Pleurisy/Plurecy [*sic*] – an infection of the lungs, it is actually the inside of the chest wall and the outside lining of the lungs or inner linings or the pleura, causing a dry cough and/or localized chest pain associated with breathing.

Pneumonia – a disease causing inflammation of the lungs, derived from various sources including, but not limited to, bacteria and viruses, which may result in death.

Poison aka Toxin – an element or a substance that when injected, inserted, introduced, absorbed, or formed in the body causes harm or damage to the body, which may lead to death or destruction of affected tissue.

Polypus – polyp.

Polypus nasc – nasal polyp.

Psoriasis – a chronic skin disease evidenced by round circumscribed patches of red, white, and dry scales.

Remittence/Remitance/Remitans/Remit Fever - a fever and/or condition which periodically ceases, but reccurs.

Resection – a surgical technique utilized later in the Civil War. Instead of amputating a wounded or infected appendage, such as a limb, the affected area between two points is severed, then the detached portion is reattached to the remaining section, resulting in a shortened length, but use of the limb is restored to some degree.

Rheumatism/Rheumatic Fever/Rheumatoid Arthritis – a painful inflammation of the joints resulting in pain and stiffness, which can lead to a fever afflicting the heart's valves and progressing to a resulting disfiguration of the joints. During the Civil War, **Rheumatism** was also synonymous with **Rheumatic Fever** and **Rheumatoid Arthritis**.

Scabies/Scabes [*sic*] – caused by mites, resulting in scratching and itching of skin, sometimes referred to as mange.

Scurvy – a nutritional disease caused by a lack of Vitamin C in the diet, symptoms are bleeding through the skin, sponge-like gums, anemia, and a general lack of energy. The consumption of citrus products such as lemons, limes, and oranges is used as a preventive measure.

Smallpox aka Variola – an acute, highly-contagious viral disease, resulting in high fever, chills, and trademarked by red skin eruptions or ulcers known as pox.

Stomatitis – any of numerous diseases of the mouth characterized by swelling, pain, and white patches (canker sores).

Surgeon – a physician who specializes in surgery. A surgeon utilizes the special skill of intrusive treatment(s) by way of a procedure commonly referred to as an operation.

Syphilis – a sexually transmitted venereal disease caused by a spirochete and containing three stages of development. The first is evidenced by chancres, followed by ulcers and lymph node enlargement, culminating in disfiguration and/or possibly death, preceded by insanity. It was formerly called **"Great Pox."**

Tetanus aka Lockjaw – an acute, extremely painful, and often fatal disease, commonly a result of wounds. Characterized by muscle spasms, contractions, seizures, and paralysis. When settled in lower jaw, can cause the jaws to lock up, muscle spasms, or the throat to close, giving it the common name of **Lockjaw**.

Tonsillitis/Toncilitis [*sic*] – an inflammation of the tonsils.

Tuberculosis aka Consumption, Phthisis – a chronic infectious disease resulting from mycobacterium lodging mainly in the lungs; can be fatal.

Typhus/Typhoid Fever aka Camp Fever– Typhus and **Typhoid** are two different diseases with characteristics confused as being the same and called **Camp Fever,** which is a fever transmitted by lice, and characterized by high fever, red spots, and depression.

Ulcer – a painful sore, an excavation, or a defect of the surface of an organ or tissue, which can be an internal or superficial infection, characterized by pain and drainage. **Ulcers** can occur from numerous conditions, infections, and/or diseases.

Venereal Warts – a sexually transmitted virus afflicting the skin of the genital areas of the body in the form of raised skin lesions.

Virus – a minute infectious agent, too small to be seen by the ordinary light microscope; a disease causing microorganism, which will reside and/or cloak itself inside a living cell as a host agent.

Vulnus/Vulmus [*sic*] – a wound.

Wound/Wounded – in most cases a penetration of the skin and/or body resulting from an injury or, in cases of war, from a bullet, bayonet, artillery shell, or other instruments intended as a means of death and destruction.

Appendix 3
Dr. Kinyoun's Medical Diary

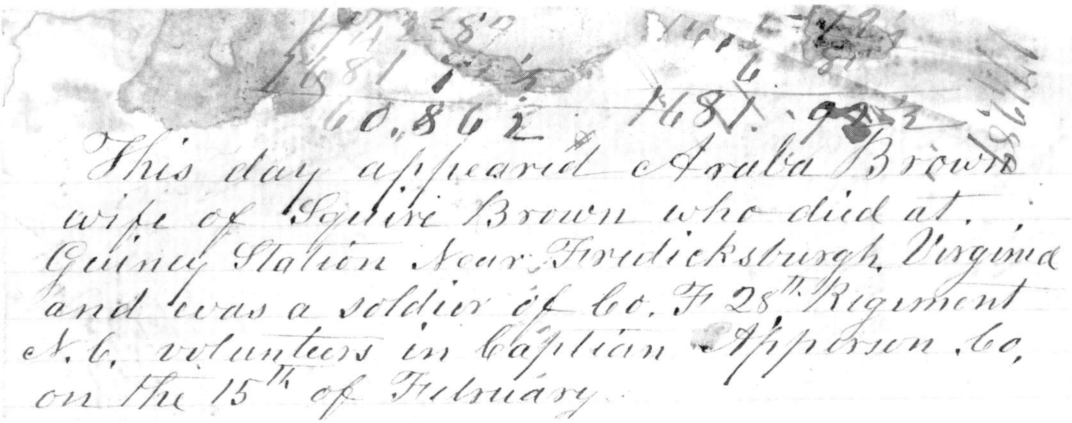

This day appeared Araba Brown
wife of Squire Brown who died at
Guiney Station Near Fredicksburgh Virginia
and was a soldier of Co. F 28th Regiment
N.C. volunteers in Captian Apperson Co.
on the 15th of Febuary

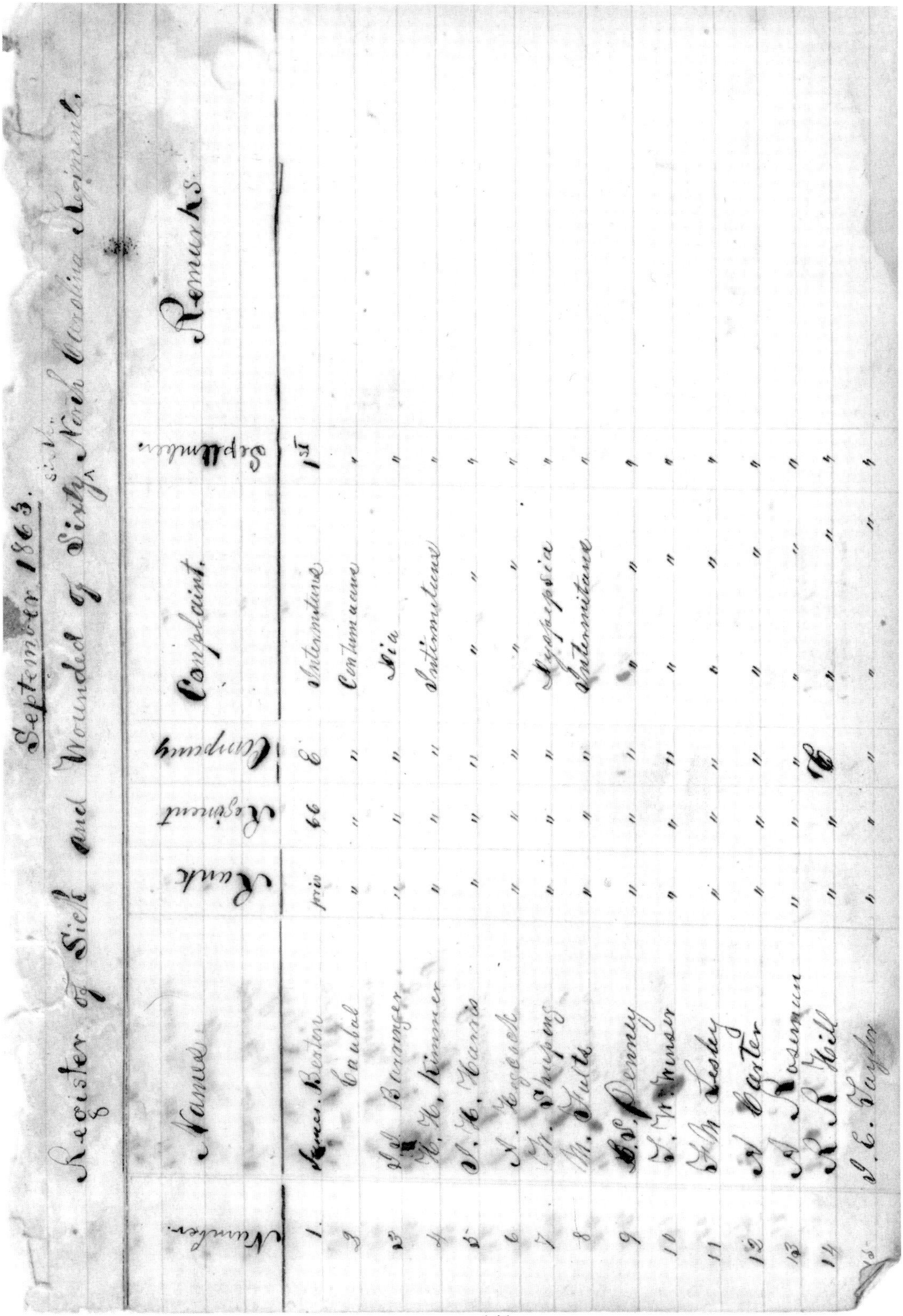

September 1863.

Register of Sick and Wounded of Sixty sixth North Carolina Regiment.

Number	Names	Rank	Regiment	Company	Complaint	September	Remarks
1.	James Bester	priv	66	E	Intermitans	1st	
2	Caubal	"	"	"	Contumacans	"	
3	J.J. Barringer	"	"	"	Dia	"	
4	H. H. Kimmer	"	"	"	Intermitans	"	
5	J. H. Harris	"	"	"	" "	"	
6	A. Hegcock	"	"	"	" "	"	
7	W. Shuping	"	"	"	Dyspepsia	"	
8	M. Fults	"	"	"	Intermitans	"	
9	B.S. Denney	"	"	"	" "	"	
10	T. W. Winser	"	"	"	" "	"	
11	F.M. Lesley	"	"	"	" "	"	
12	A. Carter	"	"	"	" "	"	
13	A. Roseman	"	"	"	" "	"	
14	R. R. Hill	"	"	C	" "	"	
15	J. C. Taylor	"	"	"	" "	"	

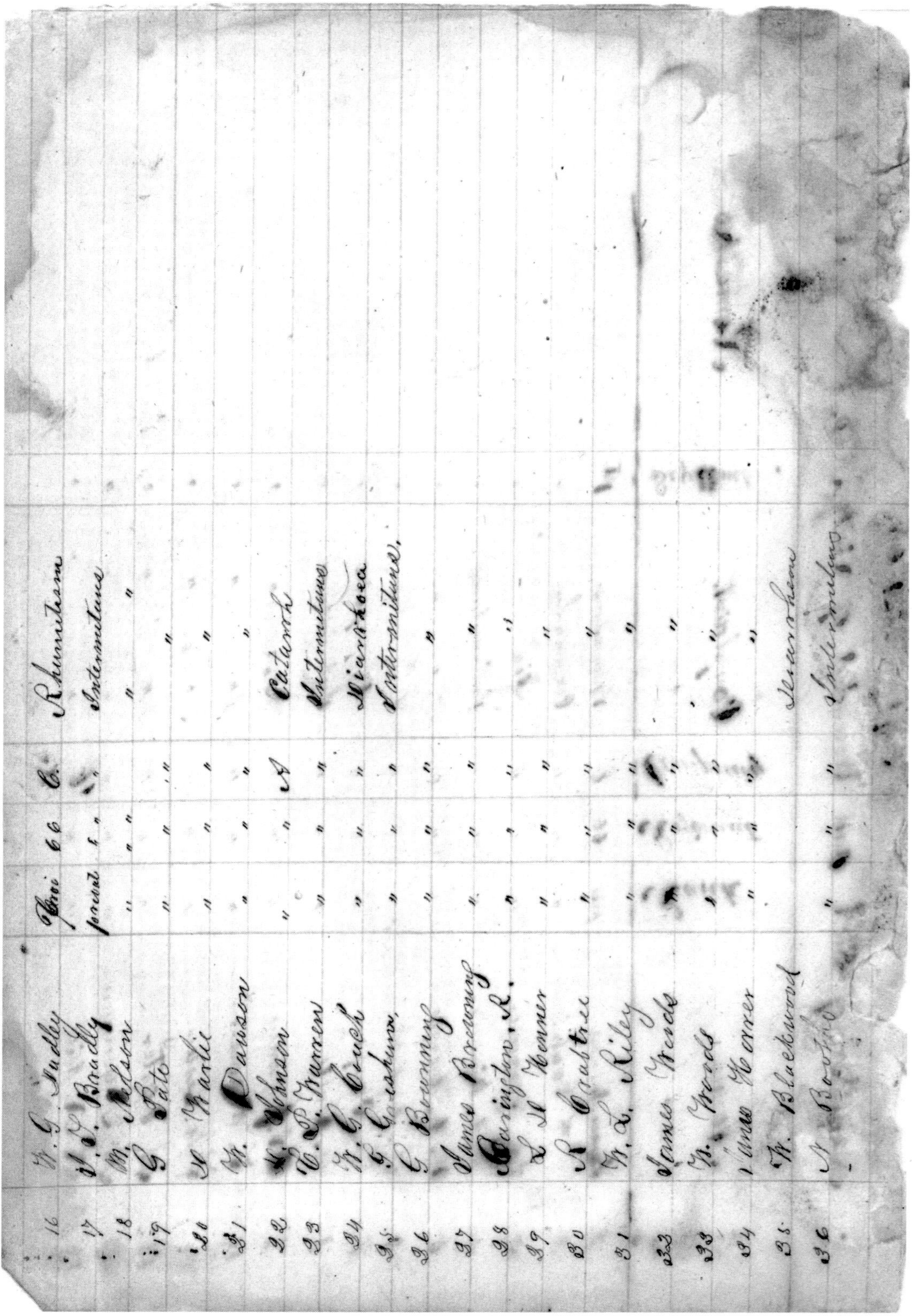

16	W. G. Sudley	Tenn	66	C	Rheumatism
17	J. J. Bradly	privat	"	"	Intermitens
18	M. Nelson	"	"	"	"
19	G. Pate	"	"	"	"
20	S. Wardie	"	"	"	"
21	W. Dawson	"	"	"	"
22	J. Johnson	"	"	A	Catarrh
23	C. P. Warren	"	"	"	Intermitens
24	J. C. Couch	"	"	"	Diarrhoea
25	G. Cashion	"	"	"	Intermittens
26	G. Browning	"	"	"	"
27	James Browning	"	"	"	"
28	Covington, R.	"	"	"	"
29	L. H. Hanner	"	"	"	"
30	R. Crabtree	"	"	"	"
31	W. L. Riley	"	"	"	"
32	James Woods	"	"	"	"
33	J. Woods	"	"	"	"
34	James Horner	"	"	"	"
35	W. Blackwood				Diarrhoea
36	N. Booth	"	"	"	Intermittens

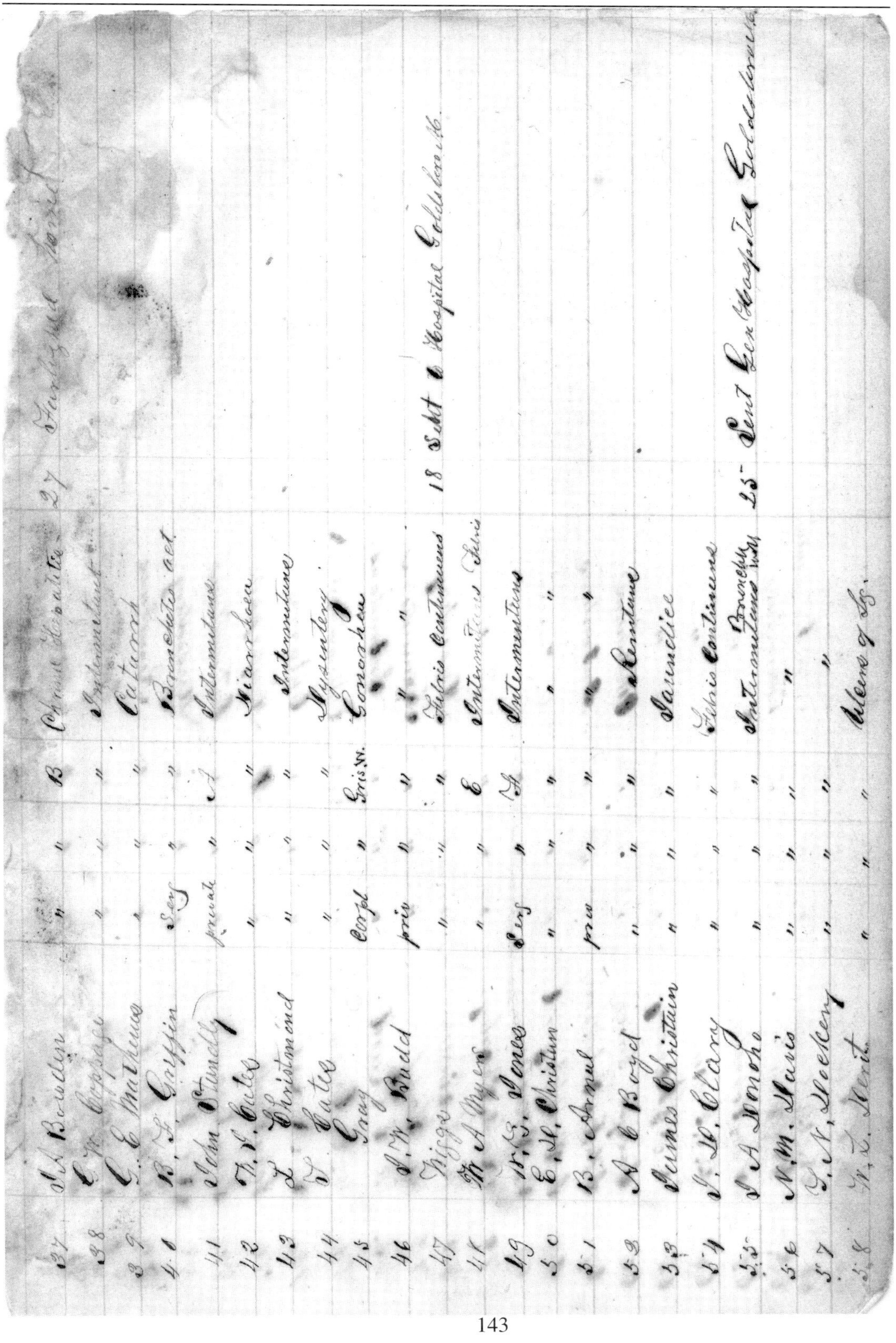

37	J. A. Bowden	"	"	B	Chronic Hepatitis	27	Furloughed home
38	C. W. Coppage	"	"	"	Intermitant		
39	G. E. Mathews	"	"	"	Catarrh		
40	B. F. Griffin	Serg	"	"	Bronchitis act.		
41	John Standly	private	"	A	Intermitans		
42	W. J. Cates	"	"	"	Diarrhoea		
43	L. Christmond	"	"	"	Intermitans		
44	J. Cates	"	"	"	Dysentery		
45	Gray	Corpl	"	Gris. W.	Gonorhea		
46	J. W. Budd	priv	"	"	" "		
47	Wiggs	"	"	"	Febris Continuens	18	Sent to Hospital Goldsboro N.
48	W. A. Myers	"	"	E	Intermitans Febris		
49	W. G. Jones	Serg	"	A	Intermentens		
50	E. W. Christian	"	"	"	" "		
51	B. Arnal	priv	"	"	" "		
52	A. C. Boyd	"	"	"	Remitans		
53	James Christain	"	"	"	Jaundice		
54	J. W. Clary	"	"	"	Febris Continens		
55	J. A. Donoho	"	"	"	Intermitans Bronchitis with	25	Sent Gen Hospital Goldsboro
56	N. M. Davis	"	"	"	"		
57	G. N. Dockery	"	"	"	"		
58	W. L. Dent	"	"	"	Ulcers of Leg.		

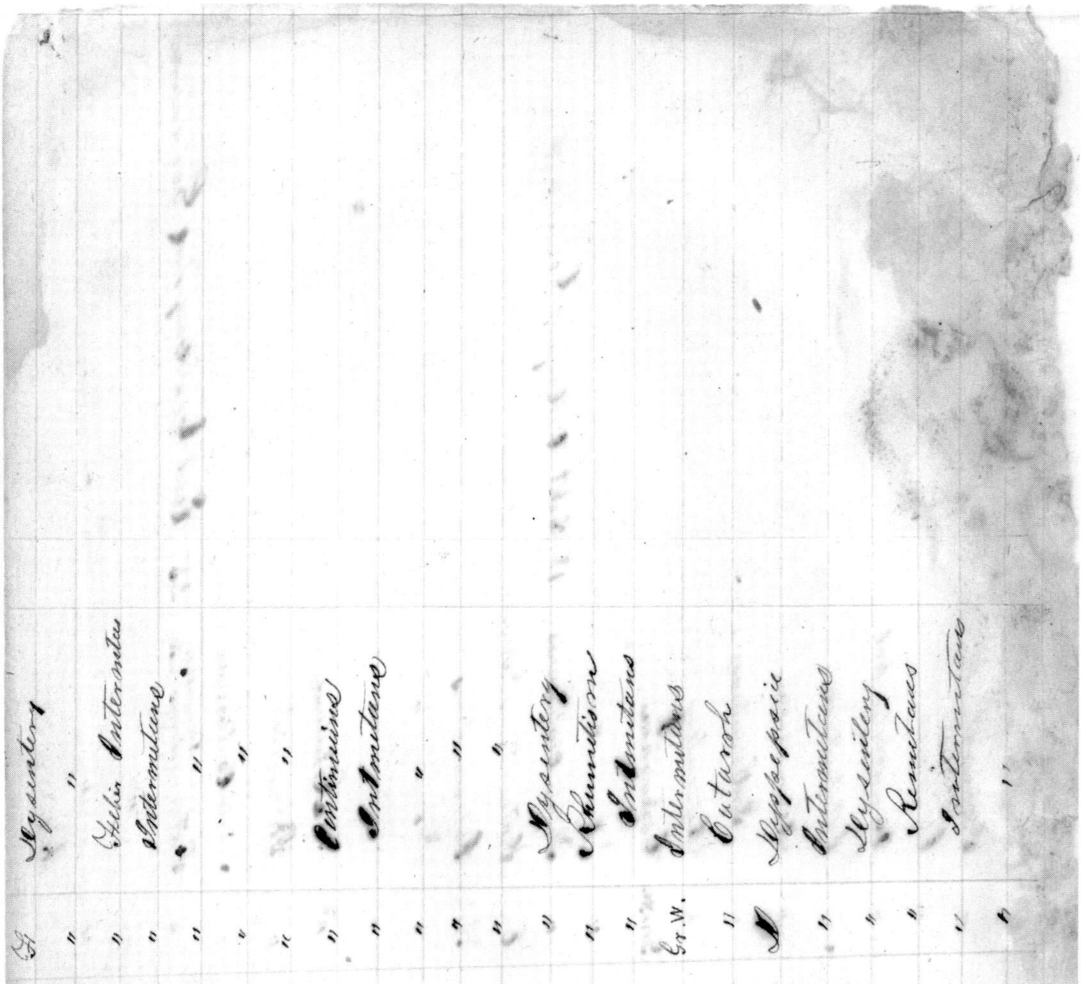

59	S C Dunn	priv	66	G	Dysentery
60	D. J Gidda	"	"	"	"
61	R. B. Hunter	"	"	"	Febir Intermitus
62	G M Hill	"	"	"	Intermitans
63	F M Johnston	"	"	"	"
64	B. J. P. Wine	"	"	"	"
65	J A Mackey	"	"	"	"
66	Joseph Price	"	"	"	Continuins
67	J H. C Robertson	"	"	"	Intmitans
68	J Shackleford	"	"	"	"
69	S. Snider	"	"	"	"
70	Robt. Sharley	"	"	"	"
71	W R Tinner	"	"	"	Dysentery
72	L Toff	"	"	"	Rheumatism
73.	W J Rush	"	"	"	Intmitans
74	W. H. Owen	"	"	Gr. W.	Intermitans
75	J. R Lee	"	"	"	Catarrh
76	John Smith	"	"	D	Dyspepsia
77	John Evans	"	"	"	Intermitans
78	R. H. Tomlin	"	"	"	Dysentery
79	Thas. Craff	"	"	"	Remitans
80	Nathan Wiggs	"	"	"	Intermitans
81	Neil Mathis	"	"	"	"

	Enlisted Men	Officers	All others	Aggregate
Oct. 31st	916	46	12	974

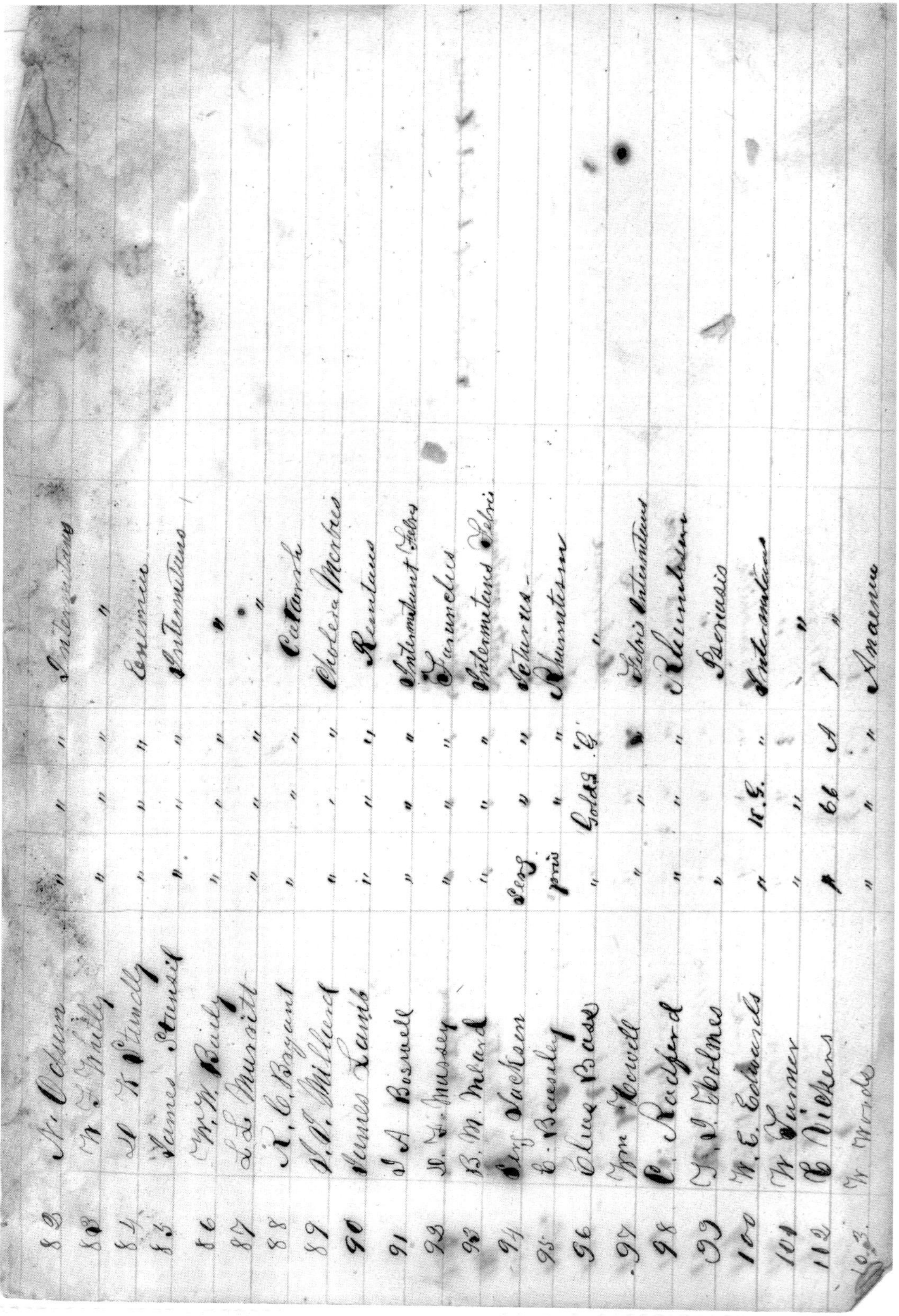

83	N. Odum	"	"	"	"	Intermittens
83	W. G. Smily	"	"	"	"	"
84	J. R. Stancil	"	"	"	"	Enemia
85	James Stancil	"	"	"	"	Intermittens
86	W. W. Bird	"	"	"	"	"
87	L. L. Messitt	"	"	"	"	"
88	R. C. Bryant	"	"	"	"	Catarrh
89	J. T. Millard	"	"	"	"	Cholera Morbus
90	James Lamb	"	"	"	"	Remittens
91	J. A. Boswell	"	"	"	"	Intermittent Febris
92	D. T. Mussey	"	"	"	"	Furunculus
93	B. M. Millard	"	"	"	"	Intermittens Febris
94	Serg Jackson	Serg.	"	"	"	Icterus
95	E. Beasley	pvt	"	"	"	Rheumatism
96	Elias Bass	"	Golds	'G'		"
97	John Howell	"	"			Febris Intermittens
98	C. Radford	"	"	"	"	Rheumatism
99	T. J. Holmes	"				Psoriasis
100	W. E. Edwards	"	18 G.	"		Intermittens
101	W. Sumner	"	"	"		"
112	E. Nickens	"	66	A		"
103	W. Woods	"	"	"		Anaemia

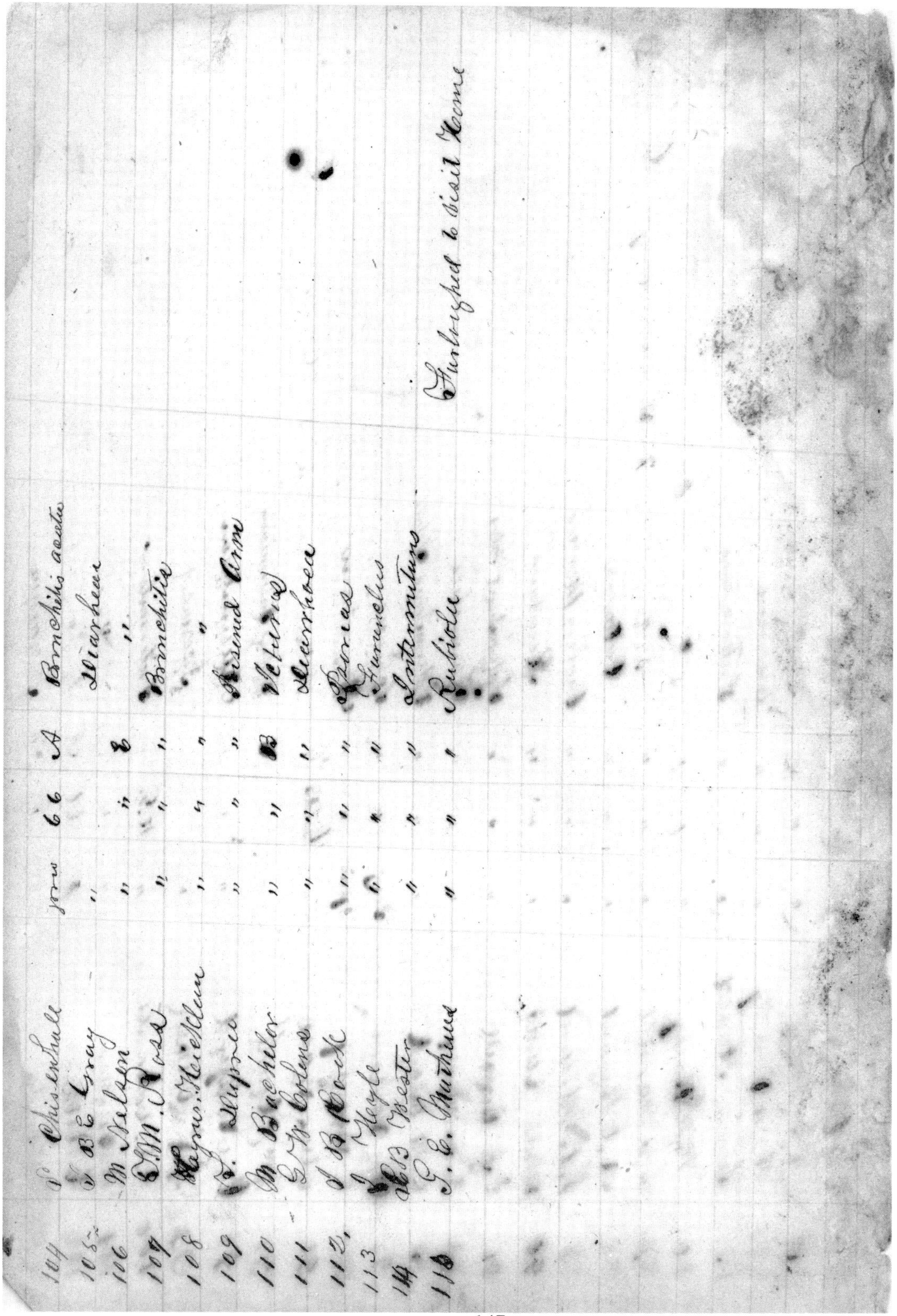

104	[illegible] Chisenhall	pvt	66	A	Bronchitis acuta
105	[illegible] B. C. Gray	"			Diarrhoea
106	M Nelson	"	"	B	"
107	D.M. Rose	"	"	"	Bronchitis
108	Hayns. Hicklin	"	"	"	"
109	[illegible]	"	"	"	Wound Arm
110	M. Bachelor	"	"	B	[illegible]
111	G. W. [illegible]	"	"	"	Diarrhoea
112	J. B. Cook	"	"	"	[illegible]
113	J. Hoyle	"	"	"	Furunculus
114	B. Bester	"	"	"	Intermittens
115	G. C. Mathews	"	"	"	Rubiola

Furloughed to visit Home

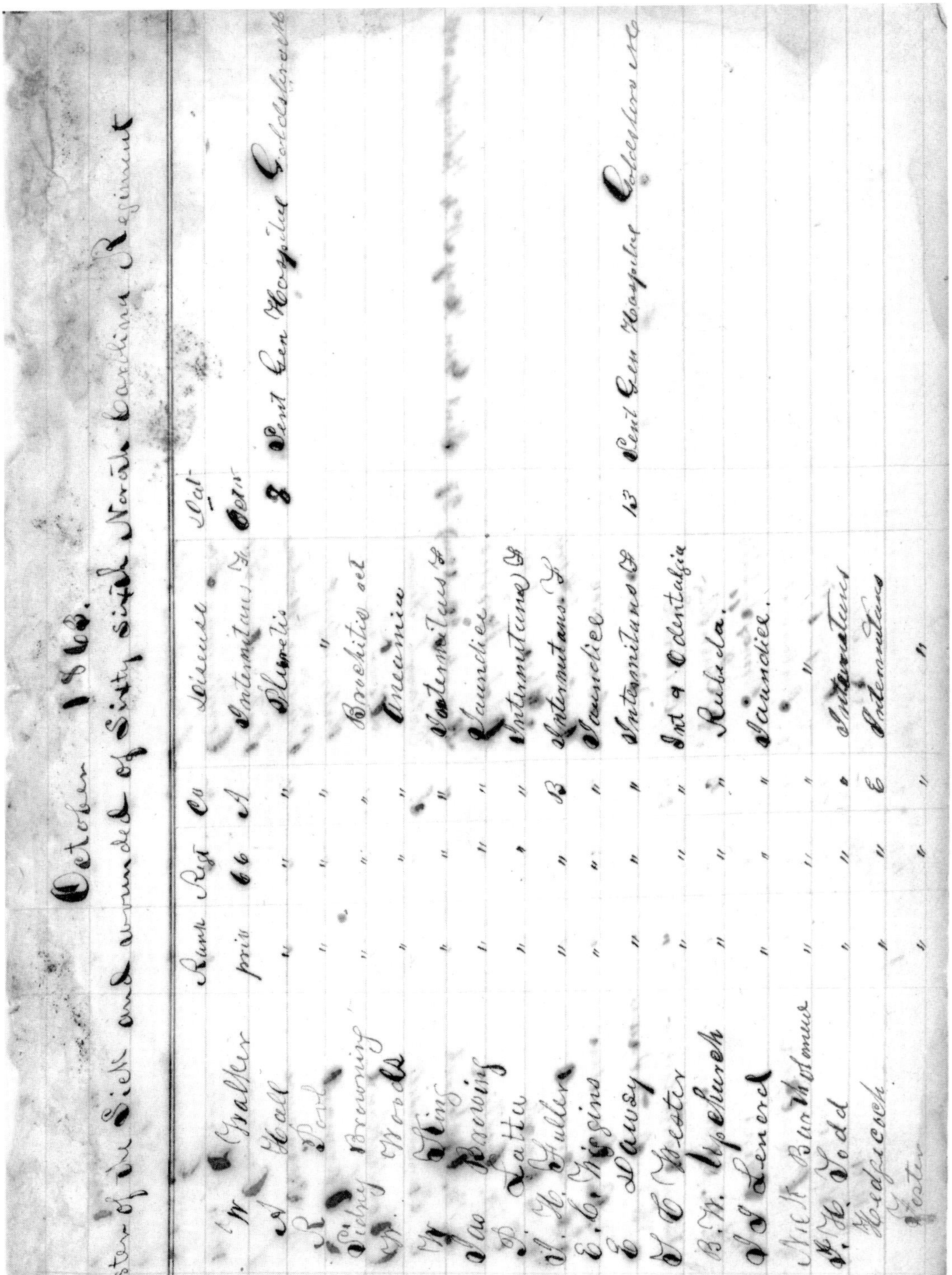

Register of the Sick and wounded of Sixty sixth North Carolina Regiment

October 1863.

	Name	Rank	Regt	Co	Disease	Dat-	
1	W Walker	priv	66	A	Intermittens F	Octr	
2	A Hall	"	"	"	Pleuritis	8	Sent Gen Hospital Goldsboro NC
3	R Pool	"	"	"	"		
4	Sidney Browning	"	"	"	Bronchitis ac		
5	G. Woods	"	"	"	Pneumonia		
6	G King	"	"	"	Intermittens F		
7	Jno Bowing	"	"	"	Jaundice		
8	B. Latta	"	"	"	Intermittens F		
9	J. H. Fuller	"	"	B	Intermittens F		
10	E. C. Higgins	"	"	"	Jaundice		
11	E Dawsy	"	"	"	Intermittens F	13	Sent Gen Hospital Goldsboro NC
12	J T Hester	"	"	"	Int q Odontalgia		
13	B. W. Upchurch	"	"	"	Rubeola		
14	J J Lenard	"	"	"	Jaundice		
15	Nick Bartholomew	"	"	"	"		
16	J. H. Todd	"	"	"	Intermittens		
17	Hedgecock	"	"	C	Intermittens		
18	G Hester	"	"	"	"		

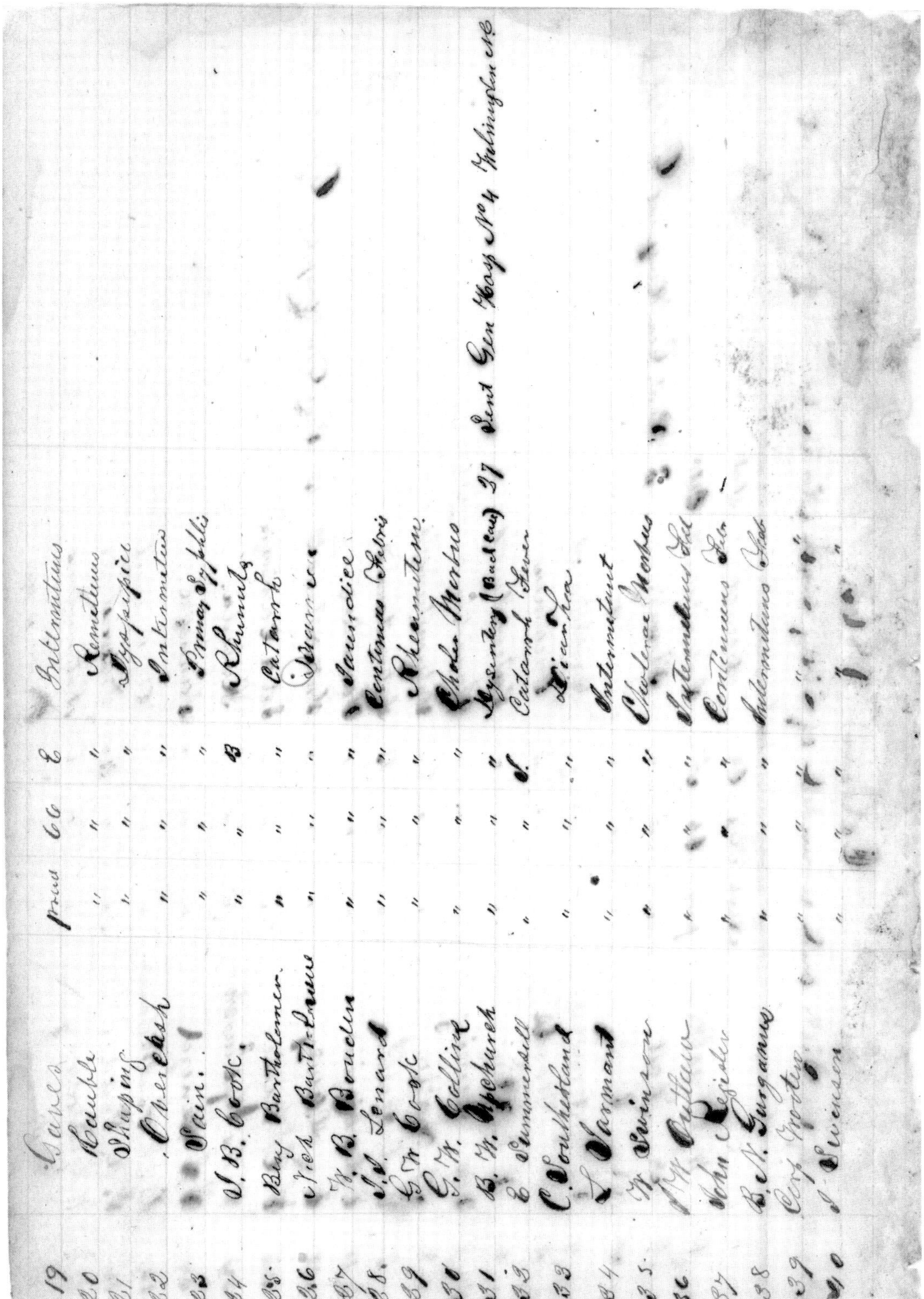

19	Gaves	prus	66	E	Intermitens	
20	Rauble	"	"	"	Remetens	
21	Shaping	"	"	"	Dyspepsia	
22	Overcash	"	"	"	Intermetens	
23	Pain.	"	"	"	Primary Syphilis	
24	J. B. Cook.	"	"	B	Rheumatis	
25	Beny Bartholomew	"	"	"	Catarrh	
26	Nick Bartholomew	"	"	"	Diarrea	
27	W. B. Bowden	"	"	"	Jaundice	
28	J. J. Lenard	"	"	"	Continuous Febris	
29	G W Cook	"	"	"	Rheumatism	
30	G. W. Collins	"	"	"	Cholera Morbus	
31	B. W. Upchurch	"	"	"	Dysentery (Bad case)	27 Sent Gen Hosp No 4 Wilmington NC
32	E Summersill	"	"	S.	Catarrh Fever	
33	C. Southerland	"	"	"	Diarrhea	
34	L Sarmant	"	"	"	Intermetent	
35	W. Swinson	"	"	"	Cholerae Morbus	
36	J W Outlaw	"	"	"	Intermetens Feb	
37	John Register	"	"	"	Continuens Feb	
38	B. N. Gurganus	"	"	"	Intermitens Feb	
39	Corp Wooten	"	"	"	"	
40	J Swinson	"	"	"	"	

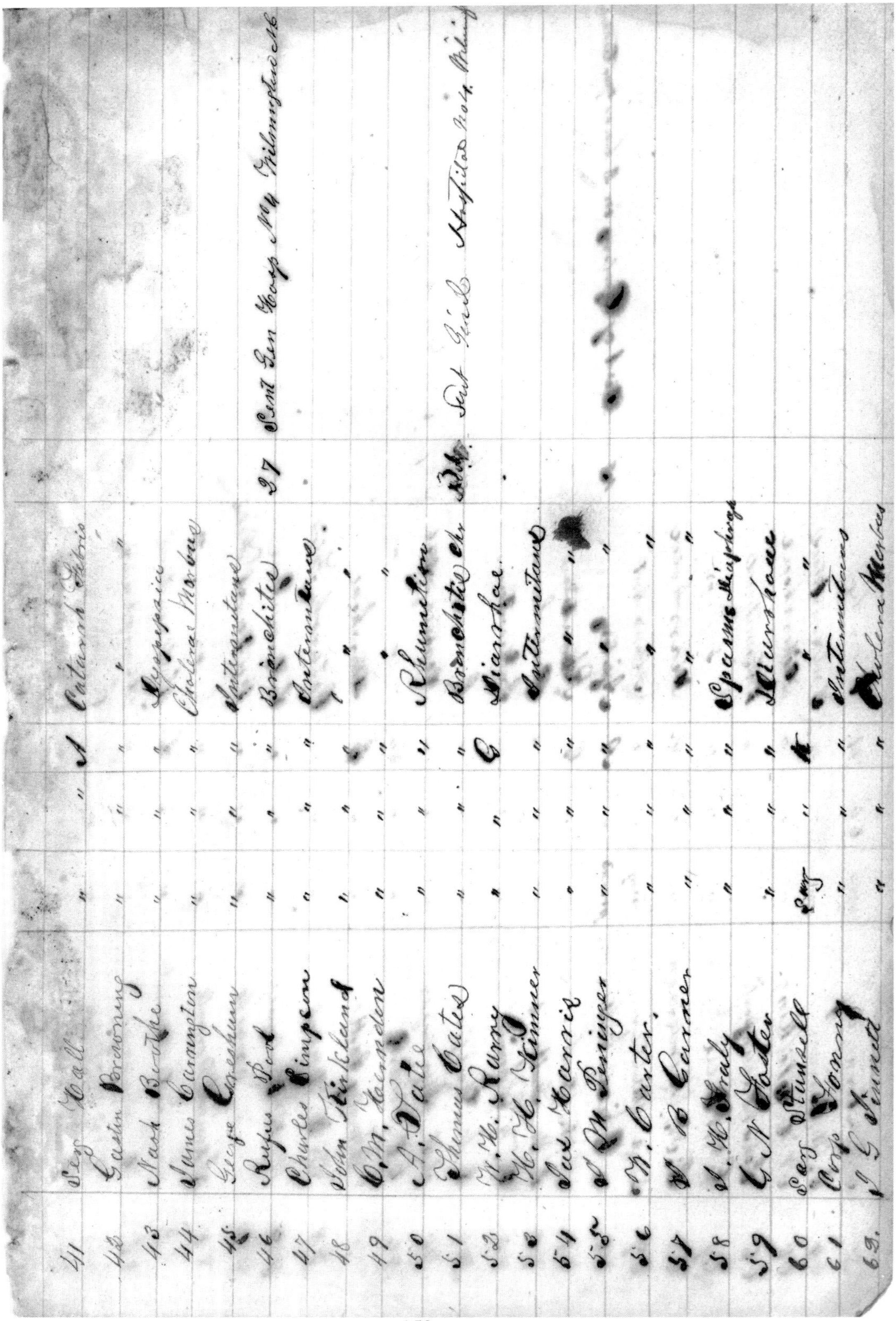

41	Serg Hall	″	″	A	Catarrh Febris		
42	Gastin Browning	″	″	″	″ ″		
43	Nash Boothe	″	″	″	Dyspepsia		
44	James Carrington	″	″	″	Cholera Morbus		
45	George Gresham	″	″	″	Intermittans		
46	Rufus Pool	″	″	″	Bronchitis	27	Sent Gen Hosp No 4 Wilmington NC
47	Charles Simpson	″	″	″	Intermittans		
48	John Kirkland	″	″	″	″ ″		
49	C.M. Herndon	″	″	″	″ ″		
50	A. Tate	″	″	″	Rheumatism		
51	Thomas Oates	″	″	″	Bronchitis Chr	[illegible]	Sent Genl Hospital No 4 Wilming[illegible]
52	W.H. Rarry	″	″	G	Diarrhae		
53	H.H. Kimner	″	″	″	Intermittans		
54	Jas Harris	″	″	″	″ ″		
55	J M Peninger	″	″	″	″ ″		
56	W. Carter	″	″	″	″ ″		
57	J B Carner	″	″	″	″ ″		
58	J. H. Graly	″	″	″	Spasms Diaphragm		
59	G N Foster	″	″	″	Diarrhoea		
60	Sarg Stunsell	Serg	″	K	″ ″		
61	Corp Fonny	″	″	″	Intermittans		
62	J G Finnell	″	″	″	Cholera Morbus		

63	A.G. Kornegay	pri	66th	H	Ulcer leg		
64	J.W. Brown	"	"	"	Intermittens		
65	N H Wilking	"	"	"	Diarrhoea		
66	John Devanport	"	"	"	Intermittens.		
67	G W Bell	"	"	"	" "		
68	J.N. Henderson	"	"	"	Diarrhoea		
69	Sergt Miller	Serg	"	"	Febris Int		
70	Chizenhall	private	"	A	Apoplexy.	13	Died of Apoplexy in 2 hours after taken
71	R H Cook	"	"	G.	Rheumatism		
72	J.M. Futts	"	"	"	Diarrhoea		
73	B.W. Simmes	"	"	"	Intermittens		
74	J.C. Griffin	"	"	"	"		
75	J.J. Barringer	"	"	"	Scabies artich		
76	C.O. Ward	"	"	"	" "		
77	Chirly Scott	"	"	E	Diarrhoea		
78	W H Ham	"	"	"	Catarrh Febris		
79	W B Balance	"	"	"	Intermittens		
80	Curtis Worrell	"	"	"	Catarrh Febris		
81	James Worrell	"	"	"	" "		
82	Lewis Edwards	"	"	L	Intermittens		
83	H Dupree	"	"	"	Diarrhoea		
84	H. B. Wilkin	"	"	W	Cystitis	27	27 Gen Hosp No 4 Wilmington N.C.
85	Lewis Ferel	"	"	"	Rheumatism		

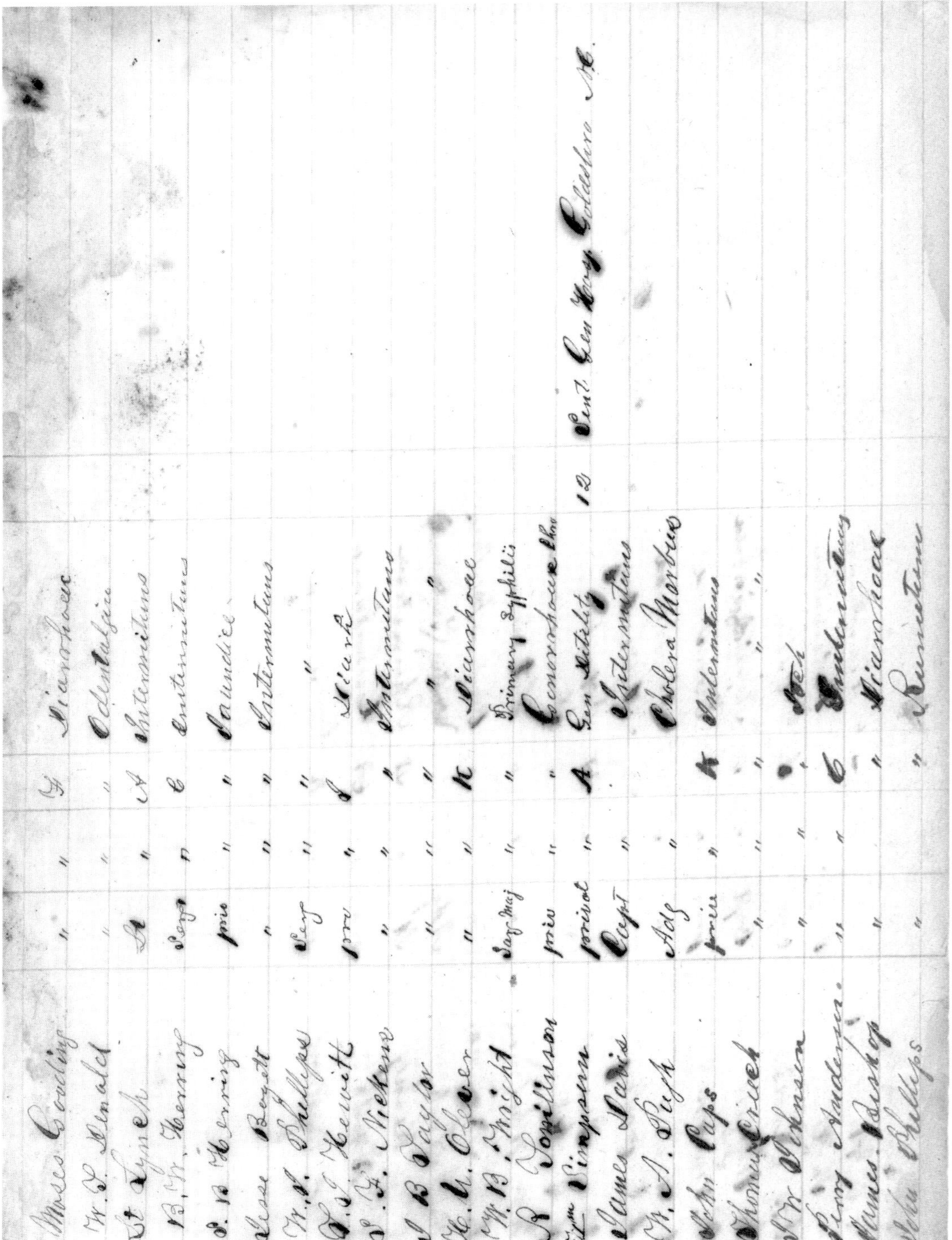

86	Moses Gooding	"	"	F	Diarrhoea		
87	W. T. Denald	"	"	"	Odontalgia		
88	Lt Lynch	Lt	"	A	Intermittens		
89.	B. W. Herring	Serg	"	C	Intermittens		
90	S. B. Herring	priv	"	"	Jaundice		
91	Jesse Bogett	"	"	"	Intermittens		
92	W. T. Phillips	Serg	"	"	"		
93	T. J. Hewitt	priv	"	I	Heart		
94	S. F. Nickens	"	"	"	Intermittens		
95	J B Taylor	"	"	"	" "		
96	H. M. Oliver	"	"	K	Diarrhoea		
97	W. B. Wright	Sarg Maj	"	"	Primary Syphilis		
98	R Tomlinson	priv	"	"	Gonorrhoea Chro		
99.	Wm Simpson	privat	"	A	Gen debility	12	Sent Gen Hosp Goldsboro NC.
100.	James Davis	Capt	"		Intermittens		
101	W. A. Pugh	Adj	"		Cholera Morbus		
102	John Caps	priv	"	K	Intermittens		
103	Thomas Creech	"	"	"	" "		
104	J W Johnson	"	"	"	Itch		
105	Perry Anderson	"	"	C	Intermittens		
106	James Bishop	"		"	Diarrhoea		
107	John Phillips	"		"	Remittens		

108	William Ware	priv	66°	B	Intermittens.
109	W B Lancaster	"	"	"	" "
110	M. C. Strickland	"	"	"	Diarrhoea
111	— Sucker	Sergt	"	"	Intermittens
112	J. G. Rhodes	Copl	"	S.	Colic
113	W Uzzell	Corpl	"	"	Nephritic or Colic
114	M. Simon	priv	"	"	Remittens
115	C. Deans	"	"	"	Diarrhoea
116	John Coley.	"	"	"	Dysentery
117	David Spence	"	"	H	Catarrh
118	J B Rhodes	"	"	"	Furunculus or Bile
119	Wm Whitman	"	"	"	Intermitten
120	J. C. Rayner	"	"	"	Cholera Morbus.
121	W. A. Pugh	Adj	"	"	Vomiting (Tartar emetic)
122	S. H. Kenny	Lt	"	B	Rheumatism
123	J. W. Smith	priv	"	A	Gonorrhoea
124	Thos Ballard	"	"	K	" "

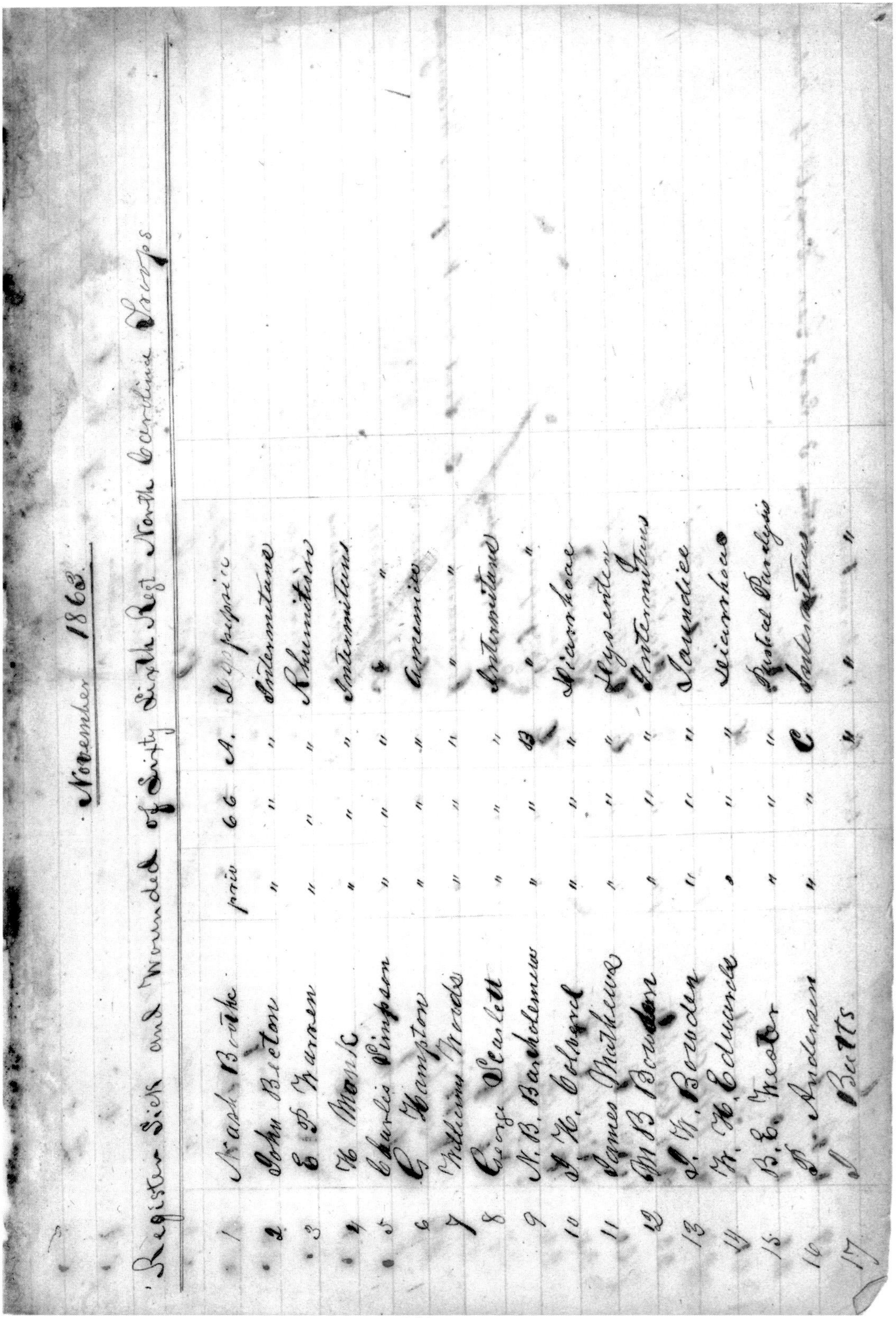

November 1863

Register Sick and Wounded of Sixty Sixth Regt North Carolina Troops

1	Mark Booth	priv	66	A.	Dyspepsia	
2	John Beeton	"	"	"	Intermitent	
3	E P Warren	"	"	"	Rheumatism	
4	H Monk	"	"	"	Intermitent	
5	Charles Simpson	"	"	"	"	
6	C Hampton	"	"	"	Anaemia	
7	William Woods	"	"	"	"	
8	George Scarlett	"	"	"	Intermitent	
9	N. B. Batchelor	"	"	B	"	
10	J H Colvard	"	"	"	Diarrhoea	
11	James Mathews	"	"	"	Dysentery	
12	M B Bowden	"	"	"	Intermitent	
13	J W Bowden	"	"	"	Jaundice	
14	W H Edwards	"	"	"	Diarrhoea	
15	B. E. Wester	"	"	"	Partial Paralysis	
16	P Anderson	"	"	C	Intermitent	
17	J Betts	"	"	"	"	"

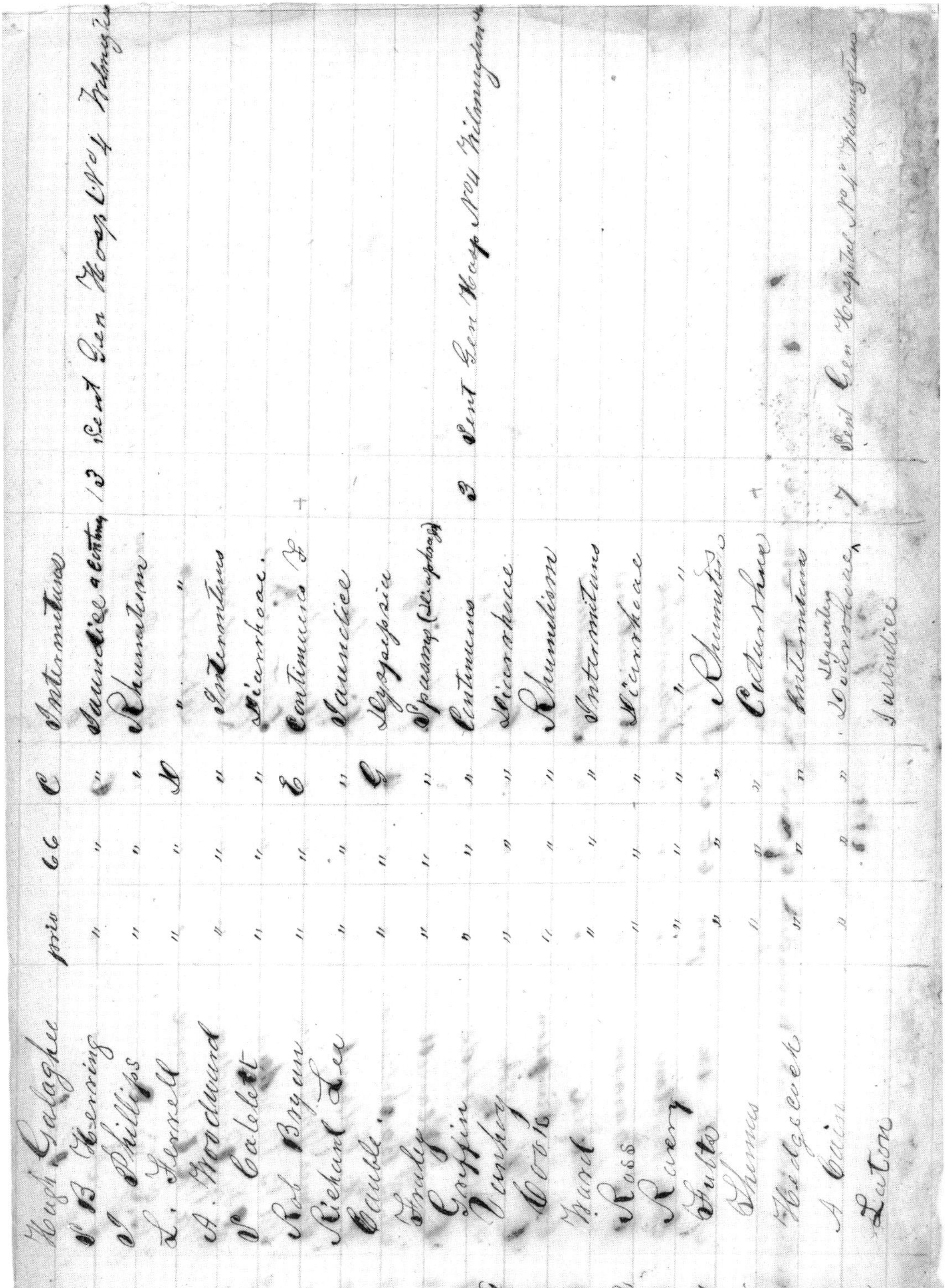

18.	Hugh Galaghee	priv	66	C	Intermitens		
19	S B Herring	"	"	"	Jaundice & Contin	13	Sent Gen Hosp No 4 Wilmington
20	J. Phillips	"	"	"	Rhumatism		
21	L. Ferrell	"	"	D	" "		
22	A. Woodward	"	"	"	Intermitens		
23	S Calclett	"	"	"	Diarrhoea.		
24	Rob Bryan	"	"	E	Continuous F		
25	Richard Lee	"	"	"	Jaundice		
26	Cauble.	"	"	G	Dyspepsia		
27	Fraley	"	"	"	Spasms (Diaphragm)		
28	Griffin	"	"	"	Continuous	3	Sent Gen Hosp No 4 Wilmington
29	Vanhoy	"	"	"	Diarrhoea		
30	Cook	"	"	"	Rhumatism		
31	Ward	"	"	"	Intermitens		
32	Ross	"	"	"	Diarrhoea		
33	Ravery	"	"	"	" "		
34	Fults	"	"	"	Rhumatism		
35	Thomas	"	"	"	Catarrhus		
36	Hedgecock	"	"	"	Intermitens		
37	A Cain	"	"	"	Dysentery Diarrhoea	7	Sent Gen Hospital No 4 Wilmington
38	Luton				Jaundice		

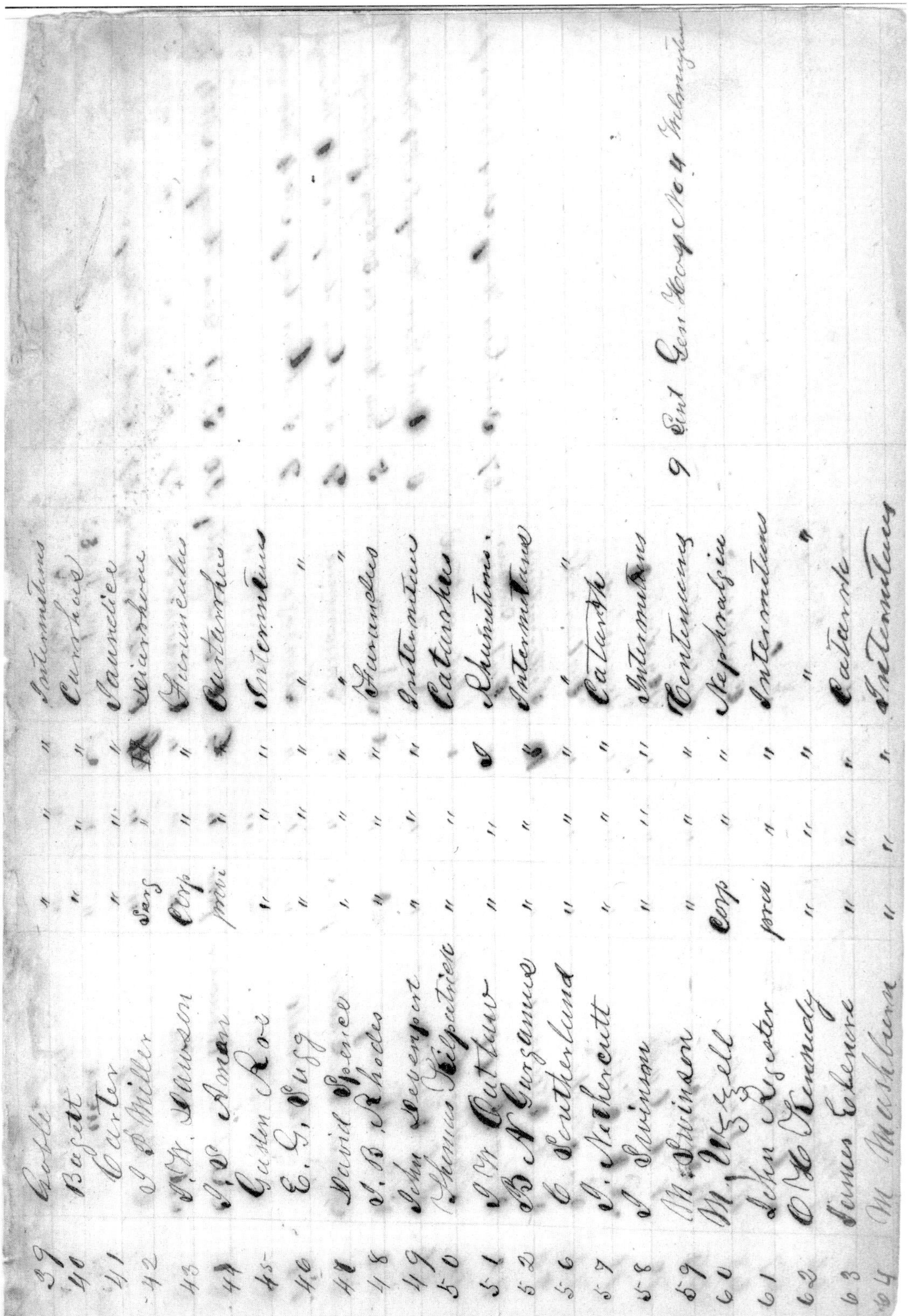

39	Cobb	"	"	"	Intermittens	
40	Bassett	"	"	"	Catarrhus	
41	Carter	"	"	"	Icterus	
42	I P Miller	Serg	"	"	Diarrhoea	
43	J. W. Dawson	Corp	"	"	Furunculus	
44	J. S. Ammon	priv	"	"	Intermittens	
45	Gustin Roe	"	"	"	Intermittens	
46	E. G. Sugg	"	"	"	"	
47	David Spencer	"	"	"	"	
48	I. B. Rhodes	"	"	"	Furunculus	
49	John Devenport	"	"	"	Intermittens	
50	Thomas Kilpatrick	"	"	"	Catarrhus	
51	J. W. Cutler	"	"	"	Rheumatism	
52	B. A. Gurganus	"	"	"	Intermittens	
56	C. Southerland	"	"	"	"	
57	J. Netherentt	"	"	"	Catarrh	
58	J. Swinson	"	"	"	Intermittens	
59	M. Swinson	"	"	"	Intermittens	9 Sent Gen Hosp No 4 Wilmington
60	M. Wezzell	Corp	"	"	Nephralgia	
61	John Register	priv	"	"	Intermittens	
62	O. M. Kennedy	"	"	"	"	
63	James Eakenore	"	"	"	Catarrh	
64	M Mashburn	"	"	"	Intermittens	

65	Rufin Hooks	prv	66	L	Diarrhoea		
66	D Worrell	"	"	"	" "		
67	S Godwin	"	"	"	Intermitans		
68	B.S. Burdin	"	"	"	Carrhus		
69	B. Smith	"	"	"	Intermitans		
70	W H Ham	"	"	"	Dysentery		
71	R S Pitts	"	"	"	Dysentery		
72	J. Parker	"	"	"	Catarrh		
73	J. H. Stansell	"	"	K	Intermitans.		
74	John Capps	"	"	"	Catarrh Ontinus	27	Sent Gen Hosp No 4 Wilmington
75	Thomas Creech			"	Intermitans		
76.	J. S. Stalling	"	"	"	Remitans	3	Sent Gen Hospt No 4 Wilmington
77	S. H. Kinney	Lt	"	D	Rhumatism	5	Gone Home on 30 days furlough
78	Rufus Bachelor	prvi	"	B	Pneumonia	9	Sent Gen Hospt No 4 Wilmington
79	Braswell	"	"	"	Lumbago	9	Sent Gen Hosp No 4 Wilmington
80	E Holland	Lt	"		Remitans		
81	Reuben Weaver	prv	"	G	Chron Dysentery	20	Sent Gen Hospt No 4 W
82	J. C. Martin	"	"	"	Continued Febris	27	" " " " "
83	O Mobley	"	"	B	Chr Diar. & Typoides	27	Sent Gen Hosp No 4 Wilmington
84	W Guess	"	"	A	Polypus Nasi		
85	G. W. Creech	"	"	"	Continus F		

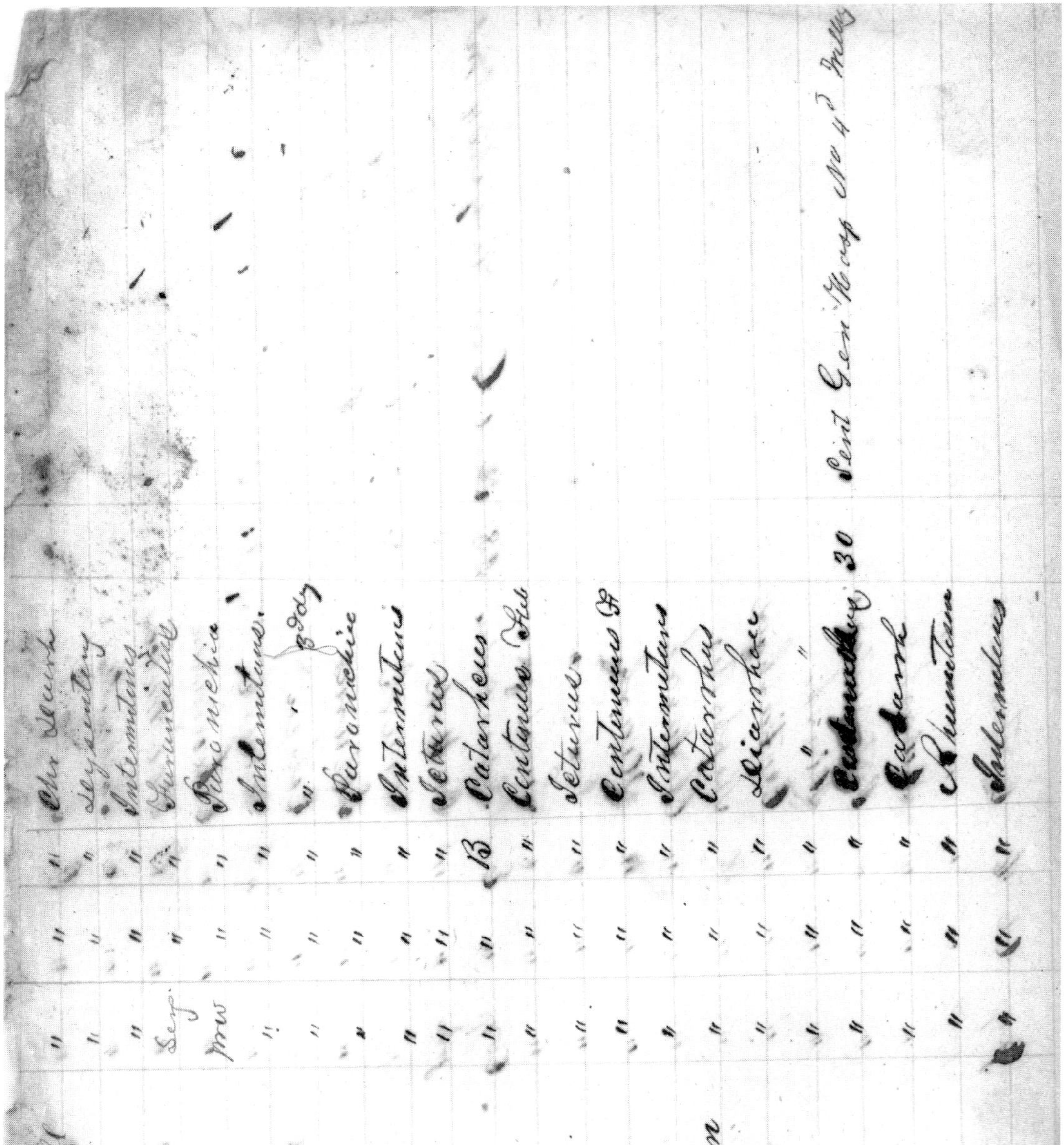

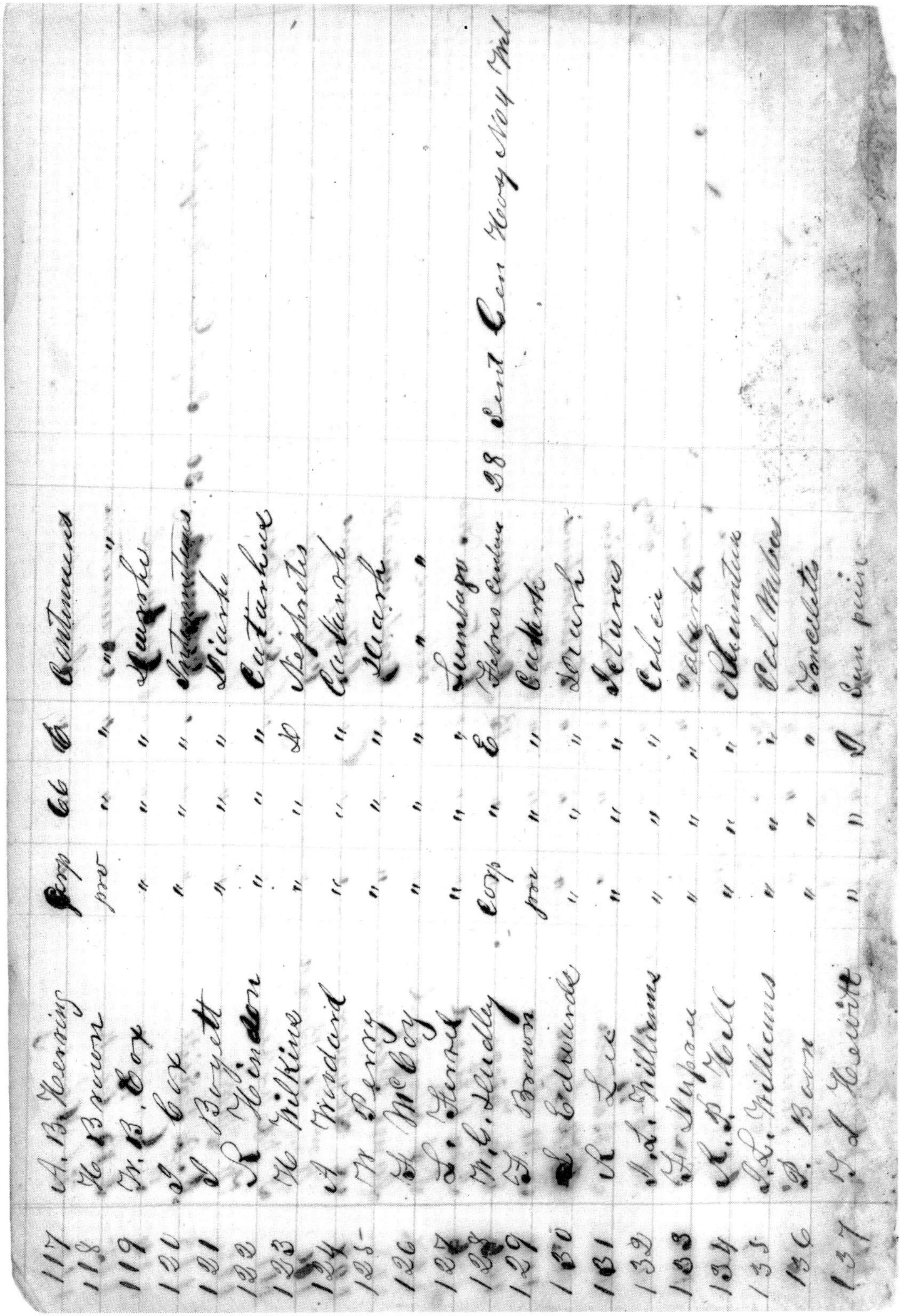

117	A. B. Herring	Corp	66	C	Continued
118	H. B. Brown	pvt	"	"	"
119	W. B. Cox	"	"	"	Neuralgia
120	J. J. Cox	"	"	"	Intermittens
121	J. J. Baggett	"	"	"	Diarrhea
122	R. Hinson	"	"	"	Catarrhus
123	M. Wilkins	"	"	D	Nephritis
124	A. Woodard	"	"	"	Catarrh
125	W. Perry	"	"	"	Headache
126	H. McCoy	"	"	"	"
127	L. L. Herod	"	"	"	Lumbago
128	W. L. Hudley?	Corp	"	E	Febris Contin
129	J. Brown	pvt	"	"	Catarrh
130	L. Edwards	"	"	"	Diarrh
131	R. Lee	"	"	"	Icterus
132	A. L. Williams	"	"	"	Colica
133	H. Nupon?	"	"	"	Catarrh
134	L. B. Hill	"	"	"	Rheumatism
135	J. L. Williams	"	"	"	Vul Vulnus
136	S. Barr	"	"	"	Tonsillitis
137	J. L. Hewitt	"	"	D	Sun [illegible]

28 Sent Gen Hosp Nov 4 ...

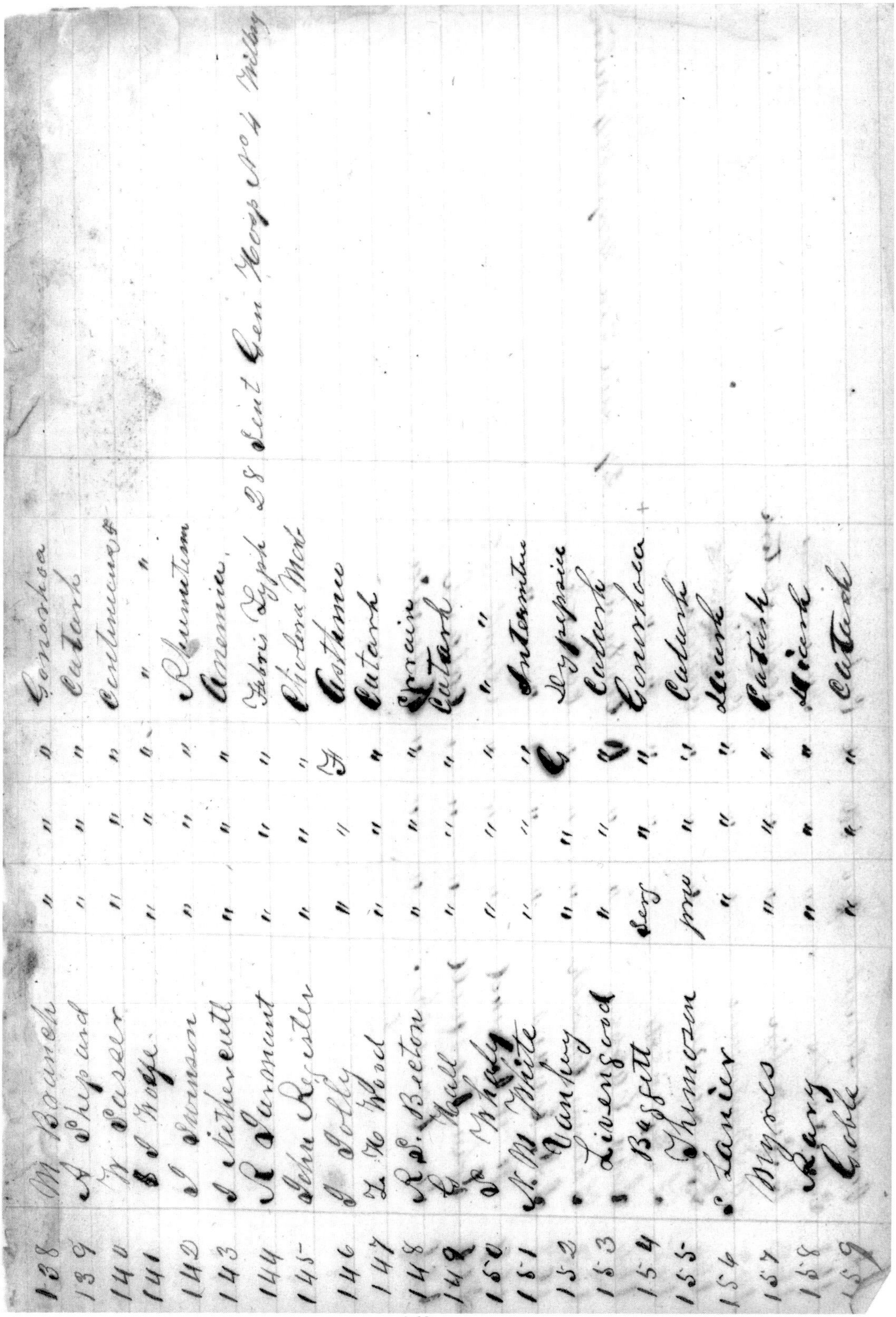

138	M Bounch	"	"	"	Gonorrhoea
139	A Shepard	"	"	"	Catarrh
140	F Cusser	"	"	"	Continued F
141	B L Hodge	"	"	"	"
142	J Swinson	"	"	"	Rheumatism
143	J Litherwell	"	"	"	Anemia
144	R Surmount	"	"	"	Febris Typh 28 Sent Gen Hosp No 4 Wilm
145	John Register	"	"	"	Cholera Mor
146	J Jolly	"	"	G	Asthma
147	L W Wood	"	"	"	Catarrh
148	R L Beeton	"	"	"	Sprain
149	G Hall	"	"	"	Catarrh
150	J Whaley	"	"	"	"
151	N M White	"	"	"	Intermittent
152	Vanhey	"	"	C	Dyspepsia
153	Livensgood	"	"	"	Catarrh
154	Bassett	Leg	"	"	Diarrhoea
155	Thomason	pre	"	"	Catarrh
156	Lanier	"	"	"	Ulcer
157	Myers	"	"	"	Catarrh
158	Raney	"	"	"	Ulcer
159	Cobb	"	"	"	Catarrh

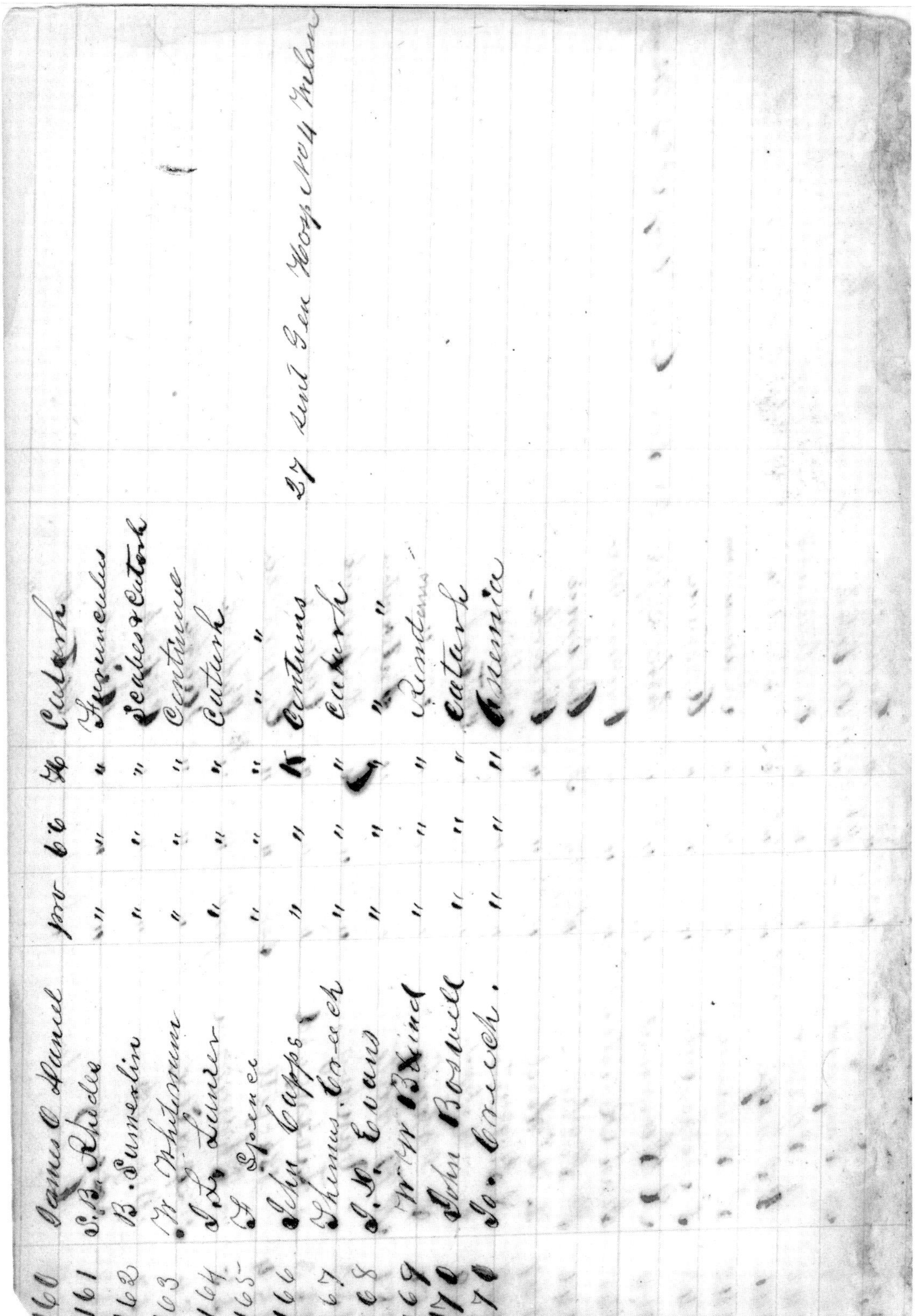

160	James O Hunnel	pvt	66	H	Catarrh	
161	S.B. Rhodes	"	"	"	Furunculus	
162	B. Sumerlin	"	"	"	Scabies & Catarrh	
163	W Whitmore	"	"	"	Contusion	
164	J.L. Linker	"	"	"	Catarrh	
165	G Spencer	"	"	"	"	
166	John Capps	"	"	K	Contusion	27 sent Gen Hosp No 4 Wilm
167	Thomas Creech	"	"	"	Catarrh	
168	J.H. Evans	"	"	"	"	
169	W W Bland	"	"	"	Contusion	
170	John Boswell	"	"	"	Catarrh	
170	Jo. Creech	"	"	"	Anemia	

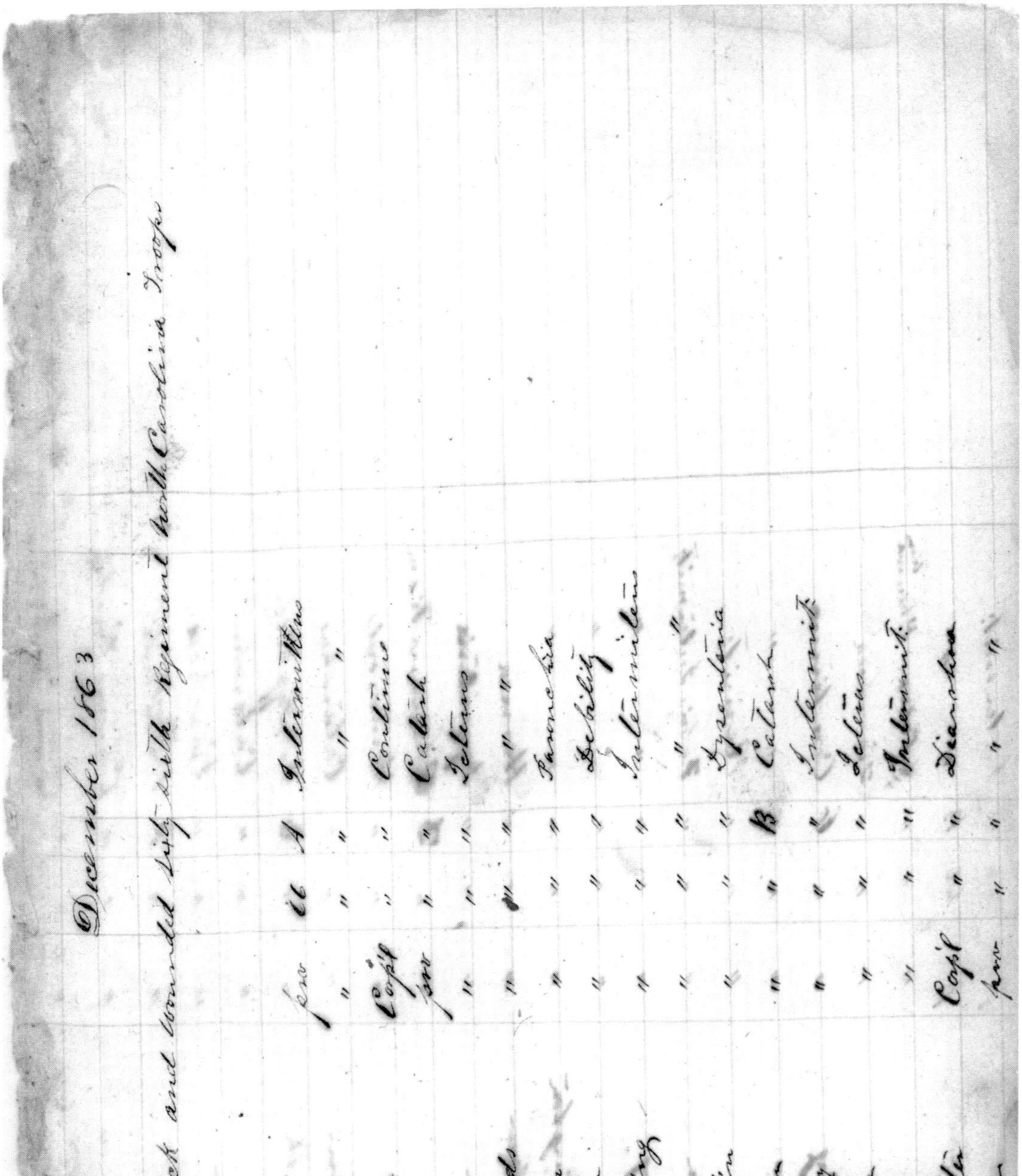

Register sick and wounded Sixty-sixth Regiment North Carolina Troops

December 1863

1	D Couch	pvt	66	A	Intermittens
2	W Couch	"	"	"	"
3	W Whitaker	Corp'l	"	"	Continua
4	Poole	pvt	"	"	Catarrh
5	S Rhew	"	"	"	Icterus
6	James Woods	"	"	"	"
7	J Baldwin	"	"	"	Pneumonia
8	H Cardin	"	"	"	Debility
9	W Browning	"	"	"	Intermittens
10	J Cates	"	"	"	"
11	Kirklin	"	"	"	Dysenteria
12	W J Bunn	"	"	B	Catarrh
13	Joseph Berry	"	"	"	Intermittens
14	W B Borden	"	"	"	Icterus
15	E Weston	"	"	"	Intermittens
16	H C Bunting	Corp'l	"	"	Diarrhoea
17	J F Tucker	pvt	"	"	"

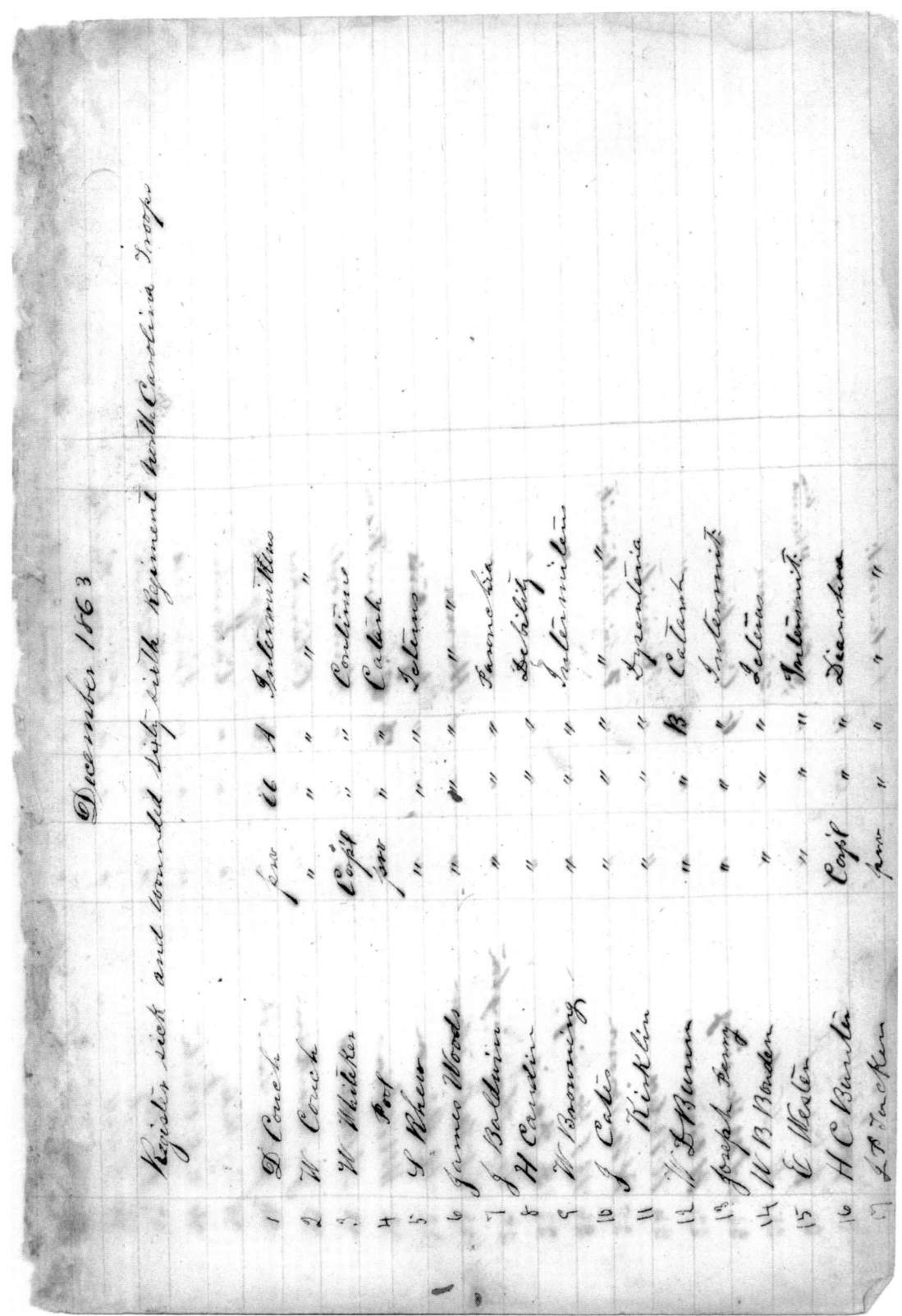

18	Harry Wood	pro	66	B	Intermit:		
19	Joseph Harper	pro	66	B	" "		
20	J Colvord	"	"	"	~~Colic~~ Rheumatism		
21	W Wood	"	"	"	Diarrhoea		
22	A B Herring	"	"	C	Continua		
23	H Brown	"	"	"	" "		
24	W B Cox	"	"	"	Remit:		
25	H M Brown	"	"	"	Febris Intermit;		
26	B J Herring	"	"	"	" "		
27	L Davis	"	"	"	" "		
28	W Tharrington	"	"	"	" "		
29	N B Outlaw	"	"	"	Hernia		
30	R Hinson	"	"	"	Dysenteria		
31	H Wilkins	"	"	D	Rheumatism		
32	A Woodsned	"	"	"	Hemoroids		
33	Jas Markam	"	"	"	Catarrhus		
34	John Smith	"	"	E	Pri; Syphilis		
35	T J Riley	"	"	"	Catarrhus		
36	L C White	"	"	"	Diarrhoea		
37	J Jolly	"	"	F	Asthma Bronchitis		
38	G Hall	"	"	"	Chronic Diarrhoea		
39	N M White	"	"	"	Diarrhoea assumed a Typhoid form	6"	Sent to Gen Hospt; No 4 at Wilmington N.C.

40	H C Gobble	pvt	"	G	Diarrhoea
41	Livengood	"	"	"	"
42	Vanhoy	"	"	"	Debility
43	Barringer	"	"	"	Erysipelas
44	Badgett	Sergt	"	"	Syphilis
45	Burton	"	"	"	
46	Griffin	Corpl	"	"	Diarrhoea
47	Payne	"	"	"	Intermitt.
48	Windsor	pvt	"	"	"
49	H S Lee	"	"	H	Remitt. fever
50	G W Pierce	"	"	"	Catarrh
51	Dawson	Corpl	"	"	Intermitt
52	J Harrison	pvt	"	"	Diarrhoea
53	Thomas King	"	"	G	Intermitt.
54	H Washburn	"	"	"	Catarrhus
55	W Harrison	"	"	"	
56	M Barrick	"	"	"	Gonorrhoea
57	C Vaughn	"	"	"	Rheumatism
58	J Rothrock	"	"	"	Anaemia
59	K Washburn	"	"	"	Intermitt.
60	Wolf	Corpl	"	"	Hemorroids
61	J W Outlaw	pvt	"	"	Hernia
62	Bennett	Sergt	"	"	Diarrhoea

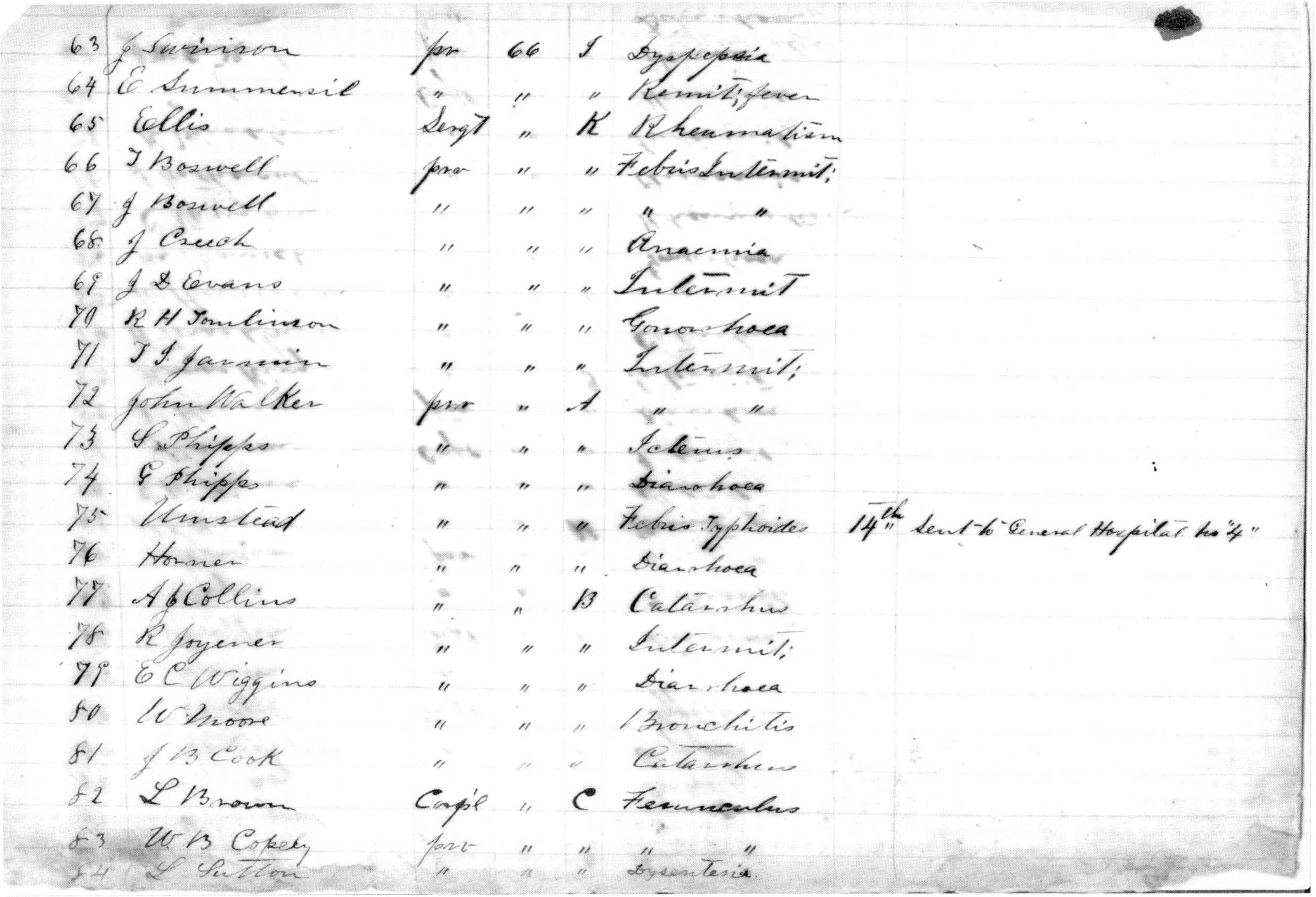

63	J Swinson	pvt	66	I	Dyspepsia	
64	E Summersil	"	"	"	Remit; fever	
65	Ellis	Sergt	"	K	Rheumatism	
66	T Boswell	pvt	"	"	Febris Intermit;	
67	J Boswell	"	"	"	" "	
68	J Creech	"	"	"	Anaemia	
69	J D Evans	"	"	"	Intermit	
70	R H Tomlinson	"	"	"	Gonorrhoea	
71	T J Jarmin	"	"	"	Intermit;	
72	John Walker	pvt	"	A	" "	
73	S Phipps	"	"	"	Icterus	
74	G Phipps	"	"	"	Diarrhoea	
75	Umstead	"	"	"	Febris Typhoides	14th " Sent to General Hospital No "4"
76	Horner	"	"	"	Diarrhoea	
77	A J Collins	"	"	B	Catarrhus	
78	R Joyener	"	"	"	Intermit;	
79	E C Wiggins	"	"	"	Diarrhoea	
80	W Moore	"	"	"	Bronchitis	
81	J B Cook	"	"	"	Catarrhus	
82	L Brown	Corpl	"	C	Furunculus	
83	W B Copely	pvt	"	"	" "	
84	L Sutton	"	"	"	Dysenteria	

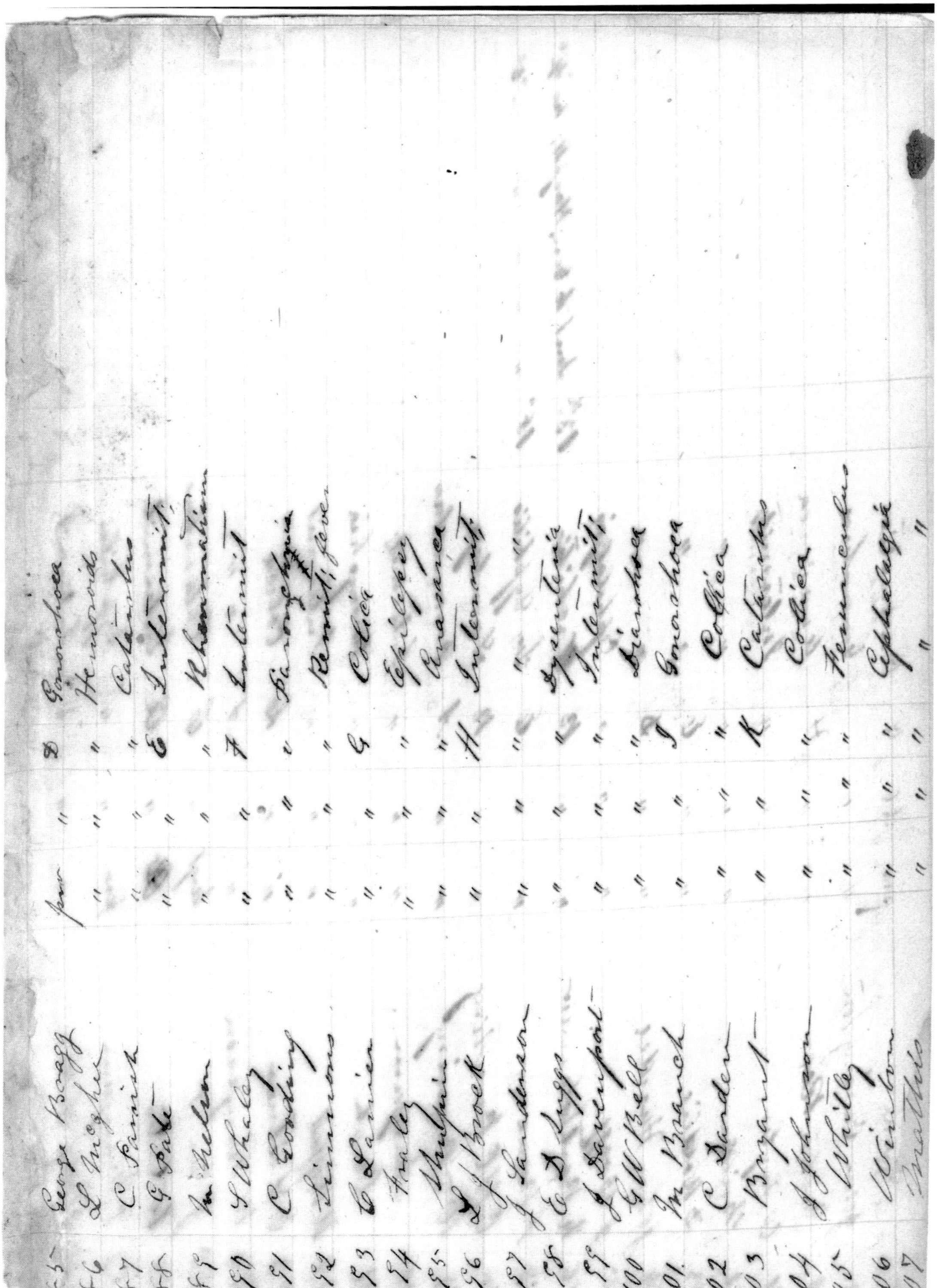

85	George Bragg	pvr	"	D	Gonorrhoea
86	L McGhee	"	"	"	Hemoroids
87	C Parrish	"	"	"	Catarrhus
88	G Pate	"	"	E	Intermit;
89	M Nelson	"	"	"	Rheumatism
90	S Whaley	"	"	F	Intermit
91	C Gooding	"	"	"	Paronychia
92	Simmons	"	"	"	Remit; fever
93	C Lanier	"	"	G	Colica
94	Fraley	"	"	"	Epilepsy
95	Sturgin	"	"	"	Anasarca
96	L J Brock	"	"	H	Intermit;
97	J Sanderson	"	"	"	" "
98	E D Suggs	"	"	"	Dysenteria
99	J Davenport	"	"	"	Intermit;
100	G W Bell	"	"	"	Diarrhoea
101	M Branch	"	"	I	Gonorrhoea
102	C Darden	"	"	"	Colica
103	Bryant	"	"	K	Catarrhus
104	J Johnson	"	"	"	Colica
105	Whitley	"	"	"	Feruunculus
106	Winborn	"	"	"	Cephalalgia
107	Mathis	"	"	"	" "

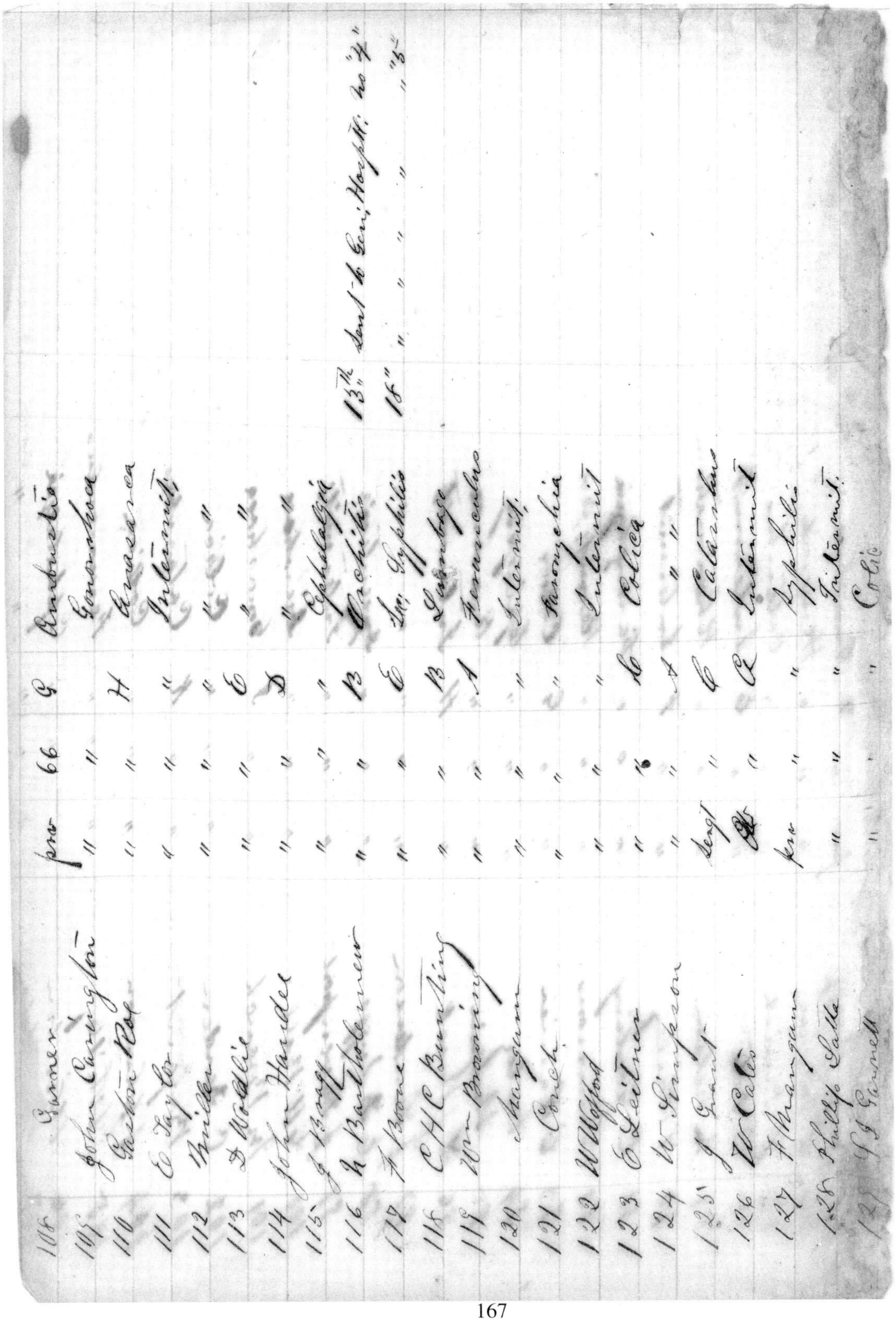

108	Garner	pvt	66	G	Combustio		
109	John Carrington	"	"		Gonorrhoea		
110	Gaston Roe	"	"	H	Anasarca		
111	E Taylor	"	"	"	Intermit;		
112	Miller	"	"	"	"		
113	D Woddie	"	"	E	"		
114	John Handee	"	"	D	"		
115	J Bragg	"	"	"	Cephalalgia		
116	R Bartholomew	"	"	B	Orchitis	13th "	Sent to Genl Hospt; no "4"
117	F Boone	"	"	E	Sec. Syphilis	18th "	" " " " "5"
118	CHC Bunting	"	"	B	Lumbago		
119	Wm Browning	"	"	A	Furunculus		
120	Mangum	"	"	"	Intermit;		
121	Couch	"	"	"	Paronychia		
122	W Wofford	"	"	"	Intermit		
123	E Leitner	"	"	C	Colica		
124	W Simpson	"	"	A	" "		
125	J Grant	Sergt	"	C	Catarrhus		
126	W Cates	Cpl	"	C	Intermit		
127	F Mangum	pvt	"	"	Syphilis		
128	Phillip Salts	"	"	"	Intermit.		
129	S J Garrett	"	"	"	Colic		

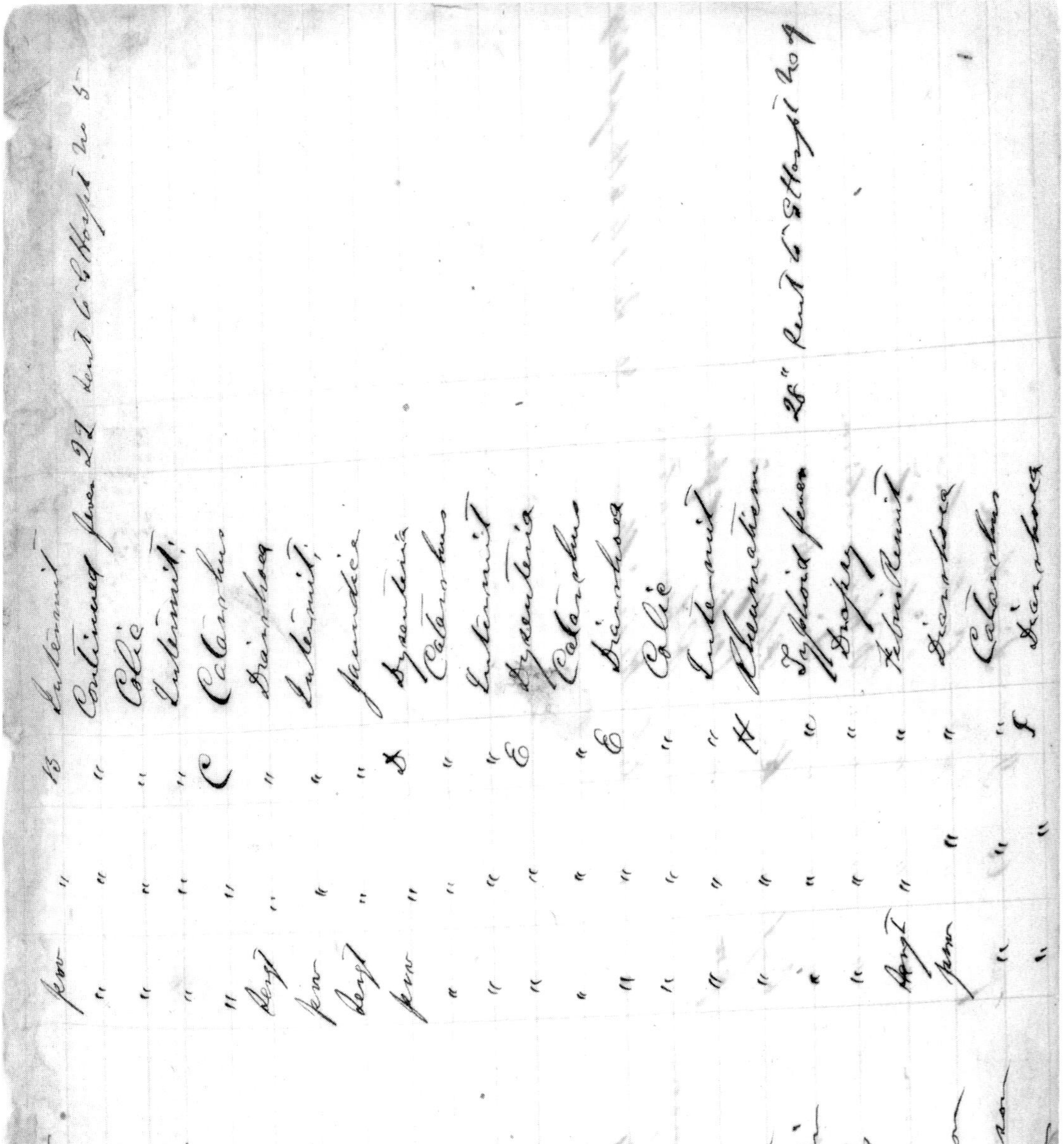

130	[illegible]	Pvt	"	13	Intermit
131	[illegible]	"	"	"	Continued fever 22 Sent to G Hospl No 5
132	J W Chapkin	"	"	"	Colic
133	[illegible]	"	"	"	Intermit
134	J Cox	"	"	C	Catarrhus
135	Grant	Sergt	"	"	Diarrhoea
136	J Waller	Pvt	"	"	Intermit
137	Philips	Sergt	"	"	Jaundice
138	L Fennel	Pvt	"	D	Dysenteria
139	L Wilson	"	"	"	Catarrhus
141	L McGhee	"	"	E	Intermit
142	J [illegible]	"	"	"	Dysenteria
143	R Lea	"	"	E	Catarrhus
144	J Barber	"	"	"	Diarrhoea
145	H Suggs	"	"	"	Colic
146	F Wolcot	"	"	"	Intermit
147	G W Reame	"	"	H	Rheumatism
148	L [illegible]	"	"	"	Typhoid fever 28 Sent to G Hospl No 9
149	W H Kennedy	"	"	"	Dropsy
150	Miller	Sergt	"	"	Febris Remit
151	J A Harrison	Pvt	"	"	Diarrhoea
152	S W Henderson	"	"	"	Catarrhus
153	C Brinson	"	"	F	Diarrhoea

#154	B N Gurganus	pr	66	I	Diarrhoea	
155	W Landing	"	"	"	Catarrhus	
156	M Mashburn	"	"	"	Intermit	
157	C Deans	"	"	"	Rheumatism	
158	N B Outlaw	"	"	"	Diarrhoea	
159	J Barnes	Sergt	"	K	Phlegmasia	
160	R Brown	pr	"	"	Continued fever	
161	E W Williamson	"	"	"	Rheumatism	
162	H P Daughtry	"	"	E	Remittens	30 Sent to G Hosp No "4"

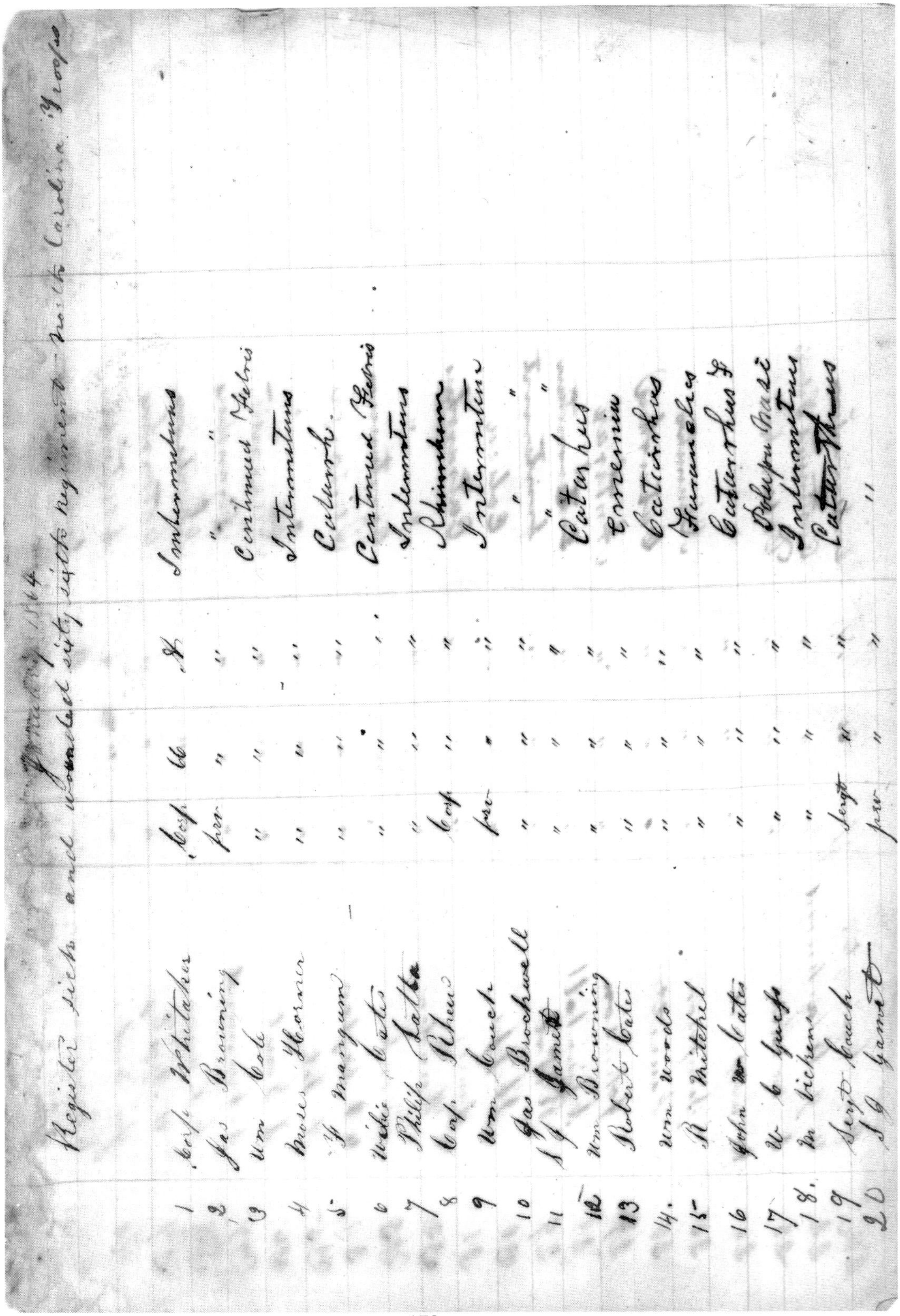
Register sick and wounded sixty sixth regiment North Carolina Troops
January 1864

1	Corp Whitaker	Corp	66	A	Intermittens
2	Jas Browning	pvt	"	"	"
3	Wm Cole	"	"	"	Continued Febris
4	Moses Horner	"	"	"	Intermittens
5	J Mangum	"	"	"	Catarrh
6	Willis Cates	"	"	"	Continued Febris
7	Philip Cates	"	"	"	Intermittens
8	Cap Rhew	Corp	"	"	Rheumatism
9	Wm Couch	pvt	"	"	Intermittens
10	Jas Brockwell	"	"	"	"
11	J G Garrett	"	"	"	"
12	Wm Browning	"	"	"	Catarrhus
13	Robert Cates	"	"	"	Emesis
14	Wm Woods	"	"	"	Catarrhus
15	R Mitchel	"	"	"	Furunculus
16	John W Cates	"	"	"	Catarrhus F
17	W C Guess	"	"	"	[illegible]
18	M Dickens	"	"	"	Intermittens
19	Sergt Couch	Sergt	"	"	Catarrhus
20	J G Garrett	pvt	"	"	"

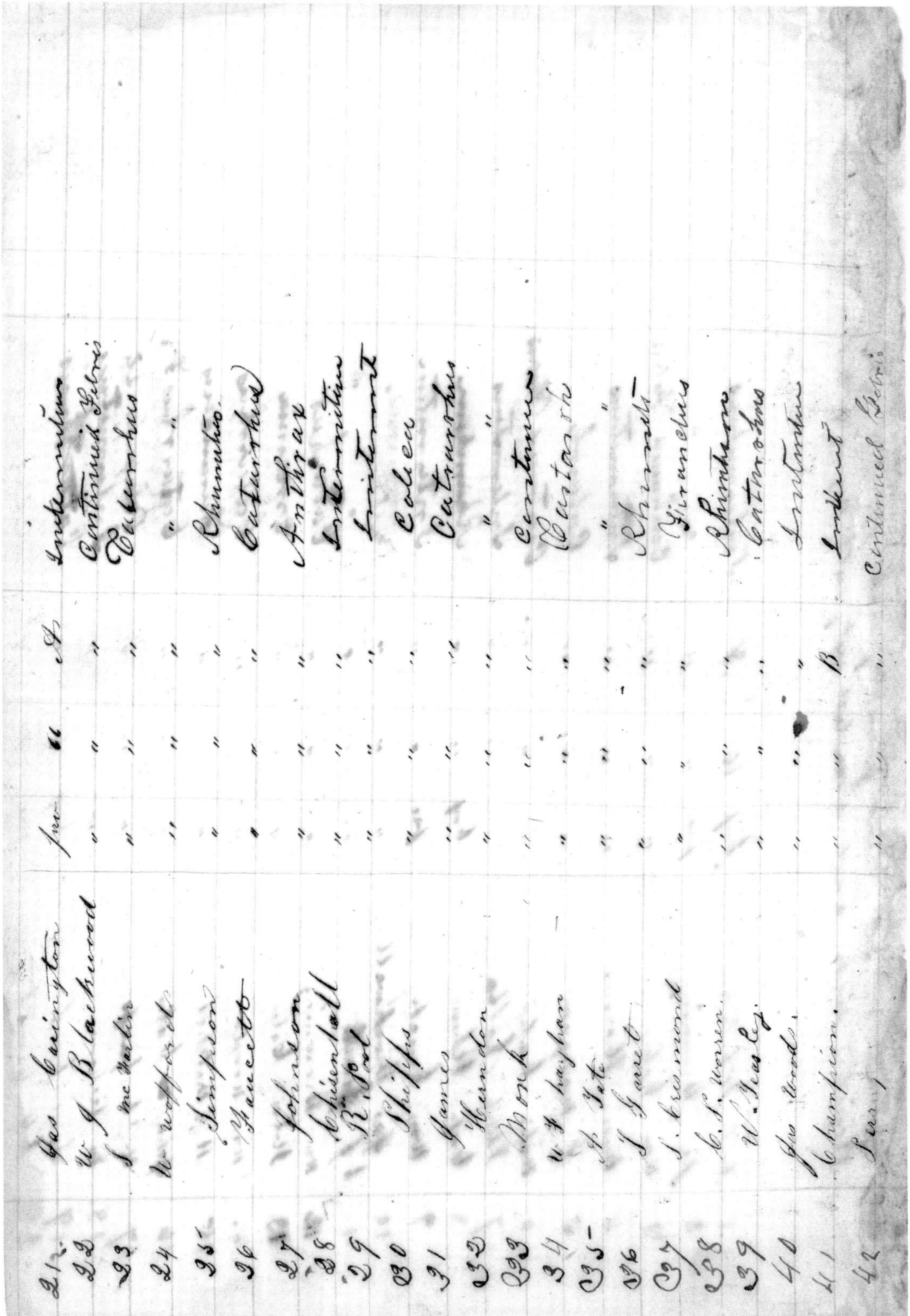

21	Jas Carrington	pvt	"	A	Intermittens
22	W J Blackwood	"	"	"	Continued Febris
23	J McFarlin	"	"	"	Catarrhus
24	W Wofford	"	"	"	" "
25	Simpson	"	"	"	Rheumatism
26	Faucette	"	"	"	Catarrhus
27	Johnson	"	"	"	Anthrax
28	Chisentall	"	"	"	Intermittens
29	R. Pool	"	"	"	Intermittent
30	Phipps	"	"	"	Colica
31	James	"	"	"	Catarrhus
32	Herndon	"	"	"	" "
33	Monk	"	"	"	Continued
34	W F Hayhan	"	"	"	Catarrh
35	A Yate	"	"	"	" "
36	J Garret	"	"	"	Rheumatism
37	S. Crismond	"	"	"	Furunculus
38	C. S. Warren	"	"	"	Rheumatism
39	W. Teasley	"	"	"	Catarrhus
40	Jas Woods	"	"	"	Intermittens
41	Champion	"	"	B	Intermittent
42	Perry	"	"	"	Continued Febris

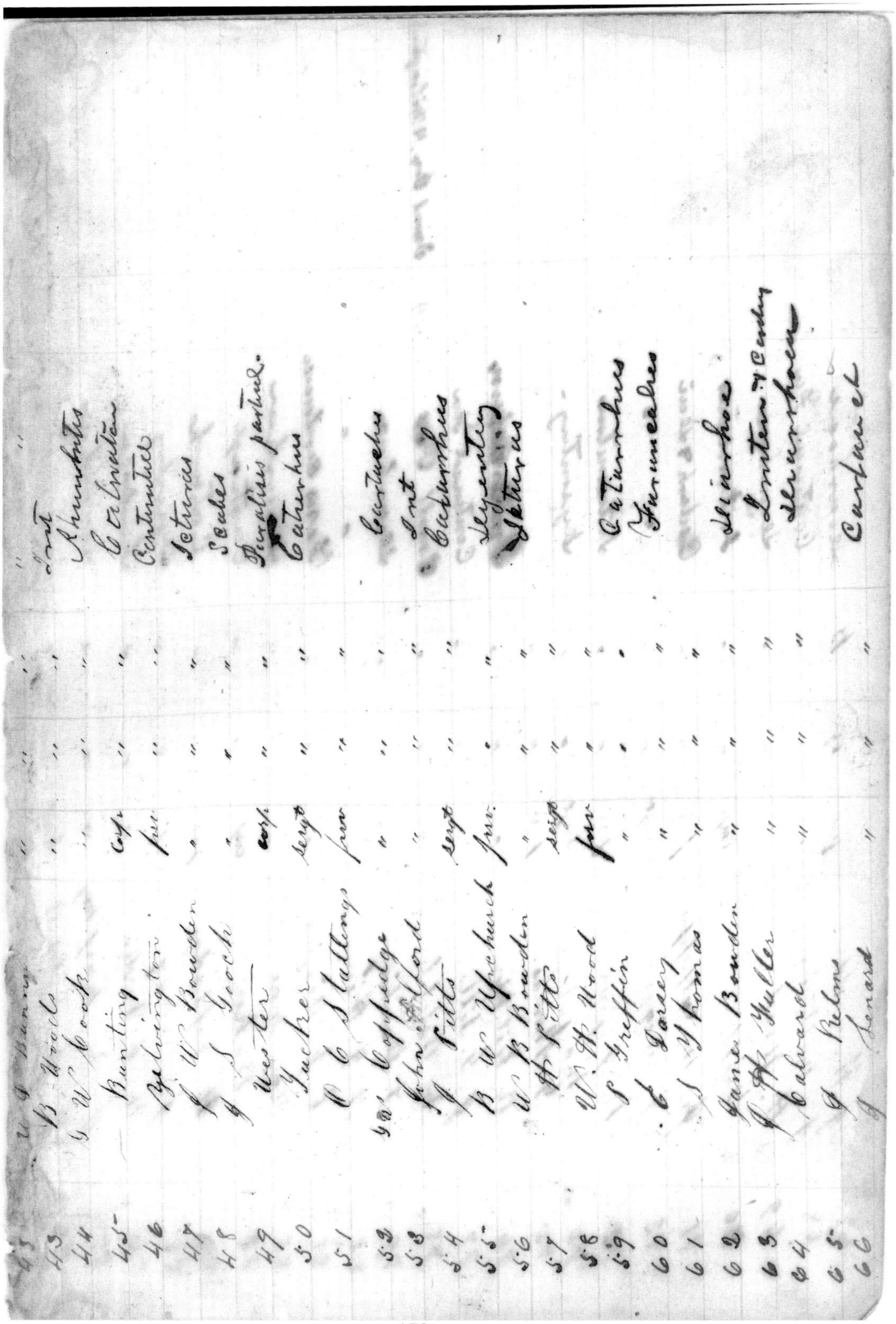

43	W J Bunn	"	"	"	"
43	B Woods	"	"	"	Int
44	G W Cook	"	"	"	Rheumatitis
45	Bunting	corp	"	"	Colivation
46	Yelvington	pvt	"	"	Contentitil
47	J W Bowden	"	"	"	Icterus
48	J S Gooch	"	"	"	Scabes
49	Wester	corp	"	"	Paralisis partial
50	Tucker	sergt	"	"	Caterrhus
51	O C Stallings	pvt	"	"	
52	Wm Coppedge	"	"	"	Cartuches
53	John Alford	"	"	"	Int
54	J Pitts	sergt	"	"	Catarrhus
55	B W Upchurch	pvt	"	"	Dysentery
56	W B Bowden	"	"	"	Icterus
57	H Pitts	sergt	"	"	
58	W H Wood	pvt	"	"	
59	S Griffin	"	"	"	Catarrhus
60	E Dorsey	"	"	"	Furunculus
61	S Thomas	"	"	"	
62	James Bowden	"	"	"	Diarrhoe
63	J H Fuller	"	"	"	Inter. & Cardy
64	Calvard	"	"	"	Diarrhoea
65	J Relms				
66	J Lenard	"	"	"	Carbuncle

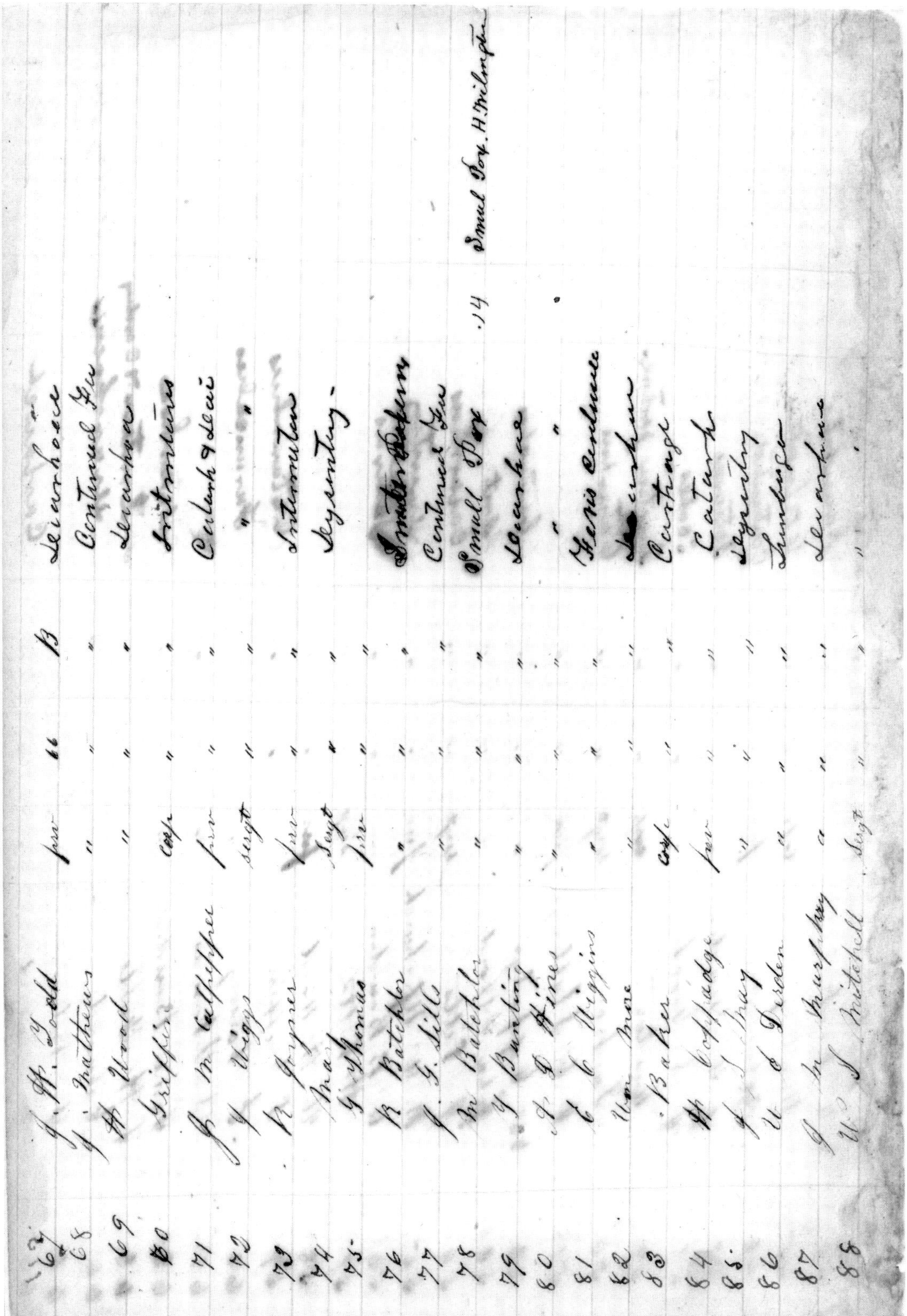

67	J. W. Todd	pvt	66	B	Diarrhoea		
68	J. Mathews	"	"	"	Continued Fev		
69	H Wood	"	"	"	Diarrhoea		
70	Griffin	corp	"	"	Intermitens		
71	J M Culpepper	pvt	"	"	Catarh & Diar		
72	J Wiggs	sergt	"	"	" "		
73	R Joyner	pvt	"	"	Intermitten		
74	May	Sergt	"	"	Dysentery		
75	G Thomas	pvt	"	"			
76	R Batchlor	"	"	"	[illegible]		
77	J. G. Sills	"	"	"	Continued Fev		
78	M Batchlor	"	"	"	Small Pox	.14	Smal Pox. H Wilmington
79	J Bunting	"	"	"	Diarhea		
80	A D Hines	"	"	"	" "		
81	E C Wiggins	"	"	"	Febris Continue		
82	Wm More	"	"	"	Diarhea		
83	Baker	corp	"	"	Carthage		
84	H Coppadge	pvt	"	"	Catarh		
85	J S May	"	"	"	Dysentery		
86	W C Derden	"	"	"	Lumbago		
87	J M Murphrey	"	"	"	Diarhea		
88	Wm S Mitchell	Sergt	"	"	"		

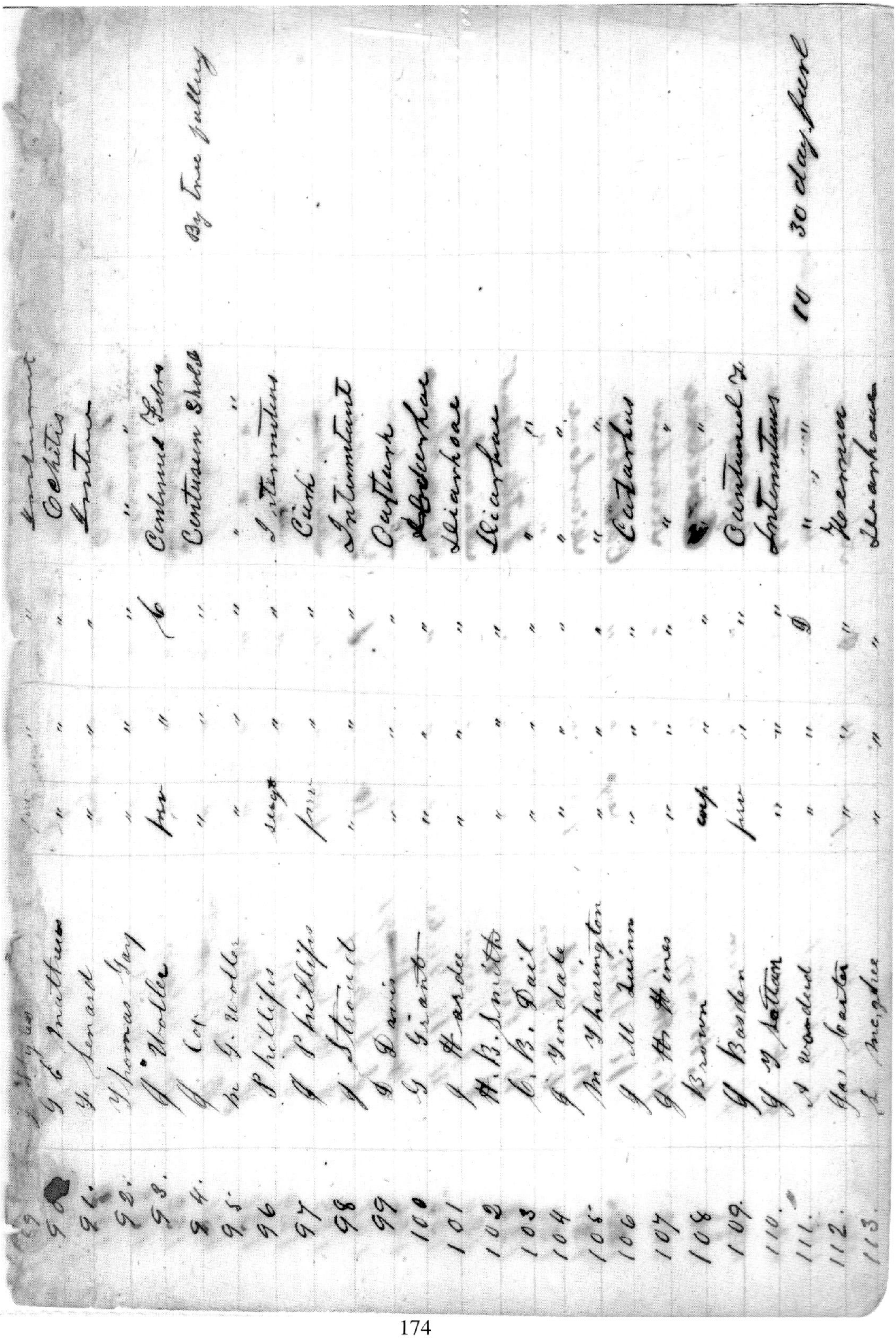

89	J. Hygus	pri	"	"	Continued	
90	G. E. Matthews	"	"	"	Orchitis	
91	J. Lenard	"	"	"	Urticaria	
92	Thomas Gay	"	"	"	"	
93	J. Waller	pri	"	6	Continued Fever	
94	J. Cox	"	"	"	Contusion Shell	By Tree falling
95	M. G. Waller	"	"	"	"	
96	Phillips	sergt	"	"	Intermittens	
97	J. Phillips	pri	"	"	Cure	
98	J. Stroud	"	"	"	Intermittent	
99	D. Davis	"	"	"	Catarrh	
100	G. Grant	"	"	"	Diarrhoea	
101	J. Hardee	"	"	"	Diarrhoea	
102	H. B. Smith	"	"	"	Diarrhoea	
103	C. B. Dail	"	"	"	"	
104	J. Yendale	"	"	"	"	
105	M. Harrington	"	"	"	"	
106	J. M. Quinn	"	"	"	Catarrhus	
107	G. H. Hines	"	"	"	"	
108	Brown	corp	"	"	"	
109	J. Barden	pri	"	"	Continued F.	
110	J. G. Cotton	"	"	"	Intermittens	
111	A. Woodard	"	"	D	" "	10 30 day furl
112	Jas. Carter	"	"	"	Pneumonia	
113	L. Megee	"	"	"	Diarrhoea	

114	S Ferrell	pvt	66	D	Rheumatism
115	C S Perrish	"	"	"	" "
116	J Fields	"	"	"	Intermittens
117	J Wilkerson	"	"	"	Cystitis
118	G. Bragg	"	"	"	Diarrhoea
119	Jas Heys	"	"	"	Diarrhea
120	R Isely	Sergt	"	"	Catarrhus
121	R May	pvt	"	"	Diarrhoea
122	C W Demon	"	"	"	" "
123	B Perry	"	"	"	Intermittent
124	C J Barrow	"	"	"	Diarrhea
125	W R Geeler	"	"	"	Diarrhoea
126	~~G M Bragg~~	"	"	"	— — —
127	J. S. May	Ctp	"	C	Typhoides
128	D Worley	pvt	"	"	Diarrhea
129	A Powell	"	"	"	" "
130	J Brattise	"	"	"	" "
131	B H Bryant	"	"	"	Cured
132	M Nelson	"	"	"	Synovitis chro
133	A Waters	"	"	"	Diarrhea
134	Taylor	Sergt	"	"	Catarrh
135	John Smith	pvt	"	"	Diarr

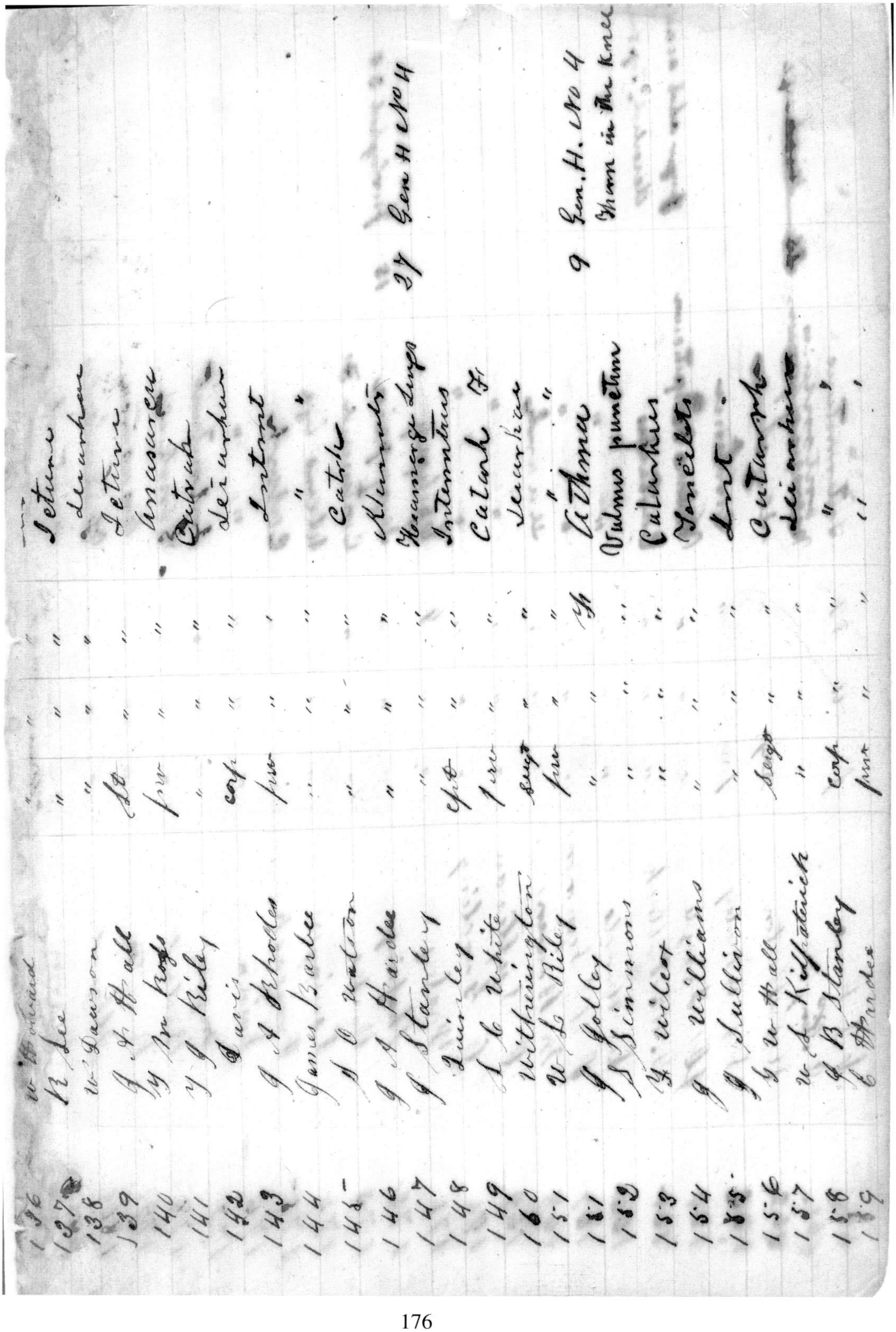

136	W Howard	"	"	"			
137	R Lee	"	"	"	Icterus		
138	W Dawson	"	"	"	diarrhea		
139	J A Hall	St	"	"	Icterus		
140	Y M Ross	prv	"	"	Anasarca		
141	Y J Riley	"	"	"	Catarrh		
142	Davis	corp	"	"	diarrhea		
143	J A Rhodes	prv	"	"	Intmt		
144	James Barbee	"	"	"	"		
145	J O Watson	"	"	"	Catarrh		
146	J A Hardee	"	"	"	Rheumatism		
147	J Stanley	"	"	"	Haemorrhage Lungs	27	Gen H No 4
148	Quinley	cpt	"	"	Intermittens		
149	A C White	prv	"	"	Catarrh F		
160	Witherington	Sergt	"	"	diarrhea		
151	W L Riley	prv	"	"	"		
151	J Jolley	"	"	Yl	Athma	9	Gen. H. No 4
152	S Simmons	"	"	"	Vulnus punctum		Thorn in the Knee
153	F Wilcox	"	"	"	Calculus		
154	J Williams	"	"	"	Tonsilitis		
155	J Sullivan	"	"	"	Int		
156	G W Hall	Sergt	"	"	Catarrh		
157	W S Kilpatrick	"	"	"	diarrhea		
158	J B Stanley	corp	"	"	"		
159	E Hardee	prvt	"	"	"		

160	C L Koonce	Pvt	66	G	Intermittens		
161	D. King	"	"	"	Intermittens ~~Necrosis of femur~~	~~15~~	~~Discharge~~
162	R S Beeton	Sergt	"	"	Diarrhea		
163	L J Whaley	Pvt	"	"	Contusio		
164	J O Frazle	"	"	"	Vulnus Sclopeticum		finger shot accidentally
165	G. W. Pollock	"	"	"	Catarrhus		deserted. Top sail
166	L Woods	"	"	"	" "		
167	J W Simmons	"	"	"	" "		
168	M Bowens	"	"	"	Scurvy		
169	O Sullivan	"	"	"	" "		
170	C Gooding	"	"	"	" "		
171	Fraley	"	"	G	Epilepsy		
172	Shaping	"	"	"	Dyspepsia	15	Furloughed 30
173	Rooks	"	"	"	Continued F.		
174	Peninger	"	"	"	Ulcers leg		
175	Overcash	"	"	"	Catarrh		
176	Quinn	"	"	"	" "		
177	Myres	"	"	"	Intermittent		
178	Badgett	"	"	"	Scorbutus		
179	Burton	"	"	"	Anasarca		
180	Allgood	"	"	"	Furunculus		
181	Garner	"	"	"	Catarrh		

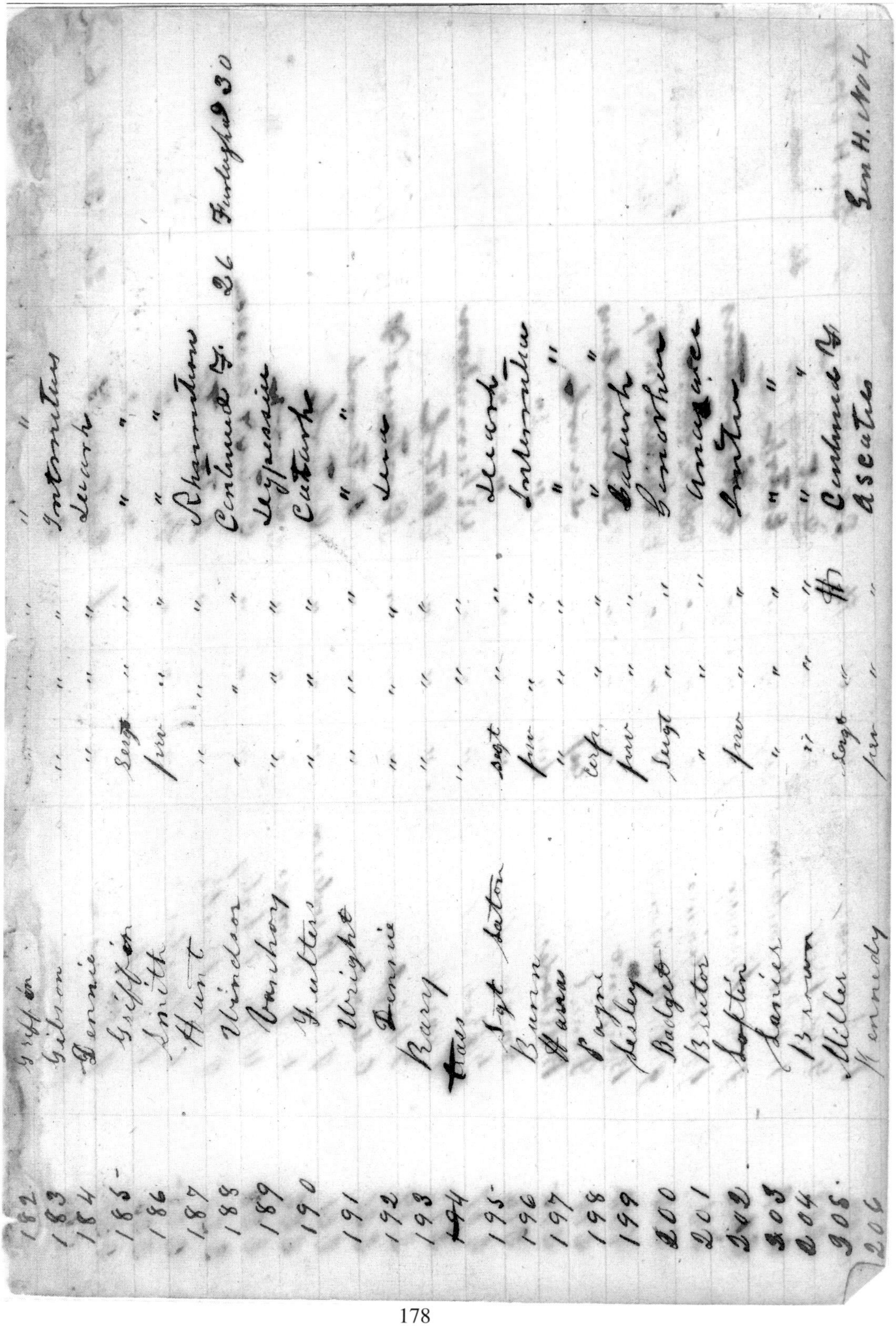

182	Griffin	"	"	"	"	
183	Gibson	"	"	"	Intermittens	
184	Dennie	"	"	"	Diarrh	
185	Griffin	Sergt	"	"	"	
186	Smith	Pvt	"	"	"	
187	Hunt	"	"	"	Rheumatism	
188	Windsor	"	"	"	Continued F. 26	Furloughed 30
189	Vanhorn	"	"	"	Dyspepsia	
190	Yatters	"	"	"	Catarrh	
191	Wright	"	"	"	"	
192	Dennie	"	"	"	Lues	
193	Rary	"	"	"		
194	Haas	"	"	"		
195	Sgt Sutton	sgt	"	"	Diarrh	
196	Bunn	Pvt	"	"	Intermittens	
197	Haas	"	"	"	"	
198	Payne	Corp	"	"	"	
199	Lesley	Pvt	"	"	Catarrh	
200	Badgett	Sergt	"	"	Gonorrhea	
201	Britton	"	"	"	Anasarca	
202	Lofton	Pvt	"	"	Icterus	
203	Lanier	"	"	"	"	
204	Brown	"	"	"	"	
205	Miller	Sergt	"	H	Continued F	
206	Kennedy	Pvt	"	"	Ascites	Gen H. No 4

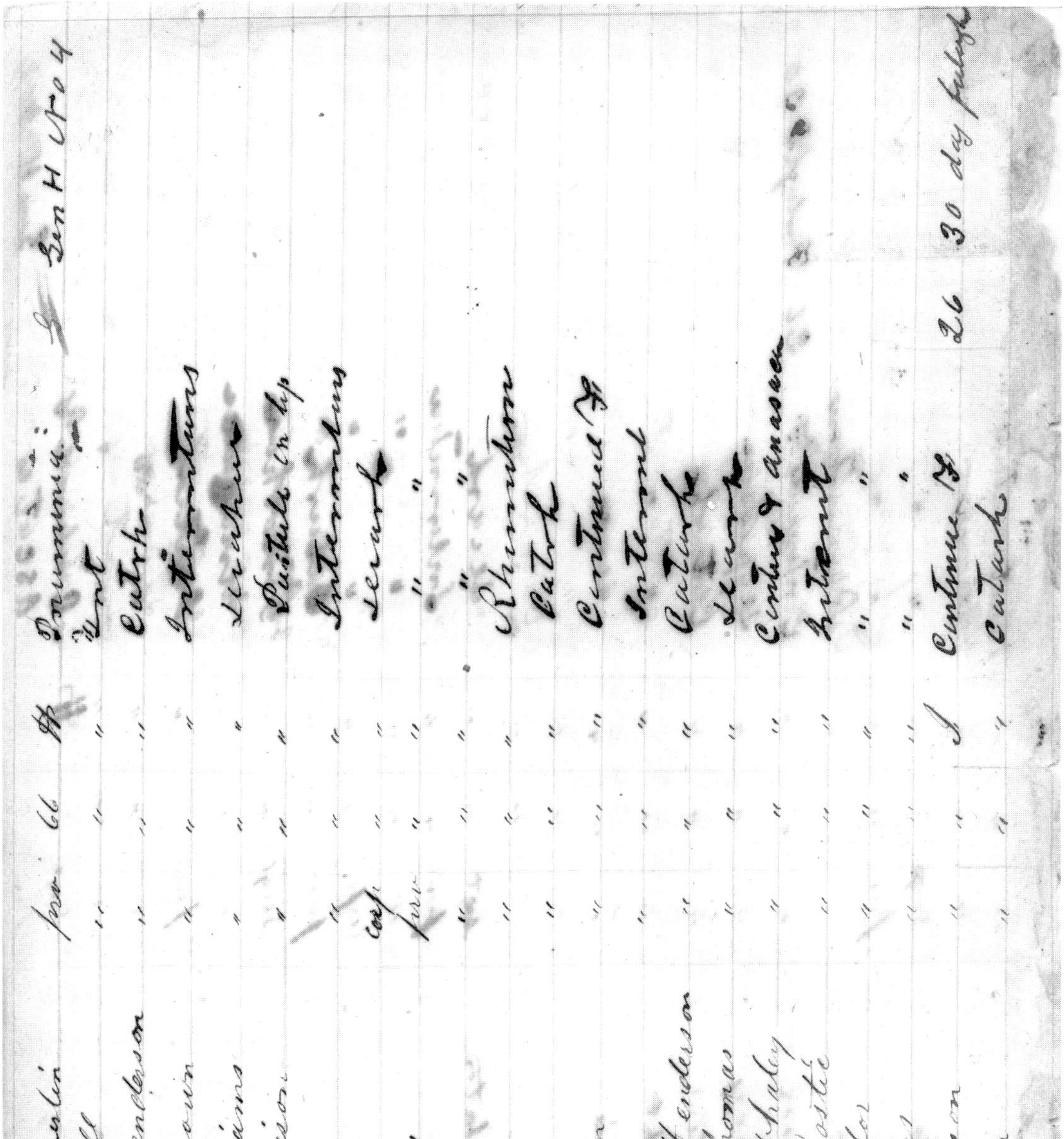

207	B Summerlin	pro	66	H	Pneumonia		Gen H No 4
208	G W Bell	"	"	"	Int		
209	S W Henderson	"	"	"	Catrh		
210	J W Brown	"	"	"	Intermittens		
211	B Williams	"	"	"	Scrabus		
212	J O Harison	"	"	"	Pustule in lip		
213	Bryant	"	"	"	Intermittens		
214	Daniel	corp	"	"	Scurvy		
215	B Rhodes	pro	"	"	" "		
216	Aman	"	"	"	" "		
217	G Roe	"	"	"	Rheumatism		
218	Pearce	"	"	"	Catrh		
219	Thigpen	"	"	"	Continued F		
220	Edwards	"	"	"	Intermit		
221	J M Henderson	"	"	"	Catarh		
222	C G Thomas	"	"	"	Scurvy		
223	W B Whaley	"	"	"	Contin & anasarca		
224	J M Bostic	"	"	"	Intermit		
225	C Taylor	"	"	"	" "		
226	C Capps	"	"	"	"		
227	J Swinson	"	"	I	Continue F	26	30 day furlough
228	H Harrison	"	"	"	Catarh		

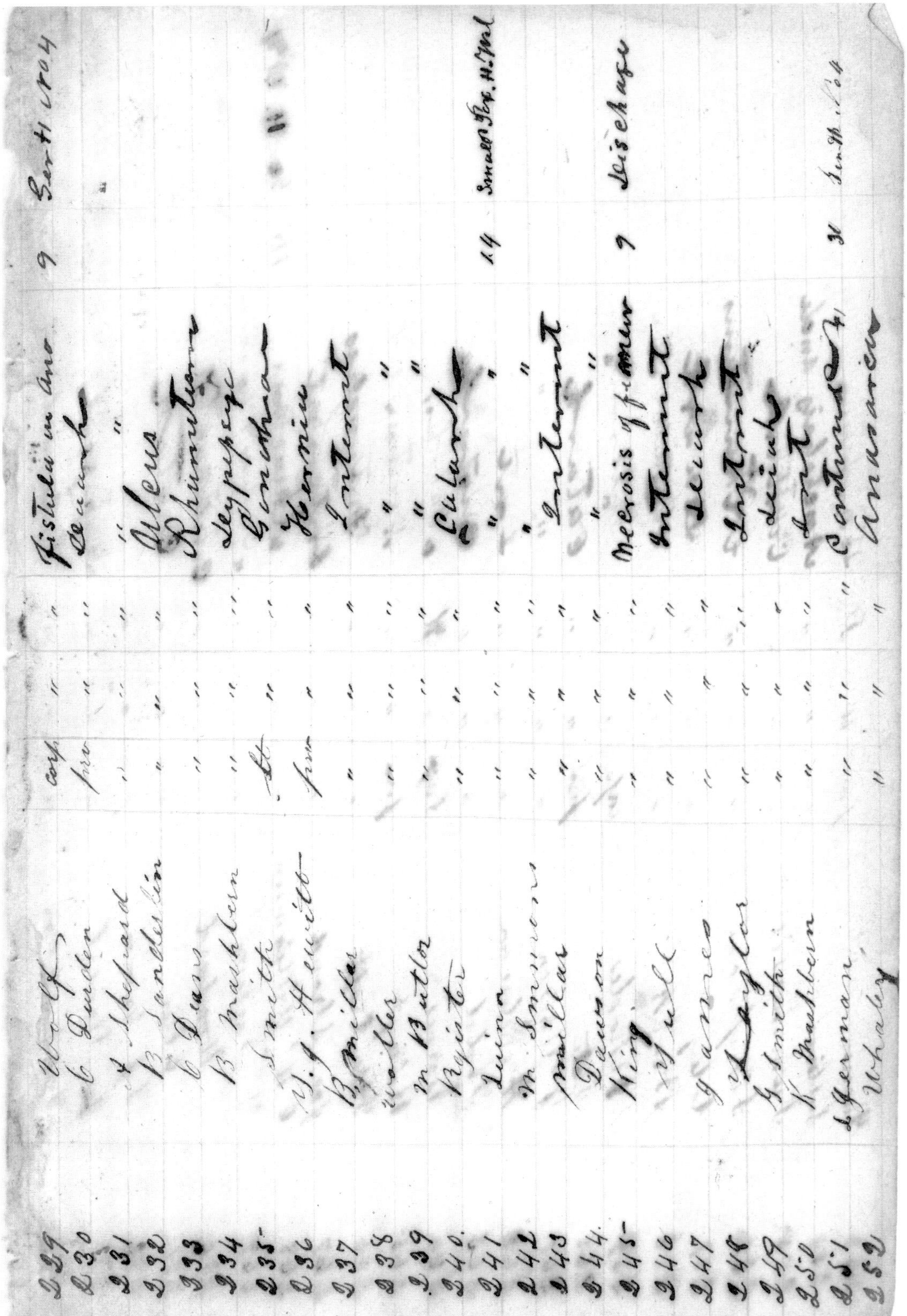

229	Wolf	corp	"	"	Fistula in Ano	9	Sep 11 1864
230	C Durden	pri	"	"	Catarrh		
231	F Shepard	"	"	"	"		
232	B Sanderlin	"	"	"	Ulcers		
233	C Dean	"	"	"	Rheumatism		
234	B Mashburn	"	"	"	Dyspepsia		
235	Smith	Lt	"	"	Gonorrhea		
236	J.J. Hewitt	pri	"	"	Hernia		
237	B Miller	"	"	"	Intermit		
238	Miller	"	"	"	"		
239	M Butler	"	"	"	"		
240	Register	"	"	"	Catarrh		
241	Luina	"	"	"	"	14	Small Pox. H. Ind
242	M Simmons	"	"	"	"		
243	Millar	"	"	"	Intermit		
244	Dawson	"	"	"	"		
245	King	"	"	"	Necrosis of femur	9	Discharge
246	Yull	"	"	"	Intermit		
247	James	"	"	"	Scurvy		
248	Taylor	"	"	"	Intermit		
249	G Smith	"	"	"	Diarrh		
250	K Mashburn	"	"	"	[illegible]		
251	L German	"	"	"	Contusion	31	Sent to [illegible]
252	Whaley	"	"	"	Anasarca		

253	Turner	pvt	66	I	Diarrhea	
254	Sullivon	"	"	"	Ancholosis ankle	
255	Summersil	"	"	"	Catarrh	
256	Simpson	"	"	"	Rheumatism	
257	Coley	"	"	"	Diarrh	
258	Brock	"	"	"	" "	
259	Rhodes	cap	"	"	" "	
260	Tate	pvt	"	"	Catarrh	
261	J Simson	"	"	"	" "	
262	Henderson	"	"	"	Int	
263	Todd	"	"	"	Catarrh	
264	Barnes	Sergt	"	K	" "	
265	Bailey	pvt	"	"	" "	
266	Thos Craft	"	"	"	Furunculus	
267	Jas Stroud	"	"	"	Intermit	
268	C W Williamson	"	"	"	Rheumatism	11 Gen H. No 4
269	W Sassem	"	"	"	" "	
270	Woodard	"	"	"	Continued F.	
271	Ellis	Sergt	"	"	Catarrh	
272	T J Lamm	pvt	"	"		
273	Jas Stansel	"	"	"	Dyspepsia	
274	Tomlinson	"	"	"	Intermitten	

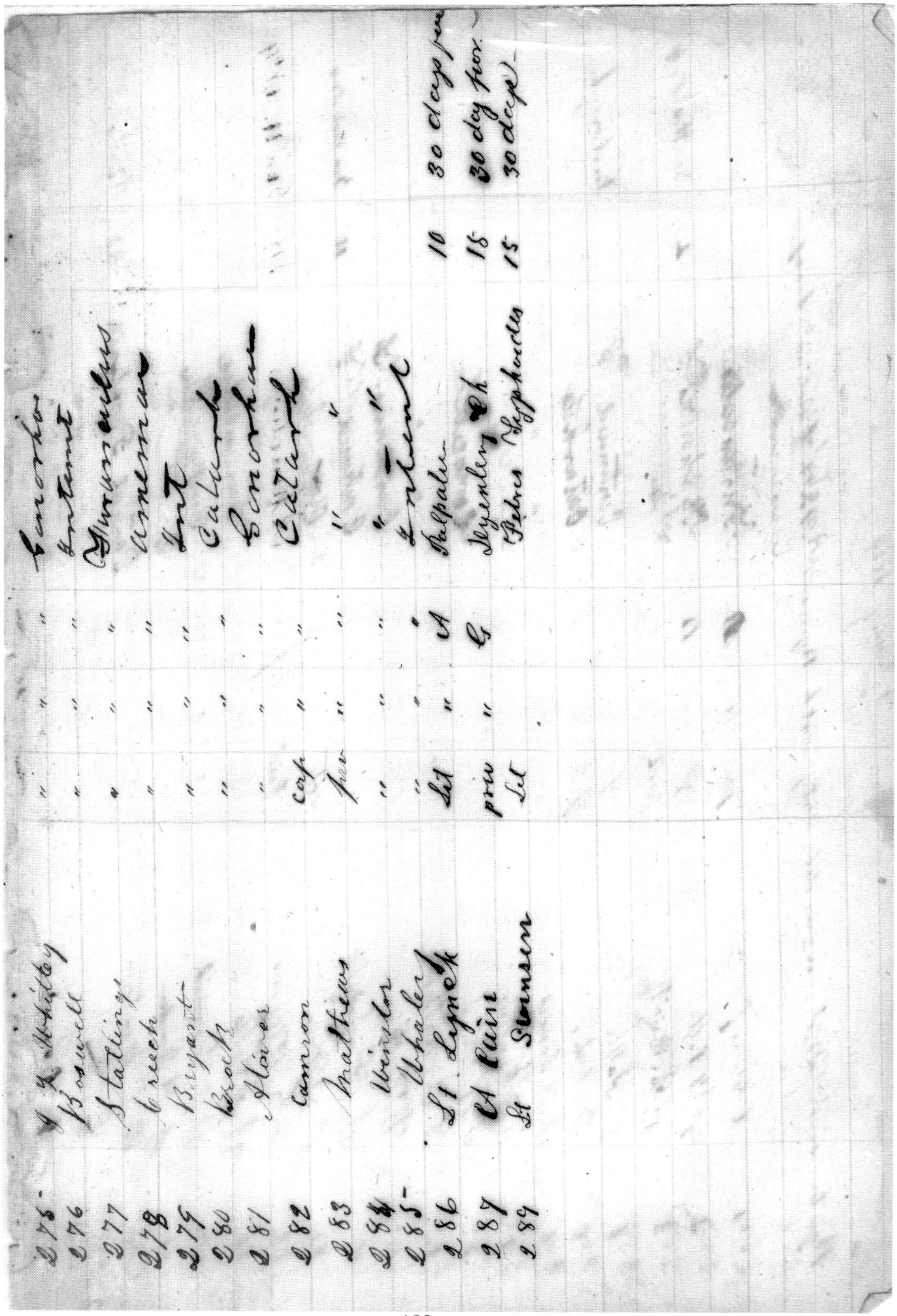

275	J. Y. Whitley	"	"	"	Gonorrhoea		
276	Boswell	"	"	"	Intermit		
277	Stallings	"	"	"	Rheumatism		
278	Creech	"	"	"	Anemia		
279	Bryant	"	"	"	Int		
280	Brock	"	"	"	Catarrh		
281	Glover	"	"	"	Gonorrhoea		
282	Cannon	corp	"	"	Catarrh		
283	Mathews	pvt	"	"	" "		
284	Winslow	"	"	"	" "		
285	Whaley	"	"	"	Intermit		
286	Lt. Lynch	Lt	"	A	Palpatio	10	30 days fur
287	Cpt Cain	priv	"	G	Dysentery Ch	15	30 day fur.
289	Lt Swanson	Lt			(Febris Syphilis	15	30 days)

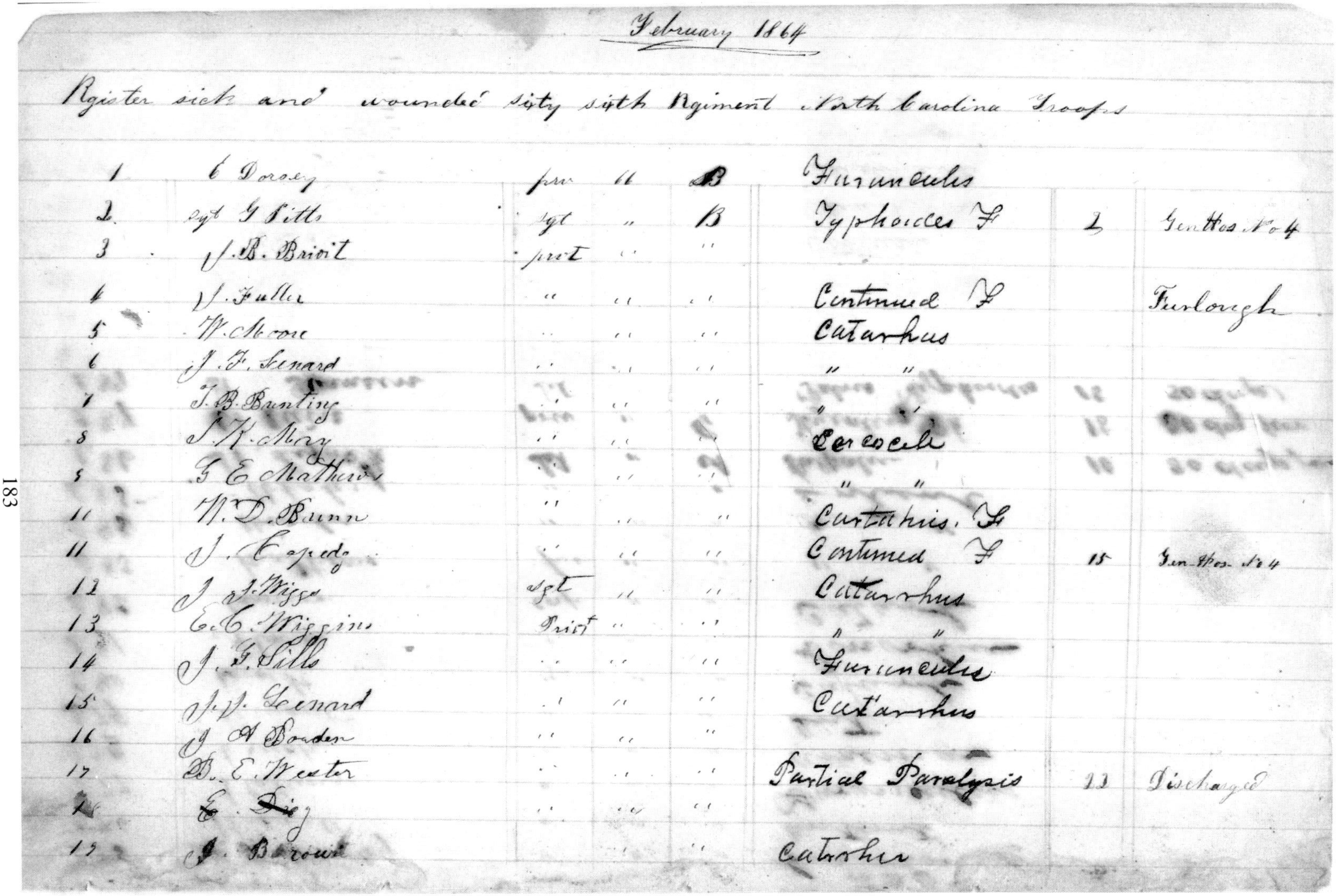

February 1864

Register sick and wounded Sixty sixth Regiment North Carolina Troops

1	C Dorsey	pvt	"	B	Furunculus		
2	Sgt G Pitts	Sgt	"	B	Typhoid F	2	Gen Hos. No 4
3	J. B. Briant	pvt	"	"			
4	J. Fuller	"	"	"	Continued F		Furlough
5	W. Moore	"	"	"	Catarrhus		
6	J. F. Lenard	"	"	"	" "		
7	T. B. Bunting	"	"	"			
8	J. K. May	"	"	"	Varicocele		
9	G. E. Mathews	"	"	"			
10	W. D. Bunn	"	"	"	" "		
11	J. Capedge	"	"	"	Continued F	15	Gen Hos. No 4
12	J. J. Wiggs	Sgt	"	"	Catarrhus		
13	E. C. Wiggins	Privt	"	"	" "		
14	J. F. Pitts	"	"	"	Furunculus		
15	J. J. Lenard	"	"	"	Catarrhus		
16	J. A. Borden	"	"	"			
17	B. E. Wester	"	"	"	Partial Paralysis	22	Discharged
18	E. Diz	"	"	"			
19	J. Brown	"	"	"	Catarrhus		

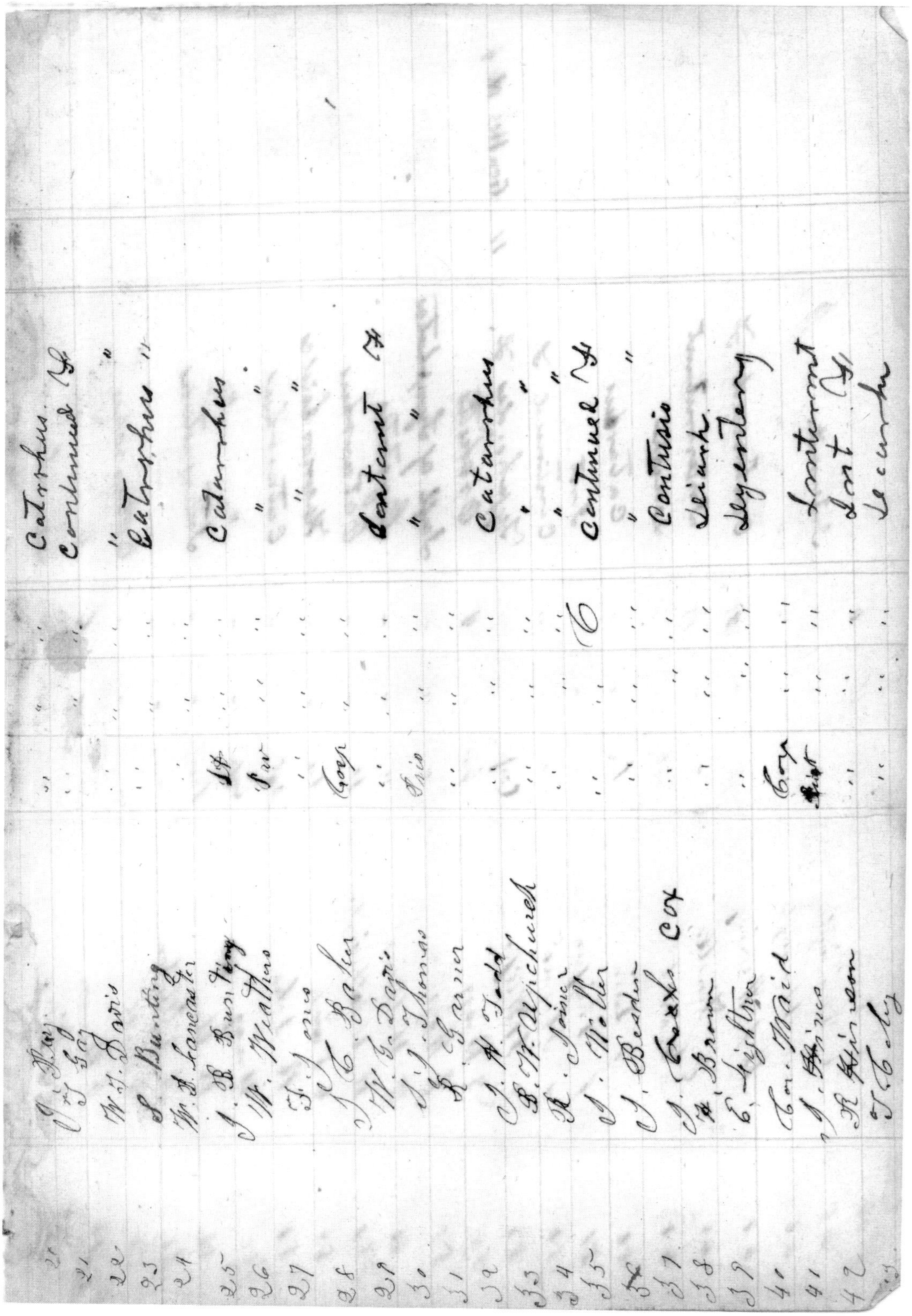

20	J. Ray	"	"	"	Catarrhus
21	J. T. Gay	"	"	"	Continued F
22	W. T. Davis	"	"	"	" "
23	S. Bunting	"	"	"	Catarrhus "
24	W. B. Lancaster	"	"		
25	J. B. Bunting	1st	"		Catarrhus
26	W. Weathers	Sar	"	"	" "
27	F. Jones	"	"	"	" "
28	J. C. Baker	Corp	"	"	
29	W. T. Davis	"	"	"	Intermit F
30	S. J. Thomas	Pri	"	"	" "
31	R. Garner	"	"	"	
32	J. H. Todd	"	"	"	Catarrhus
33	B. W. Upchurch	"	"	"	" "
34	R. Joiner	"	"	"	" "
35	J. Waller	"	"	C	Continued F
36	J. Besden	"	"	"	" "
37	J. Coates Cox	"	"	"	Contusio
38	H. Brown	"	"	"	Diarrh.
39	C. Lightner	"	"	"	Dysentery
40	Cor. Waid	Corp	"	"	
41	J. Hines	Sergt	"	"	Intermit
42	R. Hinson	"	"	"	Int. F
43	T. Coley	"	"	"	Scorbutus

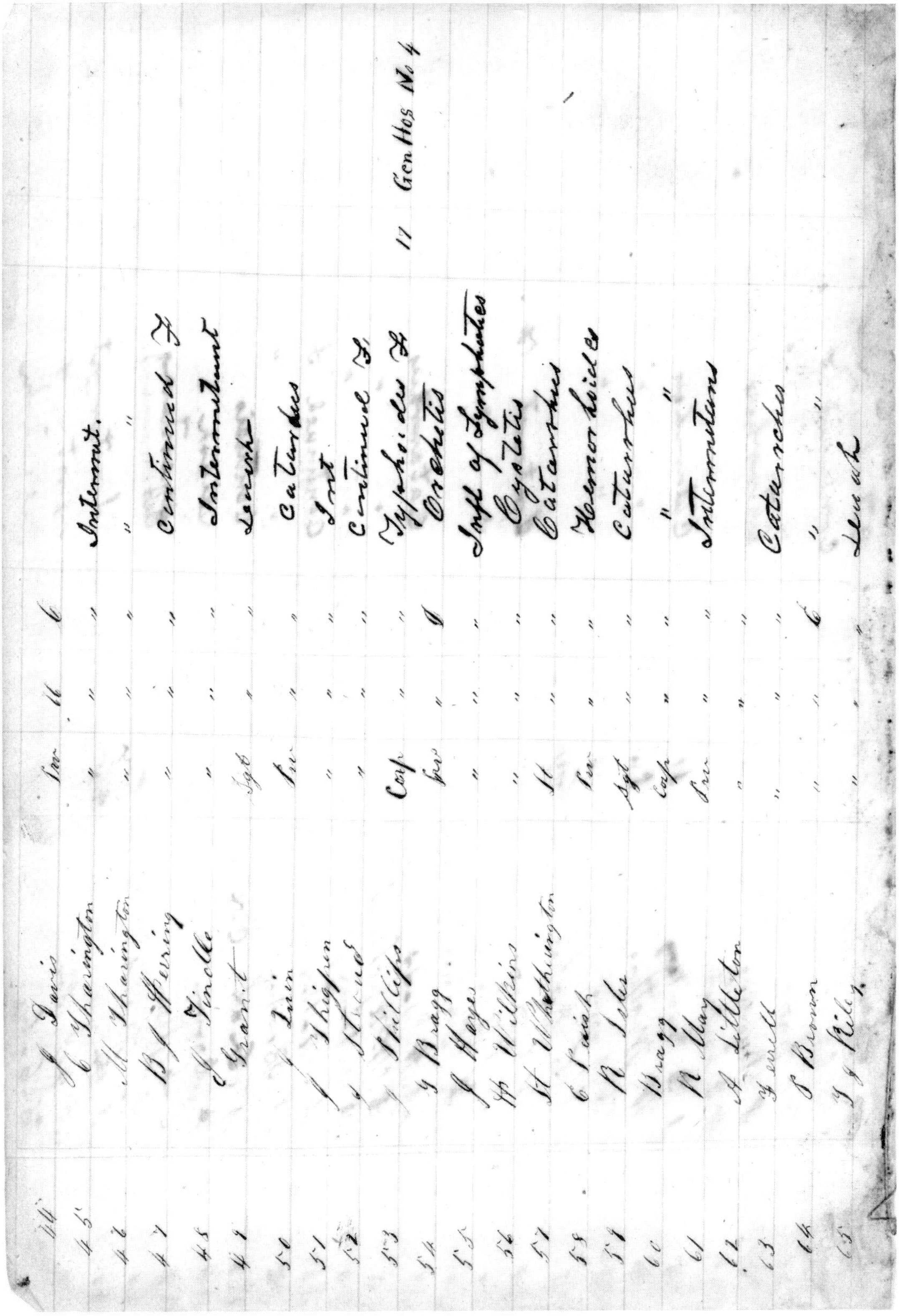

44	J Davis	Prv	11	6			
45	C Tharington	"	"	"	Intermit.		
46	M Tharington	"	"	"	" "		
47	B J Herring	"	"	"	Continued F		
48	J Tindle	"	"	"	Intermittant		
49	Grant	Sgt	"	"	Leucrh		
50	J Lain	Prv	"	"	Caturhes		
51	J Thigpen	"	"	"	Int		
52	J Stroud	"	"	"	Continued F.		
53	J Phillips	Corp	"	"	Typhoides F	17	Gen Hos No 4
54	G Bragg	Prv	"	J	Orchetis		
55	J Hayes	"	"	"	Infl of Lymphatics		
56	W Wilkins	"	"	"	Cystetis		
57	H Whitherington	Sgt	"	"	Catarrhus		
58	C Parish	Prv	"	"	Hemorhoides		
59	R Isler	Sgt	"	"	Caturrhus		
60	Bragg	Corp	"	"	" "		
61	R May	Prv	"	"	Intermitans		
62	A Littleton	"	"	"			
63	Ferrell	"	"	"	Caturrches		
64	S Brown	"	11	6	" "		
65	T J Riley	"	"	"	Leuah		

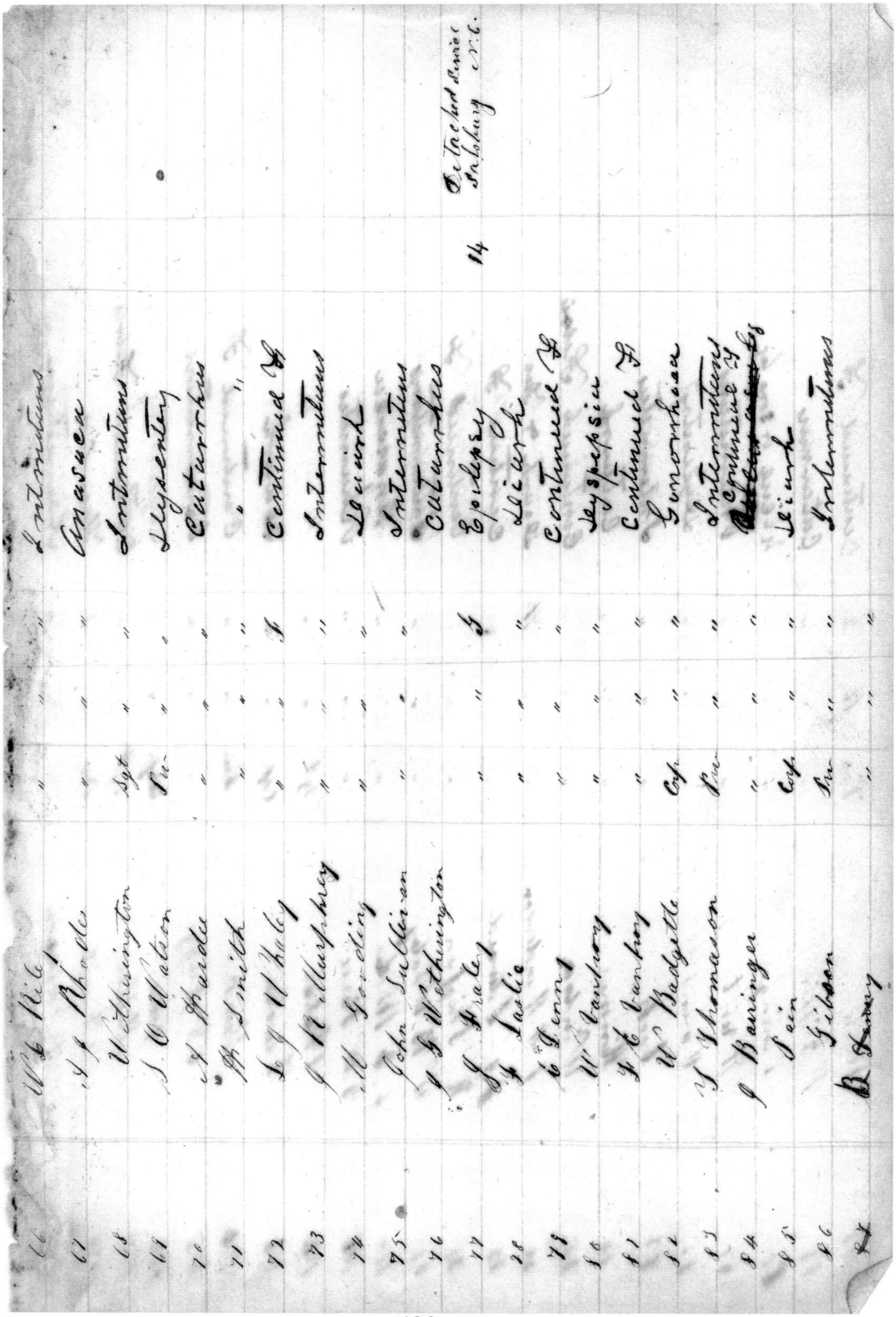

66	W L Riley	″	″	″	Intermittens		
67	A J Rhodes	″	″	″	Anasarca		
68	W Witherington	Sgt	″	″	Intermittens		
69	S O Watson	Pri	″	″	Dysentery		
70	A J Hardee	″	″	″	Catarrhus		
71	J J Smith	″	″	″	″		
72	L J Whaley	″	″	F	Continued F		
73	J R Murphrey	″	″	″	Intermittens		
74	M Gooding	″	″	″	Debility		
75	John Sullivan	″	″	″	Intermittens		
76	J G Witherington		″	″	Catarrhus		
77	J Fraley	″	″	G	Epilepsy	14	Detached Service Salisbury N.C.
78	A Laslie	″	″	″	Debility		
79	C Dennis	″	″	″	Continued F		
80	W Cantroy	″	″	″	Dyspepsia		
81	J C Cantroy	″	″	″	Continued F		
82	W Badgette	Corp	″	″	Gonorrhoea		
83	S Thomason	Pri	″	″	Intermittens		
84	J Baringer	″	″	″	Continued F ~~[illegible]~~		
85	Pein	Corp	″	″	Debility		
86	Gibson	Pri	″	″	Intermittens		
87	B [illegible]	″	″	″			

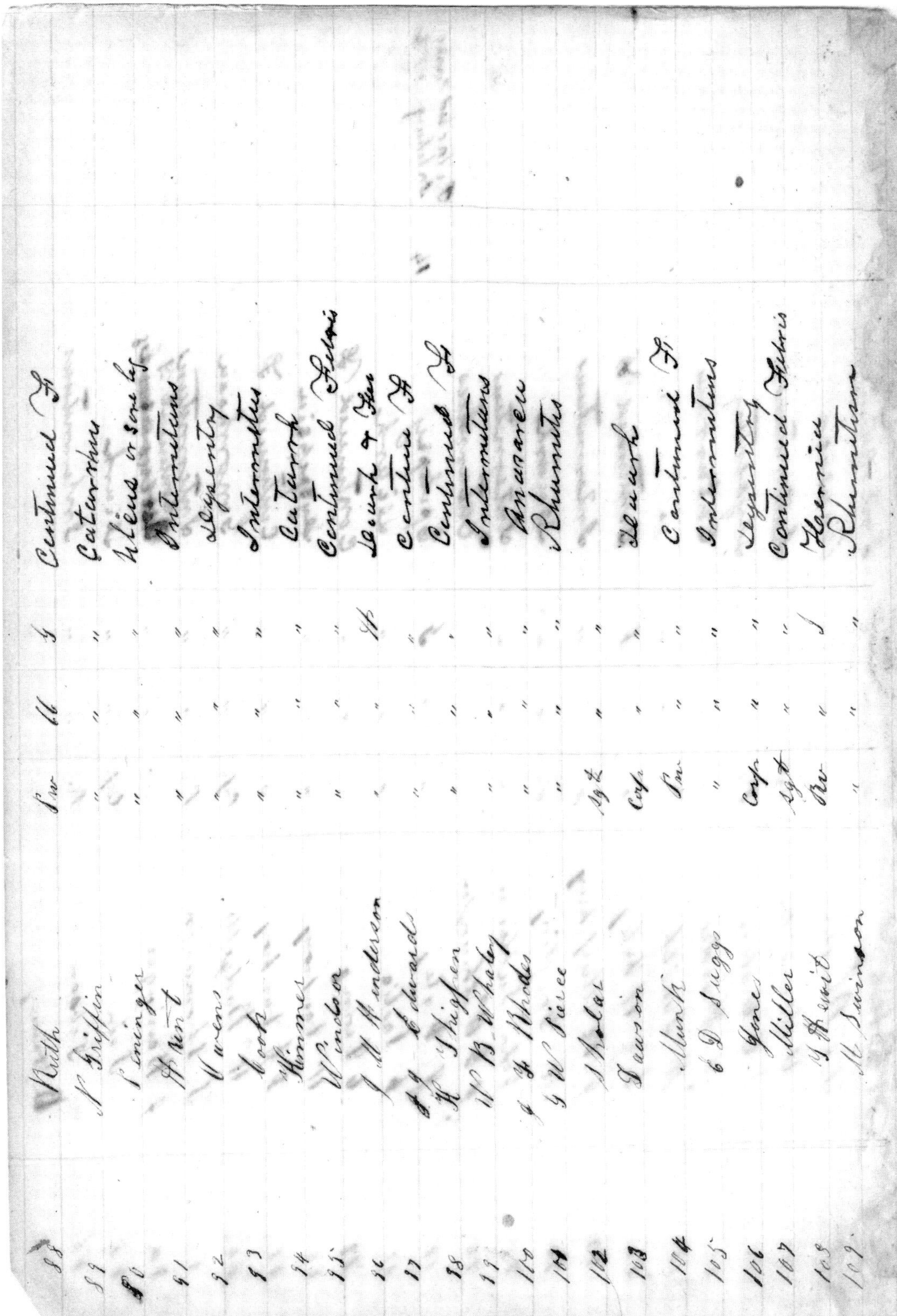

88	Ruth	Pv	66	G	Continued F
89	N Griffin	"	"	"	Catarrhus
90	Peninger	"	"	"	Ulcus or sore leg
91	Hunt	"	"	"	Intermitens
92	Owens	"	"	"	Dysentery
93	Cook	"	"	"	Intermittens
94	Kimmer	"	"	"	Catarrh
95	Windsor	"	"	"	Continued Febris
96	J M Henderson	"	"	H	Diarh & Fev
97	J G Edwards	"	"	"	Contin F
98	K Shiffen	"	"	"	Continued F
99	W B Whaley	"	"	"	Intermitens
100	J F Rhodes	"	"	"	Anasarca
101	G W Pierce	"	"	"	Rheumatis
102	Sholar	Sgt	"	"	
103	Dawson	Corp	"	"	Diarh
104	Munk	Pv	"	"	Continued F
105	C D Suggs	"	"	"	Intermitens
106	Jones	Corp	"	"	Dysentery
107	Miller	Sgt	"	"	Continued Febris
108	G Hewit	Pv	"	J	Hernia
109	M Swinson	"	"	"	Rheumatism

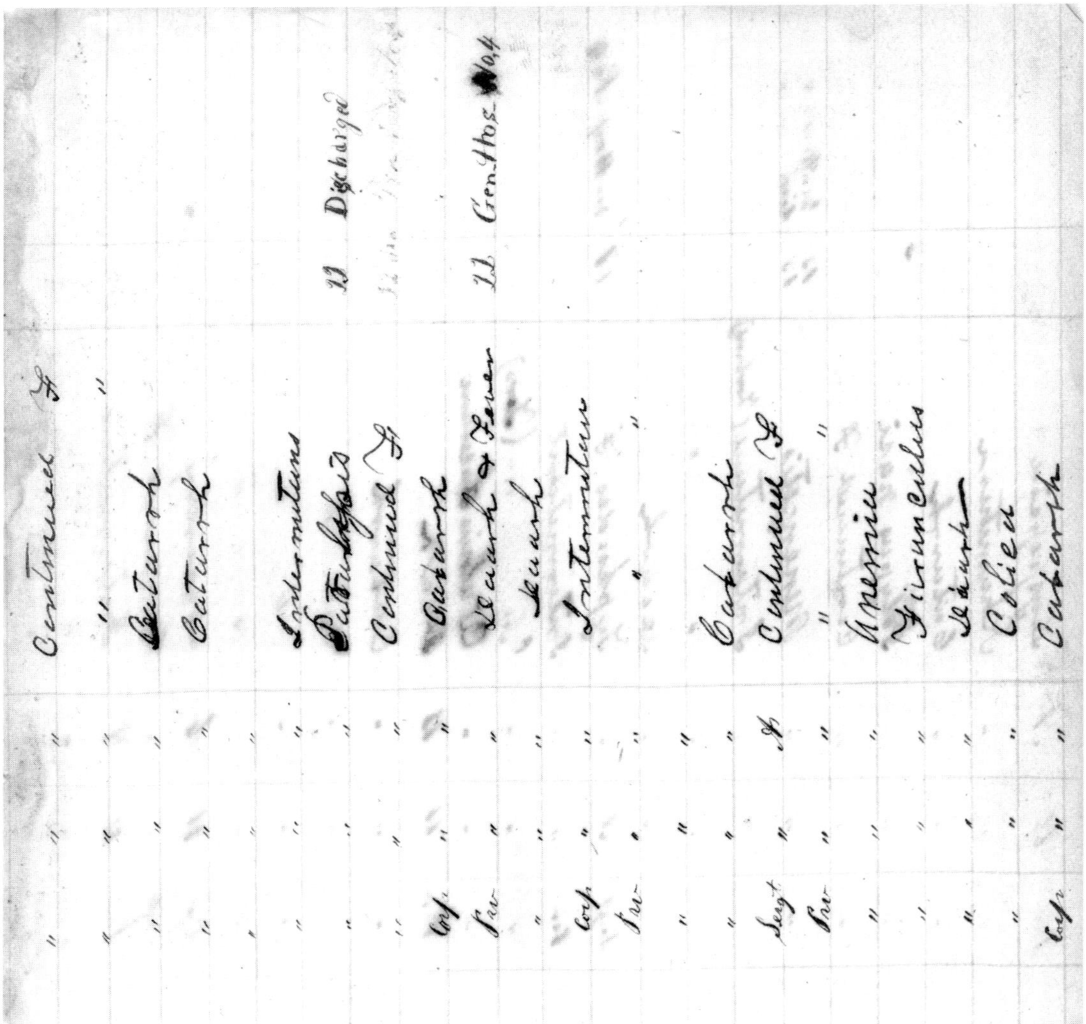

110	H Hashleen	"	"	"	Continued F	
111	H Hashleen	"	"	"	"	
112	E Summersill	"	"	"	Catarrh	
113	W Sate	"	"	"	Catarrh	
114	J G Nickins	"	"	"		
115	J Futrell	"	"	"	Intermittent	
116	W. H. Harrison	"	"	"	Pertussis	23 Discharged
117	R Gurman	"	"	"	Continued F	
118	Wooten	Corp	"	"	Catarrh	
119	Brinson	Pri	"	"	Catarrh & Fever	22 Gen Hos. No4
120	Smith	"	"	"	Catarrh	
121	Corp Woods	Corp	"	"	Intermittent	
122	Martin	Pri	"	"	"	
123	L H Lull	"	"	"		
124	L J Brock	"	"	"	Catarrh	
125	Scarlett	Sergt	"	F	Continued F	
126	H Monk	Pri	"	"	"	
127	J Woods	"	"	"	Anaemia	
128	C S Warren	"	"	"	Furunculus	
129	W Carrol	"	"	"	Catarrh	
130	S Phelps	"	"	"	Colica	
131	Proctor	Corp	"	"	Catarrh	

132	Booth	Pvt	66	I	Dyspepsia	
133	J Pool	"	"	"	Rheumatism	
134	J Hall	"	"	"	Catarrh	
135	Gress	"	"	"	Polypus nasi	
136	Cates	"	"	"	Continued F	
137	Browning	"	"	"	Meningitis	12 Gen Hosp No 4 13 died " "
138	W Wofford	"	"	"	Intermittent (Tertian)	
139	J Bushnell	"	"	"	"	
140	J Glenn	"	"	"	Catarrh	
141	John Cornel	Sergt	66	"	Typhoides F	17 Gen Hosp No 4
142	J Latta	Pvt	"	"	Intermittent	
143	J James	"	"	"	" " (Tert)	
144	W Couch	"	"	"	Vulnus Lacerum	
145	A G Fires	Pvt	66	B	Diarrh	
146	J Bartholomew	"	"	"	Catarrh	
147	W Coppedge	"	"	"	" "	
148	J W Bourden	"	"	"	" "	
149	J M Culpeper	"	"	"	"	
150	J Benton	Pvt	11	G	Dysentery	
151	J Cauley	Sergt	"	"	Continued F	
152	Le Gaffus	Pvt	66	D	Intermittens	
153	J J Clay	"	"	"	"	
154	Thos. Deyton	"	"	"	"	

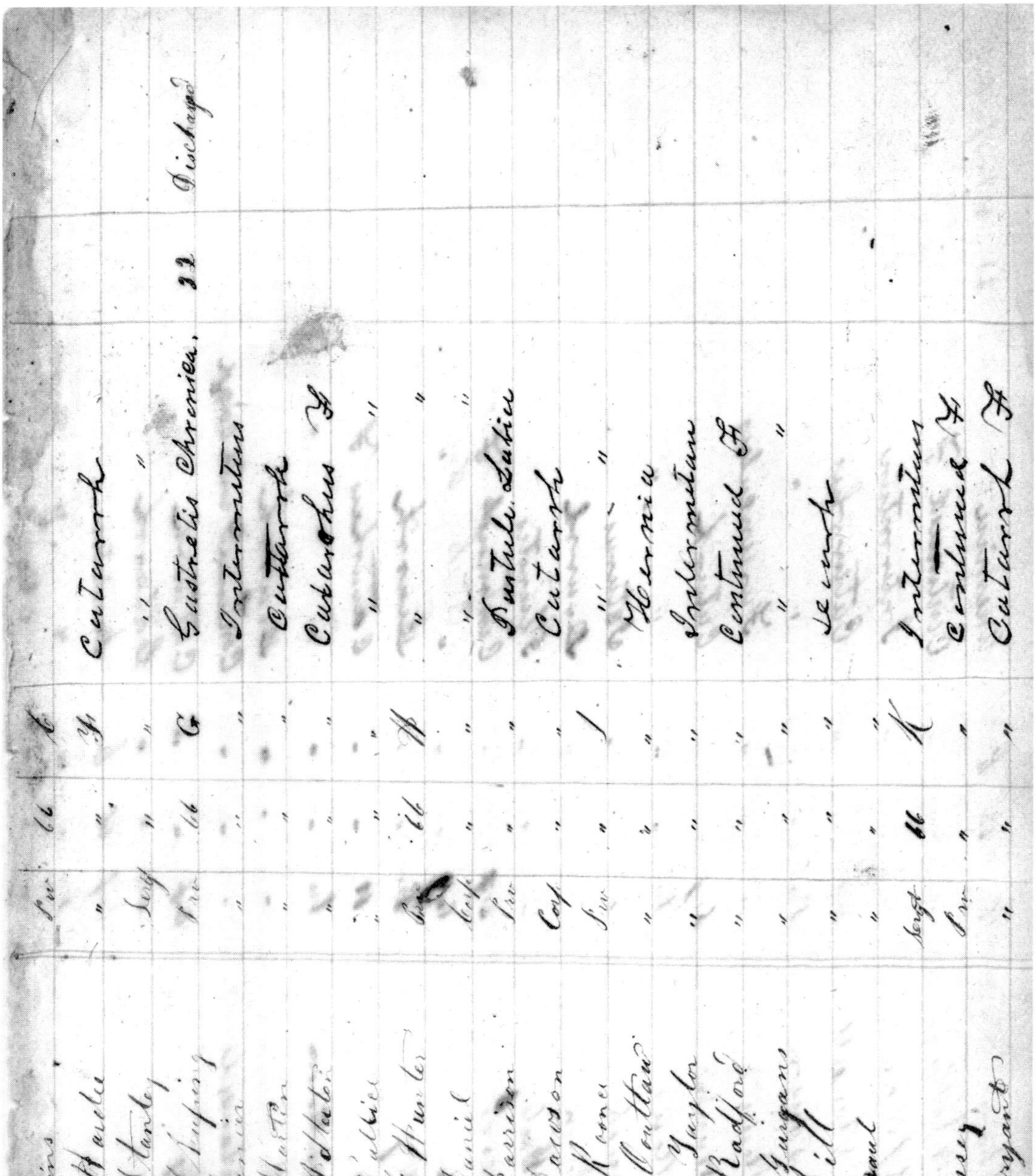

155	J J Jenkins	Pv	66	E			
156	J E Hardee	"	"	F	Catarrh		
157	J B Stanley	Serg	"	"	" "		
158	Wm. S Kuping	Pv	66	G	Gastritis Chronica.	32	Discharged
159	Lanier	"	"	"	Intermittens		
160	Martin	"	"	"	Catarrh		
161	A Staton	"	"	"	Catarrhus F		
162	Wallice	"	"	"	" "		
163	J G Hunter	Pv	66	H	" "		
164	A Daniel	Corp	"	"	" "		
165	J Harrison	Pv	"	"	Pustule Labia		
166	J Dawson	Corp	"	"	Catarrh		
167	J W Rooney	Pv	"	I	" "		
168	V B Outlaw	"	"	"	Hernia		
169	Levi Taylor	"	"	"	Intermittens		
170	H Radford	"	"	"	Continued F		
171	B N Gurgans	"	"	"	" "		
172	S Hill	"	"	"	[illegible]		
173	M Brawl	"	"	"			
174	Ellis	Sergt	66	K	Intermittens		
175	D Massey	Pv	"	"	Continued F		
176	R C Bryant	"	"	"	Catarrh F		

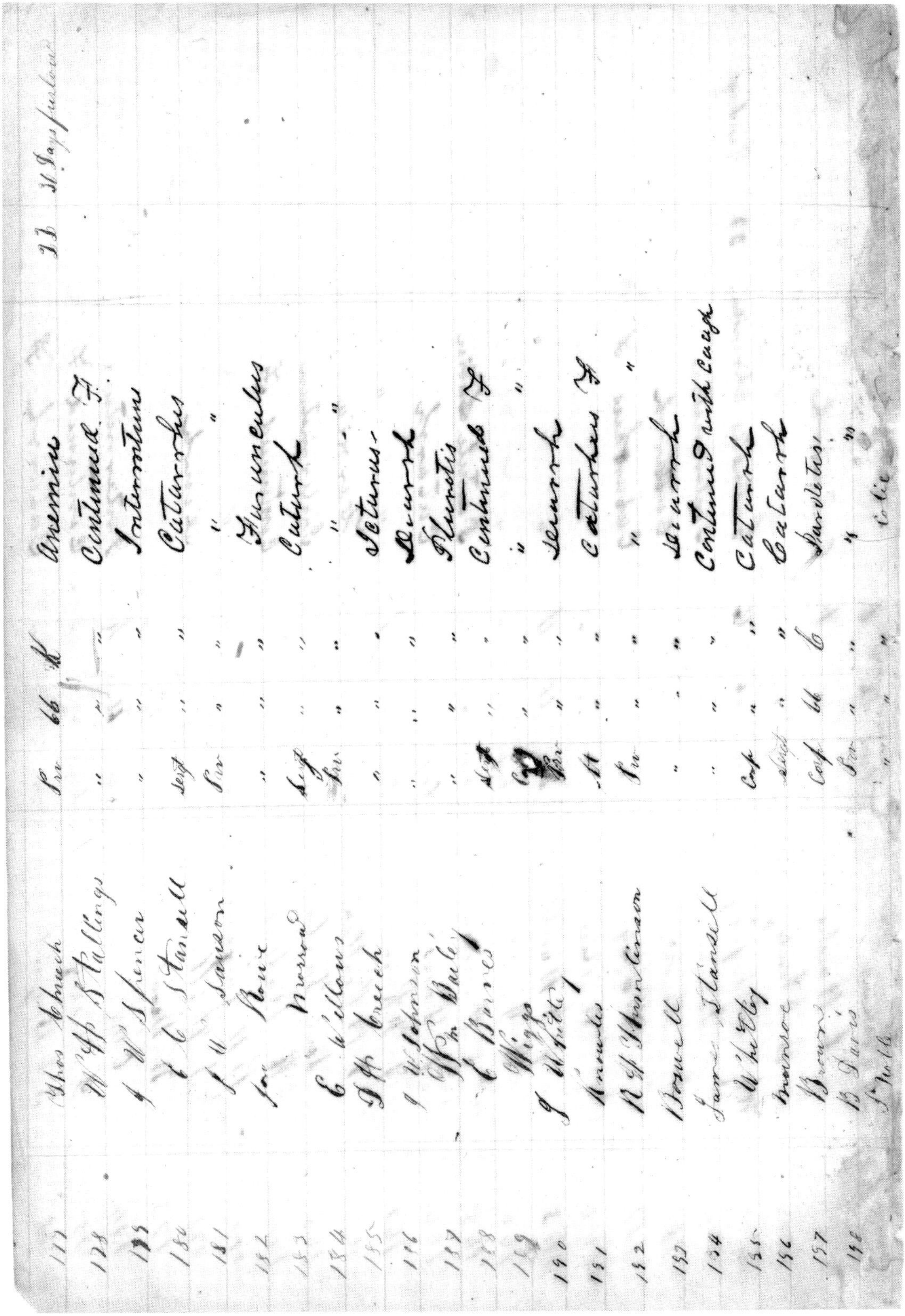

177	Thos Schuch	Pri	66	K	Anemia	33	31 Days furlough
178	W H H Stallings	"	"	"	Continued F.		
179	J W Spencer	"	"	"	Intermittent		
180	E C Stancill	Sergt	"	"	Catarrhus		
181	J H Sawson	Pri	"	"	"		
182	Jas Rowe	"	"	"	Furunculus		
183	Morrow	Sergt	"	"	Catarrh		
184	E Wellons	Pri	"	"	"		
185	D H Creech	"	"	"	Icterus		
186	J W Johnson	"	"	"	Diarrh		
187	Wm Bailey	"	"	"	Pleuritis		
188	E Barnes	Sergt	"	"	Continued F		
189	Wiggs	Corp	"	"	"		
190	J Whitley	Pri	"	"	Diarrh		
191	Knowles	"	"	"	Catarrhus F		
192	R H H Hamilton	Pri	"	"	"		
193	Boswell	"	"	"	Diarrh		
194	James Stancill	"	"	"	Continued with cough		
195	Whitley	Corp	"	"	Catarrh		
196	Munroe	Sergt	"	"	Catarrh		
197	Brown	Corp	66	C	Dysenteria		
198	B Davis	Pri	"	"	" "		
199	J. Webb	"	"	"	Colic		

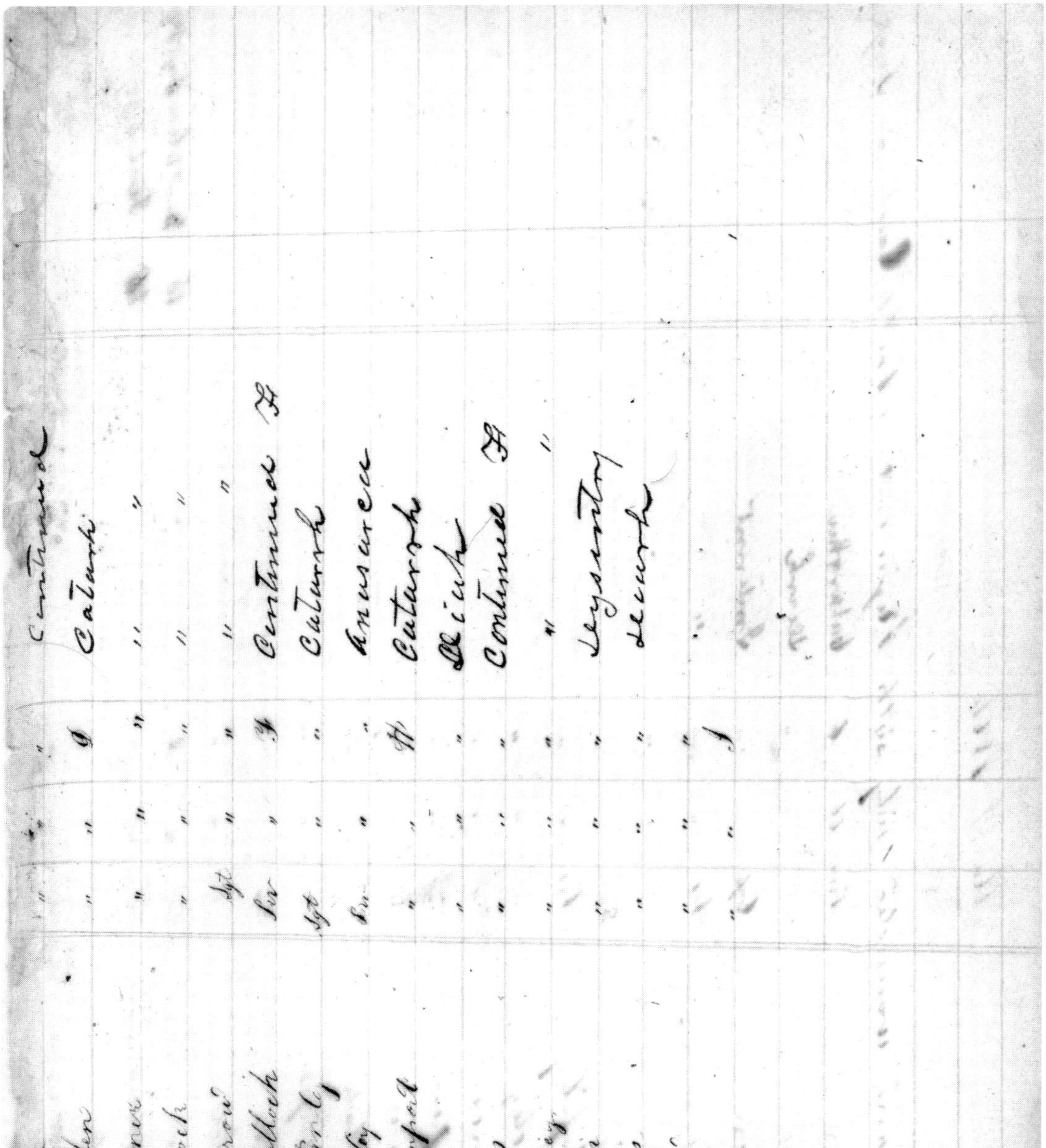

199	W Horne	"	"	"	Continued
200	J Allen	"	"	G	Catarrh
201	L Turner	"	"	"	" "
202	E A Brock	"	"	"	" "
203	E J Barrow	Sgt	"	"	" "
204	J M Pollock	Pvt	"	F	Continued F
205	J A Stanly	Sgt	"	"	Catarrh
206	C S Whaley	Pvt	"	"	Anasarca
207	John Davenport	"	"	H	Catarrh
208	C Capps	"	"	"	Diarrh
209	B Williams	"	"	"	Continued F
210	L Humphrey	"	"	"	" "
211	J J Aman	"	"	"	Dysentery
212	C J Thomas	"	"	"	Diarrh
213	C Freeman	"	"	"	
214	Lewis Taylor	"	"	J	

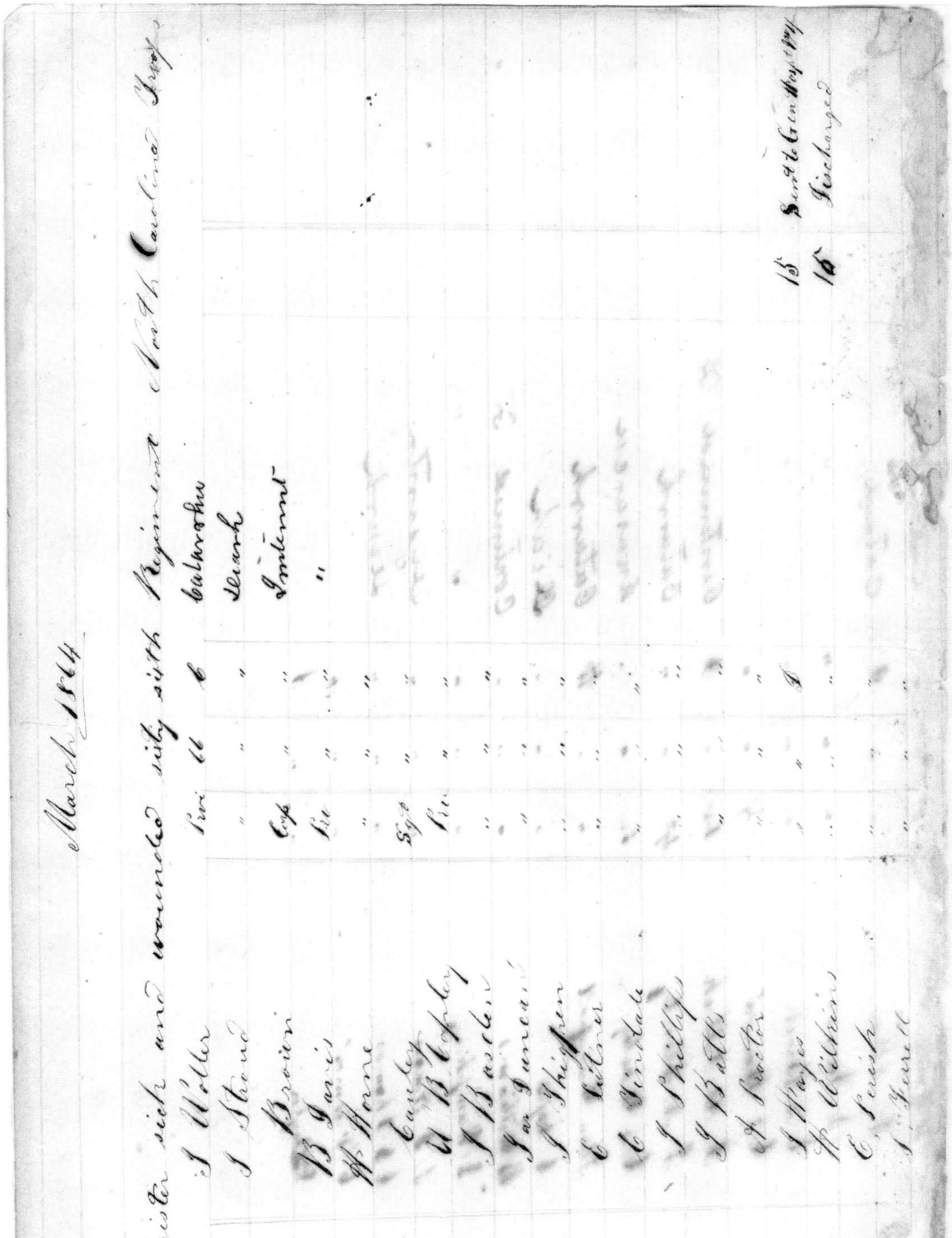

March 1864

Register sick and wounded sixty sixth Regiment North Carolina Troops

1	J Woller	Pri	66	C	Catarrhus		
2	J Strond	"	"	"	Diarh		
3	Brown	Corp	"	"	Intermt		
4	B Davis	Pri	"	"	"		
5	W Horne	"	"	"			
6	Canley	Sgt	"	"			
7	W B Copley	Pri	"	"			
8	J Basden	"	"	"			
9	Jas Duncan	"	"	"			
10	J Thigpen	"	"	"			
11	E Latner	"	"	"			
12	C Tindale	"	"	"			
13	J Phillips	"	"	"			
14	J Batts	"	"	"			
15	A Proctor	"	"	"			
16	J Hayes	"	"	D		15	Sent to Gen Hosp 1st N
17	W Wilkins	"	"	"		16	Discharged
18	E Parish	"	"	"			
19	J Ferrell	"	"	"			

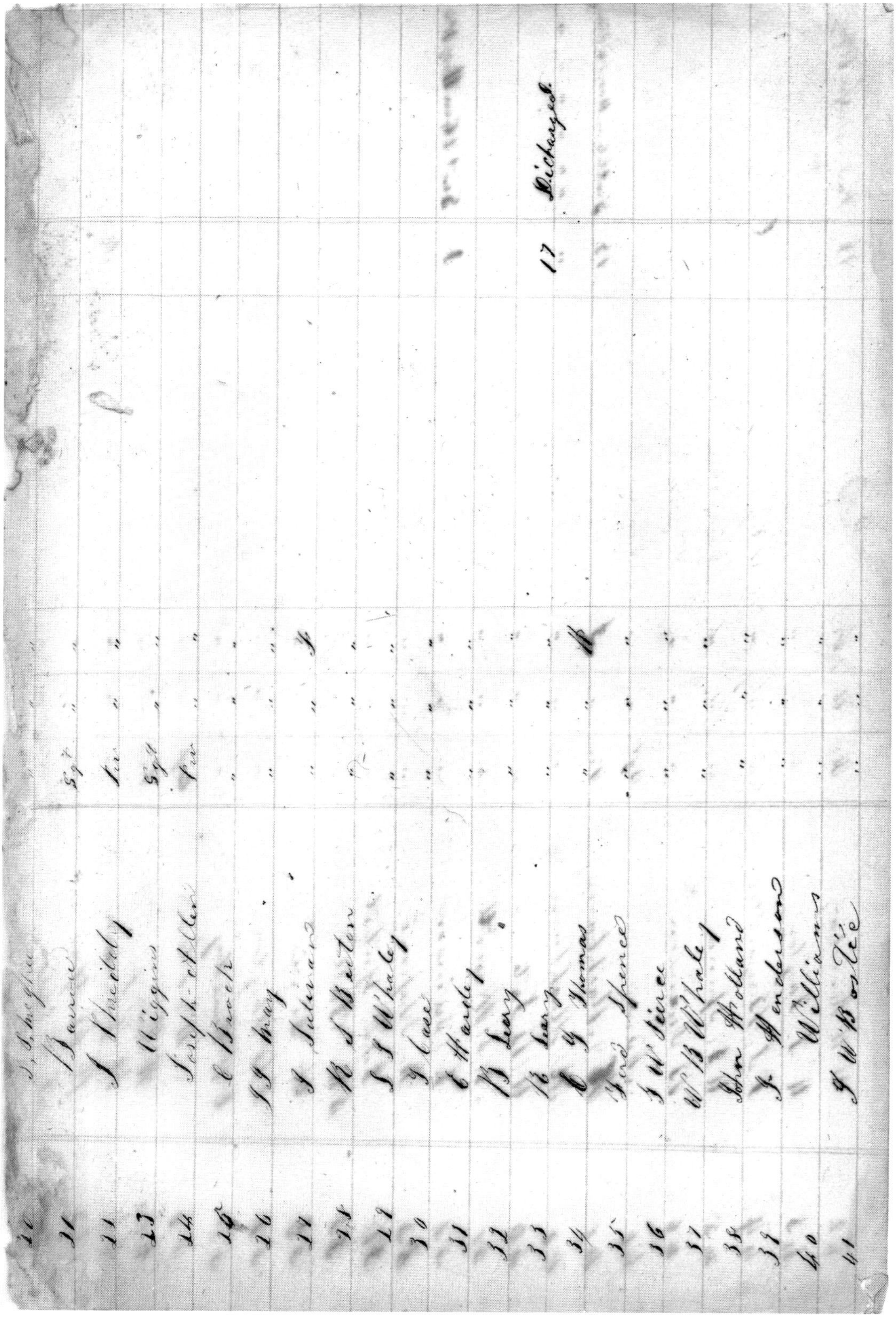

20	J. S. McGhee	″	″	″		
21	Barrow	Sgt	″	″		
22	J Shiedley	Pv	″	″		
23	Wiggins	Sgt	″	″		
24	Joseph Allen	Pv	″	″		
25	C Brock	″	″	″		
26	J J May	″	″	″		
27	J Sullivan	″	″	J		
28	R S Belton	″	″	″		
29	J J Whaley	″	″	″		
30	J Case	″	″	″		
31	E Hardey	″	″	″		
32	B Leary	″	″	″		
33	R Leary	″	″	″	17	Dicharged
34	C G Thomas	″	″	H		
35	Ford Spence	″	″	″		
36	J W Pierce	″	″	″		
37	W B Whaley	″	″	″		
38	John Holland	″	″	″		
39	J Henderson	″	″	″		
40	Williams	″	″	″		
41	J W Bostic	″	″	″		

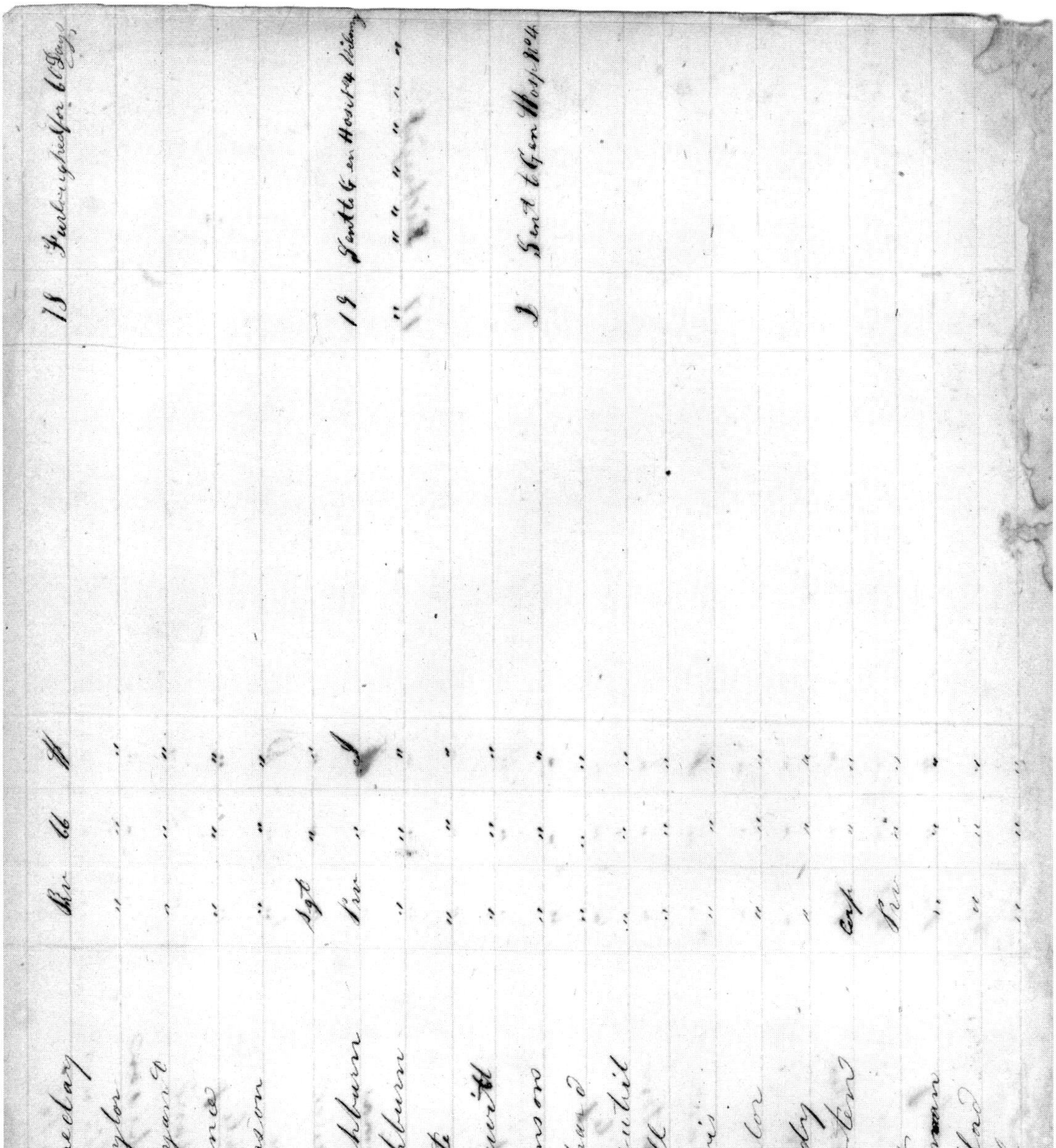

42	W H Kenedary	Pv	66	H	18	Furloughed for 60 Days
43	W T Taylor	"	"	"		
44	T T Bryant	"	"	"		
45	W D Spence	"	"	"		
46	B Swinson	"	"	"		
47	Nunn	Sgt	"	"		
48	R Mashburn	Pv	"	I	19	Sent to Gen Hosp No 4 Wilmy
49	M Mashburn	"	"	"	"	" " " " " "
50	W B Tate	"	"	"		
51	J S Hewitt	"	"	"		
52	M Swinson	"	"	"	2	Sent to Gen Hosp No 4
53	H Shepard	"	"	"		
54	John Teutil	"	"	"		
55	S H Tull	"	"	"		
56	Wm Jarvis	"	"	"		
57	T B Taylor	"	"	"		
58	O H Kenedy	"	"	"		
59	Wooten	Corp	"	"		
60	H King	Pv	"	"		
61	R Jarman	"	"	"		
62	W Radford	"	"	"		
63	L Hill	"	"	"		

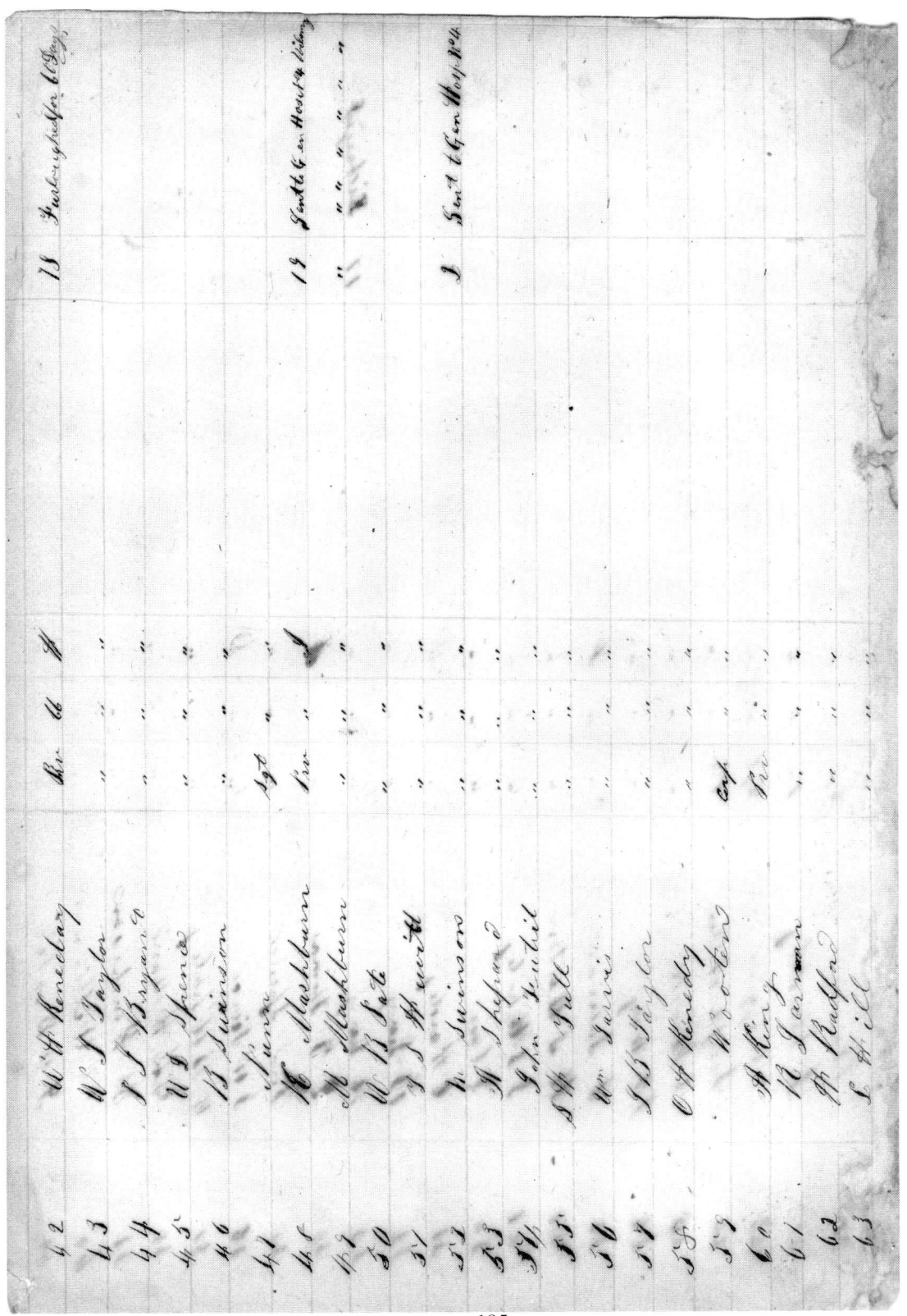

64	Jas Stansell		Priv	66	K	
65	[illegible] Ellis	Sgt	"	"	"	
66	D B Lane	Pvt	"	"	"	
67	J J Stallings	"	"	"	"	
68	Wm Sasser	"	"	"	"	
69	R C Bryant	"	"	"	"	
70	J W Whatley	"	"	"	"	
71	J J Boswell	"	"	"	"	
72	[illegible]	"	"	"	G	
73	[illegible]	Music	"	"	"	
74	Wix	Music	"	"	"	7 Sent to Gen Hosp'l [illegible]
75	J Couch	Pvt	"	"	S	
76	G Couch	"	"	"	"	
77	J Pool	"	"	"	"	
78	J Norvell	"	"	"	"	
79	J Fancett	"	"	"	"	
80	Davis	Corp	"	"	B	
81	Thomas Gay	Pvt	"	"	"	
82	J H May	"	"	"	"	
	J C Mathews	"	"	"	"	
	J W Wood	"	"	"	"	
	John Lenard	"	"	"	"	

April 1864.

Register sick and wounded of Sixty Sixth North Carolina Regim[ent]

Number	Name	Rank	Regiment	Company	Complaint	When sent to Hospital	Remarks
1	Woods J.	Prvt	66	A	Ammenea		
2	Booth A.	"	"	"	Vulnus contusum car over foot	24	Gen Hosp Tarboro N.C.
3	Carrington W.	"	"	"	Intermittens		
4	Browning S.	"	"	"	Diarh		
5	Tearley W.	"	"	"	Intermitens		
6	Couch W.	"	"	"	Countinuns Feberis		
7	Strayhorn S.	"	"	"	Catarrhus		
8	Herndon C.	"	"	"	" "		
9	Thompson F.	"	"	"	Diarh		
10	Whitaker J.	"	"	"	Catarrhus		
11	Mitchel R.	"	"	"	Intermitens		
12	[illegible] Simpson [illegible]	"	"	"	Pluritas	25	Gen Hosp Tarboro N.C.
13	Rhew W.	"	"	"	Intermitens		
14	Mangum F.	"	"	"	Catarache		
15	Cates Thos.	"	"	"	Dysentery	25	Gen Hosp Tarboro N.C.

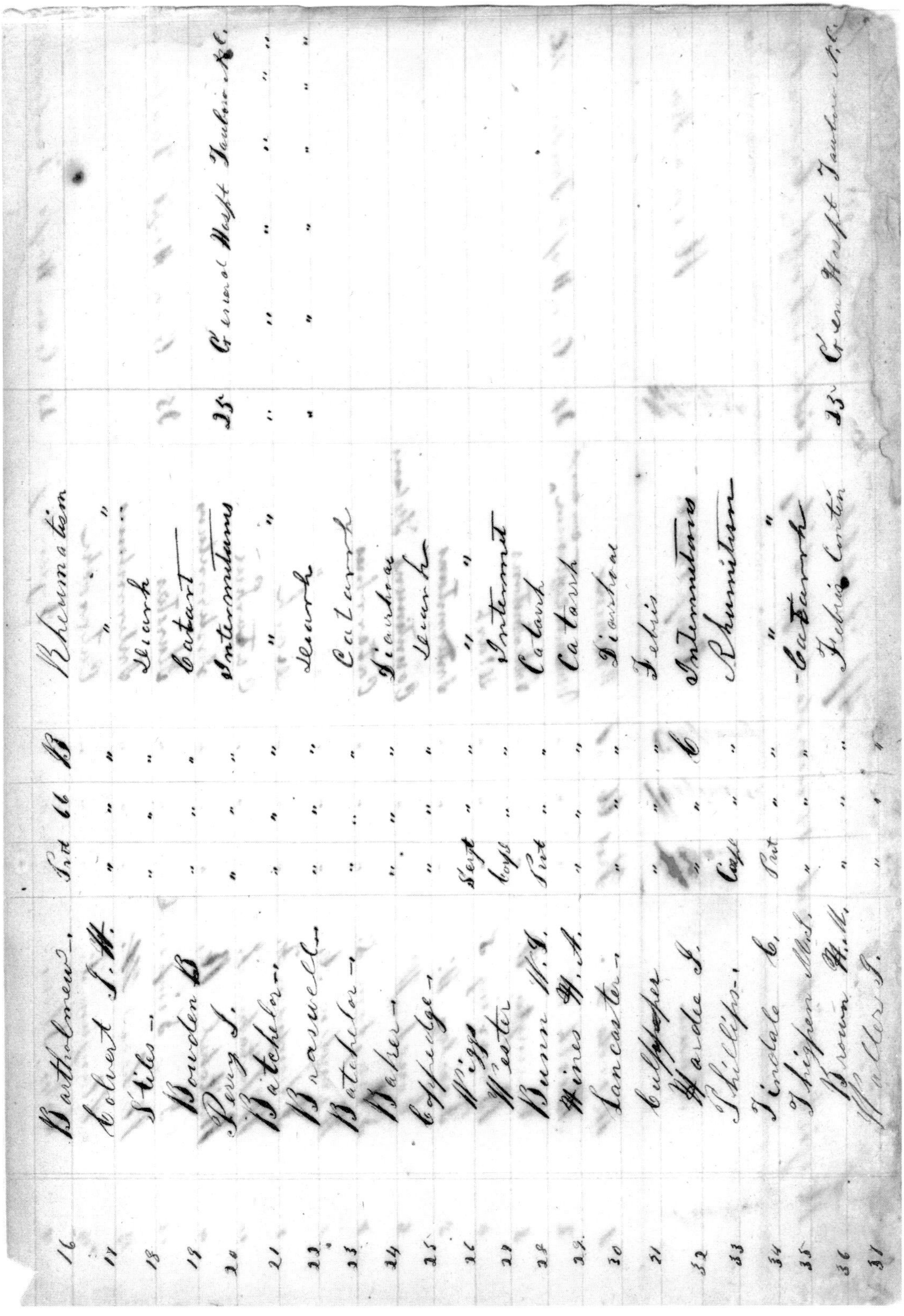

16	Barthalmew	Pvt	66	B	Rheumatism			
17	Colvert J. H.	"	"	"	"			
18	Stiles	"	"	"	Scurvy			
19	Bowden B	"	"	"	Catarrh			
20	Perry S.	"	"	"	Intermittens	25	General Hospt	Farnborough
21	Batchelor	"	"	"	"	"	"	"
22	Braswell	"	"	"	Scurvy	"	"	"
23	Batchelor	"	"	"	Catarrh			
24	Baker	"	"	"	Diarrhea			
25	Coppedge	"	"	"	Scurvy			
26	Biggs	Sergt	"	"	"			
27	Wester	Corpl	"	"	Intermit			
28	Bunn W. J.	Pvt	"	"	Catarrh			
29	Wines W. A.	"	"	"	Catarrh			
30	Lancaster	"	"	"	Diarrhea			
31	Culpeper	"	"	"	Febris			
32	Hardee J.	"	"	C	Intermittens			
33	Phillips	Capt	"	"	Rheumatism			
34	Tisdale C.	Pvt	"	"	"			
35	Thigpen M. S.	"	"	"	Catarrh			
36	Brown H. H.	"	"	"	Febris Contin	25	Gen Hospt	Farnborough
37	Wallers J.	"	"	"				

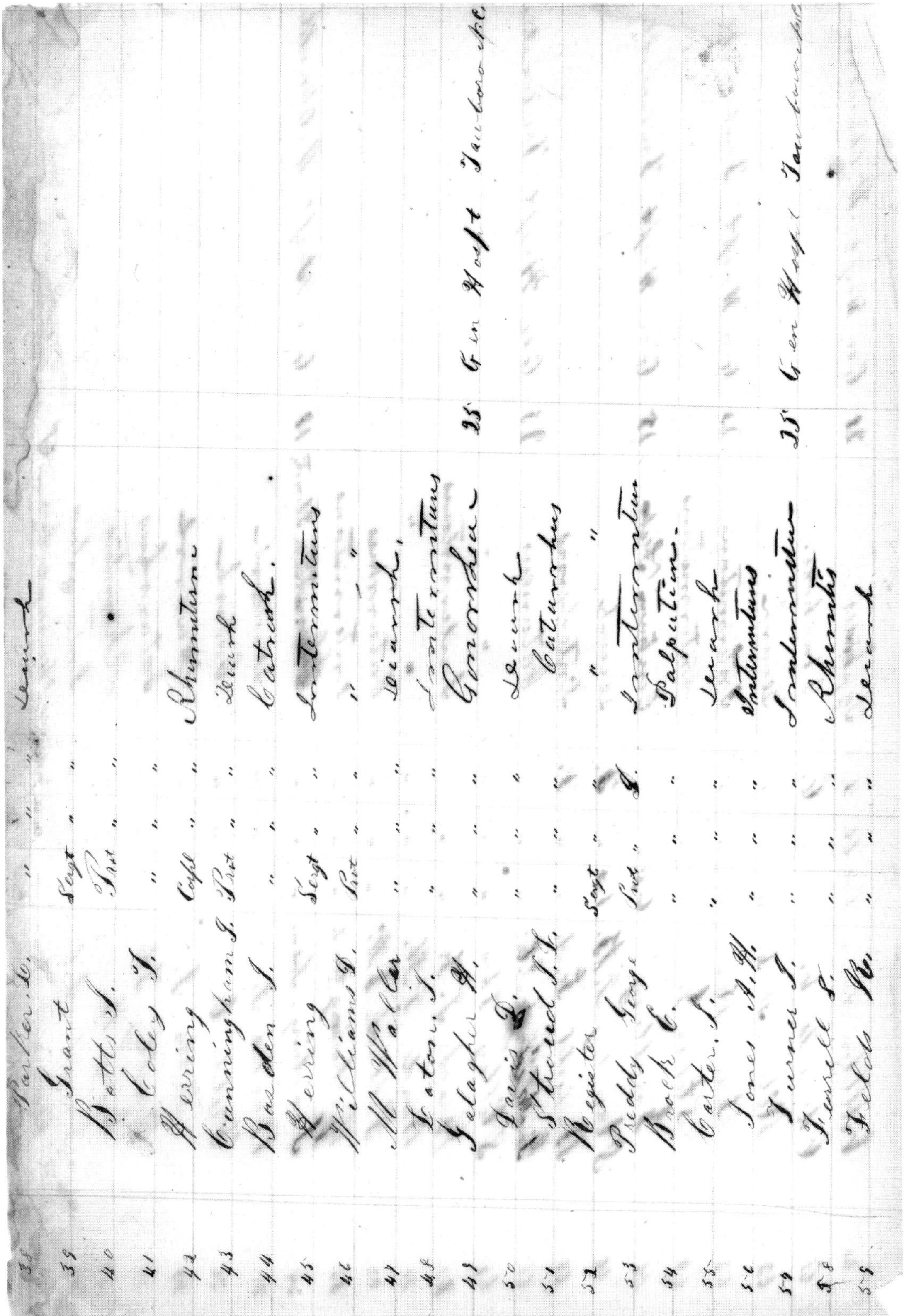

38	Parker D.	"	"	"	Diarrh			
39	Grant	Sergt	"	"				
40	Batts J.	Prvt	"	"				
41	Coley J.	"	"	"				
42	Herring	Corpl	"	"	Rheumatism			
43	Cunningham J.	Prvt	"	"	Diarh			
44	Basden J.	"	"	"	Catarrh.			
45	Herring	Sergt	"	"	Intermittens			
46	Williams D.	Prvt	"	"	" "			
47	M Waller	"	"	"	Diarrh.			
48	Eaton J.	"	"	"	Intermittens			
49	Galagher H.	"	"	"	Gonorrhea	25	Gen Hospt	Tarboro N.C.
50	Davis D.	"	"	"	Diarrh			
51	Stroud J.L.	"	"	"	Catarrhus			
52	Register	Sergt	"	"	" "			
53	Preddy George	Prvt	"	I.	Intermittens			
54	Brock E.	"	"	"	Palpitation.			
55	Carter J.	"	"	"	Diarrh			
56	Jones A.H.	"	"	"	Intermittens			
57	Turner J.	"	"	"	Intermittens	25	Gen Hospt	Tarboro N.C.
58	Ferrell S.	"	"	"	Rheumatis			
59	Fields R.	"	"	"	Diarrh			

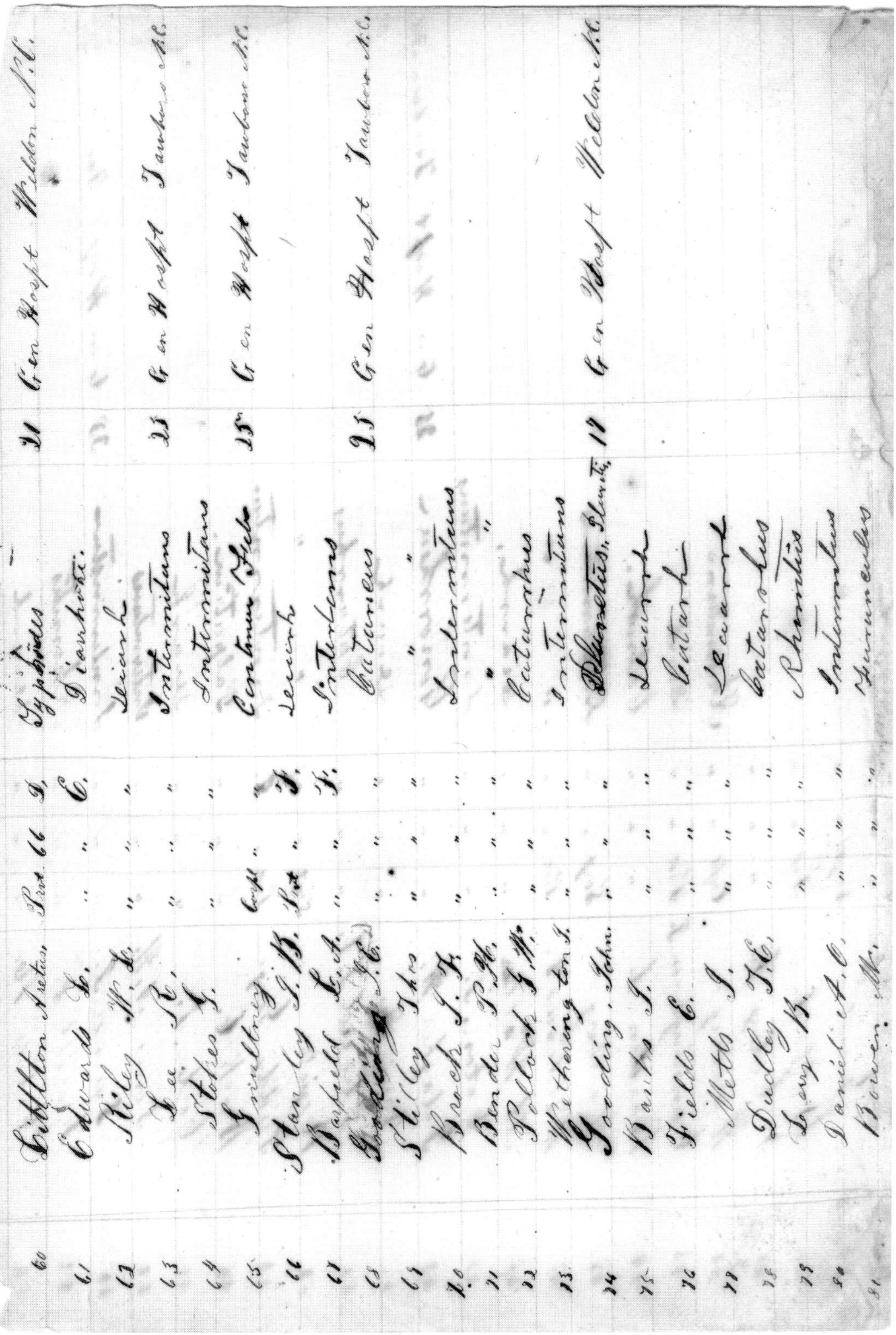

60	Littleton Aretus	Pvt.	66	D	Typhoides	21	Gen Hosp't Weldon N.C.
61	Edwards L.	"	"	C	Diarrhoea		
62	Riley W. L.	"	"	"	[illegible]		
63	Lee R.	"	"	"	Intermittens	23	Gen Hosp't Tarboro N.C.
64	Stokes J.	"	"	"	Intermittens		
65	[illegible]	Corpl	"	"	Continua Febr	15	Gen Hosp't Tarboro N.C.
66	Stanley J. B.	Pvt	"	F	[illegible]		
67	Barfield L. A.	"	"	F	Intermittens		
68	[illegible] J. C.	"	"	"	Catarrhus	25	Gen Hosp't Tarboro N.C.
69	Stilley Thos	"	"	"	"		
70	Brock J. F.	"	"	"	Intermittens		
71	Bender P. H.	"	"	"	"		
72	Pollock J. W.	"	"	"	Catarrhus		
73	Wetherington J.	"	"	"	Intermittens		
74	Gooding, John	"	"	"	Pleuritis	17	Gen Hosp't Weldon N.C.
75	Banks J.	"	"	"	[illegible]		
76	Fields E.	"	"	"	Catarrh		
77	Mills J.	"	"	"	[illegible]		
78	Dudley J. E.	"	"	"	Catarrhus		
79	[illegible] B.	"	"	"	Rheumatism		
80	Daniel A. O.	"	"	"	Intermittens		
81	Bowen M.	"	"	"	[illegible]		

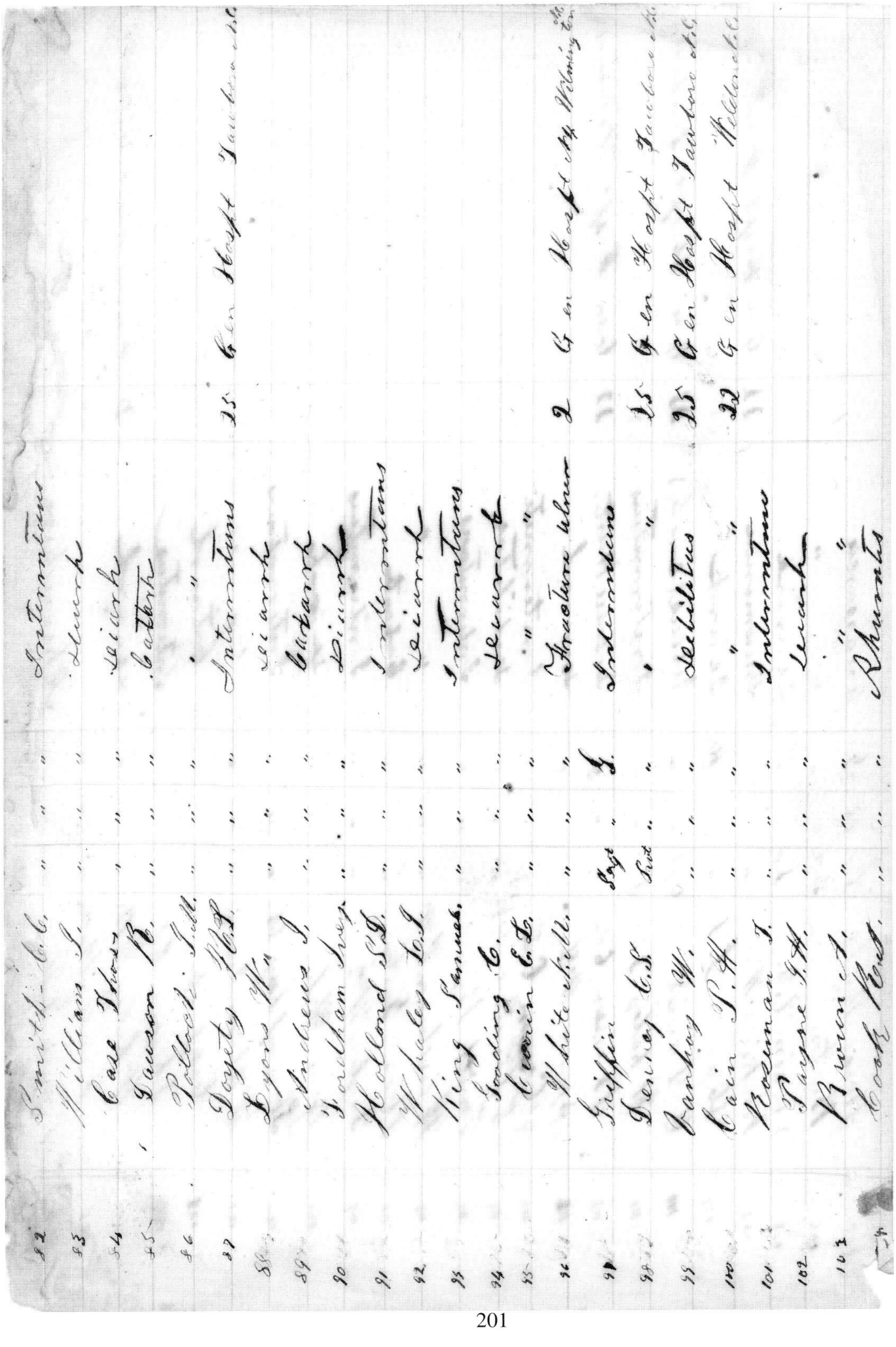

82	Smith C.C.	"	" "	Intermittens		
83	Williams J.	"	" "	Diarrh		
84	Case Thos	"	" "	Diarrh		
85	Dawson R.	"	" "	Catarrh		
86	Pollock J.H.	"	" "	"		
87	Doyety W.J.	"	" "	Intermittens	25	Gen Hospt Tarboro N.C.
88	Lyons W.	"	"	Diarrh		
89	Andrews J.	"	"	Catarrh		
90	Gorham Jas	"	"	Diarrh		
91	Holland S.D.	"	"	Intermittens		
92	Whaley L.S.	"	"	Diarrh		
93	King Samuel	"	"	Intermittens		
94	Gooding C.	"	"	Diarrh		
95	Craven E.L.	"	"	"		
96	Whitehill	"	"	Fracture ulna	2	Gen Hospt No 4 Wilmington N.C.
97	Griffin	Sergt	I.	Intermittens		
98	Dewey C.S.	Pvt	"	"	15	Gen Hospt Tarboro N.C.
99	Lankey W.	"	"	Debilitas	25	Gen Hospt Tarboro N.C.
100	Cain S.H.	"	"	"	22	Gen Hospt Weldon N.C.
101	Bozeman J.	"	"	Intermittens		
102	Payne J.H.	"	"	Diarrh		
103	Brown A.	"	"	"		
104	Cook Ed	"	"	Rheumatis		

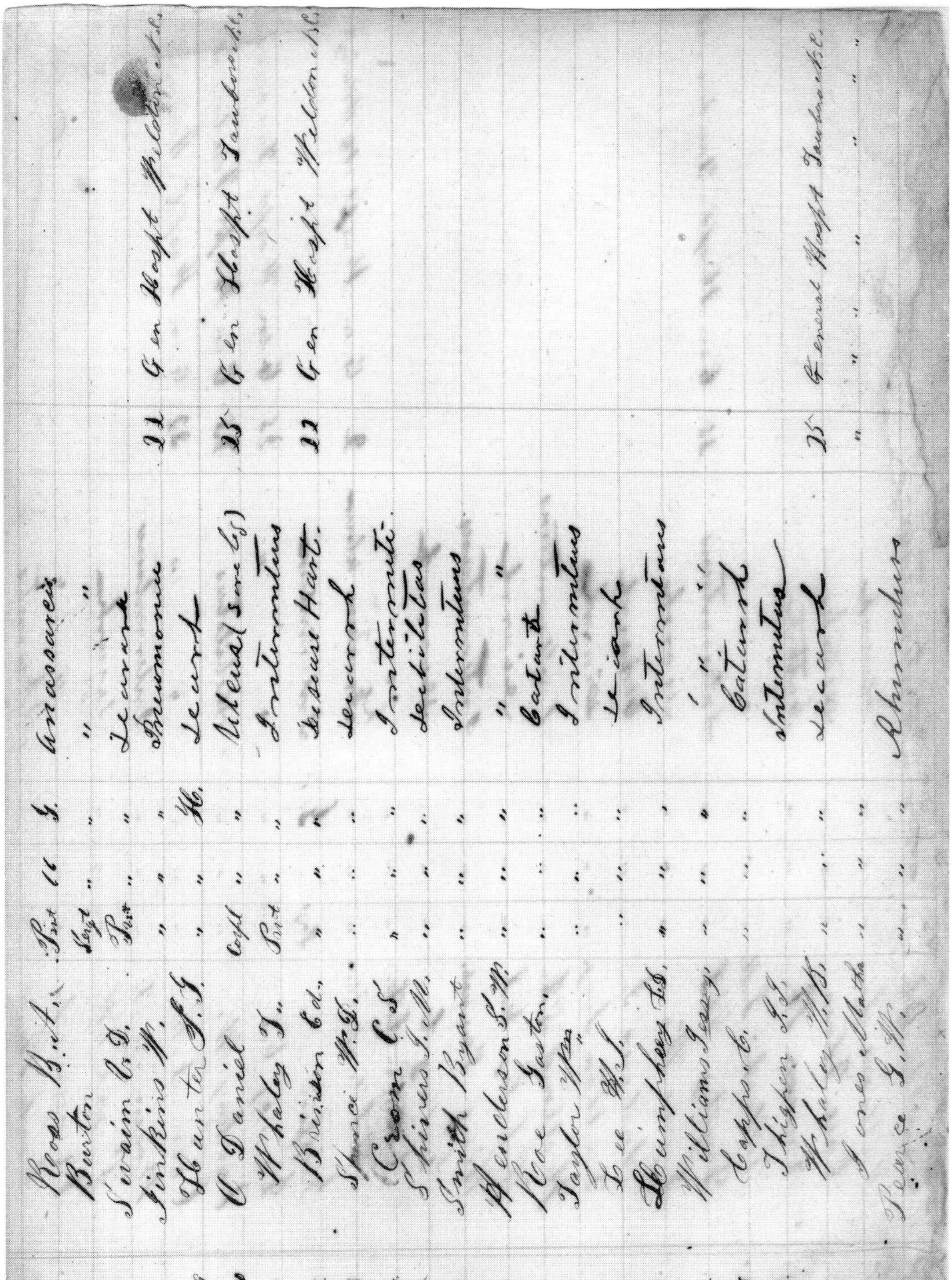

105	Ross B. A.	Pvt	16	G.	Anassarcia		
106	Burton	Sergt	"	"	" "		
107	Swaim C. D.	Pvt	"	"	[illegible]		
108	Jinkins W.	"	"	"	Pneumonia	22	Gen Hospt Weldon N.C.
109	Hunter S. G.	"	"	H.	[illegible]		
110	O Daniel	Corpl	"	"	Ulcus (sore leg)	25	Gen Hospt Tawboro N.C.
111	Whaley J.	Pvt	"	"	Intermitens		
112	Brinson Ed.	"	"	"	Disease Hart.	22	Gen Hospt Weldon N.C.
113	Spence W. D.	"	"	"	[illegible]		
114	Crom C. S.	"	"	"	Intermitti.		
115	Shivers J. M.	"	"	"	Debilitas		
116	Smith Byant	"	"	"	Intermitens		
117	Henderson S. W.	"	"	"	" "		
118	Roe Gaston	"	"	"	Catarh		
119	Taylor Wm.	"	"	"	Intermitens		
120	Lee W. S.	"	"	"	[illegible]		
121	Humphrey L. S.	"	"	"	Intermitens		
122	Williams Jessy	"	"	"	" " "		
123	Capps C.	"	"	"	Catarrh		
124	Thigpen J. J.				Intermitus		
125	Whaley W. B.	"	"	"	[illegible]	25	General Hospt Tawboro N.C.
126	Jones Matha	"	"	"		"	" " " "
127	Pearce G. W.	"	"	"	Rheumatism		

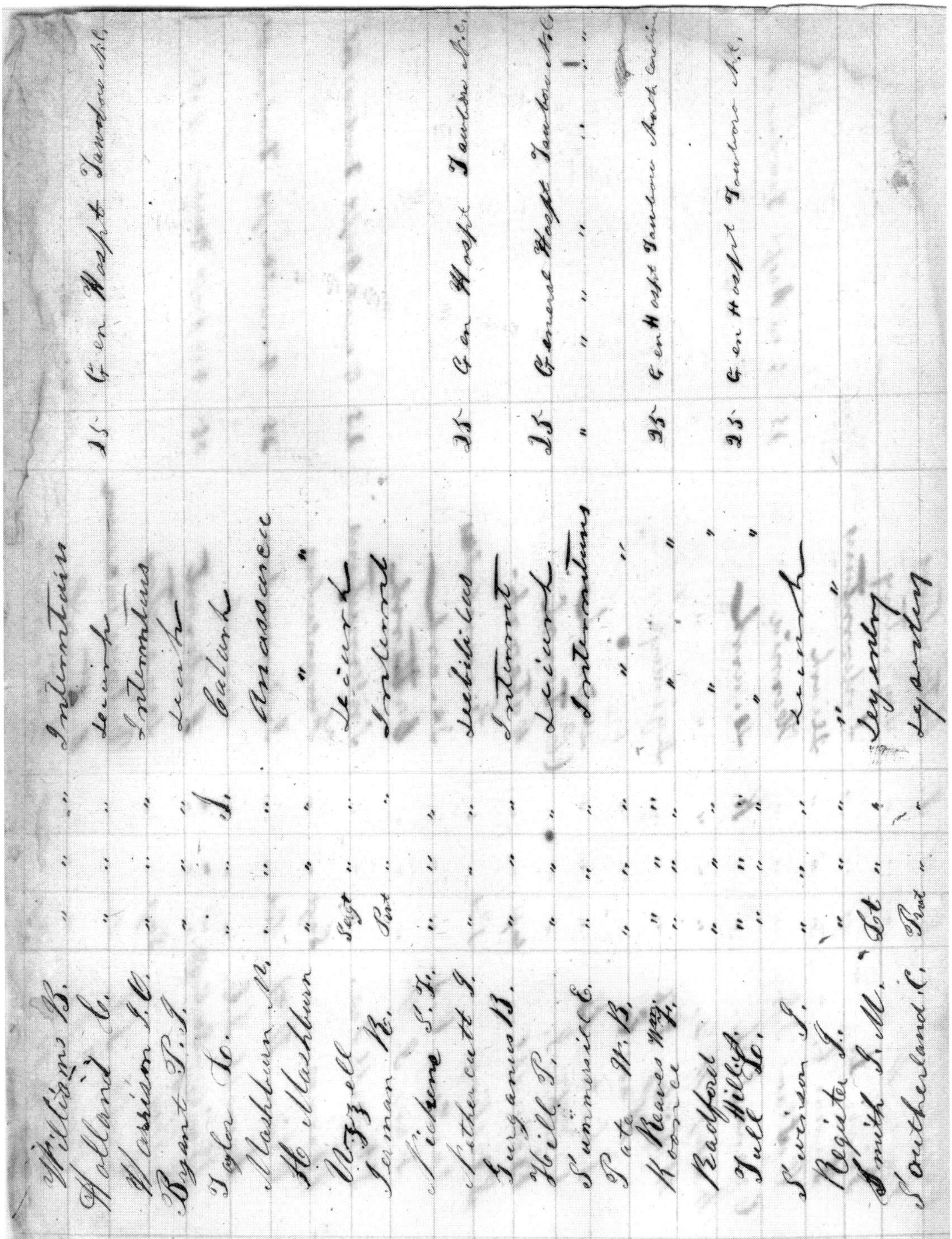

128	Williams B.	"	"	"	Intermitans		
129	Holland C.	"	"	"	Scurvh	25	Gen Hospt Tawboro N.C.
130	Warrison J.O.	"	"	"	Intermitans		
131	Bryant P.J.	"	"	"	Scurh		
132	Taylor Co.	"	"	I.	Catarh		
133	Mashburn N.	"	"	"	Anasarca		
134	H Mashburn	"	"	"	" "		
135	Uzzell	Sergt	"	"	Scurvh		
136	Jerman R.	Prvt	"	"	Interrmt		
137	Nickens S.F.	"	"	"			
138	Nethercutt J.	"	"	"	Debilitas	25	Gen Hospt Tawboro N.C.
139	Gurganus B.	"	"	"	Intermt		
140	Hill P.	"	"	"	Scurvh	25	General Hospt Tawboro N.C.
141	Summersill E.	"	"	"	Intermitans	"	" " " " "
142	Pate W.B.	"	"	"	" "		
143 / 144	Reaves Wm. / Koonce F.	"	"	"	" "	25	Gen Hospt Tawboro North Carolina
145	Radford	"	"	"	" "		
146 / 147	Hill A. / Tull Co.	"	"	"	" "	25	Gen Hospt Tawboro N.C.
148	Swinson J.	"	"	"	Scurvh		
149	Register J.	"	"	"	" "		
150	Smith J.M.	Lt	"	"	Dysentery		
151	Southerland C.	Prvt	"	"	Dysentery		

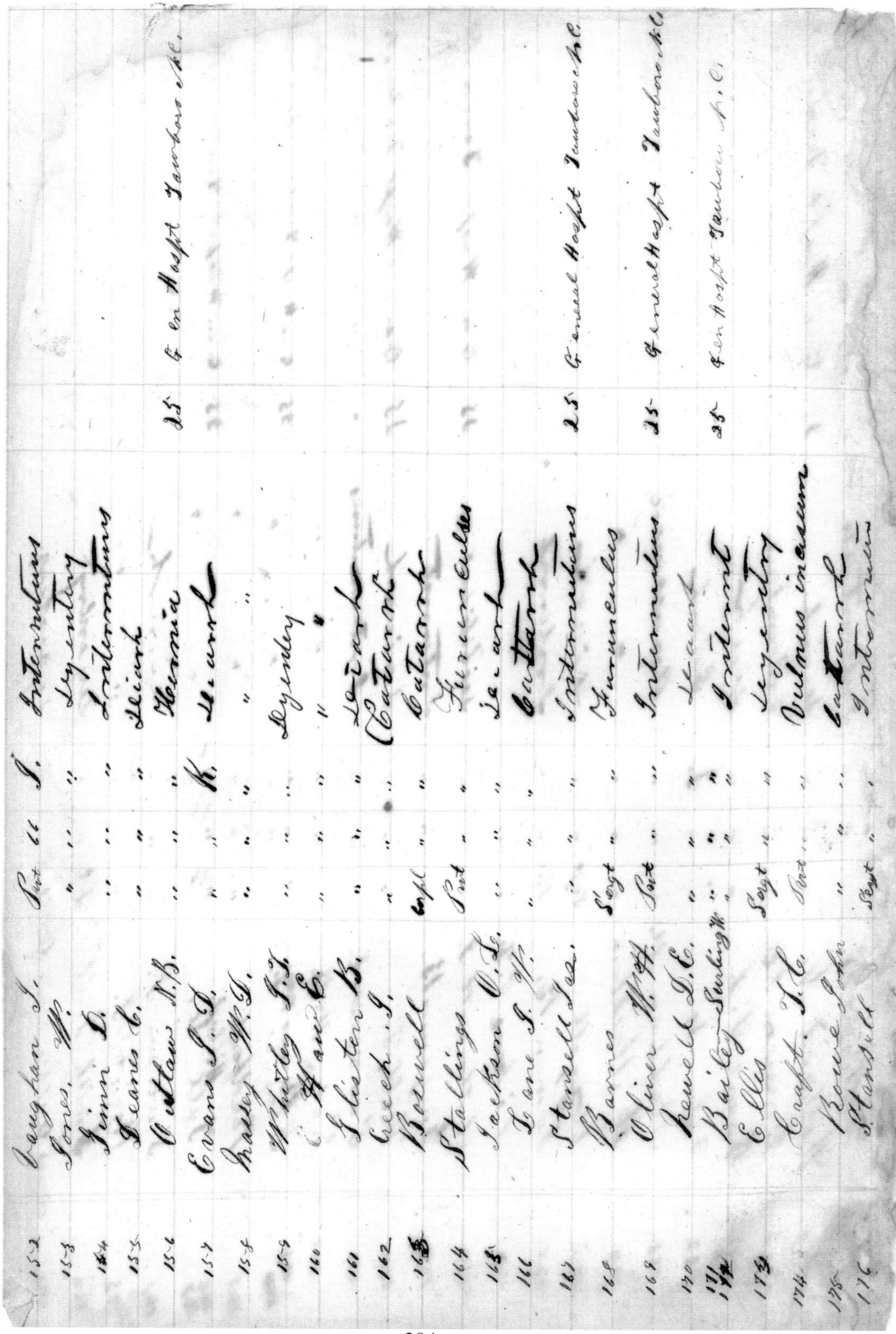

152	Vaughan J.	Prvt	66	I.	Intermittens		
153	Jones, W.	"	"	"	Dysentery		
154	Ginn D.	"	"	"	Intermittens		
155	Deanes C.	"	"	"	Diarrh		
156	Outlaw N.B.	"	"	"	Hernia	25	Gen Hospt Tarboro N.C.
157	Evans J.D.	"	"	K.	Diarrh		
158	Massey W.D.	"	"	"	"		
159	Whitley J.J.	"	"	"	Dysentery		
160	Hare E.	"	"	"	"		
161	Glisten B.	"	"	"	Diarrh		
162	Creech J.	"	"	"	Catarrh		
163	Boswell	Cpl	"	"	Catarrh		
164	Stallings	Prvt	"	"	Furunculus		
165	Jackson O.L.	"	"	"	Diarrh		
166	Lane J.W.	"	"	"	Catarrh		
167	Stansell Jas.	"	"	"	Intermittens	25	General Hospt Tarboro N.C.
168	Barnes	Sergt	"	"	Furunculus		
169	Oliver W.H.	Prvt	"	"	Intermittens	25	General Hospt Tarboro N.C.
170	Newell D.E.	"	"	"	Diarrh		
171	Bailey Sterling W.	"	"	"	Intermitt	25	Gen Hospt Tarboro N.C.
173	Ellis	Sergt	"	"	Dysentery		
174	Craft J.C.	Prvt	"	"	Vulnus incisum		
175	Rowe John	"	"	"	Catarrh		
176	Stansell	Sergt	"	"	Intermittens		

May 1864

Register of the sick and wounded of the 66 North Carolina Regt

Number	Name	Rank	Regiment	Company	Complaint	When sent to Hospital or When Wounded	Remarks
1	Carden, H. H.	Prvt	66.	A.	Febris Typhoides.	6	Hospital Plymouth N.C.
2	Faucett, J.	"	"	"	Intermitens	"	" " " "
3	Couch, G.	"	"	"	Intermitans	"	" " " "
4	Carden, W. H.	"	"	"	"	"	General " Petersburg Va
5	Rhew, Silus	"	"	"	Continuens	14	General " Petersburg Va
6	Cates, Thomas.	"	"	"	Intermitens	"	" " "
7	Mitchell – .	Lt	"	B.	Intermitans	6	" Plymouth N.C.
8	Thomas G. W.	Prvt	"	"	Febris Continued	6	" " " "
9	Mathews J. A.	"	"	"	Rubeola	"	" " " "
10	Proctor H. N.	Corpl	"	"	Febris Typhoides	"	" " " "
11	Lancaster W. B.	Prvt	"	"	Continued Febr	"	" " " "
13	Baker, Perry.	"	"	"	Rubeola	"	" " " "
13	Joiner, Samuell.	"	"	"	Continued	11	" Tawboro N.C.
14	Coppage G. W.	"	"	"	Intermitens	15	General " Petersburg Va
15	Bowden M. B.	"	"	"	Continuens	13	" Weldon N.C.
16	Hines H.	"	"	"	" "	14	General Hospital Petersburg Va
17	Woods H.	"	"	"	Rubeolia	"	" " " "
18	Bartholimew – .	"	"	"	Continsu	17	" " " "

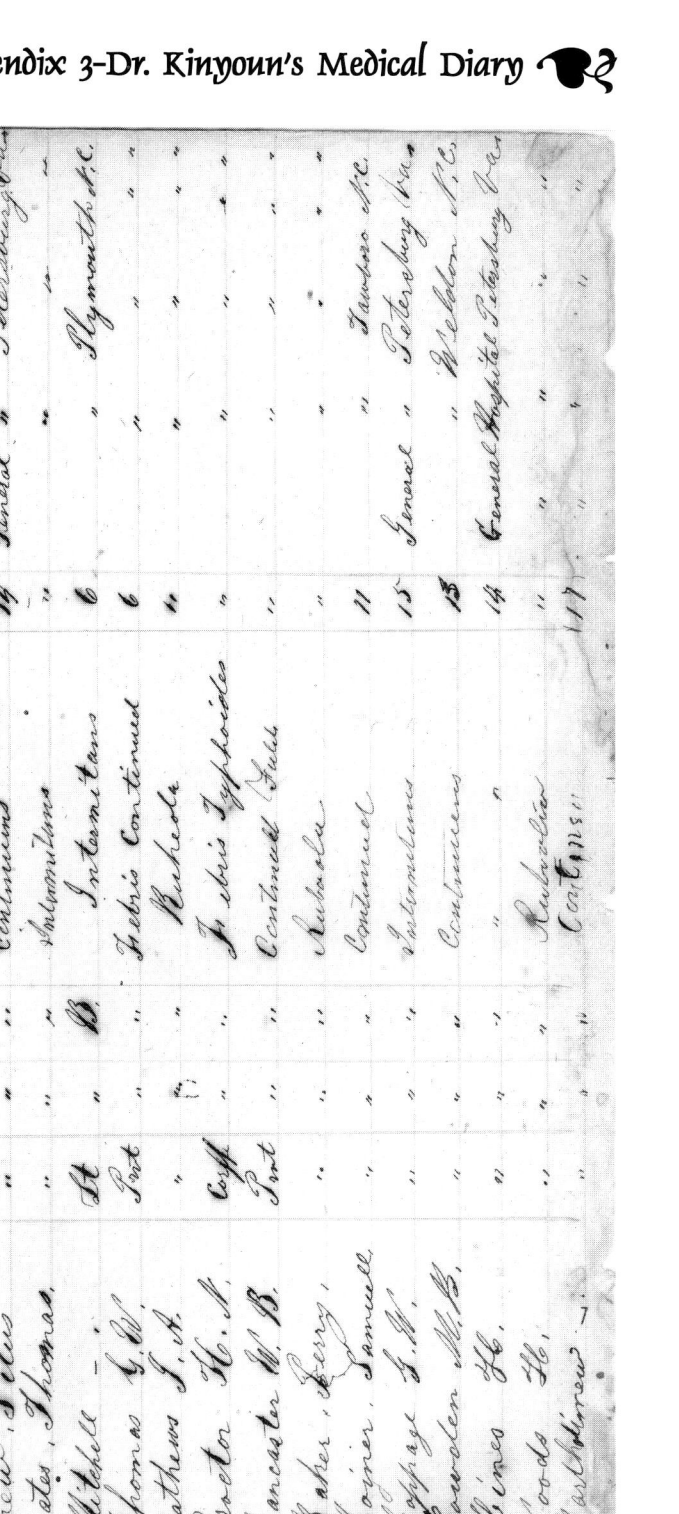

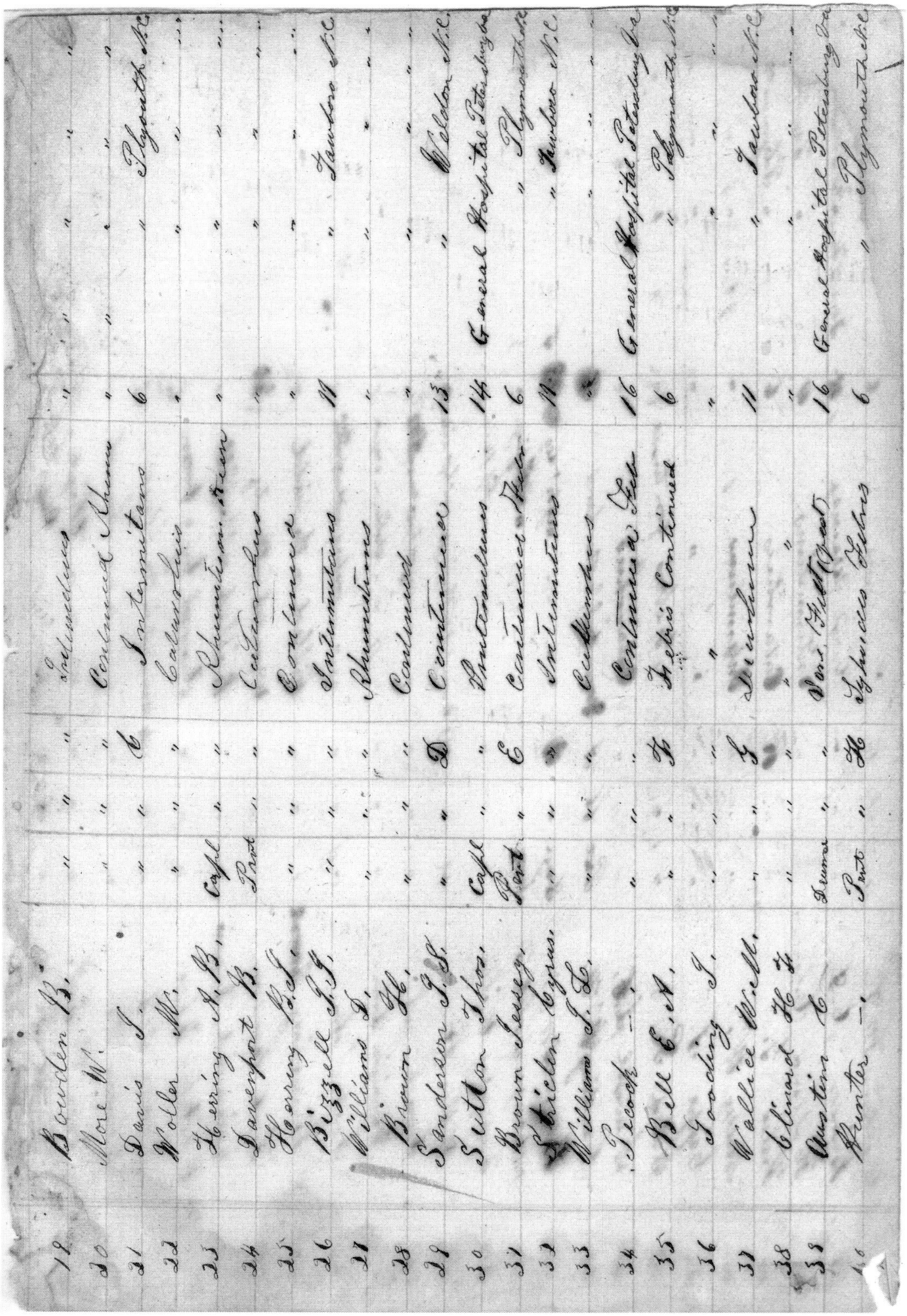

19	Bowden B.	"	"	"	Intermittens	"	"
20	More W.	"	"	"	Continued Rheum	"	"
21	Davis J.	"	"	C	Intermittens	6	Plymouth N.C.
22	Woller M.	"	"	"	Catarrhus	"	"
23	Herring A. B.	Capt	"	"	Rheumatism	"	"
24	Davenport B.	Pvt	"	"	Catarrhus	"	"
25	Herring L. L.	"	"	"	Continued	"	"
26	Bizzell J. J.	"	"	"	Intermittens	11	Tarboro N.C.
27	Williams D.	"	"	"	Rheumatism	"	"
28	Brown H.	"	"	"	Continued	"	"
29	Sanderson J. L.	"	"	D	Continued	13	Weldon N.C.
30	Sutton Thos.	Capt	"	"	Intermittens	14	General Hospital Petersburg Va
31	Brown Jessey	Pvt	"	E	Continued Febr	6	Plymouth N.C.
32	Stricklen Cyrus	"	"	"	Intermittens	11	Tarboro N.C.
33	William J. L.	"	"	"	Catarrhus	"	"
34	Pecock —	"	"	"	Continued Fev	16	General Hospital Petersburg Va
35	Bell E. A.	"	"	F	Febris Continued	6	Plymouth N.C.
36	Gooding J.	"	"	"	"	"	"
37	Wallice W. M.	"	"	G	Diarrhoea	11	Tarboro N.C.
38	Elmond H. H.	"	"	"	"	"	"
39	Austin C	Drumr	"	"	Vuln. Sclopet	16	General Hospital Petersburg Va
40	Hunter —	Pvt	"	H	Syphilis Febris	6	Plymouth N.C.

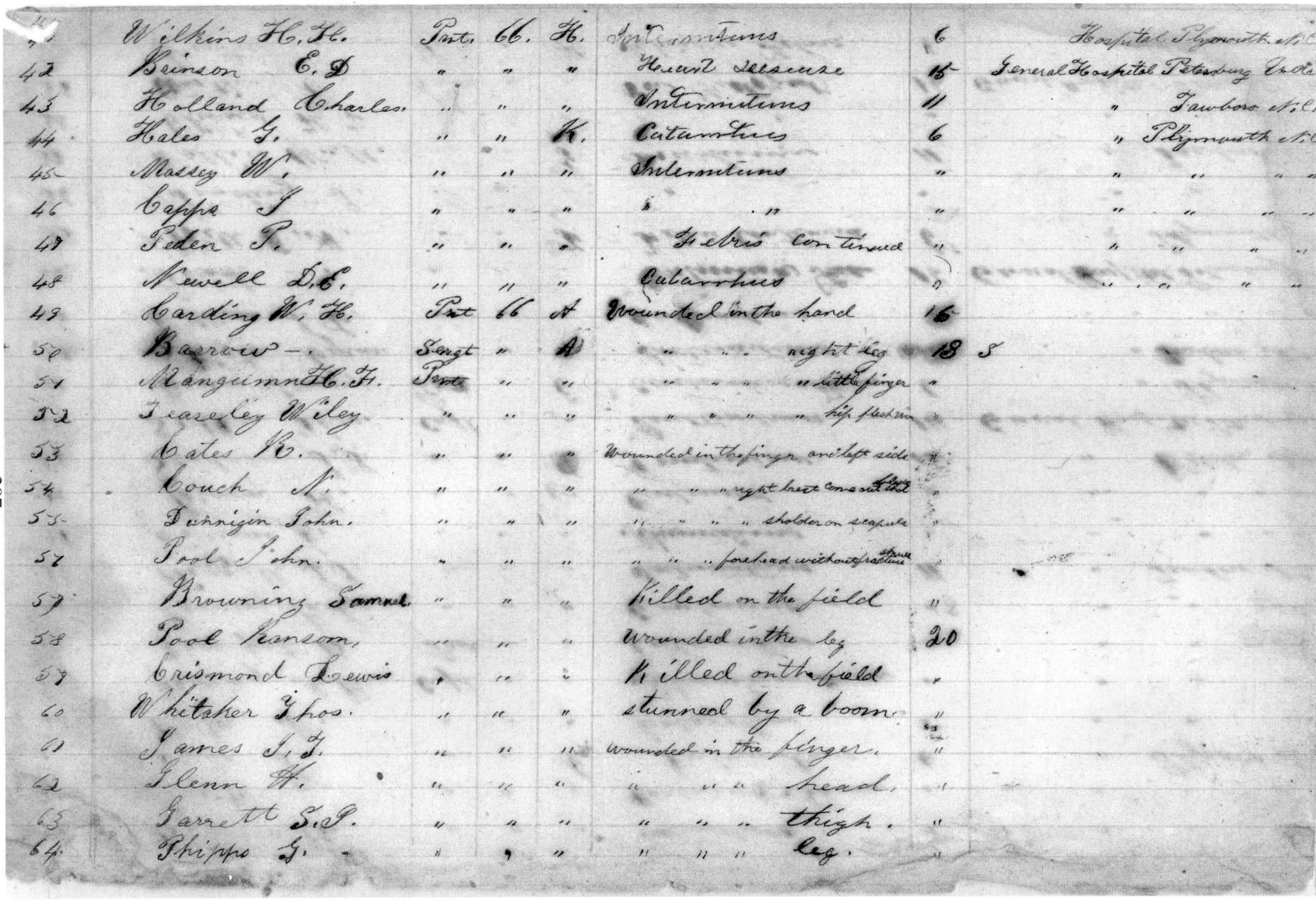

41	Wilkins H. H.	Pvt.	66.	H.	Intermittens	6		Hospital Plymouth N.C.
42	Brinson E. D	"	"	"	Heart disease	15		General Hospital Petersburg Va.
43	Holland Charles	"	"	"	Intermittens	11		" Tawboro N.C.
44	Hales G.	"	"	K.	Catarrhus	6		" Plymouth N.C.
45	Massey W.	"	"	"	Intermittens	"		" " "
46	Capps J	"	"	"	" "	"		" " "
47	Peden P.	"	"	"	Febris continued	"		" " "
48	Newell D. E.	"	"	"	Catarrhus	"		" " "
49	Carding W. H.	Pvt	66	A	Wounded in the hand	16		
50	Barrow –	Sergt	"	A	" " " right leg	18	5	
51	Manguimm H. F.	Pvt	"	"	" " " " little finger	"		
52	Feaseley Wiley	"	"	"	" " " " hip flesh	"		
53	Cates R.	"	"	"	Wounded in the finger and left side	"		
54	Couch N.	"	"	"	" " " right breast cons out the lung	"		
55	Dannigin John.	"	"	"	" " " " sholder on scapula	"		
56	Pool John.	"	"	"	" " " forehead without fracture			
57	Browning Samuel	"	"	"	Killed on the field	"		
58	Pool Ranson,	"	"	"	Wounded in the leg	20		
59	Crismond Lewis	"	"	"	Killed on the field	"		
60	Whitaker Thos.	"	"	"	stunned by a boom	"		
61	James J. T.	"	"	"	wounded in the finger.	"		
62	Glenn H.	"	"	"	" " " head.	"		
63	Garrett S. G.	"	"	"	" " " thigh.	"		
64	Phipps G.	"	"	"	" " " leg.			

65	Whitaker D.	Sergt	"	"	" " " "	"	
66	James Jesse.	Pvt	"	"	" " " wrist	"	
67	Stallings O.L.	"	"	B	" " " hand & head	16	
68	Bunting J.B.	"	"	"	" " " bowels (died)	"	
69	Horne H.D.	"	"	C	" " " head seriously	21	
70	Smith H.B.	"	"	"	" " " back "	"	
71	Smith Ira.	"	"	"	" " " left forefinger	"	
72	Robinson W.	Capt	"	D	" " " " side.	18	
73	Turner J.	Pvt	"	"	" " " flesh wound right thigh	"	
74	Wooderd Arthur.	"	"	"	" " " right thigh slightly	21	
75	Boon P.	"	"	E	" " " head seriously	20	
76	Cox Joseph.	"	"	"	" " " sholder boom slight	21	
77	Gooding C.	"	"	F	" " " sholder right	18	
78	Bowen M.	"	"	"	" " " left arm	"	
79	Stanley J.A.	Sergt	"	"	" " " "	"	
80	Lyons W.	Pvt	"	"	" " " right arm slightly	"	
81	Simmons J.	"	"	"	" " " fracture lower & upper jaw	"	
82	Brock E.A.	"	"	D	Killed on the field	18	
83	Spates Sam.	"	"	G	" " " "	20	
84	Garner J.W.	Corpl	"	"	wounded right hip	"	
85	Creech H.	Pvt	"	K	" hip Slightly	20	
86	Massey J.J.	Lt	"	"	" back near sholder	"	
87	Price D.J.	Pvt	"	"	" left forefinger	"	
88	Couch –.	"	"	A	Febris Contin	21	Gen Hospt Petersburg Va

89	Wetherington J. H.	Prvt	66	F	Wounded in right leg slight	20	
90	Lt Bagley	Lt	"	K	" " left thigh slightly	"	
91	Canon	Prvt	"	D	" " " " "	"	
92	Cox J.	"	"	E	" " right side slight	"	
93	H. Register	Sergt	"	C.	Wounded in left heel through	27	
94	Owens A.	Prvt	"	I.	" in left middle toe little finger	28	
95	Coppage Hiram	"	"	B.	Fever Typhoides	27	Sent Gen Hosp. Petersburg Va
96	Davis A.	Lt	"	C.	Dysentery act	"	" " " " "
97	Jones F.	Prvt	"	B.	Rubeola	28	" " " " "
98	Coley J.	"	"	I.	Intermittens	"	" " " " "
99	Whaley F.	"	"	H.	Anasarca		
100	Williams B.	"	"	"	Continued	28	Sent to Gen Hosp. Petersb
101	Smith G	"	"	I.	Continued Fever	"	" " " " "
102	Whaley	"	"	H.	Actis	30	" " " " "
103	Green G.W.	"	"	G.	Diarrhoea		
104	Harrison P. M.	"	"	H	" "		
105	Wade J. R.	Corpl	"	C	Catarrh		
106	Holland S. D.	"	"	F.	"		
107	Hinson R.	Prvt	"	C.	"		
108	Kornegay N. G.	"	"	H.	Abscess		
109	Spence W. D.	"	"	"	Diarrhoea		
110	Lanier J. L.	"	"	"	Catarrh		

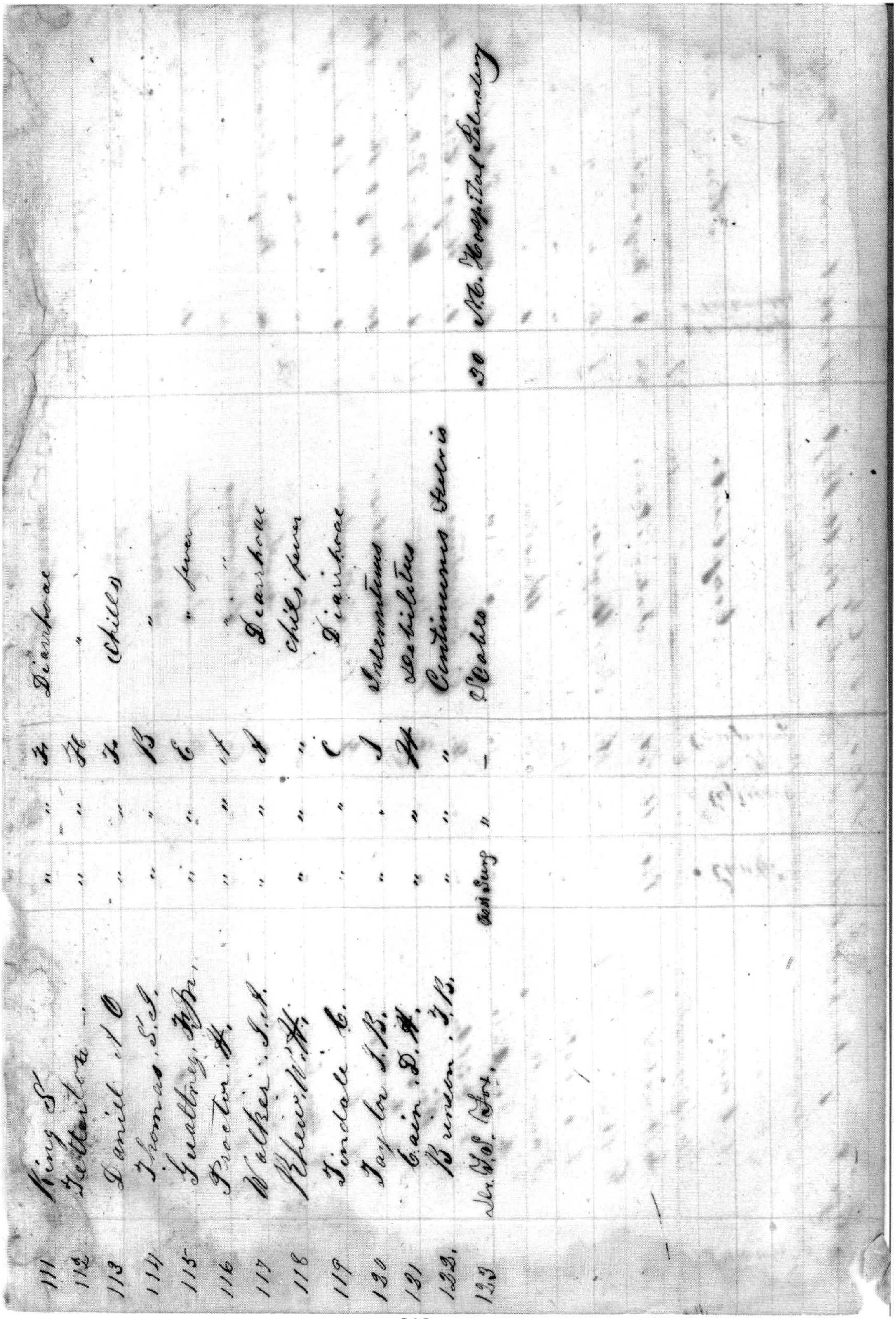

111	King S.	"	"	F	Diarrhoea			
112	Fetterton	"	"	H	"			
113	Daniel A.O.	"	"	F	Chills			
114	Thomas S.S.	"	"	B	"			
115	Gwaltney, H.M.	"	"	C	" fever			
116	Proctor, H.	"	"	F	"			
117	Walker, J.A.	"	"	A	Diarrhoea			
118	Blevins, H.H.	"	"	"	chills fever			
119	Tindale C.	"	"	C	Diarrhoea			
120	Taylor J.B.	"	"	I	Intermittens			
121	Cain D.H.	"	"	H	Debilitas			
122	Brinson, J.B.	"	"	"	Continuous Febris			
123	Mr. J.S. Cox.	Asst Surg	"	—	Scabies		30	N.C. Hospital Petersburg

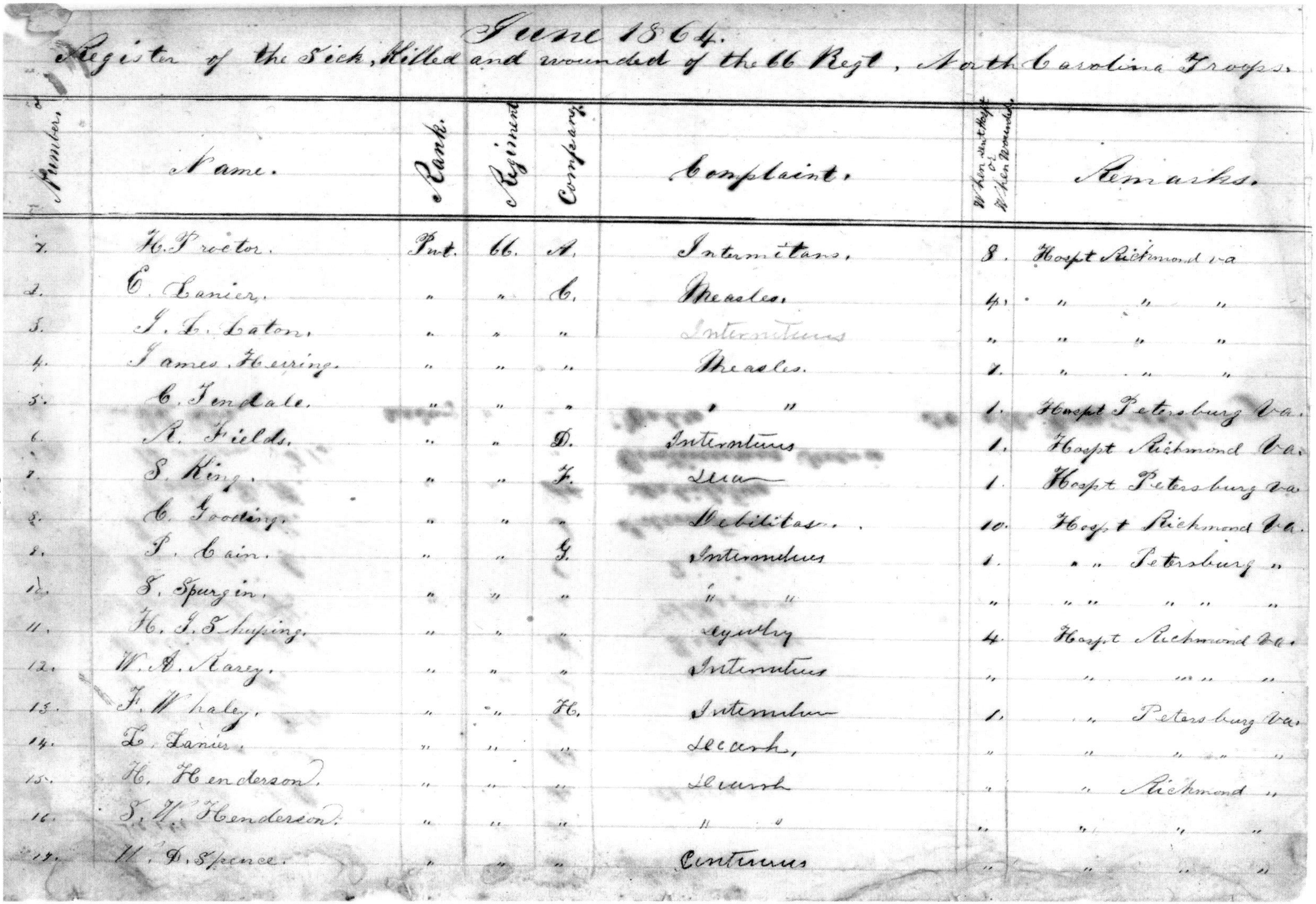

June 1864.

Register of the Sick, Killed and wounded of the 66 Regt, North Carolina Troops.

Number	Name	Rank	Regiment	Company	Complaint	When went Hospt or When Wounded	Remarks
1.	H. Proctor.	Pvt.	66.	A.	Intermitans.	8.	Hospt Richmond va
2.	C. Lanier.	"	"	C.	Measles.	4.	" " "
3.	J. L. Caton.	"	"	"	Intermittens	"	" " "
4.	James Herring.	"	"	"	Measles.	1.	" " "
5.	C. Tendale.	"	"	"	" "	1.	Hospt Petersburg Va.
6.	R. Fields.	"	"	D.	Intermittens	1.	Hospt Richmond Va.
7.	S. King.	"	"	F.	Ileu	1.	Hospt Petersburg va
8.	C. Gooding.	"	"	"	Debilitas.	10.	Hospt Richmond Va.
9.	J. Cain.	"	"	G.	Intermittens	1.	" " Petersburg "
10.	S. Spurgin.	"	"	"	" "	"	" " " " "
11.	H. J. Shuping.	"	"	"	Syphly	4.	Hospt Richmond Va.
12.	W. A. Karey.	"	"	"	Intermittens	"	" " " "
13.	F. Whaley.	"	"	H.	Intermitten	1.	" Petersburg Va.
14.	L. Lanier.	"	"	"	Diarh.	"	" " " "
15.	H. Henderson.	"	"	"	Diarrh	"	" Richmond "
16.	S. W. Henderson.	"	"	"	" "	"	" " "
17.	W. D. Spence.	"	"	"	Continuus	"	" " "

18.	J. Taylor.	"	"	J.	Continued	"	" Petersburg Va.
19.	H. Radford.	"	"	"	Remittent	"	Hospt Richmond Va.
20.	A. Wooten.	"	"	"	Fever	11.	" " " "
21.	J. W. Gurganus.	"	"	"	Typhoid Febris.	12.	" " " "
22.	J. Pittman.	"	"	"	Intermittent	1.	" " " "
23.	E. Taylor.	"	"	"	Measles.	8.	" " " "
24	W. J. Simpson.	"	"	A	wounded in left thumb slightly.	2.	
25	James Williams.	"	"	B.	" " two left little fingers severly	1.	
26	J. J. Wiggs.	Sergt.	"	"	" " lower part back slight.	3.	
27	B. W. Upchurch.	Pvt.	"	"	" " left fore arm severly.	5.	
28	J. Wilkins.	Lt.	"	C.	" in right foot 3 first toes severe	3.	
29	J. Colley.	Sergt.	"	"	" " " nee Seriously.	3.	
30	W. J. Phillips.	"	"	"	" " " arm below elbow & bruze above [illegible]	"	
31	A. P. Proctor.	Pvt.	"	"	" " left sholder slight	"	
32	J. A. Sutton.	"	"	"	" " right middle finger slight	"	
33	J. L. Herring.	"	"	"	" " " sholder severly.	6.	
34	Olen Mobley.	"	"	"	" " " side head slight	8.	
35	A. Ague.	"	"	D.	" on " " " seriously [illegible]	2.	
36	Wiley Parker.	"	"	E.	" in outer part right hand slight	3.	
37	J. Cox.	"	"	"	" " the finger slight.	4.	
38	W. J. Rasbery.	Capt.	"	F.	" " left thigh back part severe	1.	
39	S. Small.	Pvt.	"	"	" " right arm Severly.	1.	
40	A. O. Daniel.	corpl.	"	"	" " left side slight.	2.	
	E. L. Cowin.	Pvt.	"	"	" between two left little fingers severly.	8.	

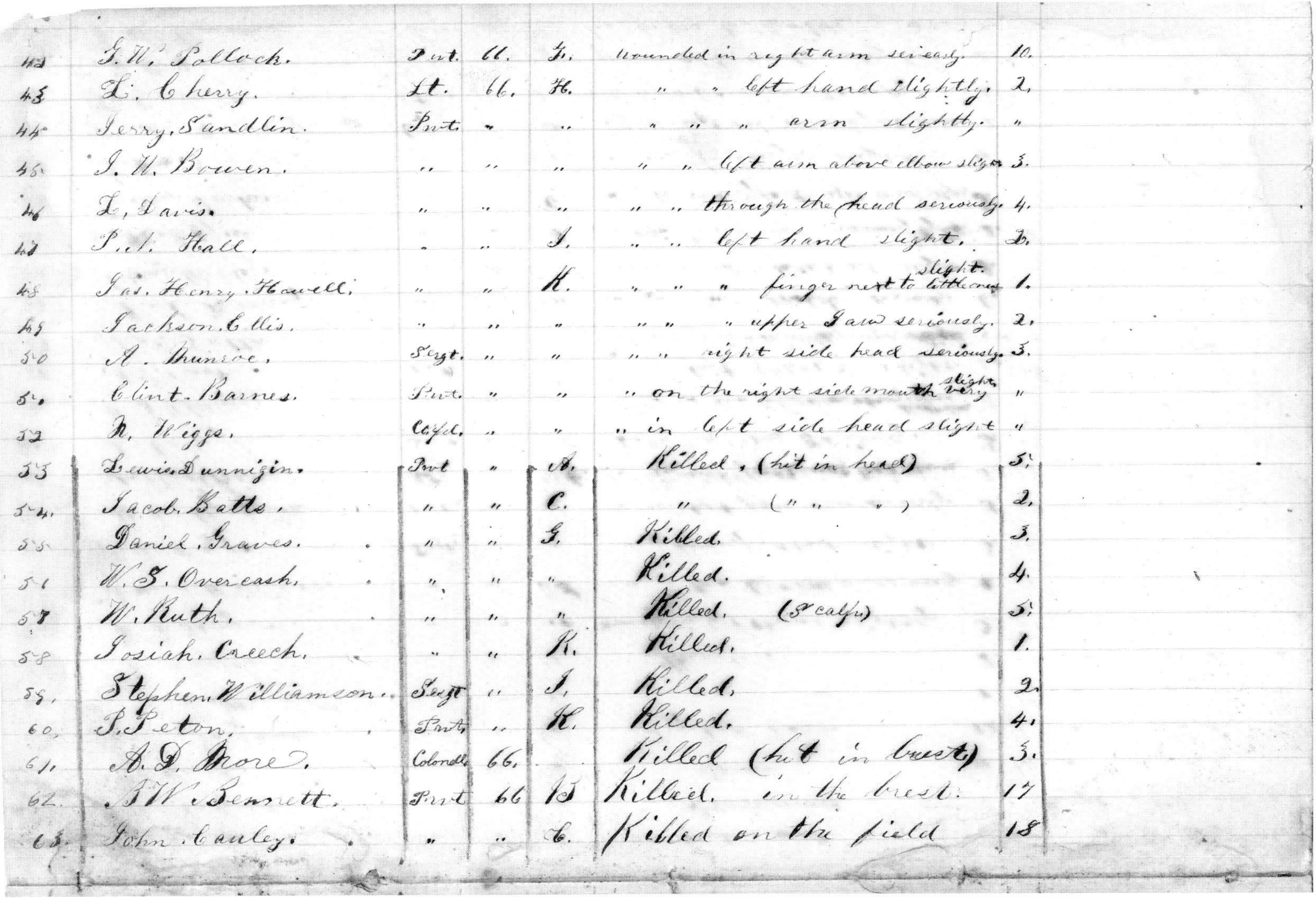

42	J. W. Pollock.	Pvt.	66.	F.	wounded in right arm seriously.	10.
43	L. Cherry.	Lt.	66.	H.	" " left hand slightly.	2.
44	Jerry. Sandlin.	Pvt.	"	"	" " " arm slightly.	"
45	J. W. Bowen.	"	"	"	" " left arm above elbow slight.	3.
46	L. Davis.	"	"	"	" " through the head seriously.	4.
47	P. A. Hall.	"	"	I.	" " left hand slight.	2.
48	Jas. Henry. Howell.	"	"	K.	" " " finger next to little one slight.	1.
49	Jackson. Ellis.	"	"	"	" " " upper Jaw seriously.	2.
50	A. Munroe.	Sergt.	"	"	" " right side head seriously.	3.
51	Clint. Barnes.	Pvt.	"	"	" on the right side mouth very slight.	"
52	R. Wiggs.	Corpl.	"	"	" in left side head slight	"
53	Lewis. Dunnizin.	Pvt	"	A.	Killed. (hit in head)	5.
54	Jacob. Batts.	"	"	C.	" (" " ")	2.
55	Daniel. Graves.	"	"	G.	Killed.	3.
56	W. S. Overcash.	"	"	"	Killed.	4.
57	W. Ruth.	"	"	"	Killed. (5th calf?)	5.
58	Josiah. Creech.	"	"	K.	Killed.	1.
59	Stephen. Williamson.	Sergt	"	I.	Killed.	2.
60	J. Peton.	Pvt.	"	K.	Killed.	4.
61	A. D. Moore.	Colonell	66.		Killed (hit in brest)	3.
62	B. W. Bennett.	Pvt	66	B	Killed. in the brest.	17
63	John. Cauley.	"	"	E.	Killed on the field	18

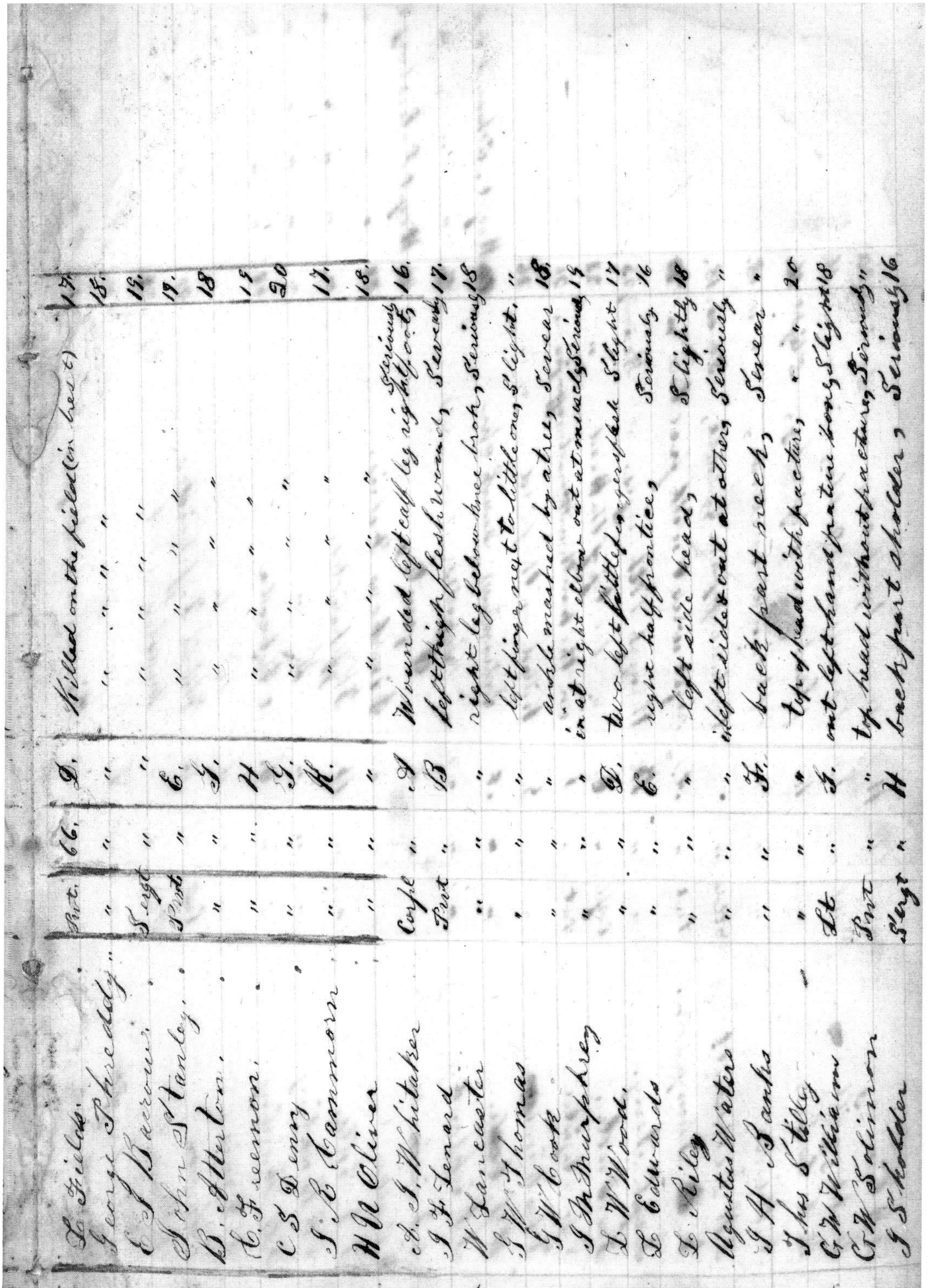

64	L Fields	Pvt.	66	D	Killed on the field (in breast)		17
65	George Threaddy	"	"	"	" " " "		18
66	E J Barrow	Sergt	"	"	" " " "		18
67	John Stanley	Pvt	"	E	" " " "		19
68	B. Atterton	"	"	G	" " " "		18
69	C. Freeman	"	"	H	" " " "		19
70	C S Denny	"	"	G	" " " "		20
71	J. E. Cannon	"	"	K	" " " "		17
72	W H Oliver	"	"	"	" " " "		18
73	A. J. Whitaker	Corpl	"	A	Wounded left calf leg right foot	Seriously	16
74	J F Lenard	Pvt	"	B	left thigh flesh wound	Severely	17
75	W Lancaster	"	"	"	right leg below knee broken	Seriously	18
76	G W Thomas	"	"	"	left finger next to little one	Slight	"
77	G W Cook	"	"	"	ankle mashed by a tree	Severe	18
78	J McMurphrey	"	"	"	in at right elbow out at muscle	Seriously	19
79	L W Wood	"	"	D	two left little fingers flesh	Slight	17
80	L Edwards	"	"	E	right half front ties	Seriously	16
81	L Riley	"	"	"	left side head	Slightly	18
82	Agustus Waters	"	"	"	left side & out at other	Seriously	"
83	J A Banks	"	"	F	back part neck	Severe	"
84	Thos Stilley	"	"	"	top of head with fracture	"	20
85	G W Wilkinson	Lt	"	G	out left hand fracture bone	Slightly	18
86	G W Soliman	Pvt	"	"	top head without fracture	Seriously	"
87	J S Holder	Sergt	"	H	back part shoulder	Seriously	16

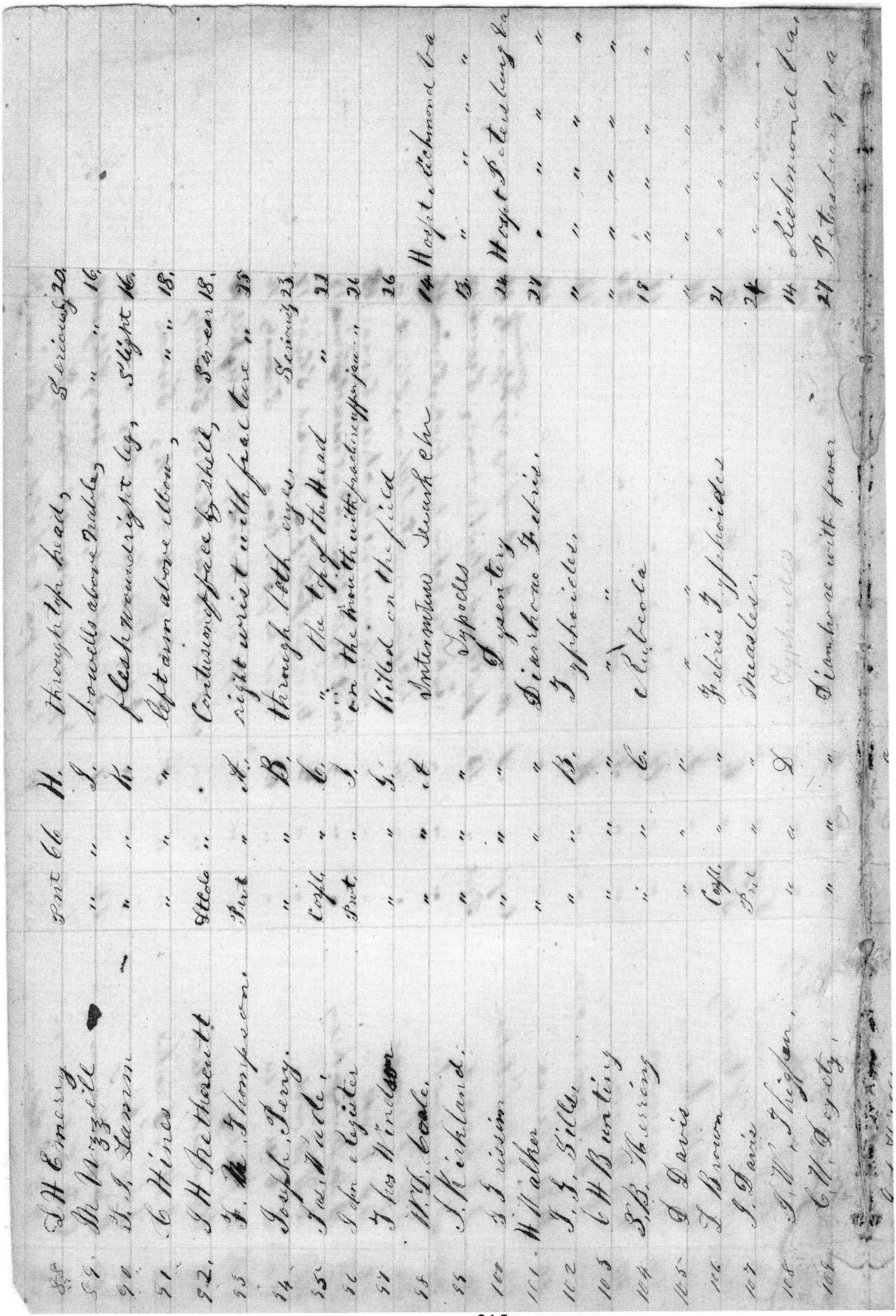

88	S H Emery	Pvt	66	H.	through top head,	Serious	20.	
89.	M Uzzell	"	"	I.	bowells above Nable,	" "	16.	
90	T. J. Lanim	"	"	K.	flesh wound right leg,	Slight	16.	
91	C Hines	"	"	"	left arm above elbow,	" "	18.	
92.	J H Netherautt	Sttdo	"		Contusion of face by shell,	Severe	18.	
93	F. M. Thompson.	Pvt	"	A.	right wrist with fracture	"	25	
94	Joseph Perry.	"	"	B.	through both eyes,	Serious	23.	
95	Jas. Wade,	Corpl.	"	C.	" the top of the Head	"	22	
96	John Register	Pvt.	"	I.	on the mouth with fracture upper jaw	"	26	
97	Thos Windsor	"	"	G.	Killed on the field		26	
98	W. D. Coale.	"	"	A	Intermitent Fever		14	Hospt Richmond Va
99	J. Kirkland.	"	"	"	Typodes		13.	" " " "
100	J J Grissim	"	"	"	Dysentery		24	Hospt Petersburg Va
101	W Walker	"	"	"	Diarrhoea Febris.		27	" " " "
102	J. J. Gills.	"	"	B.	Typhoides.		"	" " " "
103	C H Bunting	"	"	"	" "		"	" " " "
104	S. B. Herring	"	"	C.	Rubeola		18	" " " "
105	D Davis	"	"	"	" "		"	" " " "
106	J. Brown	Corpl.	"	"	Febris Typhoides		21	" " " "
107	J. Davis	Pvt	"	"	Measles.		24	" " " "
108	J. W. Thigpen.	"	"	D	Typhoides		14	Richmond Va.
109	C. W. Dogety.	"	"	"	Diarrhoea with fever		27	Petersburg Va

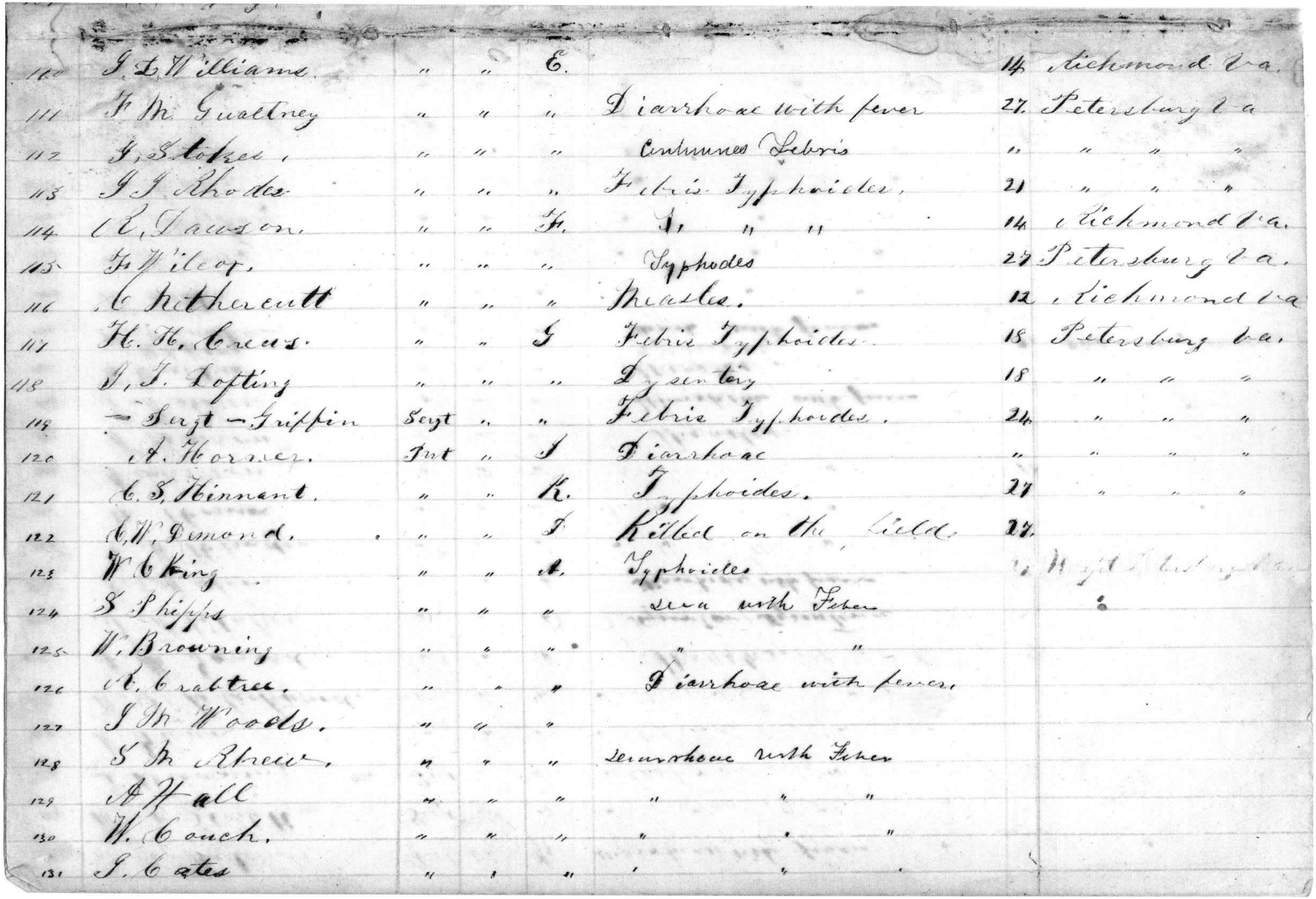

110	J. L. Williams	"	"	E.		14	Richmond Va.
111	F. M. Gualtney	"	"	"	Diarrhoea with fever	27.	Petersburg Va
112	J. Stokes	"	"	"	Continues Febris	"	" " "
113	J. J. Rhodes	"	"	"	Febris Typhoides	21	" " "
114	R. Dawson	"	"	F.	" " "	14	Richmond Va.
115	F. Wilcox	"	"	"	Typhodes	27	Petersburg Va.
116	C. Witherautt	"	"	"	Measles.	12	Richmond Va
117	H. H. Crews	"	"	G	Febris Typhoides	18	Petersburg Va.
118	J. T. Lofting	"	"	"	Dysentery	18	" " "
119	Sergt. Griffin	Sergt	"	"	Febris Typhoides.	24	" " "
120	A. Horner.	Pvt	"	I	Diarrhoea	"	" " "
121	C. S. Hinnant.	"	"	K.	Typhoides.	27	" " "
122	C. W. Demond.	"	"	I	Killed on the Field	27.	
123	W. C. King	"	"	A.	Typhoides		
124	S. Phipps	"	"	"	Diarrhoea with Fever		
125	W. Browning	"	"	"	" "		
126	R. Crabtree.	"	"	"	Diarrhoea with fever.		
127	J. M. Woods.	"	"	"			
128	S. M. Rhew.	"	"	"	Diarrhoea with Fever		
129	A. Hall	"	"	"	" " "		
130	W. Couch.	"	"	"	" " "		
131	J. Cates	"	"	"	" " "		

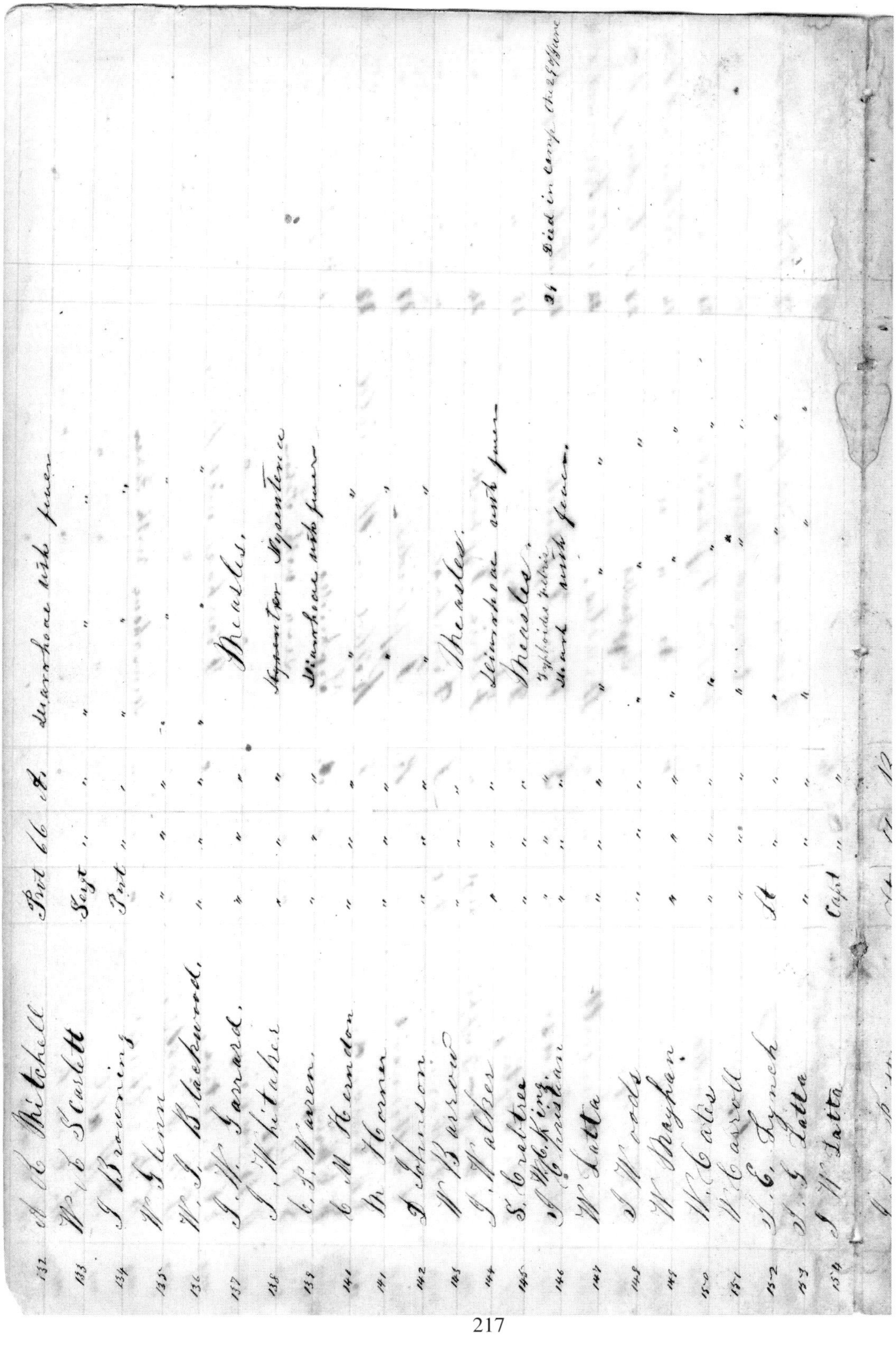

132	A. R. Mitchell	Prvt	66	A.	Diarrhoea with fever		
133	W. R. Scarlett	Sergt	"	"	" " "		
134	J Browning	Prvt	"	"	" " "		
135	W Glenn	"	"	"	" " "		
136	W. J. Blackwood.	"	"	"	" " "		
137	J. W. Garrard.	"	"	"	Measles.		
138	J. Whitaker	"	"	"	~~Dysenter~~ Dysenteria		
139	C. P. Warren.	"	"	"	Diarrhoea with fever		
140	C M Herndon	"	"	"	" "		
141	M Horner	"	"	"	" "		
142	D Johnson	"	"	"	" "		
143	W Barrow	"	"	"	Measles.		
144	J. Walker	"	"	"	Diarrhoea with fever		
145	S. Crabtree	"	"	"	Measles.		
146	W. C. King / J Christian	"	"	"	Typhoides febris / Diarh with fever.	24	Died in camp the 24 of June
147	W Latta	"	"	"	" " "		
148	J Woods	"	"	"	" " "		
149	W Mayhan	"	"	"	" " "		
150	W. Cates	"	"	"	" " "		
151	W Carroll	"	"	"	" " "		
152	J. E. Lynch	Lt	"	"	" " "		
153	J. G. Latta	"	"	"	" " "		
154	J W Latta	Capt	"	"			

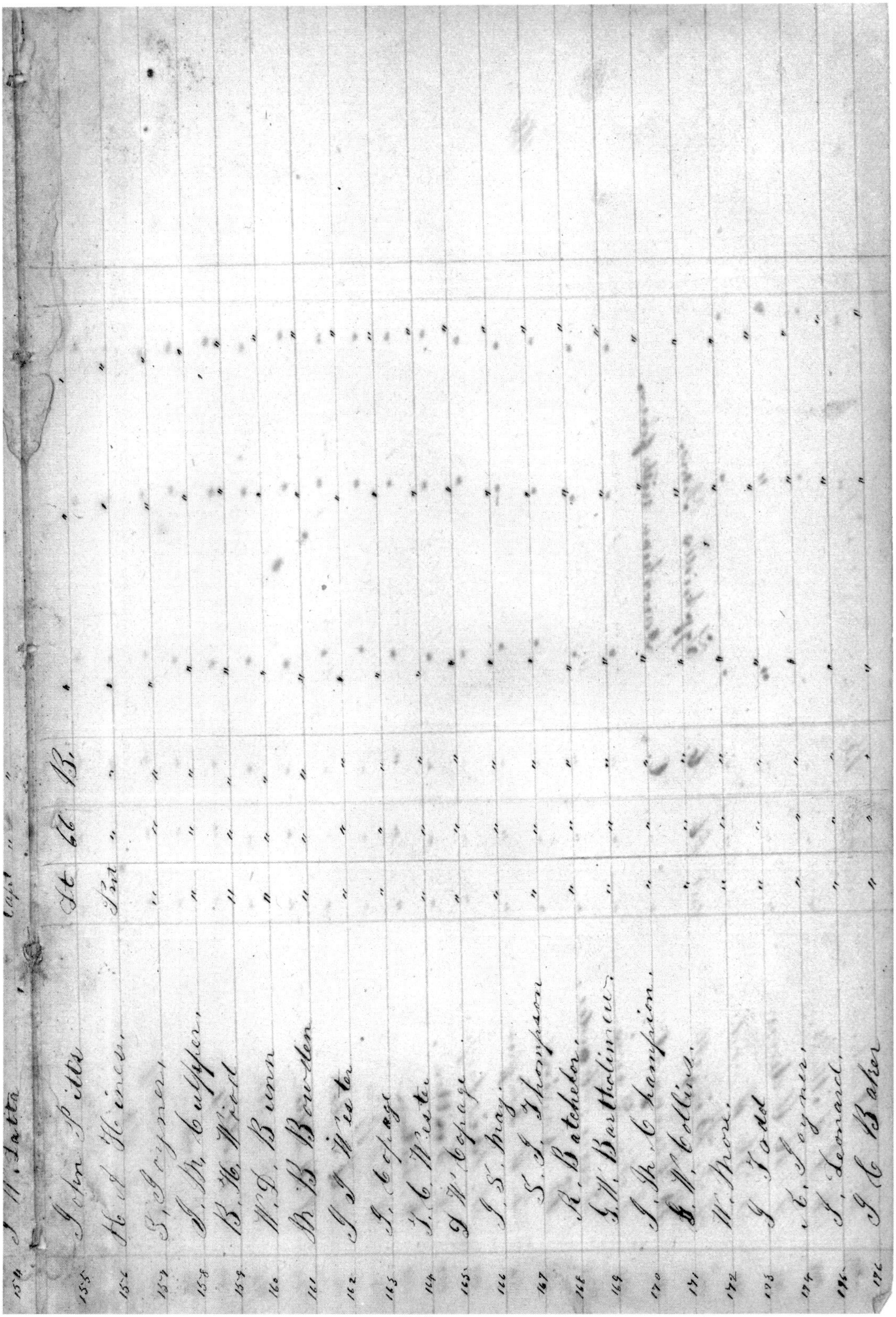
154 J. W. Latta Capt "
155 John Pitts Lt 66 B
156 H. L. Hines Pvt
157 L. Grymes
158 J. W. Culpepper
159 B. H. Wood
160 W. D. Bunn
161 R. B. Bowden
162 J. J. Wester
163 J. Copage
164 S. C. Wester
165 D. W. Copage
166 J. S. Pray
167 S. J. Thompson
168 R. Batchelor
169 J. W. Bartholomew
170 J. R. Champion
171 B. W. Collins
172 W. More
173 J. Todd
174 E. Joyner
175 J. Leonard
176 G. C. Baker

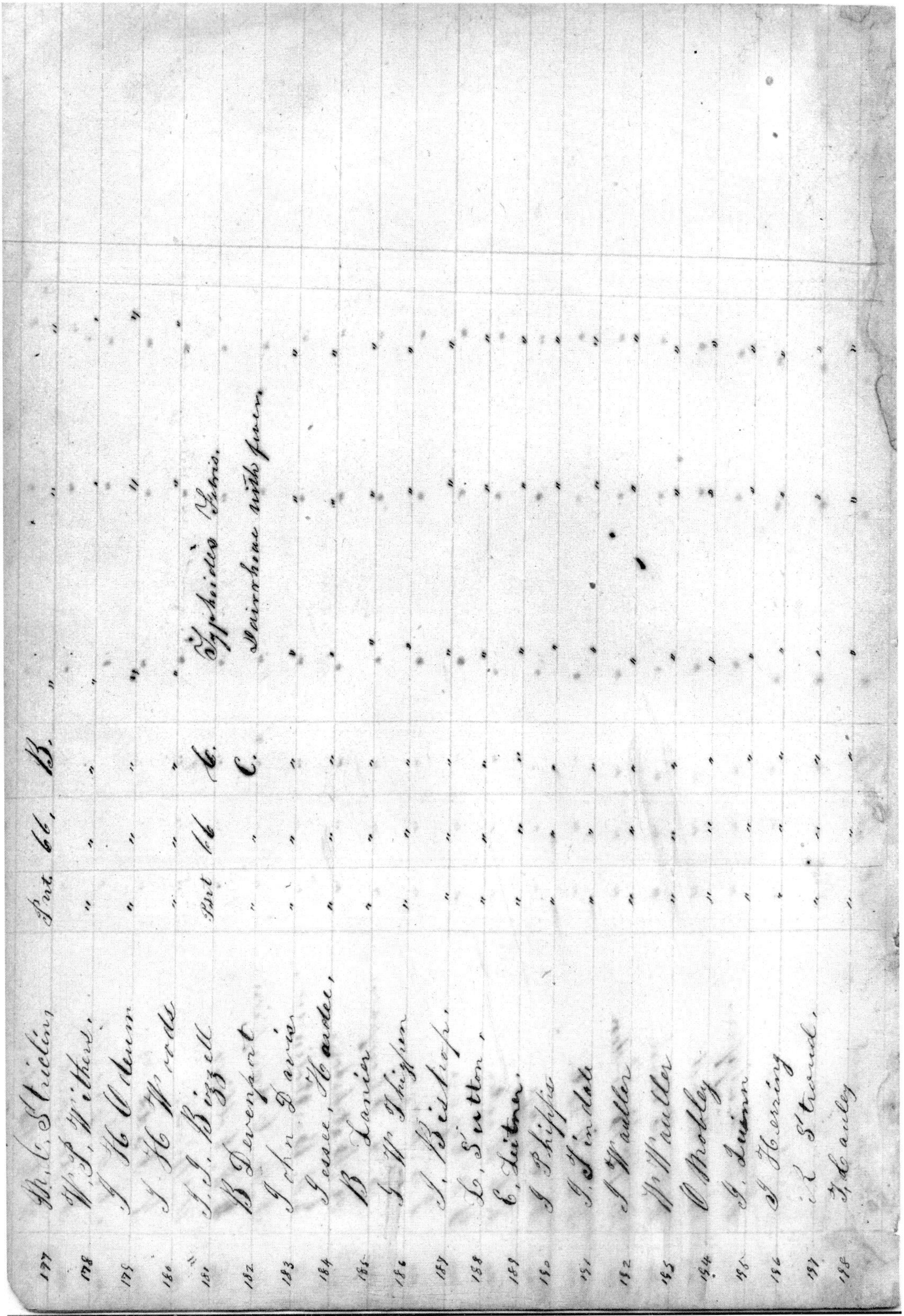

177	W. C. Stricklin	Pvt.	66,	B.	"	"
178	W. J. Withers.	"	"	"	"	"
179	J. H. Odum	"	"	"	"	"
180	J. H. Woodle	"	"	"	"	"
181	J. J. Bizzell	Pvt	66	C.	Typhoides Febris.	
182	B Devenport	"	"	C.	Diarrhoea with fever	
183	John Davis	"	"	"	"	"
184	Jessee Hardee,	"	"	"	"	"
185	B Lanier	"	"	"	"	"
186	J. W. Phipps	"	"	"	"	"
187	J. Bishop,	"	"	"	"	"
188	L. Sutton,	"	"	"	"	"
189	E. Leitner.	"	"	"	"	"
190	J Phipps	"	"	"	"	"
191	J. Tindale	"	"	"	"	"
192	J W Fuller	"	"	"	"	"
193	W Waller	"	"	"	"	"
194	O Mobley	"	"	"	"	"
195	G. Quinn	"	"	"	"	"
196	J Herring	"	"	"	"	"
197	L Stroud.	"	"	"	"	"
198	J. Bailey	"	"	"	"	"

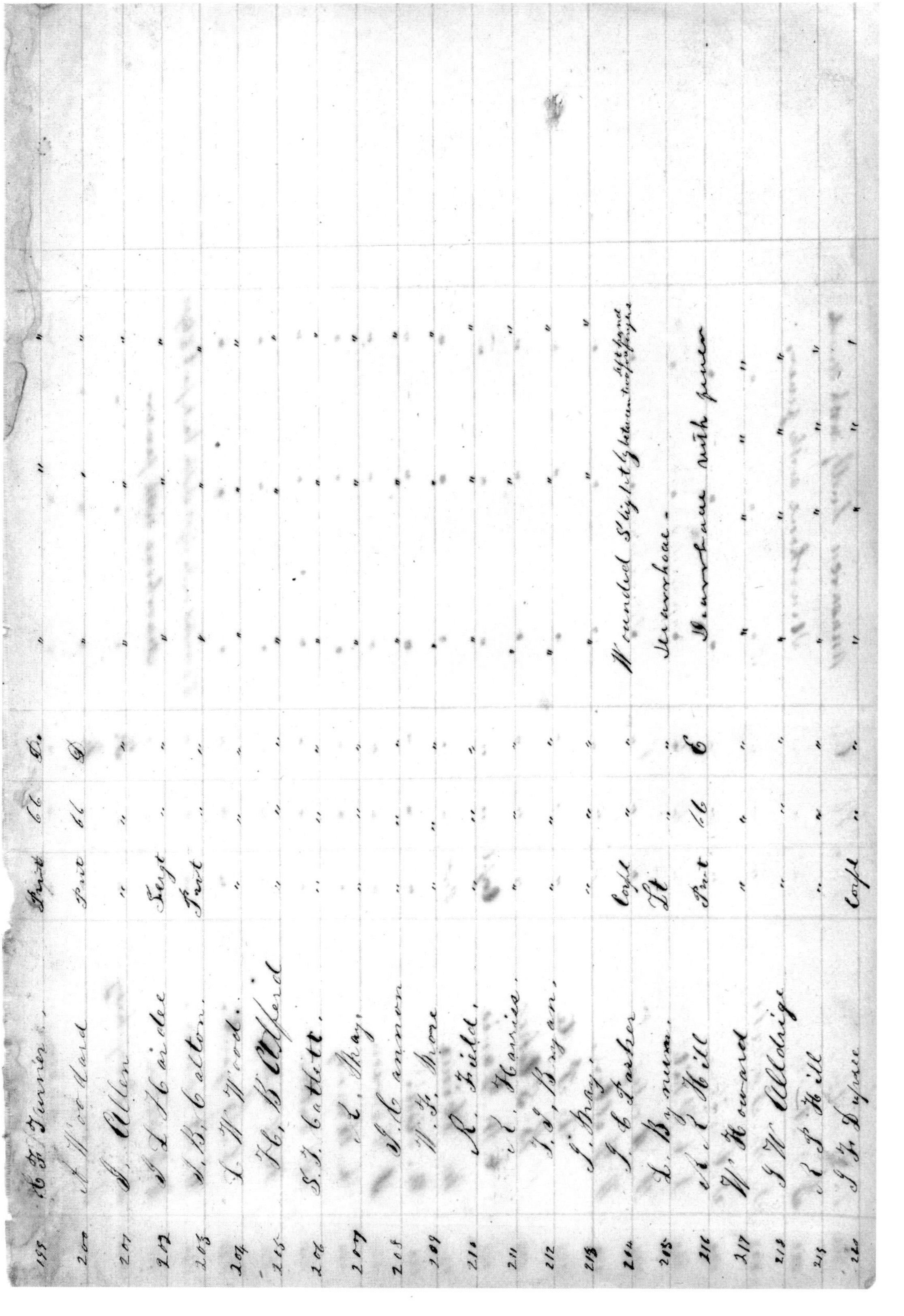

199	E F Turner.	Prvt	66	D.	"		"	"	
200	A Woodard	Prvt	66	D	"		"	"	
201	J. Allen	"	"	"	"		"	"	
202	J L Hardee	Sergt	"	"	"		"	"	
203	J. B. Calton.	Prvt	"	"	"		"	"	
204	L W Wood.	"	"	"	"		"	"	
205	H. B Alford	"	"	"	"		"	"	
206	S. J. Catlett.	"	"	"	"		"	"	
207	L. Ray.	"	"	"	"		"	"	
208	J. Cannon	"	"	"	"		"	"	
209	W. F. More	"	"	"	"		"	"	
210	R. Field.	"	"	"	"		"	"	
211	R. Harris.	"	"	"	"		"	"	
212	J. J. Bryan.	"	"	"	"		"	"	
213	J. Ray.	"	"	"	"		"	"	
214	J. C Parker	Corpl	"	"	Wounded Slightly between two fingers left hand				
215	L. Bynum.	Lt	"	"	Diarrhoea.				
216	R R Hill	Prvt	66	E	Diarrhoea with fever				
217	W Howard	"	"	"	"	"	"	"	
218	J W Alldrige	"	"	"	"	"	"	"	
219	R P Hill	"	"	"	"	"	"	"	
220	J F Dupree	Corpl	"	"	"	"	"	"	

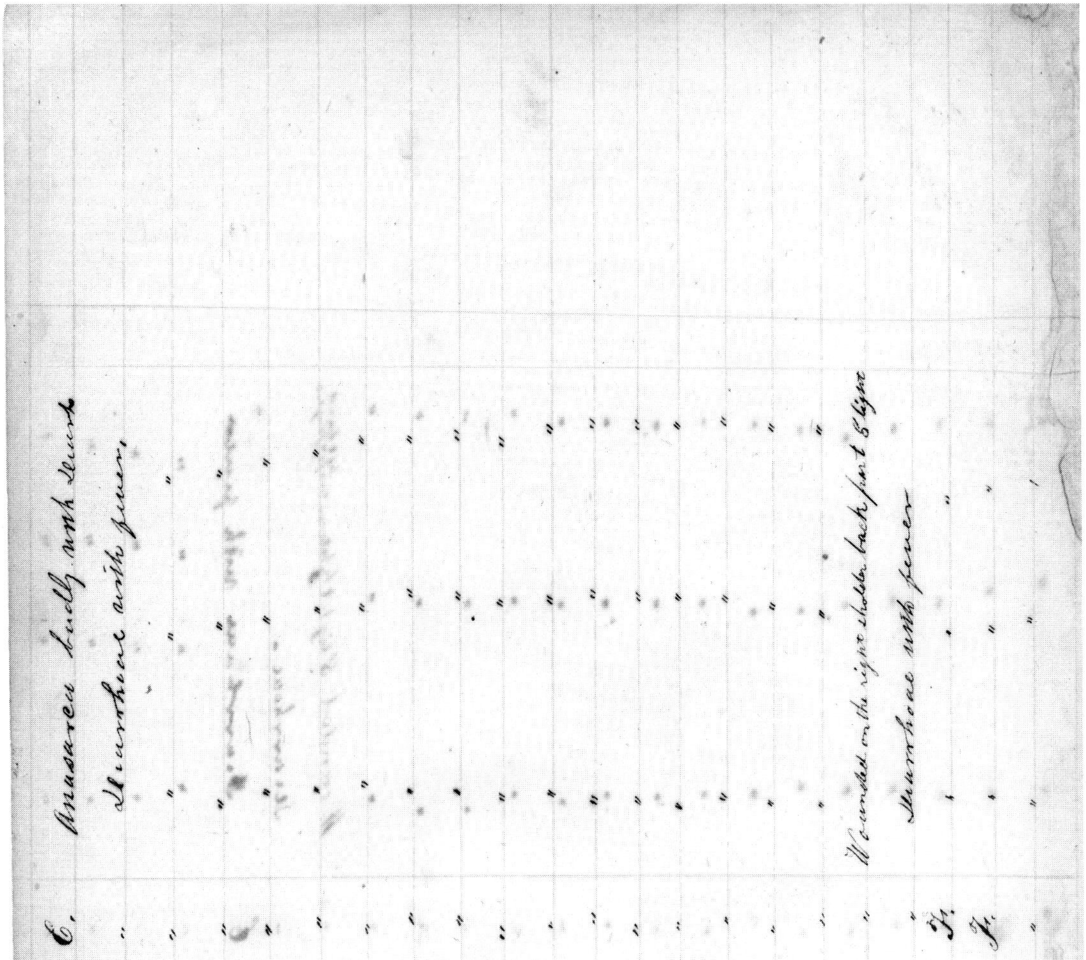

221	J. Heath,	Pvt	66	E.	Anasarca badly with Scurvy
222	G. Pate	"	"	"	Diarrhoea with fever,
223	J. M. Jarrell	"	"	"	" " "
224	J. Ervin,	"	"	"	" " "
225	L. C. White	"	"	"	" " "
226	D. Worley	"	"	"	" " "
227	W. Dalton,	"	"	"	" " "
228	L. Pate	"	"	"	" " "
229	B. Stokes	"	"	"	" " "
230	C. M. Davis	Capt	"	"	" " "
231	M. Hines	Pvt	"	"	" " "
232	M. Ross,	"	"	"	" " "
233	J. Dawson	"	"	"	" " "
234	L. Burney	"	"	"	" " "
235	A. Sutton	"	"	"	" " "
236	H. Smith,	"	"	"	" " "
237	A. Bryant,	"	"	"	" " "
238	J. Brown,	"	"	"	Wounded on the right sholder back part slight
239	W. Dawson,	"	"	"	Diarrhoea with fever
240	J. A. Murphrey	"	"	F.	" " "
241	D. King	"	"	F.	" " "
242	J. Fordham,	"	"	"	" " "

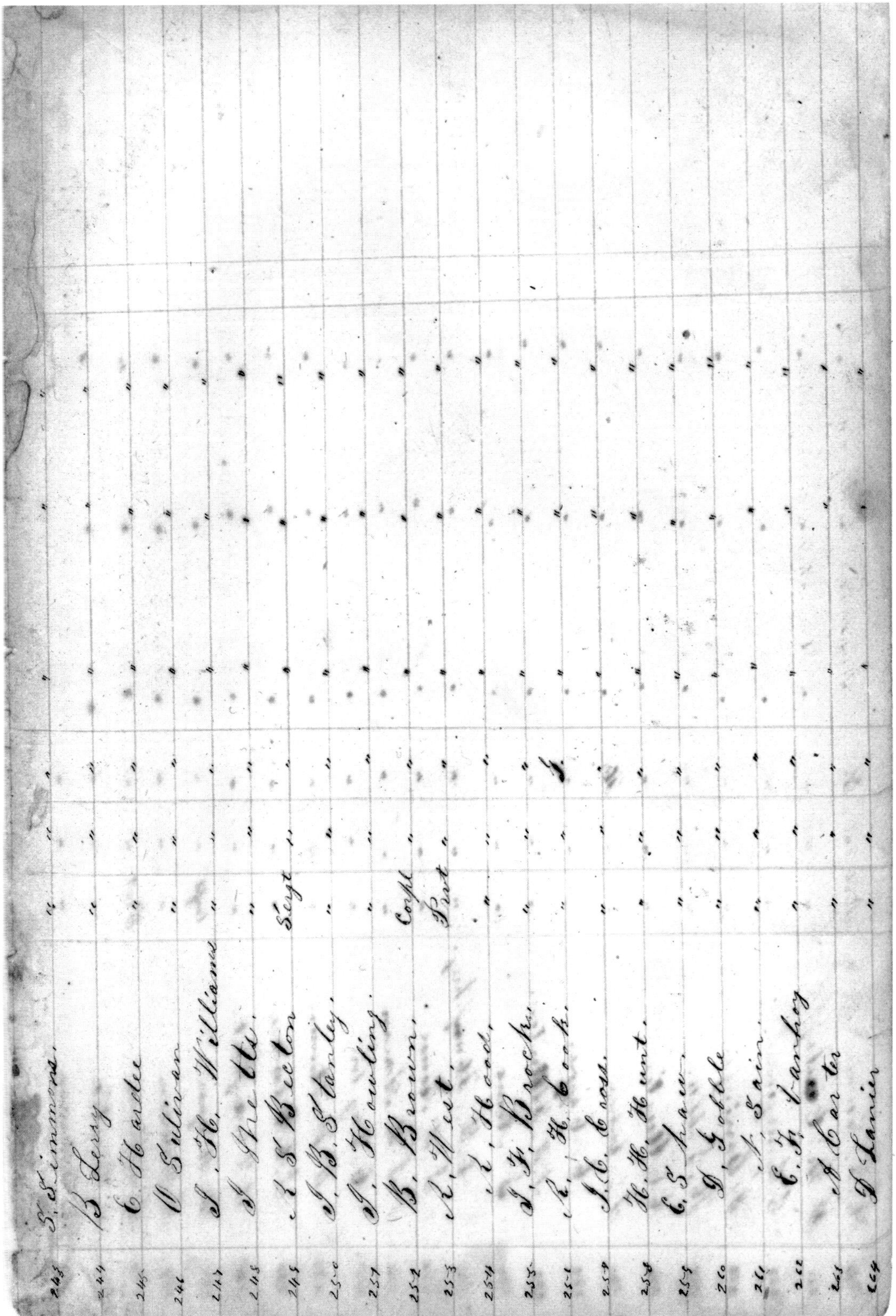

243	S. Simmons.	"	"	"	"	"	"	
244	B Lerry	"	"	"	"	"	"	
245	E. Hardee	"	"	"	"	"	"	
246	O Sulivan	"	"	"	"	"	"	
247	J. H. Williams	"	"	"	"	"	"	
248	J Shetts.	"	"	"	"	"	"	
249	A S Becton	Sergt	"	"	"	"	"	
250	J. B. Stanley.	"	"	"	"	"	"	
251	J. Howling.	"	"	"	"	"	"	
252	B. Brown.	Corpl	"	"	"	"	"	
253	A. West.	Prvt	"	"	"	"	"	
254	A. Hood.	"	"	"	"	"	"	
255	J. F. Brock.	"	"	"	"	"	"	
256	R. H. Cook.	"	"	G	"	"	"	
257	J. C. Cross.	"	"	"	"	"	"	
258	H. H. Hunt.	"	"	"	"	"	"	
259	C. S haw.	"	"	"	"	"	"	
260	D. Gobble	"	"	"	"	"	"	
261	N. Sain.	"	"	"	"	"	"	
262	E. F. Vanhoy	"	"	"	"	"	"	
263	A Carter	"	"	"	"	"	"	
264	D Lanier	"	"	"	"	"	"	

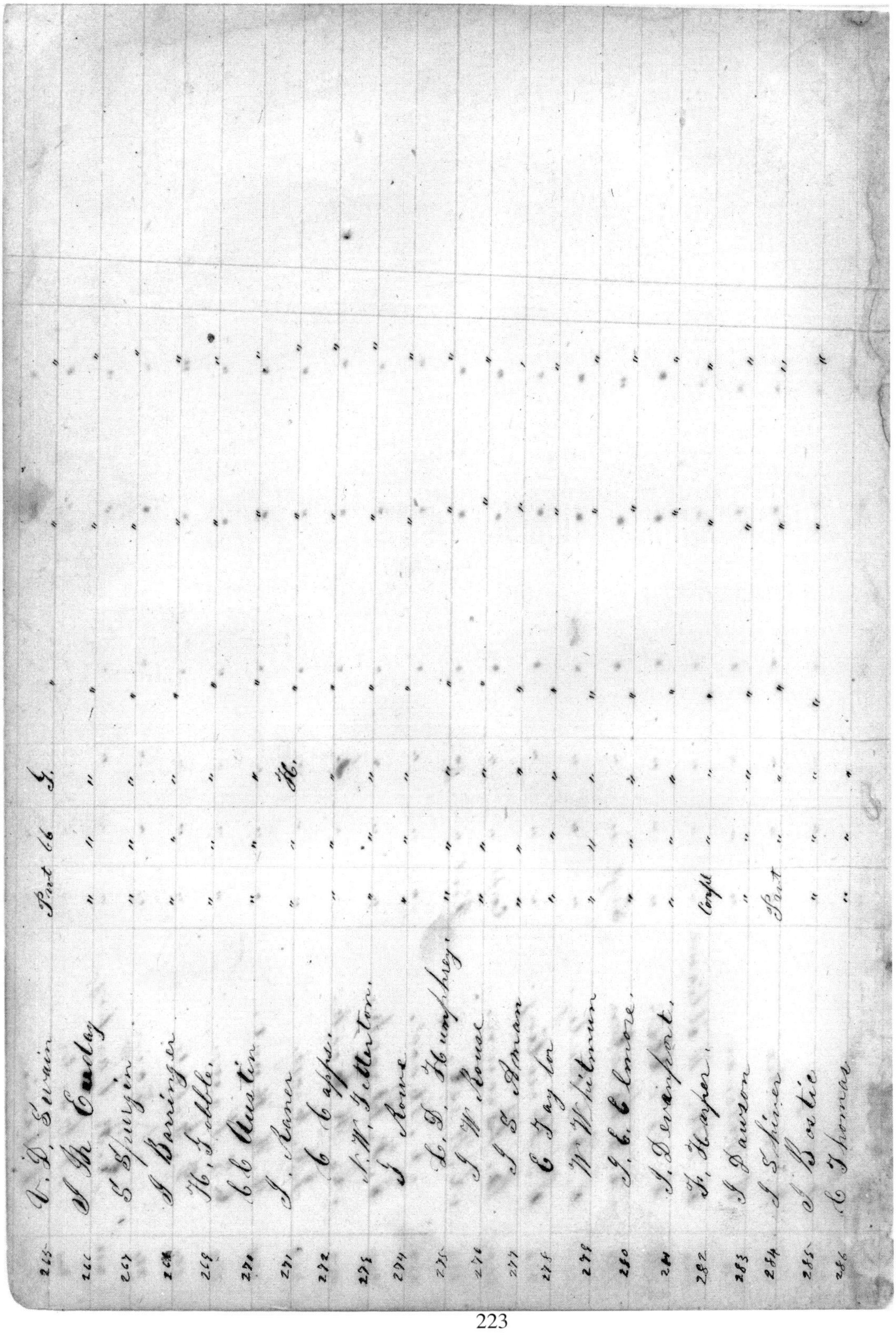

265	V. D. Swain	Pvt	66	G.	"	"	"
266	J M Eudlay	"	"	"	"	"	"
267	S Spurgin	"	"	"	"	"	"
268	J Barringer	"	"	"	"	"	"
269	H. Gobble.	"	"	"	"	"	"
270	C C Austin	"	"	"	"	"	"
271	J. Raner	"	"	H.	"	"	"
272	C Capps.	"	"	"	"	"	"
273	N. W. Fetterton.	"	"	"	"	"	"
274	J Rowe	"	"	"	"	"	"
275	L. D. Humphrey.	"	"	"	"	"	"
276	J W Rouse	"	"	"	"	"	"
277	J S Aman	"	"	"	"	"	"
278	C Taylor	"	"	"	"	"	"
279	W Whitman	"	"	"	"	"	"
280	J. E. Elmore.	"	"	"	"	"	"
281	J. Devanport.	"	"	"	"	"	"
282	F. Harper.	Corpl	"	"	"	"	"
283	J Dawson	"	"	"	"	"	"
284	J Shiver	Pvt	"	"	"	"	"
285	J Bostic	"	"	"	"	"	"
286	C Thomas	"	"	"			

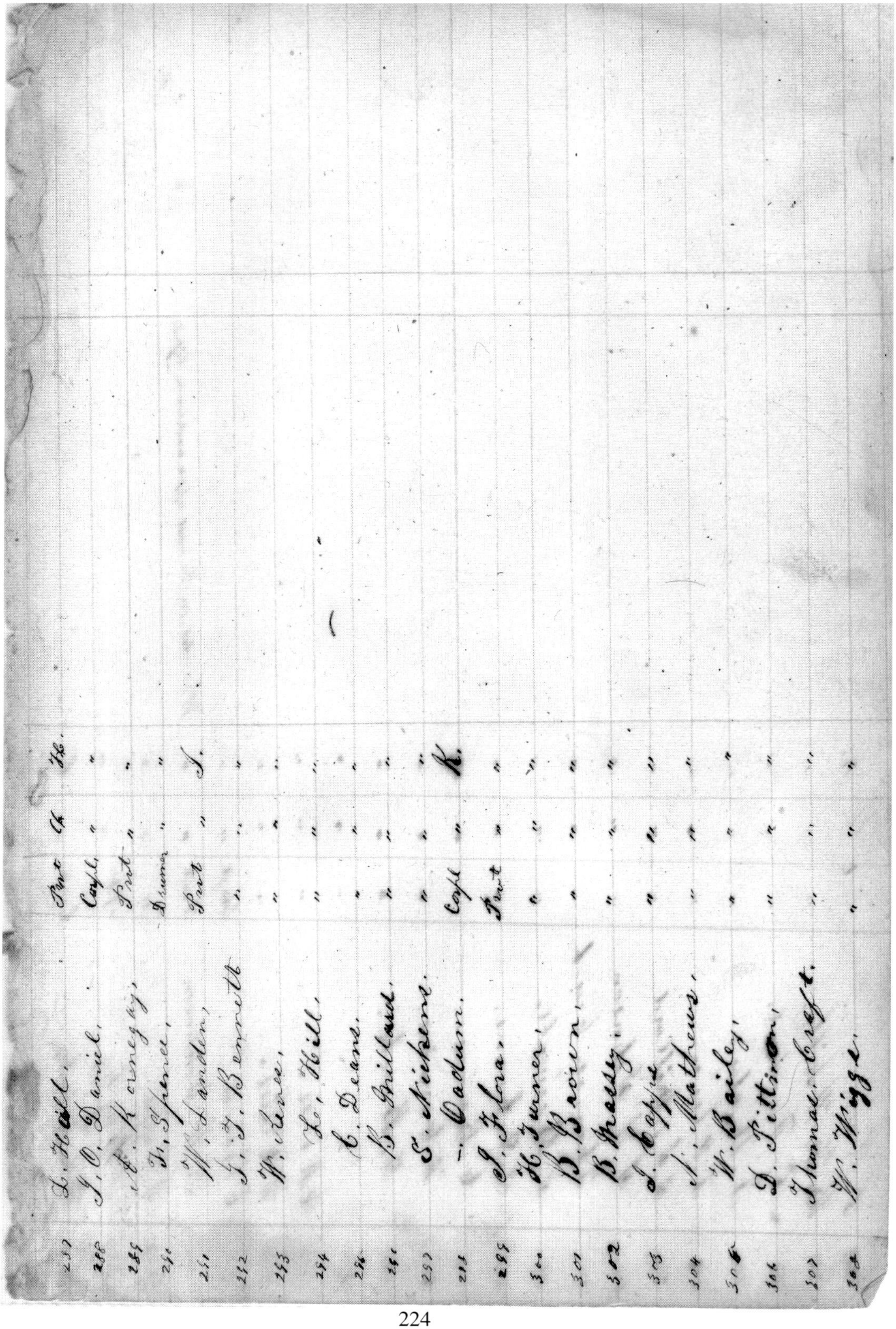

287	L. Hill.	Prvt	C.	H.
288	J. O. Daniel.	Corpl.	"	"
289	J. A. Kornegay,	Prvt	"	"
290	F. Spence,	Drumr	"	"
291	W. Landen,	Prvt	"	I.
292	J. T. Bennett	"	"	"
293	W. Lence,	"	"	"
294	L. Hill.	"	"	"
296	E. Deane.	"	"	"
295	B. Gillard.	"	"	"
297	S. Nickens.	"	"	"
298	Oadum.	Corpl	"	K.
299	J. Flora,	Prvt	"	"
300	H. Turner,	"	"	"
301	B. Brown,	"	"	"
302	B. Massey.	"	"	"
303	J. Capps	"	"	"
304	J. Mathews.	"	"	"
305	W. Bailey,	"	"	"
306	D. Pittman.	"	"	"
307	Thomas Craft.	"	"	"
308	W. Wiggs.	"	"	"

309	O. Sumlins.	Prvt	C.	K.	
310	B. F. Whitley.	"	"	"	
311.	R. Woodard.	"	"	"	
312	G. Hales.	"	"	"	
313	T. Oliver.	"	"	"	
314	J. J. Millard.	"	"	"	
315	J W Johnson.	"	"	"	
316	Thomas Creech,	"	"	"	
317	J. Boswell,	"	"	"	
318	J. D. Evans,	"	"	"	
319	C Barnes.	"	"	"	
320	W. Cornice.	"	"	"	
321	D. Brock.	"	"	"	
322	J H Stallings.	"	"	"	
323	C. Hines.	"	"	"	
324	W. Ellis.	"	"	"	
325	E Barnes	Sergt	"	"	
326	R H Tomlinson	Prvt	"	"	Wounded, on the nose upper and lower lips.
327	W Capps	"	"	"	
328	A. Bagley	Lt	"	"	
329	S. S. Quinley	Capt	"	E	

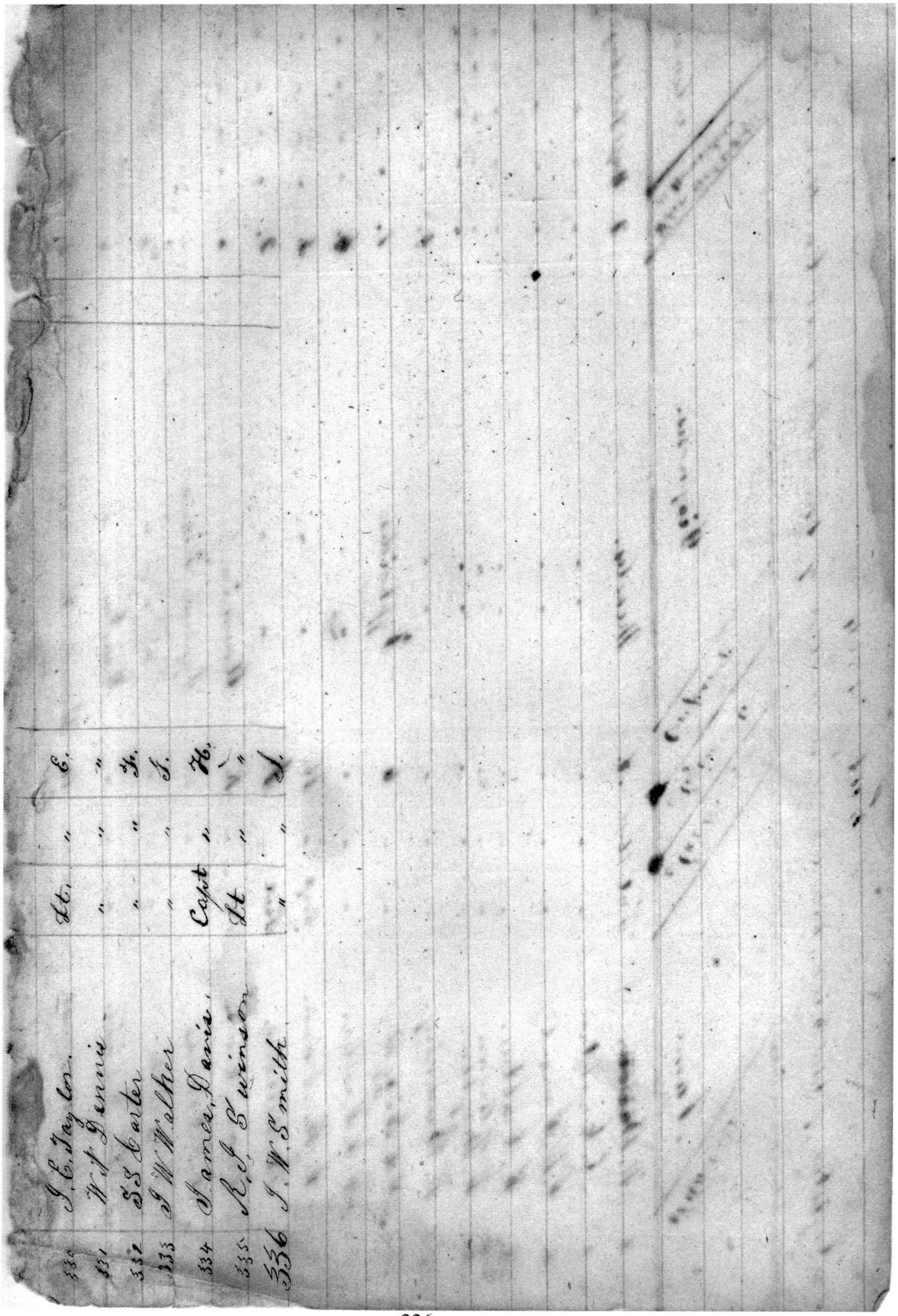

330	J. E. Taylor	Lt.	"	E.
331	W. P. Dennis	"	"	"
332	S. S. Carter	"	"	F.
333	J. W. Walker	"	"	I.
334	James Davis	Capt	"	H.
335	R. L. Swinson	Lt	"	"
336	J. W. Smith	"	"	I.

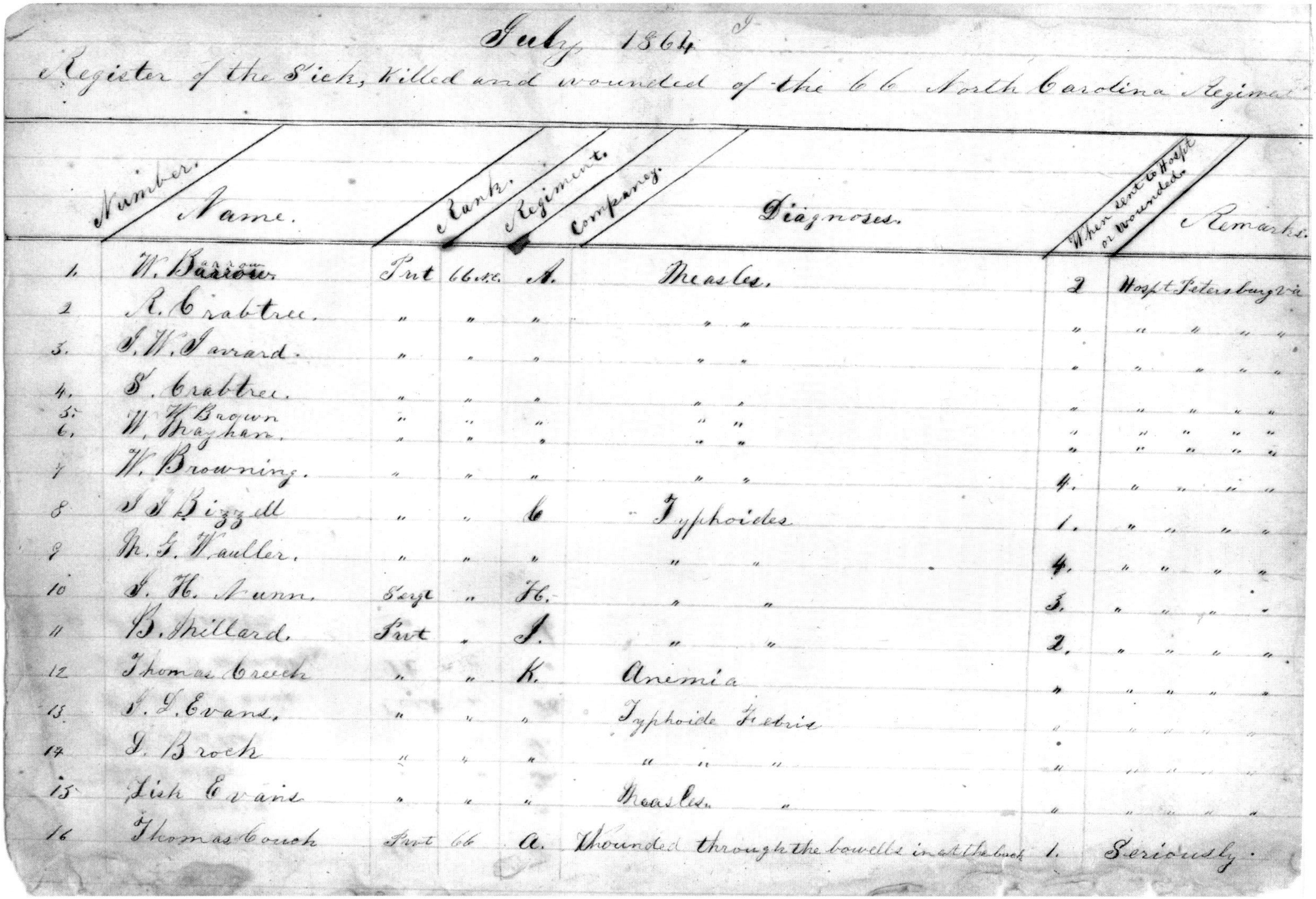

July 1864

Register of the Sick, Killed and wounded of the 66 North Carolina Regiment

Number.	Name.	Rank.	Regiment.	Company.	Diagnoses.	When sent to Hospt or wounded.	Remarks.
1.	W. Barrow	Pvt	66.N.C.	A.	Measles.	2	Hospt Petersburg Va
2	R. Crabtree.	"	"	"	" "	"	" " " "
3.	J.W. Jarrard.	"	"	"	" "	"	" " " "
4.	S. Crabtree.	"	"	"	" "	"	" " " "
5.	W. W. Brown	"	"	"	" "	"	" " " "
6.	W. Mayhan.	"	"	"	" "	"	" " " "
7	W. Browning.	"	"	"	" "	4.	" " " "
8	J.J. Bizzell	"	"	C	Typhoides	1.	" " " "
9	W.G. Waller.	"	"	"	" "	4.	" " " "
10	J. H. Nunn.	Sergt	"	H.	" "	3.	" " " "
11	B. Millard.	Pvt	"	I.	" "	2.	" " " "
12	Thomas Creech	"	"	K.	Anemia	"	" " " "
13.	J.D. Evans.	"	"	"	Typhoide Febris	"	" " " "
14	J. Brock	"	"	"	" " "	"	" " " "
15	Lish Evans	"	"	"	Measles. "	"	" " " "
16	Thomas Couch	Pvt	66	A.	Wounded through the bowells in at the back	1.	Seriously.

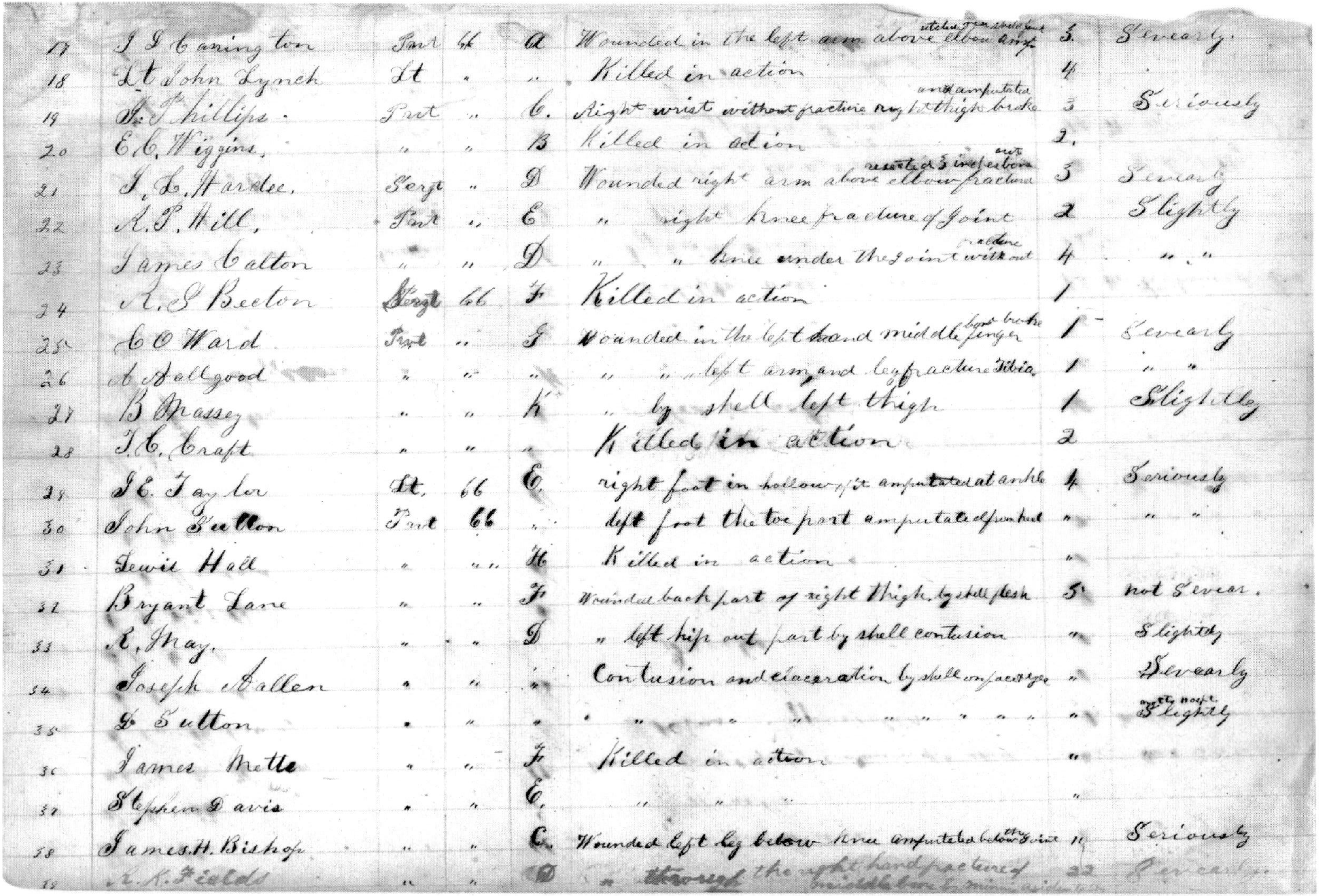

17	J J Carington	Pvt	66	A	Wounded in the left arm above elbow ampt	3.	Severaly
18	Lt John Lynch	Lt	"	"	Killed in action	4	
19	R. Phillips	Pvt	"	C.	Right wrist without fracture right thigh broke and amputated	3	Seriously
20	E. C. Wiggins,	"	"	B	Killed in action	2.	
21	J. L. Hardee,	Sergt	"	D	Wounded right arm above elbow fracture resected 3 in. of bone out	3	Severaly
22	A. P. Hill,	Pvt	"	E	" right knee fracture of joint	2	Slightly
23	James Catton	"	"	D	" " knee under the joint without fracture	4	" "
24	R. S Beeton	Sergt	66	F	Killed in action	1	
25	C O Ward	Pvt	"	G	Wounded in the left hand middle finger bone broke	1	Severaly
26	A Allgood	"	"	"	" " left arm and leg fracture tibia	1	" "
27	B Massey	"	"	K	" by shell left thigh	1	Slightly
28	T. C. Craft	"	"	"	Killed in action	2	
29	J. C. Taylor	Lt.	66	E.	right foot in hollow of it amputated at ankle	4	Seriously
30	John Fulton	Pvt	66	"	left foot the toe part amputated from heel	"	" "
31	Lewis Hall	"	"	H	Killed in action	"	
32	Bryant Lane	"	"	F	Wounded back part of right thigh by shell flesh	5	not Severe.
33	R. May,	"	"	D	" left hip out part by shell contusion	"	Slightly
34	Joseph Allen	"	"	"	Contusion and laceration by shell on face & eye	"	Severaly
35	L. Sutton	"	"	"	" " " " " " " "	"	Slightly
36	James Metts	"	"	F	Killed in action	"	
37	Stephen Davis	"	"	E.	" "	"	
38	James H. Bishop	"	"	C.	Wounded left leg below knee amputated below the joint	"	Seriously
39	R. K. Fields	"	"	D	" ~~through~~ the right hand fracture of middle bone [illegible]	22	Severaly

40.	W Latta	Pvt	6	A.	Typhoide Febris	6.	Hospitl Petersburg Va
41.	J Cross	"	"	G	Measles	"	" " " "
42.	Charles M. Herndon.	"	"	A.	Wounded on left hip by contusion of a shell	6.	Not Severe.
43.	John. Holeway.	"	"	"	~~Febris~~ Typhoidles	7.	Hospitl Richmond Va
44.	J. Leonard.	"	"	B	"	7.	" " "
45.	J.W. Cook	"	"	"	Measles	7.	" " "
46.	C F Fields.	"	"	F	" "	7.	" " " "
47.	R Woodard	"	"	K	" "	7.	" " " "
48.	C. Hines.	"	"	"		7.	" " " " "
49	D Johnson	"	"	A.	Typhoidlee	8.	Hospitl Richmond Va
50	A. Bryant	"	"	E.	" "	"	" " "
51	William Carter	"	"	G.	Killed in action	10	
52	Bryant Glysson	"	"	K	" " "	14	
53	W.B. Ferry.	"	"	D.	" " "	16	
54	W. Couch	"	"	A.	Debilitas with fever	16	H Richmond Va
55	George. Herring	Courier	"	C.	Typhoide Fever	13	" " " "
56	W.L. Thomas	Pvt	"	D.	Rubeola	"	" " " "
57	A. L. Pate	"	"	E.	Wounded through the left hand by minnie ball	2	Slightly
58	A Carter	"	"	F.	Typhoide Fever	16	H Richmond Va
59	C Vanhoy	"	"	"	Dyspepsia with fever	"	" " " "
60	J.S. Arrian	"	"	H.	Wounded through the ~~left~~ right arm by minnie flesh in above elbow	13	Severely

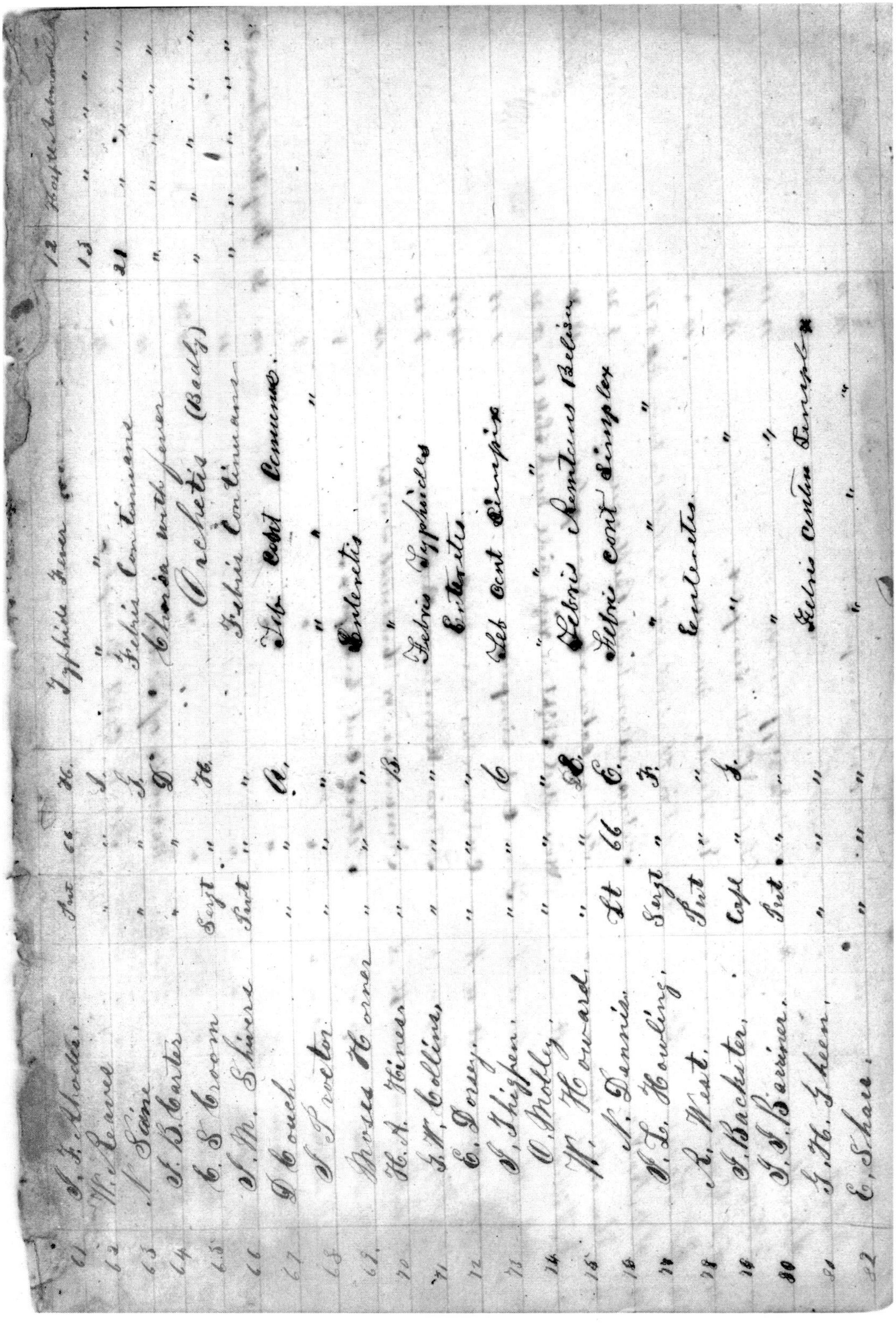

61	J. F. Rhodes.	Pvt	66	H.	Typhide Fever	12	Hosptl [illegible]
62	W. Reaves	"	"	I.	" "	13	" " " "
63	N. Sane	"	"	G.	Febris Continuans	21	" " " "
64	J. B. Carter	"	"	D	Chorea with fever	"	" " " "
65	E. S. Croom	Sergt	"	H.	Orchetis (Badly)	"	" " " "
66	J. M. Shivers	Pvt	"	"	Febris Continuans	"	" " " "
67	D Couch	"	"	A.	Feb Cont Comunis.		
68	J Proctor	"	"	"	" " "		
69	Moses Horner	"	"	"	Enteretis.		
70	H. A. Hines	"	"	B.	"		
71	G. W. Collins.	"	"	"	Febris Typhoides		
72	E. Dorsey.	"	"	"	Enteretes.		
73	J. Thigpen.	"	"	C	Feb Cont Simplex		
74	O. Mobley.	"	"	"	" " "		
75	W. Howard.	"	"	E.	Febris Remitans Belisu		
76	N. Dennis.	Lt	66	E.	Febris cont Simplex		
77	J. L. Howling.	Sergt	"	F.	" " "		
78	R. West.	Pvt	"	"	Enteretes.		
79	J. Backster.	Corpl	"	G.	" "		
80	J. J. Barriner.	Pvt	"	"	" "		
81	G. H. Gheen.	"	"	"	Febris contin Simplex		
82	E. Shaw.	"	"	"	" " "		

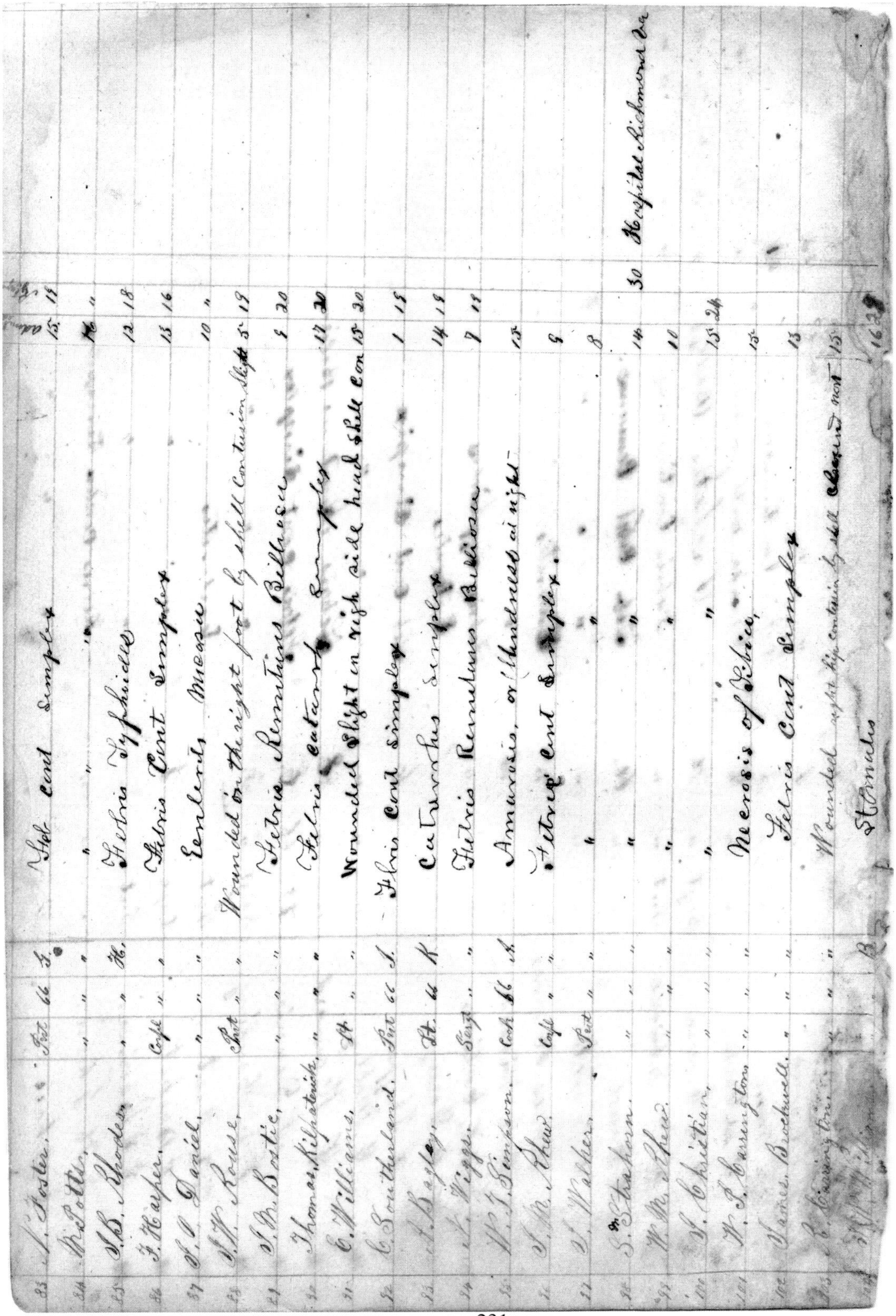

83	N. Foster.	Pvt	66	G.	Feb cont simplex	15.	18	
84	W. Potts.	"	"	"	" "	16	"	
85	J.B. Rhodes.	"	"	H.	Febris Typhoides	12	18	
86	F. Harper.	Corpl	"	"	Febris Cont Simplex	13	16	
87	J.O. Daniel.	"	"	"	Enteritis Mucosa	10	"	
88	J.W. Rouse.	Pvt	"	"	Wounded on the right foot by shell Contusion Slight	5	18	
89	J.M. Bostic.	"	"	"	Febris Remittens Billiosa	8	20	
90	Thomas Kilpatrick.	"	"	"	Febris catarrh simplex	17	20	
91	C. Williams.	Lt	"	"	Wounded Slight in righ side head Shell Con	15	20	
92	C. Southerland.	Pvt	66	I.	Febris Cont simplex	1	15	
93	A. Bagley.	Lt.	66	K	Catarrhus simplex	14	18	
94	J. Wiggs.	Sergt	"	"	Febris Remittens Billiosa	7	18	
95	W.T. Simpson.	Cook	66	A.	Amaurosis, or blindness at night	15		
96	J.M. Rhew.	Corpl	"	"	Febris Cont Simplex.	9		
97	J. Walker.	Pvt	"	"	" "	8		
98	Wm Strahorn.	"	"	"	" "	14	30	Hospital Richmond Va
99	W.M. Rhew.	"	"	"	" "	10		
100	J. Christian.	"	"	"	" "	15	24	
101	W.T. Carrington.	"	"	"	Necrosis of Tibia,	15		
102	James Brockwell.	"	"	"	Febris Cont Simplex	13		
103	R. Carrington.	"	"	"	Wounded right hip contusion by shell [illegible] not	15		
104	W.P. Williams			B	Stomatis	16	2[illegible]	

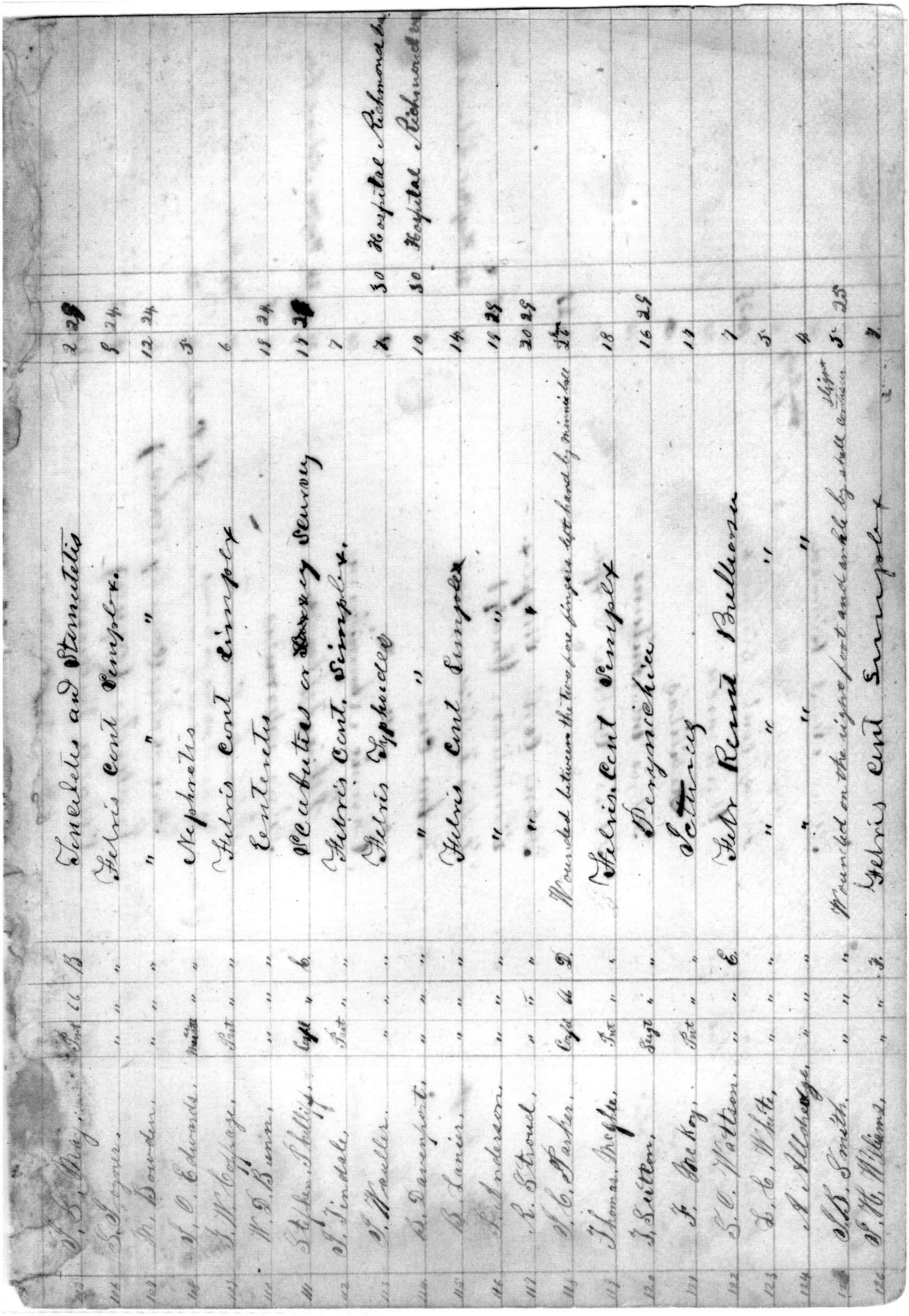

105	T. L. May	Pvt	66	B	Tonsilitis and Stomatitis	2	29		
106	S. Joyner	"	"	"	Febris Cont Simplex	8	24		
107	M. Bowden	"	"	"	" " "	12	24		
108	T. O. Edwards	Musician	"	"	Nephritis	5			
109	J. W. Coppage	Pvt	"	"	Febris Cont Simplex	6			
110	W. D. Bunn	"	"	"	Enteritis	18	24		
111	Stephen Phillips	Corpl	"	C	Scorbutus or Scurvey	17	28		
112	J. Tindale	Pvt	"	"	Febris Cont. Simplex	7			
113	J. Waller	"	"	"	Febris Typhoides	7		30	Hospital Richmond
114	B. Davenport	"	"	"	" "	10		30	Hospital Richmond
115	B. Lanier	"	"	"	Febris Cont Simplex	14			
116	P. Anderson	"	"	"	" "	19	28		
117	R. Stroud	"	"	"	" "	20	29		
118	J. C. Parker	Corpl	66	D	Wounded between the two fore fingers left hand by minnie ball	26			
119	Thomas McGhee	Pvt	"	"	Febris Cont Simplex	18			
120	J. Sutton	Sergt	"	"	Perynichia	16	29		
121	F. McKoy	Pvt	"	"	Icterus	17			
122	S. O. Wattson	"	"	E	Febr Remit Biliosa	7			
123	L. C. White	"	"	"	" " "	5			
124	A. Allbredge	"	"	"	" " "	4			
125	S. B. Smith	"	"	"	Wounded on the right foot and ankle by shell slight contusion	5	25		
126	J. H. Williams	"	"	F	Febris Cont Simplex	7			

128	J. L. Rowling,	Sergt	66	F.	Febris Cont Simplex	11			
129	C. Nethercutt.	Pvt	"	"	" " "	4			
130	T. Dudley.	"	"	"	Febris Remit Billiosa	10			
130	D. H. Harrison	Pvt	"	"	Wounded through the right thumb by minnie ball accidentally slightly	6			
131	J. B. Stanley	Sergt	"	"	Febris cont Simplex	15	28		
132	B. A. Ross,	Pvt	"	G.	Anasarca	15			
133	P. H. Cane,	Pvt	"	"	Debilitas	15			
134	B. M. Hicks.	"	"	"	Febris intermittens	15			
135	J. Lanier.	"	"	H.	Febris Continue Simplex	10			
136	John Rayner	"	"	"	" " "	20	28		
137	J. W. Bowen.	"	"	"	Febris Cont Simplex.	21			
138	W. P. Jones.	"	"	I.	Stomatitis (badly)	16	28		
139	Charles Vaughn	"	"	"	Febris Typhoides.	20		26	Hospital Richmond Va.
140	J. A. Boswell,	"	"	K.	Febris Cont	2			
141	J. H. Bailey,	"	"	"	" "	11			
142	C. W. Williamson,	"	"	"	Chronic Rheumatism	15			
143	H. Turner,	"	"	"	Febris Typhoides.	21		26	Hospital Richmond Va.
144	G. Latta.	Lt	"	A	Febris intermittens	10	28		
145	J. W. Walker,	"	"	G.	Febris Continuens.	12		24	Hospital Richmond Va.
146	P. Davis,	Capt	"	H	(Wounded left side head by peace of shell slightly he did not go to Hospt for the wound) Continued Fever	4		27	" " "
147	S. W. Ventus,	Lt	"	I	Furunculus (cause by scabes)	8			
148	J. Smith,	"	"	"	Enteretis (acute)	14	27		
149	Lewis Bynum	Lt	66	D.	Colaca Billiosa	22			
150	J. S. Bryan	Pvt	"	"	Dysentery accuta.	24		26	General Hospital Richmond [illegible]

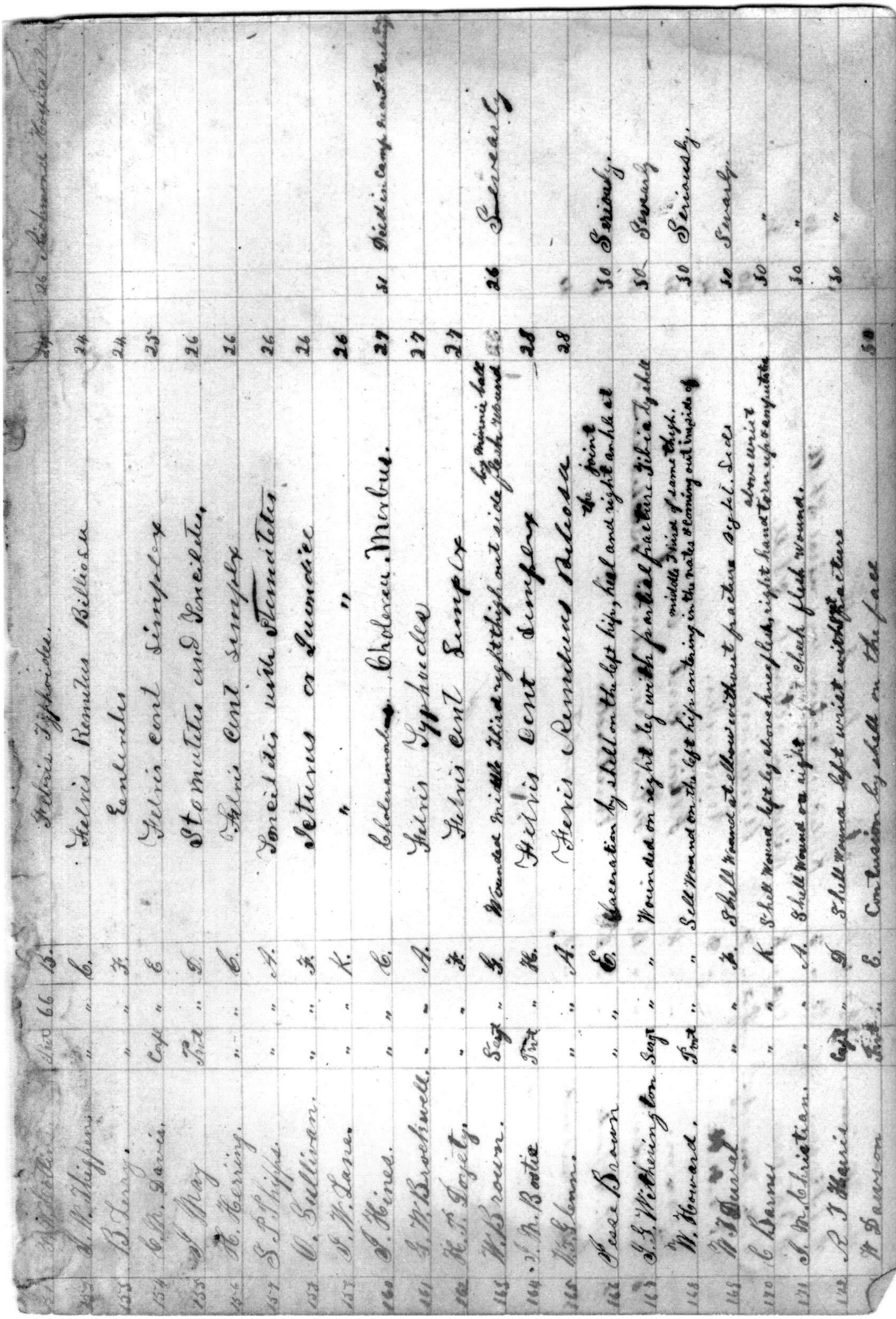

151	J. W. Collins	Pvt	66	B.	Febris Typhoides.	24	26	Richmond Hospital
152	J. W. Thippen	"	"	C.	Febris Remitus Billiosa	24		
153	B. Lerry	"	"	F.	Enteritis	24		
154	C. R. Davis	Cope	"	E	Febris cont Simplex	25		
155	J. May	Pvt	"	D.	Stomatitis and Tonsilitis	26		
156	H. Herring	"	"	C.	Febris cont simplex	26		
157	S. P. Phipps	"	"	A.	Tonsilitis with Stomatitis	26		
158	O. Sullivan	"	"	F.	Icterus or Jaundice	26		
159	J. W. Lane	"	"	K.	" "	26		
160	J. Hines	"	"	C.	Cholera Morbus	27	31	Died in Camp
161	G. W. Brockwell	-	-	A.	Febris Typhoides	27		
162	H. T. Dozety	-	-	F.	Febris cont Simplex	27		
163	W. Brown	Sergt	"	G.	Wounded middle Third right thigh out side flesh wound by minnie ball		26	Severely
164	J. M. Bostic	Pvt	"	H.	Febris Cont Simplex	28		
165	W. J. Glenn	"	"	A.	Febris Remitens Biliosa	28		
166	Jesse Brown	"	"	E.	Laceration by shell on the left hip, heel and right ankle at the joint		30	Seriously.
167	J. G. Witherington	Sergt	"	"	Wounded on right leg with partial fracture Tibia by shell		30	Severely
168	W. Howard	Pvt	"	"	Sell Wound on the left hip entering in the nates & coming out inside of middle Third of same thigh.		30	Seriously.
169	W. T. Duval	"	"	F.	Shell Wound at elbow without fracture right. Side		30	Severely.
170	C. Barnes	"	"	K.	Shell Wound left leg above knee flesh, right hand torn up & amputated above wrist		30	"
171	J. M. Christian	-	-	A.	Shell Wound on right cheek flesh wound.		30	"
172	R. T. Harris	Cept	"	D	Shell Wound left wrist with fracture		30	"
	W. Dawson	Pvt	"	E.	Contusion by shell on the face	30		

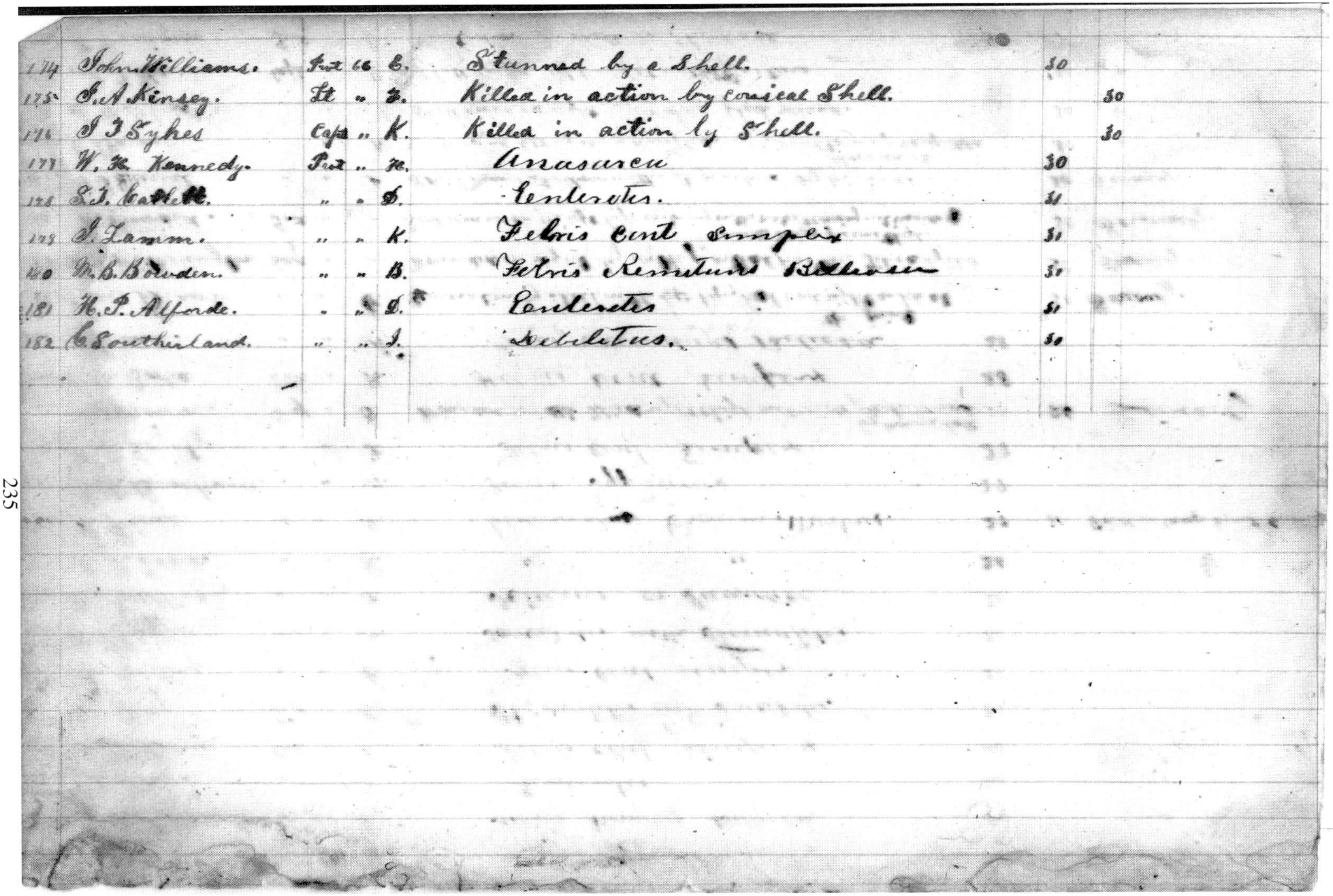

174	John Williams.	Pvt	66	E.	Stunned by a Shell.	30	
175	J. A. Kinsey.	Lt	"	F.	Killed in action by conical Shell.		30
176	J J Sykes	Capt	"	K.	Killed in action by Shell.		30
177	W. H. Kennedy.	Pvt	"	H.	Anasarca	30	
178	S. J. Cattell.	"	"	D.	Enteritis.	31	
179	J. Lamm.	"	"	K.	Febris Cont Simplex	31	
180	M. B. Bowden.	"	"	B.	Febris Remittens Biliosa	31	
181	H. P. Alforde.	"	"	D.	Enteritis	31	
182	C Southerland.	"	"	I.	Debilitas.	30	

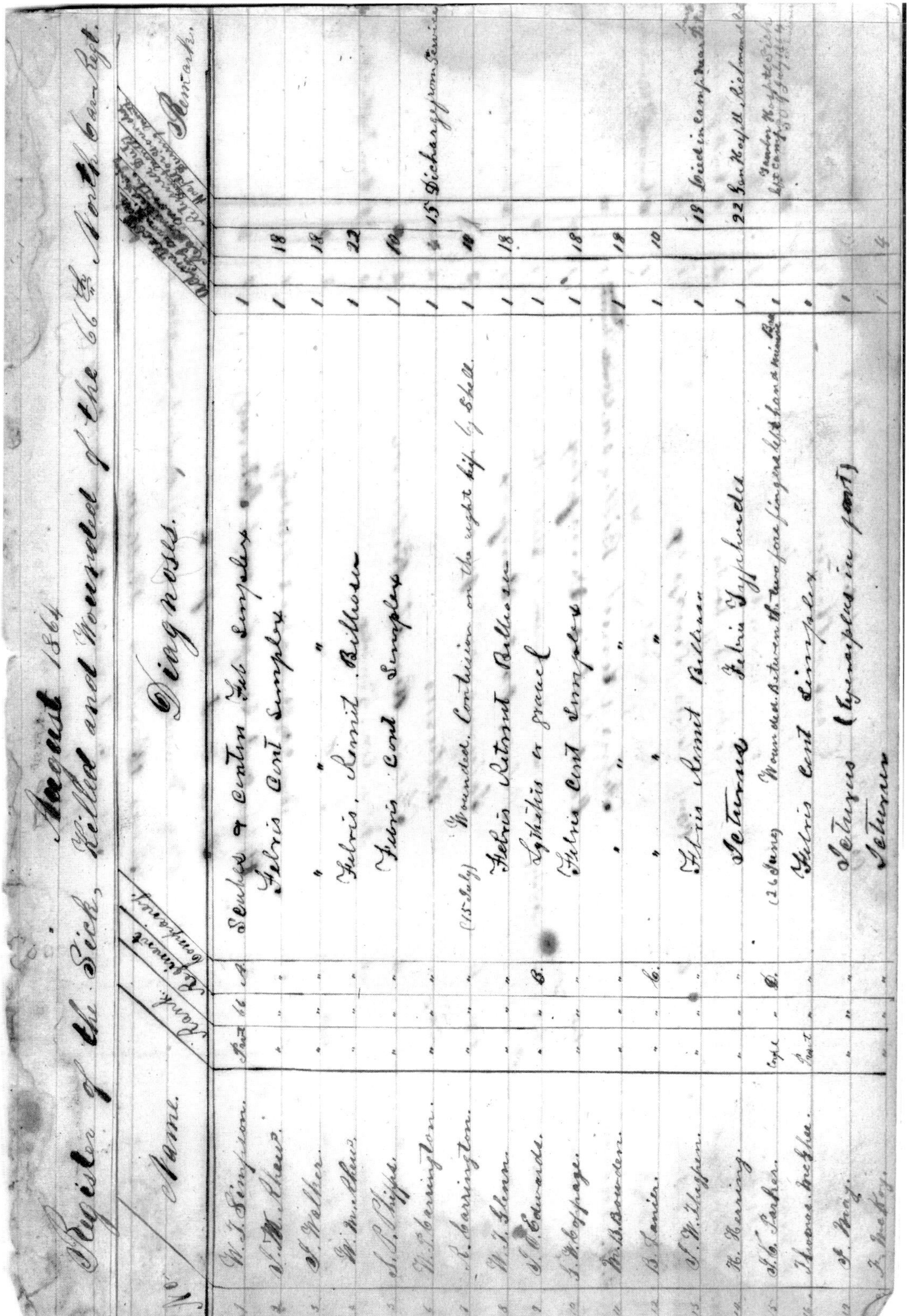
August 1864
Register of the Sick, Killed and Wounded of the 66th North Car. Regt.
No.
Name
Rank
Regiment
Company
Diagnoses
Remarks
W. T. Simpson
Scabies & Contin Feb Simplex
Febris Cont Simplex
J. Walker
W. Mathews
Febris Remit Billiosa
J. T. Phipps
W. Harrington
Discharged from Service
E. Harrington
(15 July) Wounded Contusion on the right hip by Shell
W. T. Glenn
J. Edwards
J. W. Coppage
W. B. Bowden
B. Lanier
J. W. Griffen
Died in camp near Pet.
H. Herring
Icterus
Febris Typhoides
Gen Hospl Richmond
J. C. Parker
(26 June) Wounded between the two fore fingers left hand
Thomas McGhee
J. May
Icterus (Erysipelas in foot)
Icterus

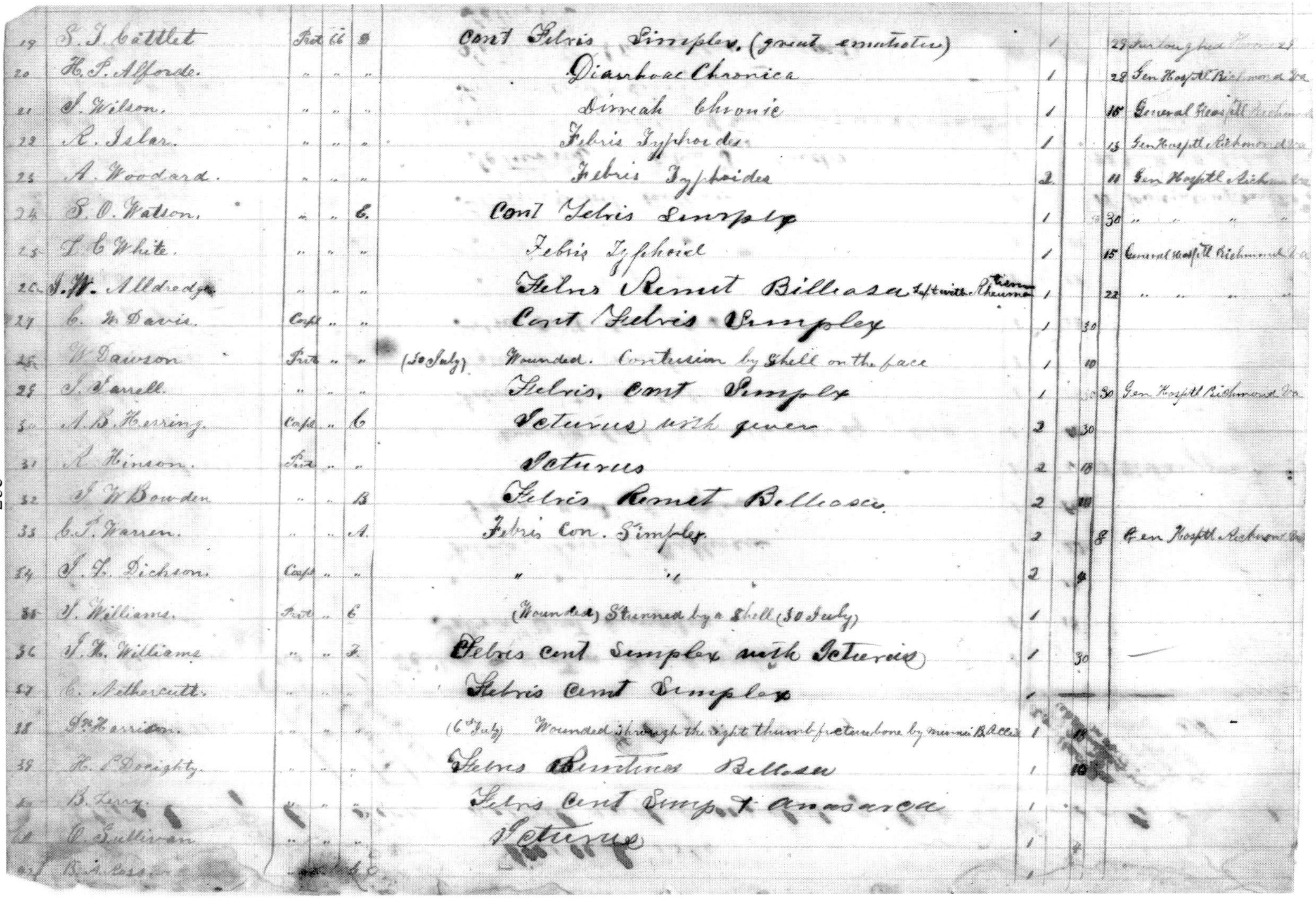

No.	Name	Rank	Regt	Co.		Disease				Disposition
19	S. J. Cattlet	Pvt	66	D		Cont Febris Simplex. (great emaciation)	1		29	Furloughed Home (?)
20	H. P. Alforde.	"	"	"		Diarrhoea Chronica	1		28	Gen Hospitl Richmond Va
21	J. Wilson.	"	"	"		Dirreah Chronic	1		15	General Hospitl Richmond
22	R. Islar.	"	"	"		Febris Typhoides	1		13	Gen Hospitl Richmond Va
23	A. Woodard.	"	"	"		Febris Typhoides	2		11	Gen Hospitl Richmond Va
24	S. O. Watson.	"	"	E.		Cont Febris Simplex	1		30	" " "
25	L. C White.	"	"	"		Febris Typhoid	1		15	General Hospitl Richmond Va
26	J. W. Alldredge.	"	"	"		Febris Remit Billiosa left with Rheumatism	1		22	" " " "
27	C. M. Davis.	Capt	"	"		Cont Febris Simplex	1	30		
28	W. Dawson	Pvt	"	"	(30 July)	Wounded. Contusion by Shell on the face	1	10		
29	J. Farrell.	"	"	"		Febris. Cont Simplex	1	30	30	Gen Hospitl Richmond Va
30	A. B. Herring.	Capt	"	C		Icterus with fever	2	30		
31	R. Hinson.	Pvt	"	"		Icterus	2	18		
32	J. W. Bowden	"	"	B		Febris Remit Belliosa	2	10		
33	C. T. Warren.	"	"	A.		Febris Con. Simplex	2		8	Gen Hospitl Richmond Va
34	J. L. Dickson.	Capt	"	"		" "	2	4		
35	J. Williams.	Pvt	"	6		(Wounded) Stunned by a Shell (30 July)	1			
36	J. H. Williams	"	"	F.		Febris cont Simplex with Icterus	1	30		
37	C. Nethercutt.	"	"	"		Febris cont Simplex	1			
38	Jn Harrison.	"	"	"	(6th July)	Wounded through the right thumb fracture bone by minnie Ballie	1	18		
39	H. L. Doughty.	"	"	"		Febris Remittens Belliosa	1	10		
40	B. Levy.	"	"	"		Febris cont Simp & Anasarca	1			
41	O. Sullivan	"	"	"		Icterus	1	4		
42	B. A. Coso	"	"	"			1			

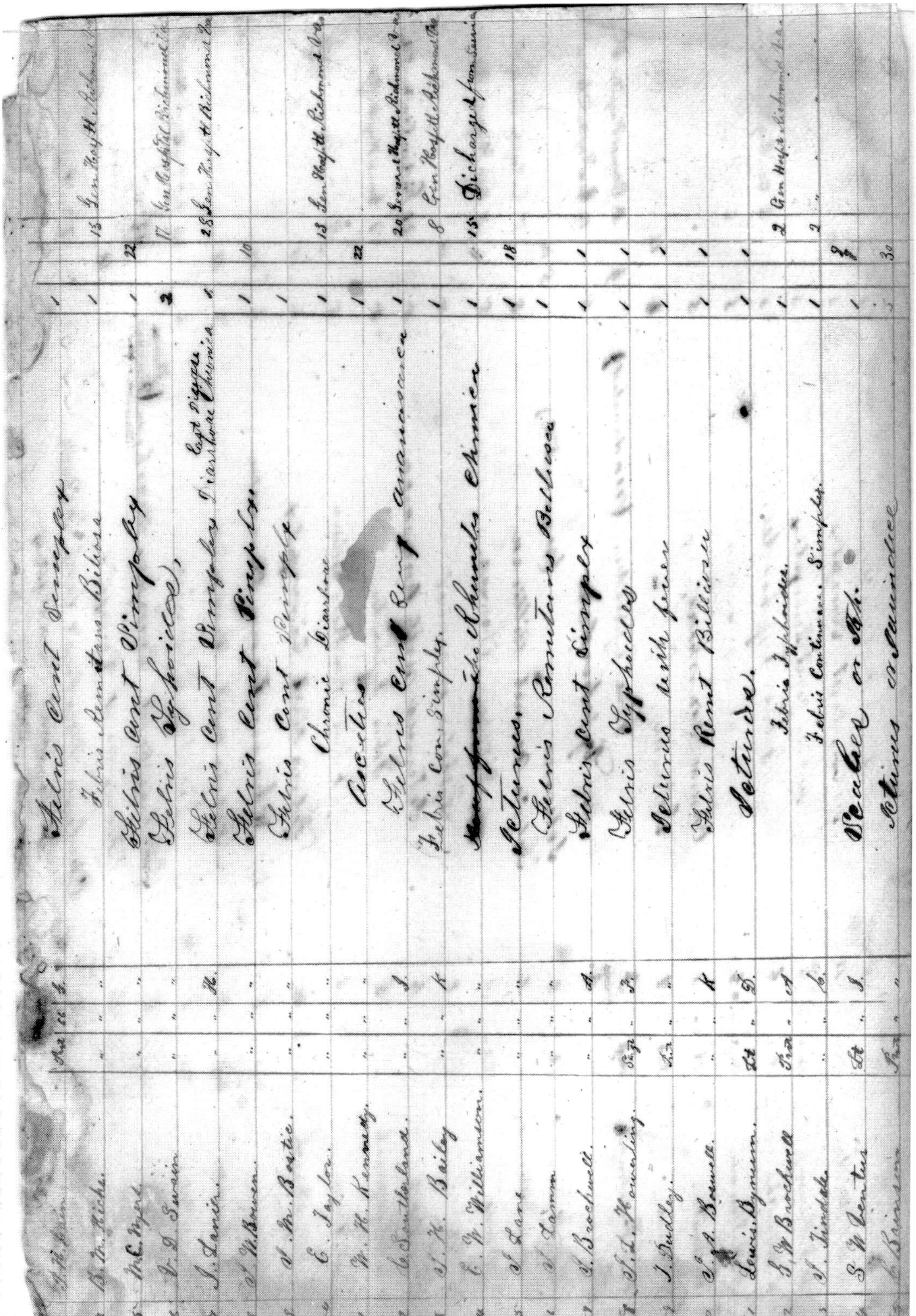

45	J. H. Kain	Pvt	11	I	Febris Cont Simplex	1			15	Gen Hosp'l Richmond
44	B. M. Hicks	"	"	"	Febris Remitens Biliosa	1			13	Gen Hosp'l Richmond Va
45	W. C. Wyatt	"	"	"	Febris Cont Simplex	1	22			
46	J. D. Swain	"	"	"	Febris Typhoides	2			17	Gen Hospital Richmond Va
47	J. Lanier	"	"	H	Febris Cont Simplex / Diarrhoea Chronica	1			28	Gen Hosp'l Richmond Va
48	J. W. Brown	"	"	"	Febris Cont Simplex	1	10			
49	J. M. Bostic	"	"	"	Febris Cont Simplex	1				
50	E. Taylor	"	"	"	Chronic Diarrhoea	1			13	Gen Hosp'l Richmond Va
51	W. H. Kennedy	"	"	"	Ascites	1	22			
52	C. Southerland	"	"	I	Febris Cont Simp / Anasarca	1			20	General Hosp'l Richmond Va
53	J. H. Bailey	"	"	K	Febris Con Simplex	1			8	Gen Hosp'l Richmond Va
54	E. W. Williamson	"	"	"	Rheumatism Chronic	1			15	Discharged from service
55	J. Lane	"	"	"	Icterus	1	18			
56	J. Lamm	"	"	"	Febris Remitens Biliosa	1				
57	J. Brockwell	"	"	A	Febris Cont Simplex	1				
58	J. L. Howerling	Sergt	"	3	Febris Typhoides	1				
59	J. Dudley	Pvt	"	"	Icterus with fever	1				
60	S. A. Boswell	"	"	K	Febris Remit Biliosa	1				
61	Lewis Bynum	Lt	"	D	Icterus	1				
62	G. W. Brockwell	Pvt	"	A	Febris Typhoides	1			2	Gen Hosp'l Richmond Va
63	J. Tisdale	"	"	C	Febris Continua Simplex	1			2	
64	S. W. Ventus	Lt	"	I	Scabies or Itch	1	9			
65	Brinson	Pvt	"	"	Icterus		30			

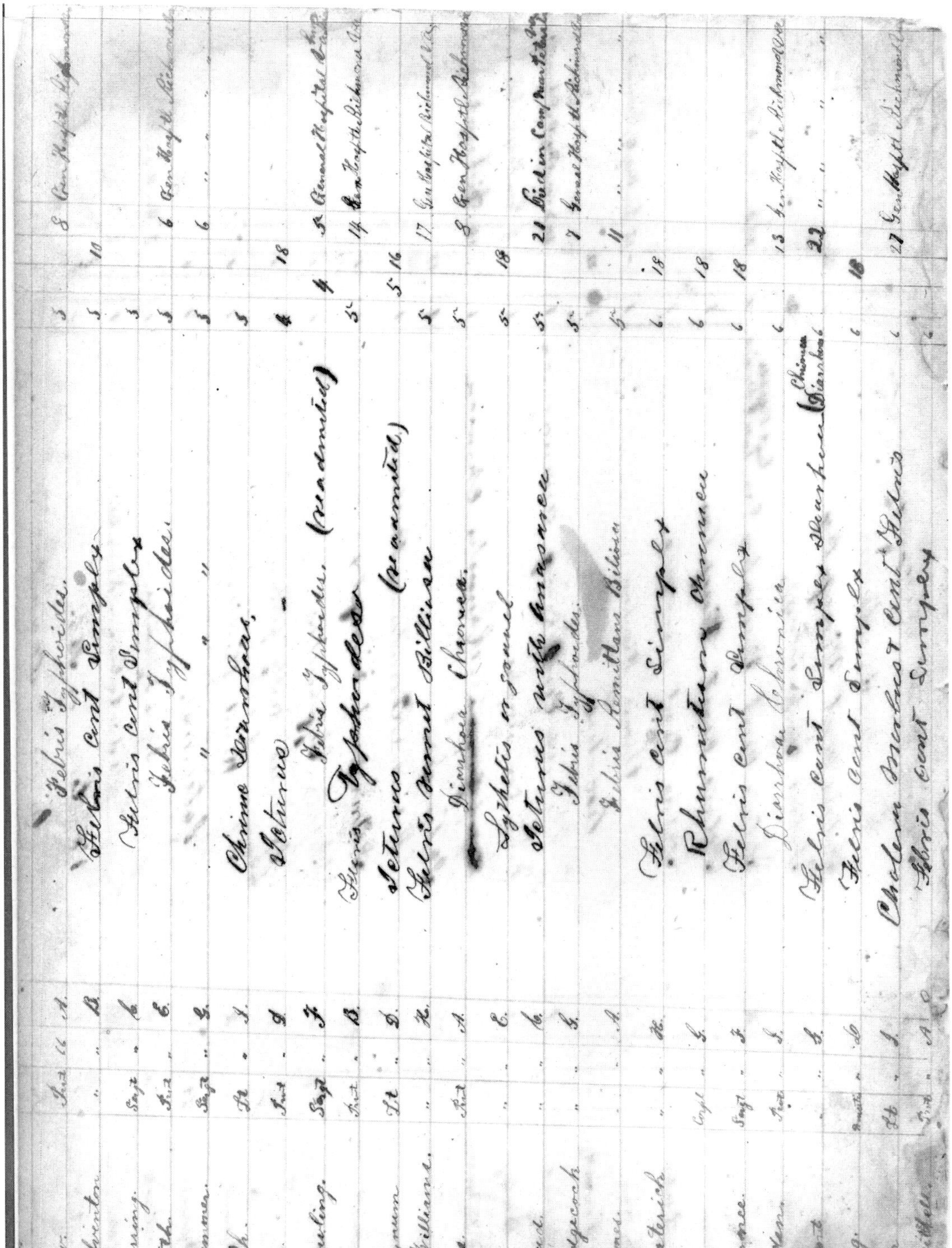

66	S. M. Chew.	Prvt	66	A.	Febris Typhoides.	5		8 Gen Hosp'tl Richmond
67	S. S. Yelventon.	"	"	B.	Febris cont Simplex	5	10	
68	B. W. Herring.	Sergt	"	C.	Febris cont Simplex	5		
69	J. W. Smith.	Prvt	"	E.	Febris Typhoides.	5		6 Gen Hosp'tl Richmond
70	R. A. Plummer.	Sergt	"	G.	" " "	5		6 " " "
71	J. Smith.	Lt	"	I.	Chronic Diarrhoea,	5		
72	E. Pearce.	Prvt	"	D.	Icterus	4	18	
73	W. L. Howling.	Sergt	"	F.	Febris Typhoides. (readmitted)	4		5 General Hospital
74	J. Baker.	Prvt	"	B.	Febris Typhoides	5		14 Gen Hosp'tl Richmond Va
75	Lewis Bynum	Lt	"	D.	Icterus (readmitted)	5	16	
76	Edward Williams.	"	"	H.	Febris remit Billiosa	5		17 Gen Hospital Richmond Va
77	J. Woods.	Prvt	"	A.	Diarrhoea Chronica.	5		8 Gen Hosp'tl Richmond
78	G. Pate.	"	"	E.	Lythetis or gravel	5	18	
79	R. Stroud.	"	"	C.	Icterus with anasarca	5		21 Died in Camp
80	A. Hedgecoch	"	"	G.	Febris Typhoides.	5		7 General Hosp'tl Richmond
81	J. N. James.			A.	Febris Remittans Biliosa	5		11 " " "
82	J. Kilpaterick	"	"	H.	Febris cont Simplex	6	18	
83	J. Payne.	Corpl	"	G.	Rheumatism Chronica	6	18	
84	J. C. Koonce.	Sergt	"	F.	Febris cont Simplex	6	18	
85	W. Landen.	Prvt	"	I.	Diarrhoea Chronica	6		13 Gen Hosp'tl Richmond Va
86	H. H. Hunt	"	"	G.	Febris cont Simplex Diarrhoea (Chronica Diarrhoea)	6		22 " " " "
87	G. Bragg.	Musician	"	D.	Febris cont Simplex	6	18	
88	J. Harper	Lt	"	I.	Cholera Morbus & cont Febris	6		27 Gen Hosp'tl Richmond Va
89	A. R. Mitchell.	Prvt	"	A.	Febris cont Simplex	6		

90	H. A. Hines	Prvt 16	B.	Febris cont Simplex	7		
91	D. Worlie	" "	C.	" "	7		
92	B. Georgenus	" "	I.	Febris Remit Billiosa	7		
93	W. S. Barrow	Sergt "	A.	Convelesent from measles	7	10	Returned from Home from [illegible]
94	J. J. James	Prvt "	A.	" " "	7	10	" " " "
95	H. Glenn	" "	A.	" " "	7	10	" " " "
96	D King	" "	F	Febris Remit Billiosa	8		
97	A. Lee	" "	E.	Febris Remit Billiosa	8		
98	B. Ham	" "	H.	Febris cont Simplex	8		
99	W. Whitmen	" "	"	Icterus	8	30	
100	J. J. Hines	" "	C	Icterus	8		Deserted 24 from the Infy near Petersburg
101	J Browning	" "	A	Febris. Remit Billiosa	8		
102	B. F. Whitley	Sergt "	K.	Icterus	8	22	
103	S. J. Phipps	Prvt "	A.	Febris Remittens Biliosa	8	11	Gen Hospt Richmond
104	B Wood	" "	B.	Icterus	8	22	Deserted 22 from the Infy near Petersburg
105	J. P. Gains	Musician "	K.	Febris cont Simplex	10		
106	C. G. Blackmer	Capt "	G.	~~[illegible]~~ Orterea	10		
107	G. W. Thomas	Prvt "	"	Poisened on arm	10	18	
108	C. A. Jenkins	" "	"	Rhumatism	10		
109	J Herring	" "	C.	Icterus	10		
110	E. Summersill	"	I	Icterus	11		
111	H. Washburn	" "	"	Febris Remt Billiosa	11		

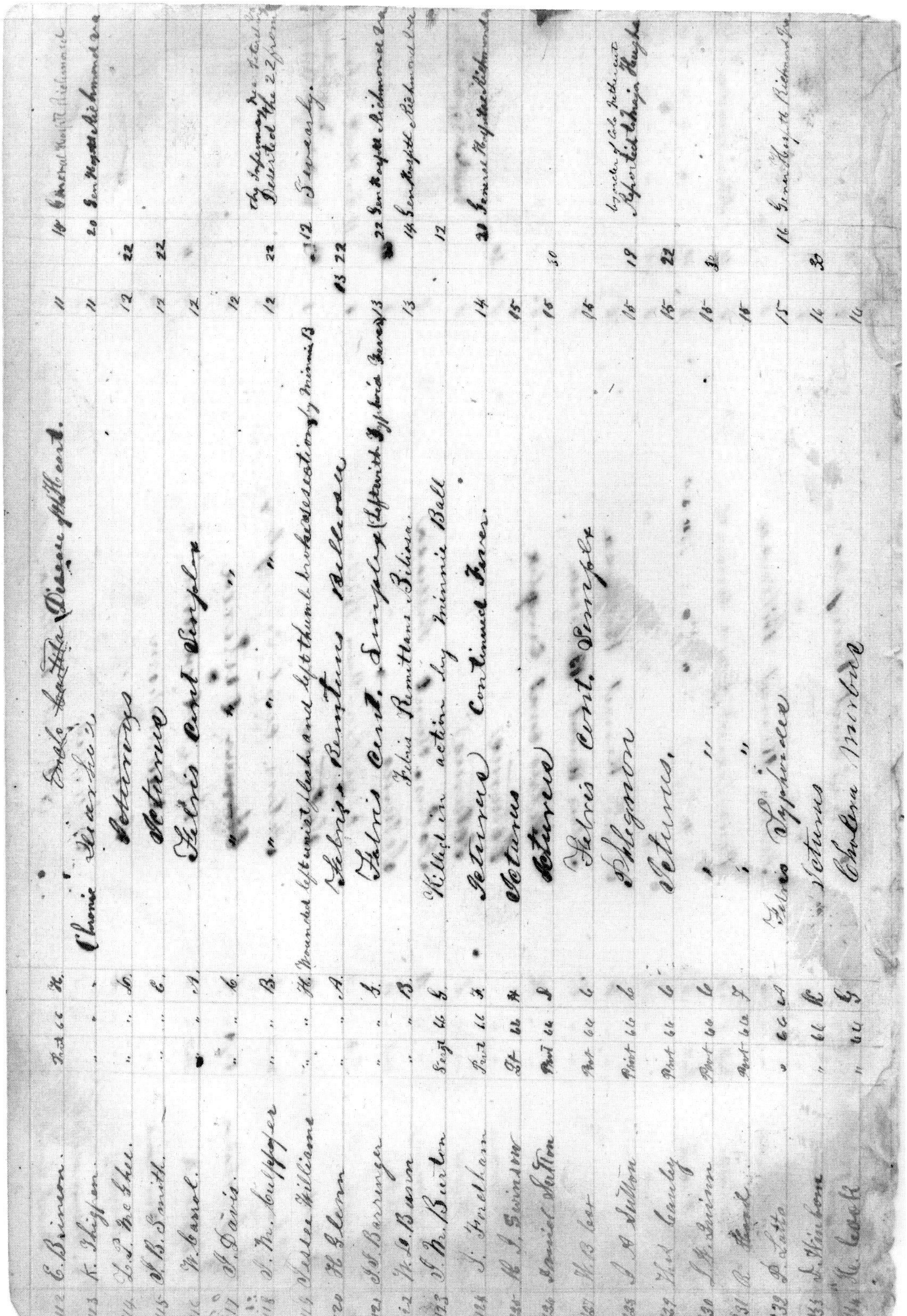

112	E. Brinson.	Pvt 66	H.	~~Endo Carditis~~ Disease of the Heart.	11		18 General Hospital Richmond
113	K. Thigpen.	" "	"	Chronic Diarrhoea	11		20 Gen Hospttl Richmond Va
114	L. P. McGhee.	" "	D.	Icterus	12	22	
115	J. B. Smith.	" "	E.	Icterus	12	22	
116	W. Carrol.	" "	A.	Febris Cont Simplex	12		
117	J. Davis.	" "	C.	" " "	12		
118	J. M. Culpepper	" "	B.	" " "	12	22	The Infirmary [illegible] Deserted the 22 from
119	Jesse Williams	" "	H.	Wounded left wrist flesh and left thumb broke resection by Minnie B		12	Severely.
120	H. Glenn	" "	A.	Febris Remittens Biliosa	13	22	
121	J. J. Barringer	" "	G.	Febris Cont. Simplex (Left with Typhoid Fever)	13		22 Gen Hospttl Richmond Va
122	W. D. Bunn	" "	B.	Febris Remittans Biliosa.	13		14 Gen Hospttl Richmond Va
123	J. M. Burton	Sergt 66	G.	Killed in action by minnie Ball			12
124	J. Fordham	Pvt 66	F.	Icterus Continued Fever.	14		20 General Hospital Richmond
125	H. J. Swinson	Lt 66	H	Icterus	15		
126	Daniel Sutton	Pvt 66	D	Icterus	15	30	
127	W. B. Lee	Pvt 66	C	Febris Cont. Simplex	15		
128	J. A. Sutton	Pvt 66	C	Phlegmon	15	18	by order of Colo Pettigrew Reported to Major Hughes
129	Thos Canley	Pvt 66	C	Icterus.	15	22	
130	L. W. Quinn	Pvt 66	C	" "	15	30	
131	R. Hood	Pvt 66	F	" "	15		
132	P. Latta	" 66	A	Febris Typhoides	15		16 Genl Hospttl Richmond Va
133	J. Winborn	" 66	K	Icterus	16	30	
134	H. Cook	" 66	G	Cholera Morbus	16		

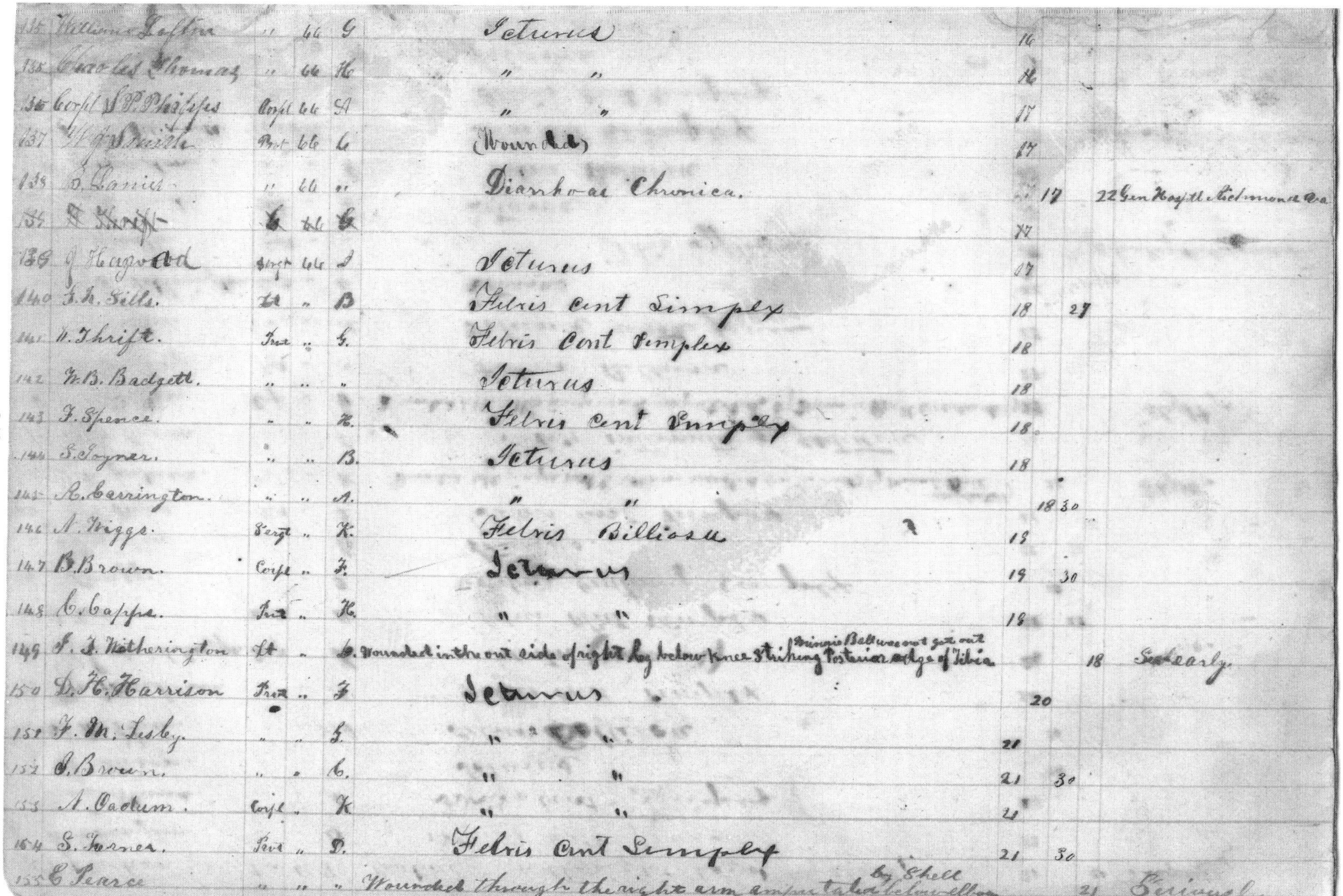

133	William Loftin	"	44	G	Icterus	16		
134	Charles Thomas	"	44	K	" "	16		
135	Corpl S.P. Phillips	Corpl	44	A	" "	17		
137	W. J. Smith	Pvt	44	C	(Wounded)	17		
138	D. Daniel	"	44	"	Diarrhoea Chronica	17		22 Gen Hosp'l Richmond Va
[illegible]	[illegible]	[illegible]	44	[illegible]		17		
139	J. Haywood	Sergt	44	I	Icterus	17		
140	J.R. Sills	Lt	"	B	Febris Cont Simplex	18	27	
141	W. Thrift	Pvt	"	G	Febris Cont Simplex	18		
142	W.B. Badgett	"	"	"	Icterus	18		
143	J. Spence	"	"	K	Febris Cont Simplex	18		
144	S. Joyner	"	"	B	Icterus	18		
145	A. Carrington	"	"	A	" "	18	30	
146	N. Wiggs	Sergt	"	K	Febris Billiosa	18		
147	B. Brown	Corpl	"	F	Icterus	19	30	
148	C. Capps	Pvt	"	K	" "	18		
149	J. J. Witherington	Lt	"	C	Wounded in the out side of right leg below knee striking posterior edge of Tibia. Minnie Ball was not got out	18		Seriously
150	D.H. Harrison	Pvt	"	F	Icterus	20		
151	J.M. Lisby	"	"	G	" "	21		
152	J. Brown	"	"	C	" "	21	30	
153	A. Oakum	Corpl	"	K	" "	21		
154	S. Turner	Pvt	"	D	Febris Cont Simplex	21	30	
155	C. Pearce	"	"	"	Wounded through the right arm amputated below elbow by Shell	21		Seriously

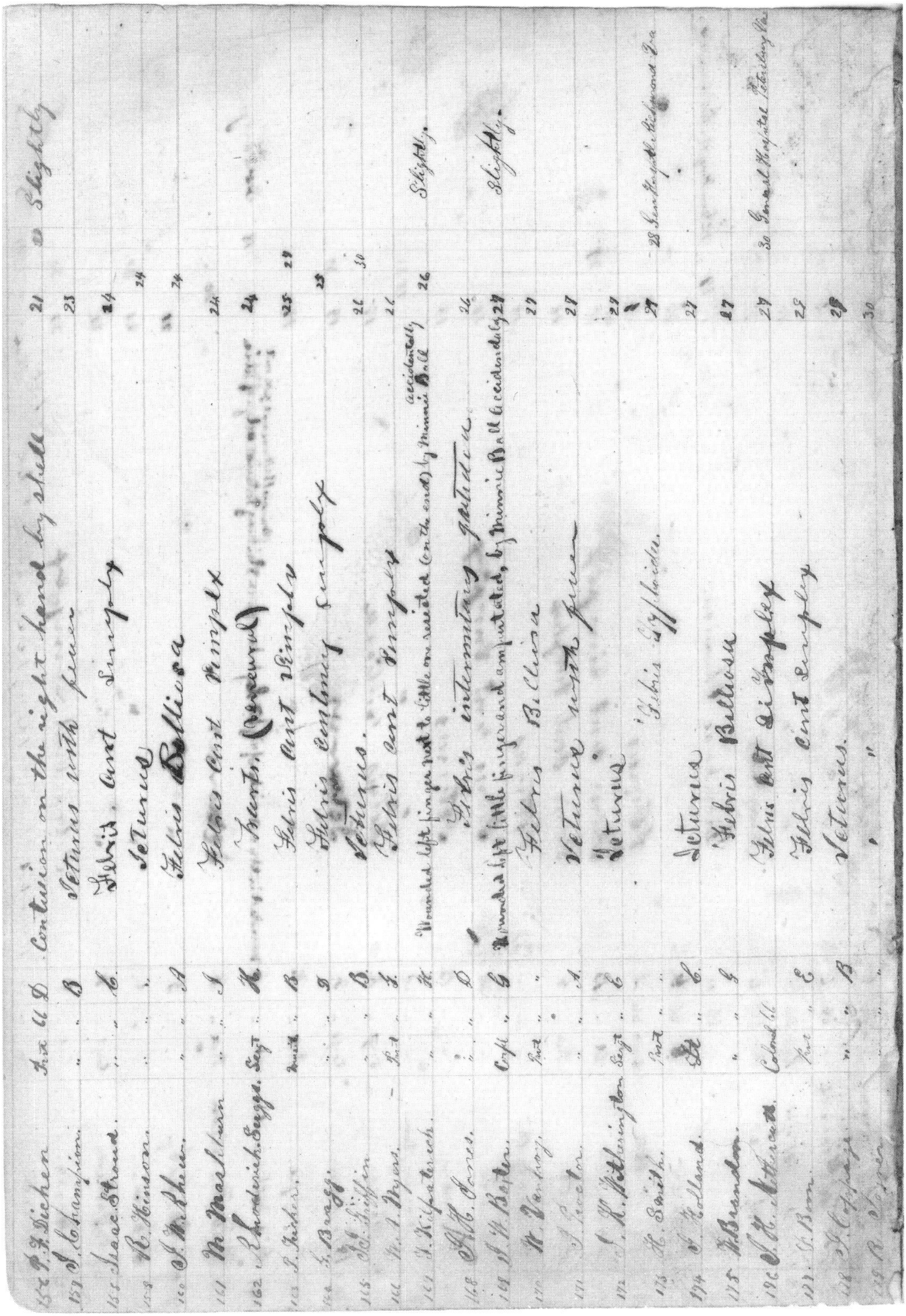

156	P. F. Dicken	Pvt 66	D	Contusion on the right hand by shell	21	[illegible]	Slightly
157	J. Champion	" "	B	Icterus with fever	23		
158	Isaac Stroud	" "	C	Febris Cont Simplex	24		
159	R. Hinson	" "	"	Icterus	24		
160	J. W. Rhew	" "	A	Febris Biliosa	24		
161	W. Washburn	" "	I	Febris Cont Simplex	24		
162	Rhoderick Suggs	Sergt	H	Vertigo (nervous)	24		
163	J. Fisher	Musik	B	Febris Cont Simplex	25	29	
164	G. Bragg	" "	D	Febris Continua Simplex	25		
165	J. C. Griffin	" "	B	Icterus	26	30	
166	W. A. Myers	Pvt	G	Febris Cont Simplex	26		
167	J. Kilpatrick	" "	H	(a) Wounded left finger next to little one resected (on the end) by Minnie Ball (accidentally)	26		Slightly
168	J. H. Jones	" "	D	Febris intermittens quotidian	26		
169	J. W. Baxter	Corpl	G	(a) Wounded left little finger and amputated, by Minnie Ball accidentaly	27		Slightly
170	W. Vanhoy	Pvt	"	Febris Biliosa	27		
171	J. Proctor	" "	A	Icterus with fever	27		
172	J. R. Witherington	Sergt	E	Icterus	27		
173	H. Smith	Pvt	"	Febris Typhoides	27	28	Gen Hospital Richmond Va
174	J. Holland	Lt	C	Icterus	27		
175	W. Brandon	" "	G	Febris Biliosa	27		
176	J. H. Nethercutt	Colonel 66		Febris Cont Simplex	27	30	General Hospital Petersburg Va
177	J. Boon	Pvt	E	Febris Cont Simplex	28		
178	J. Coppage	" "	B	Icterus	29		
179	R. Tyson	" "	"	" "	30		

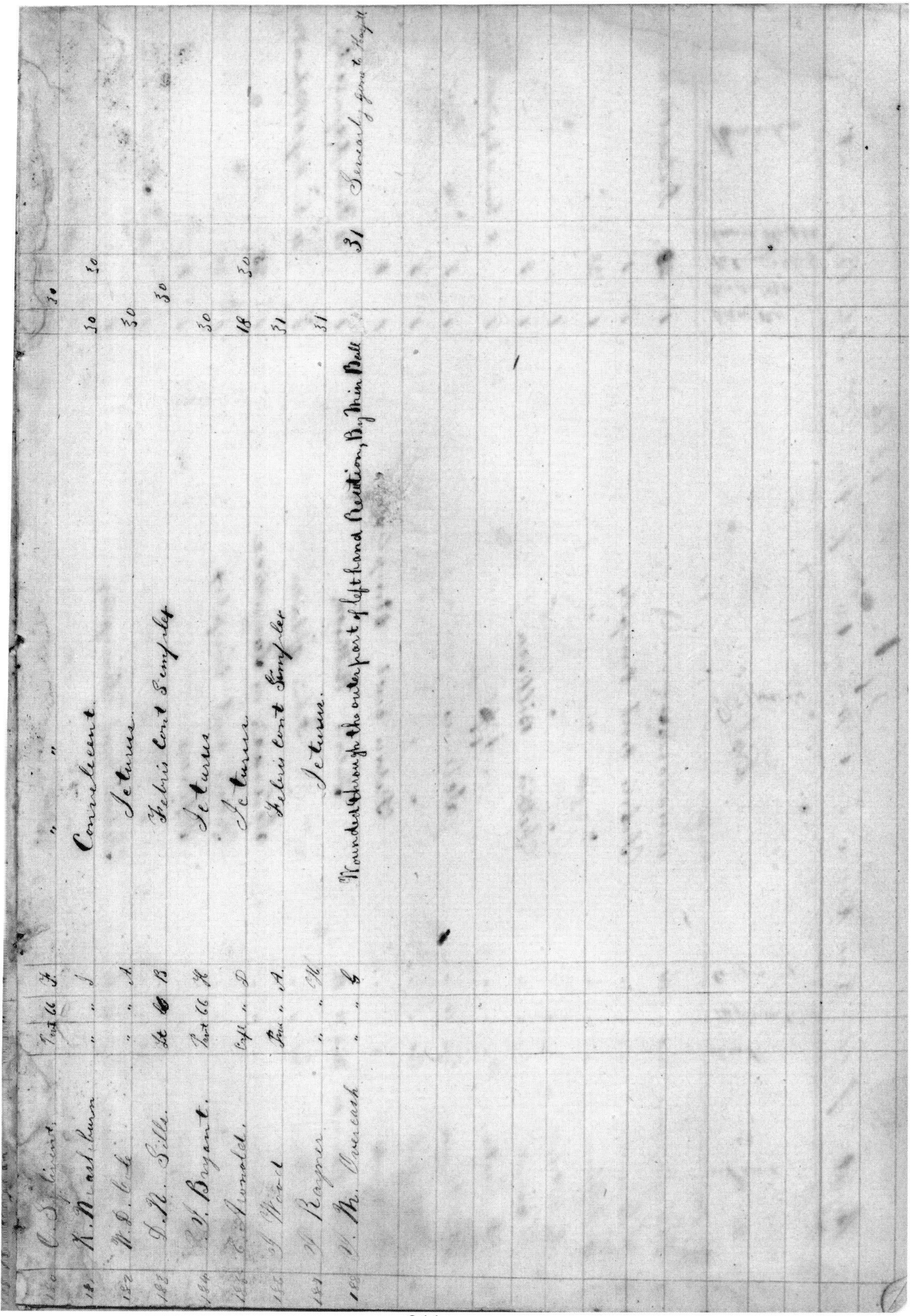

180	C. S. Vincent	Pvt	66	F	" "		30			
181	K. Washburn	"	"	I	Convalescent	30		30		
182	W. D. Cole	"	"	A	Icterus	30				
183	D. N. Sille	Lt	66	B	Febris Cont Simplex		30			
184	J. V. Bryant	Pvt	66	H	Icterus	30				
185	E. Arnold	Capt	"	D	Icterus	18		30		
186	J. Wood	Pvt	"	A	Febris Cont Simplex	31				
187	J. Rayner	"	"	K	Icterus	31				
188	V. M. Overcash	"	"	G	Wounded through the outer part of left hand Resection, By Min Ball				31	[illegible]

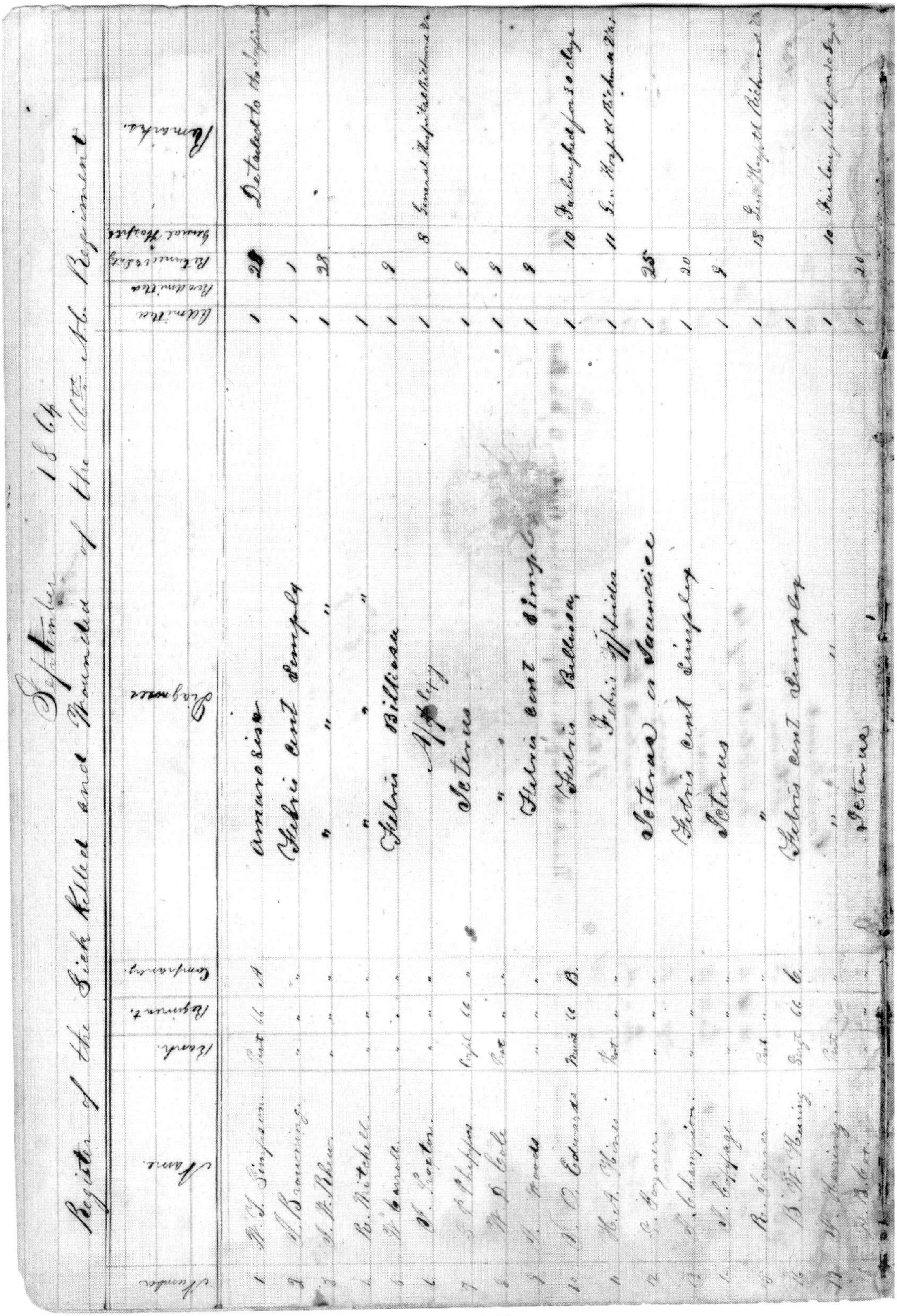

September 1864

Register of the Sick Killed and Wounded of the 66th N.C. Regiment

Number	Name	Rank	Regiment	Company	Diagnoses	Admitted	Readmitted	Returned to Duty	General Hospital	Remarks
1	W. T. Simpson.	Pvt	66	A	Amarosise	1		28		Detailed to the Infirmary
2	J. Browning.	"	"	"	Febris cont Simplex	1		1		
3	J. W. Rhew.	"	"	"	" " "	1		28		
4	R. Mitchell.	"	"	"	" " "	1				
5	W Carroll.	"	"	"	Febris Billiosa	1		9		
6	J. Proctor.	"	"	"	Apoplexy	1			8	General Hospital Richmond Va
7	S. P. Phepps	Corpl	66	"	Icterus	1		9		
8	W. D. Cole	Pvt	"	"	" "	1		9		
9	J. Woods	"	"	"	Febris cont Simplex	1		9		
10	J. O. Edwards	Music	66	B.	Febris Billiosa	1			10	Furloughed for 30 days
11	H. A. Hines	Pvt	"	"	Febris Typhoides	1			11	Gen Hospitl Richmond Va.
12	S. Joyner.	"	"	"	Icterus or Jaundice	1		25		
13	J. Champion.	"	"	"	Febris cont Simplex	1		20		
14	J. Coppage.	"	"	"	Icterus	1		9		
15	R. Joyner.	Pvt	"	"	"	1			18	Gen Hospitl Richmond Va
16	B. W. Herring	Sergt	66	C.	Febris cont Simplex	1				
17	J. Herring.	Pvt	"	"	" "	1			10	Furloughed for 30 Days
18	H. B. Cox.	"	"	"	Icterus	1		20		

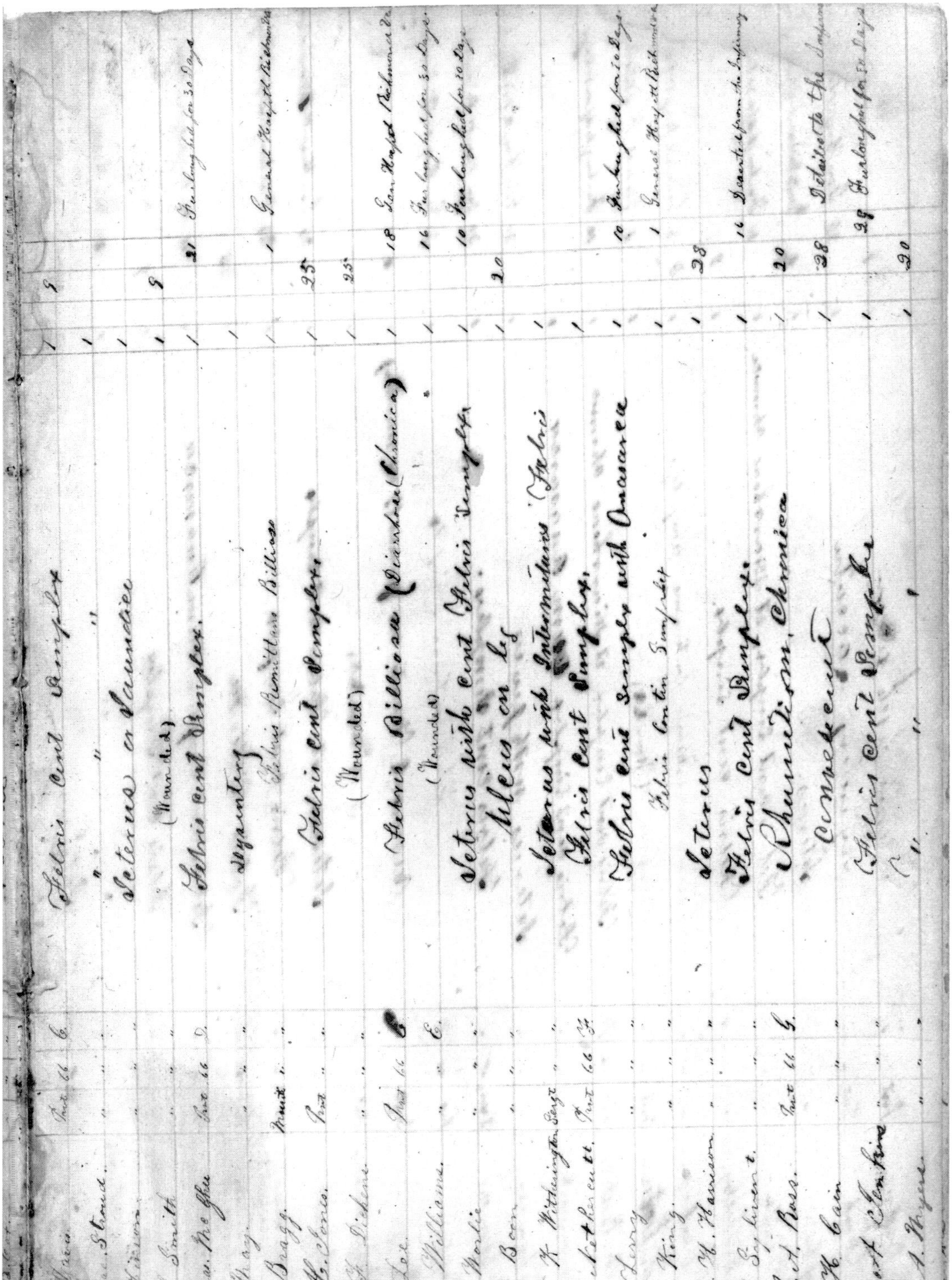

19	[illegible] Jones	Pvt	66	C	Febris Cont Simplex	1	8	
20	Isaac Strand	"	"	"	" "	1		
21	R. [illegible]	"	"	"	Icterus or Jaundice	1		
22	A.J. Smith	"	"	"	(Wounded)	1	9	
23	Thomas McGhee	Pvt	66	D	Febris cont Simplex	1	21	Furloughed for 30 Days
24	J. May	"	"	"	Dysentery	1		
25	J. Bragg	Music	"	"	Febris Remittans Billiosa	1	1	General Hospt Richmond
26	A.H. Jones	Pvt	"	"	Febris cont Simplex	1	25	
27	J.H. Dickens	"	"	"	(Wounded)	1	25	
28	C. Lee	Pvt	66	E	Febris Billiosa (Diarrhoea (Chronica)	1	18	Gen Hospt Richmond
29	J. Williams	"	"	E	(Wounded)	1	16	Furloughed for 30 Days
30	D. Worlie	"	"	"	Icterus with cont Febris Simplex	1	10	Furloughed for 20 Days
31	F. Boon	"	"	"	Ulcers on leg	1	20	
32	J.K. Witherington	Sergt	"	"	Icterus with Intermittens (Febris	1		
33	C. Netherentt	Pvt	66	F	Febris Cont Simplex	1		
34	B. Lowry	"	"	"	Febris cont simplex with Anasarca	1	10	Furloughed for 20 Days
35	D. King	"	"	"	Febris Contin Simplex	1	1	General Hospt Richmond
36	D.H. Harrison	"	"	"	Icterus	1	28	
37	O. [illegible]	"	"	"	Febris cont Simplex	1	14	Deserted from the Infirmary
38	B.A. Ross	Pvt	66	G	Rheumatism Chronica	1	20	
39	T.H. Cain	"	"	"	Convalescent	1	28	Detailed to the Infirmary
40	Burt Jenkins	"	"	"	Febris Cont Simplex	1	28	Furloughed for 30 Days
41	W.A. Wynne	"	"	"	" "	1	20	

44	W. B. Badget	Pvt	66	C	Icterus with fever	1	9		
44	W. H. Cook	Pvt	"	"	Dysentery Acute	1		28	Gen Hospital Richmond Va
44	B. Loftin	"	"	"	Icterus	1		1	Gone to Richmond after [illegible]
45	J. Thrift	"	"	"	Febris cont Simplex et Ulcerations chronic	1		10	Furloughed for 30 Days
46	J. M. [illegible]	"	"	"	Febris cont Simplex	1	9		
47	J. [illegible]	"	"	"	Febris continuous Simplex	1		8	General Hospital Richmond Va
48	J. W. Baxter	Corpl	"	"	(Wounded)	1		1	General Hospital Richmond
49	J. M. Bestie	Pvt	66	K	Febris cont Simplex et Ulcerations chronic	1		10	Furloughed for 30 Days
50	J. Davenport	"	"	"	Febris cont Simplex cum Anasarca	1			
51	C. Thomas	"	"	"	Icterus with fever	1		30	Gen Hospital Richmond Va
52	J. Spence	Drum	"	"	Febris cont Simplex	1		30	Gen Hospital Richmond Va
53	C. Capps	Pvt	66	K	Febris continuous Simplex	1		2	Gen Hospital Richmond Va
54	R. Sugg	Sergt			Venereal Ulcers on penis (? in number)	1			
55	J. Kilpatrick	Pvt	"	"	(Wounded)	1			
56	J. J. Bryant	"	"	"	Icterus et Febris cont Simplex	1		29	Gen Hospital Richmond Va
57	C. Baynes	"	"	"	Febris cont Simplex	1		29	Furloughed for 30 Days
58	B. Gurganus	Pvt	66	I	Febris Billiosa	1	25		
59	C. Cunningill	"	"	"	Febris cont Simplex cum Anasarca	1		10	Furloughed for 30 Days
60	H. Washburn	"	"	"	Febris cont Simplex	1	9		
61	B. Washburn	"	"	"	"	1		30	Gen Hospital Richmond Va
62	C. [illegible]	Sergt			Icterus	1	9		

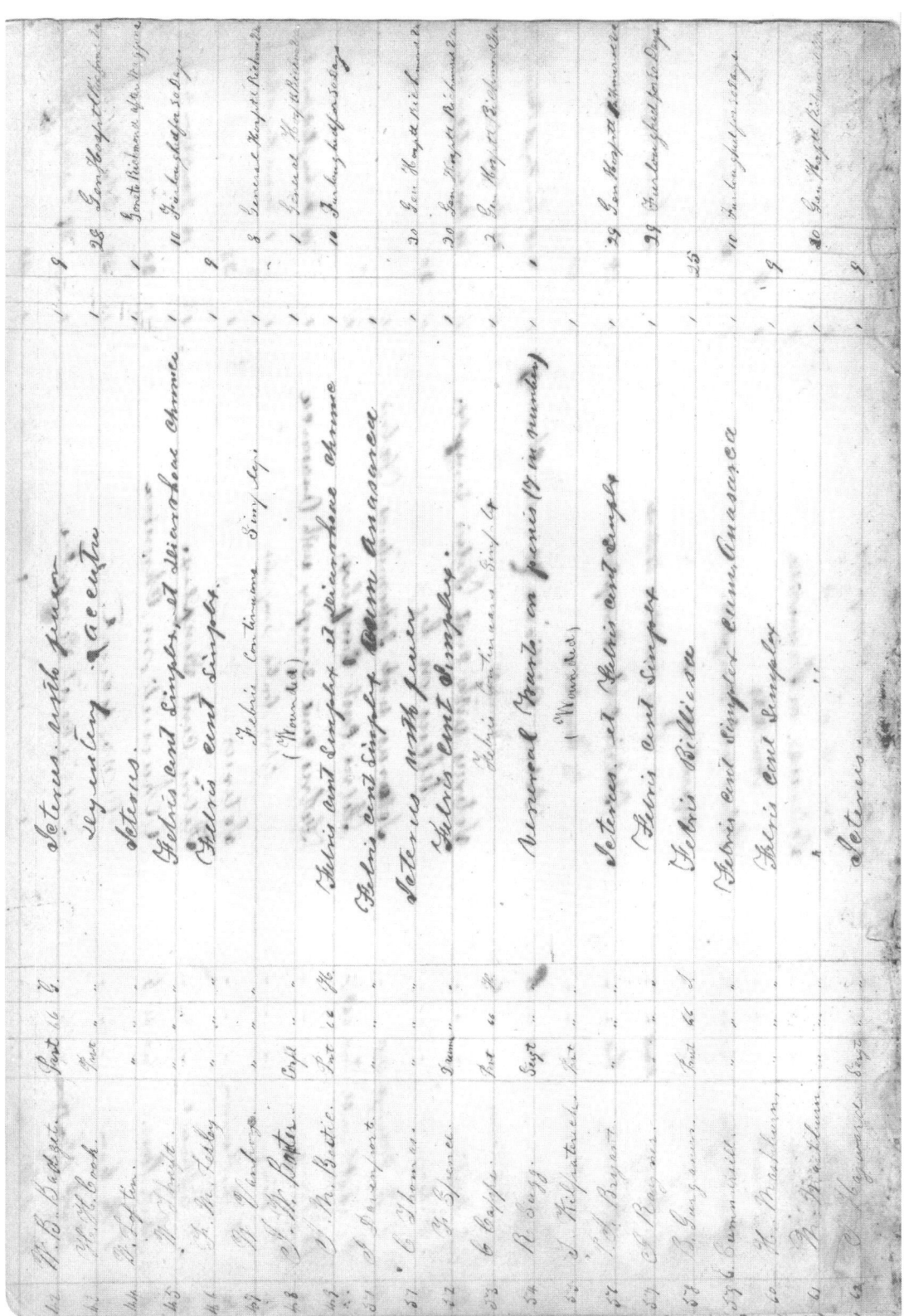

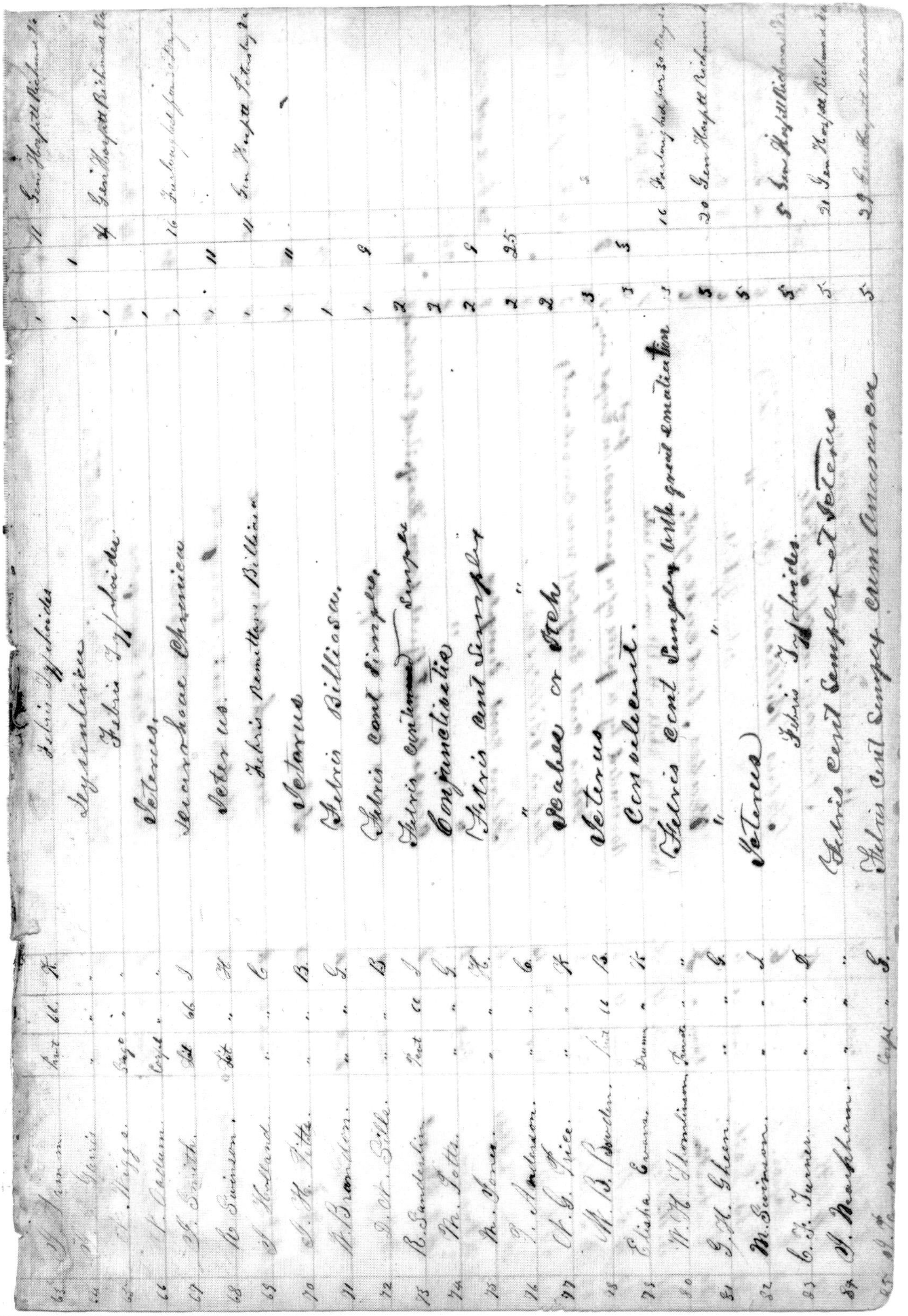

63	J. [illegible]	Pvt	66	K	Febris Typhoides	1		11	Gen Hospt Richmond Va
64	H. Geris	"	"	"	Dysenteria	1	1	4	Gen Hospt Richmond Va
65	J. Wiggs	Sergt	"	"	Febris Typhoides	1		16	Furloughed for 30 Days
66	J. Calhoun	Corpl	"	"	Icterus	1			
67	J. Smith	Lt	66	I	Diarrhoea Chronica	1	11		
68	R. Swinson	Pvt	"	H	Icterus	1	11	11	Gen Hospt Petersburg Va
69	J. Holland	"	"	C	Febris Remittens Billiosa	1			
70	J. H. Fitts	"	"	B	Icterus	1	11		
71	W. Brandon	"	"	G	Febris Billiosa	1			
72	D. W. Sills	"	"	B	Febris cont Simplex	1	9		
73	R. Sanderlin	Pvt	66	I	Febris continued Simplex	2			
74	W. Potter	"	"	G	Conjunctivitis	2			
75	W. Jones	"	"	H	Febris cont Simplex	2	9		
76	J. Anderson	"	"	C	"	2	25		
77	W. G. Price	"	"	K	Scabies or Itch	2			
78	W. B. Bowden	Pvt	66	B	Icterus	3			
79	Elisha Evans	Drum	"	K	Convalescent	3	5		
80	W. H. Tomlinson	Pvt	"	"	Febris Cont Simplex with great emaciation	3		16	Furloughed for 30 Days
81	G. H. Green	"	"	G	"	5		20	Gen Hospt Richmond
82	M. Swinson	"	"	I	Icterus	5		5	Gen Hospt Richmond Va
83	C. J. Turner	"	"	D	Febris Typhoides	5		5	Gen Hospt Richmond
84	J. Markham	"	"	[illegible]	Febris cont Simplex et Icterus	5		21	Gen Hospt Richmond Va
85	[illegible]	Corpl	"	G	Febris cont Simplex cum Anorexia	5		29	Gen Hospt Richmond

86	A. Hill	Private	66	I.	Rhumitism Chronica	5		
87	P. Whitley.	"	"	K	Neuralgia of Testicle	5	20	
88	E. Sasser.	"	"	C.	Febris Billiosa (last disease) (Febris Typhoides)	6		14 Gen Hospl Richmond
89	C.B. Dail.	Private	66	C	Febris Typhoides.	6		8 Gen Hospl Richmond Va
90	C. Austin.	Drum	"	G.	Scabes, bad case of it.	6		
91	S. Whaley.	Private	66	H.	Broozed by a shell on the left arm and side	7		Slightly.
92	W. Jenkins.	Drummer	66	G	Wounded by a piece of a percussion Capt in foot.	7	9	
93	E.G. Blackmer	Captain	"	G	Febris cont Simplex (now Convalescent)	2		6 Furloughed for 30 days
94	J.C. May	Sergt	66	B.	Febris Billiosa	8		
95	S.H. Phillips	"	"	C.	Febris cont Simplex	8		28 Gen Hospl Richmond Va
96	J Dunkin	Private	"	D	" "	8	25	
97	J.H. Stancel	"	"	K	Convalescent (just from Hospital Goldsboro)	8	20	
98	F. Foy.	Lieut	"	I	Febris cont Simplex	10		
99	W. Massey.	Private	"	K	" "	10	14	
100	J.S. Gooch.	"	"	B	Icterus	10	20	
101	J.D. Evans	Private	66	K	Diarrhoea Chronica	11		20 Gen Hospl Richmond Va
102	W.W. Williams	"	"	B.	Febris cont Simplex	11		
103	J.C. Parker	Corpl	"	I	Febris Billiosa.	11	20	
104	R. Farmon	Private	66	I.	Febris cont Simplex	11		29 Furloughed for 30 Days
105	J.W. Quinn	"	"	C	Febris Typhoides. with debilitas	11		21 Furloughed for 30 Days.
106	J Farrell	"	"	C	Debilitatis	11		21 Furloughed for 30 Days

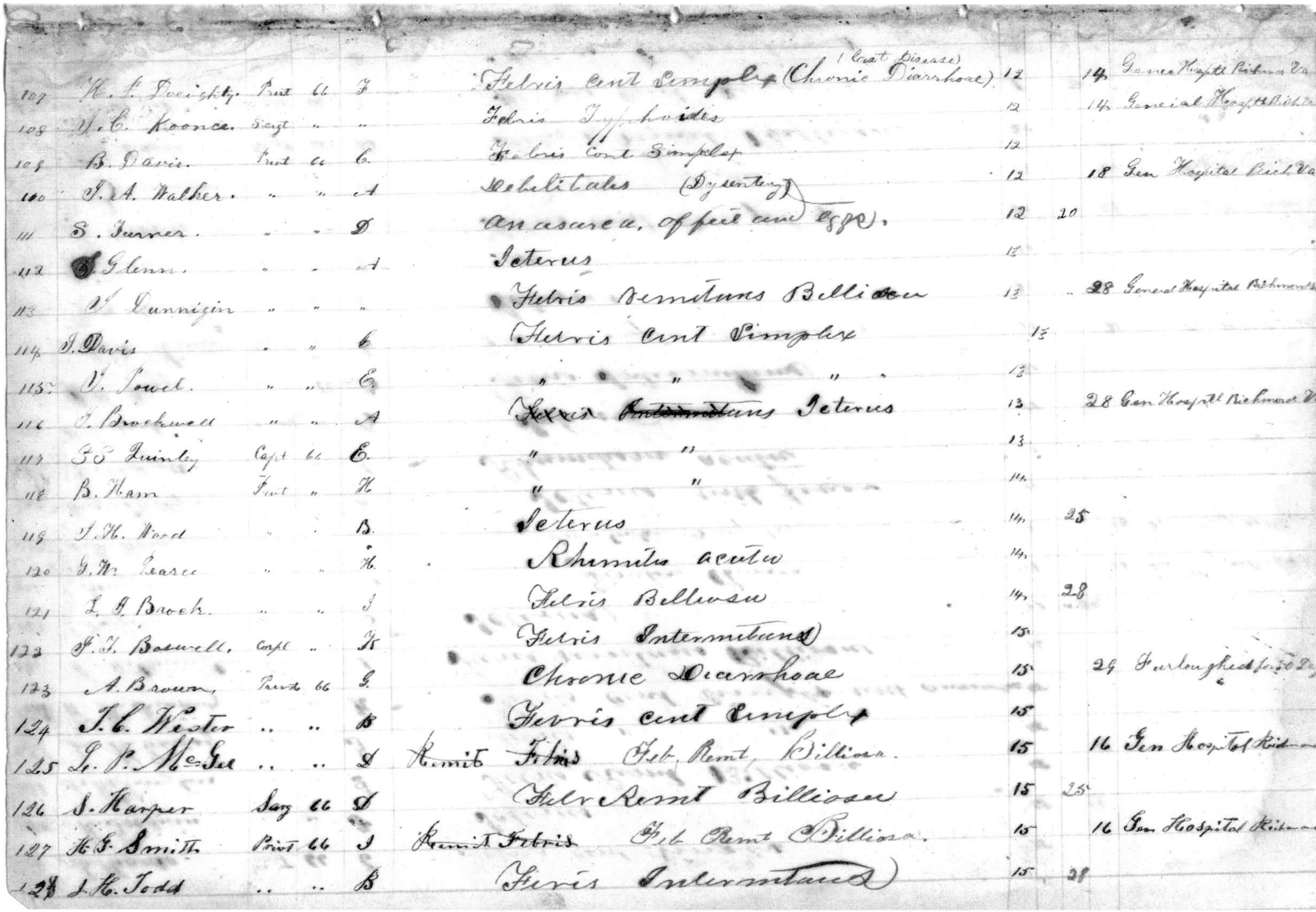

107	H. L. Doughty	Priv	66	F	Febris Cont Simplex (Chronic Diarrhoea) (Last Disease)	12		14 General Hospital Richmond Va
108	J. C. Koonce	Sergt	"	"	Febris Typhoides	12		14 General Hospital Richmond
109	B. Davis	Priv	66	C	Febris Cont Simplex	12		
110	J. A. Walker	"	"	A	Debilitas (Dysentery)	12		18 Gen Hospital Rich Va
111	S. Turner	"	"	D	Anasarca, of feet and legs	12	20	
112	J. Glenn	"	"	A	Icterus	13		
113	J. Dunnigan	"	"	"	Febris Remittens Billiosa	13		28 General Hospital Richmond Va
114	J. Davis	"	"	C	Febris Cont Simplex	13		
115	V. Powel	"	"	E	" " "	13		
116	J. Brockwell	"	"	A	~~Febris Intermittens~~ Icterus	13		28 Gen Hospital Richmond Va
117	J. S. Quinley	Capt	66	E	" "	13		
118	B. Ham	Priv	"	H	" "	14		
119	J. H. Wood	"	"	B	Icterus	14	25	
120	G. W. Pearce	"	"	H	Rheumatis acuta	14		
121	L. A. Brock	"	"	I	Febris Billiosa	14	28	
122	J. J. Boswell	Corpl	"	K	Febris Intermittens	15		
123	A. Brown	Priv	66	G	Chronic Diarrhoea	15		29 Furloughed for 30 Days
124	J. C. Wester	"	"	B	Febris Cont Simplex	15		
125	L. P. McGee	"	"	D	Remit Febris Feb Remt Billiosa	15		16 Gen Hospital Richmond
126	S. Harper	Sergt	66	D	Febr Remt Billiosa	15	25	
127	H. F. Smith	Priv	66	I	Remit Febris Feb Remt Billiosa	15		16 Gen Hospital Richmond
128	J. H. Todd	"	"	B	Febris Intermittens	15	28	

129	A. Hardo	Privt	66	E	Febris cont Simplex	15			
130	M. Goodwin	"	"	F	Icterus	15	28		
131	J. Welington	"	"	D	Febris Remt Billiosa	15			
132	J. M. Enday	"	"	G	Febris " "	15			
133	W. H. Kennedy	"	"	H	Febris cont Simplex with anasarca	15			
134	P. Witherington	Privt	66	D	Febris remitans Billiosa	16			
135	J. Griffin	Musitn	"	B	Icterus	17	24		
136	C. Simpson	Privt	66	A	Diarrhoea Chronica	18		18	Gen Hospttl Rich Va
137	W. M. Rhew	"	"	"	Febris Contin Simplex	18		18	Gen Hospttl Richmond
138	M. J. Phillips	"	"	C	Icterus with fever	18			
139	D. Padgett	"	"	H	Rhumatism acuta	18			
140	J. J. Tucker	Musitn	66	B	Icterus	19	29		
141	J. J. Wiggs	Sergt	66	B	Febris Intermitens	20			
142	A. B. Herring	Corpl	"	C	Febris Contin Simplex with Annasarca	20		21	Gen Hospttl Richmond Va
143	W. E. Morton	"	"	I	Icterus	20			
144	. Hunt	Privt	"	G	"	20			
145	G. Cobble	"	"	"	Febris cont Simplex	20		24	Gen Hospttl Richmond Va
146	B. Swinson	"	"	H	Feb Typhoides	20		22	Gen Hospttl Richm Va
147	W. J. Davis	Sergt	66	B	Febris remit Billiosa	20			
148	R. Hood	Privt	66	F	Febris cont Simplex	1	20		
149	C. L. Koonce	Musitn	"	F	Febris Intermitens	20	24		

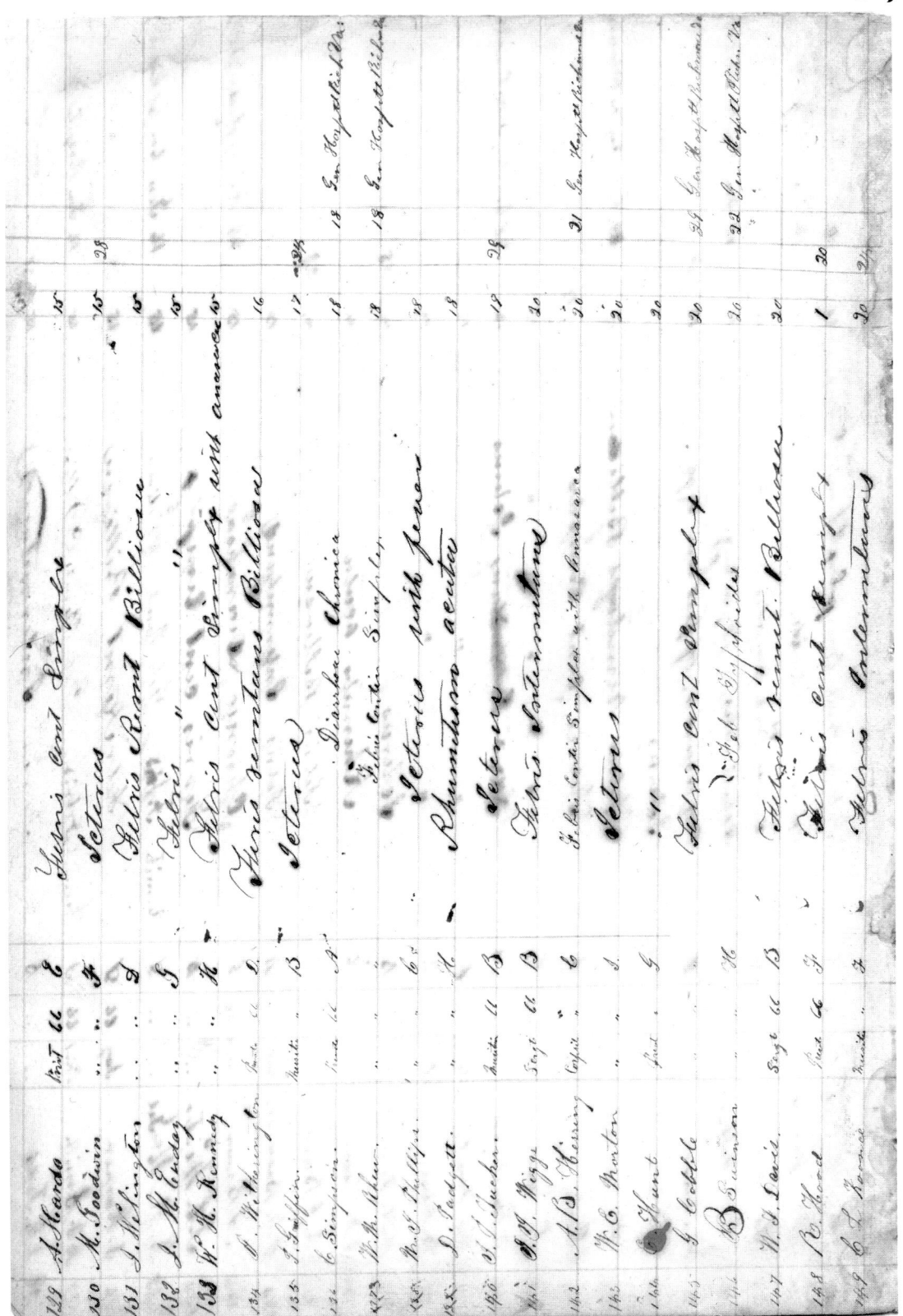

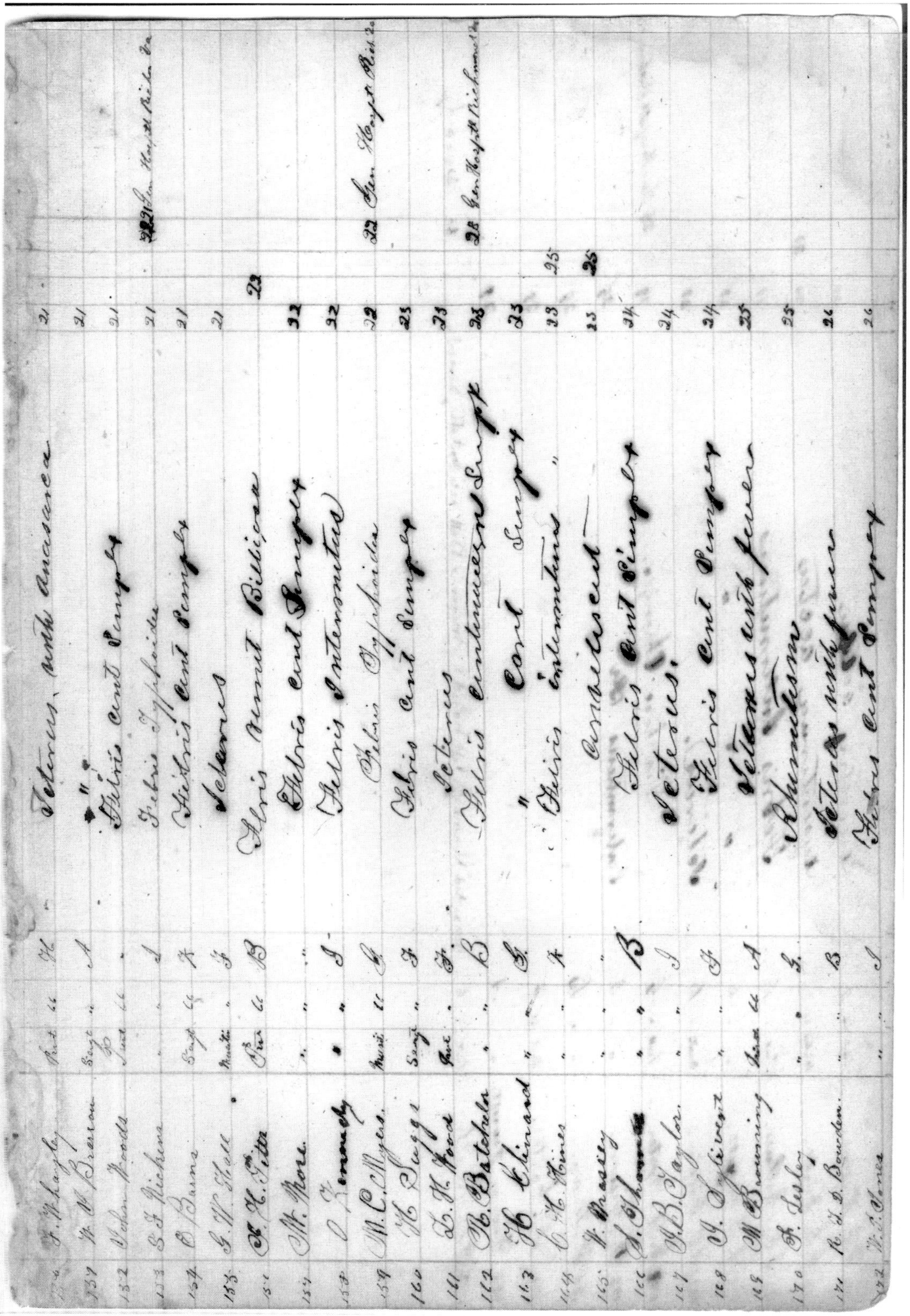

150	F. Whaply	Pvt "	H	Icterus with anasarca	21			
151	W. H. Brevon	Sergt "	A	"	21			
152	John Woods	Pvt "	"	Febris cont Simplex	21			
153	S. F. Hickens	" "	I	Febris Typhoides	21		22	Gen Hospt Rich Va
154	B Barns	Sergt "	F	Febris Cont Simplex	21			
155	G. W. Hall	Music "	F	Icterus	21			
156	F. H. Fitter	Pvt "	B	Febris remit Billiosa		23		
157	M. Moore	" "	"	Febris cont Simplex	22			
158	J. Kennedy	" "	I	Febris Intermittens	22			
159	M. C. Myers	Music "	G	Febris Typhoides	22		22	Gen Hospt Rich Va
160	H. Suggs	Sergt "	F	Febris cont Simplex	23			
161	L. H. Wood	Pvt "	F	Icterus	23			
162	H. Batchela	" "	B	Febris continua Simplex	23		23	Gen Hospt Richmond Va
163	H. Klinard	" "	G	" Cont Simplex	23			
164	C. H. Hines	" "	F	Febris intermittens "	23	25		
165	W. Massey	" "		Anasarca	23	25		
166	J. Thomas	" "	B	Febris Cont Simplex	24			
167	H. B. Taylor	" "	I	Icterus	24			
168	J. Sylvester	" "	F	Febris Cont Simplex	24			
169	M. Browning	Sergt "	A	Icterus with fever	25			
170	F. Lesley	" "	G	Rheumatism	25			
171	R. H. D. Bowden	" "	B	Icterus with fever	26			
172	W. S. Jones	" "	I	Febris Cont Simplex	26			

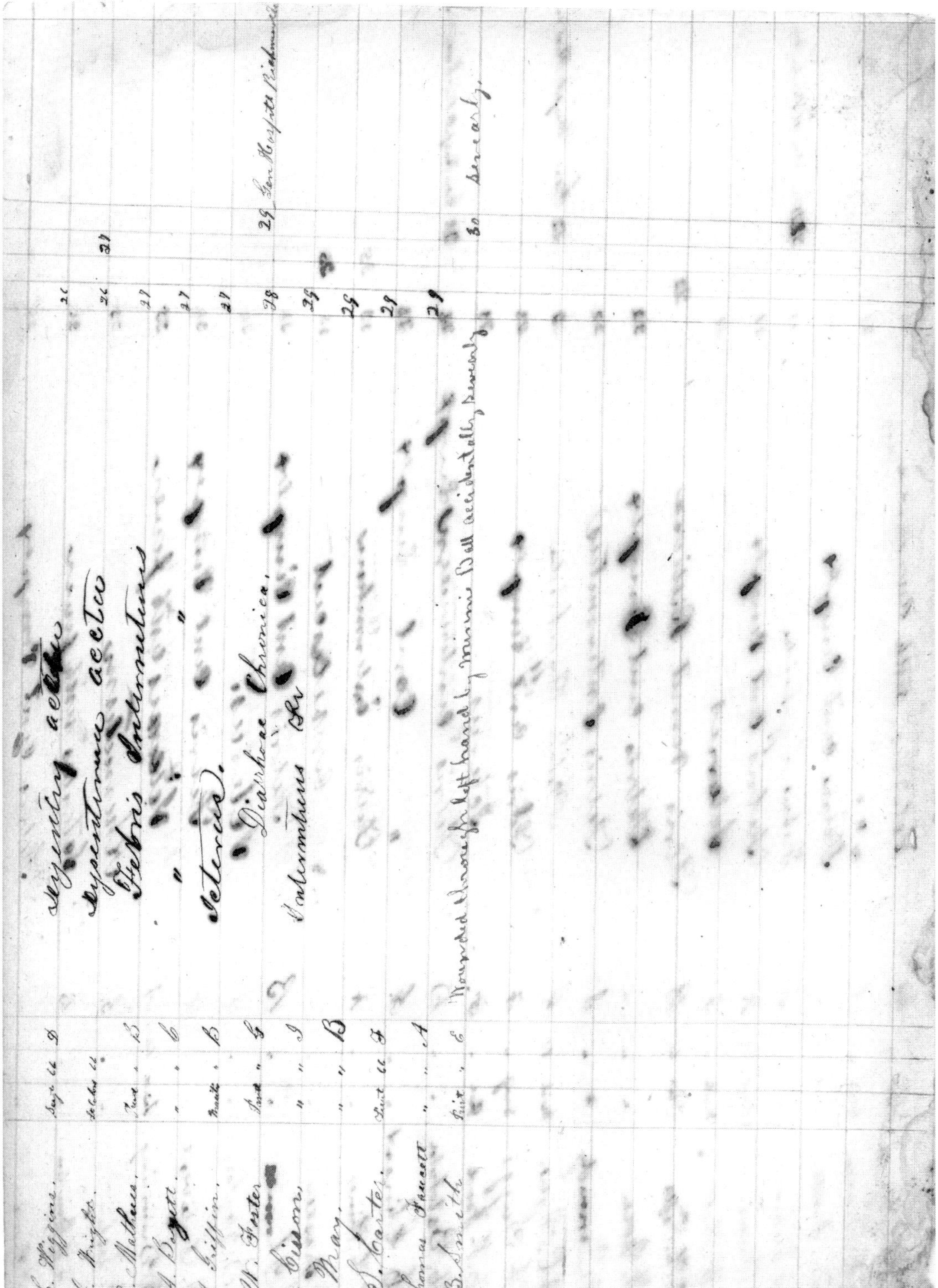

173	W.L. Wiggins.	Sergt 66	D	Dysentery acute	26		
174	C.G. Wright.	Sd Color 66		Dysenteria acuta	26	27	
175	G.E. Mathews.	Priv't "	B	Febris Intermittens	27		
176	W.A. Boyett.	" "	C	" "	27		
177	J.J. Griffin.	Music "	B	Icterus.	27		
178	G.W. Foster	Priv't "	G	Diarrhoea Chronica.	28	29	Gen Hospital Richmond Va
179	J. Cisson.	" "	I	Intermittens Fev	29		
180	J. May.	" "	B		29		
181	S.S. Carter.	Lieut 66	F		29		
182	Thomas Faucett	" "	A		29		
183	J.B. Smith	Priv't "	E	Wounded through left hand by minnie Ball accidentally severely		30	severely.

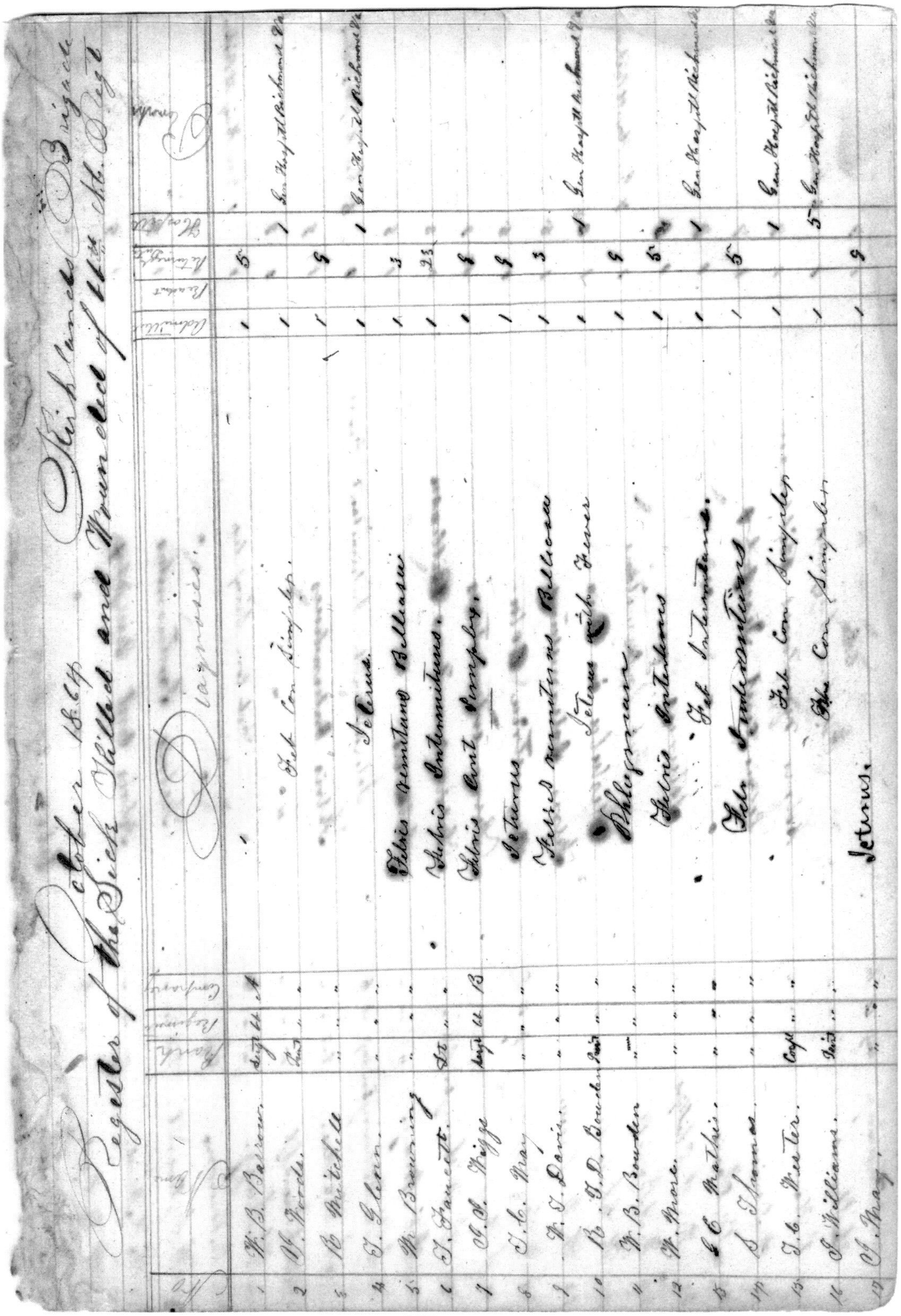
October 1864 Kirkland's Brigade
Register of the Sick Killed and Wounded of 44th N.C. Regt
Diagnosis
W. B. Barrow
B. Mitchell
T. Fawcett
W. B. Bowden
W. More
J. C. Wester
J. Williams

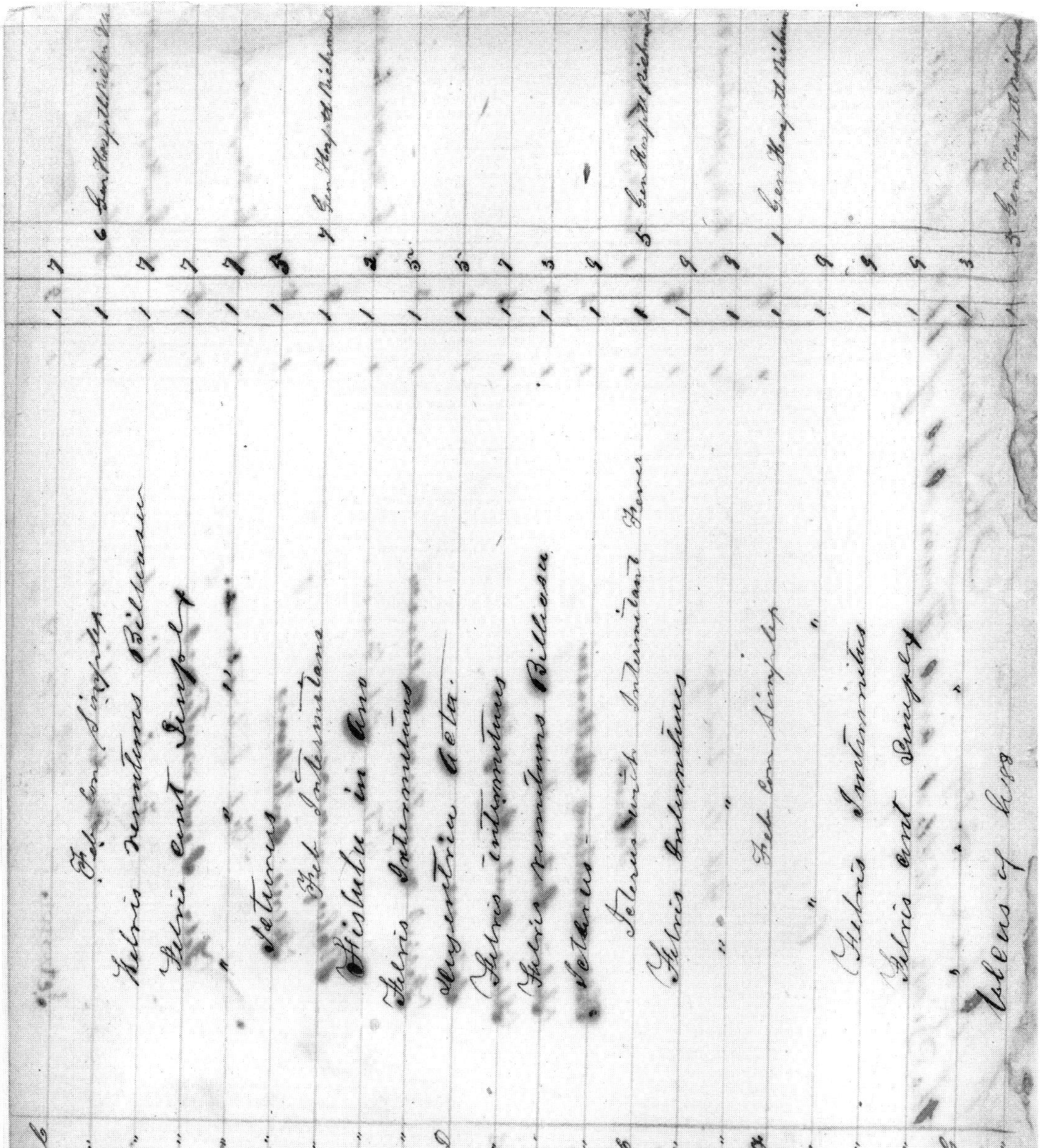

18	B. W. Herring.	Sergt	66	C		1	7	
19	Geo Stroud.	Privt	"	"	Feb Con Simplex	1		6 Gen Hospt Richm Va
20	B. Hinson.	"	"	"	Febris remittens Billiosa	1	7	
21	J. Davis.	"	"	"	Febris cont Simplex	1	7	
22	B. Davis.	"	"	"	" " "	1	7	
23	M. J. Phillips.	"	"	"	Icterus	1	5	
24	W. A. Boyett.	"	"	"	Feb Intermitans	1		7 Gen Hospt Richmond
25	H. Ghalagher	"	"	"	Fistula in Ano	1	2	
26	H. M. Brown	"	"	"	Febris Intermittens	1	5	
27	W. L. Wiggins.	Sergt	66	D	Dysentria Acta.	1	5	
28	S. Harper.	"	"	"	Febris intermittens	1	7	
29	J Witherington	Privt	"	"	Febris remittens Billiosa	1	3	
30	J. V. May.	"	"	"	Icterus	1	9	
31	J. K. Witherington	Sergt	66	C	Icterus with Intermitant Fever	1		5 Gen Hospt Richmond
32	A. Hardee.	Privt	"	"	Febris Intermittens	1	9	
33	J. A. Powell	"	"	"	" "	1	9	
34	H. Sugg.	"	"	G	Feb Con Simplex	1		1 Gen Hospt Richmond
35	B. Brown.	Corpl	"	"	" "	1	9	
36	J. Sylivant.	Privt	"	"	Febris Intermittens	1	9	
37	L. H. Wood.	"	"	"	Febris cont Simplex	1	9	
38	J M Euday	"	"	G	" " "	1	3	
39	[illegible] C Austin	"	"	"	Ulcers of Leg	1		5 Gen Hospt Richmond

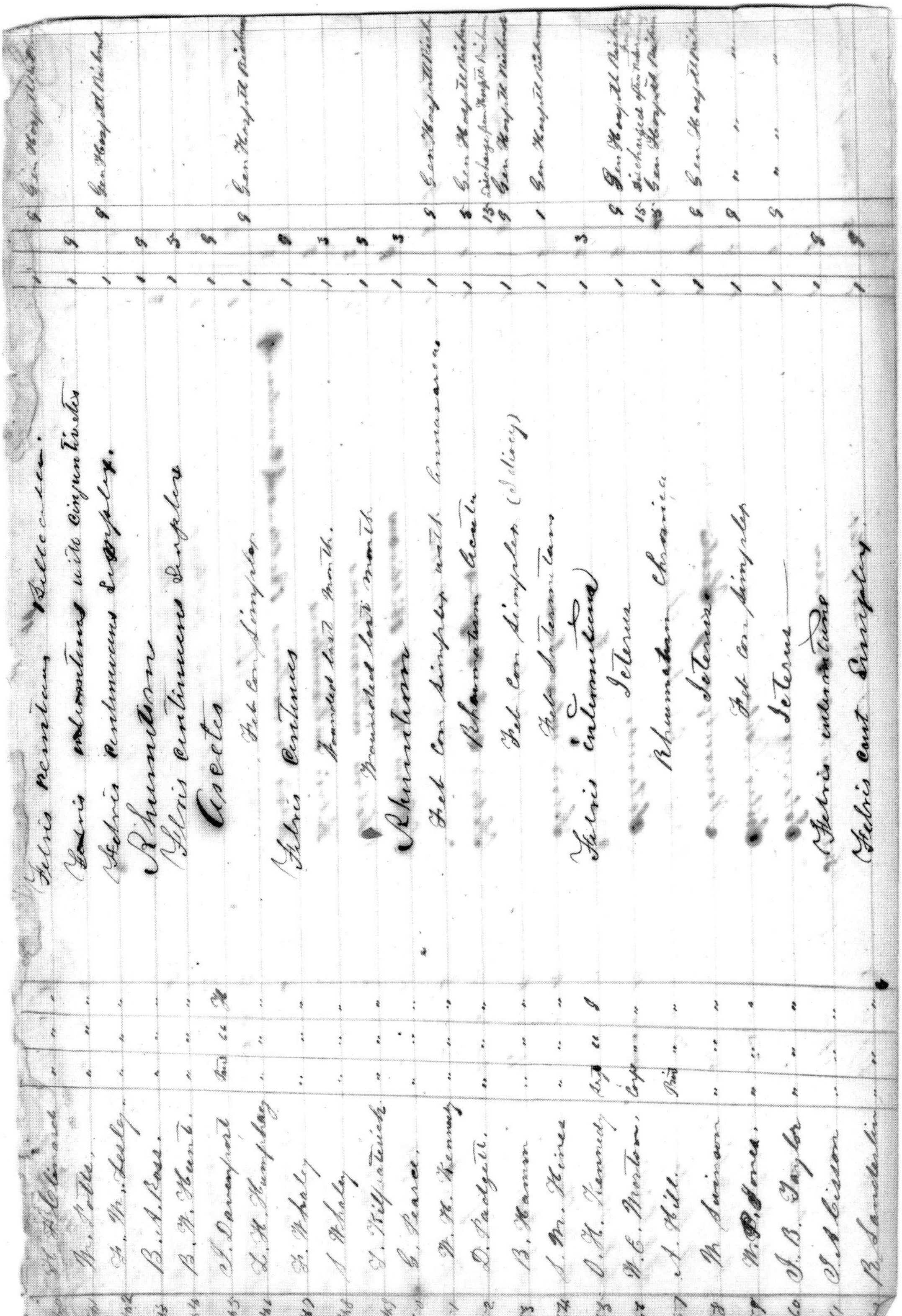

40	H. F. Clinard	"	"	"	Febris remittens Billiosa	1		9 Gen Hospitl Rich
41	W. Potts.	"	"	"	Febris intermittens with cinjunctivitis	1	9	
42	F. M. Lesly.	"	"	"	Febris continuens simplex.	1		9 Gen Hospitl Richmd
43	B. A. Ross.	"	"	"	Rheumatism	1	9	
44	B. W. Hunt.	"	"	"	Febris continuens simplex	1	5	
45	J. Davenport	Serg	66	H	Ascites	1	9	
46	L. H. Humphrey	"	"	"	Feb con simplex	1		9 Gen Hospitl Richmd
47	F. Whaley	"	"	"	Febris continues	1	9	
48	S. Whaley	"	"	"	Wounded last month.	1	3	
49	J. Kilpatrick.	"	"	"	Wounded last month	1	3	
50	G. Pearce.	"	"	"	Rheumatism	1	3	
51	W. H. Kennedy	"	"	"	Feb con simplex with Annasarca	1		9 Gen Hospitl Rich
52	D. Padgett.	"	"	"	Rheumatism Acuta	1		5 Gen Hospitl Richm 15 Discharge from Hospitl Richm
53	B. Hamm	"	"	"	Feb con simplex (Idiocy)	1		9 Gen Hospitl Richmd
54	S. M. Hines	"	"	"	Feb Intermittens	1		1 Gen Hospitl Richm
55	O. H. Kennedy	Serg	"	I	Febris intermittens	1	3	
56	W. E. Morton.	Corp	"	"	Icterus	1		9 Gen Hospitl Richm
57	A. Hill.	Priv	"	"	Rheumatism Chronica	1		15 Discharged after ... 5 Gen Hospitl Rich
58	M. Swinson	"	"	"	Icterus	1		9 Gen Hospitl Rich
59	W. P. Jones.	"	"	"	Feb con simplex	1		9 " " "
60	J. B. Taylor	"	"	"	Icterus	1		9 " " "
61	J. A. Cisson	"	"	"	Febris intermittens	1	9	
62	R. Sanderlin	"	"	"	Febris cont simplex	1	9	

63	E. Barnes.	Sgt	"	F	Feb Con Simplex	1	9	Gen Hospital Richmond
64	J. T. Boswell.	Corpl	"	"	Febris remit Billiosa	1	9	
5	N. Oadum	"	"	"	Icterus	1	9	
66	N. J. Price.	Prvt	"	"	Inter Febs	1	9	
67	B. F. Whitley	Sgt	"	"	Neuralgia of Testis.	1	9	
68	W. Bailey.	Prvt	"	"	Diarrhoea Chronica	1	4	Gen Hospital Richmond
69	J. J. Griffin	Music	"	B	Icterus.	1	9	
70	G. E. Hall.	"	"	F	" "	1	9	
71	B. F. Stansell.	"	"	K	Febris intermitans.	1	9	
72	S. S. Gurnley	Capt	"	C	Feb Con Simplex	1	5	Gen Hospital Richmond
73	F. Fry	Lieut	"	G	Febris Cont Simplex	1	1	
74	W. Brandon.	"	"	G	Feb Remit Billiosa	1	9	Gen Hospital Richmond
75	A. H. Pitts	"	"	B	Febris remit Billiosa	1	9	
76	S. S. Carter.	"	"	F	Febris intermitans	1	3	
77	A. Bagley.	"	"	K	Febris intermitans	1	9	
78	S. Holland.	"	"	C	Febris remitans Billiosa (Convalescent)	1	9	
79	G. B. Cook.	Prvt	"	B	Rheumatism.	1	2	Gen Hospital Richmond
80	D. J. Pitman.	"	"	K	Feb Remit Billiosa	1	3	Gen Hospital Richmond
81	J. Cox.	"	"	C	Feb Remit Billiosa	3	8	" " " "
82	S. Joyner.	"	"	B	Feb Remit Billiosa	3	8	" " " "
83	J. Brown.	"	"	C	Feb Remit Billiosa	8	10	" " " "
84	B. E. Little	Lt.	"	B	Febris Typhoides.	1	10	" " " "

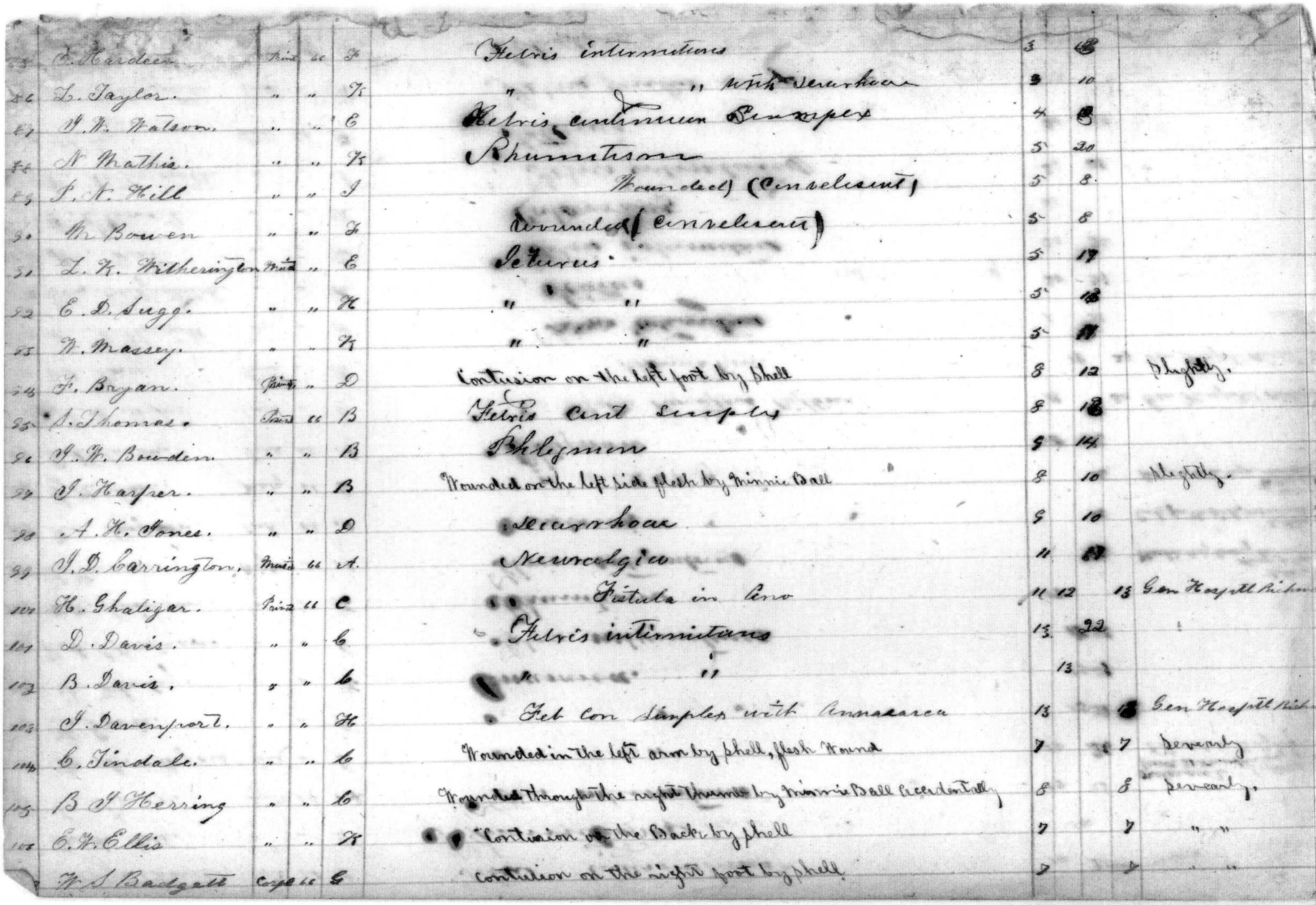

85	E. Hardee	Priv	"	F	Febris intermittens	3	[illegible]		
86	L. Taylor	"	"	K	" " with Diarrhoea	3	10		
87	J. W. Watson	"	"	E	Febris continua Simplex	4	[illegible]		
88	N. Mathis	"	"	K	Rheumatism	5	20		
89	J. N. Hill	"	"	I	Wounded (Convalescent)	5	8		
90	W. Bowen	"	"	F	Wounded (Convalescent)	5	8		
91	L. K. Witherington	Musn	"	E	Icterus	5	17		
92	E. D. Sugg	"	"	H	" "	5	18		
93	W. Massey	"	"	K	" "	5	17		
94	F. Bryan	Priv	"	D	Contusion on the left foot by shell	8	12		Slightly.
95	J. Thomas	Priv	"	B	Febris Cont Simplex	8	18		
96	J. W. Bowden	"	"	B	Phlegmon	8	14		
97	J. Harper	"	"	B	Wounded on the left side flesh by Minnie Ball	8	10		Slightly.
98	A. H. Jones	"	"	D	Diarrhoea	9	10		
99	J. D. Carrington	Musn	"	A	Neuralgia	11	[illegible]		
100	H. Ghaligar	Priv	"	C	Fistula in Ano	11	12	13	Gen Hospitl Richm
101	D. Davis	"	"	C	Febris intermittens	13	22		
102	B. Davis	"	"	C	" "		13		
103	J. Davenport	"	"	H	Feb Con Simplex with Anasarca	13		13	Gen Hospitl Rich
104	C. Tindale	"	"	C	Wounded in the left arm by shell, flesh wound	7		7	Severely
105	B. J. Herring	"	"	C	Wounded through the right thumb by Minnie Ball accidentally	8		8	Severely.
106	E. W. Ellis	"	"	K	Contusion on the Back by shell	7		7	" "
	W. S. Badgett	Corpl	"	G	Contusion on the right foot by shell	7		7	" "

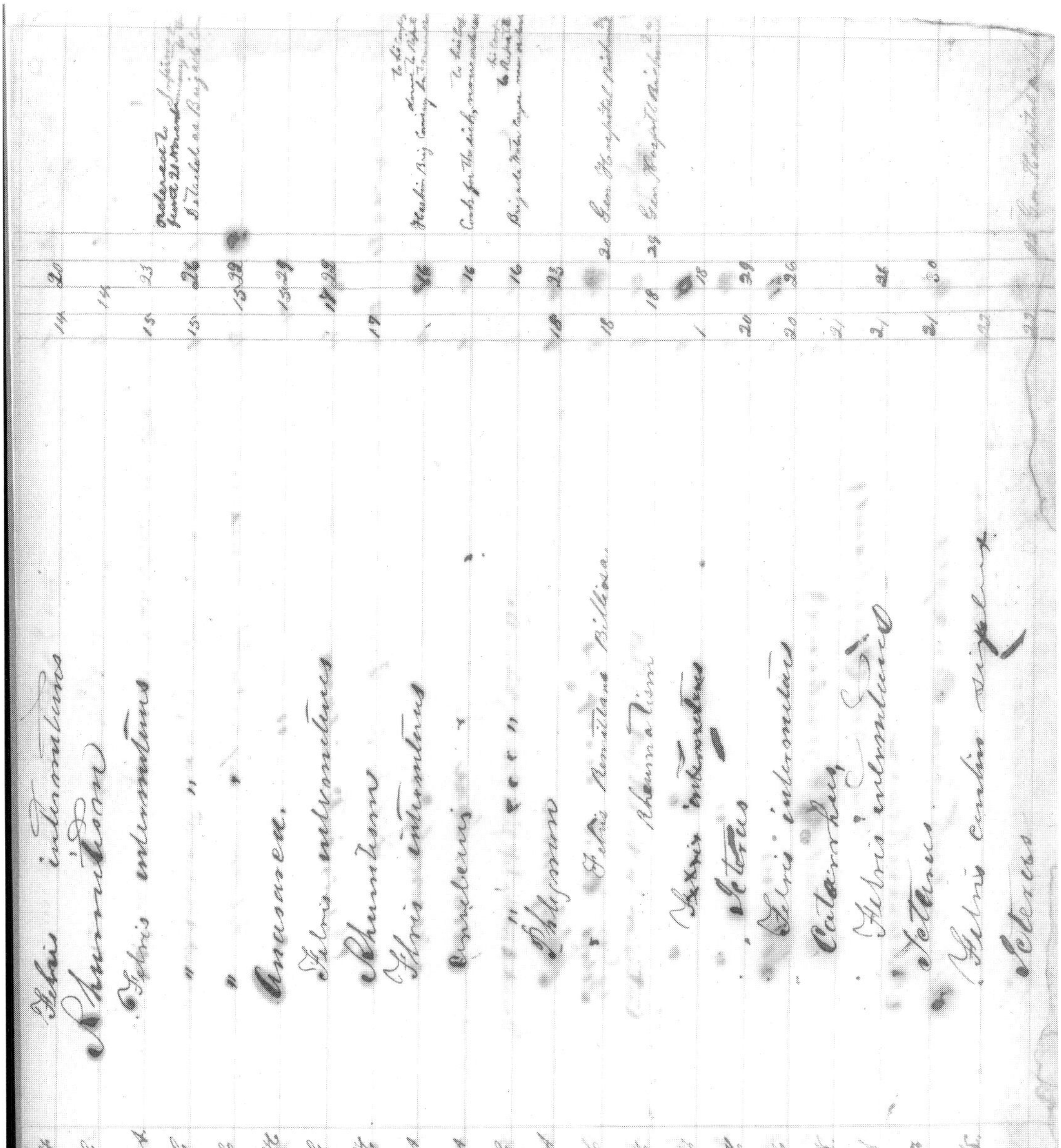

108	F. Sylceant	Privt	"	F	Febris intermittens	14	20	
109	B. A. Ross.	"	"	G	Rheumatism		14	
110	G. Pierce.	Lieut	"	A.	Febris intermittens	15	23	Ordered to Infirmary [illegible]
111	M. C. Myers	Privt	"	G	" "	15	26	Detailed as Brigade [illegible]
112	G. Davis.	"	"	C	" "	15	22	
113	F. Whaley.	"	"	H	Anasarca.	15	29	
114	J. A. J. Roseman.	"	"	G	Febris intermittens	18	22	
115	B. F. Swinson.	"	"	H.	Rheumatism	17		
116	S. Horner.	Brig Com	"	A	Febris intermittens		26	Hospital Brig Commissary [illegible]
117	W. J. Simpson.	Cook	"	A	[illegible]		16	Cook for the sick, now [illegible]
118	J. H. Cain.	[illegible]	"	G	" "		16	Brigade Water Carrier [illegible]
119	D. Johnson.	Private	"	A	Phlegmon	18	23	
120	A. W. Taylor	Corpl	"	C	Febris Remittans Billiosa.	18	20	Gen Hospital Richmond
121	G. W. Pierce.	Private	"	H	Rheumatism	18	29	Gen Hospital Richmond
122	C. Wethercutt	"	"	F	Febris intermittens	1	18	
123	Thos. Kilpatrick.	"	"	H	Icterus	20	29	
124	R. West.	"	"	F	Febris intermittens	20	26	
125	O. Stancil.	"	"	K.	Catarrhus	21		
126	O. Wethercutt.	"	"	I	Febris intermittens	21	26	
127	A. Fog.	Lieut	"	F	Icterus	21	30	
128	R. C. Bryant.	Privt	"	K.	Febris continua simplex	22		
129	C. G. Wright.	[illegible]	"		Icterus	22	22	Gen Hospital [illegible]

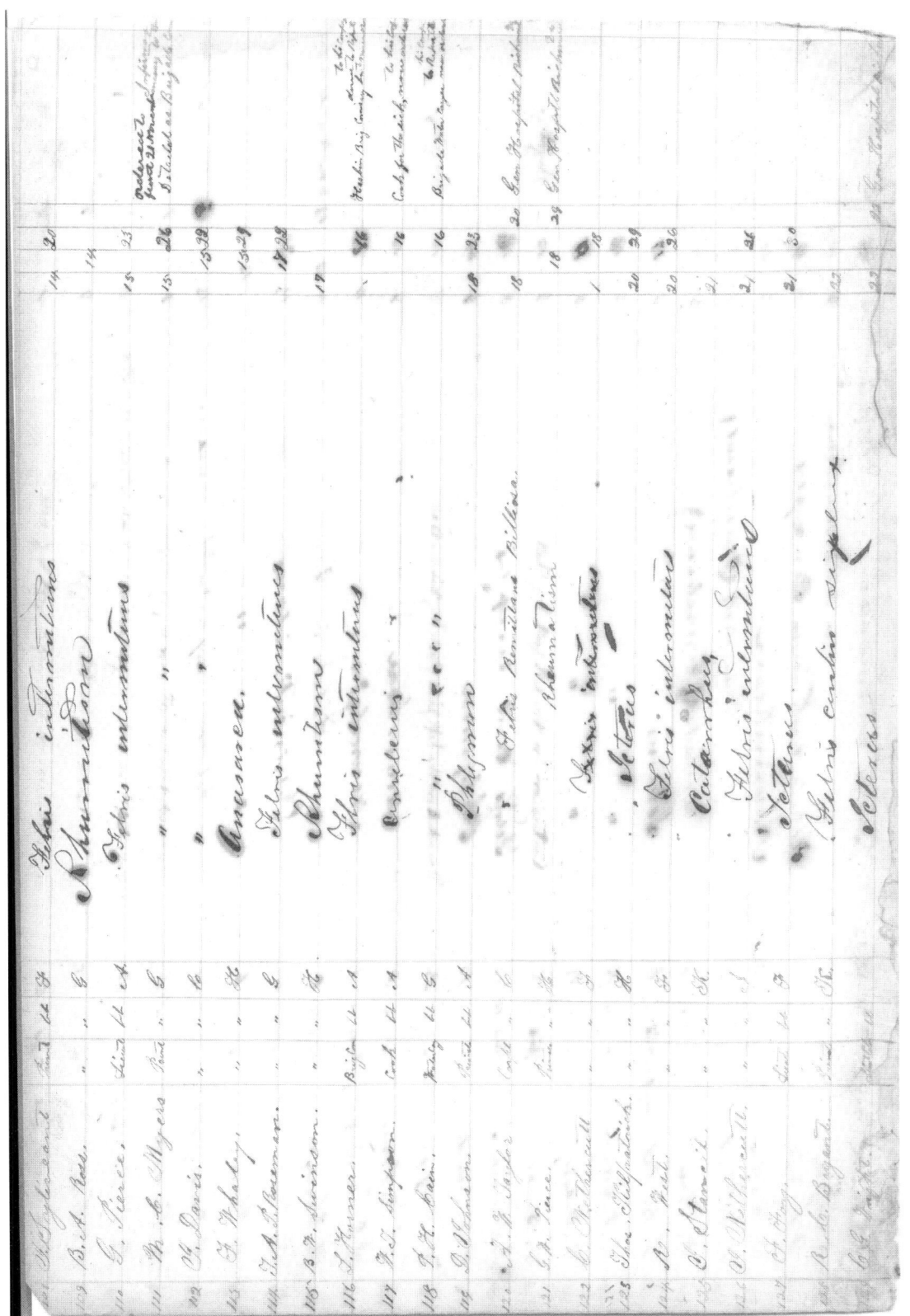

130	J. Davis	Priv.	12	C	Febris cont simplex	29	29
131	H. Munk	"	"	A	Intermittens	24	
132	A. J. Faucett	Capt	"	A	Paralysis in the face.	24	27 Gen Hospt Richmond Va
133	B. Davenport.	Priv	"	C	Anasarca	25	
134	G. G. Bennett.	Sergt	12	I	Febris cont simplex	26	
135	J. Lamm.	Priv	"	K	" " "	27	
136	L. J. Brock.	"	"	I	Intermittens	27	
137	J. W. Leonard.	"	"	B.	Pneumonia	27	28 Gen Hospt Richmond
138	J. B. Stanley.	Priv [illegible]		G	Diarrhoea Chronica.	27	29 Gen Hospt Richmond Va
139	W. Lyons.	Priv	66	F	Orchitis	28	29 Gen Hospt Richmond
140	Scissom J. A.	"	"	I	Icterus	28	
141	M. C. Stricklin	"	"	B	Wounded in the Bowells Ball did not come out [illegible] Seriously.	28	28 Seriously.
142	J. M. Hayes.	"	"	D	Epilepsia	24	
143	J. Massey.	Music	66	K	Intermittens) Febris	25	
144	D. J. Pitman.	Priv	66	K		31	

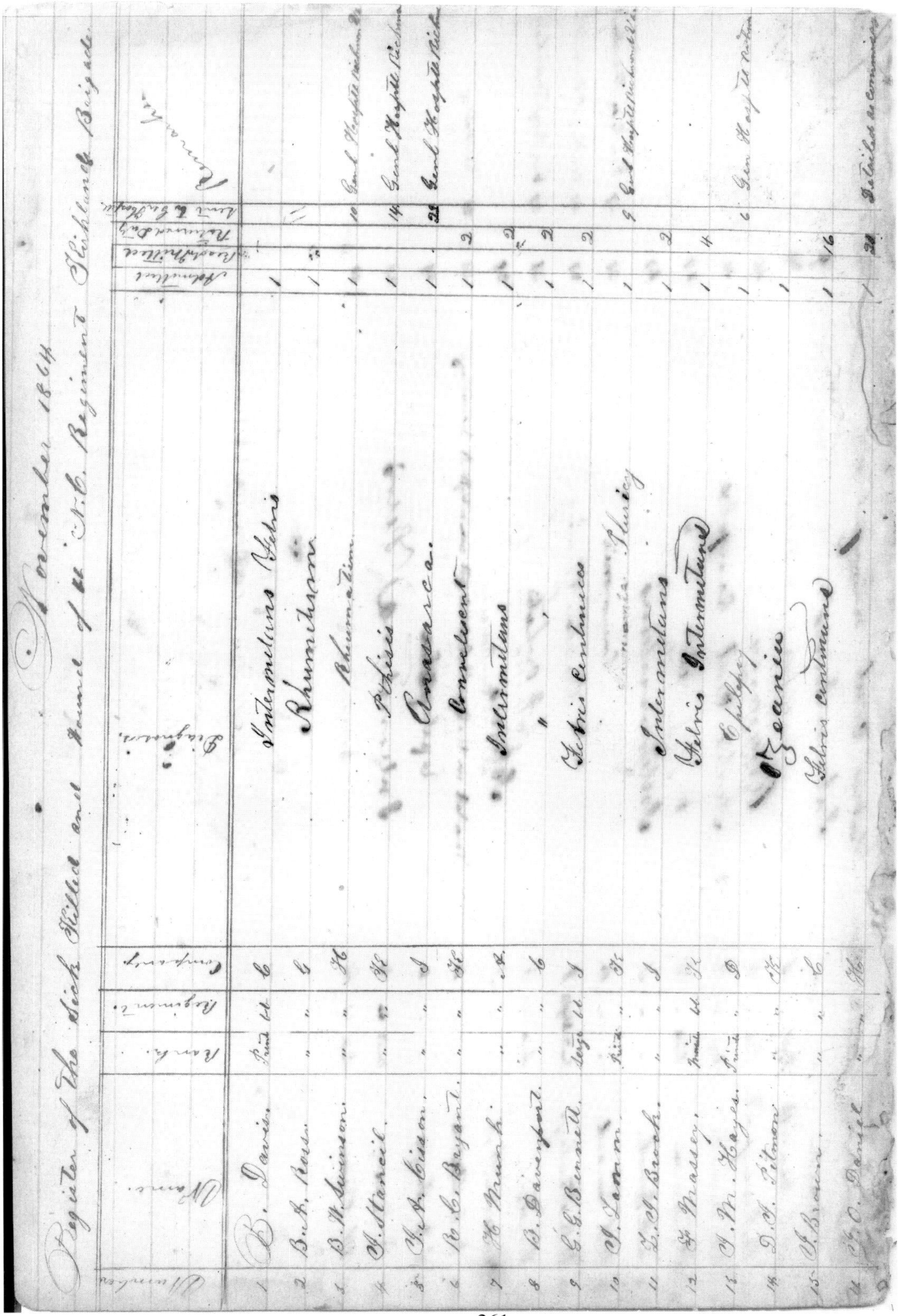

November 1864

Register of the Sick Killed and Wound of 66 N.C. Regiment Kirkland's Brigade

Number	Name	Rank	Regiment	Company	Diagnosis	Admitted	Readmitted	Returned to Duty	Sent to Gen Hospt	Remarks
1	B. Davis.	Privt	66	C	Intermetans Febris	1				
2	B. A. Ross.	"	"	G	Rhumetism	1				
3	B. W. Swinson.	"	"	H	Rheumatism	1			10	Genl Hospital Richmond Va
4	J. Stancil.	"	"	H	Pthisis	1			14	Genl Hospital Richmond
5	J. A. Cisson.	"	"	I	Anasarca.	1			29	Genl Hospital Richmond
6	R. C. Bryant.	"	"	H	Convelescent	1		2		
7	H Munk	"	"	A.	Intermetans	1		2		
8	B. Davenport.	"	"	C	"	1		2		
9	G. G. Bennett.	Serge	66	I	Febris Continuus	1		2		
10	J. Lamm.	Privt	"	H	Pluricy	1			9	Genl Hospital Richmond Va
11	L. J. Brock.	"	"	I	Intermetans	1		2		
12	F Massey.	Musician	66	H	Febris Intermetans	1		4		
13	J. M. Hayes.	Privt	"	D	Epilepsy	1			6	Gen Hospital Richmond
14	D. J. Pitmon	"	"	H	Ozeania	1				
15	J. Brown.	"	"	C	Febris continuus	1		16		
16	J. O. Daniel	"	"	H		1		20		Detailed as Commissary

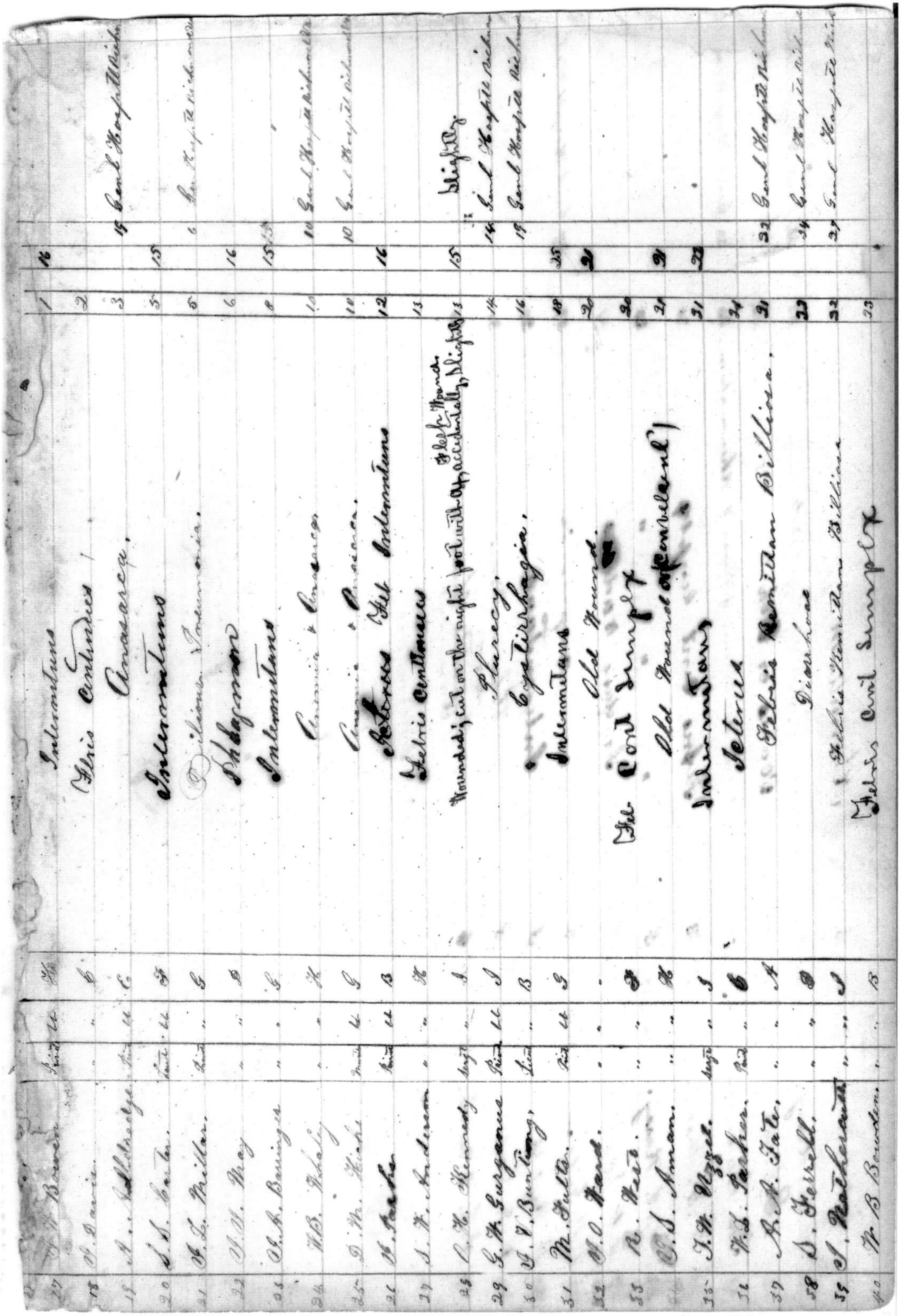

17	J. W. Bowen	Privt	"	K	Intermitens	1	16		
18	J. Davis	"	"	C	Febris Continues	2			
19	A. Alldredge	Privt	"	C	Anasarca.	3		19	Genl Hospitl Richm
20	S. S. Carter	Privt	"	F	Intermitens	5	15		
21	J. L. Millar	Privt	"	G	Bilious Pneumonia.	5		6	Genl Hospitl Richmond Va
22	J. H. May	"	"	B	Phlegmon	6	16		
23	A. A. Barringer	"	"	G	Intermitans	8	15		
24	W. B. Whaley	"	"	K	Anemia & Anasarca	10		10	Genl Hospitl Richmond Va
25	D. M. Hicks	Music	"	G	Anemia & Anasarca.	10		10	Genl Hospitl Richmond Va
26	H. Parks	Privt	"	B	Icterus Fel Intermitens	12	16		
27	S. W. Anderson	"	"	K	Febris Continues	13			
28	O. H. Kennedy	Sergt	"	I	Wounded; cut on the right foot with Ax, accidentally, Slightly (Flesh Wound)	13	15		Slightly
29	G. W. Gurganus	Privt	"	I	Plurecy.	14		14	Genl Hospitl Richm
30	J. V. Bunting	Lieut	"	B	Cystirrhagia.	16		19	Genl Hospitl Richm
31	M. Fulta	Privt	"	G	Intermitans	18	25		
32	J. O. Ward	"	"	"	Old Wound.	20	21		
33	R. West	"	"	F	Fel Cont Simplex	20			
34	G. S. Aman	"	"	K	Old Wound (Convalescent)	21	21		
35	J. W. Uzzel	Sergt	"	I	Intermitans	21	22		
36	W. L. Parker	Privt	"	C	Icterus	24			
37	A. A. Tate	"	"	A	Febris Remittan Billiosa.	21		22	Genl Hospitl Richm
38	D. Ferrell	"	"	D	Diarrhoea	22		24	Genl Hospitl Rich
39	J. Matheraut	"	"	I	Febris Remittan Billiosa	22		27	Genl Hospitl Rich
40	W. B. Bowden	"	"	B	Febris Cont Simplex	23			

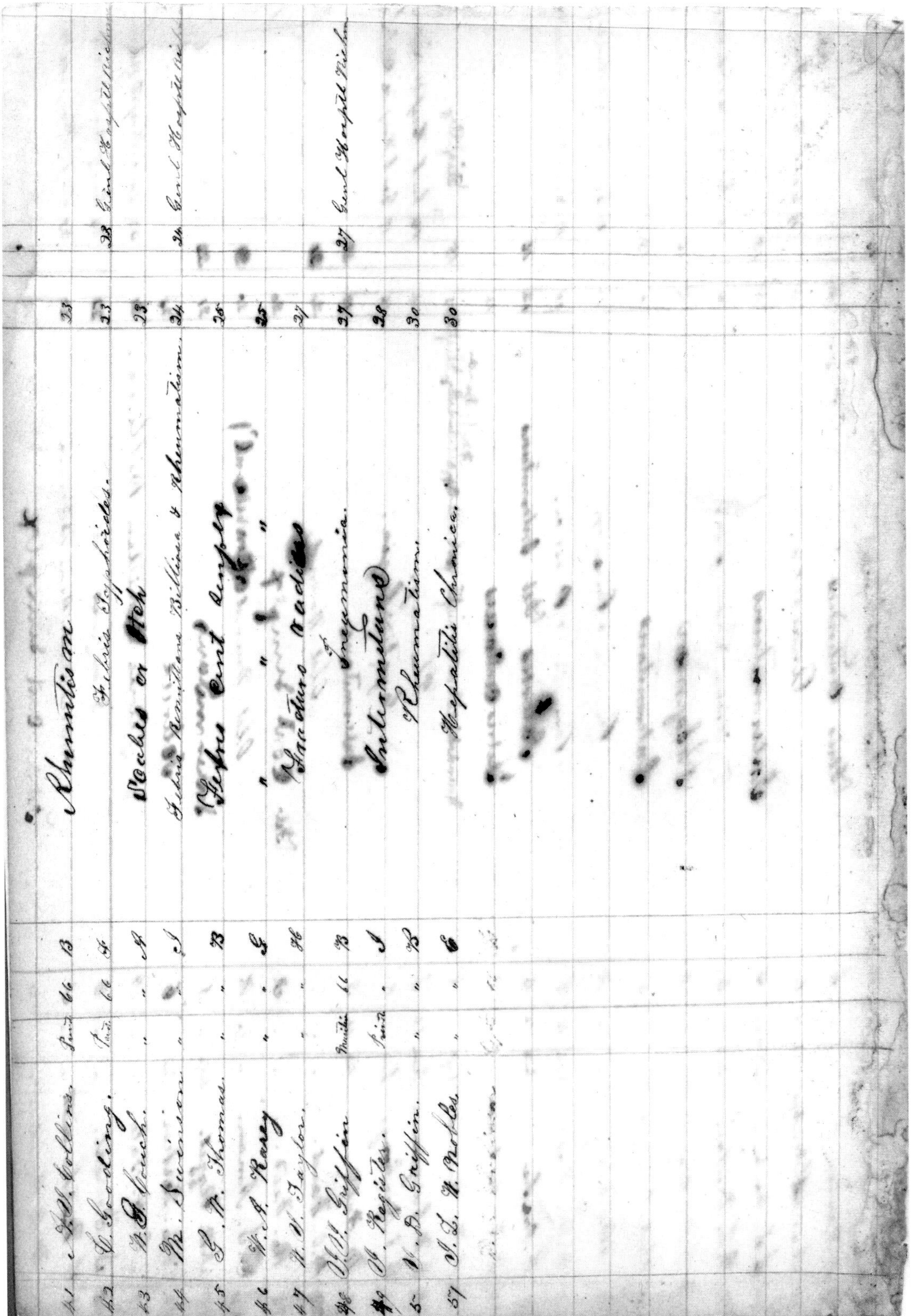

41	A. V. Collins.	Priv.	66	B	Rheumatism	23		
42	C. Gooding.	Priv.	66	F	Febris Typhoides.	23	28	Genl Hospitl Rich
43	W. P. Couch.	"	"	A	Scabies or Itch	23		
44	M. Swinson.	"	"	I	Febris Remittans Billiosa & Rheumatism.	24	24	Genl Hospitl Rich
45	G. W. Thomas.	"	"	B	Febris Cont Simplex	25		
46	W. A. Rarey	"	"	G	" " "	25		
47	W. V. Taylor.	"	"	H	Fractura radius	27		
48	V. V. Griffin	Muscn.	66	B	Pneumonia.	27	27	Genl Hospitl Richm
49	J. Register.	Priv.	"	I	Intermitans	28		
5	V. D. Griffin.	"	"	B	Rheumatism.	30		
57	J. L. W. Nobles	"	"	E	Hepatitis Chronica.	30		

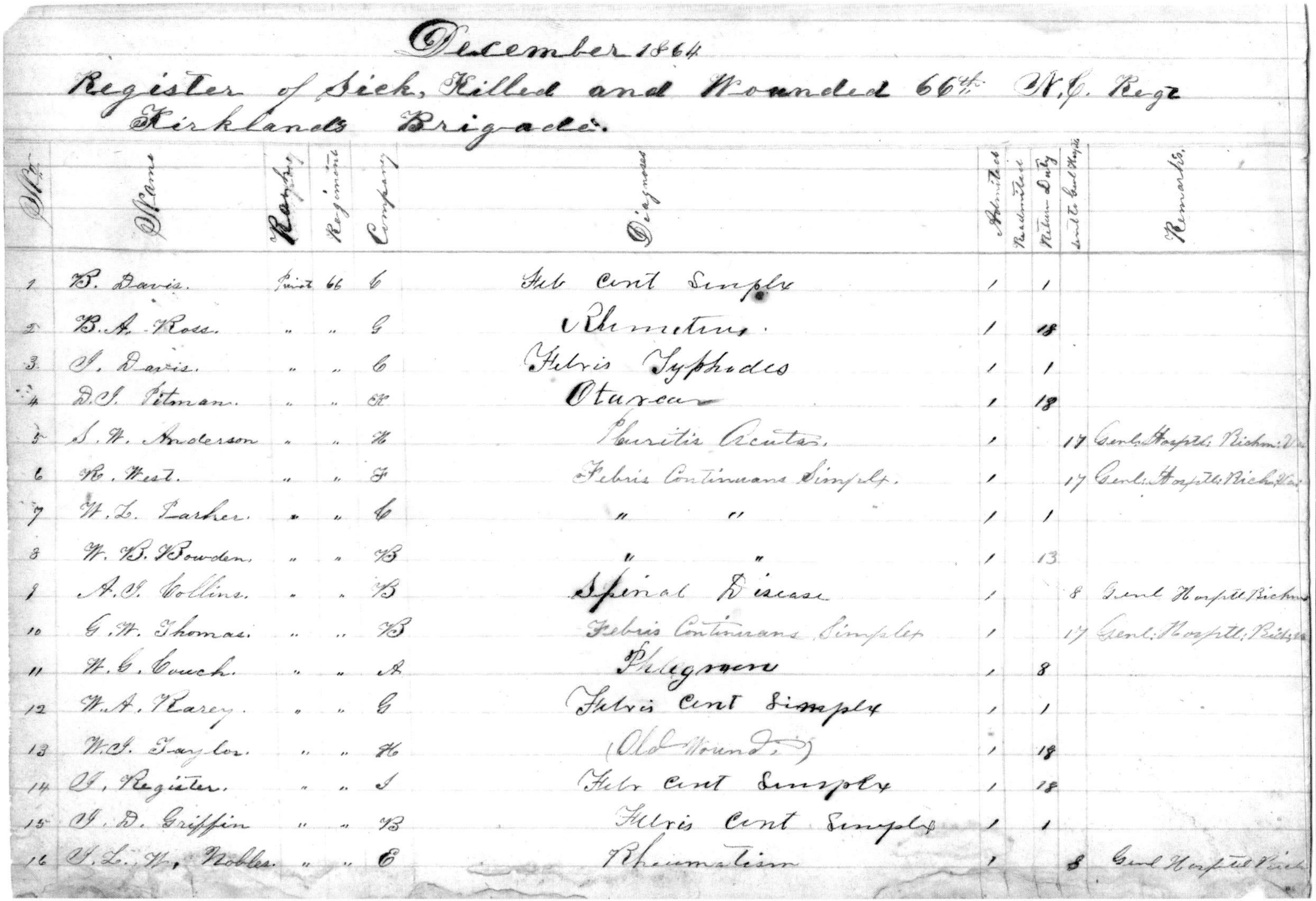

December 1864

Register of Sick, Killed and Wounded 66th N.C. Regt Kirklands Brigade.

No.	Name	Rank	Regiment	Company	Diagnoses	Admitted	Readmitted	Return Duty	Sent to Genl Hospl	Remarks
1	B. Davis.	Privt	66	C	Feb Cont Simplex	1		1		
2	B. A. Ross.	"	"	G	Rheumatism.	1		18		
3	J. Davis.	"	"	C	Febris Typhodes	1		1		
4	D. J. Pitman.	"	"	K	Otarrea	1		18		
5	S. W. Anderson	"	"	H	Pleuritis Acuta.	1			17	Genl. Hospt. Richm. Va
6	H. West.	"	"	F	Febris Continuans Simplex.	1			17	Genl. Hospt. Richm. Va
7	W. L. Parker.	"	"	C	" "	1		1		
8	W. B. Bowden.	"	"	B	" "	1		13		
9	A. J. Collins.	"	"	B	Spinal Disease	1			8	Genl Hospt Richm
10	G. W. Thomas.	"	"	B	Febris Continuans Simplex	1			17	Genl. Hospt. Richm
11	W. C. Couch.	"	"	A	Phlegmon	1		8		
12	W. A. Karey.	"	"	G	Febris Cont Simplex	1		1		
13	W. J. Taylor.	"	"	H	(Old Wound.)	1		18		
14	J. Register.	"	"	I	Febr Cont Simplex	1		18		
15	J. D. Griffin	"	"	B	Febris Cont Simplex	1		1		
16	J. L. W. Nobles.	"	"	E	Rheumatism	1			8	Genl Hospt Rich

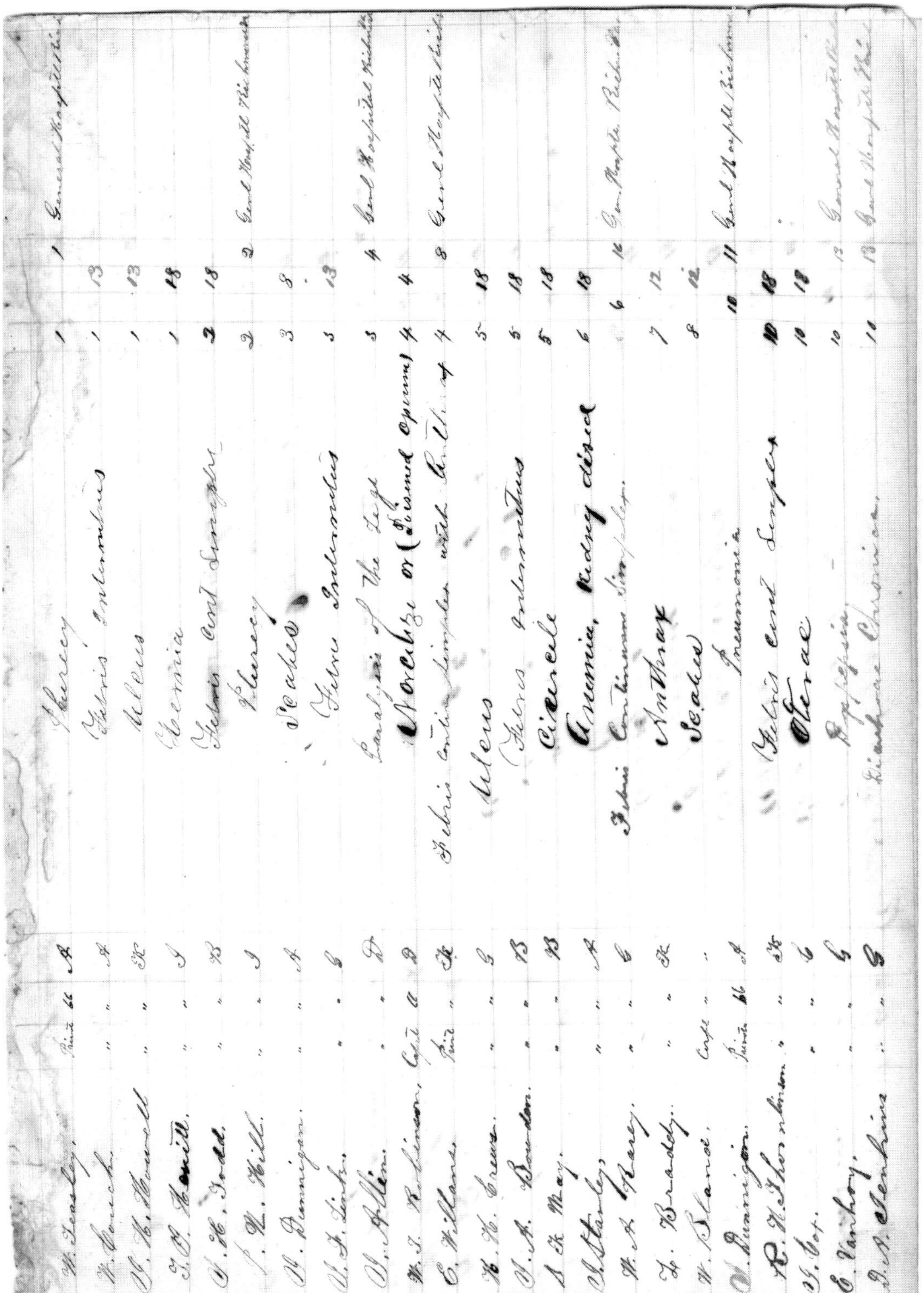

17	W. Teasley.	Privt 66	A	Pleurecy	1	1	General Hospitl Rich
18	W. Couch.	" "	A	Febris Intermitens	1	13	
19	J. H. Howell	" "	K	Ulcers	1	13	
20	J. O. Hewitt.	" "	I	Hernia	1	18	
21	J. H. Todd.	" "	B	Febris Cont Simplex	2	18	
22	J. W. Hill.	" "	I	Pleurecy	2	2	Genl Hospitl Richmond
23	J. Dunnigan.	" "	A	Scabies	3	8	
24	J. F. Link.	" "	G	Febris Intermitens	3	13	
25	J. Allen.	" "	D	Paralysis of the Legs	3	4	Genl Hospital Richmd
26	W. T. Robinson,	Capt A	D	Narcotize or (Poisoned Opium)	4	4	
27	E. Willans.	Privt "	K	Febris Contin Simplex with Anth of	4	8	Genl Hospitl Rich
28	H. H. Crews.	" "	G	Ulcers	5	18	
29	J. A. Bowden.	" "	B	Febris Intermitens	5	18	
30	S. K. May.	" "	B	Circocele	5	18	
31	J. Stanley,	" "	A	Anemia, Kidney disea	6	18	
32	W. A. Rarey.	" "	C	Febris Continuous Simplex.	6	16	Gen. Hosptl. Rich.
33	L. Braddy.	" "	K	Anthrax	7	12	
34	W. Bland.	Corpl "		Scabies	8	12	
35	J. Dunnigan.	Privt 66	A	Pneumonia	10	11	Genl Hosptl Richmn
36	R. H. Thornlinson	" "	K	Febris Cont Simplex	10	18	
37	J. Cox.	" "	C	Ulcerae	10	18	
38	E. Vanhoy.	" "	G	Dyspepsia.	10	13	General Hospitl Rich
39	D. A. Jenkins	" "	G	Diarrhoe Chronica.	10	13	Genl Hospitl Rich

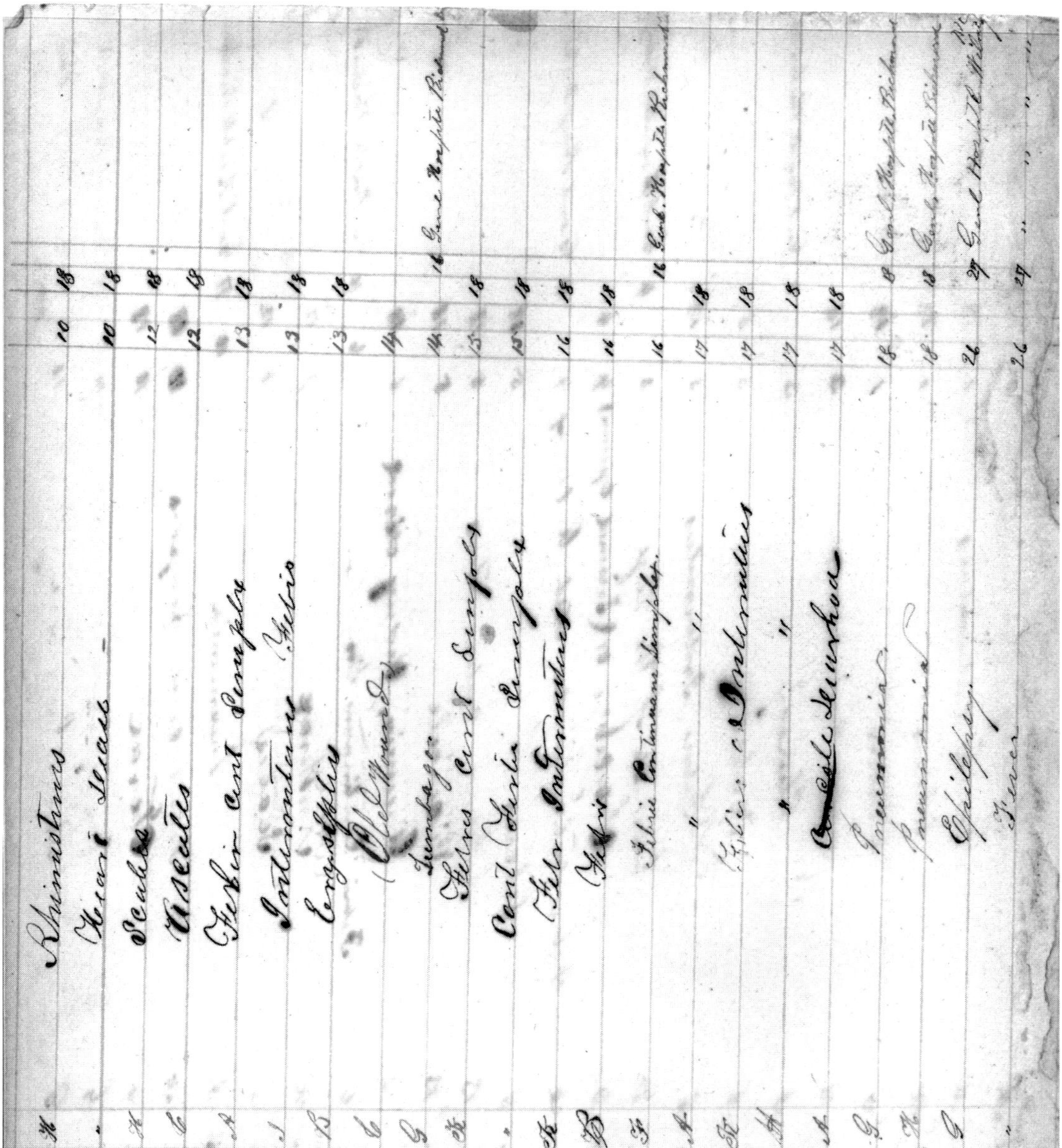

40	B. W. Swinson	Priv 66	H	Rheumatismus	10	18	
41	E. Brinson	" "	"	Heart Disease	10	18	
42	W. Fullerton	" "	H	Scabies	12	18	
43	W. Walter	" "	C	Ascites	12	18	
44	W. Browning	" "	A	Febris cont Simplex	13	18	
45	J. Wetherell	" "	I	Intermittens Febris	13	18	
46	W. Harper	" "	B	Erysipelas	13	18	
47	E. Tindale	" "	C	(Old Wound)	14		
48	Rich. Plummer	Sergt 66	G	Lumbago	14	16	Genl Hospital Richmond
49	W. Coahun	Corpl "	H	Febris Cont Simplex	15	18	
50	W. W. Bailey	Priv "	"	Cont Febris Simplex	15	18	
51	W. Bailey	" "	H	Febr Intermittens	16	18	
52	J. Parks	" "	B	Febris	16	18	
53	D. J. Warrison	" "	F	Febris Continuus Simplex	16	16	Genl Hospital Richmond
54	J. W. Christian	" "	A	"	17	18	
55	J. Smeland	" "	F	Febris Intermittens	17	18	
56	E. L. Ing	" "	H	"	17	18	
57	W. May	" "	A	Acute Diarrhoea	17	18	
58	M. Petty	" "	G	Pneumonia	18	8	Genl Hospital Richmond
59	J. Hunter	" "	H	Pneumonia	18	8	Genl Hospital Richmond
60	H. H. Kealy	" "	G	Epilepsy	26	27	Genl Hospital Wilm
61	W. H. Browning	" "		Fever	26	27	" " "

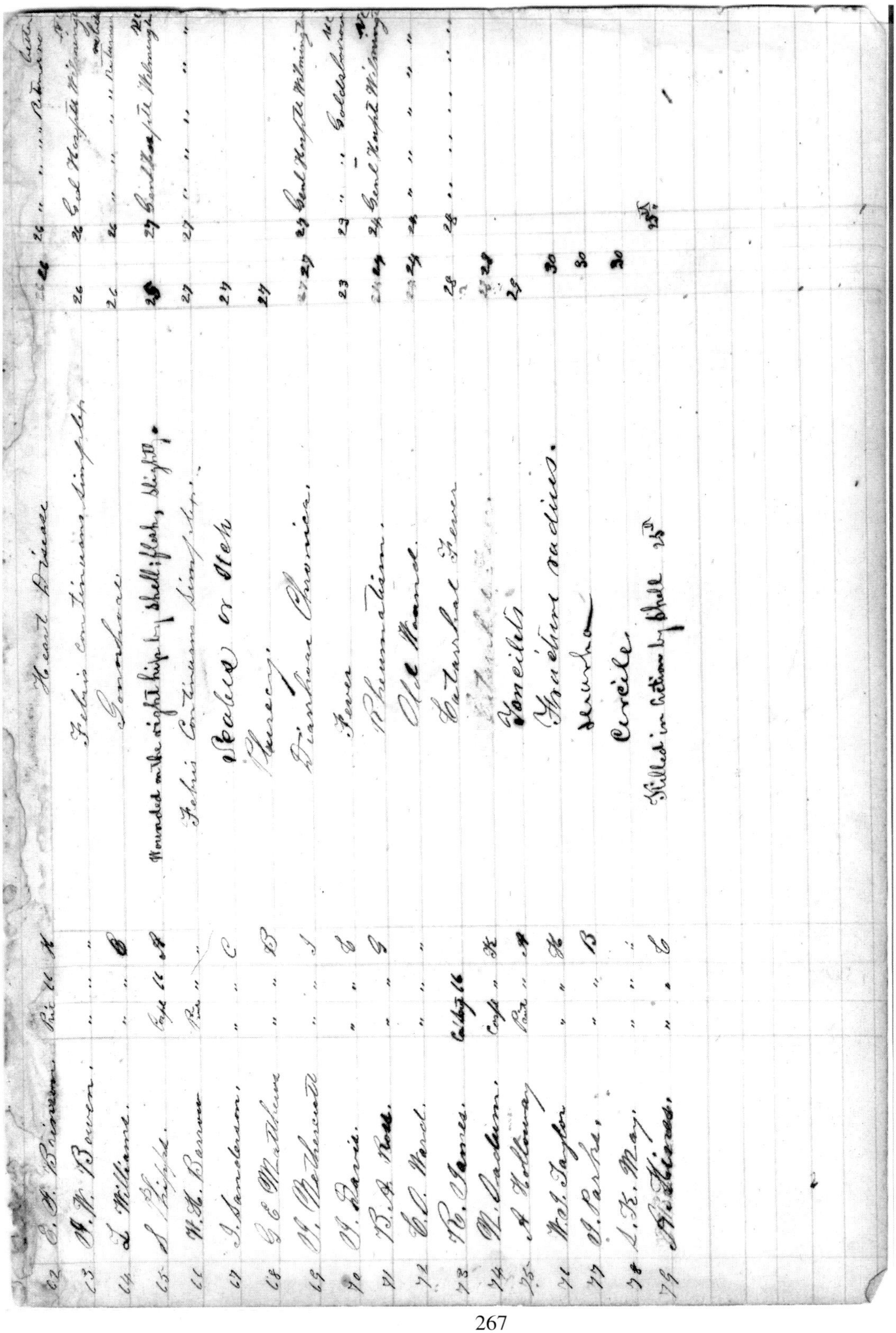

62	E. F. Brinson	Pvt 11	K	Heart Disease	26 26	26 " " " "	Returned to duty
63	W. W. Bowen	" "	"	Febris continuans simplex	26	26	Genl Hospital Wilmington
64	L. Williams	" "	B	Gonorrhoea	26	26 " " " "	Returned
65	S. Phipps	Corpl 11	A	Wounded on the right hip by shell; flesh, slightly.	25	27	Genl Hospital Wilmington
66	W. H. Barrow	Pvt "	"	Febris Continuans Simplex.	27	27 " " " "	
67	J. Sanderson	" "	C	Scabies or Itch	27		
68	G E Matthews	" "	B	Pleurecy	27		
69	J. Nethercutt	" "	I	Diarrhoea Chronica.	27 27	27	Genl Hospital Wilmington
70	J. Davis	" "	E	Fever	23	23 " "	Goldsboro
71	B. A. Ross	" "	G	Rheumatism	24 24	24	Genl Hospital Wilmington
72	C. O. Ward	" "	"	Old Wound	24 24	24 " " " "	
73	R. James	Col Sergt 16		Catarrhal Fever	28	28 " " " "	
74	W. Oadum	Corpl "	K	Catarrhal Fever	28 28		
75	A Holloway	Pvt "	A	Tonsilitis	29		
76	W. J. Taylor	" "	K	Fracture radius.	30		
77	J. Parks	" "	B	Diarrhoea	30		
78	L. K. May	" "	"	Cercile	30		
79	A. Hines	" "	E	Killed in action by shell 25th		25th	

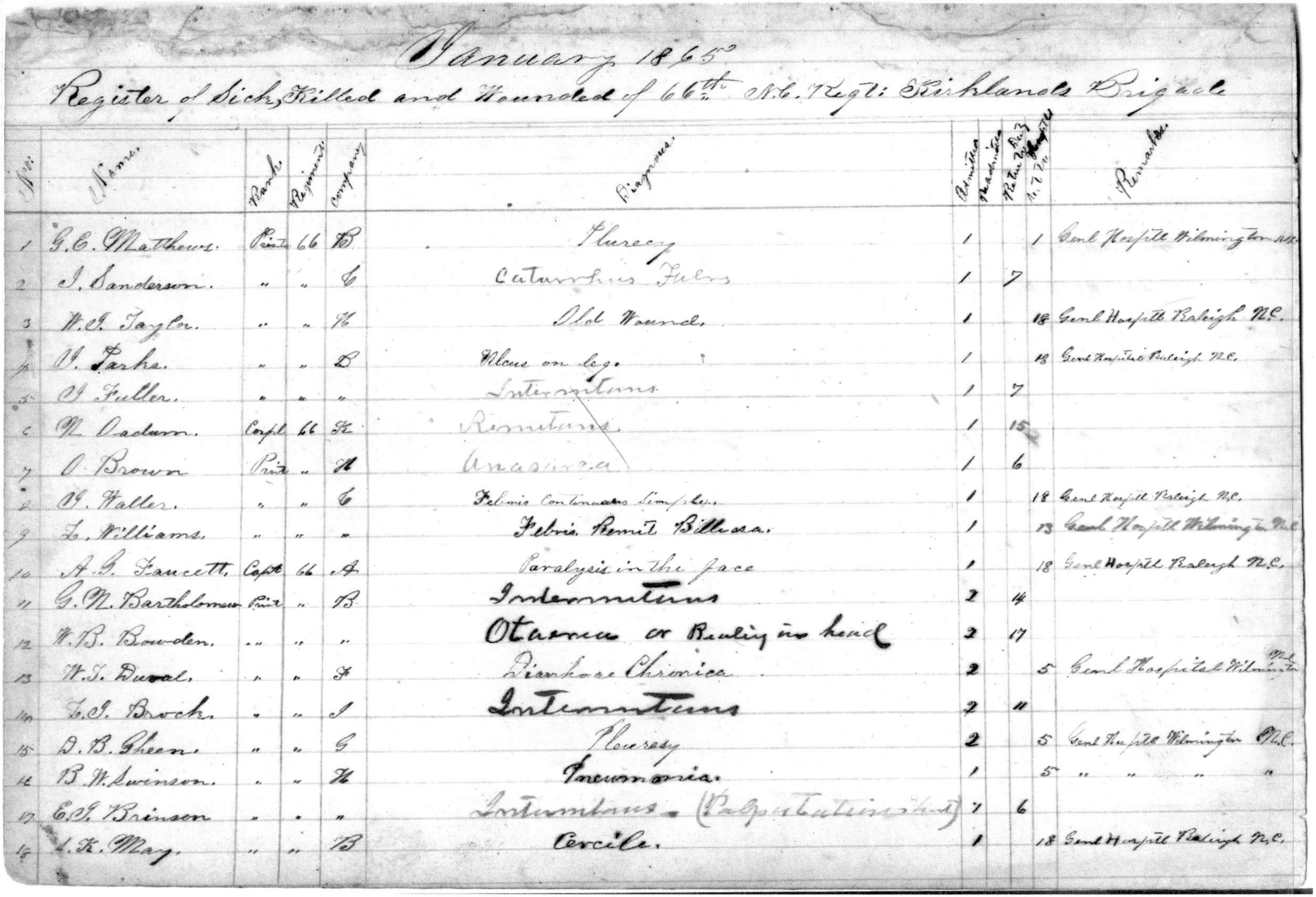

January 1865

Register of Sick, Killed and Wounded of 66th N.C. Regt: Kirklands Brigade

No.	Name	Rank	Regiment	Company	Diagnosis	Admitted	Readmitted	Return to Duty	Sent to Hospital	Remarks
1	G.C. Mathews.	Privte	66	B	Plurecy	1			1	Genl Hospitl Wilmington N.C.
2	J. Sanderson.	"	"	C	Caturrhus Febris	1		7		
3	W.J. Taylor.	"	"	H	Old Wound.	1			18	Genl Hospitl Raleigh N.C.
4	J. Parks.	"	"	D	Ulcus on leg.	1			18	Genl Hospital Raleigh N.C.
5	J. Fuller.	"	"	"	Intermittens	1		7		
6	M. Oadum.	Corpl	66	K	Remitens	1		15		
7	O. Brown	Priv	"	H	Anasarca	1		6		
8	J. Waller.	"	"	C	Febris Continuus Simplex.	1			18	Genl Hospitl Raleigh N.C.
9	L. Williams.	"	"	"	Febris Remit Billiosa.	1			13	Genl Hospitl Wilmington N.C.
10	A.G. Faucett.	Capt	66	A	Paralysis in the face	1			18	Genl Hospitl Raleigh N.C.
11	G.N. Bartholomew	Priv	"	B	Intermittens	2		14		
12	W.B. Bowden.	"	"	"	Otaorrea or Realiz in head	2		17		
13	W.J. Duval.	"	"	F	Diarrhoea Chronica	2			5	Genl Hospital Wilmington N.C.
14	L.J. Brock.	"	"	I	Intermittens	2		11		
15	D.B. Gheen.	"	"	G	Pleuresy	2			5	Genl Hospitl Wilmington N.C.
16	B.W. Swinson.	"	"	H	Pneumonia.	1			5	" " " "
17	E.J. Brinson	"	"	"	Intermitens. (Palpitation of Heart)	1		6		
18	J.K. May.	"	"	B	Cercile.	1			18	Genl Hospitl Raleigh N.C.

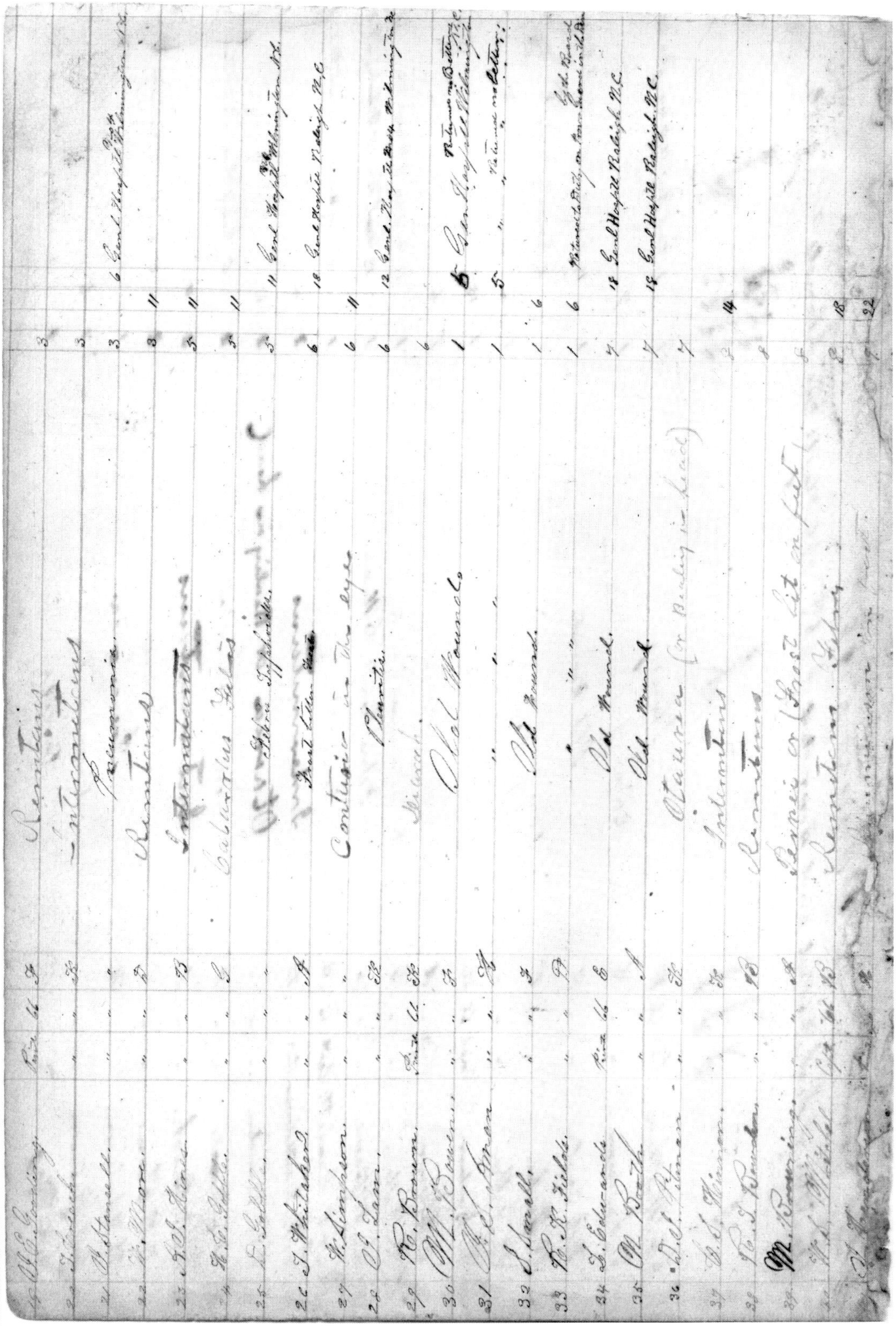

19	W. E. Gooding	Private 66	F	Remittens	3		
20	T. Beach	" "	K	Intermittens	3		
21	B. Stancell	" "	"	Pneumonia	3		6 Genl Hospitl No 4 Wilmington N.C.
22	W. More	" "	D	Remittens	3	11	
23	A. J. Hines	" "	B	Intermittens	5	11	
24	H. C. Gobble	" "	G	Catarrhus Febris	5	11	
25	E. Gobble	" "	"	Febris Typhoides	5		11 Genl Hospitl No 4 Wilmington N.C.
26	J. Whitaker	" "	A	Frost bitten feet	6		18 Genl Hospitl Raleigh N.C
27	W. Simpson	" "	"	Contusio in the eye	6	11	
28	J. Lam	" "	K	Pleuritis	6		12 Genl. Hospitl No 4 Wilmington N.C
29	R. Brown	Private 66	K	Diarrh.	6		
30	M. Bowen	" "	F	Old Wounds	1		5 Genl Hospitl Wilmington N.C. Returned no Better
31	A. S. Aman	" "	H	" "	1		5 " " Returned no better
32	S. Small	" "	F	Old wound	1	6	
33	R. K. Fields	" "	P?	" "	1	6	Returned to duty on Recommend by the Board in the [illegible]
34	L. Edwards	Private 66	E	Old Wound	7		18 Genl Hospitl Raleigh N.C.
35	M. Booth	" "	A	Old Wound	7		18 Genl Hospitl Raleigh N.C.
36	D. J. Pitman	" "	K	Otaurea (or Bealing in head)	7		
37	C. S. Winnon	" "	K	Intermittens	8	14	
38	R. J. Bowden	" "	B	Remittens	8		
39	M. Browning	" "	A	Pernio or (Frost bit on feet)	8		
40	W. L. Mitchel	Capt 66	B	Remittens Febris	8	18	
41	J. Henderson	[illegible]	K	[illegible] in feet	[illegible]	22	

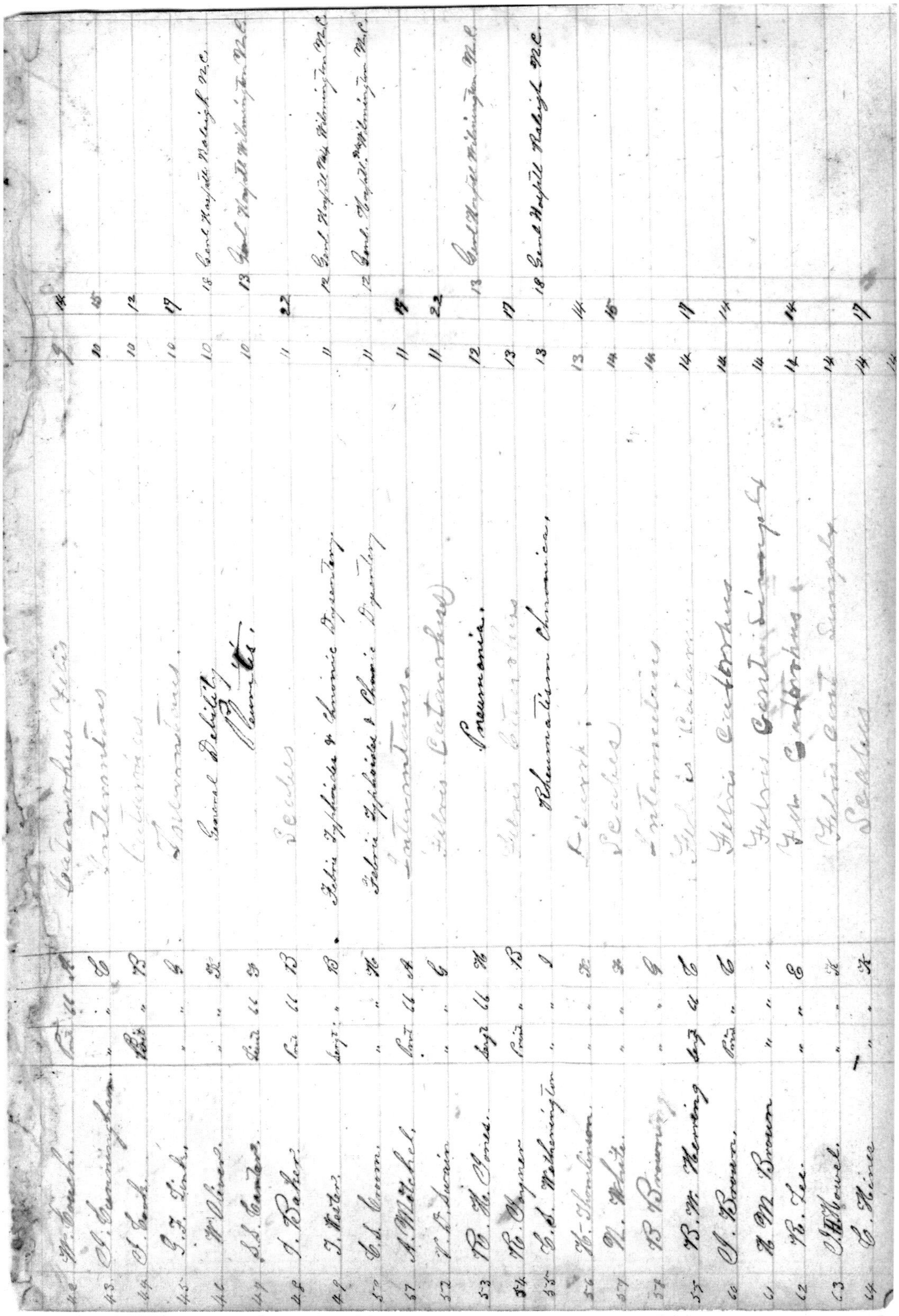

42	W. Leach	Pvt	"	F	Catarrhus [illegible]	9	14	
43	A. Cunningham	"	"	E	Intermittens	10	15	
44	J. Cook	Pvt	"	B	[illegible]	10	12	
45	G. F. Link	"	"	G	Intermittens	10	17	
46	W. Oliver	"	"	K	General Debility	10	18	Genl Hospital Raleigh N.C.
47	S. S. Eanes	Corpl	"	F	[illegible]	10	13	Genl Hospital Wilmington N.C.
48	J. Baker	Pvt	"	B	Scabies	11	22	
49	J. Wester	Sergt	"	B	Febris Typhoides & Chronic Dysentery	11	12	Genl Hospital Wilmington N.C.
50	C. L. Crum	"	"	H	Febris Typhoides & Chronic Dysentery	11	12	Genl Hospital Wilmington N.C.
51	A. Mitchel	Corpl	"	A	Intermittens	11	17	
52	W. F. Swain	"	"	G	Febris Catarrhus	11	22	
53	B. H. Jones	Sergt	"	H	Pneumonia	12	13	Genl Hospital Wilmington N.C.
54	W. Joyner	Pvt	"	B	Febris Intermittens	13	17	
55	E. S. Wetherington	"	"	I	Rheumatism Chronic	13	18	Genl Hospital Raleigh N.C.
56	W. Tomlinson	"	"	K	Icterus	13	14	
57	N. White	"	"	K	Scabies	14	15	
58	B. Browning	"	"	G	Intermittens	14		
59	B. W. Herring	Sergt	"	C	Febris Catarrhus	14	17	
60	S. Brown	Pvt	"	C	Febris Catarrhus	14	14	
61	H. M. Brown	"	"		Febris Continua Simplex	14		
62	W. Lee	"	"	E	Febris Catarrhus	14	14	
63	J. H. Howell	"	"	K	Febris Continua Simplex	14	17	
64	E. Hines	"	"	K	Scabies	14		

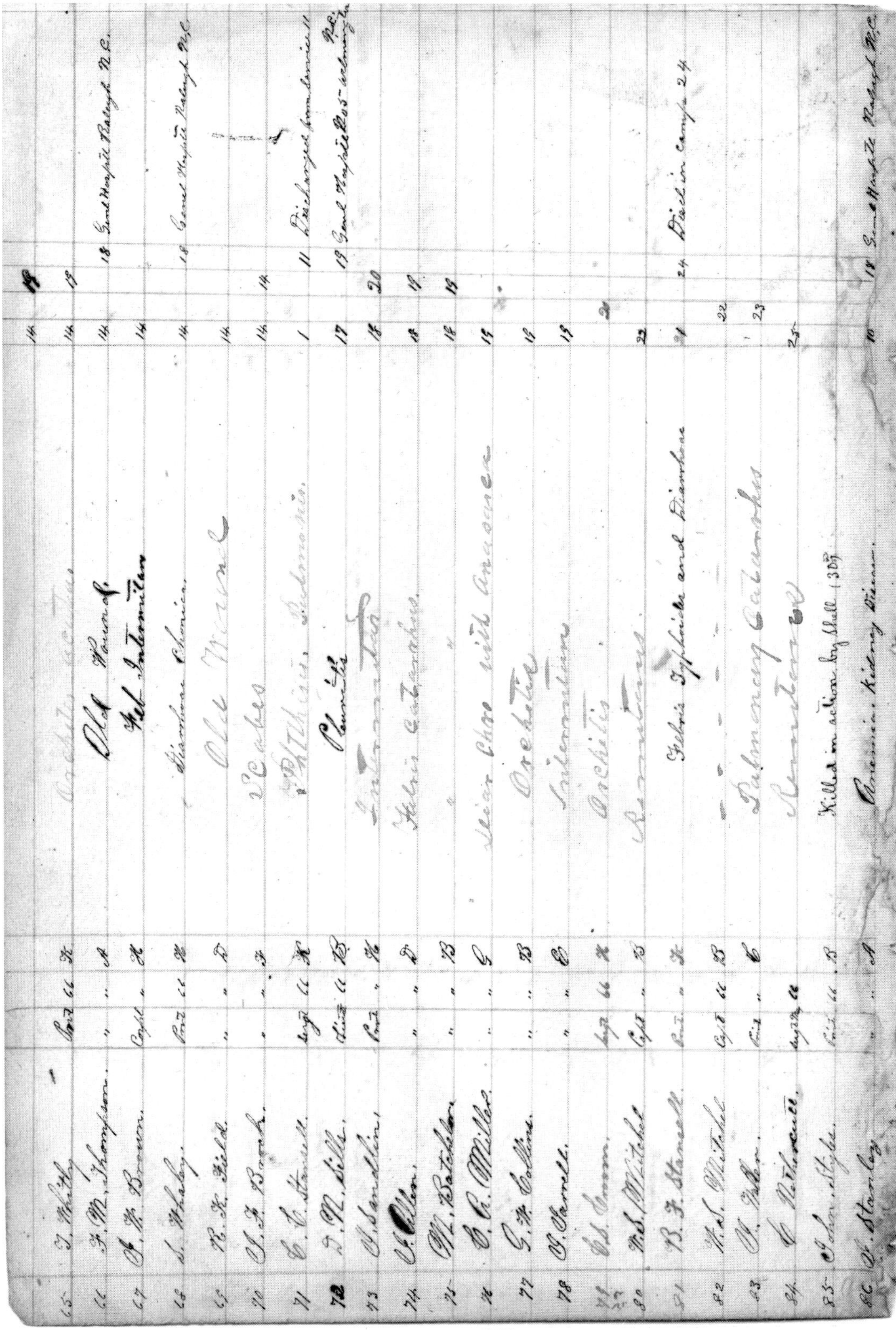

						14	19	
65	J. Whitly	Pvt	66	K	Orchitis acutus	14	19	
66	F. M. Thompson	"	"	A	Old Wound	14		18 Genl Hospitl Raleigh N.C.
67	J. W. Brown	Corpl	"	H	Feb Intermitten	14		
68	S. Whaley	Pvt	66	H	Diarrhoea Chronica	14		18 Genl Hospitl Raleigh N.C.
69	R. K. Field	"	"	D	Old Wound	14		
70	J. F. Brock	"	"	F	Scabes	14	14	
71	C. C. Stansell	Sergt	66	K	Phthisis Pulmonis	1		11 Discharged from Service 11
72	D. N. Sills	Lieut	66	B	Pleuritis	17		19 Genl Hospitl No 5 Wilmington N.C.
73	J. Sandlin	Pvt	"	K	Intermitten	18	20	
74	J. Allen	"	"	D	Febris Catarrhus	18	19	
75	M. Batchelor	"	"	B	" "	18	19	
76	C. C. Miller	"	"	G	Diar Chro with Anasarca	19		
77	G. W. Collins	"	"	B	Orchitis	19		
78	J. Sarrell	"	"	E	Intermitten	19		
79	C. S. Croom	Sergt	66	K	Orchitis		20	
80	W. S. Mitchel	Capt	"	B	Remittens	22		
81	B. F. Stansell	Pvt	"	K	Febris Typhoides and Diarrhoea	21		24 Died in camp 24
82	W. S. Mitchel	Capt	66	B	- - - - -		22	
83	J. Miller	Pvt	"	C	Pulmonary Catarrhus		23	
84	C. Nethercutt	Sergt Maj	66		Remittens	25		
85	John Styles	Pvt	66	B	Killed in action by Shell (30th)			
86	J. Stanley	"	"	A	Anemia, Kidney Disease	10		18 Genl Hospitl Raleigh N.C.

87	C. M. Herndon.	Pvt	44	A	Old Wound.	10		18	Genl Hospital Raleigh N.C.
88	T. Stilley.	"	"	F	" " "	10		18	" " " " "
89	James Wilkins.	Pvt	44	C	" " "	10		18	" " " " "
90	M. Bowen.	Pvt	"	F	" " "		15	18	" " " " "
91	J. S. Aman.	"	"	H	" " "		15	18	" " " " "
92	E. Pearce.	"	"	D	" " "	12		18	" " " " "
93	B. Jeffreys.	"	"	A	Killed in Action by Shell. (13th ")				

February 1865

Register of Sick, Killed and Wounded of 66th N.C. Regt. Kirklands Brigade

No.	Name	Rank	Regiment	Company	Diagnosis	Admitted	Readmitted	Returned to Duty	Sent to Hospital	Remarks
1	B. Brown.	Privt	66	G	Febris Intermittens	1		6		
2	J. E. Gooding.	"	"	F	Febris Remitans	1		20		
3	J. Creech.	"	"	K	Debilitas.	1			20	Genl Hosptl Wilmington N C
4	H. Brown.	"	"	"	Diarrhoae.	1		9		
5	R. J. Bowden	"	"	B	Otaurea.	1		14		
6	M. Browning.	"	"	A	Frost bit on feet.	1		14		
7	H. M. Brown.	"	"	C	Feb Contin Simplex.	1			20	Genl Hosptl Wilmington N.C.
8	J. H. Howell.	"	"	K	Debilitas	1			20	" " " "
9	J. W. Brown.	Copl	66	H	Heart Disease.	1			20	" " " "
10	C. A. Miller.	Privt	"	G	Diarrhoae Chronica.	1			(8th)	Furloughed for 30 days 8th
11	G. W. Collins.	"	"	B	Orchetis.	1			21	Genl Hosptl Wilmington N.C.
12	J. Farrell.	"	"	E	Diarrhoae	1		12		
13	C. S. Croom	Sergt	66	H	Orchetis Chronica	1		11		
14	D. J. Pitman	Privt	"	K	Otaurea	1				
15	W. S. Mitchel.	Copl	66	B	Feb Remitans Billiosa.	1		14		
16	J. Waller.	Privt	66	C	Phthisis Pulmonia	1		21		

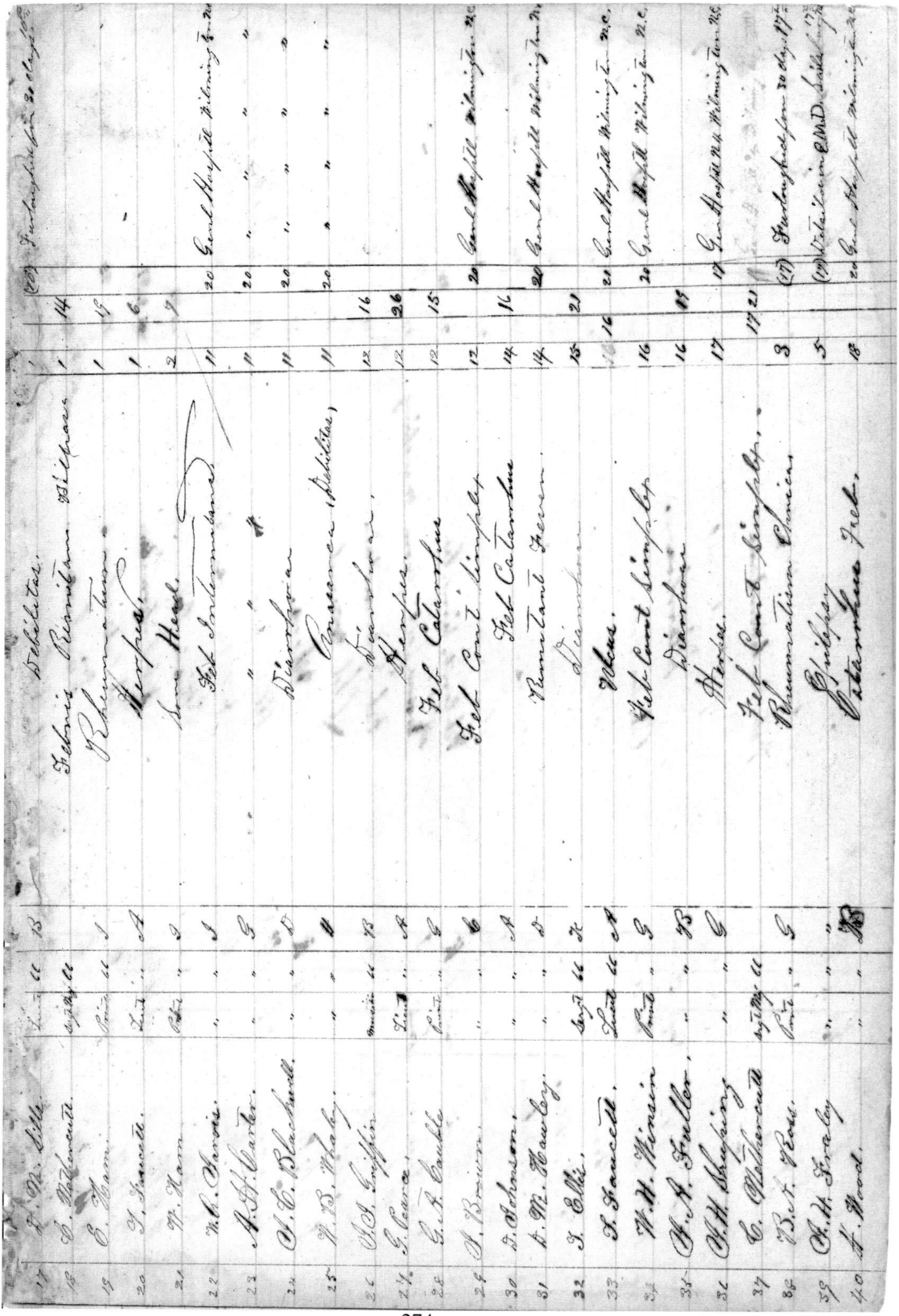

17	D. M. Sille.	Lieut	66	B	Debilitas.	1		(10)	Furloughed for 30 days 10th
18	C. Nethercutt.	Sgt Maj	66		Febris Remittens Billiosa	1	14		
19	E. Ham.	Privt	66	I	Rheumatism.	1	19		
20	J. Faucett.	Lieut	"	A	Herpes.	1	6		
21	W. Ham	Privt	"	I	Sore Head.	2	7		
22	W. R. Jarvis.	"	"	I	Feb Intermittens	11		20	Genl Hospitl Wilmington NC
23	A. H. Carter.	"	"	G	" " "	11		20	" " " "
24	J. C. Blackwell.	"	"	D	Diarrhoea	11		20	" " " "
25	W. B. Whaley.	"	"	H	Anasarca (Debilitas)	11		20	" " " "
26	J. J. Griffin	musician	66	B	Diarrhoea.	12	16		
27	G. Pearce.	Lieut	"	A	Herpes.	12	26		
28	G. A. Cauble	Privt	"	G	Feb Catarrhus	12	15		
29	J. Brown.	"	"	C	Feb Cont Simplex	12		20	Genl Hospitl Wilmington NC
30	D. Johnson.	"	"	A	Feb Catarrhus	14	16		
31	D. M. Hawley.	"	"	D	Remittant Fever.	14		20	Genl Hospitl Wilmington NC
32	J. Ellis.	Sergt	66	K	Diarrhoea	15	21		
33	J. Faucett.	Lieut	66	A	Ulcus.	16	16	21	Genl Hospitl Wilmington N.C.
34	W. H. Winsin	Privt	"	G	Feb Cont Simplex	16		20	Genl Hospitl Wilmington N.C.
35	J. A. Fuller.	"	"	B	Diarrhoea	16	19		
36	J. H. Shuping	"	"	G	Herpes.	17		17	Gen Hospitl No 4 Wilmington NC
37	C. Nethercutt	Sgt Maj	66		Feb Cont Simplex.	17	21		[illegible]
38	B. A. Ross.	Privt	"	G	Rheumatism Chronic	3		(17)	Furloughed for 30 days 17th
39	J. H. Fraley	"	"	"	Epilepsy	5		(17)	Detailed in C.M.D. Sailsbury 17th
40	H. Wood.	"	"	B	Catarrhus Feb.	18		20	Genl Hospitl Wilmington NC

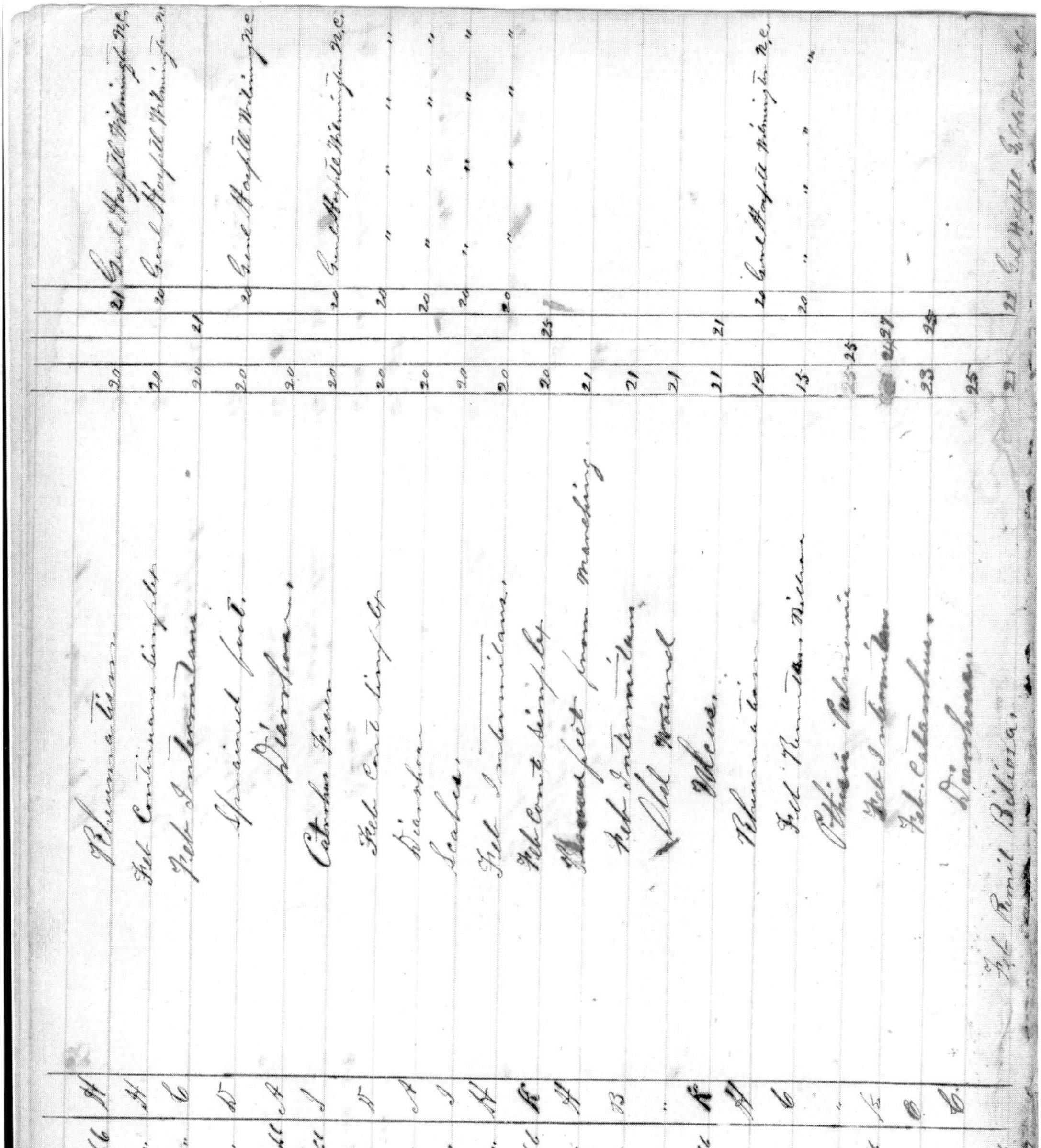

41	J. M. Henderson	Pt	66	H	Rheumatism	20		21	Genl Hospitl Wilmington N.C.
42	O. Harrison	"	"	H	Feb Continuans simplex	20		20	Genl Hospitl Wilmington N.C.
43	J. Hardee	"	"	C	Feb Intermitans	20	21		
44	J. G. Dalrymple	"	"	D	Sprained foot.	20		20	Genl Hospitl Wilmington N.C.
45	S. T. Phipps	Corpl	66	A	Diarrhoea.	20			
46	W. Wilkerson	Pvt	66	I	Catarrhus Fever	20		20	Genl Hospitl Wilmington N.C.
47	W. T. Jones	"	"	D	Feb Cont simplex	20		20	" " " "
48	R. Crabtree	"	"	A	Diarrhoea	20		20	" " " "
49	A B. Watson	"	"	I	Scabes.	20		20	" " " "
50	W. D. Spence	"	"	H	Feb Intermitans.	20		20	" " " "
51	J. P. Garris	Music	66	K	Feb Cont simplex	20	25		
52	F. G. Spence	Pvt	"	H	Sore feet from marching	21			
53	G. W. Coppage	"	"	B	Feb Intermitans	21			
54	J. D. Griffin	"	"	"	Old wound	21			
55	J. Whitley	Sergt	66	K	Ulcus.	21	21		
56	G. Pearce	Pvt	"	H	Rheumatism	12		20	Genl Hospitl Wilmington N.C.
57	B. J. Herring	"	"	C	Feb Remittans Billious	13		20	" " " "
58	J. Walker	"	"	"	Phthisis Pulmonia	25	25		
59	J. Ellis	Sergt	66	E	Feb Intermitans	[illegible]	24	27	
60	J. Hall	Lieut	"	C	Feb. Catarrhus	23	25		
61	J. Hardee	Pvt	"	C	Diarrhoea.	25			
62	John H. Witherington	Col	66		Feb Remit Billiosa.	21		22	Genl Hospitl Goldsboro N.C.

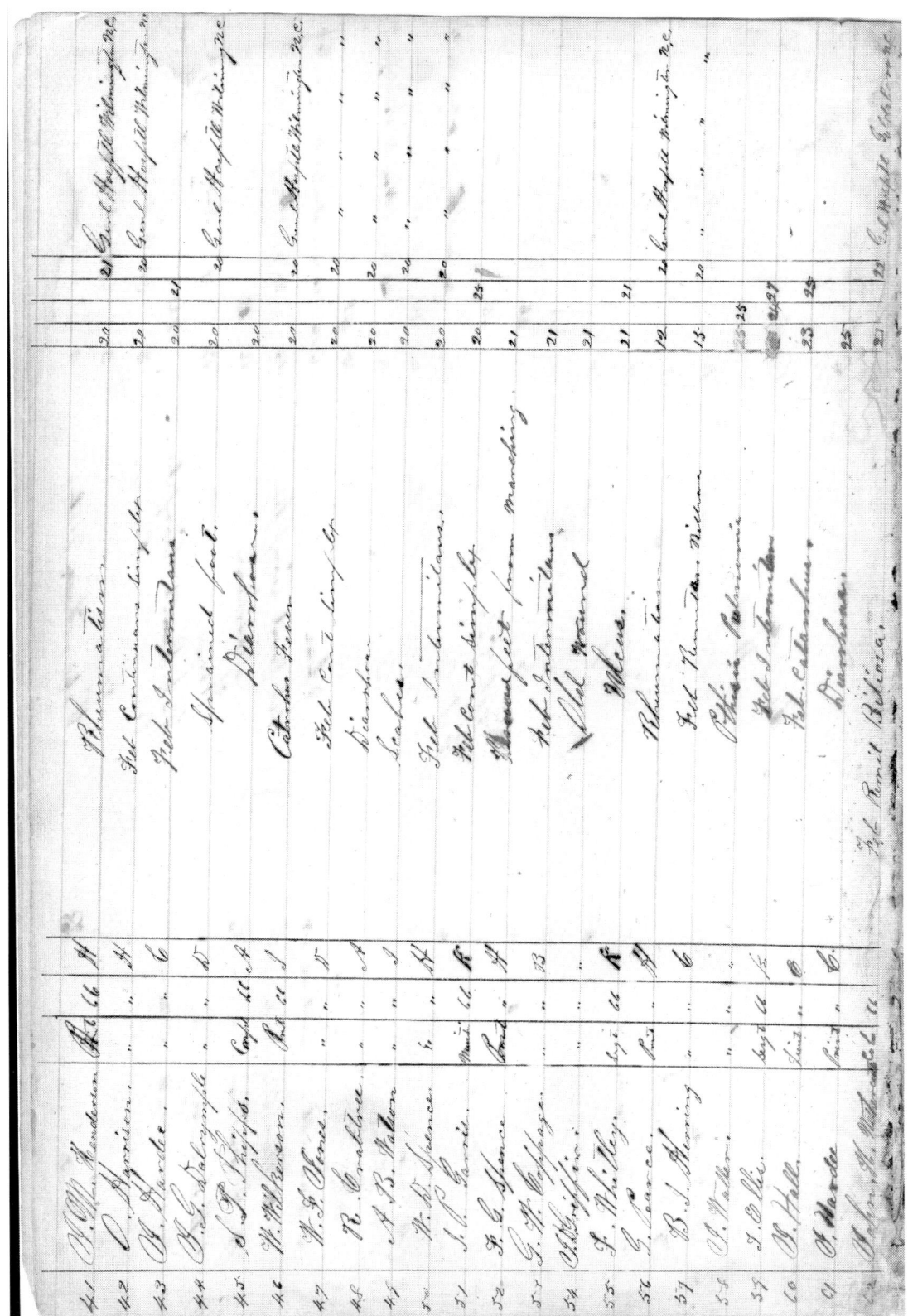

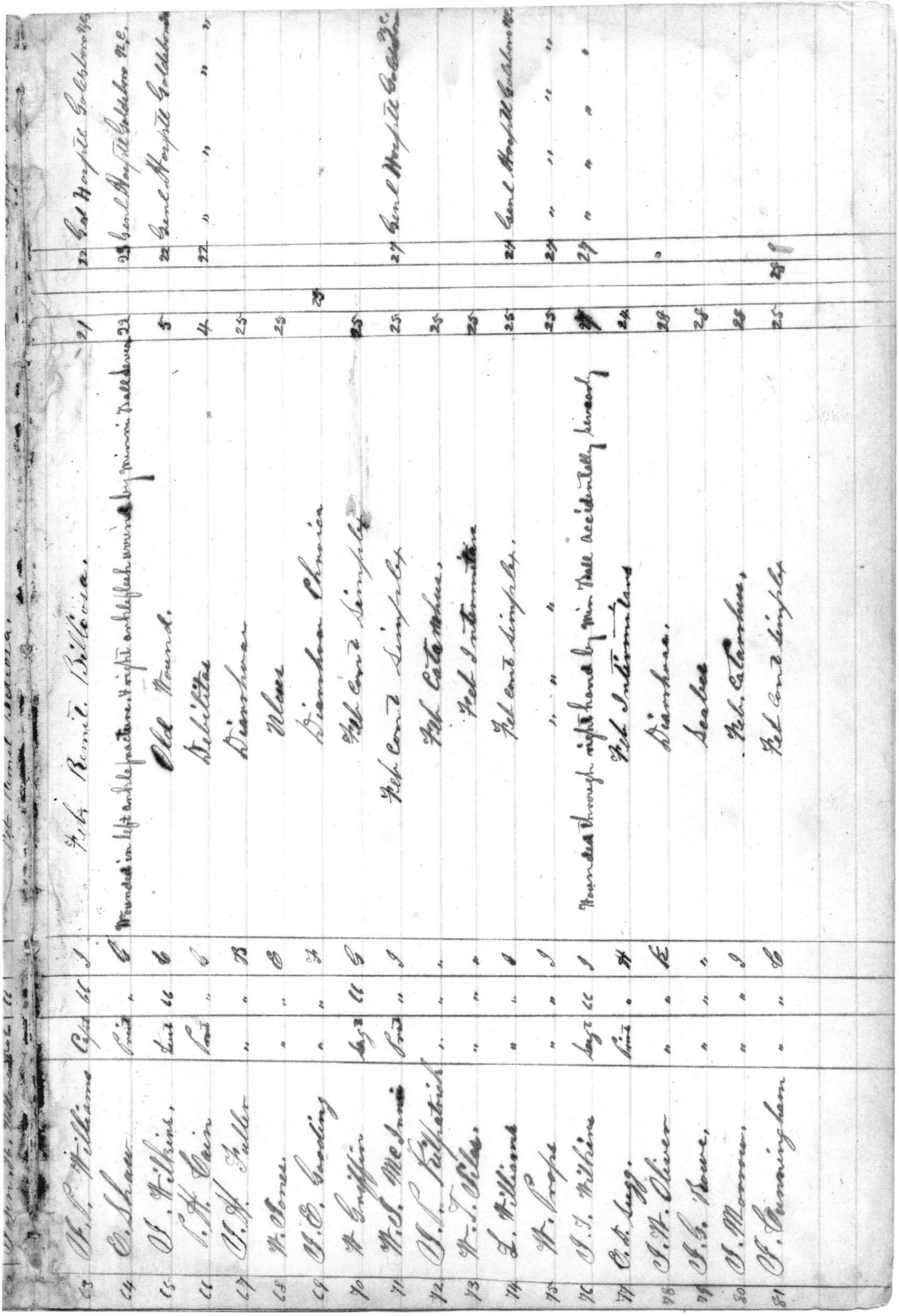

62	[illegible]		"		Feb Remit Billoosa.					[illegible]
63	F. L. Williams	Capt	66	I	Feb. Remit. Billoosa.	21			22	Gel Hospitl Goldsboro N.C.
64	E. Shaw	Privt	"	G	Wounded in left ankle fracture, & right ankle flesh wound by minnie ball severe	22			23	Genl Hospitl Goldsboro N.C.
65	J. Wilkins	Lieut	66	C	Old Wound.	5			22	Genl Hospitl Goldsboro
66	J. H. Cain	Privt	"	C	Debilitas	4			22	" " " "
67	J. H. Fuller	"	"	B	Diarrhoea	25				
68	W. Jones	"	"	E	Ulcus	25				
69	J. E. Gooding	"	"	F	Diarrhoea Chronica		23			
70	W Griffin	Sergt	66	G	Feb Cont Simplex	25				
71	W. J. McInnis	Privt	"	I	Feb Cont Simplex	25			27	Genl Hospitl Goldsboro N.C.
72	J. L. Kilpatrick	"	"	"	Feb Catarrhus.	25				
73	W. J. Siles	"	"	"	Feb Intermittens	25				
74	L. Williams	"	"	I	Feb cont Simplex.	25			27	Genl Hospitl Goldsboro N.C.
75	W. Props	"	"	I	" " "	25			27	" " " "
76	J. J. Wilkins	Sergt	66	I	Wounded through right hand by min Ball accidentally severely	27			27	" " " "
77	C. L. Sugg	Privt	"	H	Feb Intermittens	24				
78	J. W. Oliver	"	"	K	Diarrhoea.	28				
79	J. G. Rowe	"	"	"	Scabies	28				
80	J. Morrow	"	"	I	Feb. Catarrhus.	28				
81	J. Cunningham	"	"	C	Feb cont Simplex	25		28		

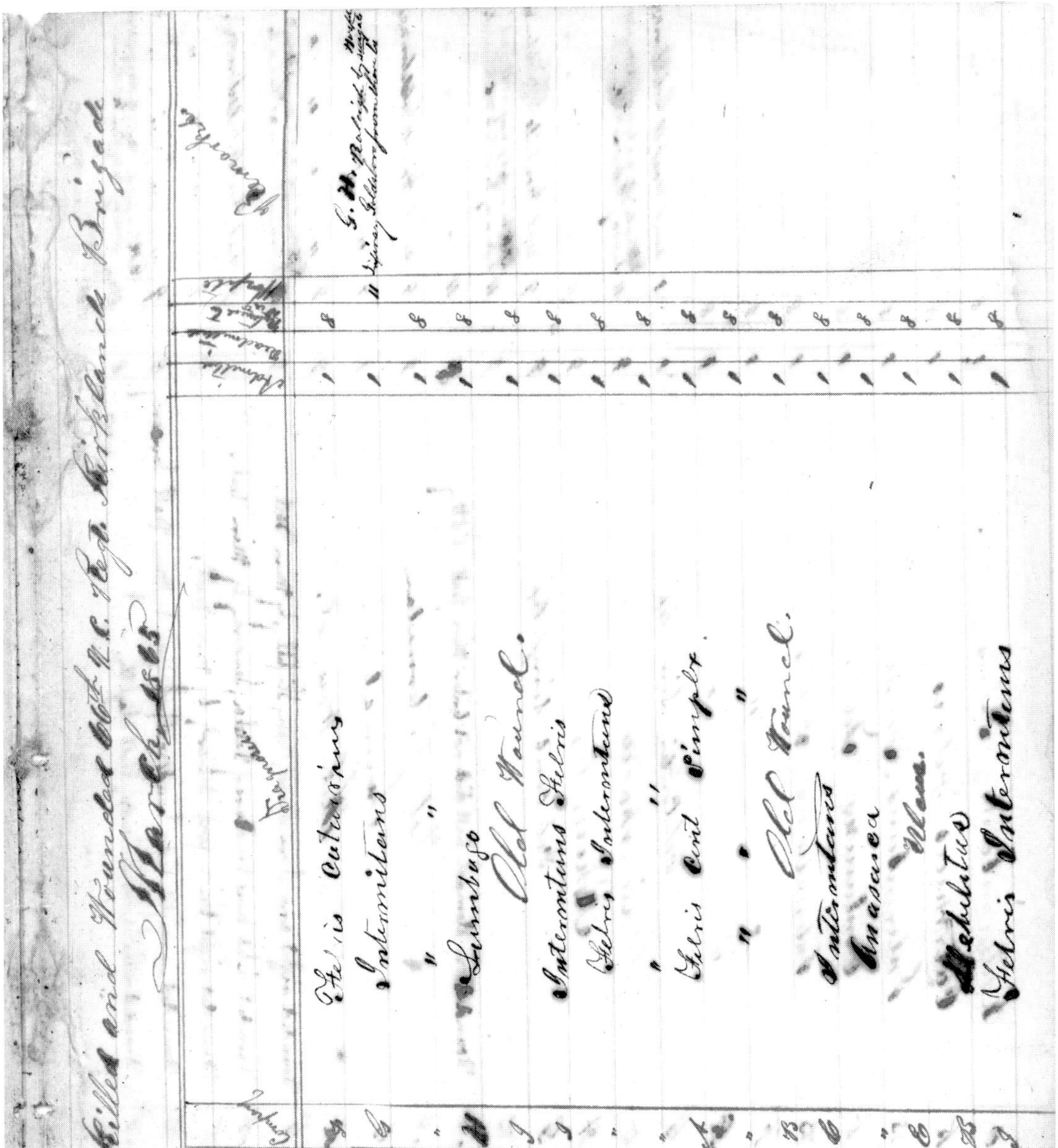

Register of Sick, Killed and Wounded 66th N.C. Regt. Kirklands Brigade
March 1865

No	Name	Rank	Regt	Company	Diagnosis	Admitted	Dead	Returned to Duty	Hospital	Remarks
1	V. E. Gooding	Pvt	66	D	Febris [illegible]	1		8		
2	G. T. Link	"	"	G	Intermittens	1			11	G. H. Raleigh by [illegible] Goldsboro from there to [illegible]
3	V. C. Martin	"	"	"	" "	1		8		
4	C. D. Sugg	"	"	H	Lumbago	1		8		
5	V. Rhodes	Corpl	66	I	Old Wound.	1		8		
6	V. P. Kilpatrick	Pvt	"	I	Intermittens Febris	1		8		
7	W. Giles	"	"	"	Febris Intermittens	1		8		
8	V. Morrow	"	"	"	" "	1		8		
9	S. T. Phipps	Corpl	66	A	Febris Cont Simplex	1		8		
10	J. S. Whitaker	Pvt	"	"	" " "	1		8		
11	V. D. Griffin	"	"	B	Old Wound.	1		8		
12	V. Hardee	"	"	C	Intermittens	1		8		
13	V. Waller	"	"	"	Anasarca	1		8		
14	W. Jones	"	"	E	Ulcers	1		8		
15	H. Fuller	"	"	B	Debilitas	1		8		
16	O. Baker	"	"	I	Febris Intermittens	1		8		

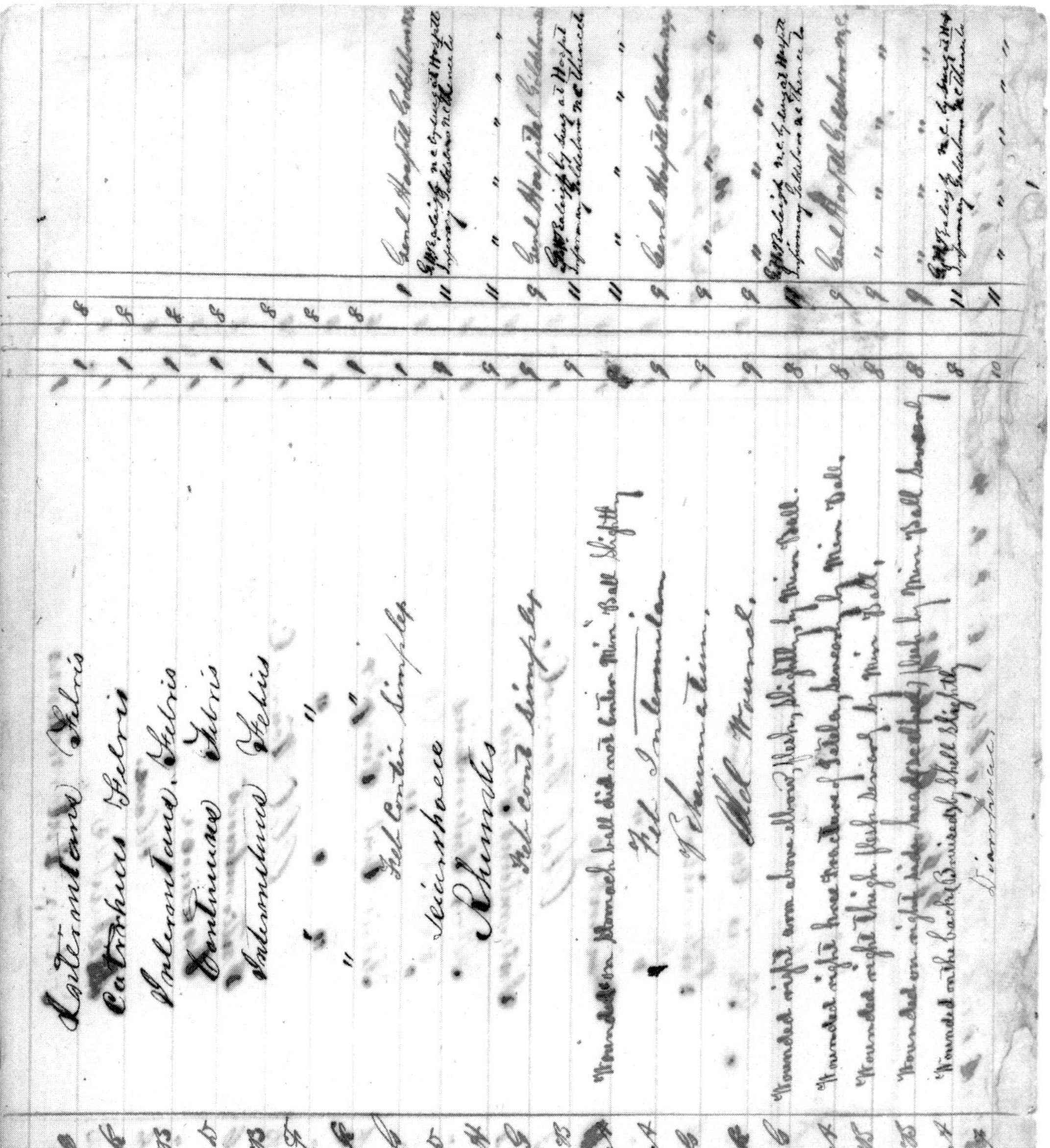

No.	Name	Rank	Regt	Co.	Disease / Wound
17	H. Wilmington	Sgt	16	C	Intermittent Febris
18	J. W. Oliver	Pvt	"	E	Catarrhus Febris
19	R. J. Bowden	"	"	B	Intermittent Febris
20	J. Mariner	"	"	D	Continued Febris
21	W. B. Batchelor	"	"	B	Intermittent Febris
22	H. E. Parham	"	"	F	"
23	J. G. Rowe	"	"	[illegible]	"
24	W. Griffin	Sgt	16	C	"
25	L. J. Catlett	Pvt	16	D	Feb Contin Simplex
26	G. W. Pearce	"	"	H	Diarrhoea
27	[illegible]	"	"	G	Rheumatis
28	W. A. Matthews	"	"	B	Feb cont Simplex
29	[illegible]	"	"	A	Wounded in Stomach ball did not enter Min Ball Slightly
30	W. Cook	"	"	A	Feb Intermitten
31	Lt. W. H. Brandon	Lt	16	C	Rheumatism
32	J. J. Ollis	Pvt	"	[illegible]	Old Wound
33	J. M. Eudy	"	"	C	Wounded right arm above elbow, flesh, slightly, by min ball
34	J. H. Christian	"	"	A	Wounded right knee fracture of patella, severely, by min ball
35	J. J. Wiggs	Sgt	16	B	Wounded right thigh flesh severely by min ball
36	J. T. Bunting	Pvt	"	B	Wounded on right side [illegible] by min ball severely
37	J. Whitaker	Pvt	"	A	Wounded on the back bruised by shell slightly
38	W. L. Christman	"	"	[illegible]	Diarrhoea

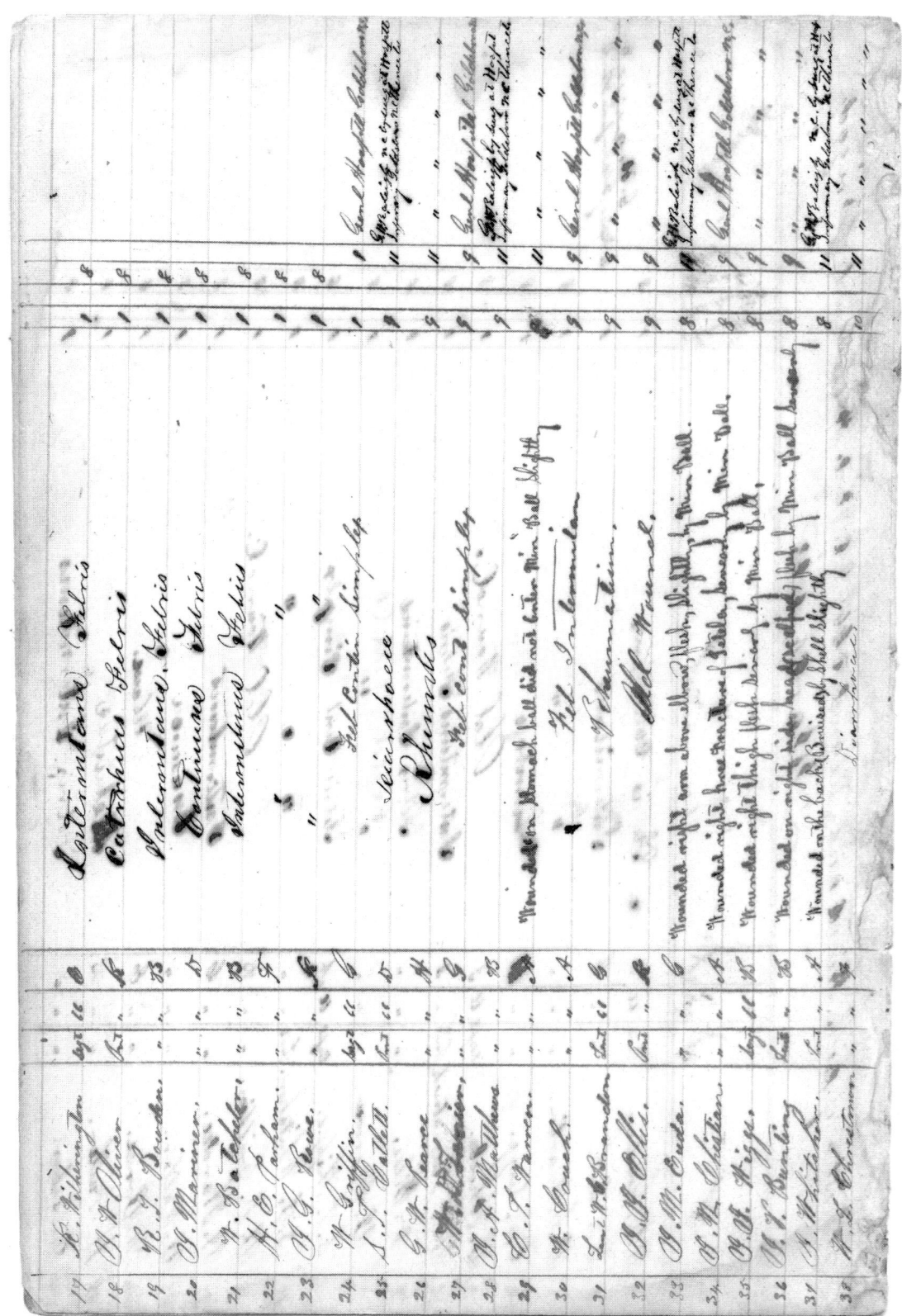

Continued

Names of Disease	Seat of Disease	Special Diseases.	Original Admissions Cases	Original Admissions Death	Admitted During the Cases	Admitted During the Death
Are inflammation but frequently attended / inflammation During their course	Accidents, Injuries &c.	Contusio.				
		Vulnus Incisum.				
		" Lateratum.	28			
		" Punctum.				
		" Slop.	11			
		Erysipelas Traum.				
		Luxatio Simplex.				
		" Composita.				
		Fractura Simplex.				
		" Composita.				
		Subluxatio.				
		Prolapsus Ani.				
		Hernia Inguinalis.				
		" Femoralis.				
		Concussio Cerebri.				
		Compressio Cerebri.				
		Suicidium.				
		Asphyxia:				
		By Hanging.				
		Drowning.				
		Irrespirable Air.				
		Military Execution.				
		Total.				

General Summary.

	Remaining last Report: Sick.	Remaining last Report: Wounded	Remaining last Report: Total	Taken Sick or Wounded during Month: Taken Sick or Wounded during month.	Supervening diseases.	Aggregate.	Returned to Duty.	Sent to General Hospital	Dismissed cured - to be returned.	On Furlough.	Discharged.	Deserted.	Died.	Remaining: Sick	Remaining: Wounded.	Remaining: Total.	Mean: Month.	Mean: Officers.	Mean: Enlisted Men.
July	155	5	160	200		360.	262	45.					1	47	5	52.		30	501
August	73	3	76.	208		368	343	41		1	2	3	2	73	5	76			
September	67	3	70	175			123	42		18		1		64	3	67		26	460
October.	14	0	14	143		213	150	47			3			14		14	Octob.	32	540
November	15	1	16	51		65	32	17						15	1	16	Nov	37	624
December 1864	27	1	28	78		84	37	29						27	1	28	Decem	35	620
January 1865	27		27	85		113	50	34			1		1	27		27	Janry	36	630

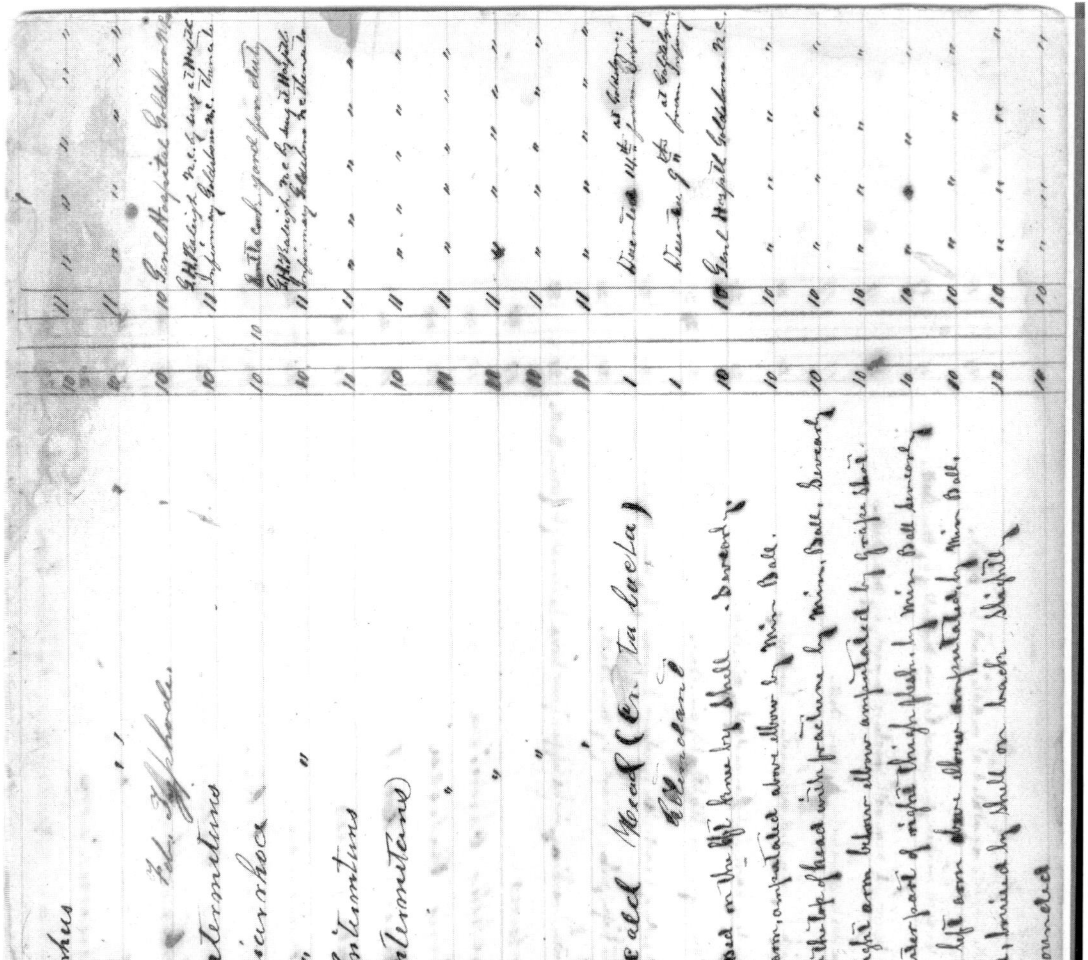

39	W. Cox.	Pvt	66	C	Catarrhus	10	11	" " " " "
40	W. Woodshee	"	"	B	"	10	11	" " " " "
41	R. Hinson.	"	"	C	Feb. Typhoide.	10	10	Genl Hospital Goldsboro N.C.
42	A. R. Mitchel	"	"	A	Intermitens	10	11	G.H. Raleigh N.C. by surg at Hospital Infirmary Goldsboro N.C. thence to
43	J. W. Brown	Corpl	66	H	Diarrhoea	10	10	Sent to cook yard for duty
44	P. Anderson	"	"	C	" "	10	11	G.H. Raleigh N.C. by surg at Hospital Infirmary Goldsboro N.C. thence to
45	G. B. Guffy	Pvt	66	I	Intermitens	10	11	" " " " "
46	C. H. Lyon.	"	"	A	Intermitens)	10	11	" " " " "
47	M. B. Bowden	"	"	B	" "	11	11	" " " " "
48	J. Tindal	"	"	C	" "	11	11	" " " " "
49	D. Johnson.	"	"	A	" "	11	11	" " " " "
50	J. Sumlin.	"	"	K	" "	11	11	" " " " "
51	W. Ham.	"	"	I	Scald Head (Cr. ta lacta)	1		Deserted 14th at Goldsboro from Infirmary
52	R. Brown.	Cook	66	K	Attendant	1		Deserted 9th at Goldsboro from Infirmary
53	J. Alforde.	Pvt	"	B	Wounded, Bruised on the left knee by Shell. Severely	10	10	Genl Hospital Goldsboro N.C.
54	N. Matthews	"	"	K	Wounded left arm, amputated above elbow by Min Ball.	10	10	" " " "
55	N. White.	"	"	F	Wounded on the top of head with fracture by Min. Ball. Severely	10	10	" " " "
56	S. S. Carter.	Lieut	66	F	Wounded right arm below elbow amputated by Grape Shot.	10	10	" " " "
57	J. Barlee.	Pvt	"	C	Wounded outer part of right thigh flesh. by Min Ball Severely	10	10	" " " "
58	J. M. Ross.	"	"	E	Wounded left arm above elbow amputated by Min Ball.	10	10	" " " "
59	H. A. Hines	"	"	B	Wounded, bruised by Shell on back Slightly	10	10	" " " "
60	Mc Farlin				Wounded	10	10	" " " "

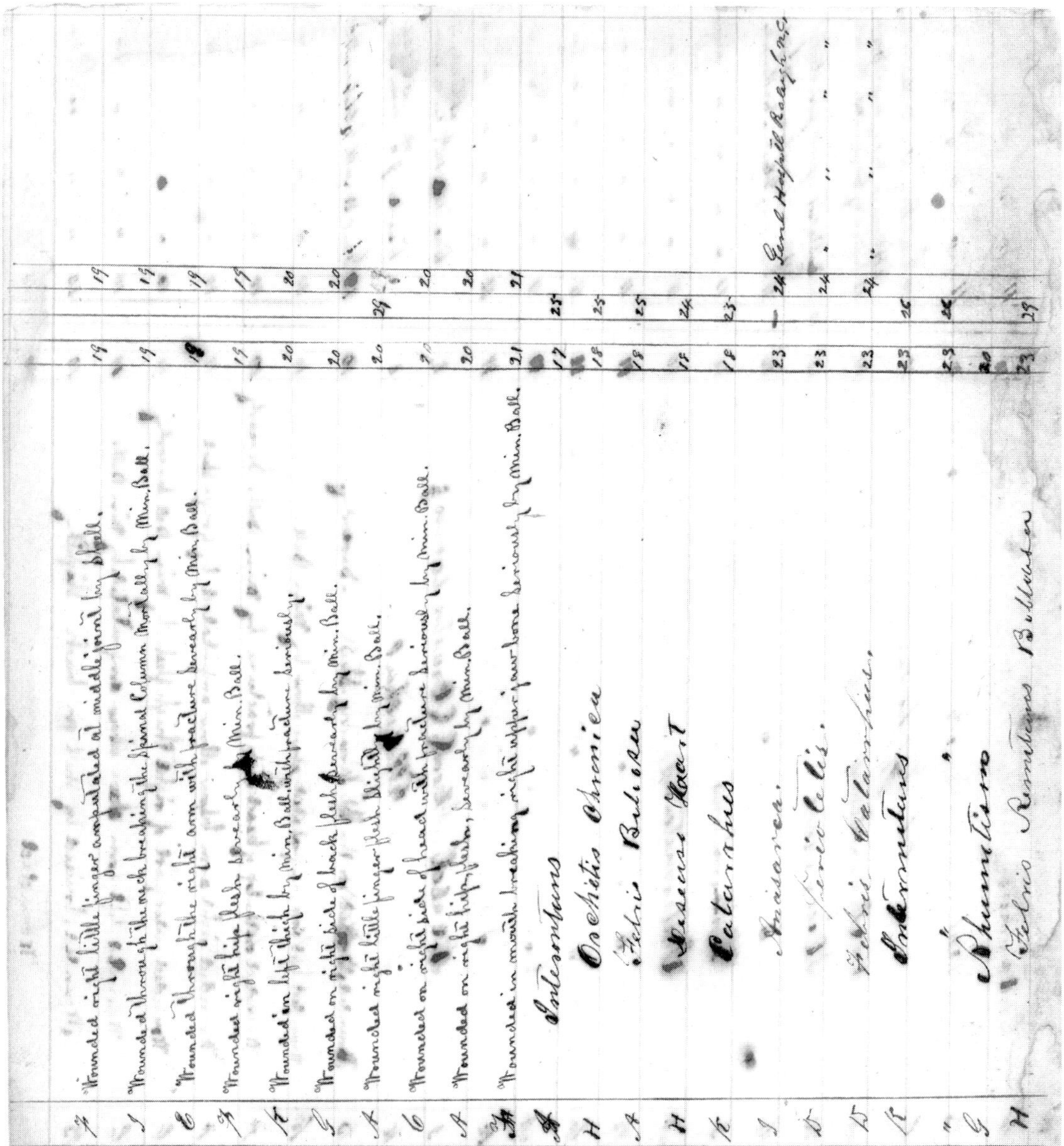

61	H. B. London.	Prvt	66	F	Wounded right little finger amputated at middle joint by Shell.	19		19	
62	A. Wooten.	Corpl	"	I	Wounded through the neck breaking the Spinal Column Mortally by Min. Ball.	19		19	
63	J. Braxton.	Prvt	66	E	Wounded through the right arm with fracture Severely by Min. Ball.	19		19	
64	L. M. Paton.	"	"	F	Wounded right hip flesh severely by Min. Ball.	19		19	
65	J. A. Boswell.	"	"	K	Wounded in left thigh by Min. Ball with fracture Seriously.	20		20	
66	B. Brown.	"	"	G	Wounded on right side of back flesh Severely by Min. Ball.	20		20	
67	J. W. Garrard	"	"	A	Wounded right little finger flesh Slightly by Min. Ball.	20	29		
68	J. Stroud.	"	"	C	Wounded on right side of head with fracture Seriously by Min. Ball.	20		20	
69	W. R. Scarlett.	Sergt	66	A	Wounded on right hip flesh, Severely by Min. Ball.	20		20	
70	J. Whitaker.	Prvt	"	H	Wounded in mouth breaking right upper jaw bone Seriously by Min. Ball.	21		21	
71	F. Mangrum.	"	"	A	Intermittens	17	25		
72	C. S. Croom.	Sergt	66	H	Orchitis Chronica	18	25		
73	Lieut Latta.	Lieut	"	A	Febris Biliosa	18	25		
74	J. Brown.	Corpl	"	H	Disease Heart	18	24		
75	H. Thomlinson.	Prvt	66	K	Catarrhus	18	23		
76	W. J. More.	"	"	I	Anasarca.	23	—	24	Genl Hospitl Raleigh N.C.
77	J. G. Dalrymple	"	"	D	Periolitis.	23		24	" " " "
78	J. C. Perry	"	"	D	Febris Catarrhus.	23		24	" " " "
79	R. Bailey	"	"	K	Intermittens	23	26		
80	J. D. Evans	"	"	"	" "	23	26		
81	B. A. Ross	"	"	G	Rheumatism	20			
82	J. W. Rouse.	"	"	H	Febris Remittens Bilious	23	29		

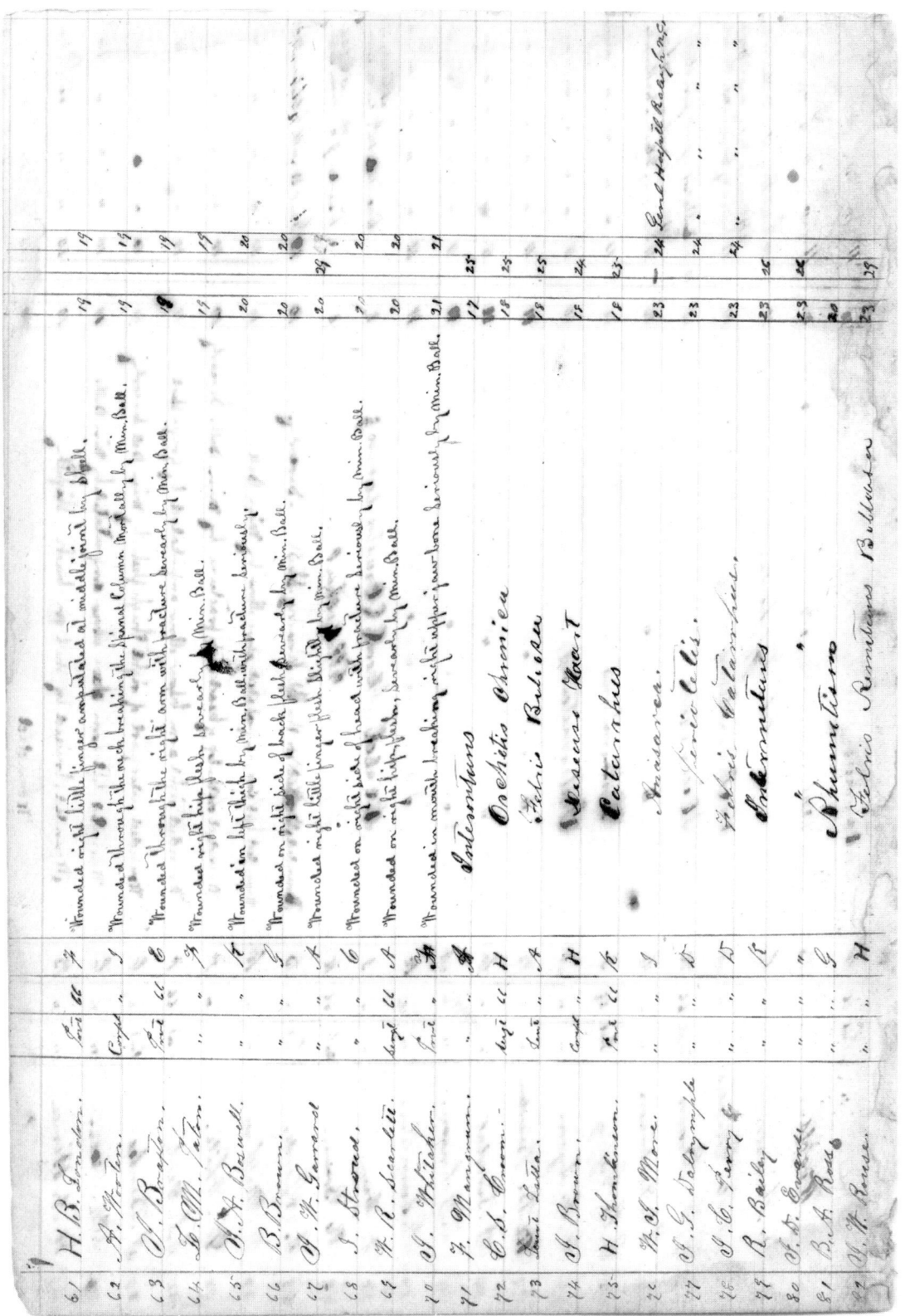

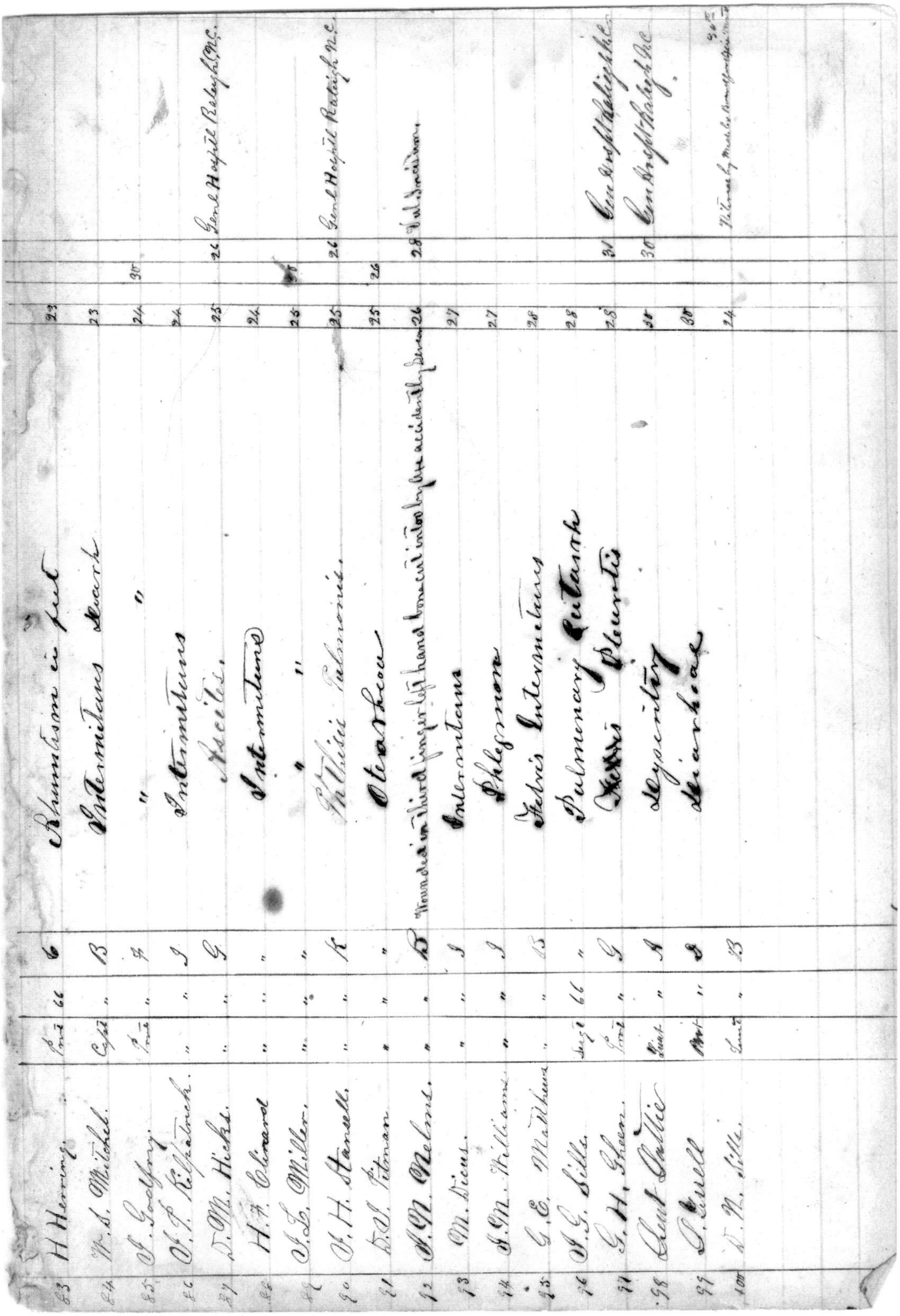

83	H Herring	Pvt	66	C	Rheumatism in feet	23			
84	W. S. Mitchel	Capt	"	B	Intermitans Quart	23			
85	J. Godfrey	Pvt	"	F	" "	24	30		
86	J. P. Kilpatrick	"	"	I	Intermitens	24			
87	D. M. Hicks	"	"	G	Ascites	25		26	Genl Hospitl Raleigh N.C.
88	H. F. Clinard	"	"	"	Intermitens	24			
89	J. L. Miller	"	"	"	" "	25	30		
90	J. H. Stansell	"	"	K	Phthisis Pulmonis	25		26	Genl Hospitl Raleigh N.C.
91	D. J. Pitman	"	"	"	Otorrhoea	25	26		
92	J. N. Nelms	"	"	B	Wounded in third finger left hand bone cut in two by axe accidently Severe	26		28	Vul. Incision
93	M. Dicus	"	"	I	Intermitans	27			
94	J. M. Williams	"	"	I	Phlegmon	27			
95	G. E. Matthews	"	"	B	Febris Intermitens	28			
96	J. G. Sills	Sergt	66	"	Pulmonary Catarrh	28			
97	G. H. Green	Pvt	"	G	~~Febris~~ Pleuritis	28		31	Gen Hospt Raleigh N.C
98	Lieut Dattie	Lieut	"	A	Dysentery	30		30	Gen Hospt Raleigh N.C
99	P. Lurell	Pvt	"	D	Diarrhoea	30			
100	D. N. Sills	Lieut	"	B		24			Returned by Med. Ex Board [illegible] 30th

April 1865

Register of Sick Killed and Wounded of 66th N.C. Regiment

No.	Name	Rank	Regiment	Company	Diagnosis	Admitted	[illegible]	Returned to Duty	Hosp. [illegible]	Remarks
1	B. A. Ross.	Privt	66	G		1				
2	H Herring.	"	"	C		1		9		
3	W. S. Mitchel	Capt	"	B		1		9		
4	J. J. Kilpatrick.	Privt	"	I		1				
5	H. F. Clinard.	"	"	G		1		4		
6	M. Ficus.	"	"	I		1		3		
7	J. M. Williams.	"	"	"		1		3		
8	G. E. Matthews.	"	"	B.		1		6		
9	J. G. Sills	Sergt	"	B		1		6		
10	S. Ferrell	Privt	"	D		1				
11	C. Simpson.	"	"	A		1				
12	L E Pence	Sergt	"			2				
13	I S Veach	Privt	"	A		2		3		
14	J R Griffin	Sergt	"	C		2		6		
15	John Johnson	Privt	"	D	Febris Typhoides.	2			3	Genl Hospital Raleigh N.C.
16	R. Johnson	"	"	C		3		8		

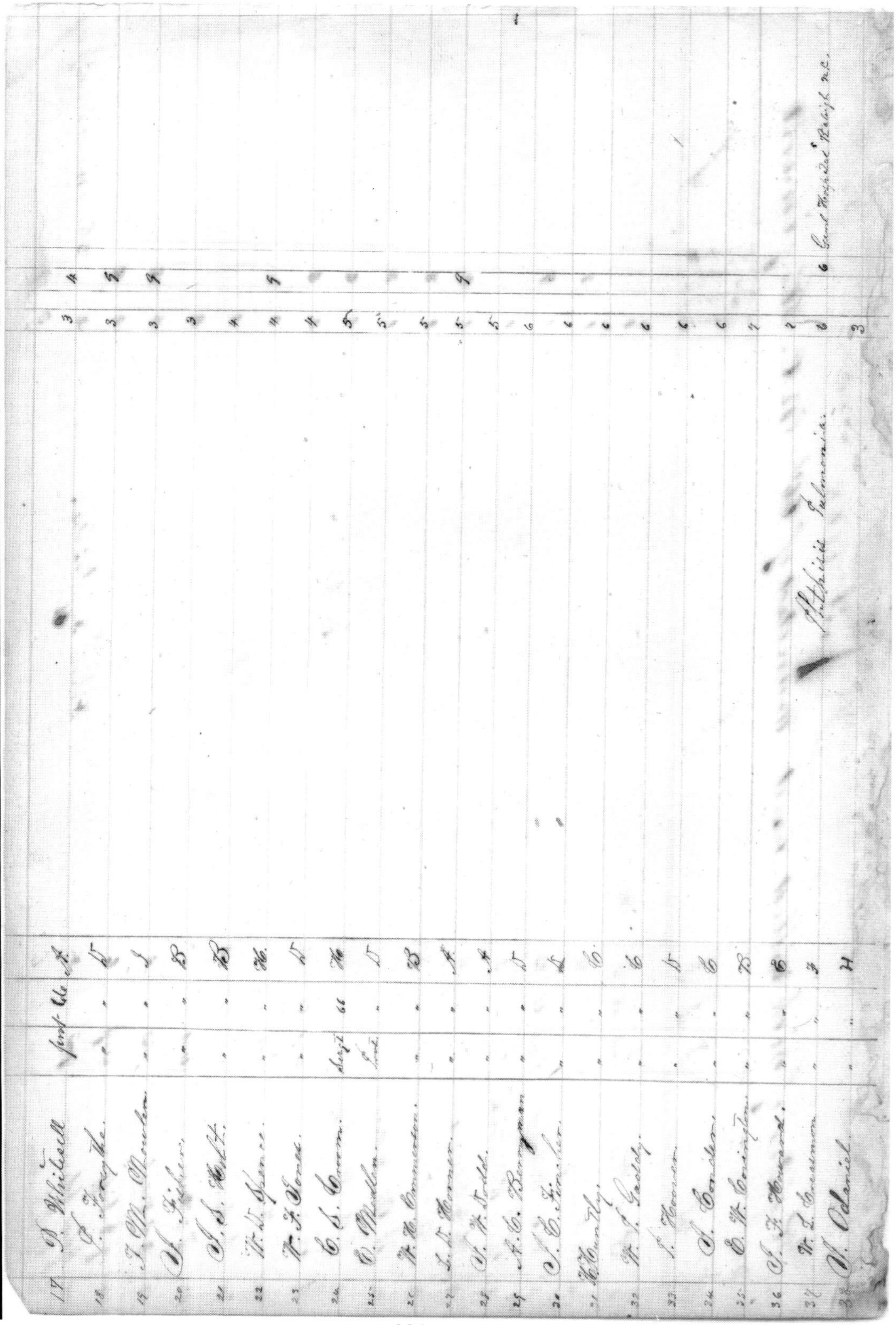

17	A. Whitesell	Priv	66	A	3	4	
18	J. Forsythe	"	"	D	3	5	
19	J. M. Moulon	"	"	I	3	9	
20	J. Fisher	"	"	B	3		
21	J. S. Holt	"	"	B	4		
22	W. D. Spence	"	"	H	4	9	
23	W. F. Jones	"	"	D	4		
24	C. S. Crows	Sergt	66	H	5		
25	C. Mullen	Corpl	"	D	5		
26	W. H. Emmerton	"	"	B	5		
27	L. D. Horner	"	"	F	5	9	
28	J. W. Dodd	"	"	F	5		
29	A. C. Berryman	"	"	D	6		
30	J. C. Fincher	"	"	L	6		
31	H. Huntly	"	"	C	6		
32	W. J. Gaddy	"	"	C	6		
33	J. Hoover	"	"	D	6		
34	J. Conder	"	"	C	6		
35	E. W. Covington	"	"	B	7		
36	J. F. Howard	"	"	C	7		
37	W. L. Ensmon	"	"	F	6	6	Phthisis Pulmonalis. Genl Hospital Raleigh N.C.
38	J. Odaniel	"	"	H	3		

39	W. Tarlton.	Pvt	66	C	8
40	L. Yelton.	"	"	D	9
41	J. A. Withrow.	"	"	I	9
42	H. B. Alford	"	"	D	9

Continued.

Non-inflammatory Diseases, the forms of Inflammation occasionally attendant on them

Non-inflammatory, but frequently attended by Inflammation during their Course.

Seat of Disease	Special Diseases.	Original Admission: Cases	Original Admission: Deaths	Readmitted during month: Cases	Readmitted during month: Deaths
Abdomen Disease	Vermes.				
	Ischuria vera.				
	Enuresis.				
Organs of Special Sense.	Amaurosis.	2			
	Hemeralopia.				
	Nyctalopia.				
	Cataracta.				
	Otalgia.				
	Otorrhea.				
	Surditas.				
	Ozaena.				
Arteries and Veins.	Aneurisma verum.				
	" Spurium				
	Varicocele.				
	Venae varicosae.				
Skin and Cellular Tissue.	Scabies.				
	Eczema.				
	Impetigo.				
	Psoriasis.				
	Urticaria.				
	Lepra.				
	Herpes.				
	Anasarca.				
	Ulcus.				
	Fistula in Ano.				
	Gangrena Sicca.				
	" Humida.				
	Phagedena Gangrenosa.				
Urinary and Genitial Organs.	Gonorrhoea Simplex.				
	Strictura Urethrae.				
	Phymosis.				
	Paraphymosis.				
	Bubo Simplex.				
	Ulcus Penis Simp.				
	Hydrocele.				
	Haematocele.				
	Gonorrhoea virulenta.				
	Syphilis Primitiva.				
	Bubo Specific.				
	Sarcocele Syphilit.				
	Calculus.				
[illegible]	Morsus Serpentis.				
	Pustula Maligna.				
	Equinia				
	Uraemia.				
Blood Affected or addition of certain Specifics.	Pyaemia.				
	Plethora.				
	Anaemia.				
	Scorbutus.				
	Purpura.				
	Struma.				
	Syphilis Consecutiva				
	Podagra.				
Malignant Disease.	Scirrhus.				
	Fungus Haematodes.				
	Melanosis.				
Accid. [illegible]	Ambustio.				
	Gelatio.				
	Toxicum.				

Continued.

Forms of Disease	Seat of Disease (Organs & tissues)	Special Diseases	Original Admission Cases	Original Admission Deaths	Admitted During Month Cases	Admitted During Month Deaths
		Ophthalmia Tarsi.				
Phlegmasiae	Various organs and tissues.	Rheumatismus Acutus.				
		" Chronicus.				
		Synovitis Acuta.				
		" Chronica.				
		Osteitis.	1			
		Periosteitis.				
		Arteritis.				
		Phlebitis.				
		Orchitis.	1			
		Abscessus Acutus.				
		" Chronicus.				
		Phlegmon.	2			
		Anthrax.				
		Paronychia.	1			
		Onychia Maligna.				
		Prostatitis.				
Non-inflammatory Diseases of Great Cavities.	Cranium and Spinal Cavity	Cephalalgia.				
		Chorea.	1			
		Delirium Tremens.				
		Apoplexia.				
		Epilepsia.				
		Paralysis.				
		Neuralgia.				
		Ictus Solis.				
		Mania.				
		Nostalgia.				
		Tetanus Idiopathic.				
		" Traumaticus.				
		Melancholia.				
		Irritatio Spinalis.				
		Debilitas.	2			
		Ebrietas.				
		Alcoholismus Chronic.				
Noninflammatory Diseases or Inflammation occasionally attended upon them.	Thorax.	Haemoptysis Simp.				
		" Tuberculosa.				
		Phthisis.				
		Asthma.				
		Hydrothorax.				
		Hydrops Pericardii.				
		Hypertrophia Cordis.				
		" Falsa.				
		Dilatatio Passiva.				
		" Activa.				
		Angina Pectoris.				
		Aneurisma Aortae.				
		Pertussis.				
	Abdomen.	Constipatio.				
		Colica.				
		" Pictonum.				
		Ileus.	1			
		Cholera Sporad.				
		" Epidemic.				
		Haematemesis.				
		Hemorrhois.				
		Diarrhoea Acuta.				
		" Chronica.				
		Dyspepsia.	1			
		Icterus.				
		Ascites.				
		Diabetes Mellitus.				
		Marasmus.				

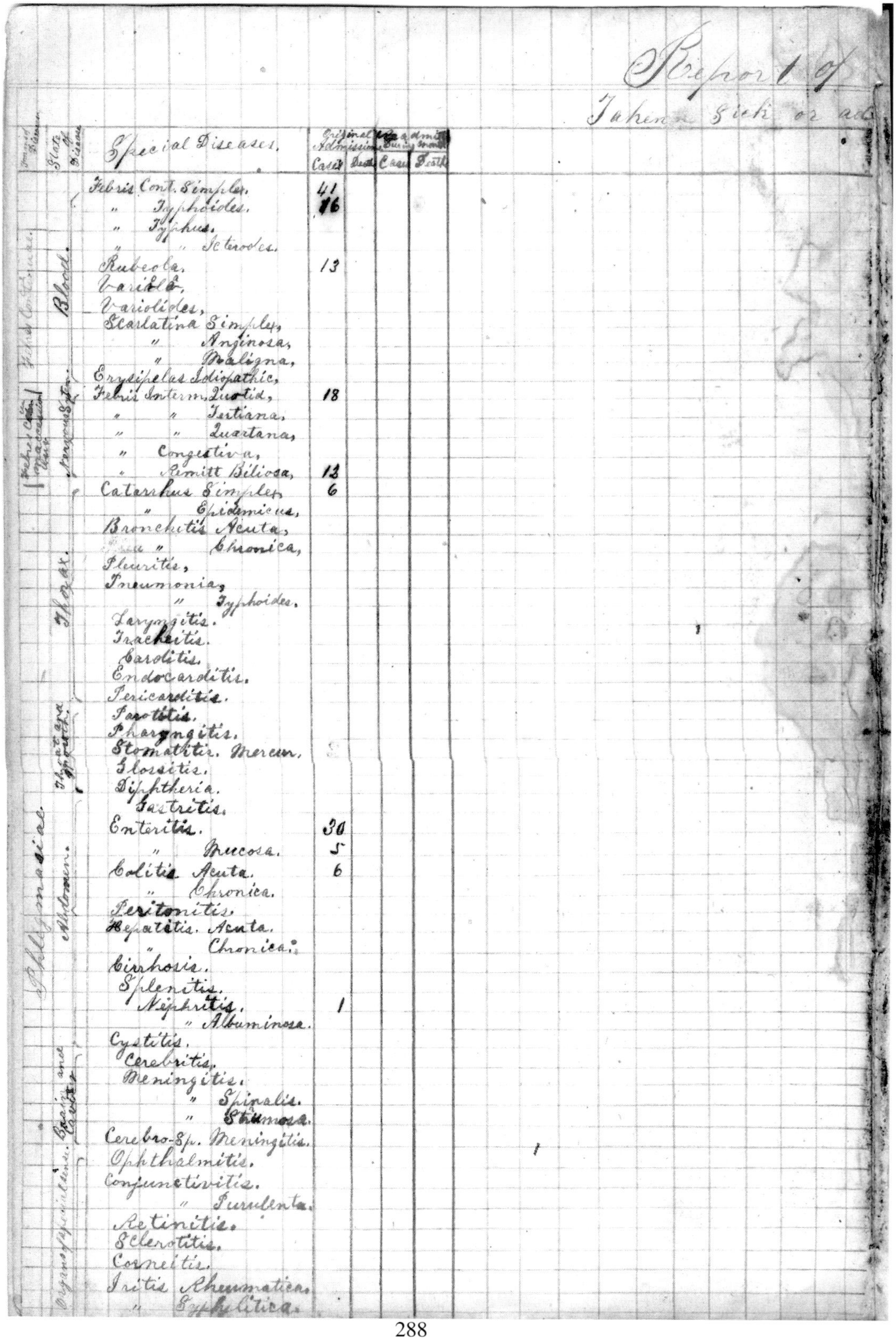

Report of

Taken sick or ad

Seat of Disease	Special Diseases.	Original Admission Cases	Original Admission Deaths	Readmitted Cases	Readmitted Deaths
Blood.	Febris Cont. Simplex.	41			
	" Typhoides.	16			
	" Typhus.				
	" " Icteroides.				
	Rubeola.	13			
	Variola.				
	Varioloides.				
	Scarlatina Simplex.				
	" Anginosa.				
	" Maligna.				
	Erysipelas Idiopathic.				
Nervous Sys.	Febris Interm. Quotid.	18			
	" " Tertiana.				
	" " Quartana.				
	" Congestiva.				
	" Remitt Biliosa.	12			
Thorax.	Catarrhus Simplex.	6			
	" Epidemicus.				
	Bronchitis Acuta.				
	" Chronica.				
	Pleuritis.				
	Pneumonia.				
	" Typhoides.				
	Laryngitis.				
	Tracheitis.				
	Carditis.				
	Endocarditis.				
	Pericarditis.				
Throat and Mouth.	Parotitis.				
	Pharyngitis.				
	Stomatitis. Mercur.				
	Glossitis.				
	Diphtheria.				
Abdomen.	Gastritis.				
	Enteritis.	30			
	" Mucosa.	5			
	Colitis Acuta.	6			
	" Chronica.				
	Peritonitis.				
	Hepatitis. Acuta.				
	" Chronica.				
	Cirrhosis.				
	Splenitis.				
	Nephritis.	1			
	" Albuminosa.				
	Cystitis.				
Brain and Cord.	Cerebritis.				
	Meningitis.				
	" Spinalis.				
	" Strumosa.				
	Cerebro-Sp. Meningitis.				
Organs of Special Sense.	Ophthalmitis.				
	Conjunctivitis.				
	" Purulenta.				
	Retinitis.				
	Sclerotitis.				
	Corneitis.				
	Iritis Rheumatica.				
	" Syphilitica.				

Sick and Wounded.

mitted in to Hospital during month.

Tabular Statement

	Seat and Character	Side of body: Right	Side of body: Left	How Received: In Battle	How Received: By Accident & otherwise	Nature of Missile: Round Lead or Bullet	Nature of Missile: Conical Lead or Bullet	Nature of Missile: Shell	Nature of Missile: Round Shot	Nature of Missile: Other Missiles
Shot Wounds	Of Head.	4	3	7				7		
	Of Neck.									
	Of Trunk.									
	Of External Genitals.									
	Of Upper Extremities.	3	2	3	3		2	3		
	Of ~~Brain.~~ Lower Extremities.	7	6	13	[illegible]		1	10		2
Wounds of Cavities.	Of Lungs.									
	Of Heart.									
	Of Stomach.									
	Of Intestines.									
	Of Bladder.									
	Other Wounds of Cavities.									
Gunshot Fractures.	Of Cranium									
	Of Facial Bones.									
	Of Clavicle.									
	Of Scapular.									
	Of Humerus.	[illegible]	1	2			2			
	Of Forearm.	2		2			2			
	Of Femur.	1		1			1			
	Of Legs.	1	2	3				3		
	Of Ribs.									
	Of Vertebrae.									
	Of other Bones.									
Gunshot Wounds of Joints.	Of Sholder Joint.									
	Of Elbow.									
	Of Wrist.									
	Of Hip.									
	Of Knee.									
	Of Ankle									
	Of other Joints.									
Contusions and Wounds by Spent Balls	3 in face	1	2	3		1	2			
	1 on side trunk	1	1	[illegible]						

General Summary.

Strength	Number Admitted								Average Number on Sick report Daily.		
	Commissioned Officers.				Enlisted Men.						
	Sick.		Wounded		Sick.		Wounded				
Total.	Cases.	Deaths.	Cases.	Deaths.	Cases.	Deaths.	Cases.	Deths.	In Hospital	In Quarters	Total.
331	15		3		146	1	36		58.67	58.67	58.67
	9		1		352		6		66.7		66.7
486	5				167		8		71.50		71.50
572	13				128		7		14		14
661	2				47		2		14		14
655	1				76		1		15		15
666	4				107	1	1		20		20

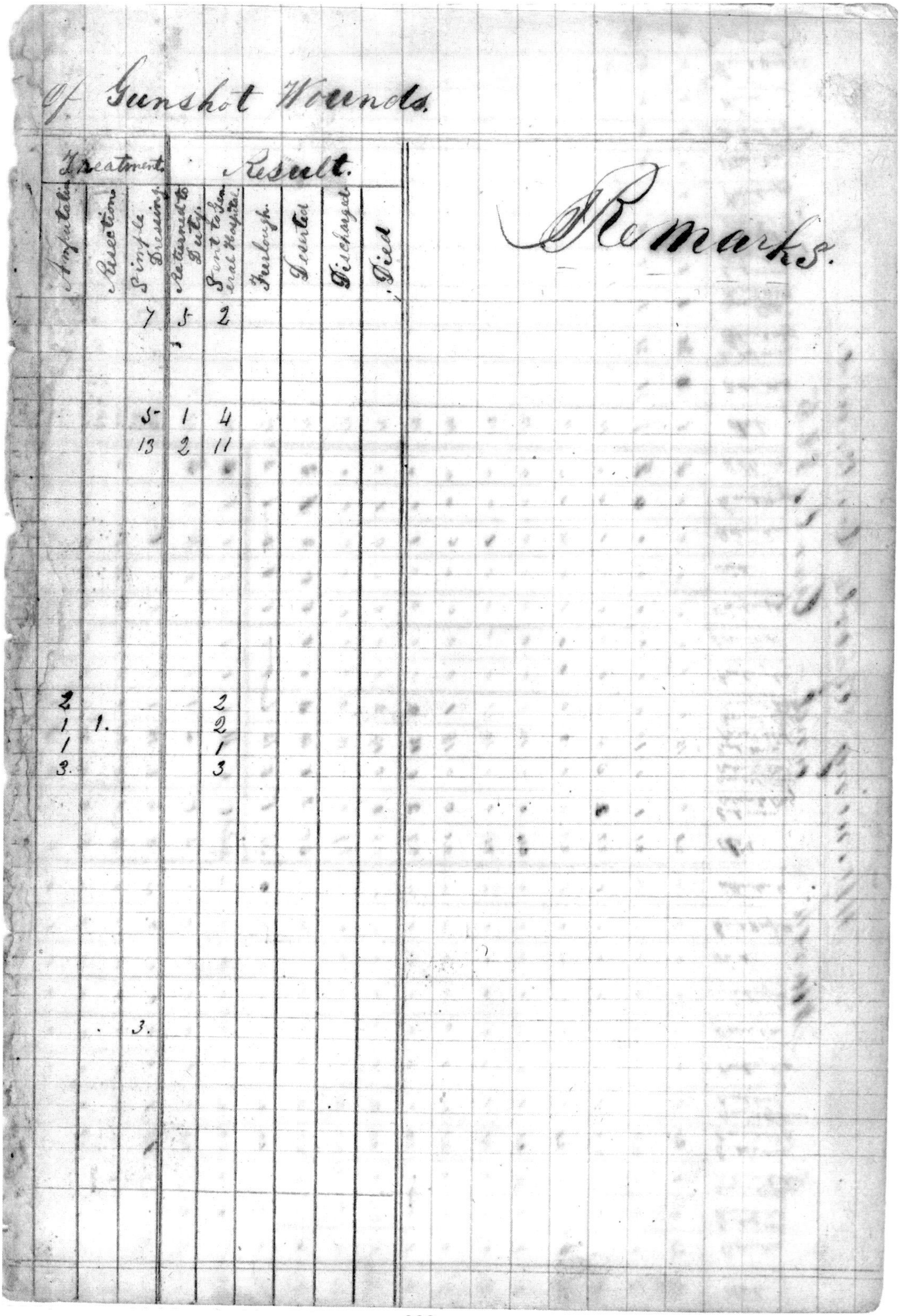

Of Gunshot Wounds.

Treatment			Result.						Remarks.
Amputation	Resection	Simple Dressing	Returned to Duty	Sent to General Hospital	Furlough	Deserted	Discharged	Died	
		7	5	2					
		5	1	4					
		13	2	11					
2				2					
1	1.			2					
1				1					
3.				3					
		3.							

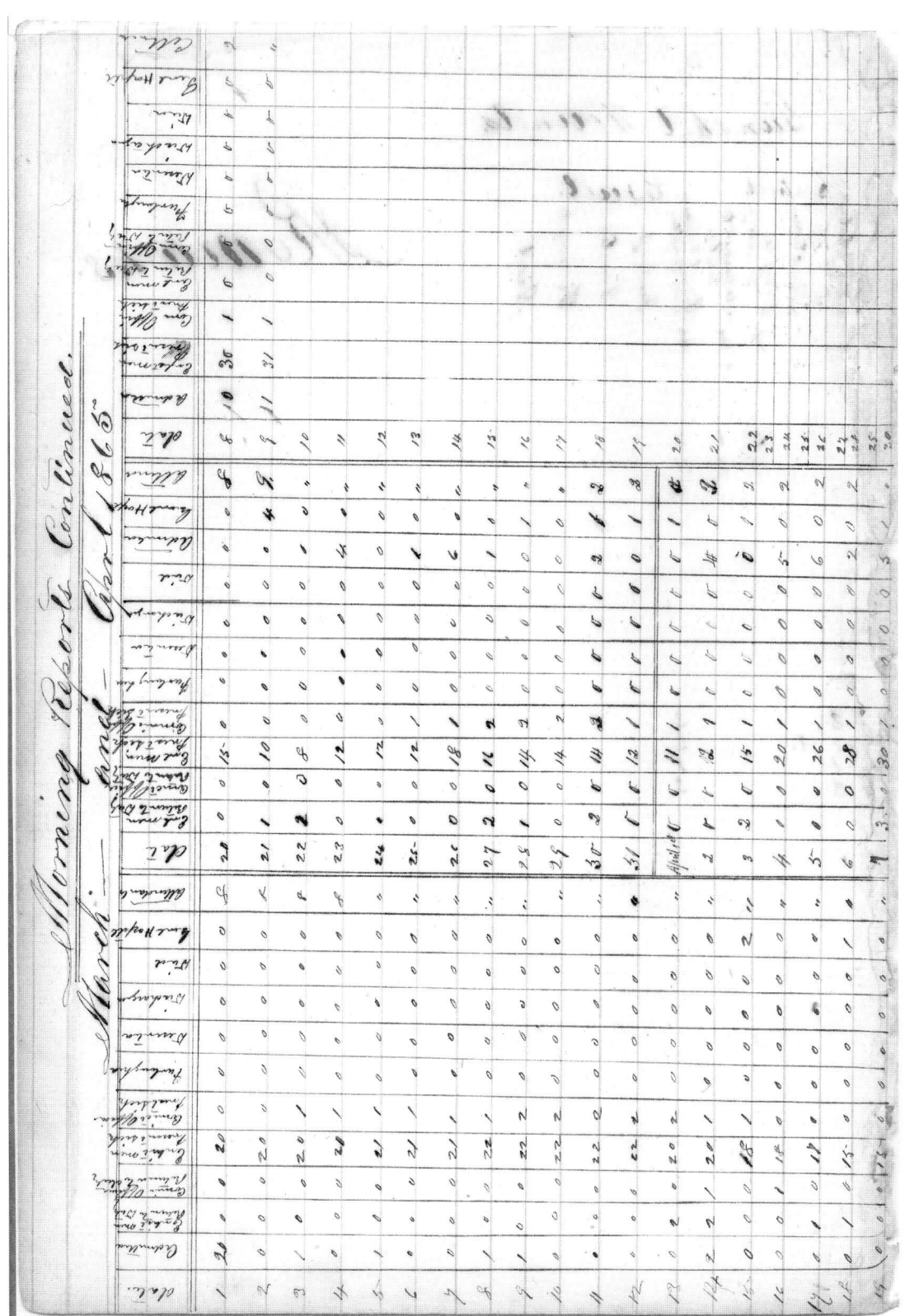

Morning Reports Continued.

March — and — April 1865

Date	Admitted	Enlisted men Return to Duty	Comm. Officers Return to Duty	Enlisted men Remaining sick	Comm. Officers Remaining sick	Furloughed	Deserted	Discharged	Died	Genl Hospital	Attendants
1	20	0	0	20	0	0	0	0	0	0	8
2	0	0	0	20	0	0	0	0	0	0	8
3	1	0	0	20	1	0	0	0	0	0	8
4	0	0	0	20	1	0	0	0	0	0	8
5	1	0	0	21	1	0	0	0	0	0	"
6	0	0	0	21	1	0	0	0	0	0	"
7	0	0	0	21	1	0	0	0	0	0	"
8	1	0	0	22	1	0	0	0	0	0	"
9	1	0	0	22	2	0	0	0	0	0	"
10	0	0	0	22	2	0	0	0	0	0	"
11	0	0	0	22	2	0	0	0	0	0	"
12	0	0	0	22	2	0	0	0	0	0	"
13	0	2	0	20	2	0	0	0	0	0	"
14	2	2	1	20	1	0	0	0	0	0	"
15	0	0	0	18	1	0	0	0	0	2	"
16	0	0	1	18	0	0	0	0	0	0	"
17	0	1	0	17	0	0	0	0	0	0	"
18	0	1	0	15	0	0	0	0	0	1	"
19	0	0	0	15	0	0	0	0	0	0	"

Date	Enlisted men Return to Duty	Comm. Officers Return to Duty	Enlisted men Remaining sick	Comm. Officers Remaining sick	Furloughed	Deserted	Discharged	Died	Admitted	Genl Hospital	Attendants
20	0	0	15	0	0	0	0	0	0	0	8
21	1	0	10	0	0	0	0	0	0	4	8
22	2	0	8	0	0	0	0	0	1	0	"
23	0	0	12	0	0	0	1	0	4	0	"
24	0	0	12	0	0	0	0	0	0	0	"
25	0	0	12	1	0	0	0	0	1	0	"
26	0	0	18	1	0	0	0	0	6	0	"
27	2	0	16	2	0	0	0	0	1	0	"
28	1	0	14	2	0	0	0	0	0	1	"
29	0	0	14	2	0	0	0	0	0	0	"
30	2	0	14	2	0	0	0	0	2	1	2
31	0	0	12	1	0	0	0	0	0	1	2
April 1st	0	0	11	1	0	0	0	0	0	1	2
2	0	0	12	1	0	0	0	0	4	0	2
3	2	0	15	1	0	0	0	0	0	1	2
4	0	0	20	1	0	0	0	0	5	0	2
5	0	0	26	1	0	0	0	0	6	0	2
6	0	0	28	1	0	0	0	0	2	0	2
7	3	0	30	1	0	0	0	0	5	1	"

Date	Admitted	Enlisted men Remaining sick	Comm. Officers Remaining sick	Enlisted men Return to Duty	Comm. Officers Return to Duty	Furloughed	Deserted	Discharged	Died	Genl Hospital	Attendants
8	10	30	1	0	0	0	0	0	0	0	2
9	11	31	1	0	0	0	0	0	0	0	"
10											
11											
12											
13											
14											
15											
16											
17											
18											
19											
20											
21											
22											
23											
24											
25											
26											
27											
28											
25											
30											

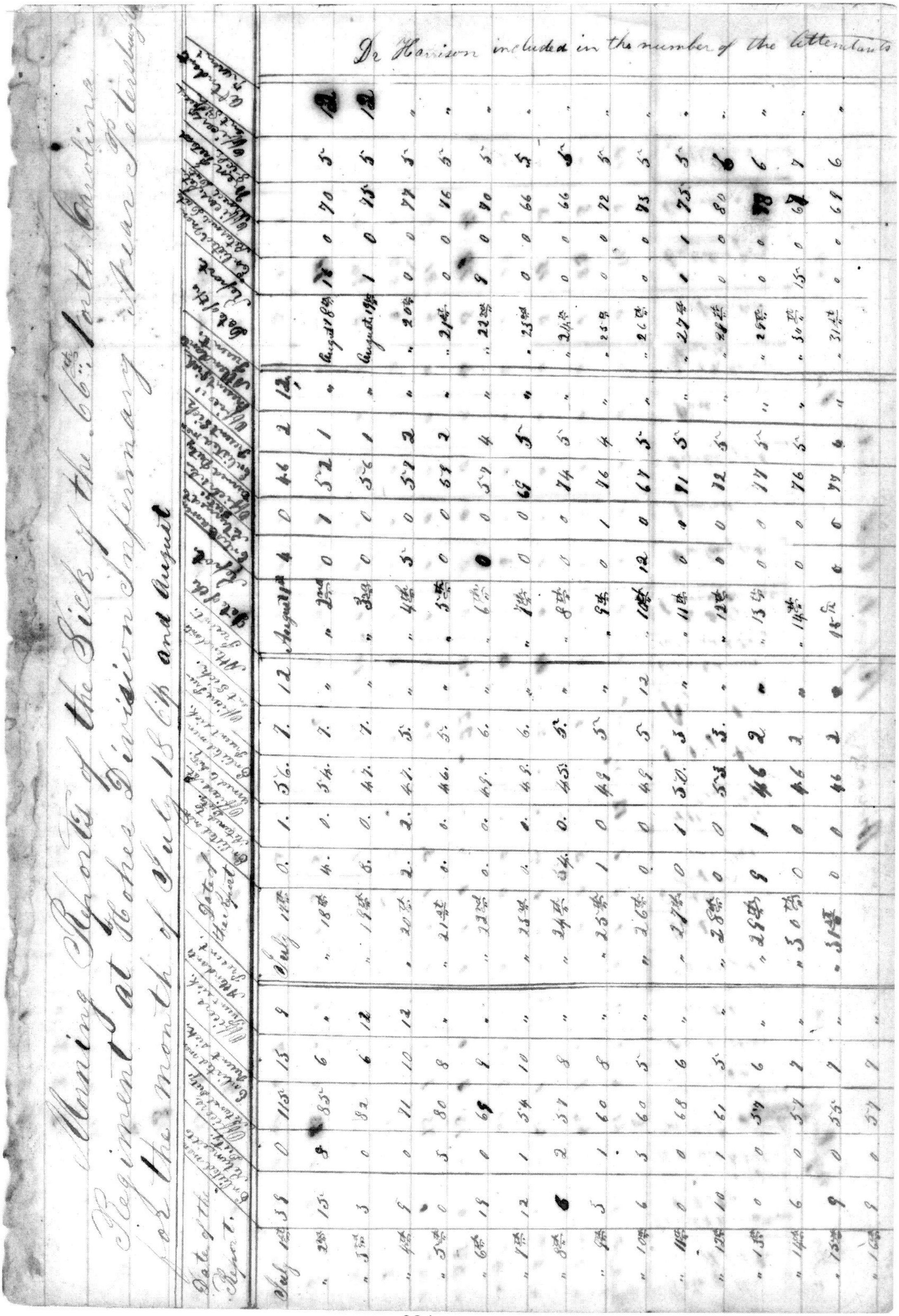

Morning Reports of the Sick of the 66th North Carolina Regiment at Hokes Division Infirmary Near Petersburg for the month of July 1864 and August

Date of the Report	Enlisted men Returned to Duty	Officers Returned to Duty	Enlisted men Present sick	Officers Present sick	Attendants Present
July 1st	38	0	115	15	9
" 2nd	15	8	85	6	"
" 3rd	3	0	82	6	12
" 4th	8	0	71	10	12
" 5th	0	5	80	8	"
" 6th	18	0	69	9	"
" 7th	12	1	54	10	"
" 8th	6	2	57	8	"
" 9th	5	1	60	8	"
" 10th	6	5	60	5	"
" 11th	0	0	68	6	"
" 12th	10	1	61	5	"
" 13th	0	0	57	6	"
" 14th	6	0	57	7	"
" 15th	9	0	55	7	"
" 16th	8	0	57	7	"

Date of the Report	Enlisted men Returned to Duty	Officers Returned to Duty	Enlisted men Present sick	Officers Present sick	Attendants Present
July 17th	0.	1.	56.	7.	12
" 18th	4.	0.	54.	7.	"
" 19th	8.	0.	47.	7.	"
" 20th	2.	2.	47.	5.	"
" 21st	0.	0.	46.	5.	"
" 22nd	0.	0.	49.	6.	"
" 23rd	0.	0.	48.	6.	"
" 24th	34.	0.	45.	5.	"
" 25th	1	0	49	5	"
" 26th	0	0	49	5	12
" 27th	0	1	50.	3	"
" 28th	0	0	53	3.	"
" 29th	9	1	46	2	"
" 30th	0	0	46	2	"
" 31st	0	0	46	2	"

Date of the Report	Enlisted men Returned to Duty	Officers Returned to Duty	Enlisted men Present Sick	Officers Present Sick	Attendants Present
August 1st	4	0	46	2	12
" 2nd	0	1	52	1	"
" 3rd	0	0	56	1	"
" 4th	5	0	58	2	"
" 5th	0	0	58	2	"
" 6th	0	0	57	4	"
" 7th	0	0	69	5	"
" 8th	0	0	74	5	"
" 9th	0	1	76	4	"
" 10th	12	0	67	5	"
" 11th	0	0	71	5	"
" 12th	0	0	72	5	"
" 13th	0	0	77	5	"
" 14th	0	0	76	5	"
15th	6	6	77	6	"

Date of the Report	Enlisted men Returned to Duty	Officers Returned to Duty	Men Present Sick	Officers Present Sick	Attendants Present
August 18th	18	0	70	5	12
August 19th	1	0	75	5	12
" 20th	0	0	77	5	"
" 21st	0	0	76	5	"
" 22nd	9	0	70	5	"
" 23rd	0	0	66	5	"
" 24th	0	0	66	5	"
" 25th	0	0	72	5	"
" 26th	0	0	73	5	"
" 27th	1	1	75	5	"
" 28th	0	0	80	6	"
" 29th	0	0	78	6	"
" 30th	15	0	67	7	"
" 31st	0	0	68	6	"

Dr Harrison included in the number of the attendants

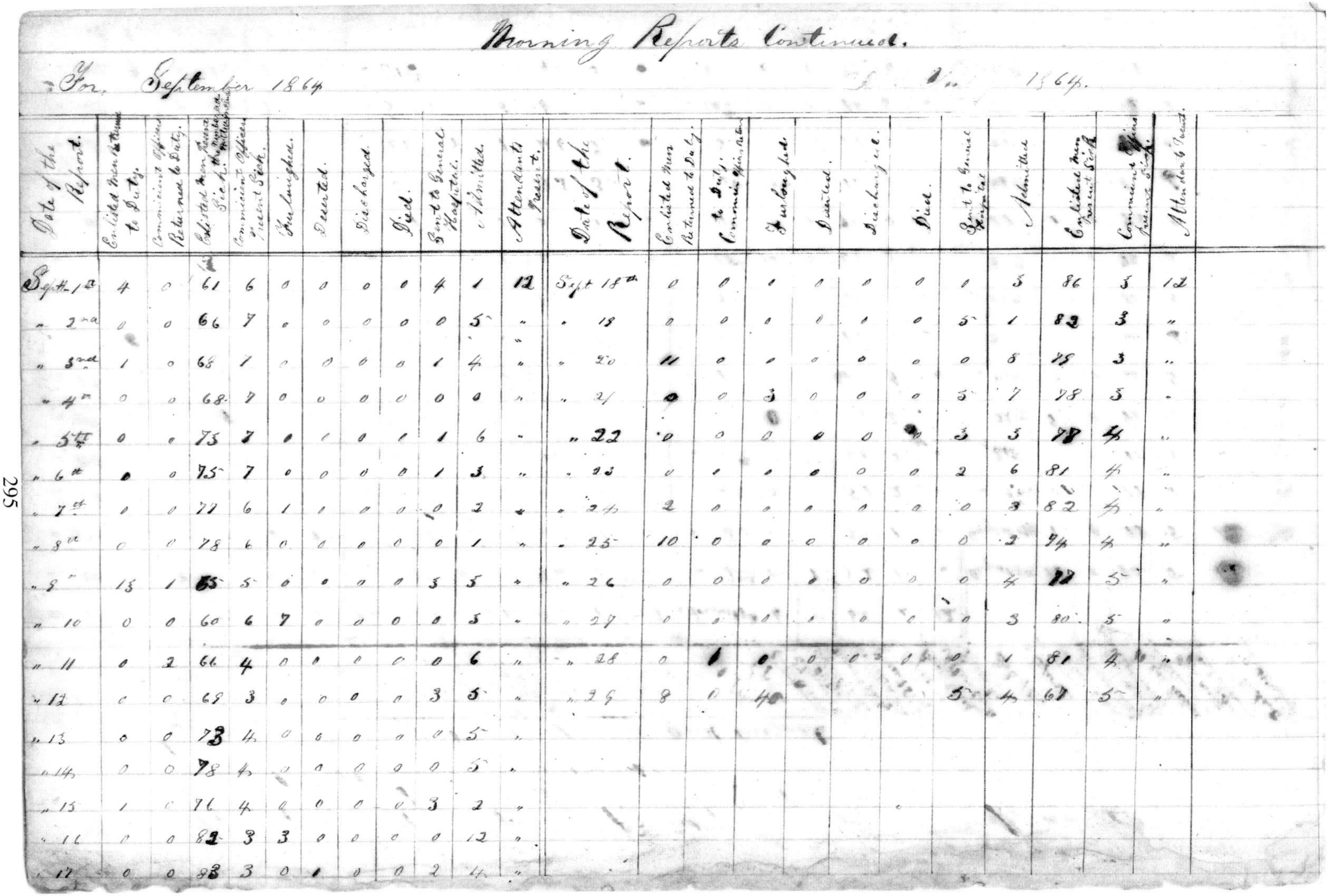

Morning Reports Continued.

For September 1864 ... 1864.

Date of the Report.	Enlisted men returned to Duty.	Commissioned Officers Returned to Duty.	Enlisted men remaining Sick.	Commissioned Officers Present Sick.	Furloughed.	Deserted.	Discharged.	Died.	Sent to General Hospital.	Admitted.	Attendants Present.
Sept. 1st	4	0	61	6	0	0	0	0	4	1	12
" 2nd	0	0	66	7	0	0	0	0	0	5	"
" 3rd	1	0	68	7	0	0	0	0	1	4	"
" 4th	0	0	68	7	0	0	0	0	0	0	"
" 5th	0	0	73	7	0	0	0	1	1	6	"
" 6th	0	0	75	7	0	0	0	0	1	3	"
" 7th	0	0	77	6	1	0	0	0	0	2	"
" 8th	0	0	78	6	0	0	0	0	0	1	"
" 9th	13	1	65	5	0	0	0	0	3	5	"
" 10	0	0	60	6	7	0	0	0	0	5	"
" 11	0	2	66	4	0	0	0	0	0	6	"
" 12	0	0	69	3	0	0	0	0	3	5	"
" 13	0	0	73	4	0	0	0	0	0	5	"
" 14	0	0	78	4	0	0	0	0	0	5	"
" 15	1	0	76	4	0	0	0	0	3	2	"
" 16	0	0	82	3	3	0	0	0	0	12	"
" 17	0	0	83	3	0	1	0	0	2	4	"

Date of the Report.	Enlisted men Returned to Duty.	Commissioned Officers Returned to Duty.	Furloughed.	Deserted.	Discharged.	Died.	Sent to General Hospital.	Admitted.	Enlisted men present Sick.	Commissioned Officers present Sick.	Attendants Present.
Sept 18th	0	0	0	0	0	0	0	3	86	3	12
" 19	0	0	0	0	0	0	5	1	83	3	"
" 20	11	0	0	0	0	0	0	8	75	3	"
" 21	0	0	3	0	0	0	5	7	78	3	"
" 22	0	0	0	0	0	0	3	3	78	4	"
" 23	0	0	0	0	0	0	2	6	81	4	"
" 24	2	0	0	0	0	0	0	3	82	4	"
" 25	10	0	0	0	0	0	0	2	74	4	"
" 26	0	0	0	0	0	0	0	4	77	5	"
" 27	0	0	0	0	0	0	0	3	80	5	"
" 28	0	1	0	0	0	0	0	1	81	4	"
" 29	8	0	4	[illegible]	[illegible]	[illegible]	5	4	67	5	"

Morning Reports Continued
October 1864

Date of the Report	Enlisted Men Returned to Duty	Commissioned Officers Returned to Duty	Enlisted Men Present Sick	Commissioned Officers Present Sick	Furloughed	Deserted	Discharged	Died	Sent to Gen. Hospitals	Admitted	Attendants
10	3	0	10	1	0	0	0	0	0	0	13
11	0	0	12	1	0	0	0	0	0	3	13
12	1	0	12	1	0	0	0	0	0	1	13
13	7	0	15	1	0	0	0	0	1	3	"
14	1	0	12	1	0	0	0	0	2	2	"
15	0	0	13	2	0	0	0	0	0	2	"
16	1	0	15	2	0	0	0	0	0	2	"
17	3	0	11	2	0	0	0	0	0	2	11
18	0	0	12	3	0	0	0	0	0	1	"
19	0	0	13	2	0	0	0	0	0	1	"
20	2	0	13	2	0	0	0	0	1	2	"
21	0	0	14	3	0	0	0	0	0	3	"
22	0	0	15	3	0	0	0	0	0	1	"
23	4	2	11	1	0	0	0	0	1	0	"
24	0	0	13	2	0	0	0	0	0	3	13
25	0	0	14	2	0	0	0	0	0	1	"
26	0	0	15	2	0	0	0	0	0	1	"
27	4	0	15	2	0	0	0	0	0	4	13
28	0	0	16	1	0	0	0	0	0	3	"
29	2	0	15	1	0	0	0	0	2	3	"
30	0	0	13	1	0	0	0	0	2	0	"
31	0	1	14	1	0	0	0	0	0	1	"

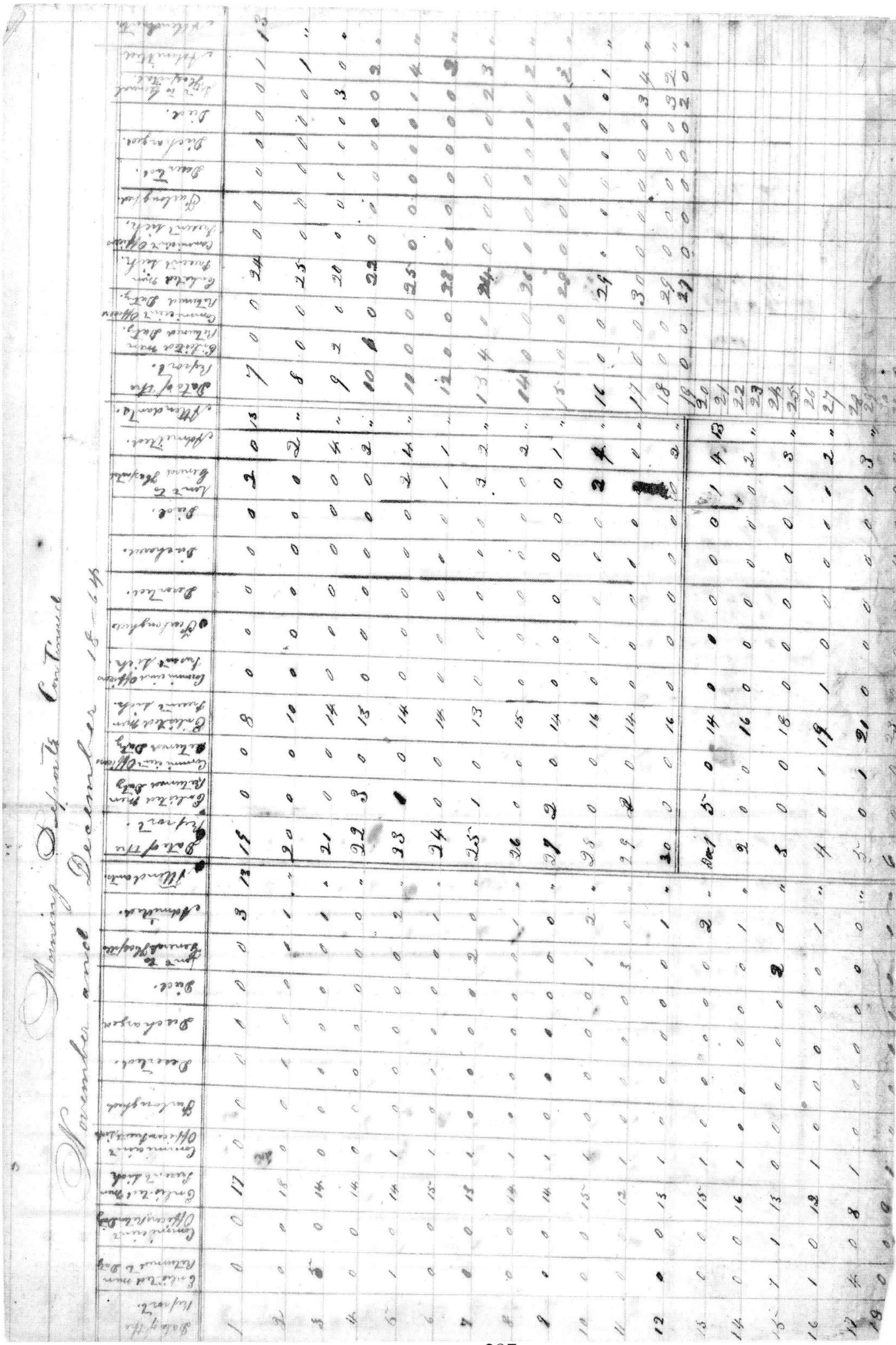

Morning Reports Continued
November and December 1864

Date of the Report	Enlisted men Returned to Duty	Commissioned Officers returned to Duty	Enlisted men Present Sick	Commissioned Officers Present Sick	Furloughed	Deserted	Discharged	Died	Sent to General Hospital	Admitted	Attendants
1	0	0	17	0	0	0	0	0	0	3	13
2	0	0	18	0	0	0	0	0	1	1	"
3	5	0	14	0	0	0	0	0	0	1	"
4	0	0	14	0	0	0	0	0	0	0	"
5	1	0	14	1	0	0	0	0	0	2	"
6	0	0	15	1	0	0	0	0	0	1	"
7	0	0	13	1	0	0	0	0	2	0	"
8	0	0	14	1	0	0	0	0	0	1	"
9	0	0	14	1	0	0	0	0	0	0	"
10	0	0	15	1	0	0	0	0	1	2	"
11	0	0	12	1	0	0	0	0	3	0	"
12	0	0	13	1	0	0	0	0	0	1	"
13	0	0	15	1	0	0	0	0	0	2	"
14	0	0	16	1	0	0	0	0	0	1	"
15	7	1	13	0	0	0	0	0	2	0	"
16	1	0	12	1	0	0	0	0	0	1	"
17	4	0	8	1	0	0	0	0	0	0	"
18	0	0	0	1	0	0	0	0	0	1	"

Date of the Report	Enlisted men Returned to Duty	Commissioned Officers Returned to Duty	Enlisted men Present Sick	Commissioned Officers Present Sick	Furloughed	Deserted	Discharged	Died	Sent to General Hospital	Admitted	Attendants
19	0	0	8	0	0	0	0	0	2	0	13
20	0	0	10	0	0	0	0	0	0	2	"
21	0	0	14	0	0	0	0	0	0	4	"
22	3	0	13	0	0	0	0	0	0	2	"
23	1	0	14	0	0	0	0	0	2	4	"
24	0	0	14	0	0	0	0	0	1	1	"
25	1	0	13	0	0	0	0	0	3	2	"
26	0	0	15	0	0	0	0	0	0	2	"
27	2	0	14	0	0	0	0	0	0	1	"
28	0	0	16	0	0	0	0	0	2	4	"
29	2	0	14	0	0	0	1	0	[illegible]	0	"
30	0	0	16	0	0	0	0	0	0	2	"
Dec 1	5	0	14	0	0	0	0	0	1	4	13
2	0	0	16	0	0	0	0	0	0	2	"
3	0	0	18	0	0	0	0	0	1	3	"
4	0	1	19	1	0	0	0	0	1	2	"
5	0	1	21	0	0	0	0	0	1	3	"
6	0	0	23	0	0	0	0	0	0	2	"

Date of the Report	Enlisted men Returned to Duty	Commissioned Officers Returned to Duty	Enlisted men Present Sick	Commissioned Officers Present Sick	Furloughed	Deserted	Discharged	Died	Sent to General Hospital	Admitted	Attendants
7	0	0	24	0	0	0	0	0	0	1	13
8	0	0	25	0	0	0	0	0	0	1	"
9	2	0	20	0	0	0	0	0	3	0	"
10	0	0	22	0	0	0	0	0	0	2	"
11	0	0	25	0	0	0	0	0	1	4	"
12	0	0	28	0	0	0	0	0	0	3	"
13	4	0	24	0	0	0	0	0	2	3	"
14	0	0	26	0	0	0	0	0	0	2	"
15	0	0	28	0	0	0	0	0	0	2	"
16	0	0	29	0	0	0	0	0	0	1	"
17	0	0	30	0	0	0	0	0	3	4	"
18	0	0	29	0	0	0	0	0	3	2	"
19	0	0	27	0	0	0	0	0	2	0	"
20											
21											
22											
23											
24											
25											
26											
27											
28											
29											
30											

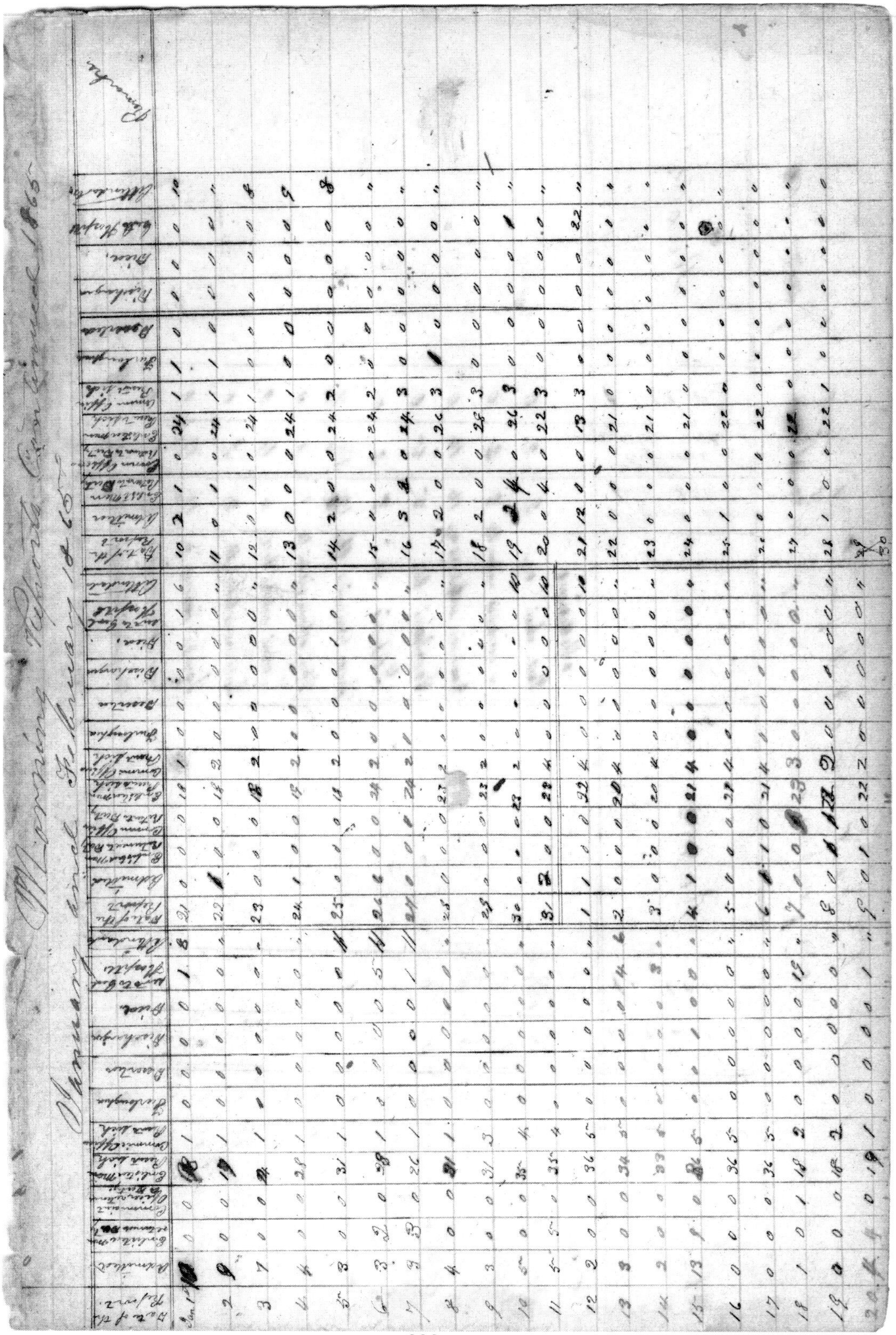

Morning Reports Continued 1865
January and February 1865

Date of the Report	Admitted	Enlisted Men returned to duty	Commissioned Officers returned to duty	Enlisted Men Present Sick	Commissioned Officers Present Sick	Furloughed	Deserted	Discharged	Died	Sent to Genl Hospital	Attendants
Jan 1st	10	0	0	18	1	0	0	0	0	1	8
2	9	0	0	19	1	0	0	0	0	0	"
3	7	0	0	24	1	0	0	0	0	0	"
4	4	0	0	28	1	0	0	0	0	0	"
5	3	0	0	31	1	0	0	0	0	0	11
6	3	2	0	28	1	0	0	0	0	5	11
7	3	3	0	26	1	0	0	0	0	1	11
8	4	0	0	31	1	0	0	0	0	0	"
9	3	0	0	31	3	0	0	0	0	0	"
10	5	0	0	35	4	0	0	0	0	0	"
11	5	5	0	35	4	0	0	0	0	0	"
12	2	0	0	36	5	0	0	0	0	0	"
13	3	0	0	34	5	0	0	0	0	4	6
14	2	0	0	33	5	0	0	0	0	3	"
15	13	1	0	36	5	0	0	1	0	0	"
16	0	0	0	36	5	0	0	0	0	0	"
17	0	0	0	36	5	0	0	0	0	0	"
18	1	0	1	18	2	0	0	0	0	19	"
19	0	0	0	18	2	0	0	0	0	0	"
20	4	4	0	19	1	0	0	0	0	1	"

Date of the Report	Admitted	Enlisted Men returned to duty	Commissioned Officers returned to duty	Enlisted Men Present Sick	Commissioned Officers Present Sick	Furloughed	Deserted	Discharged	Died	Sent to Genl Hospital	Attendants
21	0	0	0	18	1	0	0	0	0	1	6
22	1	0	0	18	2	0	0	0	0	0	"
23	0	0	0	18	2	0	0	0	0	0	"
24	1	0	0	17	2	0	0	0	0	0	"
25	0	0	0	18	2	0	0	0	1	0	"
26	6	0	0	24	2	0	0	0	0	0	"
27	0	0	0	24	2	0	0	0	0	0	"
28	0	0	0	23	2	0	0	0	0	0	"
29	0	0	0	23	2	0	0	0	0	0	"
30	0	0	0	23	2	0	0	0	0	0	10
31	2	0	0	23	4	0	0	0	0	0	10
1	1	0	0	22	4	0	0	0	0	0	10
2	0	0	0	20	4	0	0	0	0	0	"
3	0	0	0	20	4	0	0	0	0	0	"
4	1	0	0	21	4	0	0	0	0	0	"
5	0	0	0	22	4	0	0	0	0	0	"
6	1	1	0	21	4	0	0	0	0	0	"
7	0	0	0	23	3	0	0	0	0	0	"
8	0	0	1	22	2	0	0	0	0	0	"
9	0	1	0	22	2	0	0	0	0	0	"

Date of the Report	Admitted	Enlisted Men returned to duty	Commissioned Officers returned to duty	Enlisted Men Present Sick	Commissioned Officers Present Sick	Furloughed	Deserted	Discharged	Died	Sent to Genl Hospital	Attendants	Remarks
10	2	1	0	24	1	1	0	0	0	0	10	
11	0	1	0	24	1	1	0	0	0	0	"	
12	0	1	0	24	1	0	0	0	0	0	8	
13	0	0	0	24	1	0	0	0	0	0	9	
14	2	0	0	24	2	0	0	0	0	0	8	
15	0	0	0	24	2	0	0	0	0	0	"	
16	3	2	0	24	3	0	0	0	0	0	"	
17	2	0	0	26	3	1	0	0	0	0	"	
18	2	0	0	28	3	0	0	0	0	0	"	
19	2	4	0	26	3	0	0	0	0	1	"	
20	0	4	0	22	3	0	0	0	0	0	"	
21	12	0	0	13	3	0	0	0	0	22	"	
22	0	0	0	21	0	0	0	0	0	1	0	
23	0	0	0	21	0	0	0	0	0	0	0	
24	0	0	0	21	0	0	0	0	0	0	0	
25	1	0	0	22	0	0	0	0	0	0	0	
26	0	0	0	22	0	0	0	0	0	0	0	
27	0	0	0	22	0	0	0	0	0	0	0	
28	1	0	0	22	1	0	0	0	0	0	0	

Return of Medical and Hospital Property received, expended, and remaining on hand at for the month ~~[illegible]~~ ending Sept 1863

Articles	Recd. since last return	Expended with the sick	On Hand	Remarks	Articles	Received since last return	Expended with the sick	On Hand	Remarks
Medicines					Medicines				
Acaciae lb.	2	1 3/4	1/4		Pul. rhei oz.	2	2	0	
Acidi nitrici "	1/2	1/4	1/4		" sinapis nigrae lb.	3	3	0	
" tannici oz.	3	3	0		Quiniae sulphatis oz.	16	16	0	
Alcoholis bott.	3	3	0		Sacchari lb.	5	5	0	
Aluminis lb.	1	1/2	1/2		Saponis lb.	3	3	0	
Argenti nitratis (crystals	0	0	0		Sodae bicarbonatis lb.	1 1/2	1 1/4	1/4	
" " (fused) oz.	1	3/4	1/4		Spir. aetheris nitrici lb.	1	1	0	
Camphorae lb.	2 1/2	2	1/2		" vini gallici bott.	6	4	2	
Cerati resinae lb.	1	1/2	1/2		Sulphuris loti lb.	2	2	0	
" simplicis lb.	1	1/2	1/2		Syrupi scillae "	1 1/2	1 1/2	0	
Chloroformi lb.	2	1 1/2	1/2		Tinc. ferri chloridi "	3/4	3/4	0	
Copaibae lb.	3	3	0		Unguenti hydrarg. "	3/4	1/2	1/4	
Cupri sulphatis oz.	2	2	0		Vini colchici seminis "	1/2	1/2	0	
Emplastri adhaesivi yds.	1	1/4	3/4		Zinci acetatis	2	1 1/2	1/2	

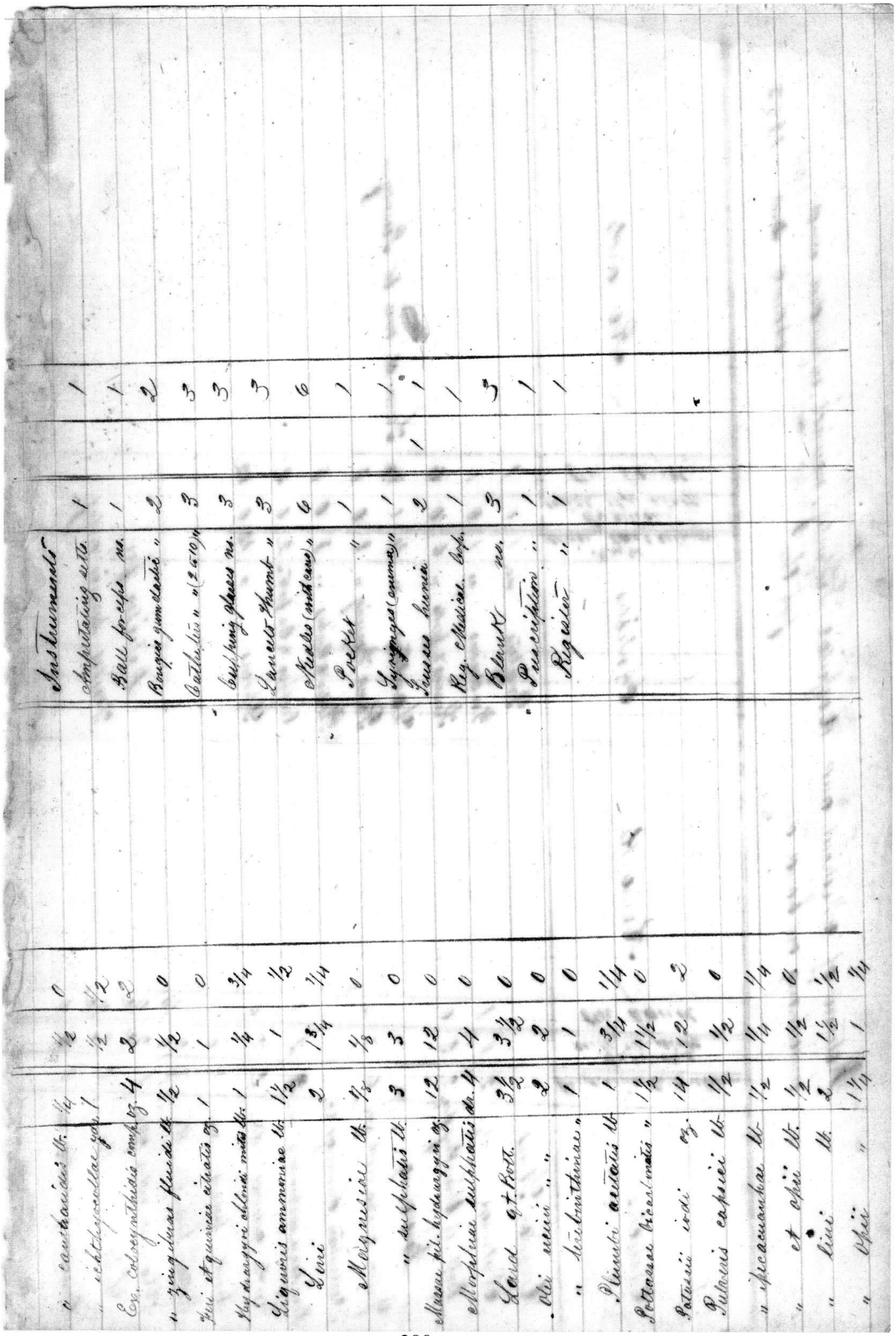

" cantharidis lb.	1/4	1/2	0
" ichthyocollae ℥	1	1/2	1/2
Ex. colocynthidis comp. oz.	4	2	2
" zingiberas fluidi lb.	1/2	1/2	0
Feri et quiniae citratis oz.	1	1	0
Hydrargyri chloridi mitis lb.	1	1/4	3/4
Liquoris ammoniae lb.	1 1/2	1	1/2
Lini	2	1 3/4	1/4
Magnesiae lb.	1/8	1/8	0
" sulphatis lb.	3	3	0
Massae pil. hydrargyri oz.	12	12	0
Morphiae sulphatis dr.	4	4	0
Lard qt. Bott.	3 1/2	3 1/2	0
Olei ricini " "	2	2	0
" terebinthinae "	1	1	0
Plumbi acetatis lb.	1	3/4	1/4
Pottassae bicarbonatis "	1 1/2	1 1/2	0
Potassii iodi oz.	14	12	2
Pulveris capsici lb.	1/2	1/2	0
" ipecacuanhae lb.	1/2	1/4	1/4
" et opii lb.	1/2	1/2	0
" lini lb.	2	1 1/2	1/2
" opii "	1 1/4	1	1/4

Instruments			
Amputating setts.	1		1
Ball forceps no.	1		1
Bougies gum elastic "	2		2
Catheters " "(2 to 10)"	3		3
Cupping glasses no.	3		3
Lancets thumb "	3		3
Needles (with case) "	6		6
Pocket "	1		1
Syringes (enema) "	1		1
Trusses hernia	2	1	1
Reg. Medical Cop.	1		1
Blank no.	3		3
Prescription "	1		1
Register "	1		1

Return of Medical and Hospital Property, received, expended, and remaining on hand at for the ending Dec 1863

Articles	Rec'd since last return	Expended within the date	On hand	Remarks	Articles	Rec'd since last return	Expended within the date	On hand	Remarks
Hospital Stores									
Nutmegs oz.	2	1	1		Graters no.	1	0	1	
Bott. of Whiskey doz.	2	2	0		Gridirons "	1	0	1	
Bedding					Knives & forks "	6	0	6	
Gutta percha cloth yds.	6	3	3		Lanterns "	4	0	*	Turned over to Purveyor
Furniture dressings &c.					Pans Frying "	1	0	1	
Bandages, suspensory no.	3	2	1		Plates & dishes "	8	0	8	
Corks assorted doz.	2	2	0		Coffee & tea pots "	2	0	2	
Cork Screws no.	1	0	1		Spoons "	12	0	12	
Cotton batting lb.	1/2	1/4	1/4						
Flannel (red) yds.	1	1/2	1/2		Articles for				
Lint lbs	1	1/2	1/2		Field Service only				
Measures graduated no.	3	3	0						

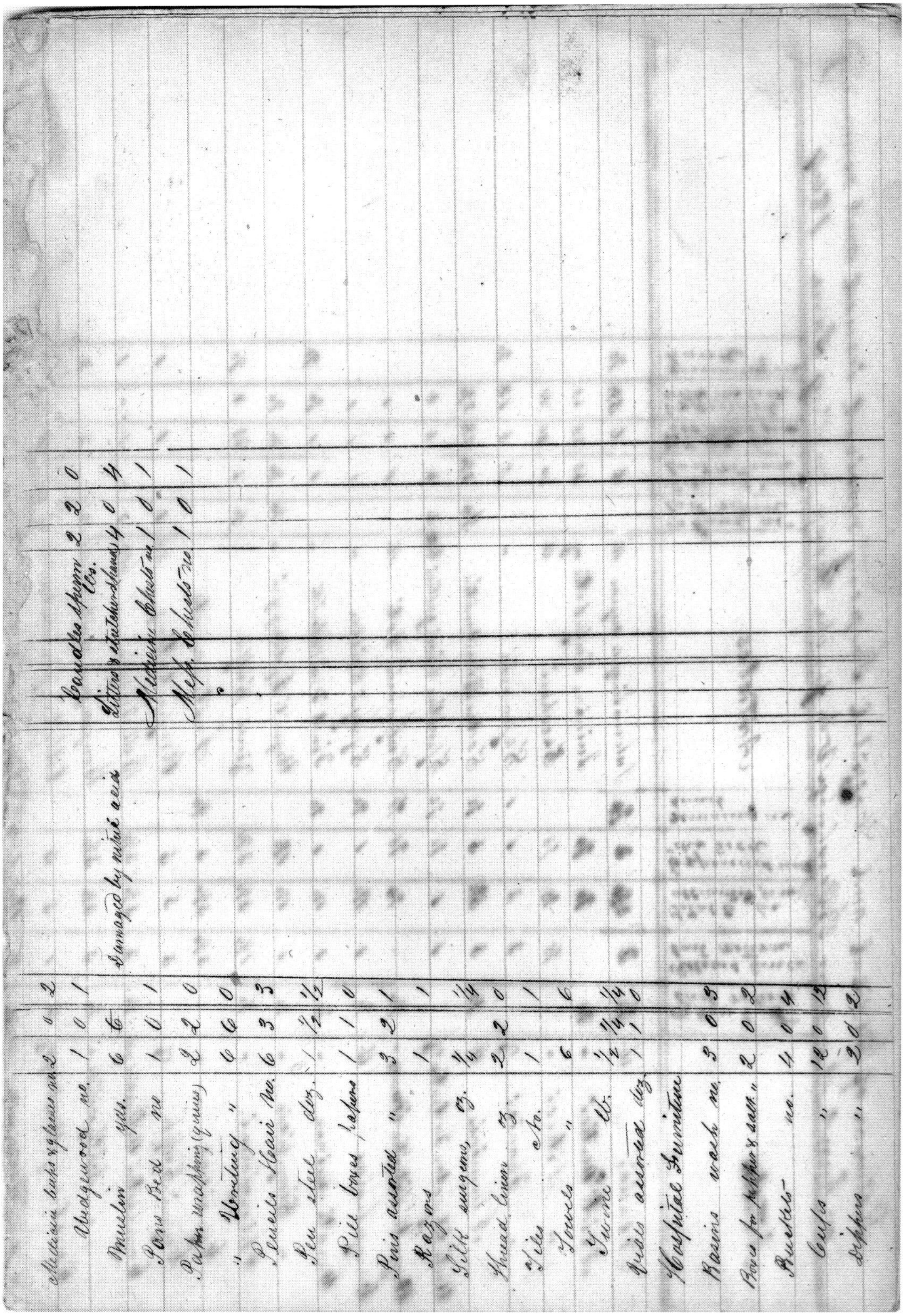

Medicine cups & glasses no.	2	0	2	
Wedgewood no.	1	0	1	
Muslin yds.	6	6		Damaged by nitric acid
Pans Bed no	1	0	1	
Paper wrapping (quires)	2	2	0	
" Writing "	6	6	0	
Pencils Hair no.	6	3	3	
Pen steel doz.	1	1/2	1/2	
Pill boxes papers	1	1	0	
Pins assorted "	3	2	1	
Razors	1		1	
Silk surgeons, oz.	1/4		1/4	
Thread linen oz.	2	2	0	
Tiles No.	1		1	
Towels "	6		6	
Twine lb.	1/2	1/4	1/4	
Vials assorted doz.	1	1	0	
Hospital Furniture				
Basins wash no.	3	0	3	
Boxes for pepper & salt "	2	0	2	
Buckets no.	4	0	4	
Cups "	12	0	12	
Dippers "	2	0	2	

Candles sperm lbs.	2	2	0
Litters & stretchers hand	4	0	4
Medicine Chests no.	1	0	1
Mess Chests no.	1	0	1

Return of Medical and Hospital Property received, issued and remaining on hand at or near Petersburg Va for the Month ending June 1864

Articles		On hand at last return	Received since last return	Total to be accounted for	Expended with the Sick	remaining on hand
Acacia,	lb	1/4	2	2 1/4	2	1/4
Acidi Acetici	"	1/4		1/4	1/4	
" Nitrici	"		1/8	1/8	1/8	
" Tannici	℥		2	2	1	1
Aluminis,	lb	1/2	3	3 1/2	3	1/2
Anti et potas Tartratis	℥		1	1	1/2	1/2
Argenti Nitratis (Fused)	"	1/4		1/4	1/8	1/8
Camphorae	lb	1/2	1	1 1/2	1	1/2
Cerati Resinae	"	1/2	1	1 1/2	1	1/2
" Simplicis	"	1/2	1	1 1/2	1 1/2	
Chloroformi,	"	1/2	1 3/4	2 1/4	2 1/4	
Copaibae	"		3 3/4	3 3/4	3	3/4
Cupri Sulph	℥		3	3	3	
Emplastri Adhaesivi	yds	3/4	2	2 3/4	2 3/4	
" Ichthyocollae	"	1/4	3	3 1/4	3 1/4	
Extrat Colocynthidis Comp	℥	2	1	3	3	
Hydrarg Chloridi Mitis	lb	3/4	1/2	1 1/4	1	1/4

Articles		on hand at last return	Received since last return	Total to be accounted for	Expended with the Sick	remaining on hand
Pulveris sinapis nigrae	lb		6	6	5 1/2	1/2
Quiniae Sulphatis	℥		38	38	38	
Sacchari	lb		10	10	10	
Saponis	"		8	8	7 1/2	1/2
Sodae Bicarbonatis		1/4	2 1/4	2 1/2	2 1/2	
Spiritus vini gallici	bottl	2	4	6	6	
Sulphuris Loti	lb		1	1	1	
Syrupi Scillae	"		1	1	1	
Tinct Ferri Chloridi	"		1	1	1/2	1/2
Urgenti hydrargyri	"	1/4	1/4	1/2	1/2	
Zinci Sulph		1/2	2	2 1/2	2	1/2
Instruments						
Amputating	Sets	1		1		1
Ball Forceps	No	1		1		1
Bougies gum elastic (1 to 12)	"	2		2		2
Catheters gum elastic (1 to 10)	"	3		3		3
Cupping Glasses or tins	No	3		3		[illegible]

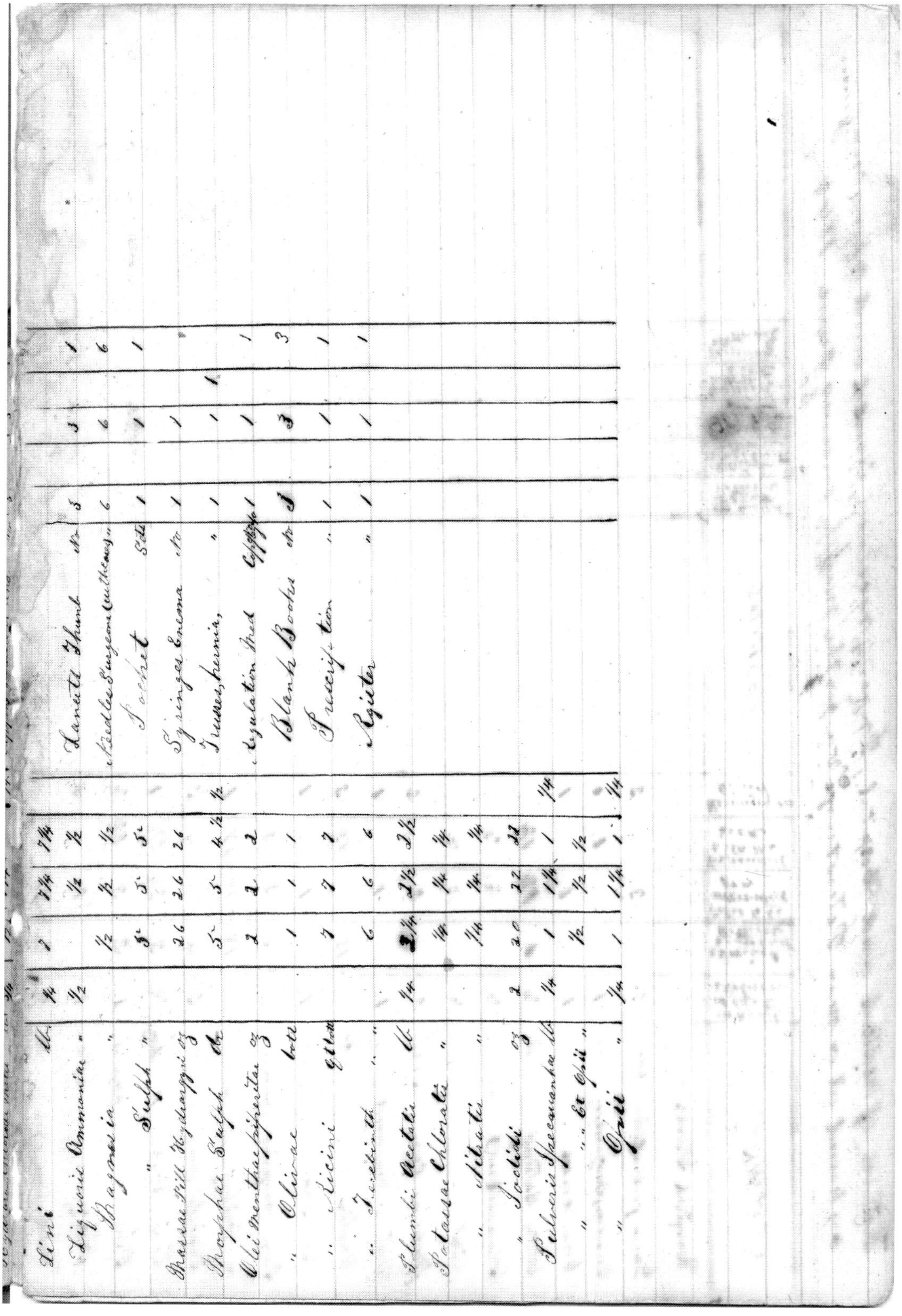

Lini	lb	1/4	7	7 1/4	7 1/4	
Liquoris Ammoniae	"	1/2		1/2	1/2	
Magnesia	"		1/2	1/2	1/2	
" Sulph	"		5	5	5	
Massae Pill Hydrargyri	oz		26	26	26	
Morphae Sulph	dr		5	5	4 1/2	1/2
Olei menthae piperitae	oz		2	2	2	
" Olivae	bott		1	1	1	
" Ricini	qt bott		7	7	7	
" Terebinth	" "		6	6	6	
Plumbi Acetatis	lb	1/4	2 1/4	2 1/2	2 1/2	
Potassae Chloratis	"		1/4	1/4	1/4	
" Nitratis	"		1/4	1/4	1/4	
" Iodidi	oz	2	20	22	22	
Pulveris Ipecacuanhae	lb	1/4	1	1 1/4	1	1/4
" " Et Opii	"		1/2	1/2	1/2	
" Opii	"	1/4	1	1 1/4	1	1/4

Lancets Thumb	No	3		3		1
Needles Surgeons (with cases)	"	6		6		6
Pocket	Sets	1		1		1
Syringes Enema	No	1		1		
Trusses, hernia,	"	1		1	1	
Regulation Med	Copy	1		1		1
Blank Books	No	3		3		3
Prescription	"	1		1		1
Register	"	1		1		1

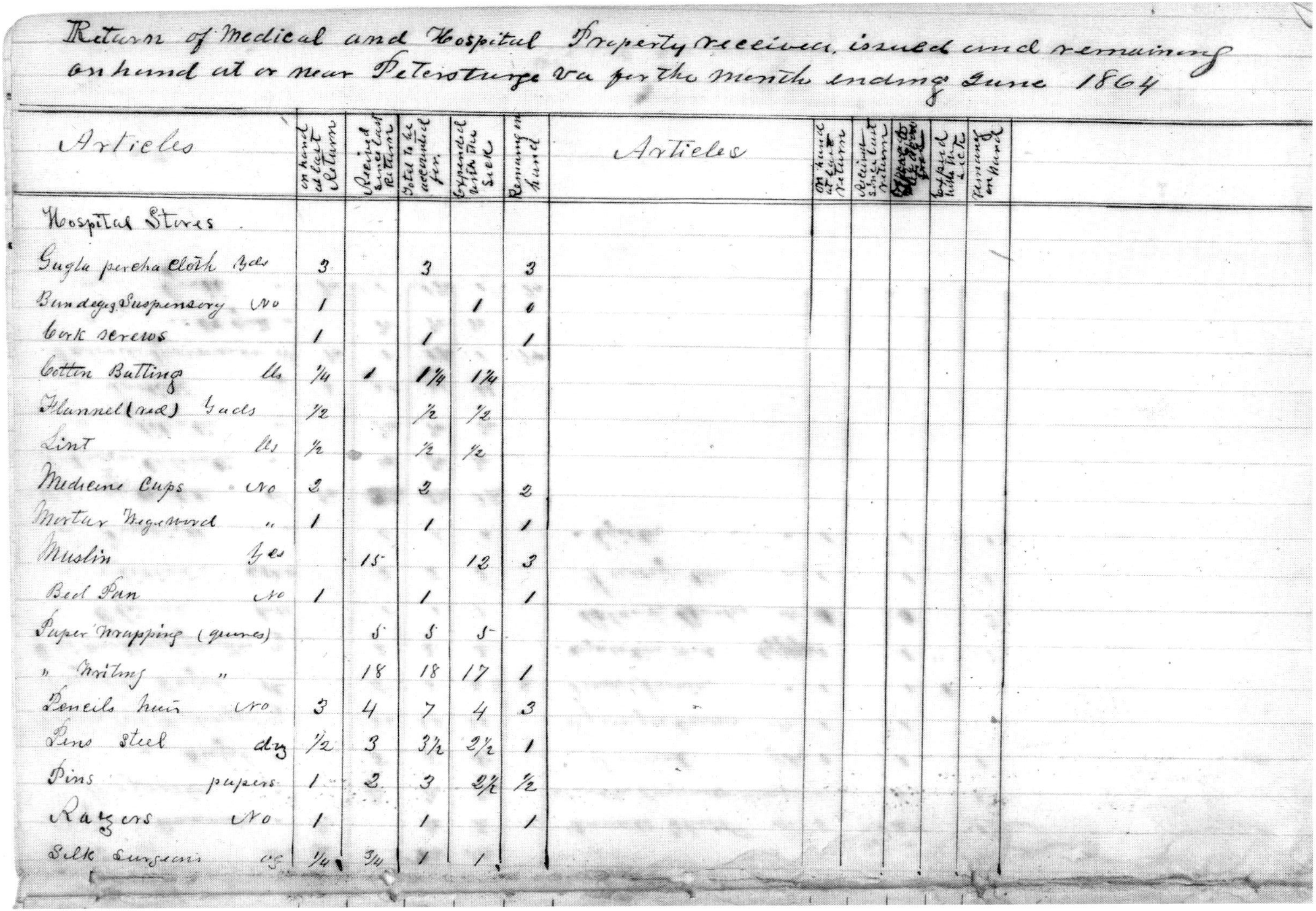

Return of Medical and Hospital Property received, issued and remaining on hand at or near Petersburg Va for the month ending June 1864

Articles		on hand at last Return	Received since last Return	Total to be accounted for	Expended with the sick	Remaining on hand	Articles	On hand at last return	Received since last return	[illegible]	Expended with the sick	Remaining on hand
Hospital Stores												
Gugla percha Cloth	yds	3		3		3						
Bandages Suspensory	No	1			1	0						
Cork screws		1		1		1						
Cotton Batting	lbs	1/4	1	1 1/4	1 1/4							
Flannel (red)	yards	1/2		1/2	1/2							
Lint	lbs	1/2		1/2	1/2							
Medicine Cups	No	2		2		2						
Mortar Wegewood	"	1		1		1						
Muslin	yds		15		12	3						
Bed Pan	No	1		1		1						
Paper Wrapping (quires)			5	5	5							
" Writing	"		18	18	17	1						
Pencils hair	No	3	4	7	4	3						
Pins steel	doz	1/2	3	3 1/2	2 1/2	1						
Pins	papers	1	2	3	2 1/2	1/2						
Razers	No	1		1		1						
Silk Surgeons	oz	1/4	3/4	1	1							

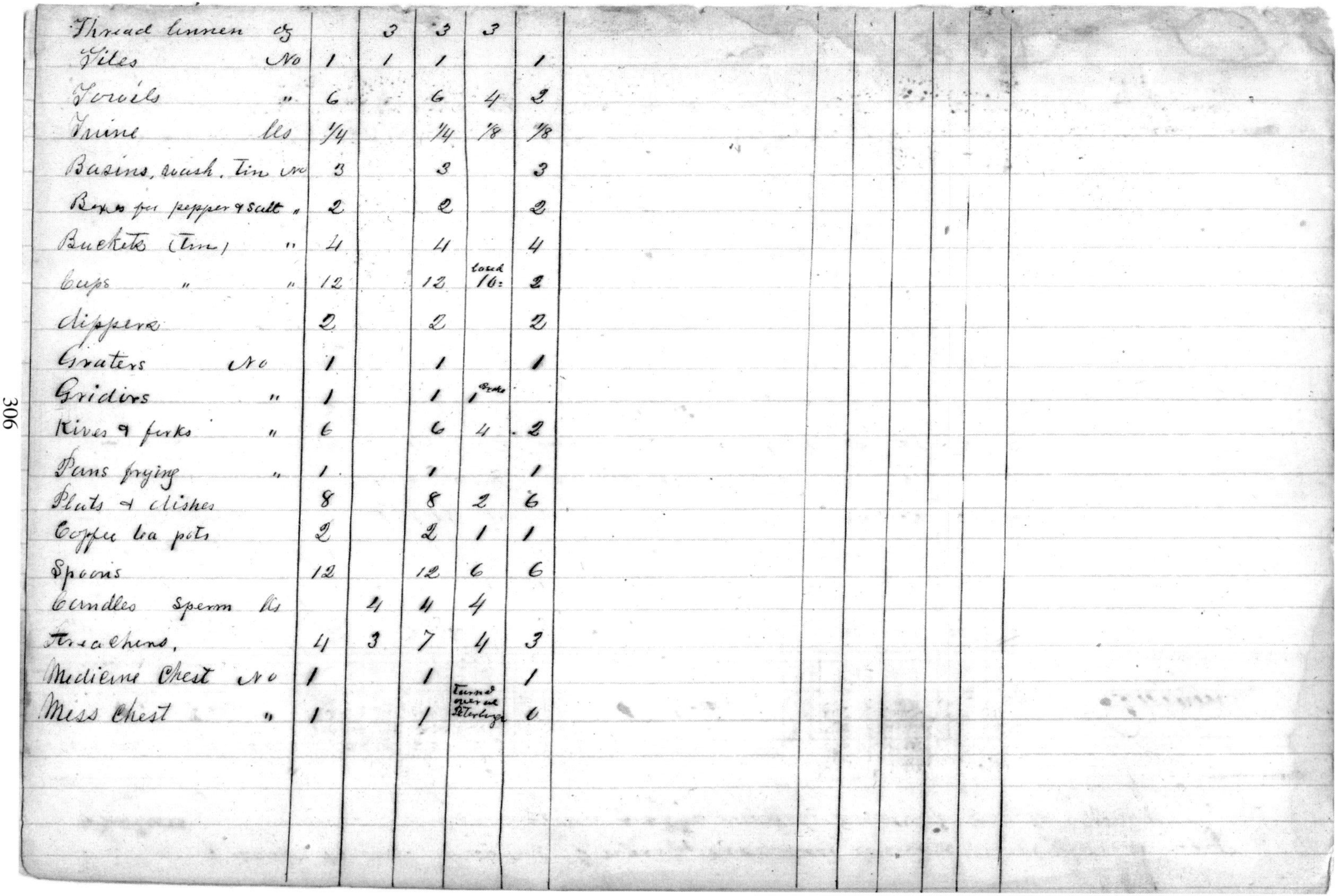

Thread linnen	oz		3	3	3	
Files	No	1	1	1		1
[illegible]	"	6		6	4	2
Twine	lbs	1/4		1/4	1/8	1/8
Basins, wash. Tin	No	3		3		3
Boxes for pepper & salt	"	2		2		2
Buckets (Tin)	"	4		4		4
Cups "	"	12		12	lost 10:	2
Dippers		2		2		2
Graters	No	1		1		1
Gridirons	"	1		1	1 Broke	
Knives & forks	"	6		6	4	2
Pans frying	"	1		1		1
Plates & dishes		8		8	2	6
Coffee tea pots		2		2	1	1
Spoons		12		12	6	6
Candles Sperm	lbs		4	4	4	
[illegible]		4	3	7	4	3
Medicine Chest	No	1		1		1
Mess Chest	"	1		1	Turned over at Petersburg	0

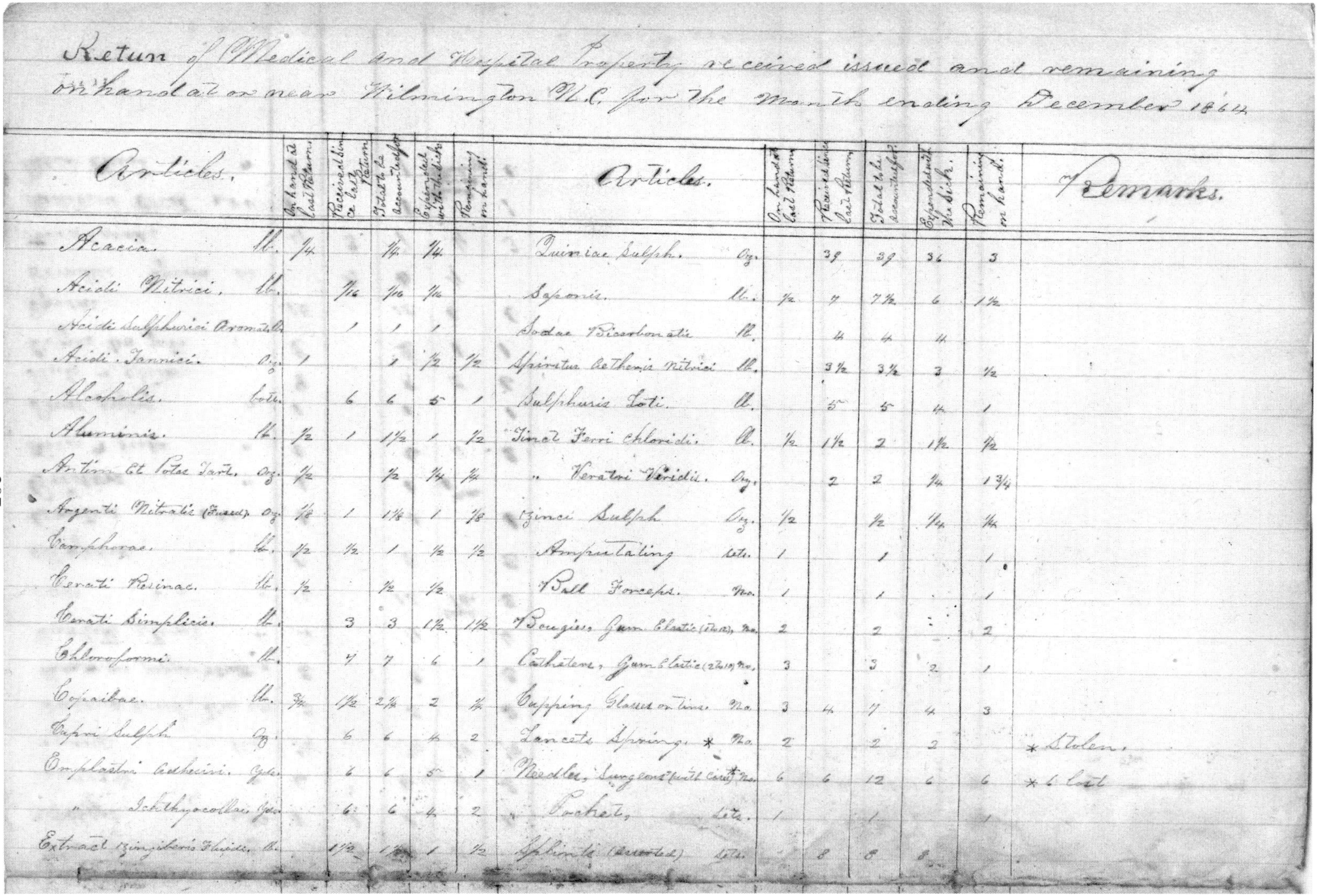

Return of Medical and Hospital Property received issued and remaining on hand at or near Wilmington N.C. for the month ending December 1864

Articles.		On hand at last Return	Received since last Return	Total to be accounted for	Expended with the sick	Remaining on hand	Articles.		On hand at last Return	Received since last Return	Total to be accounted for	Expended with the sick	Remaining on hand	Remarks.
Acacia	lb.	1/4		1/4	1/4		Quiniae Sulph.	Oz.		39	39	36	3	
Acidi Nitrici.	lb.		1/16	1/16	1/16		Saponis.	lb.	1/2	7	7 1/2	6	1 1/2	
Acidi Sulphurici Aromatic	lb.		1	1	1		Sodae Bicarbonatis	lb.		4	4	4		
Acidi Tannici.	Oz.	1		1	1/2	1/2	Spiritus Aetheris Nitrici	lb.		3 1/2	3 1/2	3	1/2	
Alcoholis.	bots.		6	6	5	1	Sulphuris Loti.	lb.		5	5	4	1	
Aluminis.	lb.	1/2	1	1 1/2	1	1/2	Tinct Ferri Chloridi.	lb.	1/2	1 1/2	2	1 1/2	1/2	
Antim et Potas Tart.	Oz.	1/2		1/2	1/4	1/4	" Veratri Viridis.	Oz.		2	2	1/4	1 3/4	
Argenti Nitratis (Fused)	Oz.	1/8	1	1 1/8	1	1/8	Zinci Sulph	Oz.	1/2		1/2	1/4	1/4	
Camphorae.	lb.	1/2	1/2	1	1/2	1/2	Amputating	Sets.	1		1		1	
Cerati Resinae.	lb.	1/2		1/2	1/2		Ball Forceps.	No.	1		1		1	
Cerati Simplicis.	lb.		3	3	1 1/2	1 1/2	Bougies, Gum Elastic (Ass'd),	No.	2		2	:	2	
Chloroformi.	lb.		7	7	6	1	Catheters, Gum Elastic (2 to 10)	No.	3		3	2	1	
Copaibae.	lb.	3/4	1 1/2	2 1/4	2	1/4	Cupping Glasses or tins.	No.	3	4	7	4	3	
Cupri Sulph	Oz.		6	6	4	2	Lancets Spring. *	No.	2		2	2		* Stolen.
Emplastri Adhesivi.	Yds.		6	6	5	1	Needles, Surgeons (with case) *	No.	6	6	12	6	6	* 6 lost
" Ichthyocollae	Yds.		6	6	4	2	" Pocket,	Sets.	1		1		1	
Extract Zingiberis Fluidi	lb.		1 1/2	1 1/2	1	1/2	Splints (Assorted)	Sets.		8	8	8		

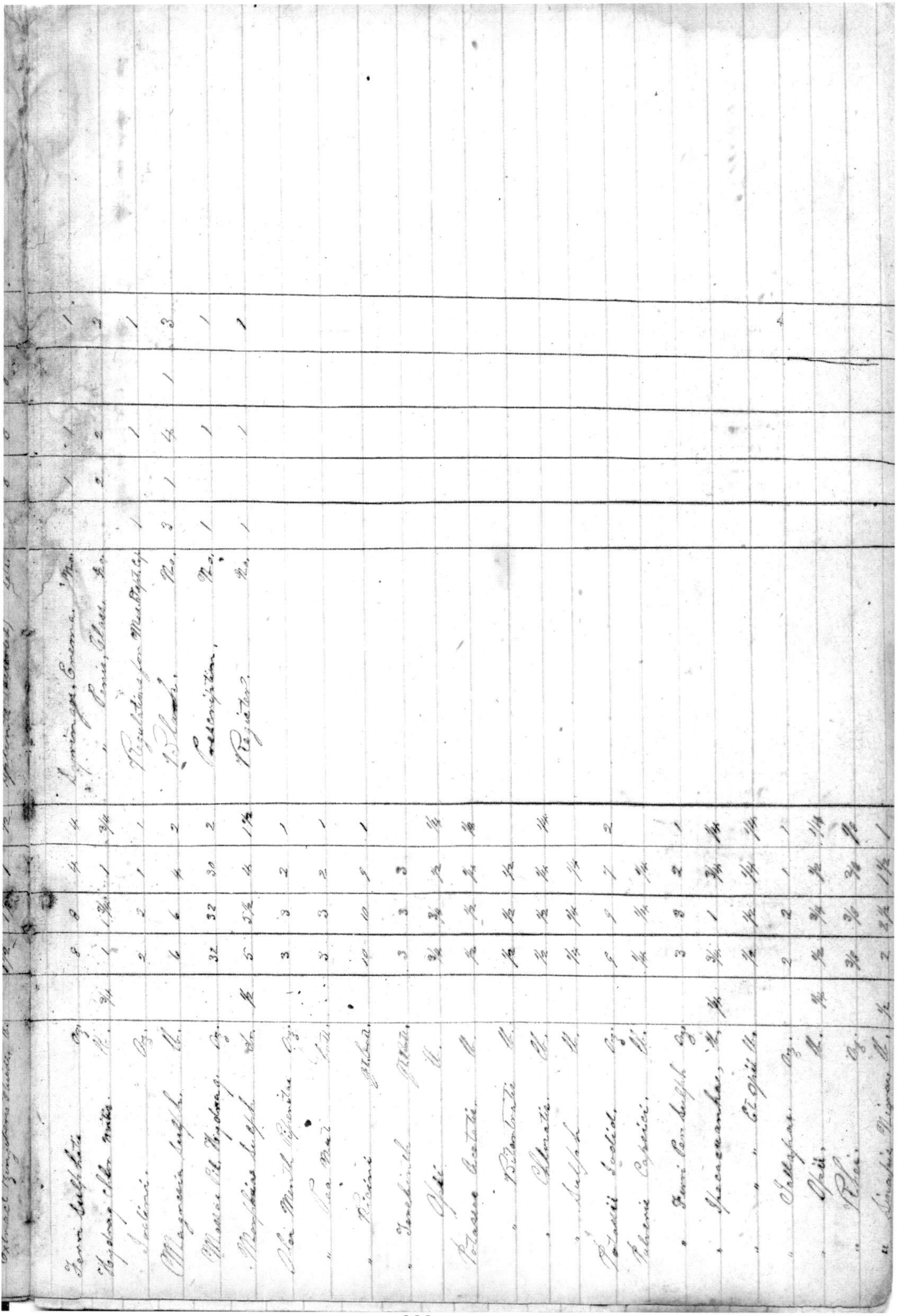

Extract Zingiberis Fluidi.	lb.		1/2	1/2	1	1/2
Ferri Sulphatis	Oz.		8	8	4	4
Hydrarg Chlor mitis.	lb.	3/4	1	1 3/4	1	3/4
Iodini.	Oz.		2	2	1	1
Magnesia Sulph.	lb.		6	6	4	2
Massae Pil. Hydrarg.	Oz.		32	32	30	2
Morphiae Sulph.	dr.	1/2	5	5 1/2	4	1 1/2
Olei Menth Piperitae	Oz.		3	3	2	1
" Pea Nut	bott.		3	3	2	1
" Ricini	gt. bott.		10	10	9	1
" Terebinth	gt. bott.		3	3	3	
Opii	lb.		3/4	3/4	1/2	1/4
Potassae Acetatis.	lb.		1/2	1/2	1/4	1/8
" Bitartratis	lb.		1/2	1/2	1/2	
" Chloratis.	lb.		1/2	1/2	1/4	1/4
" Sulph	lb.		1/4	1/4	1/4	
Potassii Iodid.	Oz.		9	9	7	2
Pulveris Capsici.	lb.		1/4	1/4	1/4	
" Ferri Per Sulph	Oz.		3	3	2	1
" Ipecacuanhae,	lb.	1/4	3/4	1	3/4	1/4
" " " Et Opii	lb.		1/2	1/2	1/4	1/4
" Jallapae.	Oz.		2	2	1	1
" Opii.	lb.	1/4	1/2	3/4	1/2	1/4
" Rhei.	Oz.		3/8	3/8	3/8	1/8
" Sinapis Nigrae	lb.	1/2	2	2 1/2	1 1/2	1

Splints (assorted)	Sets	[illegible]	6	6	6	[illegible]
Syringes, Enema	No.		1	1		1
" Penis, Glass.	No.		2	2		2
Regulations for Med. Dept. Cop.		1		1		1
Blanks.	No.	3	1	4	1	3
Prescription.	No.	1		1		1
Register.	No.	1		1		1

Return of Medical and Hospital Property received, expended, issued and remaining on hand at or Near Wilmington N.C. for the Month ending December 1864

Articles.		On hand at last Return	Received since last Return.	Total to be accounted for.	Expended with the Sick.	On hand.	Articles.		On hand at last Return.	Received since last Return.	Total to be accounted for.	Expended with the Sick.	On hand.	Remarks.
Nutmegs.	Oz.		2	2	2		Pots. Coffee, and Tea.	No.	1		1		1	
Tea.	lb.		1	1	1/2	1/2	Spoons.	No.	6		6		6	
Whiskey	Galls.		15	15	15		Pil: Cathartic: Comp: (Pills) doz.			22	22	22		
Gutta Percha Cloth.	Yds.	3		3		3	Tinct. Opii	Oz.		29	29	21	8	
Bandages, Suspensory,	No.		6	6	6		Candles, Sperm.	lbs.		7	7	6	1	
Cork Screws.	No.	1		1		1	Ink (2 oz Bott),	No.		10	10	7	3	
Cotton Batting	lb.		2	2	2		Litters and Stretchers (hand) *	No.	3		3	1	2	* 1 lost or worn out.
Flannel, red.	Yds.		2	2	2		Medicine chest,	No.	1		1		1	
Hones (in wood),	No.		1	1		1	Tinct. Indigimus,	Galls.		2	2	2		
Lint,	lb.		3	3	2	1	Bottles of all kinds	No.		113	113	113		
Medicine cups & Glasses	No.	2	2	4	2	2	Boxes.	No.		7	7	7		
Mortars & Pestles. Wedgewood	No.	1		1		1	Canisters.	No.		2	2	2		
Muslin	Yds.	3	12	15	12	3	Jars.	No.		4	4	4		
Needles, sewing.	No.		37	37	12	24								
Pans, Bed. *	No.	1		1	1									* Burned By the Enemy at Stony Creek
Paper Envelopes.	No.		175	175	150	25								
Paper, Writing.	Qrs.	1	22	23	21	2								

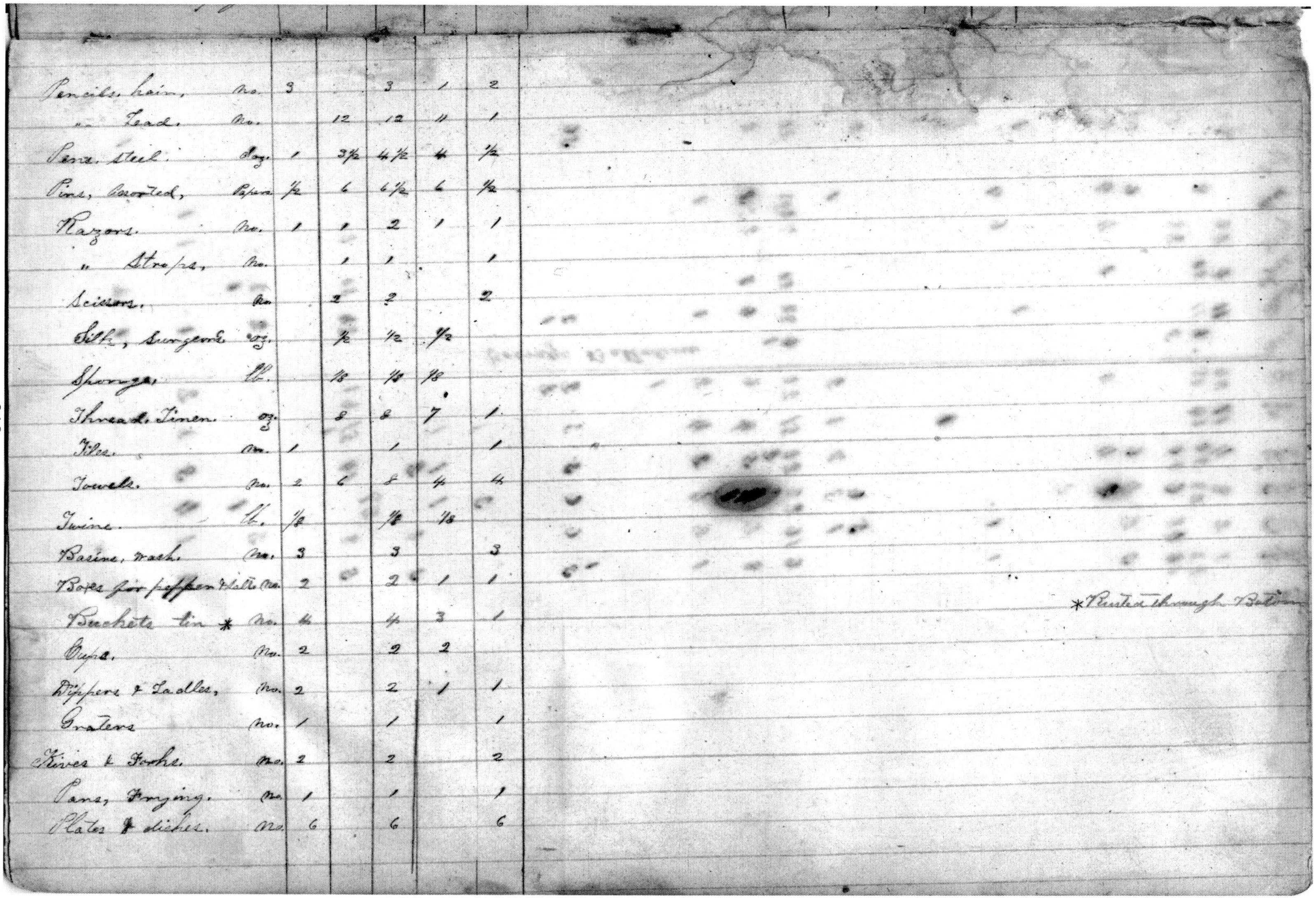

Pencils, hair,	no.	3		3	1	2
" Lead.	no.		12	12	11	1
Pens, steel.	Doz.	1	3½	4½	4	½
Pins, assorted,	Papers	½	6	6½	6	½
Razors.	no.	1	1	2	1	1
" Straps,	no.		1	1		1
Scissors,	no.		2	2		2
Silk, Surgeons	oz.		½	½	½	
Sponge,	lb.		1/8	1/8	1/8	
Thread, Linen.	oz.		8	8	7	1
Files.	no.	1		1		1
Towels.	no.	2	6	8	4	4
Twine.	lb.	1/8		1/8	1/8	
Basins, wash.	no.	3		3		3
Boxes for pepper & salt	no.	2		2	1	1
Buckets tin *	no.	4		4	3	1
Cups.	no.	2		2	2	
Dippers & Ladles,	no.	2		2	1	1
Graters	no.	1		1		1
Knives & Forks.	no.	2		2		2
Pans, Frying.	no.	1		1		1
Plates & dishes.	no.	6		6		6

*Rusted through Bottom

CLASSES OF DISEASES.	SPECIFIC DISEASES.	1863	Sept	Oct	Nov	Dec	Jan	Feb	March	March	April	May	June	July	Aug	Sept	Oc
FEVERS.	Febris Congestiva,																
	Febris Continua Communis,		4	2	8	4	17	34		11	4	22			58		
	Febris Intermittens Quotidiana,		43		28	30	64	45	.6	11	50		8				
	Febris Intermittens Tertiana,		16	48	6	10	-		3			28			5		
	Febris Intermittens Quartana,																
	Febris Remittens,		3	2	4	6							6		23		
	Febris Typhoides,				2	4		4	–		1	4	9		16		
	Febris Typhus,																
	Febris Typhus Icterodes,				2												
	All other diseases of this class,																
ERUPTIVE FEVERS.	Erysipelas,									1					1		
	Rubeola,		1	1								6	9				
	Scarlatina,																
	Variola,						1										
	Varioloides,																
	All other diseases of this class,																
DISEASES OF THE ORGANS CONNECTED WITH THE DIGESTIVE SYSTEM.	Cholera Asiatica,																
	Cholera Morbus,			5	6										2		
	Colica,			1	3	7	1	2					1				
	Constipatio,																
	Diarrhœa Acuta,		6	16	22	20	51	20	6	32	51	7	205		10		
	Diarrhœa Chronica,				2	2			1								
	Dysenteria Acuta,		8	2	2	5	4	6		6	7	2	2[illegible]		2		
	Dysenteria Chronica,				2												
	Dyspepsia,		1	2	4	2	4	2		1			1				
	Enteritis,																
	Gastritis,							1									
	Hæmatemesis,																
	Hepatitis Acuta,																
	Hepatitis Chronica,		1														
	Icterus,		3	6	6	5	3	2		2					56		
	Parotitis,							2		1							
	Peritonitis,																
	Splenitis,																
	Tonsillitis,				3		1										
	All other diseases of this class,																
DISEASES OF THE RESPIRATORY SYSTEM.	Asthma,				1	1	1										
	Bronchitis Acuta,		3	3		2											
	Bronchitis Chronica,																
	Catarrhus Epidemicus,				29												
	Catarrhus,		5	8		14	51	61		24	30	5					
	Hæmoptysis,						1										
	Laryngitis,																
	Phthisis Pulmonalis,																
	Pleuritis,			2						.2	2						
	Pneumonia,				1						1						
	All other diseases of this class,																
DISEASES OF THE CIRCULATORY SYSTEM.	Anæmia,		4	1	4	3	2	2		1		1	1				
	Aneurisma,																
	Angina Pectoris,																
	Carditis,									1	2				1		
	Endocarditis,																
	Pericarditis,																
	Phlebitis,																

Youngs Battalion

Diseases.	Specific Diseases.	186[illegible]	Sept	Oct	Nov	Dec	Jan	Feb	Mar	March	April	May	June	July	Augt	Sept	Oct
	Brought forward,						201				148						
Diseases of the Circulatory System.	Varicocele,																
	Varix,																
	All other diseases of this class,																
Diseases of the Brain and Nervous System.	Apoplexia,			1						1							
	Cephalalgia,					4											
	Cerebritis,																
	Chorea,																
	Delirium Tremens,																
	Epilepsia,						1	1		1							
	Ictus Solis,																
	Irritatio Spinalis,																
	Mania,																
	Melancholia,																
	Meningitis,							1									
	Neuralgia,																
	Paralysis, partial				1		1	3									
	Tetanus,																
	All other diseases of this class,			1													
Diseases of the Urinary and Genital Organs, and Venereal Affections.	Bubo Syphiliticum,																
	Calculus,																
	Cystitis,			1			1	1									
	Diabetes,																
	Enuresis,																
	Gonorrhœa,		3	2	2	4	5	1	1	1	1						
	Ischuria et Dysuria,																
	Nephritis,			1	2												
	Orchitis,					1	1	1									
	Sarcocele,							2		2							
	Strictura Urethræ,																
	Syphilis Primitiva,			2		3											
	Syphilis Consecutiva,																
	Ulcus Penis Non Syphiliticum,																
	All other diseases of this class,																
Diseases of the Serous Exhalant Vessels.	Anasarca,					4	3	3		1	2	1	1		15		
	Ascites,					1	2					2			1		
	Hydrarthrus,																
	Hydrocele,																
	Hydrothorax,																
	All other diseases of this class,																
Diseases of the Fibrous and Muscular Structures.	Lumbago,						1			1							
	Podagra,																
	Rheumatismus Acutus,		4	7													
	Rheumatismus Chronicus,			[illegible]	12	6	13	3		6	8		2		4		
	All other diseases of this class,						1										
Abscesses and Ulcers.	Abscessus,							4		3	6						
	Anthrax,						1										
	Fistula, ani						1										
	Paronychia,				2	3											
	Phlegmon,		3	1	7	6	5		1						2		
	Ulcus,		3	1	1		2	2			1		2				
	All other diseases of this class,						1										

Young's Battalion

1863	Remaing last Report: Sick	Convalescent	Total	Taken Sick during the Month	Aggregate	Sent Gen Hospital	Returned to Duty	On Furlough	Discharged	Deserted	Died or Killed	Remaing: Sick	Convalescent	Total	Officers / Enlisted men / Total
Sept.				115	115	2	72	2				29	10	39.	~~740 : 72 :: 1000~~ : 1554
Oct	29	[illegible]	[illegible]	124	165	7	94				1.	20	41.	61.	38.597. 884 mean
Nov	15	49	54	171	210	14	141	1							[illegible] } 846 mean single
Decd	20.	44.	64.	162.	216.	8.	144.								6[illegible] : 645
Jan 1864	20	42	62	259	323	8	245	7	1						
~~Feb~~	~~20~~	~~44~~	~~64~~	~~259~~	~~323~~	~~8~~	~~245~~	~~7~~							
Feb	12	18	30	210.	272.	6.	231	2	3						
Yeuns Bal				21	26	1	11					5	3	8:	(116) : 20 :: 1000 : 172.414
April	6	18	24.	174	184	34	126 :					6,	18	24 :	699 : 184 : 1000
May	20	11.	30	124	148	42	76				4	20.	11.	30	546. 271.066
June	155	—	155.	306	336	99.	82				21	155	0	155	: 529 : 336 : 1000 = 635.160

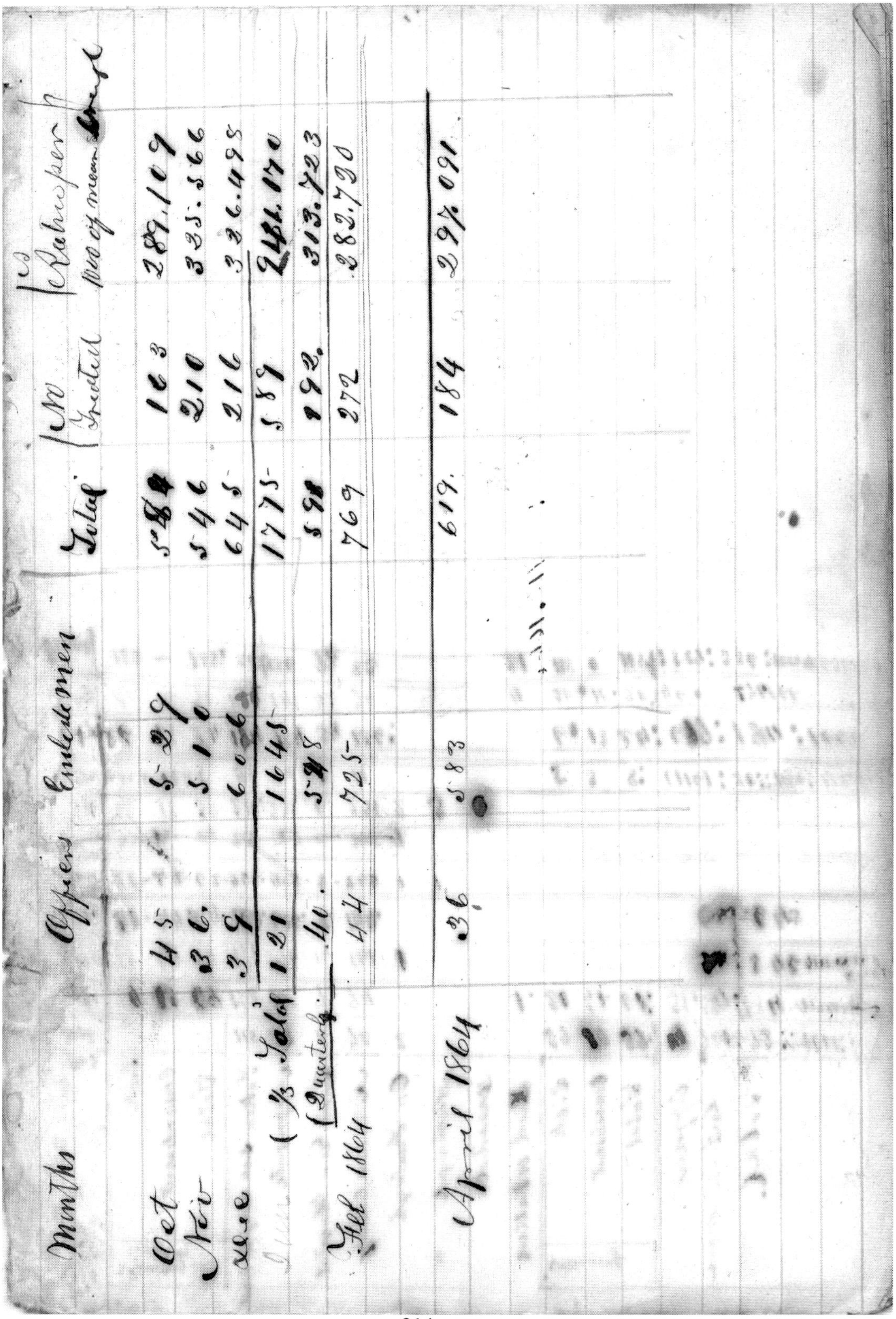

Months	Officers	Enlisted men	Total	No. Treated	Ratio per 1000 of mean strength
Oct	45	529	584	163	289.109
Nov	36.	510	546	210	335.566
Dec	39	606	645	216	336.498
(⅓ Total	121	1645	1775	589	2481.170
(Quarterly	40.	548	598	192.	313.723
Feb 1864	44	725	769	272	282.720
April 1864	36	583	619.	184	297.091

Quarterly report ending December 31st 1863.
Taken sick during the Quarter 480
Aggregate 480
Sent Gen Hospital 29
Returned to duty 387
Remaining sick end of the Quarter 19
Convalescent 44
Mean strength for the Quarter
Officers 40
Enlisted men 634-
Then 674: 480 :: 1000: 712.166+

Appendix 4
Photographs

Tintype of Capt. John Hendricks Kinyoun in his Confederate uniform while serving in Company F, Twenty-Eighth North Carolina Infantry Regiment, CSA. 1861
From the author's collection.

Sash worn by Captain Kinyoun with uniform in above tintype.
From the author's collection.

Button from Captain Kinyoun's uniform worn in above tintype.
From the author's collection.

Tintype of Captain Kinyoun with his son, Joseph James Kinyoun. In 1887, Joseph Kinyoun founded the National Institutes of Health, Staten Island, New York.
From the author's collection.

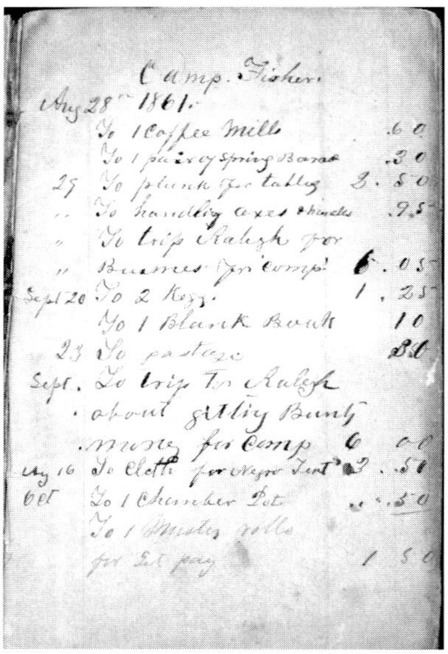

Camp. Fisher.
Aug 28th 1861.
To 1 Coffee mill .60
To 1 pair of Spring Barrs .30
25 To plank for tables 3.50
" To handling axes & hinds .95
" To trip Raleigh for
" Business for Camp 6.05
Sept 20 To 2 Kegs 1.25
To 1 Blank Book 10
23 To postage .30
Sept. To trip To Raleigh
about getting Bounty
money for Camp 6.00
Aug 16 To Cloth for Negro Tent 3.50
Oct To 1 Chamber Pot .50
To 1 Muster rolls
for Sd pay 1.50

Camp Fisher Supply & Travel Log. August-October 1861. Belonged to Dr. Kinyoun.
From the author's collection.

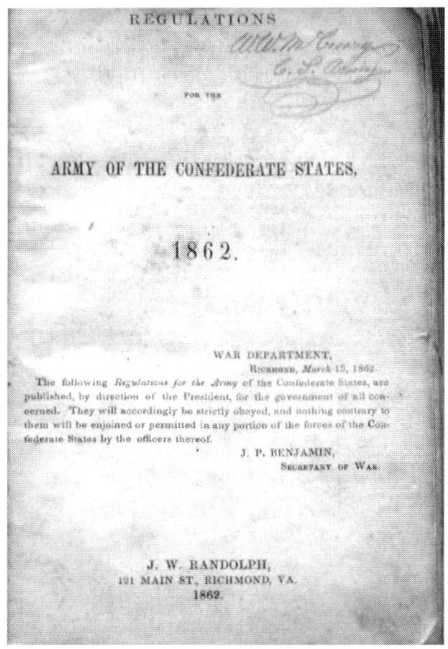

REGULATIONS

FOR THE

ARMY OF THE CONFEDERATE STATES,

1862.

WAR DEPARTMENT,
RICHMOND, *March* 13, 1862.

The following *Regulations for the Army* of the Confederate States, are published, by direction of the President, for the government of all concerned. They will accordingly be strictly obeyed, and nothing contrary to them will be enjoined or permitted in any portion of the forces of the Confederate States by the officers thereof.

J. P. BENJAMIN,
SECRETARY OF WAR.

J. W. RANDOLPH,
121 MAIN ST., RICHMOND, VA.
1862.

Confederate Regulations Manual, 1862. Belonged to Dr. Kinyoun.
From the author's collection.

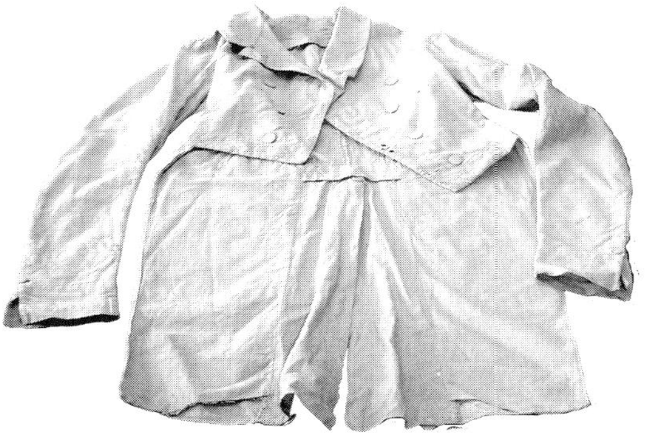

Wartime Surgical Uniform worn by Dr. Kinyoun while serving as Regimental Surgeon of the Sixty-sixth North Carolina Infantry Regiment.
From the author's collection.

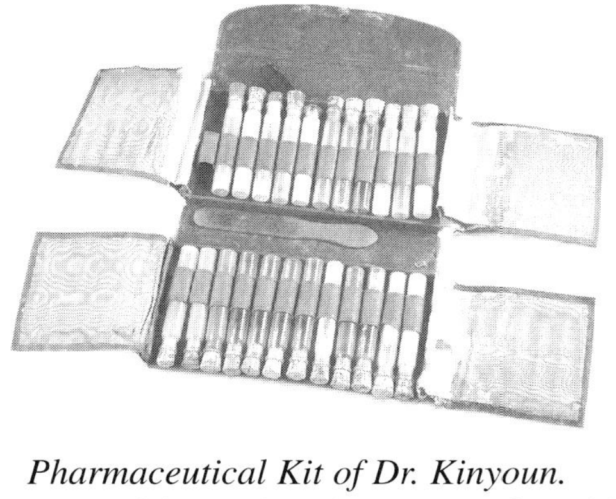

Pharmaceutical Kit of Dr. Kinyoun.
Courtesy of the National Museum of Health and Medicine, Armed Forces Institute of Pathology, Washington, D.C. (M-660 00344)

Tintype of Dr. Aylett, one of Dr. Kinyoun's medical instructors at New York Medical School, 1857-1859
From the author's collection.

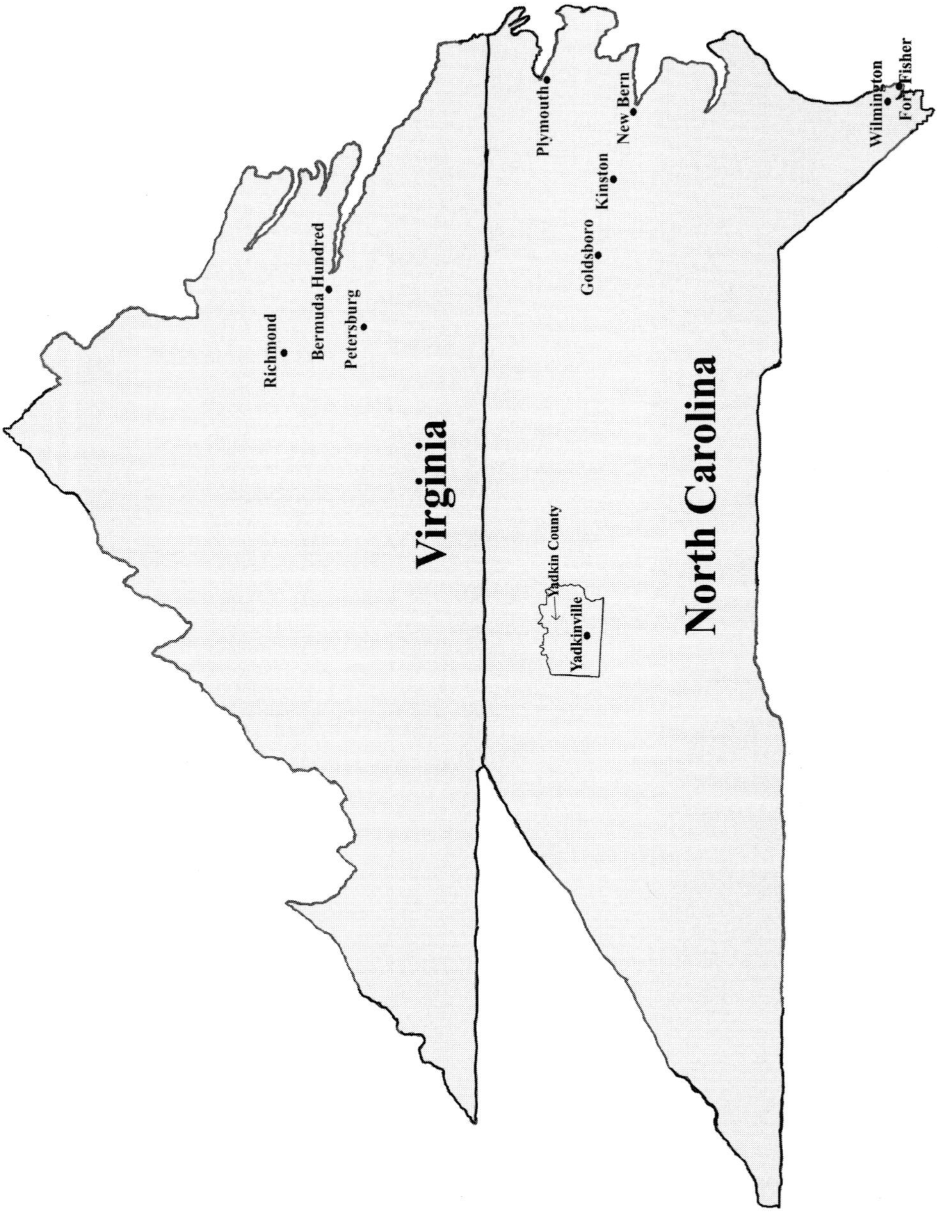

Map of Virginia and North Carolina with selected battles fought by the Sixty-Sixth North Carolina Infantry Regiment.
Map by Sarah Elder, Curator, St. Joseph Museums Inc.

Wartime Travel Chest belonging to Dr. Kinyoun. Initials "JK" carved on lid. Originally used as either a Confederate munitions case or an artillery limber chest.
From the author's collection.

Confederate Currency. The first two $10 bills on the third row from the top are in sequence; #50969 and #50970. Belonged to Dr. Kinyoun.
From the author's collection.

Assorted Confederate Currency. Belonged to Dr. Kinyoun.
From the author's collection.

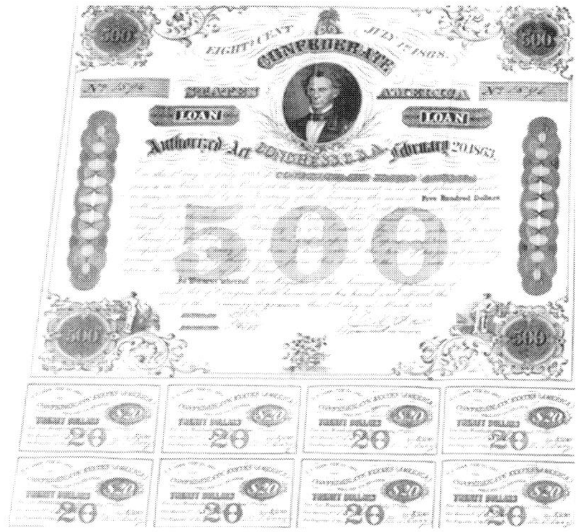

$500 Confederate War Bonds.
Belonged to Dr. Kinyoun.
From the author's collection.

Left: Front of Southern Cross of Honor. Presented to Dr. Kinyoun by the United Daughters of the Confederacy. Given to Confederate soldiers for Meritorious Service. c. 1890.
From the author's collection.

Bottom: Back of Southern Cross.

Seal of the Confederate States of America. Reproduction. Belonged to Dr. Kinyoun.
From the author's collection.

Dr. Joseph H. Kinyoun. c. 1890
From the author's collection.

Dr. Joseph H. Kinyoun and his second wife, Martha (seated). Their daughter is standing. c. 1890
From the author's collection.

Dr. Joseph H. Kinyoun. Taken on his seventy-fourth birthday, October 4, 1899.
From the author's collection.

Kinyoun Family Home. Centerview, Missouri. c. 1890
From the author's collection.

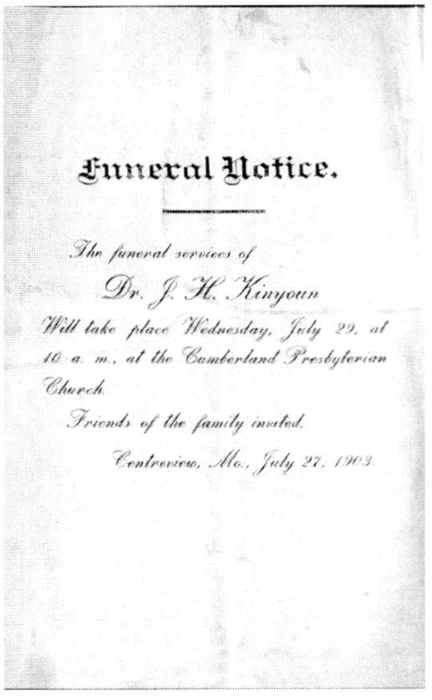

Funeral Notice.

The funeral services of

Dr. J. H. Kinyoun

Will take place Wednesday, July 29, at 10 a. m., at the Cumberland Presbyterian Church.

Friends of the family invited.

Centreview, Mo., July 27, 1903.

Funeral Notice of the death of Dr. Kinyoun, July 27, 1903. Services were conducted July 29, 1903

From the author's collection.

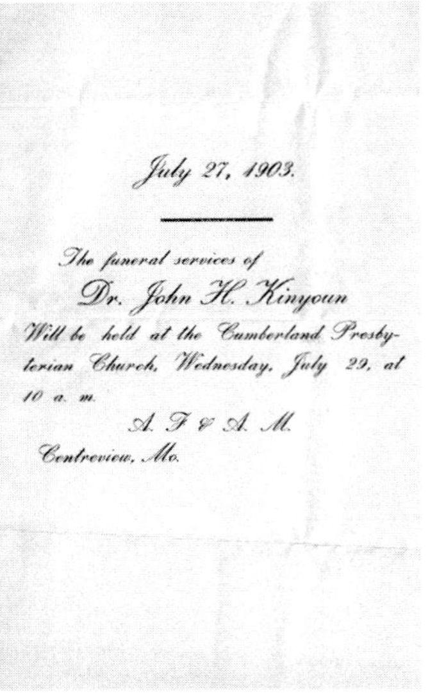

July 27, 1903.

The funeral services of

Dr. John H. Kinyoun

Will be held at the Cumberland Presbyterian Church, Wednesday, July 29, at 10 a. m.

A. F. & A. M.

Centreview, Mo.

Masonic Funeral Notice of the death of Dr. Kinyoun.

From the author's collection.

Tombstone of Dr. John Hendricks Kinyoun between the tombstones of both wives, Elizabeth at left, and Martha at right.

From the author's collection.

Notes
Bibliography
Index

NOTES

CHAPTER I "A DARKNESS"

1. Corporal Isaiah B. Keuppers and Isaiah Benjamin Keuppers are purely fictional characters.

2. Josiah Keuppers is a purely fictional character.

3. H. H. Cunningham, *Doctors In Gray* (Baton Rouge: Louisiana State University Press, 1993), 129.

4. Ralph Chester Williams, *The United States Public Health Service 1798-1950* (Washington, D.C.: Commissioned Officers Association of the United States Public Health Service, 1950), 180.

5. Dr. Wallace McDonald, "The Life and Times of Dr. Silas McDonald" (Speech, Pony Express Museum, St. Joseph, MO, February 19, 2002).

6. Cunningham, *Doctors In Gray,* 9, 247.

7. Susan Provost Beller, *Medical Practices in the Civil War* (Cincinnati, OH: Betterway Books, 1992), 22.

8. Williams, *The United States Public Health Service 1798-1950*, 177.

9. E. B. Long and Barbara Long, *The Civil War Day by Day: An Almanac 1861-1865* (Garden City, NY: Doubleday & Co. , 1971), 99.

10. Ibid., 711-12.

11. Cunningham, *Doctors In Gray*, 3.

12. Ibid., 17-18.

13. Ibid., 18.

14. Glenna R. Schroeder-Lein, *Confederate Hospitals On The Move* (Columbia, South Carolina: University of South Carolina Press, 1996), 68.

15. Cunningham, *Doctors In Gray*, 21-22.

16. David S. Heidler and Jeanne T. Heidler, *Encyclopedia of the American Civil War* (New York: W. W. Norton & Company, 2000), 603; Long and Long, *The Civil War: Day By Day An Almanac 1861-1865,* 712; George Washington Adams, *Doctors In Blue* (Baton Rouge: Louisiana State University Press, 1996), 13-15.

17. Geoffrey C. Ward, Ric Burns, and Ken Burns, *The Civil War* (New York: Alfred A. Knopf, Inc., 1990), 296.

18. Long and Long, *The Civil War Day by Day: An Almanac 1861-1865*, 712.

19. Ward, Burns, and Burns, *The Civil War*, 184.

20. Cunningham, *Doctors In Gray*, 85, 163, 184.

21. Ibid., 168, 180-81.

22. Glenna R. Schroeder-Lein, *Confederate Hospitals on the Move*, 44.

23. Cunningham, *Doctors In Gray* 181-82, 184.

24. Heidler and Heidler, *Encyclopedia of the American Civil War*, 1336.

25. Adams, *Doctors In Blue*, 114.

26. Francis A. Lord, *Civil War Collector's Encyclopedia* (Secaucus, New Jersey: Castle Books a division of Book Sales, Inc., 1979), 19-29, 237-55.

27. Adams, *Doctors In Blue*, 114.

28. Beller, *Medical Practices in the Civil War,* 69.

29. Cunningham, *Doctors In Gray*, 21-22.

30. Ibid., 22.

31. Ibid., 24-25.

32. Ibid., 26.

33. Ibid.

34. Ibid., 32-33.

35. Ibid., 36-37.

36. Ibid., 43.

37. Ibid., 47.

38. Ibid., 73.

39. Schroeder-Lein, *Confederate Hospitals On The Move*, 42, 44.

40. Cunningham, *Doctors In Gray*, 50.

41. Ibid.

42. Heidler and Heidler, *Encyclopedia of the American Civil War,* 1353.

43. Schroeder-Lein, *Confederate Hospitals On The Move*, 120.

44. Ward, Burns and Burns, *The Civil War*, 298.

45. Jefferson Davis, *The Rise And Fall of the Confederate Government* (New York: D. Appleton And Company, 1881), 310; Heidler and Heidler, *Encyclopedia of the American Civil War,* 1353.

46. Schroeder-Lein, *Confederate Hospitals On The Move*, 192.

47. Cunningham, *Doctors In Gray*, 30.

48. Heidler and Heidler, *Encyclopedia of the American Civil War,* 1353.

49. Cunningham, *Doctors In Gray*, 254-55, 259.

50. Ibid., 259.

51. Ibid., 256.

52. Schroeder-Lein, *Confederate Hospitals On The Move*, 63.

53. Ibid.

54. Cunningham, *Doctors In Gray*, 260-61, 263.

55. Ibid., 262.

56. Ibid., 263.

57. Ibid., 266.

58. Ibid., 221.

59. Ibid., 130-31.

60. Adams, *Doctors In Blue*, 3-9; Heidler and Heidler, *Encyclopedia of the American Civil War*, 1303-10.

61. Ibid., 30-32, 39-41.

62. William E. Parrish, "The Western Sanitary Commission," *Civil War History*, Vol. 36, March 1990, 17-35.

63. Adams, *Doctors In Blue* 28-31; Parrish, "The Western Sanitary Commission," 21-23.

64. Cunningham, *Doctors In Gray*, 26-31.

65. Adams, *Doctors In Blue*, 25-32.

66. Ibid., 9.

67. Sheridan A. Logan, *Old Saint Jo*, (St. Joseph, MO: John Sublett Logan Foundation, 1979), 304-9.

68. Adams, *Doctors In Blue*, 228-30.

CHAPTER II "YADKIN COUNTY BOY"

1. William E. Rutledge, Jr. and Max O. Welborn, *An Illustrated History of Yadkin County 1850-1965* (Yadkinville, NC: 1965), 7.

2. Ibid.

3. Frances Harding Casstevens, Editor, *The Heritage Of Yadkin County* (Yadkinville, North Carolina: Published By The Yadkin County Historical Society, 1981), 3.

4. Ibid.

5. Ibid., 2..

6. Rutledge and Welborn, *An Illustrated History of Yadkin County 1850-1965,* 7.

7. Casstevens, *The Heritage Of Yadkin County*, 7.

8. Rutledge and Welborn, *An Illustrated History of Yadkin County 1850-1965*, 7.

9. Ibid., 8-9.

10. John Mack Faragher, *Daniel Boone,* (New York: Henry Holt Company, Inc., 1992), 76-77.

11. Rutledge and Welborn, *An Illustrated History of Yadkin County 1850-1965*, 9.

12. Casstevens, *The Heritage Of Yadkin County*, 3.

13. Rutledge and Welborn, *An Illustrated History of Yadkin County 1850-1965*, 8.

14. Casstevens, *The Heritage Of Yadkin County,* 6.

15. Ibid., 7.

16. Ibid., 1.

17. Ibid., 7.

18. Kinyoun Genealogical Papers, *Ancestral Record,* Alice Kinyoun Houts.

19. Ibid.

20. "In Memoriam," *The Atlantic Messenger*, New Bern, N. C.

21. Kinyoun Genealogical Papers, *Ancestral Record.*

22. Ibid.

23. Ibid.

24. Alice Kinyoun Houts to Joseph Kinyoun Houts, Jr., 6 March 1968

25. Rutledge and Welborn, *An Illustrated History of Yadkin County 1850-1965*, 84.

26. Ibid., 31.

27. Ibid.

28. Kinyoun Genealogical Papers.

29. Ibid.

30. Frances H. Casstevens, *The Civil War And Yadkin County, North Carolina* (Jefferson, North Carolina, and London: McFarland & Company, Inc., Publishers, 1997), 18.

31. Kinyoun Genealogical Papers.

32. Casstevens, *The Civil War And Yadkin County, North Carolina* 11.

33. Kinyoun Genealogical Papers, Alice Kinyoun Houts.

34. *The Real American Tragedy* (Oklahoma City, Oklahoma: Homsey-Simon Production Co., 1977), 30.

35. Joseph K. Houts, Jr., *Quantrill's Thieves* (Kansas City, Mo: Truman Publishing Company, 2002), 10.

36. Ibid., 11.

37. Ibid.

38. Long and Long, *The Civil War Day By Day An Almanac 1861-1865,* 12-13.

39. Heidler and Heidler, *Encyclopedia of the American Civil War*, 1426-28.

40. Mrs. Hale Houts, "Yadkin Boys," *Journal of North Carolina Genealogy* Vol. IX No.2 (North Carolina State Library Raleigh: Summer 1863), 1131-35.

41. Ibid.

42. Ibid.

43. Ibid.

44. Walter Clark, Editor, *Histories of the Several Regiments And Battalions from North Carolina in the Great War 1861-65*, Vol. 2 (Published By The State), 469.

45. Ibid., 466.

46. Casstevens, *The Civil War And Yadkin County, North Carolina* 38-39.

47. Ibid.

48. Clark, *Histories of the Several Regiments And Battalions from North Carolina in the Great War 1861-65*. Vol. 2., 478.

49. Ibid.

50. Mark Mayo Boatner III, *The Civil War Dictionary* (New York: Vintage Books, 1991), 400.

51. Kinyoun Genealogical Papers.

52. Interview by author with Jesse Poindexter, Colorado Springs, 28 September 2002.

53. Clark, *Histories of the Several Regiments And Battalions from North Carolina in the Great War 1861-1865*, Vol. 2, 467.

54. Ibid., 468.

55. Cunningham., *Doctors In Gray,* 52.

56. Ibid.

57. Ibid., 88-89.

58. Ibid., 85.

59. Ibid., 64.

60. Ibid., 45.

61. Weymouth T. Jordan, Jr., *North Carolina Troops 1861-1865: A Roster,* Vol. 15 (Raleigh, NC: Raleigh, North Carolina, Office Of Archives and History, Courtesy State Library Of North Carolina, 2003), 277-78.

62. Walter Clark, ed., *Histories of the Several Regiments And Battalions from North Carolina in the Great War 1861-1865*, Vol. 3, (Published by the State), 685.

63. Ibid., 687.

64. Boatner, *The Civil War Dictionary*, 163.

65. Clark, *Histories of the Several Regiments And Battalions from North Carolina in the Great War 1861-1865*, Vol. 3, 688-89.

66. Jordan, *North Carolina Troops 1861-1865 A Roster*, Vol. 15, 286-89.

67. Ibid.

68. John H. Kinyoun to Elizabeth Conrad Kinyoun, 17 June 1864

69. Clark, *Histories of the Several Regiments And Battalions from North Carolina in the Great War 1861-1865*, Vol. 3, 690; Jordan, *North Carolina Troops 1861-1865: A Roster 1861-1865*, Vol. 15, 291-92.

70. Ibid., 692-95.

71. Ibid., 696-99.

72. Ibid., 699-700.

73. Ibid., 700-01.

74. Dr. John Hendricks Kinyoun, "An Incident of the Emancipation," Undated.

75. Ibid.

76. Heidler and Heidler, *Encyclopedia of the American Civil War*, 1873-75

77. Kinyoun Genealogical Papers.

78 Heidler and Heidler, *Encyclopedia of the American Civil War*, 1583.

79. Kinyoun Genealogical Papers.

80. Ibid.

81. "Centerview Woman Found Dead," *Journal Democrat*, February 14, 1923.

82. Ibid.

83. Kinyoun Genealogical Papers.

84. Ibid.

85. "Death of Dr. J. H. Kinyoun," *The Centerview Record*, July 31, 1903; "In Memoriam," *The Atlantic Messenger*, New Bern, NC; Kinyoun Genealogical Papers.

86. "Death of Dr. J. H. Kinyoun," *The Centerview Record,* July 31, 1903.

87. "In Memory of Dr. Kinyoun," *Journal Democrat*, August 7, 1903.

88. "Death of Dr. J. H. Kinyoun," *The Centerview Record*, July 31, 1903; "In Memory of Dr. Kinyoun," *Journal Democrat*, August 7, 1903.

89. "In Memory of Dr. Kinyoun," *Journal Democrat*, August 7, 1903.

CHAPTER III "ABRAHAM THE FIRST"

1. Ward, Burns, and Burns, *The Civil War,* 325, 340-42.

2. Ezra J. Warner, *Generals In Gray*, (Baton Rouge and London: Louisiana State University Press, 1959), 213-14

3. Heidler and Heidler, eds., *Encyclopedia of the American Civil War*, 1910-12.

4. Ibid., 411-15.

5. Frances H. Casstevens to Joseph K. Houts, Jr., 17 December 2003.

6. Ward, Burns and Burns, *The Civil War*, 340-42.

7. Heidler and Heidler, eds., *Encyclopedia of the AmericanCivil War,* 18.

8. Ibid., 41-42, 1309-1403.

9. Long and Long, *The Civil War Day by Day An Almanac*, 577.

10. Boatner, *The Civil War Dictionary* 218-19, 459-61; Heidler and Heidler, *Encyclopedia of the American Civil War* 1122-26.

11. Boatner, *The Civil War Dictionary*, 866; E. B. Long and Barbara Long, *The Civil War Day By Day An Almanac 1861-1865*, 408, 691.

12. Ruthridge and Welborn, *An Illustrated History of Yadkin County 1850-1965,* 31, 84.

13. Long and Long, *The Civil War Day by Day: An Almanac 1861-1865*, 49.

14. Heidler and Heidler, *Encyclopedia of the American Civil War,* 2119-21.

15. Warner, *Generals In Gray*, 140-41.

16. Heilder and Heidler, *Encyclopedia of the American Civil War*, 1591-98.

17. Heidler and Heidler, *Encyclopedia of the American Civil War*, 1494-1504.

18. Ibid., 799-803, 1481-84.

19. Lord, *Civil War Collector's Encyclopedia*, 20, 30, 196.

20. Chris Calkins to Joseph K. Houts Jr., 14 January 2004.

21. Warner, *Generals In Gray,* 157-58.

22. Chris Calkins to Joseph K. Houts, Jr., 14 January 2004.

23. Jordan, *North Carolina Troops 1861-1865: A Roster.* Vol. 15, 291.

24. Chris Calkins to Joseph K. Houts, Jr., 14 January 2004.

25. Ibid.

26. Boatner, *The Civil War Dictionary*, 644-47.

27. Heidler and Heidler, *Encyclopedia of the American Civil War*, 1349-50.

28. Ward, Burns, and Burns, *The Civil War*, 295, 308-09.

29. Chris Calkins to Joseph K. Houts, Jr., 14 January 2004.

CHAPTER IV "IN DIES"

1. Cunningham, *Doctors In Gray* 242-243.

2. Ruthledge and Welborn, *An Illustrated History of Yadkin County 1850-1965*, 31, 84.

3. Schroeder-Lein, *Confederate Hospitals On The Move*, 17-18.

4. Ibid.

5. Clark, *Histories of the Several Regiments and Battalions from North Carolina of the Great War 1861-65*. Vol. 3, 687-89.

CHAPTER V "ABLAZE"

1. Cunningham, *Doctors In Gray,* 106, 108-109, 242-43.

2. Kinyoun Genealogical Papers.

3. Schroeder-Lein, *Confederate Hospitals On The Move,* 18

APPENDIX I - ROSTERS

1. John W. Moore, *Roster of North Carolina Troops in the War Between The States* (Raleigh: Ashe & Gatling, State Printers and Binders, Presses of Edwards, Broughton & Co., 1882)

2. Ibid.

BIBLIOGRAPHY

BOOKS

Adams, George Worthington. *Doctors In Blue*. Baton Rouge: Louisiana State University Press, 1996.

Barnett, D. Christopher and Dr. T. Adrian Wheat. *Hospital Life Within The Confederate Medical Department*. Richmond, Virginia: The Museum of The Confederacy.

Barnett, Joseph H. *Life of Abraham Lincoln*. New York: Moore, Wilstach & Baldwin, 1865.

Beller, Susan Provost. *Civil War Medicine in the Civil War*. Cincinnati, Ohio: Betterway Books, 1992.

Boatner, III, Mark Mayo. *The Civil War Dictionary*. New York: Vintage Books, 1988.

Buchanan, Lamont. *A Pictorial History of the Confederacy*. New York: Crown Publishers, Inc., 1951.

By A Distinguished Southern Gentleman. *The Early Life, Campaigns, And Public Service of Robert E. Lee; With A Record Of The Campaigns And Heroic Deeds of His Companions in Arms*. New York: E. B. Treat & Co., Publishers, 1870.

Cane, Philip and Nisenson, Samuel. *Giants of Science*. New York: Grosset & Dunlap, Inc., 1959.

Cartwright, Frederick F. *Disease and History*. New York: Thomas Y. Crowell Company, 1972.

Casstevens, Frances H. *The Civil War And Yadkin County, North Carolina*. Jefferson, North Carolina, and London: McFarland & Company, Inc., Publishers, 1997.

Casstevens, Frances H. *Yadkin County The First One Hundred Years*. Dover, New Hampshire, Great Britain: Arcadia Publishing, 1996.

Casstevens, Frances Harding. *The Heritage Of Yadkin County*. Yadkinville, North Carolina: The Yadkin County Historical Society, 1981.

Castel, Albert. *William Clarke Quantrill*. New York: Frederick Fell, Inc., Publishers, 1961.

Cattell, J. McKeen. *American Men Of Science*. New York: The Science Press, 1906.

Catton, Bruce. *A Stillness at Appomattox*. Garden City, New York: Doubleday & Company, Inc., 1953.

Clark, Walter. *Histories of the Several Regiments And Battalions from North Carolina in the Great War 1861-65*. Vol. 2. Published By The State.

Clark, Walter. *Histories of the Several Regiments And Battalions from North Carolina in the Great War 1861-65*. Vol. 3. PublishedBby The State.

Coggins, Jack. *Arms And Equipment Of The Civil War*. New York: The Fairfax Press, 1983.

Commager, Steele and Erik Brunn. *The Civil War Archive*. New York, NY: Black Dog & Leventhal Publishers, Inc., 2002

Cunningham, H. H. *Doctors In Gray*. Baton Rouge: Louisiana State University Press, 1993.

Davis, Charles C. *Clark's Regiments: An Extended Index*. Gretna, Louisiana: Pelican Publishing Company, 2001.

Davis, Jefferson. *The Rise And Fall of the Confederate Government* Volume 1. New York: D. Appleton and Company, 1881.

—. *The Rise And Fall of the Confederate Government* Volume 2. New York: D. Appleton and Company, 1881.

Dickey, Thomas S., and Peter C. George. *Field Artillery Projectiles of The American Civil War*. Mechanicsville, Virginia: Arsenal Publications II, 1993.

Faragher, John Mack. *Daniel Boone*. New York: Henry Holt and Company, Inc., 1992.

Grant, Ulysses S. *Personal Memoirs of U. S. Grant*. New York: Charles L. Webster & Company, 1886.

Heidler, David S. and Jeanne T. Heidler. *Encyclopedia of the American Civil War*. New York London: W. W. Norton & Company, Inc., 2000.

The Holy Bible. Toronto, New York, and Edinburgh: Thomas Nelson & Sons, 1952.

Houts, Alice Kinyoun. *Ancestral Record*. Kinyoun Genealogical Records.

Houts, Jr., Joseph K. *Quantrill's Thieves*. Kansas City, Missouri: Truman Publishing Company, 2002.

Johnson, Clint. *Civil War Blunders*. Winston-Salem, North Carolina: John F. Blair, Publisher, 1997.

Jordan, Jr., Weymouth T. *North Carolina Troops 1861-1865: A Roster*. Vol. 15. Raleigh, North Carolina, 2003.

Lawlor, Laurie. *Daniel Boone*. Niles, Illinois: Albert Whitman & Company, 1989.

Lewis, Charlton T. *An Elementary Latin Dictionary*. Oxford: Clarendon Press, 1966.

Logan, Sheridan A. *Old Saint Jo*. John Sublett Logan Foundation: St. Joseph, Missouri, 1979.

Long, E. B. and Barbara Long. *The Civil War Day By Day-An Almanac 1861-1865*. Da Capo, 1971.

Lord, Francis A. *Civil War Collector's Encyclopedia*. Castle Books, Secaucus, New Jersey: Book Sales, Inc., 1979.

Melton, Jr., Jack W. and Lawrence E. Pawl. *Introduction to Field Artillery Ordnance 1861-1865*. Kennesaw, Georgia: Kennesaw Mountain Press, Inc., 1994.

Miller, Judith, Stephen Engleberg, and William Broad. *Germs*. New York, NY: A Touchstone Book Published by Simon & Schuster, 2002.

Moore, John W. *Roster of North Carolina Troops in the War Between The States.* Raleigh: Ashe & Gatling, State Printers and Binders, Presses of Edwards, Broughton & Co., 1882.

Nelson, Clark W. *Mayo Roots.* Rochester, Minnesota: Mayo Foundation, 1990.

Parsons, Robert P. *Trial To Light.* Indianapolis, Indiana, and New York: The Bobbs-Merrill Company, Cornwall, N. Y.: The Cornwall Press, Inc., 1943.

Photographic History Of The Civil War: Armies and Leaders, Vol. 5. Secaucus, NJ: The Blue & Gray Press, 1987.

Richardson, Albert D. *A Personal History of Ulysses S. Grant.* Hartford, Connecticut; American Publishing Company, 1868.

Robbin, Irving and Nisenson, Samuel. *Giants of Medicine.* New York: Grosset & Dunlap, Inc., 1962.

Rutledge, Jr., William E., and Max O. Wellborn. *An Illustrated History of Yadkin County 1850-1965.* Yadkinville, North Carolina, 1965.

Snell, Mark A. *A Journal of the American Civil War.* Volume 6, Number 1. Campbell, California: Regimental Studies, Inc., an affiliation of Savas Publishing Company, 1998.

The Real American Tragedy. Oklahoma City, Oklahoma: Homsey-Simon Production Co., 1977.

Thorne, John and Paul Mandel, eds. *Great Battles of the Civil War.* New York: Time Incorporated, 1961.

United Sates War Department. *The War of the Rebellion: A Compilation of the Official Records if the Union and Confederate Armies.* 128 Volumes. Washington, D.C.: 1880-1912.

Wall, James W. *Davie County: A Brief History.* Raleigh, North Carolina: North Carolina Department of Cultural Resources, Division of Archives and History, 1976.

—. *History of Davie County.* Spartanburg, South Carolina: The Reprint Company, Publishers, 1985.

Ward, Geoffery C., Ric Burns, and Ken Burns. *The Civil War-An Illustrated History.* New York: Alfred A. Knopf, Inc., 1990.

Warner, Ezra J. *Generals In Gray.* Baton Rouge Louisiana, and London, England: Louisiana State University Press, 1997.

Williams, Ralph Chester. *The United States Public Health Service 1798-1950.* Washington D.C.: Commissioned Officers Association of the United States Public Health Service, 1950.

Woodhead, Henry, ed. *Echoes of Glory-Arms and Equipment of The Confederacy.* Alexandria, Virginia: Time-Life Books, 1991.

—. *Echoes of Glory-Arms and Equipment of The Union.* Alexandria, Virginia: Time-Life Books, 1991.

ESSAYS

Kinyoun, John Hendricks. "An Incident of the Emancipation." Undated.

GENEALOGICAL

Houts, Alice Kinyoun. Conrad Genealogical Papers

Houts, Alice Kinyoun. Harding Genealogical Papers

Houts, Alice Kinyoun. Kinyoun Genealogical Papers.

INTERVIEWS

Poindexter, Jesse. Interview by Joseph K. Houts,Jr., Colorado Springs, Colorado; September 28, 2002

JOURNALS

Houts, Mrs. Hale. "Yadkin Boys." *Journal of North Carolina Genealogy.* (Summer 1963)

LEGAL DOCUMENTS

Kinyoun, John H. Will and Testament, dated December 24, 1892

LETTERS

Calkins, Chris. Letter to Joseph K. Houts, Jr. 14 January 2004.

Casstevens, Frances H. Letter to Joseph K. Houts, Jr. 17 December 2003.

Houts, Alice Kinyoun. "Dr. John Hendricks Kinyoun." Letter to Joseph Kinyoun Houts, Jr., 6 March 1968.

Kinyoun, J H. Letter to Elizabeth Conrad Kinyoun, his wife, concerning state of the war, focusing on the fall of Chattanooga, Tennessee and personal issues. 29 November 1863.

—. Letter to Elizabeth Conrad Kinyoun, his wife, concerning state of the war. January 1864.

—. Letter to Elizabeth Conrad Kinyoun, his wife, concerning state of the war. 8 March 1864.

—. Letter to Elizabeth Conrad Kinyoun, his wife, concerning state of the war. March 1864.

—. Letter to Elizabeth Conrad Kinyoun, his wife, concerning state of the war, focusing on the battle of Petersburg. 17 June 1864.

—. Letter to Elizabeth Conrad Kinyoun, his wife, concerning state of the war, focusing on the battle of Petersburg. 19 July 1864.

Parrish, William E. Letter to Joseph K. Houts, Jr. 2 January 2004.

MAGAZINES

Parrish, William E., "The Western Sanitary Commission," *Civil War History* March 1990.

MILITARY DOCUMENTS

Kinyoun, John Hendricks. "Medical Diary of the Sixty-Sixth North Carolina Infantry Regiment". August 1863 to April 1865.

NEWSPAPERS

Atlantic Messenger, "In Memoriam," undated, New Bern, North Carolina.

Centerview Record, "Death of Dr. J. H. Kinyoun," July 31, 1903, Centerview, Missouri.

Journal Democrat, "Centerview Woman Found Dead," February 14, 1923.

—. "In Memory of Dr. Kinyoun." August 7, 1903.

"Death Of Mrs. E. Conrad." Undated.

SPEECHES

McDonald, Dr. Wallace. "The Life and Times of Dr. Silas McDonald." Presentation, Tuesday Night Talks, Pony Express Museum. St. Joseph, Missouri, February 19, 2002.

Index

I

J

K

L

M

Y

About the Author

Joseph Kinyoun Houts, Jr., is a resident of St. Joseph Missouri. He is the author of *Quantrill's Thieves*, which was published in August 2002. Mr. Houts is a graduate of Westminster College, in Fulton, Missouri, where he received his Bachelor of Arts degree in May 1975, majoring in History. In 1978, he graduated from Lewis University College of Law in Glen Ellyn, Illinois, now Northern Illinois College of Law, with his Juris Doctor degree. Mr. Houts has been in banking for twenty-six years and works at the Commerce Bank as a Vice-President in charge of Community Development.

Besides his passion for writing history, he is very involved in his community, having served twenty-five years on The Salvation Army Advisory Board of Directors, ten years as member of the Board of Trustees of the Pony Express National Museum, Advisory Board member of the Heartland Foundation emPower Plant, Publications Committee of the Oregon-California Trails Association in Independence, Missouri, Board member of the Mount Mora Preservation and Restoration Cemetery Association Foundation, Board member of the Buchanan County conventions and Visitors Bureau, which serves the greater St. Joseph Metropolitan Area, and Chairman of the St. Joseph Civil War Sesquicentennial Commemoration Committee.

Mr. Houts is married to Noreen Mahoney Houts and has two children, Joseph Kinyoun Houts III and Katherine Mahoney Houts.